More comments about *The Baja Adventure Book*:

"...it's a wonderful, well written publication, the most complete Baja information and guide book I have ever seen."   Bill Johnson, Diving Charters, Inc., San Diego.

"...a must-have [book] for cruisers who explore ashore."   Captain John Rains, *San Diego Log.*

"Without question, this is the most informative and factful work on Baja that exists."   Neal Allen, eleven-year resident of Baja.

"...we were delighted...intensely detailed...we were [also] delighted by the wonderful black-and-white photos..."   *San Francisco Letter.*

"[*The Baja Adventure Book*] is by far the most informative and enjoyable book on Baja that I have ever seen."   Barbara Littlemore, Baja California Tours, Inc.

"For kayakers and smallboaters, this book is a gold mine of information on little-used beach access roads, launching sites, unspoiled camping and the best diving and fishing 'secret spots' in Baja...an indispensable companion on any Baja trip."   Ed Gillet, Southwest Sea Kayaks.

"...a unique contribution to the literature on Baja...readable, well organized and offers a sensible view regarding the need for conservation of natural resources."   Dr. José A. Mercadé, Professor, Glendale Community College.

"As 'first-timers' setting out on a two month voyage of discovery in Baja, we felt like we had a friend and Baja expert along with us. *The Baja Adventure Book* became our single most-used reference...Mr. Peterson's humorous asides and personal encounters gave us many hearty laughs en route."   Nancy Lattier Nash, video producer, *"On The Road in Baja."*

"...[this] handsome new...book is about the most comprehensive we've ever seen."   *AIM*, Mexico retirement and travel newsletter.

"...an almost awe-inspiring effort."   Sharon Wootton, *The Herald* (Lynwood, WA).

Peter Kuhn makes friends with a very relaxed upside-down manta.

The BAJA ADVENTURE Book

Walt Peterson

WILDERNESS PRESS
Berkeley

FIRST EDITION July 1987
Second printing July 1989
SECOND EDITION January 1992

Copyright © 1987, 1992 by Walt Peterson

Design by Thomas Winnett and Roslyn Bullas
Cover design by Michael Powers/Kris, and Larry Van Dyke

Maps by Judith Peterson
Photos by author except as noted

Library of Congress Card Number 91-36330
International Standard Book Number 0-89997-130-X

Manufactured in the United States of America

Published by   Wilderness Press
                2440 Bancroft Way
                Berkeley, CA 94704
                (510) 843-8080
                Write for free catalog

Library of Congress Cataloging-in-Publication Data

Peterson, Walt.
    The Baja adventure book / Walt Peterson. — 2nd ed.
            p. cm.
    Includes bibliographical references and index.
    ISBN 0-89997-130-X
        1. Outdoor recreation—Mexico—Baja California—Guide-books
2. Natural history—Mexico—Baja California. 3. Automobile
travel—Mexico—Baja California—Guide-books. 4. Baja California (Mexico)—Description and travel—Guide-books. I. Title.
        GV191.48.M6199
        917.22—dc20   91-36330
                                            CIP

CONTENTS

USING THE BAJA ADVENTURE BOOK

Operating instructions

An assumption has been made that the reader has a basic knowledge of his or her outdoor activity or sport and is well versed in safety and conservation matters. However, where certain Baja activities are likely to be outside the experience of many readers, such as off-road driving in two-wheel-drive vehicles, launching trailerboats over sand beaches and making friends with whales, some basic materials are included.

Regional and topographic maps in the book are based on Mexican and U.S. topographic maps and marine charts, updated and corrected with information from many sources. A small number of maps, labeled "sketch maps," were developed from aerial photographs and personal observations. All maps are oriented with true north at the top, but compass roses showing magnetic bearings and local variation are provided on the regional and topographic maps. None of the maps are intended to replace official government-issued charts and pilots for the purpose of air or marine navigation, and they should be used for planning purposes only. Official Spanish place names from the Mexican topographic maps have been used, although a few have been converted to their English equivalent to promote euphony and brevity. Alternate names used locally are provided in the text in some cases. The State of Baja California is referred to as "Baja Norte" or "Baja California Norte" throughout the book to avoid confusion with the popular name of the peninsula. Unofficial names assigned by surfers, climbers, cave explorers and fishermen, like "Zippers," "Gorin's Gully," "Cueva Tres Pisos" and "6 1/2 Spot," are placed in quotation marks when first used and should be obvious. Ranches and small settlements shown on the maps may be abandoned or in operation only seasonally, and their names change frequently. Only those mountains discussed in the text are shown on the maps.

Most road travel directions are keyed to the kilometer markers found on virtually all paved highways and on many unpaved roads. WAIT! THERE IS NO CAUSE FOR PANIC! THIS SYSTEM REQUIRES NO KNOWLEDGE OF THE METRIC SYSTEM! Just look at each KM marker as a little lighthouse, providing unmistakable identification as to geographic location. A "+" after a kilometer number means that the site occurs about half-way between that marker and the next higher marker. Where markers are not available, the distances cited were measured with a calibrated odometer, but to take full advantage of them readers must know the error rate of their own odometers. Distances over land are given in statute miles, except those pertaining to backpacking and hiking trips, which are expressed in the amount of time, in minutes, normally required of persons in good physical condition carrying packs and equipment appropriate to the venture being described. Distances over water are given in nautical miles. Coastal routes are measured closely following the shoreline. All compass bearings in the text are magnetic, and all elevations are in feet. Temperatures are expressed in degrees Fahrenheit.

Chapters 9 through 16 classify unpaved roads as sedan, pick-up or four-wheel-drive. The ratings have nothing to do with comfort, but rather with the physical ability of the vehicle to get down the road. They are subjective, and your own experience with individual roads may differ. Equally important, time will bring change to the roads. Most unpaved roads in Baja are either poorly culverted or not culverted at all, and a major storm can change everything. On the other hand, road crews are busier than ever, and you may be pleasantly surprised. Use the ratings as rough guides and remember the Baja adventurer's motto, "Remain rigidly flexible."

The addresses of most businesses and organizations mentioned by name in the text are contained in Appendix A. A number in parentheses following a name indicates that its location is shown by that number on the accompanying city map. Many businesses and services not specifically mentioned in the text, such as grocery stores and bus stations, also are shown on the city maps with a two-character alphabetical key, described in Appendix B. Mention of providers of travel services has mostly been limited to those utilizing their own equipment and facilities, although some organizations providing biologists, guest speakers, etc., on otherwise brokered trips are included, as are a small number of brokers specializing in Baja travel. There is considerable ebb and flow in this business, so expect change.

Since this is a book on adventure, not conventional tourism, information on hotels, resorts, RV parks and restaurants is limited. Additional information is provided in cases where hotels and resorts provide a sportfishing fleet, sailboard rentals, a dive shop or other facilities or services relevant to the adventure theme of the book.

The border cities

The border cities Tijuana, Tecate and Mexicali are sizable modern cities having many of the services, facilities and businesses found in cities of similar size in the United States. However, their urban nature and close proximity to the border render them of limited interest in a book on adventure, at least the type of adventure discussed in *The Baja Adventure Book*. In addition, each city and each state has a tourist bureau that can provide information by mail or telephone, the addresses and phone numbers of which are found in Appendix A. Thus, other than providing border crossing information, and the location of consulates, legal assistance offices and places where local information can be obtained, *The Baja Adventure Book* does not describe these cities.

Caveats

Sincere efforts have been made to insure that *The Baja Adventure Book* is current and correct. However, to err is human, and Baja California is a land of rapid change. Readers anticipating activities that are regulated, such as fishing and diving, should obtain current information from the sources listed. Although the author and the publisher cannot be responsible for the consequences of errors, the author will gladly receive corrections, comments and constructive suggestions.

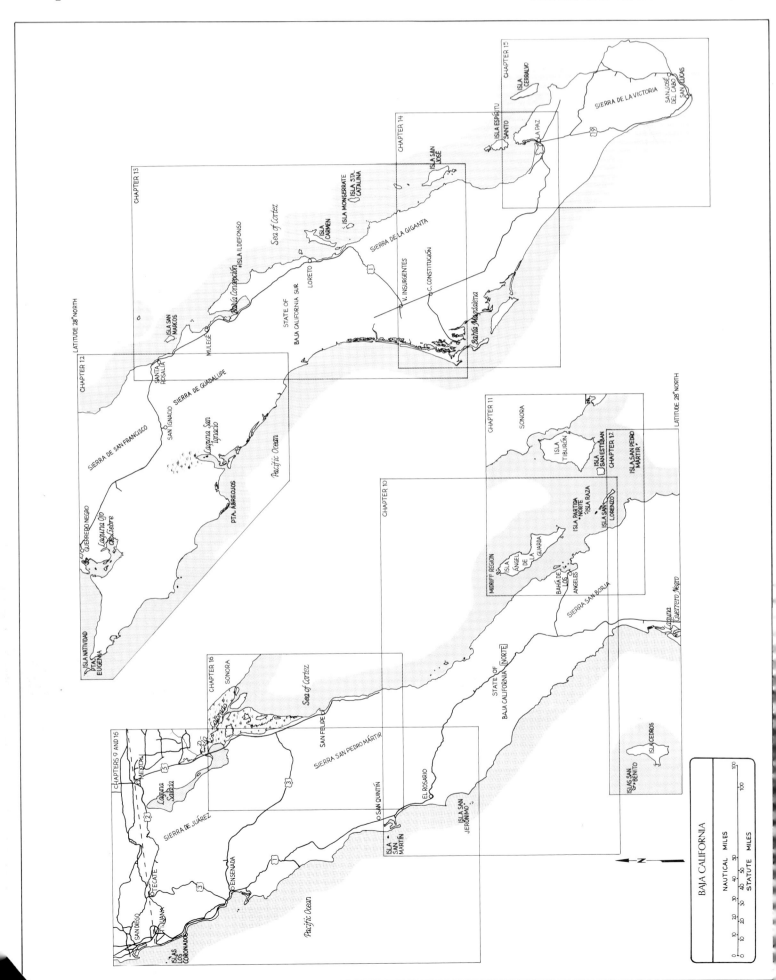

BAJA CALIFORNIA

NAUTICAL MILES

STATUTE MILES

CHAPTER 1
NATURAL WONDERS

Every adventure described in this book depends in many ways on what Mother Nature provided when she designed Baja California, so a basic knowledge of the natural history of the peninsula and nearby islands and waters will contribute greatly to the enjoyment of everyone traveling there.

The lay of the land

Five million years ago the land mass of today's Baja California was firmly attached to what is now mainland Mexico. However, the Pacific Plate, on which Baja and all the land west of the San Andreas Fault lie, eventually separated from the North American Plate. Today the peninsula and the deep gulf to the east that were formed are among the most striking geologic features on earth. The Kamchatka, Malay and Antarctic peninsulas are longer, but none is so narrow in relation to its length. Baja averages less than 70 miles in width along its 798-mile length, the narrowest part being 26 miles from the Pacific to the western shore of the bay near La Paz, and the greatest being 144 miles at the latitude of Punta Eugenia. Land area is about 53,280 square miles, and the shoreline on both coasts totals 1,980 miles, excluding the interiors of large enclosed bays. The southernmost extent of the peninsula is an unnamed and otherwise undistinguished point 2 1/2 miles west of Los Frailes, the famed rocks at Cabo San Lucas that are incorrectly granted that honor by many T-shirt and postcard artists.

There are seven principal mountain ranges. The Sierra de Juárez and Sierra San Pedro Mártir, extending south about 160 miles from the border, form the backbone of the northern part of the peninsula. The western slopes of both ranges are fairly gentle and descend to coastal plains along the Pacific. The eastern slopes, however, are mostly steep escarpments plunging down to sweltering lowlands along the Río Colorado and the Sea of Cortez. Both escarpments have been eroded into a series of major canyons. The massive double peak called Picacho del Diablo, at 10,154 and 10,152 feet Baja's highest, rises just east of the San Pedro Mártir escarpment. A broken series of mountain ranges runs south from the Sierra San Pedro Mártir, including the Sierra San Borja, the Sierra de San Francisco, the Sierra de Guadalupe and the

Sierra de la Giganta, ending north of La Paz. The central part of the Cape region south of La Paz is mountainous. This area is part of a single fault block, but erosion and movement along transverse faults have created two major ranges, the Sierra de la Laguna to the north, and the Sierra de la Victoria to the south. Since most geologists refer to the complex by the latter name, it will be used throughout this book.

There are three great lowland areas: the area east of the escarpments of the Sierra de Juárez and Sierra San Pedro Mártir, the area south of Guerrero Negro stretching along the

Rick Tinker and Will Ashford hike up the mouth of one of the great canyons in the escarpment of the Sierra San Pedro Mártir.

Pacific coast past Laguna San Ignacio, and the area around Bahía Magdalena.

The Sea of Cortez

The Cortez is the scene of some of the world's greatest oceanographic extremes. Its long, narrow configuration produces one of the largest tidal ranges in the world, up to thirty-one feet at the north end. Materials eroded out of today's Grand Canyon and surrounding lands over millions of years have been deposited at the north end of the Cortez by the Río Colorado, and low tides uncover mud flats up to three miles wide. Until it was tamed by dams, the tidal bore that ran up the Colorado was so powerful that it once sank a sizable ship. Tidal currents form huge whirlpools and rips in the Midriff region of the central Cortez, and velocities of over six knots have been recorded. Because there is no long fetch, large swells do not build up as they do in the ocean and there is little surge.

The Cortez has deep basins in its central and lower parts, some over 10,000 feet deep. Variations in water temperature also are extreme, inshore surface waters reaching 91° in the south during summer and 47° in the north during winter. Since freshwater transport into the Cortez is less than evaporation, it is more saline than the Pacific.

Pacific coastal waters

The southern sweep of the California Current carries cool water from more northerly regions, and surface water temperatures range between 50° and 75°. Northern coastal areas are characterized by cool water, ocean swells, heavy surge and upwellings of nutrient-laden deep water, producing an underwater environment almost indistinguishable from that of Southern California. To the south the California Current eventually becomes submerged under the Davidson Current, a body of warm water moving north during part of the year.

Climatic conditions

Baja's Pacific coastal areas have generally mild weather, and a number of fairly dependable seasonal patterns are recognizable. In winter, winds offshore tend to be steady from the northwest, averaging about seven knots and occasionally reaching twenty-five, with lesser velocities toward the southern end of the peninsula. Winds near the coastline are moderated by the influence of land, and nights and early mornings tend to be calm, northwest winds beginning in late morning and blowing until sunset or even two or three hours into the night. Fog and overcast are common around Isla Cedros and Bahía Magdalena.

North Pacific cold fronts disrupt this pattern, primarily between November and February. Fronts often bring winds from the southeast to southwest quadrants which rise in velocity, sometimes carrying driving rain, later shifting to northwest, moderating and then clearing. Strong north winds generally lasting two or three days are common in December and January. A high often forms over the interior of the southwestern United States, creating a strong, persistent northeasterly wind. Known in Southern California as the Santa Ana, it can affect the coast from Tijuana to the Cape, with winds strongest near shore and lessening south of Cedros. Strong northwesterlies are common in the spring and early summer, but as summer wears on, wind strength drops.

Tropical storms, known locally as *chubascos*, form far to the south and affect the southern part of the peninsula and surrounding waters from mid-May to mid-November, peak-

A large sea cave on the north coast of Isla Carmen.

ROB WATSON

ing in August and September, although abnormal water temperatures can cause exceptions. Most such storms affect only the southern part of the peninsula, but a few extend far to the north, occasionally moving up the Cortez to go ashore at San Felipe or into Sonora. Prodded by their insurance companies to be elsewhere during the *chubasco* season, many yachtsmen follow a migratory pattern as regular as any swallow, leaving San Diego after Thanksgiving with fair winds and following seas, and slogging back against the prevailing winds and the California Current before Memorial Day.

Between November and May prevailing winds in the Cortez are northerly, generally light and unpredictable, often following coastlines, and sailing yachts become festooned with cans of fuel. However, the winds are strong and dependable enough in the Punta Chivato and East Cape areas that thriving boardsailing operations have been established. ("East Cape" is an unofficial name for the area between Punta Pescadero and somewhere short of San José del Cabo.) In the summer most winds are from the south or southeast, but in the spring and fall the winds become variable. Calms are frequent all year and fog is uncommon. However, wide changes in wind velocity and direction occur over short

periods of time, and prevailing oily calms can turn into cauldrons of whitecaps in minutes. Most of these winds do not last long, but during winter ridges of high pressure often lie over the southwestern U.S., causing cool, dry winds to rip down the Cortez, sometimes lasting more than a week and bringing joy to boardsailors looking for speed sailing, and gloom to fishermen, divers, kayakers and cruisers.

There are other, more local, weather patterns. The *cordonazo* is a short but severe storm encountered in the Cortez, generally developing in the summer months during periods of southerly winds and often accompanied by lightning. A breeze known as the *coromuel* blows from the south in the La Paz area almost every day from late spring to early fall, starting in the late afternoon and continuing until morning. Thermal winds, created when air rushes in to fill the partial vacuum created by rising air currents over land heated by the sun, can occur anywhere. Mountains along Baja's eastern coast often cool rapidly at night, causing gravity to funnel strong winds through arroyos. Termed gravity—more properly katabatic—winds, they cause discomfort in villages and anchorages along the shore. Bahía de los Angeles is famous for gale-force gravity winds, sometimes lasting a week while

A *chubasco* devastates the Cape Region (satellite photo).

COURTESY NOAA

surrounding areas remain relatively calm. Local topography can influence the strength and direction of winds in other ways, and prominent capes along the Pacific coast like Punta Eugenia often see heavy weather.

Much of the peninsula lies between two rainfall zones. Winter storms provide northwest Baja with up to twelve inches per year, while summer storms account for much of the eight to sixteen inches received annually by the Cape region, micro-climates in the Sierra de la Victoria receiving up to thirty inches. A few storms stray from their normal routes and provide rain in the central zone, but between El Rosario and La Paz rainfall is extremely low, averaging as little as two to four inches a year, sometimes only traces for years at a time. The pattern of rainfall is complicated by the ranges of mountains, which form an almost unbroken barrier up to 2,000 feet, half the length of the peninsula being blocked up to 3,000 feet. Adiabatic cooling of damp westerly winds causes them to lose much of their moisture over western slopes, leaving the eastern slopes much drier. Higher areas of the Sierra de Juárez and Sierra San Pedro Mártir receive enough rain to support sizable pine forests, the latter accumulating up to 8 feet of snow in winter, while the coastal area in the "rain shadow" to the east is among the driest in North America.

Except for the Río Colorado, now reduced to a relative trickle because of increasing human demands, only about a half-dozen small streams flow into the sea on a more-or-less permanent basis along Baja's entire coastline. The famous "river" at Mulegé is actually an estero, although springs above a dam near the highway bridge provide a small flow of fresh water. There are only two sizable lakes in Baja. Laguna Salada, in the lowlands south of Mexicali, receives widely differing amounts of water from the Río Colorado from year to year; in 1987 the lake was sixty miles long, but by 1991 the drought prevalent in the Southwest had reduced it to perhaps twenty. Laguna Hanson in the Sierra de Juárez is less than a mile across and is shallow and muddy.

Air temperatures along the Pacific coast are moderated by prevailing winds and the California Current, providing cool-to-moderate shirt-sleeve weather most of the year. In contrast, the Mexicali region, with an average summer maximum of 104-108° and extreme highs of 120°, is the hottest on the continent. The Cortez coast lacks the moderating influences of the ocean and can become very hot in summer. On a windless summer day Santa Rosalía can seem as hot as a blast from the town's copper smelters. The Cape region at the southern end of the peninsula tends to have moderate temperatures year-round. Mountain areas can be downright cold in winter; five-gallon water jugs can freeze solid overnight at the 8,000-foot level west of Picacho del Diablo. As in desert areas elsewhere, day-to-night temperature variations are extreme, and it is not uncommon for well-equipped RVers to run their heaters early in the morning and their air conditioners in the afternoon.

Living things

The peninsula is rich in native and introduced plants; 2,958 species, subspecies and varieties of vascular plants have been recorded. The number of endemic species (found only in one area on earth) is lower than what might be expected in a long,

narrow peninsula, only 23% of the total. The reason for this appears to be that the peninsula split off from the mainland relatively recently, so isolation has been limited. In addition, its mountains are not very high, snow and freezing temperatures are uncommon, and rainfall is low.

The plants of northern Baja are closely related to those of Southern California. Much of the land below 3,000-5,000 feet west of the Juárez and San Pedro Mártir escarpments is covered by chaparral consisting of chamise, manzanita, laurel sumac, sage and other plants, giving way at lower elevations to a coastal scrub of agave, cliff spurge, buckeye, buckwheat and bladderpod. Juniper-pinyon woodlands are found at higher elevations, and some mountain areas have forests of pine, cedar, fir, aspen and oak. The highest areas of the Sierra San Pedro Mártir even have an impoverished version of a Canadian boreal forest, with lodgepole pine, white fir and an endemic cypress. Plants in the Cape region and the Sierra de la Giganta are closely related to those of the nearest areas on the mainland, with oak-pinyon woodlands at high elevations and complex communities of cacti, yuccas, various shrubs and trees like palo blanco and palo verde below. Between these two northern and southern areas many familiar desert plants are found, including ocotillo, ironwood, cholla, creosote bush, mesquite, agave and various cacti, along with a number of striking plants adapted to extreme dryness such as boojum, cardón, copalquín and torote.

Rob Watson studies a Rubenesque "elephant tree" on Isla Cerralvo.

A verdant palm oasis in Cañon San Pablo, Sierra de San Francisco.

endemics. Xanthus hummingbird is a common resident of the Cape region north to San Ignacio. Mangrove yellow warblers are found in mangrove lagoons from the Cape region to as far north as Estero la Bocana and Caleta San Lucas. The gray thrasher is common along the Pacific coast south from Punta Cabras and throughout Baja California Sur in desert scrub at low elevations. San Lucas robin, a colorfully feathered sub-species of American robin, is common in the Sierra de la Victoria. Two subspecies of Belding's yellowthroat are found, the northern from San Ignacio to Comondú, the south-ern from La Paz south, both normally seen in marshy loca-tions. The yellow-legged gull breeds entirely within the Cortez and its range is almost, but not quite, limited to those waters; some get as far north in summer as the Salton Sea, and several have been recorded in the Bahía Magdalena area, so it perhaps could be termed a Cortez "almost-endemic." There are odd habitat-species relationships—places where birds appear though not expected—and unusual species com-positions—birds keeping unusual avian company. Even after more than a hundred years of professional studies, Baja's birds are not well known, and although the place is not likely to appeal to the birding-from-the-bumper crowd, amateurs might be able to make real contributions.

A number of prominent bird areas are described in Chap-ters 9 through 16, including Laguna Hanson, Bahía San Quintín, Bahía de los Angeles, Laguna Ojo de Liebre (Scammon's Lagoon), Laguna San Ignacio, Bahía Magda-lena, La Laguna, the south end of Isla San José, and Islas Ángel de la Guardia (Guardian Angel Island), San Pedro Mártir, San Esteban, Partida Norte, Raza, San Lorenzo and Ildefonso. Use great care when visiting these places, espe-cially when in the vicinity of nesting seabirds. Most species

An osprey feeds its young in a nest built in an unlikely place.

These distinctions are not sharp, and there are transition zones combining features of the communities on both sides. In addition, scattered accidents of geology and meteorology provide micro-environments containing interesting plant communities, including the verdant palm groves of the east-side canyons of the Sierra de Juárez and Sierra San Pedro Mártir; the park-like meadows of the higher reaches of the Sierra San Pedro Mártir; the complex plant communities of La Laguna, a meadow high in the Sierra de la Victoria; the fresh- and saltwater marshes along the Colorado; the man-grove lagoons along the Pacific and Cortez coasts, and the pines of Cedros, surviving on the moisture provided by fog. Chapters 9 through 16 describe a number of the more inter-esting plants and plant communities.

Large land mammals include only mule deer, mountain lion, bighorn sheep and a few antelope, but there are many smaller mammal species, including coyote, fox, rabbit, bob-cat, skunk, badger, raccoon, ring-tailed cat, ground squirrel, chipmunk, gopher, mouse and rat, plus feral goat, cat and pig.

Well-adapted to Baja's climates, many reptile species inhabit the peninsula, including such familiar and expected animals as various species of rattlesnake and whiptail, king and gopher snakes, and numerous iguanids, geckos and liz-ards. Tree frog, salamander and pond turtle don't seem to be the sort of animal species you would encounter in Baja, but they are present, along with a number of species of toad.

Baja's diverse mix of deserts, bays, mangrove lagoons, forested peaks and remote islands, together with its strategic location on many flyways, promotes an equally diverse mix-ture of bird life. Check lists differ, but some identify over 400 species that live in, breed in or pass through Baja and over surrounding waters. Extended isolation has produced five react to humans as if they were large ground predators, and if disturbed adults may abandon their eggs and chicks, leaving them vulnerable to hypo- and hyperthermia, falling off ledges and other accidents. Gulls are major predators of eggs and chicks, and since they are less afraid of humans than other species are, they can be seen escorting visitors through nesting colonies, darting in to take advantage of every opportunity. Stay at least a hundred yards away and use binoculars. You will have an adequate view of the birds going about their natural business of raising their young, rather than of frightened parents poised to take flight. Never allow a pet near a nesting area. The check lists in later chapters were developed from those of professional ornithologists, who can't be everywhere and see everything, and there are undoubtedly many additional species.

The Mexican Galapagos

From a distance many of the hundred or so islands and islets in the Cortez seem almost barren, little more than scattered desert scrub and a few cactus and agave being visible to the average person. However, a trained naturalist can find more diversity than most people would dream possible. Tiburón, for instance, has 298 species of vascular plants, Guardian Angel 199, Espíritu Santo 168 and Carmen 163. Isla las Ánimas Sur, little more than a rock sticking out of the sea northeast of Isla San José, has 11. Even Isla San Pedro Mártir, with its seemingly impenetrable covering of guano, has 24. The islands have the most spectacular concentrations of nesting southern seabirds on the west coast of North America, San Pedro Mártir, Partida Norte, Raza and San Lorenzo being among the most important. Reptiles and amphibians thrive, with 25 species on Tiburón, 20 on San Marcos, 16 on Carmen and 15 on Guardian Angel. Even some of the tiniest islets have one; Islotes las Galeras, a group of small islets north of Isla Monserrate, have a species of lizard. Many islands have land mammals; Tiburón has 13 species, San José 7, Espíritu Santo 6, Carmen 4, and even tiny Mejía, located at the north end of Guardian Angel, has 3. Larger mammals such as ring-tailed cat, fox, coyote, brush rabbit and jackrabbit are found only on Espíritu Santo, Tiburón and San José, and mule deer only on the last two.

Freed from many of the predators and competitors found on the mainland, the species that have become established on the islands have evolved under very different conditions from their mainland ancestors, some to the point that they are now considered separate species. Of about 581 plants found on the islands, 18 are endemic. The more curious animals include the "rattle-less" rattlesnake of Santa Catalina and the black jackrabbit of Espiritu Santo. As noted earlier, the yellow-legged gull seldom leaves the Cortez area except for forays to the Salton Sea in California. In addition, there are three other species of seabirds whose breeding ranges are almost totally confined to the islands of the Cortez: Heermann's gull, elegant tern and Craveri's murrelet. The last is the southern-most member of a family of cold-water birds, an example of the curious mix of the temperate and tropical found in the Cortez area. Raza is the nesting site for over 90% of the world's Heermann's gulls and elegant terns.

The Cortez islands are a treasure of genetic diversity and scientific interest, and it has been suggested that had Charles

One of the famous Espíritu Santo black jacks. Can you spot it?

Darwin visited them instead of the Galapagos he would have arrived at the same conclusions. Even today they are incompletely explored biologically, and the inventory of their terrestrial, avian and marine life is far from complete. In the past the islands have been preserved by a blessing in disguise; they had little in the way of direct economic potential other than fishing, seabird eggs, salt, guano and gypsum, and except on several of the largest islands, no potable water was present. There has been some damage: seabird rookeries have been subject to heavy pressure by egg collectors; green turtle and totuaba (a large fish) have been taken to near-extinction; there is a major gypsum mine on San Marcos; salt works have been in operation on Carmen and San José; and some guano collecting still goes on, especially on Patos. However, most communities of flora and fauna have remained largely intact, and many scientists consider the Cortez islands, especially those in the Midriff region, to be among the world's last major refuges of relatively undisturbed island life.

In recent years the islands have become popular stops for yachtsmen, boaters and tourists on natural-history tours, and increased numbers of outboard motors have made possible more frequent visits by the local people. While all or most of these visitors may be caring and well-meaning, their mere presence on the islands sometimes has hidden consequences that work against the preservation of the natural order. Some islands are more sensitive than others, and laws have been passed controlling many activities. Raza became a seabird sanctuary in 1964, and in 1978 all Cortez islands were granted wildlife-refuge status. Hunting and foraging are prohibited, and a permit is needed to collect or otherwise disturb the flora and fauna. Proposals have been made to include many of the islands in a national park.

Marine life

Along the northern part of the Pacific coast divers and fishermen will be hard-pressed to differentiate the flora and fauna from those of Southern California. At Isla San Martín, however, cool-water plants and animals start to disappear and more tropical forms are increasingly common, and south of Punta Abreojos the underwater environment becomes distinctly tropical, although some cool-water life like abalone can be found all the way to the Cape. The diversity of fish in the Cortez is also extreme due to its great variations in water temperature and depth, and great range of bottom topography, from great shallows with flat, silty bottoms to vertical rock walls. In the north end there are isolated assemblages of cool-water fish that seem to have been taken from the Pacific—white sea bass, ocean whitefish, several species of rockfish and even sheephead and California halibut. At the southern end of the Cortez, Indo-Pacific species like Moorish idols and longnose butterfly fish can be seen, and there is even a sizable coral reef. Blooms of plankton occasionally become so dense that large areas of the Cortez are colored deep red, accounting for one of its early names, the Vermilion Sea.

The Pacific coast and the Cortez are home to over 800 species of fish. Three species, Pacific manta, whale shark and hammerhead shark, have become the object of attention by divers and are described in the following chapter, and Chapters 9 through 16 describe a number of underwater communities. A few of the more than one hundred species pursued by sportfishermen are discussed in Chapter 3.

While a visitor to Baja is unlikely to see a large, wild land mammal—the four-legged kind anyway—the waters surrounding the peninsula contain an abundance of marine mammals. Over twenty species of cetaceans (whales, porpoises and dolphins) have been identified. The most numerous large whales in Baja waters are the gray whales, discussed in the following section. A full-time resident population of fin whales lives in the Cortez, often concentrated in the Midriff region, and others can be seen in the Pacific in winter. Fin whales are large; at up to eighty feet they are second only to blue whales. They sometimes swim in groups of two to ten, their spouts shooting up like geysers, followed by the slow roll of dark backs, with a small tell-tale fin set well aft. On rare occasions they get together in larger groups; twenty-seven have been seen feeding together in the Cortez. Similar

in appearance but smaller and less gregarious than fin whales, Bryde's whales are also seen along the Pacific coast and throughout the Cortez. In 1980 boaters in a twenty-four-foot cruiser were crossing Bahía de los Angeles when a large whale, possibly an adult fin or Bryde's whale, breached next to the boat. (During a breach a whale "jumps," so that all or most of its body is out of the water.) It landed across the bow, driving the boat down to the gunnels and leaving several pounds of hide aboard as it slid off. The boat was a shambles, with a smashed bow and a two-foot crack in its hull, but it did not sink and no one was hurt.

Humpbacks, with their long white flippers and musical talents, inhabit the Cortez and waters off the Cape in winter, especially the latter. Blue whales, at 100 feet and 150 tons the largest animals ever to live on earth, cruise off the Pacific coast, some visiting the Cortez between late winter and late spring. A "school," or better yet a "university," of twelve blues was recently seen feeding west of Cedros. Other whales that might be encountered include Sei, Minke, Cuvier's beaked, sperm, pygmy sperm, northern pilot, orca and false killer. Orcas often stay near the Islas San Benito, where they are attracted by large numbers of sea lions, a favorite delicacy. In 1978 a pod of forty orcas was seen attacking a blue whale off Cabo San Lucas, biting its lips and flukes for over an hour. Sperm whales are seen occasionally, sometimes traveling in large groups. Fifty-two of them stranded on a beach north of Mulegé in 1979 and died in the hot sun.

The smaller cetaceans in Baja waters include harbor porpoise, Dall's porpoise, common dolphin, Risso's dolphin, Pacific white-sided dolphin, Eastern Pacific spotted dolphin, spinner dolphin, Pacific bottlenose dolphin and Gulf of California harbor porpoise. Bottlenose and common dolphins are abundant, often racing at the bows of passing boats. Several friends and I were rounding the south cape of a small island south of Tiburón when we came upon an unbelievable sight to the west: although the Cortez was flat calm, an area of about ten acres was being churned into whitecaps. Only when great numbers of black and white shapes leaped into the air did we

A fin whale almost engulfs a brown pelican while feeding on krill.

BERNIE TERSHY/CRAIG STRONG

A troop of passing acrobats puts on an impromptu circus for author's wife Judy and niece Suzy Peterson.

realize that it was a group of a hundred or more common dolphins. At the other end of the spectrum, the Gulf of California harbor porpoise, found only in the northern Cortez, has the smallest range of any cetacean and is one of the least-known marine mammals on earth.

Pinnipeds (seals and sea lions) are common in Baja waters. California sea lions, elephant seals and harbor seals breed and calve on the larger islands along the Pacific coast. California sea lions frequently seem quite friendly and accompany divers on the reefs at Isla San Jerónimo and the Benitos, to the great disgust of spearfishermen. There is a very large rookery of sea lions on the San Benitos. Sea lions are the only pinnipeds common to the Midriff region, and often haul out on beaches at San Lorenzo and San Pedro Mártir and at Puerto Refugio at the north end of Guardian Angel. They entertain human divers at the islands north of La Paz with barrel-rolls and somersaults. The best place to meet an elephant seal is at the San Benitos, although they haul out on the Islas los Coronados, San Jerónimo and San Martín as well. Harbor seals often can be seen on San Martín, San Jerónimo and the Coronados, and occasionally on the Islas de Todos Santos west of Ensenada. Steller sea lions and northern fur seals are seen from Cedros north, but only rarely.

Be extremely careful when in the vicinity of pinnipeds, for their sake and as well as yours. In the wild they can be extremely shy and if frightened may stampede for the safety of the sea, crushing pups and seriously injuring adults, some even throwing themselves off cliffs. If they feel cornered they may defend themselves, moving with unexpected swiftness on land. California sea lions occasionally nip at the fins of

divers in a seemingly playful way. Elephant seals may appear largely indifferent toward people, but during the breeding season males can be very aggressive. Although there seem to be no reports of attacks of humans, local commercial divers at the San Benitos give elephant seals healthy respect and a wide berth.

The gray whale

No aspect of Baja California's natural history has been the subject of more public attention than the life and times of the California gray whale. The first years of this attention nearly resulted in their extermination.

Gray whales make a variety of sounds, and many people believe they communicate with one another by verbal means. If so, today's mariners and yachtsmen are fortunate that they do not seem to have an oral history to be passed from generation to generation. In the mid-1800s large-scale whaling began in the eastern Pacific. Whales found in Bahía Magdalena were taken in such large numbers that the business soon became unprofitable. In 1857 Captain Charles Scammon rediscovered a lagoon visited by Juan Rodríguez Cabrillo in 1542, which became known as Scammon's Lagoon. Due to their large size, slow movements and frequent surfacing habits, the whales inside the lagoon were highly vulnerable, and Scammon returned home with a full cargo of oil after a short voyage. It was not long until the secret was out, and a large-scale slaughter began again. Whalers often harpooned the babies first, knowing that their mothers would return to defend them and offer a second target. Scammon later discovered a similar lagoon to the south, now known as

A male sea elephant exercises his territorial rights to a few square yards of Isla Benito Este.

Laguna San Ignacio. Between whales taken by ships in the lagoons and those taken along the coast by shore-based operations, the number of grays declined rapidly. Scammon estimated the gray whale population at between 30,000 and 40,000 in 1853; twenty-eight years later it was between 5,000 and 9,000 (these estimates were little more than educated guesses). Many naturalists thought the species was headed for extinction, but in 1937 the grays were given legal protection and by the early 1990s the population had increased to perhaps 21,000.

In recent years gray whales have become the subject of public interest of a more gentle nature, occasioned by two aspects of their behavior: their annual breeding migration and the fact that some are "friendly." Most grays inhabit the protein-rich waters of the Chukchi and Bering seas between April and October. Early in October they start the 5,000-mile journey south to Laguna Guerrero Negro, Scammon's Lagoon, Laguna San Ignacio and Bahía Magdalena, the longest migration of any mammal. A small number continue on to the western coast of mainland Mexico, and a few end up in the Cortez. Some females return consistently to the same lagoon year after year, others return to different lagoons, and still others circulate among the lagoons during the same season. Whales begin to arrive in the lagoons in late November, stragglers arriving as late as February. About half of the mature females conceived the prior year and are about to give birth. Most others are ready for breeding, many having given birth the previous year, while some are in season for the first time. They are hotly pursued by amorous adult males and precocious adolescents, who outnumber receptive females

two to one. Like most mammals, males compete hotly for females, who, like most mammals, respond with feigned disinterest. The whales are promiscuous, copulating with a number of partners. At times the event turns into a free-for-all, with as many as twenty individuals involved.

A few calves are born along the migration route, but most births occur in the lagoons, where warm, safe waters insure a high success rate. Approximately 1,500 grays are born each year, about half in Scammon's. A whale calf is about fifteen feet long and weighs between 1,500 and 2,000 pounds. The mother nurses it from two nipples, providing up to fifty gallons of milk a day. Containing 53% fat, the milk enables a calf to grow rapidly, and within several months it may reach twenty feet and 4,000 pounds. The return migration to Arctic waters begins in late-January, a few mothers and calves remaining as late as May or June. Those leaving early may encounter stragglers still heading south.

This annual migration has become the object of a great deal of attention. Large numbers of people watch from shore or go out on private boats, hundreds of commercial craft offer daily whale-watching trips out of coastal ports, and trips to the lagoons are offered on large sportfishing boats out of San Diego. It is estimated that over a million humans see the whales each year, making them the "most-seen" whales in the world.

A phenomenon that began in 1976 caused a new surge of interest, the "friendly" whales. A whale thought by some to be Gigi, a gray captured in 1971 and studied at Sea World in San Diego until she was released a year later, surfaced next to the vessel *Royal Polaris* while it was in Laguna San

A friendly whale pays a call in Laguna San Ignacio.

Ignacio. When everyone rushed to the side to see her, she submerged and caused another rush when she came up on the other side. She did this more than a dozen times and observers became convinced she was a tease. She was so curious about inflatable boats that she would lift them with bursts of exhaled bubbles and balance them on her head or back, always being careful to do this only when passengers were not aboard. Other whales have apparently learned that humans can be trusted, some of them anyway, and the number of such incidents increases each year. Perhaps calves once petted by tourists have grown up and now allow their youngsters the same experience. Originally observed only in Laguna San Ignacio, these encounters have occurred recently in Bahía Magdalena, near Vancouver Island, and in the Bering Sea.

Whale fans with their own boats can see grays at many coastal locations, and a yacht trip down the Baja coast in midwinter will result in dozens, perhaps hundreds, of sightings. Boaters anchoring just inside the entrance to Bahía Magdalena may be treated to an incredible sight: two, three or even four whales breaching or spy-hopping at the same time. (A spy-hopping whale vigorously beats its flukes, or if in shallow water pushes its flukes against the bottom, so that its body is vertical and about a third out of the water.) Another good place is the inside waterway running north from Bahía Magdalena, where Jacques Cousteau filmed his television program "Desert Whales." My son Mike and I were fishing in our cartopper on a calm day north of Isla San Martín when a gray appeared on the horizon, showing his flukes every three or four minutes. We could hear his pulsing sounds when he was still a hundred yards away and soon had the wonderful thrill of seeing him pass directly under our boat. There are occasional surprise encounters: I was diving in a kelp bed south of Punta Eugenia when a gray plowed through only yards away.

To see a whale traveling offshore, first look for a "blow," and start timing the rhythmic breathing pattern to predict when it will surface. The powerful flukes disturb the water, leaving what appear to be oil slicks on the surface, showing its course. To avoid harassing the whale and exposing yourself to danger, your boat should not be operated at speeds faster than the whale when paralleling it and within a hundred yards. If more than one is present go no faster than the slowest. Never try to overtake a whale from behind or to drive or herd it, and keep your speed and course as steady as possible. Take no action which causes it to use escape tactics, such as frequent changes in direction or rapid swimming at the surface, prolonged diving or underwater course changes, or which causes underwater exhalation. Never separate a calf from adults or cause a female to shield her calf by tail swishing or other maneuvers.

Whales can be encouraged to come right up to a boat in the lagoons and in Bahía Magdalena. The Mexican boatmen of Laguna San Ignacio say that grays are attracted by the sound of outboard engines and that they have a definite preference for the sound of certain engines, or possibly engine sounds of certain pitches. This seems to be true, perhaps because the sounds generated by outboards are of about the same frequency as those emitted by the whales themselves, so to encourage a visit by a "friendly," the boatmen stop their boats, but leave their engines running in neutral. This also keeps the whales informed of where the boats are, an obvious safety precaution among breaching whales. If nothing happens, they alter the idling speed of their engines. They do not use their engines to get closer; when the whales want to visit they will come to the boats, sometimes from quite a distance. The lagoons are closed to private power boats without permits, although paddled and rowed boats are permitted, including kayaks and canoes. At present there are no restrictions on boats in Bahía Magdalena. Regulations on boat usage in these areas may change in future years, so it would be well to check first with the nearest Captain of the Port (see the index for their locations). A visit with the "friendly" whales of Laguna San Ignacio is described beginning on page 168.

Great caution must be exercised while visiting the whales, for not all have such easy-going dispositions. During a whale-watching expedition to Laguna San Ignacio in 1982, a gray slapped a boat with its fluke. All thirteen passengers were dumped into the water, and two hit their heads and were killed. In March 1983 Sue Dippold and Bernie Eskesen were off Punta Abreojos in their Islander 30 when they heard a loud blow and a gray surfaced with its flukes raised. It returned twice, raising the boat partly out of the water, causing a great list and damaging the rudder. They attempted to steer with the sails, but kept spinning around in circles. Finally Bernie fashioned a temporary rudder and they made it to Punta Abreojos.

Several years ago two divers in an inflatable were approached by an apparently friendly whale who seemed to want a backrub, when suddenly they found themselves, their equipment and their boat "flying like leaves in a storm." Yet, on another occasion, one of these divers spent a great deal of time in the water with a mother and her calf, all three swimming peacefully together. However, a diver later made the mistake of swimming directly at a whale and got a tremendous whack from a well-aimed fluke, causing broken bones. Other people have encountered "bumpers" and "thrashers," males who play a rough game with inflatables and skiffs, slamming into them repeatedly with considerable force, often for as long as an hour. This sport seems to be be something other than simple light-hearted highjinks, and if these animals were human, we would call them bullies.

By far the best location to see whales from shore is at Laguna San Ignacio. Grays also can be seen from Parque Natural de la Ballena Gris on the northern shore of Scammon's, from the beaches along the waterway north of Bahía Magdalena and from the old salt pier at Guerrero Negro. Although you will probably need binoculars to get a good look from these places, grays have occasionally cruised within twenty yards of the salt pier.

Given the popularity of the whales and the many dollars expended in seeing them, it seems only a matter of time until the economic value of live whales will exceed everything ever realized by killing them. There is still plenty of time; the Pacific Plate is being carried to the northwest, and in about forty million years Baja California will be part of an island lying off British Columbia. One wonders whether the gray whales knew something about this when they selected the lagoons for the end of their annual migration; after all, the route is getting shorter every year.

Natural history trips and courses

Nature lovers have a virtual cornucopia of choices. Many organizations offer vessel-based trips, most with qualified naturalists aboard to present programs and answer questions. Baja Expeditions offers a number of natural history trips that visit Islas Espíritu Santo, San José, Santa Catalina, Ildefonso, Raza, San Francisquito and Partida Sur. The company also offers a gray whale trip to Bahía Magdalena, another trip to Magdalena and south to the Cape to see blues and humpbacks, and still another in the Cortez for blues and finbacks. Thompson Voyages offers a "Baja Whales & Wildlife Adventure" aboard a large San Diego long-range boat, visiting the Islas San Benito, Laguna San Ignacio, Isla Cedros and either Isla San Jerónimo, Isla San Martín or the Islas de Todos Santos, depending on the time of the year. Biological Journeys has a variety of vessel-based natural history trips, some ranging down the Pacific coast from San Diego to visit Todos Santos, San Martín, the Benitos, Cedros, Laguna San Ignacio, Bahía Magdalena and the Cabo San Lucas area, some ending in La Paz. Others begin in La Paz and make trips to many prime locations in the southern Cortez such as Islas San Esteban, Raza, San José, Santa Catalina and Cerralvo, some getting as far north as Puerto Refugio on Guardian Angel.

Special Expeditions offers trips on the motor vessels *Sea Lion* and *Sea Bird*, visiting Bahía Magdalena, the southern Cortez, Islas Espíritu Santo, Santa Catalina and Ildefonso, the Midriff region and other locations, with stops at Cabo San Lucas, La Paz and Loreto. The American Cetacean Society sponsors vessel-based trips to Laguna San Ignacio, with stops at many islands en route, all beginning in San Diego, some returning to San Diego, others ending in La Paz. Another trip, beginning and ending in La Paz, explores the southern Cortez. Some Pacific Sea Fari Tours trips visit San Martín, the Benitos, Scammon's, Laguna San Ignacio, Cedros and Todos Santos, while others range down the Pacific coast, stopping at many of the same places and going on into the Cortez, visiting Islas Espíritu Santo, San José, Santa Catalina and Ildefonso. Oceanic Society Expeditions sponsors a variety of trips, including a Bahía Magdalena whale-watching and camping trip, and vessel trips to Laguna San Ignacio, the

southern Cortez, the Midriff and elsewhere. Some of the long-range fishing boats working out of Fisherman's Landing in San Diego also make independent natural history trips.

Day-trips are offered in many locations. Ensenada Clipper Fleet often takes whale-watchers on local trips from Ensenada. Raul Perez and Alberto Lucero take visitors on trips in the Bahía de los Angeles and Bahía San Francisquito areas, respectively. Three-hour whale-watching trips on an outboard-powered barge are offered daily during the season at Guerrero Negro, departing from the old salt pier. Viajes Mario's in Guerrero Negro offers similar trips. Fishermen at Puerto Lopéz Mateos, Puerto San Carlos, Scammon's and Laguna San Ignacio are often willing to take people out to see the whales. Cabo Acuadeportes and Amigos del Mar in Cabo San Lucas offer whale-watching trips.

A number of organizations combine nature-watching with other pursuits, so a rich diversity of interests can be accommodated. Baja Discovery has a tent camp at Laguna San Ignacio where visitors can meet the whales, expand their birding check lists and do some local exploring. The camp is equipped with a solar-powered bathroom and showers. Some Wilderness: Alaska/Mexico kayak trips visit Bahía Magdalena. Baja Expeditions offers kayak trips to Bahía Magdalena to see the whales at close quarters. The National Outdoor Leadership School "Semester in Mexico" course visits Bahía Magdalena by kayak and focuses on the gray whales, birds and local ecology, and their sea kayaking, backpacking and rock-climbing ventures head for other prime areas. Touring Exchange has a natural history camping trip to the desert around Cataviña, guided by a naturalist. Cirilo Manriquez Trasviña offers mule trips to La Laguna in the Victorias.

There are no current trips devoted exclusively to birding, but the National Audubon Society offers vessel-based natural-history trips led by ornithologists, and Raul Perez takes people on *panga* trips to Raza. Foundation for Field Research provides opportunities to participate in various scientific expeditions. The programs change, but in recent years the subjects have included island mammals of the Cortez, and marine biology and mule deer at Cedros, as well as the archaeology of Bahía de los Angeles. Glendale Community

Two kayakers venture close to a gray whale.

RON YARNELL

College offers courses in marine biology, natural history, marine vertebrates and other subjects at their field station in Bahía de los Angeles. The new museum at Bahía de los Angeles has natural history exhibits, including the skeleton of a baby whale.

****

A GLOW-RIOUS OCCASION. Perry Studt, my brother Reeve and I launched our Columbia 22 sailboat at San Felipe and headed south, encountering fierce winds almost immediately. Several days later our prayers were answered, too well in fact, and we had to resign ourselves to the noise of the outboard. At midnight I relieved Perry at the helm and soon lapsed into a reflective mood, wodering how such absolute peace could be possible in such a turbulent world. Our passage through the water was the only detectable motion, and even the sound of the engine did not seem to intrude into the silence. Gradually I became aware that something had been added to the velvety darkness of the water and the moonless sky. A dull glow of indefinite proportions could be seen to port. My eyes struggled to focus on the object, but due to its lack of form and substance I could not get a fix on it. Faint apprehensions began to stir; a gigantic glowing object was coming closer, and it was on a collision course. Thoughts raced through my mind, but evasion did not occur to me. No ripple or wake was evident and it appeared to be below the surface. Sorting through all the possibilities I hit on the absurd: a giant squid! Captain Nemo! It shot toward the boat like an oversized torpedo, and as I braced for the crash, I realized I had not warned Perry and Reeve. Too late! At the last possible moment the object dove and then reappeared some distance to starboard. My mind still had not caught up with events as the glow faded in the distance, and it wasn't until my heartbeat returned to normal that the obvious became apparent: it was a whale. Perhaps with amorous designs on the shapely hull of our sailboat, he had homed in on the sound of the outboard engine. Finding the boat unresponsive, he dove under us and continued on his way, with billions of the famous Cortez bioluminescent plankton signaling their objections to his passage by switching on their tiny lanterns. Relieved, I laughed so loudly that Reeve and Perry started from their bunks and fell into a heap on the cabin sole. We spent the rest of the dark night in quiet speculation on the wonders of Baja, the only other sounds being the purr of the engine and the gurgle of the coffee pot.

****

I found wonderfully sculpted rock formations on Isla Espíritu Santo.

CHAPTER 2

THE BOTTOM LINE

Baja California has the most diverse and interesting diving attractions found almost anywhere in the world. On a single trip a diver can hunt for ling cod in a cool-water kelp environment, visit a coral reef, make friends with a huge manta ray, hitch a ride on the fin of a gigantic whale shark, watch sand cascade down steep underwater canyons, and photograph such Indo-Pacific beauties as Moorish idols and longnose butterfly fish. A visit to a mysterious Pacific seamount, where life competes so vigorously for living space that not a square inch of bare rock can be seen, may be followed days later by a dive on a pristine sand bottom devoid of life; devoid, that is, unless you approach slowly and quietly, to find hundreds of slim garden eels swaying in the underwater breezes, ready to disappear instantly into the sand. Individually, these marvels are found elsewhere; collectively they make Baja unique.

Favorite dive locations

A dive trip to Baja, perhaps more than most places, requires careful planning, plenty of time and a high degree of flexibility. Many of the best locations on the Pacific coast are around offshore islands and can be reached only by boat, or are in exposed locations, where wipeout conditions can prevail for weeks at a time. The greatest attractions in the Cortez lie far to the south, or are otherwise hard to reach. Although the peninsula's extreme length and narrow configuration create problems of distance and access, they also provide an advantage shared by few areas in the world: widely divergent weather and water conditions are only a short-to-moderate distance apart. If Sacramento Reef is a wipeout, entirely different conditions are only 189 road miles away at Bahía de los Angeles, and if the surf is up at Cabo San Lucas, Pulmo Reef is probably calm.

The Islas de Todos Santos and the Punta Banda peninsula near Ensenada and the Islas los Coronados west of Tijuana traditionally attract more divers than all other areas of Baja combined. They have much to recommend them: close proximity to the border, easy access and a variety of underwater life. However, people able to make a greater investment in time and effort will find far more beautiful and exotic loca-

tions farther south. Roca Ben and Johnston's Seamount, jutting up almost to the surface south of Isla San Martín, mark the first really unusual dive sites south of the border. Surrounded by marvelously clear deep blue water, their soaring walls and jagged pinnacles are celebrated for their beauty.

If these are beyond the safe limits of your boat or your diving ability, you can get a fair idea of what they are like by visiting Rocas Soledad, 1 1/4 miles off Punta Santo Tomás. At Sacramento Reef and the Islas San Benito, divers will encounter marine life so dense that the areas have been called "biological miracles." The Cape region has good beach access, underwater sandfalls, a number of wrecks and exotic fish. Pulmo Reef, around the turn of the Cape into the Cortez, is one of the few coral reefs on the west coast of North America. Most of the islands along the coast between La Paz and Mulegé and those in the Midriff region are among the finest and least spoiled in the world, especially less accessible spots like Isla las Ánimas Sur. Chapters 9 through 16 contain detailed information on these and many other dive sites.

Diving with the mantas

In 1863 Baja explorer J. Ross Browne summarized the then-current understanding of the Pacific manta ray: "The manta ray is an immense brute of great strength, cunning and ferocity, and is more the terror of the pearl divers than any other creature of the sea...The habit of the animal is to hover at the surface over the pearl divers, obstructing the rays of the sun, and moving as the diver moves, and, when he is obliged to come up for breath, hugging him in his immense flaps until he is suffocated, when the brute, with his formidable teeth and jaws, devours him with gluttonous voracity. Many fishermen and pearl divers have been killed by them."

Recent events at Marisla Seamount (El Bajo Seamount), located northeast of the north end of Isla Espíritu Santo in the Cortez, have shown mantas to be something entirely different from what Browne would lead us to believe. In September 1980 a boat carrying a television crew was anchored on the seamount, filming an American Sportsman show about schooling hammerhead sharks. Aboard were Stan Waterman, Howard Hall, Ted Rulison, Marty Snyderman and novelist

MARTY SNYDERMAN/BAJA EXPEDITIONS

Tim and Nora Means hitch a fantastic ride at Marisla Seamount.

Peter Benchley, of *Jaws* fame. Soon a sixteen-foot manta came by, swimming slowly, something obviously wrong; ropes were fouled around its left wing and ala, a hornlike appendage used to sweep food into its mouth. Closer inspection showed it also had a number of fish hooks embedded in its wings, and a rope had cut deeply near an eye. Sensing the divers wanted to help, the manta let them come close, cut off the rope and remove the hooks. It began swimming more vigorously and allowed one of the divers to climb on its back, taking him for a swooping, soaring ride. Returning the first diver, the fish gave the others a chance, and if a diver dropped off, it would circle back and pick him up. It hung around the entire time the crew was on the seamount, offering rides to whoever wanted them.

No one knows whether the manta knew that humans like to go for rides and was rewarding them, or whether it considered the divers a species of cleaner fish, a sort of giant black wrasse useful for removing hooks and line. In any event, it was not an isolated incident; other Cortez divers have had similar experiences with a number of different mantas. Trips were offered to Marisla Seamount for visits with the mantas until 1984, when the fish became scarce, possibly due to a change in water temperatures induced by El Niño. They returned unexpectedly during the summer of 1989, and perhaps it will again be possible to go for a fantastic ride on the back of a manta.

A dive with the mantas is always an interesting experience,

even if you can't get a ride. They are common along the coast from Loreto to La Paz, especially between July and October. There is no certain way to get close to a manta. They are aware of your presence long before you are of theirs, and may turn before you come into view. They often nose over in an outside loop, perhaps to see an approaching diver better. Occasionally they will move straight in, make a ninety-degree turn at the last moment and glide away. Chasing them is futile, for they can swim far faster than any diver; when they want to play they will come to you. Some have gray backs, with lighter, V-shaped markings, and are generally less skittish than darker fish (this color difference may be sexual). They quiver all over when touched, and a few seem playful, or at least curious. Divers have hand-fed them with small fish and the mantas soon begin to hang around like hungry dogs.

If they are shy and won't let you near, it may be possible to at least get a look at them. When they are feeding at the surface, their wing tips can be seen some distance away. Since they tend to swim in straight lines, you can maneuver your boat to where you think they will be in five minutes, shut the engine off and quietly slip into the water.

Diving with the hammerheads

Schooling hammerhead sharks have been another major attraction at Marisla. Up to a hundred have been seen swimming in synchronized fashion in large, endless circles. There seems to be little survival value in schooling for a fish at the top of the food chain, and no one has figured out why they do this. At intervals they conduct maneuvers described as "body tilting, head shaking and corkscrewing." They look tough, but are very shy and will flee en masse at the pop of a strobe. Most seem disturbed by the noise a SCUBA regulator makes, and free-divers have a better chance of approaching them than tankers. The sharks appear to present little danger, but there have been minor incidents. During a study a number of years ago, six snorkelers were in the water with about five hundred hammerheads for a week, and several bumping incidents occurred. No damage was done, but the sharks apparently wanted to get a message across. Recently a diver, accompanied by his wife, was photographing the hammerheads when she nudged him to get his attention. Too intent on the sharks to be distracted, he ignored her, generating another nudge, and then another. Finally he turned around and found it wasn't his wife at all! The best time to visit the sharks is late summer and early fall, although evidence is accumulating that they may be present year-round.

Diving with the biggest fish in the sea

Because they do not breach or spy-hop like gray whales, making them difficult to spot, whale sharks have been considered rare in Baja. However, recent organized efforts to locate them have proved that they are more common than was once believed, and they have become the object of a good deal of interest. A small number of Baja divers have been able to approach them, sometimes spending considerable periods of time swimming alongside, and a lucky few have had the extraordinary experience of riding on their huge dorsal fins like jockeys.

Adult whale sharks can approach forty-five feet in length, and there have been reports of fish seventy feet long. They are among the few sharks whose mouth is located at the end of the snout, rather than being underslung, making them look like wingless underwater 747s. With their six-foot-wide mouths open, they swim at about three knots, collecting vast quantities of plankton, crustaceans and small fish with sievelike gill rakers, straining almost a million gallons of water an hour. They prefer deep water, and surface only occasionally to bask and feed, often at rips where currents meet. Small schools have been seen, but they tend to be solitary animals.

In the summer of 1977, two twenty-footers grazed off Puerto Escondido for several hours, allowing snorkelers to ride their great dorsal fins and causing a great commotion ashore. Dawn Breese was able to ride a plankton-grazing female for twenty minutes in Bahía las Ánimas in August 1984. One event has suggested that there may be more to their intellect than might be believed. Ted Rulison and Flip Nicklin were riding on the dorsal of a forty-footer when it stopped and rested its chin on their vessel's anchor chain. Using its great weight, it pressed down until finally the chain was curved in a U-shape. Then it slowly swam forward, dragging chain along its entire underside. It was scratching its tummy! Not so dumb!

There seems to be no great difficulty in approaching a whale shark once one is located. When it wishes to break off

Two divers record the passage of a gigantic whale shark.

JIM TOBIN/BAJA EXPEDITIONS

the encounter it will make a steep dive, as if it knew the tiny creature clinging to it is an air-breathing mammal. In spite of its bulk, a whale shark can move fast when spooked; Sigurd Tesche bumped a twenty-footer with a camera, and within seconds it was out of sight. The only danger encountered by divers has occurred when they have attempted to hang onto the tail and have been violently swished back and forth in a fifteen-foot arc, tearing off fins, masks and SCUBAs.

Because of their habits and relatively small numbers, a dive with a whale shark is largely a target of opportunity. Fishermen have reported them to be most numerous off the Cape region, especially around the Bancos Gorda, between May and October. As many as a dozen have been spotted in a single day in this area, although this is highly unusual. They also have been seen around Marisla Seamount, primarily in August and September.

Spearfishing locations

Baja California has many fine spearfishing areas. On the Pacific side the Benitos have the best white sea bass and yellowtail hunting found anywhere, and Sacramento Reef has moderate numbers of black sea bass. The Midriff region, especially around the southwest coast of Isla Tiburón, probably has the best spearfishing in the Cortez. In 1972 Don Barthman bagged a 550 pound jewfish off Punta Willard on Tiburón, the largest ever taken free-diving. Punta Púlpito,

Barthman's big fish. Left to right: Gary Faulkner, Bill Bishopp, Bob Jackson and Don Barthman (hand on spear).

LLOYD WHITENECK

south of Mulegé, has exciting spearfishing for grouper and yellowtail.

The above areas are relatively difficult to reach, but there are many other places where off-the-beach divers and those with only small cartop boats or inflatables can find good spearfishing. Large gamefish sweep into the deep water at Cabo Frailes, located south of Pulmo Reef, which can be reached by sedan. Los Candeleros, a group of rocky islets south of Loreto, have many fish and are only a few miles off a beach with close road access. The reef areas centered around Roca Lobos south of Isla San Marcos are within easy range of a boat launched at Caleta San Lucas. Several new roads and improvements to existing roads now provide easy access to a number of fine spearfishing areas, including that from KM 63+ on the Transpeninsular Highway south of Loreto to Bahía Agua Verde. The road from Bahía de los Angeles to Bahía San Francisquito allows cartoppers and small trailerboats relatively easy access to Islas Salsipuedes and San Lorenzo in the Midriff. On the Pacific coast, Isla Asunción and the reefs off Punta Abreojos are much easier to approach since road improvements were completed.

Spearfishermen should avoid a few places. Pulmo Reef, the harbor at Cabo San Lucas and Scammon's Lagoon are underwater parks. Many biologists and sport divers believe certain other areas should also be given park status because of their profusion of underwater life (not necessarily big fish) and unspoiled nature, including the reef southeast of Isla la Ventana in Bahía de los Angeles, Isla las Ánimas Sur and the wreck of the *Salvatierra* near La Paz. Foragers should avoid removing slow-growing shellfish and other sessile life from the tiny diveable areas of seamounts like Rocas Soledad, Roca Ben, Johnston's Seamount, Roca Pináculo (the one at the Benitos) and Marisla Seamount, for this quickly destroys their beauty and their value to others.

Licensing requirements, species, seasons and so forth described in the following chapter generally apply to spearfishermen as well. Specific bag limits apply to spearfishing, and the taking of corals and gorgonians is prohibited. In early 1991 new regulations adopted by the Mexico Department of Fisheries limited spearfishing to free-diving and rubber- or spring-powered guns only. These regulations change frequently, and it is essential that divers get a current copy and study it. Mexico enforces wastage laws, and due to the remoteness of many spearfishing locations it is often difficult or impossible to place fish under refrigeration, so limit what you shoot to fish that can be consumed right away.

A fine collection of wrecks

During Baja's four-hundred-year maritime history, over 800 vessels, and possibly twice that number, have been lost along its Pacific coast and in the Cortez—a wonderful array of barks, barges, barkentines, brigs, tugs, ferryboats, full-rigged ships, junks, LCIs, Liberty ships, paddlewheel steamers, schooners, screw steamers, sloops, sportfishing vessels, submarines, tuna clippers, yachts, subchasers and a destroyer. Their nationalities include the United States, Mexico, Canada, Colombia, England, Denmark, Japan, Greece, Ecuador and Peru. Many sank in deep water and are beyond reach, but some are in known locations shallow enough that they can be reached by divers. Many lie in remote areas and others require decompression diving, but some are easy to get to and a few can even be explored with mask and snorkel.

The sea has strange habits, and a few wrecks in the most exposed locations on the west coast of North America still have major parts visible, like the tanker *Swift Eagle*, run ashore on Benito Oeste in 1934. Many others lying in protected locations are quickly reduced to rubble, such as the shrimper *San Gabriel*, sunk in placid Bahía Concepción in 1981. Novice divers often have unrealistic expectations about what they will encounter—an almost intact "Hollywood" wreck sitting sedate and upright on a flat bottom—and will almost certainly be disappointed, for these are rarities in Baja, and the term "wreckage" diving is often more appropriate. It often takes careful examination even to tell that anything is there at all, such as the remains of the paddlewheel steamer *Sacramento*, lost on Sacramento Reef in 1872.

Although most Baja wrecks are widely scattered, a few areas contain the bones of many ships. The outer shores of islands forming Bahías Magdalena and las Almejas contain more major shipwrecks than anywhere else in Baja, including the steamers *Indiana*, *Colombia* and *Westbank Park*, and the U.S. submarine *H-1*, as well as lesser wrecks like the fishing vessel *Shasta*. Although not diveable, the great paddlewheel

Joe Harold Brown investigates a "blip" near the wreck of the sailing ship *John Elliott Thayer*.

steamers *Independence* and *Golden City* were also lost there, and there are a number of sizable wrecks on the beaches north of Cabo San Lázaro. Another interesting site is Sacramento Reef, where dozens of vessels have been lost, the schooner *Goodwill* and the *Sacramento* being of prime interest. The San Roque/Asunción area also has a number of wrecks, including the steamer *San José*, aground on Isla San Roque in 1921. The Midriff region and Canal San Lorenzo near La Paz each has one major wreck, the great sailing ship *John Elliott Thayer* and the ferry *Salvatierra*.

The descriptions in this book have been limited to wrecks of interest to divers and a few of historical or human interest. Maritime histories usually include only vessels above a given size, say fifty tons, but no limit has been made here, because some very small wrecks, such as that at Isla el Racito, provide better diving than larger ones, like the steamer *San José*. If you locate a wreck and can't put a name on it or would like to know something of its history, I have a computerized file of 840 Baja wrecks and would be happy to exchange information. Write in care of the publisher.

Mexico has strict laws concerning salvage diving, especially on wrecks of historical or archaeological interest. In addition, the United States is a signatory to a United Nations multilateral convention on cultural property, and U.S. law prohibits importation of certain objects of historical or archaeological value. There seems to be no law restricting casual hands-off visits to wrecks, but unless you are part of an authorized expedition having the required permits, you would be well advised to touch or remove nothing. You may be judged by the equipment you carry; possession of air lifts and sand blasters may be taken as prima facie evidence of intent.

Sales, service and air

As *The Baja Adventure Book* went to press, independent dive shops were in operation in Ensenada (Almar, El Yaqui), La Bufadora (La Bufadora Dive), Mulegé (Mulegé Divers), Loreto (Deportes Blazer), La Paz (Baja Diving & Service, Baja Sur Internacional) and Cabo San Lucas (Amigos del Mar). Hotel/resort shops were in operation at the Baja Beach & Tennis Club near Ensenada, the Stouffer Presidente Hotel near Loreto (Fantasia Destinations), Hotel Punta Pescadero, Rancho Leonero (East Cape Divers), the Hotel Palmilla (Dive Palmilla), the Hotel Cabo San Lucas (Cabo Acuadeportes) and the Hotel Hacienda Beach Resort (Cabo Acuadeportes), the last five all in the Cape region. Even though they may lack an in-house dive shop, most beach-front hotels and resorts have snorkeling equipment available for guests and can arrange dive trips.

In past years Punta San Francisquito Resort maintained a small dive shop, but as of press time, its status was unclear. The dive operation at Bahía de los Angeles has closed, and although Loreto Divers is out of business, there is a new dive shop in town (Deportes Blazer, included in the summary above).

Further information on dive shops can be found in Chapters 9, 13, 14 and 15. Most of these businesses are not the full-service dive shops you may be used to. Sales and rentals are normally confined to basic equipment and then not in all sizes, styles and types, and few regulators are available.

REEVE PETERSON

Ramon Carballo tells of wrecks that occurred near Bahía Magdalena when he was a young man.

Repairs and spare parts are virtually nonexistent. Some hotel/resort operations limit sales, rentals and services to guests only and a few close during the off-season. Several independent shops operate at the whim of the owner, who may be off chasing turtles when you need to have your tanks pumped. None of the shops will pump out-of-hydro tanks, and a few ask for VIP. All require certification from those requesting air, SCUBA equipment sales or rentals and SCUBA trips. Few have more than one compressor, and since parts are difficult to obtain, a breakdown can leave a shop without air for months. Air is not subject to periodic testing, and a visiting diver cannot assess its quality, so it is advisable to ask to see the compressor. While a clean and obviously well-maintained compressor does not guarantee good air, the reverse is frequently true. Many sporting goods stores, hardware shops and supermarkets carry masks, snorkels and fins.

Boats and diving equipment

Excellent off-the-beach diving with good road access is available, especially at Punta Banda, south of Ensenada, at San Sebastián, south of Mulegé, and in the Cape region at Pulmo Reef and between San José del Cabo and Cabo San Lucas, and a number of the dive shops noted above offer day-trips on *pangas*, cruisers, platform boats, etc. However, true to the Protestant work ethic, almost all of the most interesting and least picked-over dive sites are in remote and inaccessible areas, and a boat is almost a necessity for full enjoyment of Baja diving. Because distances from launch to dive site are generally too great, paddleboards have limited usefulness, although in a few compact locations with close road access, like Punta Banda, San Sebastián and Pulmo, they

can be great fun. See Chapter 4 for information on bringing your own boat to Baja.

Traditional twelve-foot aluminum boats are too small for most Baja diving conditions, lacking the seaworthiness, speed, range and load-carrying ability necessary to make them useful in any but the most limited circumstances. Years ago Reeve and I made a night dive off Punta Banda in a twelve-footer. Arriving alongside at the same time with a huge bag of goodies, and not realizing the other person was there, each of us tried to hoist himself aboard, tipping the boat over. It was rough and we could not bail, and we had to free-dive to the ocean floor to recover our equipment. I had dropped my light, but fortunately it was turned on, and I could see the shaft of light on the bottom. It took almost an hour to collect our gear and swim the sodden mess to shore. The goodies were recovered and shortly thereafter were boiled and served with garlic butter and Chianti.

While they do not normally have diving platforms or boarding ladders, local *pangas* and cruisers discussed in the next chapter are otherwise suitable for diving. Along Cortez coasts, the owner-guide is almost always a fisherman, and few have much to offer divers beyond advice on geography and weather conditions, although local dive shops can often provide qualified guides. Mexican abalone and sea urchin divers along the Pacific coast are knowledgeable about local conditions, dive sites and wrecks, and make excellent guides. However, they tend to ignore technicalities like decompression procedures, and their hooka compressors are usually castoffs from refrigerators, so bring your own equipment and

Reeve suits up for a night dive.

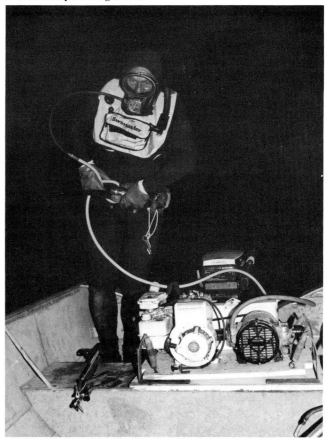

keep your own counsel as to bottom times and surface intervals.

Divers traveling by private vehicle have a great deal of mobility and may encounter a wide variety of conditions, requiring a full range of equipment. Most people need a full quarter-inch wet suit year-round along the Pacific coast south to Abreojos, and in the Cortez south to the Midriff region from late fall to late spring. Lighter suits may be in order elsewhere, depending on your metabolism and the thickness of your subcutaneous fat. In protected areas of the Cortez even shorty suits may not be necessary during summer. There is no ready access to a SCUBA compressor in vast areas of Baja, but a portable compressor or hooka will provide complete flexibility in the location and duration of dives. Take special precautions to protect such equipment from dust. Since you will probably end up doing a lot of free-diving, a low-volume mask and a shotgun snorkel are assets. A supply of batteries, bulbs, O-rings, rubbers, wishbones and wet suit cement is essential.

Underwater photography

The realities of Baja diving are such that you will probably be happier with the reliability, simplicity and small size of a Nikonos rather than a big pressure cooker with your Nikon F inside. Because of the great tides in the northern Cortez, visibility can change radically in a short time, and a variety of lenses is needed, especially wide-angle. Dust is pervasive, so every piece of camera equipment should be sealed in a Ziploc bag, and accessible O-rings should be checked before each dive. Bring all the film you plan to use, for selection in Baja is limited, especially medium-format films like 120 and 220. Common camera batteries and flashlight batteries for strobes can usually be found, but the chance of finding a high-voltage battery used on some older strobes is zero. If you use rechargeables, bring a charger; RV parks, hotels, resorts and dive boats operate on 110-volt 60-cycle. Processing for C-41 color print film is available in most larger towns, but other films can take a great deal of time. Polaroid's 35mm transparency film and processor can provide valuable feedback early in the trip.

Dive safety

Heavy kelp, ocean waves, surge and currents occur along the Pacific coast. Although kelp is absent and heavy surge is uncommon in the Cortez, strong tidal currents are frequently encountered, especially in the northern and Midriff regions. When diving out of a boat, always leave someone aboard who knows how to operate it, and use a long trailer line. A diver's knife is essential; there has been an explosive growth of fishing in most of Baja's waters, and there is a remote danger of becoming entangled in a length of monofilament or a gill net. Although shark incidents are remarkably few, there are large numbers present in some locations, and standard avoidance techniques found in any good dive manual should be followed. All in all, the greatest dangers to divers in Baja are self-inflicted: inadequate equipment, poor training, overexertion and foolishness—and running into cows while unwisely driving at night on the Transpeninsular.

Divers working Baja's Pacific coast for sea urchin and abalone.

Decompression facilities

The laws of physics and physiology have not been repealed, and divers can get the bends as easily in Baja as anywhere else; in 1987 a diver doubled over in pain soon after two or three dives to about 100 feet at Marisla Seamount and had to be flown to San Diego. The nearest available U.S. decompression chamber is at the Hyperbaric Medicine Center of the University of California, San Diego. Chambers also exist at El Rosario, Isla Cedros, Isla Natividad and Bahía Tortugas. A chamber has been received at the health clinic at Puerto San Carlos, but as of early 1991 it was not yet in operation. Except in a dire emergency, they should be avoided, and an ailing diver should be rushed to the UCSD facility. The Baja chambers are owned by fishing cooperatives, which may not operate year-round, and their compressors use locally generated electricity or small gasoline engines. Many are in a state of disrepair and are not equipped with filters, heating or intercoms, and qualified operators and adequate medical attention are virtually nonexistent. However, since no one can foresee all possible circumstances, directions to these chambers will be found in Chapters 10, 12 and 14. The village near Punta Eugenia also has a chamber, but when last seen it appeared to be permanently non-operational and had been converted into a playhouse knee-deep in Tonka trucks, plastic bazookas and a foam rubber Miss Piggy.

Dive boat trips

A multi-day trip on a vessel operating out of San Diego or La Paz is a fine introduction to Baja diving. They visit the best areas and provide comfortable accommodations, lots of good diving and minimum hassle. *Sand Dollar* and *Bottom Scratcher* out of San Diego (Diving Charters, Inc.) make trips down the Pacific coast to the Coronados, San Martín, Sacramento Reef and the Benitos. Baja Expeditions offers trips that visit Los Islotes, Marisla Seamount, Isla las Ánimas Sur, the Midriff and other diving attractions in the Cortez, as well as Isla Socorro, 322 miles to the south. *Marisla* offers dive trips throughout the southern Cortez. See & Sea Travel Service, Inc. has trips to Las Ánimas Sur, the reef at Isla San Diego, Marisla Seamount and other locations aboard the schooner *Elias Mann*. She also makes trips to Socorro. Ocean Voyages offers charters out of La Paz on the compressor-equipped sailboat *Pacemaker*. Fraser Charters, Inc. offers charters on the seventy-two-foot compressor-equipped cruiser *Ambar III* out of La Paz.

All boats operate seasonally, so get a schedule before your plans get too far along. If you are a spearfisherman or a shell collector ask first; some boats encourage it, some don't. There is often an unwritten rule: no large groupers or jewfish. Most boats supply tanks, weights and backpacks, but check before going. All limit SCUBA diving to certified divers.

****

FOUR HARD LESSONS. Some learn about diving at a NAUI or PADI course, others attend the school of hard knocks. Many years ago I learned four hard lessons at this school during a dive trip with Dick Mandich and Reeve to Isla Turners in the Midriff. On the first day we were exploring a cave when we saw two groupers, one behind the other. Wow, we thought! What a chance—two fish with one shot! Urged on by my brother, I aimed and pulled the trigger, and the six-foot shaft shot through both fish and hit the back of the cave. Unfortunately, the three heavy rubber slings had not ended their travel, and they drove the gun backwards, dealing a sharp blow to my chin. I saw stars for a few minutes, but when I recovered I found I still had both fish and the only damage was a painful jaw. Had the gun hit my faceplate things would have been quite different. The fish were not as big as they seemed and we ate them for supper.

The next day we went for a night dive, and in the first cave our lights shone on an almost unbelievable object, a giant, fluorescent goldfish. About 3 or 4% of leopard groupers assume this coloration when they reach ten inches, for reasons not understood. Suddenly, it spooked and came rushing out of the cave, its nose dealing a painful blow to the inside of my leg, avoiding major tragedy only by inches.

Although I could barely walk the next morning and my jaw was so sore I could hardly hold a snorkel in my mouth, we decided to do some foraging. We kicked north toward a large bird rock several hundred yards away. Visibility had decreased and we could not see the bottom, a clue that we carelessly ignored. Like three black submarines with their sonars out of operation, we blindly proceeded. Uneasy feelings finally descended on us, and when we looked up to get our bearings we knew we were in big trouble; a strong current was sweeping us away from the island. Kicking against the current proved futile, so we turned in hopes that we could reach the edge of the current. Although we knew we could outflank it sooner or later, we faced a long swim, and no one was around to help if we cramped up or became exhausted.

Waltraude Kuhn spots a playful octopus at Los Islotes.

HELMET HORN

We were about to abandon our goody bags when we began to make some progress, and we finally arrived back at camp cold, extremely tired and considerably smarter.

It was time for more innocent pursuits, so I rigged up my F in its housing and attached a big strobe. Cruising along, I hyped up, kicked down and started to take photographs of beautiful nudibranchs. There were some great scenes through the viewfinder, and I began to fantasize I was no longer man-the-hunter but an artist, paying homage to beauty. However, on the tenth dive I learned something about human nature, mine at least. A lobster convention was in progress in a cave, which was chock-full of them. Did I back off, focus the lens, set the f-stop, compose the picture and take a marvelous photograph of this amazing scene? No! I threw my $1,500 rig aside, shot to the surface and raced back to the boat to get Reeve and several gunny sacks. Within twenty minutes we were back in the boat with two bulging sacks (we didn't know at the time that the Mexican Fish and Game frowns on such conduct), celebrating our luck with cold cervezas, when I suddenly remembered my camera. It took a dozen free-dives to find it, and as I lay panting in the bottom of the boat, sore jaw throbbing and leg aching, I realized I could have had it all: I could have taken some great photos and THEN bagged the bugs.

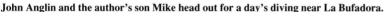

John Anglin and the author's son Mike head out for a day's diving near La Bufadora.

CHAPTER 3
FISHING FUNDAMENTALS

"Fish pileup!" "A . . . continuous school [of tuna] . . . a hundred miles long!" "Acres of roosterfish!" "Terms such as 'schools,' 'shoals,' or even 'armies' are inadequate to convey the enormity of a ten-mile-long horde of gamefish feeding on a still larger body of forage fish." Like thousands of others, I can still remember the first time I read Ray Cannon's marvelous tales of Baja fishing in his classic 1966 book, *The Sea of Cortez*. Today they provide a magical spice that flavors fond memories of long-ago trips to the Sea.

It is hard to comprehend the changes that have occurred since Ray's book was published. At that time paved roads heading south from the U.S. border ended at San Felipe and north of San Quintín. Fishing in the western and southern Cortez was limited largely to fly-in anglers and those who came in off-road vehicles, although if you had the time you could drive to Mazatlan and take a ferry to La Paz. Fishing along the Pacific coast south of the roadhead was limited to off-road drivers and those with the price of a trip on a long-range boat or access to a yacht. In those days you had to be either rich or rugged, and for the average man a Baja fishing trip was the stuff of dreams.

All this changed when the Transpeninsular Highway opened in 1973, making it possible to fish Baja waters without a huge outlay of time or money. Dozens of hotels and resorts, ranging from modest to magnificent, now cater to fishermen, and rental and charter boats are available in many locations, from humble skiffs to fine diesel fishing cruisers. Ramps for trailerboats have been constructed in a number of key locations, and cartoppers and inflatables can be launched across hundreds of beaches. Although paved roads still reach Pacific shores in only a handful of locations between El Rosario and the Cape, and facilities are extremely limited, drivers with ordinary pickups can now fish hundreds of miles of remote coast, and trailerboat sailors have access to huge Bahía Magdalena and its rich offshore banks, and to Bahía Tortugas and the islands to the northwest.

The big eight

Eight of the most sought-after gamefish in Baja's waters are black, blue and striped marlin, sailfish, wahoo, rooster-fish, dolphin and yellowtail. The sources of their popularity are threefold: they are powerful, often spectacular fighters; they exist in fairly large numbers; and they are found in waters close enough to shore that fishermen with trailerboats, cartoppers and inflatables can reach them safely.

Billfish

To many people, when you talk Baja fishing, you are talking about billfishing in the Cape region, which offers a world-class fishery for these magnificent fighters. In fact, striped marlin fishing at the Cape is almost four times better than in Southern California, requiring an average of only 1.95 days of effort per fish as opposed to 7.29. These results were last tabulated in 1984, and conditions in the Cape region have often been even more favorable in recent years.

Billfish feed on almost anything in the sea, including squid, yellowfin tuna, albacore, mullet, mackerel, dolphin, flying fish, paper nautilus and their own kind. Although most are caught on surface baits, they feed at any depth, even taking such bottom-dwellers as octopus. When hungry they are fearless, and have been known to use their bills to stun and stab. They have poor memories, proved by the fact that there are many records of individual fish being hooked over and over again. Most large "bills" are females.

Black marlin are among the most prized gamefish in the world. Large, powerful and determined, they have been called "the bulls of the sea." They can be differentiated from other marlin by the fact that their pectoral fins cannot be folded flat against the body, and by relatively small, rounded anal and first dorsal fins. Mackerel and squid are favorite foods. Found in tropical parts of the Indian and Pacific oceans, the biggest fish come from Australia, with no current (1991) International Game Fish Association (IGFA) records from Baja. Blacks are encountered from June to December in the Cape region, and off Isla Cerralvo in May and June, although their appearance is erratic and there are a number of year-round residents.

Found in the Cape region primarily from June through the fall, Pacific blue marlin are the strongest fighters of all billfish. They are more acrobatic than blacks, often jumping and sounding to great depths, and probably no more than one out of ten hookups is boated. More numerous and slightly slimmer than blacks, their anal and first dorsal fins are more pointed and proportionately longer, and their pectoral fins can fold flat against the body. Their food is largely offshore fish, especially skipjack. Five current IGFA records are from Baja, including a 315-pound fish caught on 8-pound test line at East Cape in 1990, an astounding weight/test ratio of over 39:1. Baja's memorable "Year of the Blues" was 1983, when daily catches of as many as four 300-pound blues per boat were recorded.

There are probably more stuffed striped marlin hanging on the barbershop walls of America than all other billfish combined. The most abundant and frequently caught of all Baja billfish, they are fantastic jumpers, often wearing themselves out more with their leaps, pirouettes and greyhounding (swimming rapidly while breaking the surface with a series of long, low jumps) than in fighting the drag, a few jumping more than a hundred times. They can be distinguished from other marlin by an obvious lateral line and vertical stripes, and their high, pointed first dorsal fin, which is usually equal to or slightly longer than the greatest body height. They are primarily surface feeders. Stripers are found in the Cape region all year, and they migrate as far north as the Midriff region and San Diego in the warm months, often coming close to shore. Four current IGFA records are from Cabo San Lucas, one from Las Cruces. One is a dazzler—a 132-pounder taken off Cabo San Lucas in 1989 on 2-pound test, a remarkable 66:1 weight/test ratio.

Easily identified by a prominent lateral line and tremendous first dorsal fin, Pacific sailfish are a favorite with fishermen because of their hard fight and acrobatic skills, although light tackle is preferred since they lack the staying power of their marlin cousins. They feed at all hours, but are most active at night. They tend to form schools, sometimes with as many as forty members. Sailfish are common between June and the end of December from Bahía Magdalena to the Midriff, with some year-round fish in the Cape region. Two current IGFA records are from Baja, both set more than twenty years ago. The most durable of all world records from Baja waters is the women's 50-pound-line-class sailfish, set at La Paz in 1950 with a 192-pound fish.

Sailfish can drive men to a certain madness. A number of years ago Rich Brown was fishing off Loreto in a *panga* when he hooked a big one. He finally got it alongside, but when the guide whacked it with a billy, the leader broke and the fish started to sink. Fully clothed and wearing boots, Rich dove in and caught it about thirty feet down. On the way back to town Rich and his partner toasted their good luck with a six-pack of Tecate. Their guide joined in, but his toasts were to luck of a different sort. Because the guide could not speak English, it was not until they returned to the hotel that they learned that three days earlier a customer in the same boat had also caught a sailfish, but only the bloody front half.

Since they are pursued by legions of skilled sportfishermen, a great deal is known about baits and techniques for billfish. While there are differences among the four species, it all boils down to just two basic methods: drifting a live bait

A magnificent striped marlin loses a fight.

GARY KRAMER

or trolling with a large whole bait like bonito, mackerel or ballyhoo or an artificial lure specially designed for bills. A marlin lure is generally about a foot long and has a clear plastic head with large eyes and prismatic strips of color embedded inside, and a brightly colored vinyl skirt. A heavy fifteen-foot monofilament (mono) leader runs through the head to a hook hidden in the skirt. Record marlin have been caught with everything from 2-pound "button thread" to 130-pound "telephone cable," so there is hope for fishermen using almost any type of tackle, but those after blues and blacks probably will be better off with the heavy-duty trolling rig described later, those after stripers and sailfish with the medium-duty trolling rig. Use a ball-bearing swivel and a heavy mono leader, with the drag set at one-quarter to one-third of line test.

Since bills tend to be unevenly distributed, asking around for recent information before you go out often pays off. They don't move far during the night, so if you find them one day, they should not be far away the next. Different species have slightly different habitat preferences. Blacks are sometimes found near seamounts and pinnacles, stripers a half-mile or so away, and blues in deeper water still farther away. Search for an area of clean, clear, warm water, determine its limits, and stay there by trolling in large circles or back and forth in straight lines. Troll an artificial just past the wake, at a speed high enough that it occasionally breaks the surface, probably about six knots. If a fish follows an artificial but won't take it, slow down, reel in and simultaneously let out a live bait on another line. They have color vision, so experiment with different colors if you are using artificials.

Stripers, and to a lesser extent other species, will "fin" or "sleep" on the surface with the top of their dorsal and caudal (tail) fins exposed, especially in calm weather. Binoculars are thus a vital piece of equipment. In good years it is not unusual to see twenty or thirty finning stripers in a day of fishing at the Bancos Gorda off San José del Cabo, often keeping company in groups of two or three. Careful helmsmanship can place a bait in an irresistible position. When you see a fish, put on a live bait, let it out sixty or seventy yards and troll slowly in a large circle, with no changes in throttle. Try to place it within sight of the fish, then stop and let the bait swim freely. Stripers are sometimes not too concerned about boats and may let you troll within twenty or thirty yards without spooking. However, avoid putting a wake over a finning or sleeping fish. If this scheme doesn't work and you have heavy casting gear aboard, stop the engine, drift down on the fish from upwind, and drop a bait or lure right in front of it.

Sometimes "tailing" fish are seen, swimming with the swell, at about the same speed. This usually occurs in the late afternoon when the winds have come up. The most effective way to handle such fish is to get well ahead, start trolling a lure or bait and then slow down, letting the fish catch up.

You don't have to be an experienced fisherman to get a shot at a billfish, and you don't need a yacht equipped with outriggers, a fighting chair and a spotting tower. A modest trailerboat, an inflatable or even a cartopper will do. In addition to rod and reel and other tackle, bring a large cooler and a bucket. Get up early and launch in the inner harbor at Cabo San Lucas. Fill your cooler with sea water and buy live

mackerel offered from boats in the harbor; four or five per person should last for an entire day. The bait should stay frisky if you drain half the water every half-hour and refill. Run between three and six miles south of Cabo Falso and shut off the engine. Rig a hook and leader, but do not use a weight. Hook a mackerel through the nose, damaging it as little as possible, and simply let it swim about sixty or eighty yards away from the boat before setting the drag, and wait.

It might take five minutes, five hours or five days, but your chances of getting a hookup using this method are excellent, the most likely fish being a striper of between 125 and 150 pounds. When it happens, your modest boat has a number of distinct advantages over larger craft: your engine can be tilted up, the shallow hull offers few opportunities for snags, and if

John Anglin's striper was over half the length and three-quarters the weight of our cartop boat.

the fish runs under the hull you can put the tip of your rod underwater if necessary to keep the line from touching the hull. A fish may drag you for miles, but it will be a fight to remember. Release the fish unharmed if you can, but if it is too badly injured, don't believe the rumor that stripers are poor eating. Like all marlin, they are excellent, especially if they are bled by cutting the gills and quickly cooled.

Wahoo!!

It has been claimed that the name is derived from the shouts of people who catch them, for wahoo are among the swiftest fish in the sea, capable of reaching fifty miles an hour, and they can spool you before you know what happened. Related to mackerel and tuna, they inhabit tropical and warmer temperate waters. Their bodies are slim and powerful, with a shape like barracuda, except that the first dorsal fin of a wahoo is much longer. They are pelagic and tend to swim alone or in small groups. Their migratory habits are hard to pin down. Wahoo like to winter at the Cape, returning to more northerly locations off Bahía Magdalena and in the southern Cortez in warmer months. Off Bahía Magdalena and at Banco Thetis they are found from June to December, off Cabo San Lucas all year, being most numerous from December to April, and from East Cape to north of La Paz from June to November. However, water temperatures can alter this pattern drastically, and during El Niño years, wahoo have been caught at the Islas los Coronados. Most are taken in water of at least seventy-six degrees. Although they grow to over 155 pounds in the Atlantic, Baja waters typically produce fish from 30 to 60 pounds, and no current IGFA world records are from Baja.

Wahoo feed on almost anything they can catch, which is almost everything, but they prefer flying fish, mullet, ballyhoo, mackerel and squid, and will take artificials, especially those that make surface noise. Trolling or casting vinyl-skirted and natural feather lures and jigs are the most popular methods, but on long-range trips down the Pacific coast between half and three-quarters of all wahoo are taken on live bait. They are not plentiful, but good numbers are taken at Banco Thetis and Rocas Alijos off Baja's Pacific coast, in the Cape region, especially at Bancos San Jaime and Gorda, at the south tip of Cerralvo, and off the east side of Isla Espíritu Santo. Wahoo are notorious morning-biters, and the best time of day is from first light until two hours after dawn. Since the hotel boats get going too late, plan to use your own. Because they have bony mouths and they often shake their heads violently when they feel the hook, a relatively stiff rod and dacron line are best, and hooks must be needle-sharp. A wire leader is necessary, but avoid bright-finish snaps and swivels. Make sure swivels do not ride at the surface, for wahoo will strike at the trail of bubbles, cutting the line. Because they are attracted by turbulence, place your lure at the end of the wake and be ready for close-in strikes. Wear shoes and use a billy at the first opportunity, for a wahoo will bite you if given the chance.

Wahoo are great jumpers, sometimes causing surprises. Many years ago a fisherman trolling for marlin in an outboard at Banco Gorda reeled in his lure to clear a foul. This done, he started to let out, when all hell broke loose; a wahoo grabbed the lure only thirty feet out, dove straight down, turned under the boat and headed for the sky, flying right over

the boat, the line making a full circle. The fisherman instantly considered the alternatives and dove in with rod in-hand, coming up on the other side of the boat. The fish started to tow him away, but someone managed to snag him by the collar with a boat hook. His efforts were not in vain, and the fish ended up on the barbecue that night. A number of years ago another wahoo was similarly unlucky when it smashed through the galley window of the long-range boat *Red Rooster* during lunch and landed on a table in front of a group of startled fishermen. It too ended up on the barbecue. They are fine eating, with firm, fine-grained white flesh. Wahoo don't always come out on the short end—several years ago a fisherman aboard the *Royal Star* was attacked by a wahoo while on a long-range trip and had to be flown back to San Diego, where surgeons reattached three ligaments in his left arm. To make it worse, the wahoo had not even been hooked! While chasing another fisherman's lure, it jumped twelve feet into the air, smashed into the unlucky man, landed on the deck and escaped over the side with a tale to tell its children!

A wahoo comes over the rail.

Roosterfish

Roosterfish have gray and silver bodies, with spectacular dorsal rays, which they erect when excited. Voracious predators of small fishes, they generally are found on shallow reefs and sandy bottoms from the surf line out to very moderate depths, usually no more than fifteen feet, especially where shallow rocky bottoms come up to meet sandy beaches. Fishable populations extend from Bahía Magdalena to the Cape and as far north as Mulegé, the greatest concentrations being at East Cape. Baja is the best place in the world to fish for large roosters. Of nineteen current IGFA records from throughout the world, five are from La Paz, four from East Cape, two from Cabo San Lucas and one from Loreto, a total of twelve. The all-tackle record is a 114-pound fish taken at La Paz in 1960.

Fishing for these finicky, exciting fish is a real challenge. Often reputed to take only live bait, they will sometimes fall for artificials, especially in the surf or during a feeding frenzy. However, no single artificial produces consistently, and most fish are taken by slow trolling live bait, especially ladyfish, needlefish, halfbeaks, grunts and mullet, the last being the bait of choice. Roosters have no sharp teeth, so metal leaders are unnecessary. Live baits tend to be too large for roosters to swallow immediately, so they drop them and hit again, especially if a feeding frenzy is not going on, making it difficult to know when to strike. Trollers often proceed at about one or two knots with the reel clutch out, the spool held with a thumb. When a strike is felt, the spool is released, allowing the fish to take the bait without resistance, and after five or ten seconds the hook is set. Once a school is located, usually involving less than a dozen fish, it pays to stop and drift a live bait. Roosters hit hard and are powerful, long-range fighters, often greyhounding with their great dorsal fins raised, and some have been known to beach themselves in an effort to get away.

Favorite areas include the coast south from La Paz to Cabo Pulmo, especially Punta Arena de la Ventana and Punta Colorada, and the best months are May through October, primarily July and August, the very best usually being the last two weeks of July and the first two of August. The older fish disappear in the cold months and no one seems to know where they go. Opinion is divided as to their culinary value, but some claim they are good eating if bled and cooled quickly.

A roosterfish comes aboard off Punta Colorada.

GARY KRAMER

Dolphin

Dolphins are the perfect gamefish; they take artificials readily, put on a fantastic aerial ballet of leaps, flips, twists, somersaults and tailwalks when hooked, and if these efforts fail, they provide fine eating. Found throughout the world in tropical and warm temperate seas, they are migratory and tend to be found in schools. Extremely beautiful, they have iridescent blue backs and compressed flanks. Freshly caught dolphins often turn the color and sheen of gold lamé, with waves of blue and green shimmering over their entire bodies.

Their favorite diet consists of squid, flying fish and other small fish, and they can be taken in many ways, primarily by fast trolling dead or strip baits or artificials such as Rapalas or silver spoons fifty or sixty feet back of the boat, or by drifting live bait. Marlin fishermen often catch dolphins, but they are at their best on light tackle—a big meat stick takes the fun out of it. Individuals and small schools sometimes hang around floating objects like oil drums, forklift pallets, planks, logs or seaweed, a habit of great usefulness to fisherman. They are not afraid of boats; it is often possible to look down and see schools milling about, and double and triple hookups are common. They can be chummed, and chunk or strip bait works well once a school has been attracted. It often pays to let them have a free spool for a five-count before clutching in and setting the hook, but from that point on never give a dolphin an inch of slack line. When a fish is caught, his fellows often will escort him to the boat, and they can be taken by casting vinyl skirt or feather lures, especially those with a red and white color scheme. You don't always need a hook and line; in 1986 Sue Dippold and Bernie Eskesen were hiking on a beach south of Bahía Agua Verde when they saw some fish feeding in the clear water of the shallow bay. To their surprise one large fish became so intent on chasing his lunch that he ran right up on the beach! Bernie threw off his pack and scrambled down the cliff in a matter of seconds. The prize? A beautiful three-foot dolphin.

Dolphin are found primarily from Bahía Magdalena to Mulegé in the hot months, although some stay off Cabo San Lucas and East Cape all year. Dolphin pileups have been reported in the Midriff, especially around Isla San Pedro Mártir. In years with unusually warm water they are found as far north as Bahía de los Angeles, but occasionally things are so cool that few are taken in Baja waters. Superb eating (probably sold as mahi-mahi in your local fish market), dolphins do not keep well and should be consumed immediately. Two current IGFA records come from Baja, the men's 4-pound-line-class, 52-pounds 14-ounces, taken at Cabo San Lucas in 1989, and the women's 30-pound-line-class, 73-pounds 11-ounces, taken at Cabo San Lucas in 1962.

Reeve, John Anglin and I were drifting live bait for stripers off the Cape one year when John hooked a dolphin. After a lengthy battle he began to gain some line, his eyes all aglow and war-whoops resounding across the water—his first dolphin! The fish spooked when it saw the boat, and spooked again and then a third time. Finally it was alongside, but just as I bent down to scoop it up with the net, the line broke. I was blamed, of course, and had to endure an hour of criticism and heated instruction. Finally satiated, Reeve and John dozed off, but I kept scanning the horizon for marlin fins. About twenty minutes later I saw something out of the corner

LARRY RAUEN

Gary Kramer displays a dolphin taken off Buena Vista.

of my eye—a large dolphin trailing a line was jumping repeatedly a hundred yards away. Reeve and John leaped up and began to reel in, but they soon found their lines were in a terrible tangle. Efforts to straighten out the mess were futile, and the two of them finally agreed that Reeve's line should be the one to be cut away—it was the one with no tension on it. As the last cut was made John's line went limp—they had cut the wrong one! This two-part tale has been repeated endlessly around campfires ever since, but guess which half?

Yellowtail

The California yellowtail is one of the most abundant and popular gamefish in Baja's Pacific and Cortez waters. In fact, Baja is the California yellowtail capital of the world, for of sixteen current IGFA records, nine are from Baja waters. The location of these records illustrates the wide distribution of the fish: two are from the Coronados, two from Isla San

Martín, one from the Islas San Benito, three from Loreto, and one from La Paz. Of four flyrod world records, two are from Loreto.

Related to amberjack, yellowtail are blue-gray to olive above and silver-white below, and have yellow-tinged fins and a yellow stripe down their sides. Large fish tend to be solitary and often stay in one area, but smaller ones usually join schools and migrate in season. "Psyching" out these migratory patterns is the key to productive fishing. March through December is often best on the Pacific coast south to Bahía Magdalena. In the Cortez their migratory pattern is regular but the dates are hard to predict. As the northern Cortez cools down in winter, yellows head south, leaving Bahía de los Angeles and showing up at Santa Rosalía, then Mulegé and so on, and in summer the migration is reversed. From San Felipe to the Midriff the warmer months are thus often the best, but from Mulegé to La Paz best is often winter and early spring. In the Cape region large numbers are found from January to May. To complicate things, small groups of year-round fish provide good fishing in many locations any time of year. Because of these tendencies it does not pay to

Reeve and I took a fine pair of yellowtail off Isla San Esteban.

PERRY STUDT

fish one area too long; if you are not getting bites, move on.

Yellows are structure-oriented, hanging around rocky points, headlands and reefs, rather than flat, featureless underwater terrain, and are often found under kelp paddies. They feed in the morning and late afternoon on small fish, crabs and other invertebrates, and will take live, strip or chunk bait and cast, trolled or yoyoed jigs, and trolled or cast chrome spoons or swimmer-style lures like Rapalas. Live bait or slabs fished on the bottom in deep water with plenty of lead often take the largest fish. Yellowtail can be strangely unpredictable; when crazed by the sight of squid, they will hit anything in the water, but sometimes they carefully ignore anything with even a suggestion of a protruding hook as they gobble up chum. When schools are "breezing"—swimming at the surface and creating a slight disturbance that looks like a wind ruffle—they may go into a frenzy of competition to see who can get to the bait first, may follow it without biting, or may spook and disappear. A full moon often, but not always, shuts off the bite. They are masters at taking advantage of propellers, rudders, kelp and rocks to break lines. If one tries this, give him a free spool, deceiving him into thinking he has escaped. Yellows hit hard, make long sizzling runs and provide excellent eating.

Favorite spots along the Pacific coast include San Martín and the San Benitos, the latter being the most consistent yellowtail fishery on the west coast of North America. In the Cortez, the chain of islands in the Midriff from Partida Norte to San Lorenzo is highly productive, as is the Loreto area. A washrock 200 yards west of the north tip of Isla Turners may be the most productive location in the Cortez.

A mixed bag

Although the eight species just described are the most popular with small-boat fishermen, there are many others that deserve attention. In fact, many fishermen head for Baja without any specific type of fish in mind, seeking a mixed bag of edible, sporty fish like sierra, grouper, or any of a hundred species. Some of these are of modest size and fighting ability, but others are large, first-rate gamefish. In fact, in addition to the IGFA records noted above, Baja has produced world records for giant sea bass (four), Pacific bonito (two), Pacific jack crevalle (ten, including the all-tackle record), Pacific dog snapper (one), white sea bass (two, including the all-tackle record), black skipjack (nine), spearfish (one), swordfish (one), Pacific bigeye tuna (one), California halibut (three) and rainbow runner (one). In addition, flyrod records have been set for Pacific bonito (one), California halibut (four), Pacific jack crevalle (two), and black skipjack (one).

Some of these migrate seasonally, others are permanent residents; some inhabit rocky caves and reefs, others sandy bottoms, and still others are pelagic, roaming the seas. This diversity, however, makes it highly likely that a fisherman who visits almost any location on Baja waters any time of the year will find at least one species available and reasonably willing. When is the best time of year for the mixed-bag fisherman? If you ask the question at Gordo's Sportfishing office in Ensenada you will get an inevitable answer, "Today! Today is best!" However, if the last boat has already left, the best time of year becomes "Tomorrow!" There is a certain logic to this—any day is good to go fishing—but there are definite seasonal aspects to mixed-bag fishing, and the best months are the hot ones, June to October, although there are fine fisheries during the entire year in some locations, especially in the Cape region. Chapters 9 through 16 provide additional information on locations, species and seasons.

Rods, reels and equipment

Because Baja is home to several hundred species of gamefish, ranging from delicate ladyfish to great black marlin, a one-rod fisherman is likely to be disappointed. To take full advantage of what is available you will need four rigs: a heavy-duty trolling rod with roller guides and a 6/0 revolving-spool reel loaded with 50- to 80-pound mono; a medium-duty six-foot trolling rod with ceramic guides and a 4/0 reel loaded with 30-pound mono; a medium-duty eight- or nine-foot spinning outfit handling 20-pound mono; and a light spinning outfit with 8-pound mono. This array will handle almost any fish Baja has to offer and permit almost any technique except fly fishing and surf casting.

Be prepared to fish both natural and artificial baits. Your tackle box should include shrimp-fly rigs and small shiny lures for catching live bait, and you should have a bait tank or large cooler to keep it alive. A shovel is useful for taking clams and other tidal critters. The vast assortment of trinkets turned out by tackle manufacturers is proof that no artificial works all of the time everywhere, and specific advice as to make, model and color has filled generations of fishing magazines. However, the basic guidelines are simple: you will need a variety of colors, types and sizes of artificial baits, and those imitating natural foods, such as feathers, plastic shrimp, leadheads, chrome spoons and candybars, continue to be sold year after year, while highly publicized gimmicks usually disappear in a year or two. Probably the most effective all-around lures are the jointed Rebel plug and its look-alikes; one in my tackle box has worked so well that all the paint is gone and the underlying plastic is grooved by teeth marks, in some places so deeply that the eyes holding the hooks are in danger of pulling out. They come in a variety of sizes and three types, surface, medium depth and deep-diving. Krocodile spoons also produce. Chapters 9 through 16 list a small number of sources of tackle in Baja, but full-service tackle shops are few and far between, so bring extra snaps, swivels, weights, leader, line, hooks, lures and spare parts.

Binoculars, preferably 7 x 50s, are a great asset, since they can be used to spot schools of baitfish, feeding fish and birds, especially frigates, boobies, gulls and pelicans. In addition, they can save you time by letting you determine whether a commotion on the surface is being caused by seals or sea lions instead of fish.

Staying legal

Licenses are available for periods of one week, one month and one year. All persons aboard a boat must have a fishing license if any fishing tackle is aboard—even if it's just fish hooks and line in life rafts. Licenses can be obtained by mail from the Mexico Department of Fisheries office in San Diego and from the Mexico West Travel Club, and in person from *Oficinas de Pesca* in Baja. The latter offices, referred to from this point on simply as "Pesca offices," are found in numerous locations in Baja, many of which are identified in Chapters 9

through 16. Allow at least two weeks when obtaining licenses by mail. Special excursion permits are available for those fishing from party-boats, one type good for up to five days, the other for over five days. Long-range boats usually provide these aboard at cost. Some fishing operations in Baja include the cost of an excursion license in their fee, but make sure you get a copy to avoid problems at the border if you intend to bring fish back. Baja Outfitter, located just north of the San Ysidro border crossing on Via de San Ysidro, sells tackle, frozen bait, camping gear, Mexican fish licenses and boat permits, making it a handy last stop before heading south.

Only one rod per person is allowed, and no "long-lines" with multiple hooks, nets or explosives can be used. Specific bag and possession limits are established. Pismo clams, oysters, abalone, lobster, shrimp, cabrilla and totuaba are reserved for the Mexican fishing cooperatives and may not be taken by sportfishermen, and no turtles may be taken by anyone, Mexican or American. If you purchase seafood, make sure you get a receipt. Cleaning and filleting fish for storage and transportation are permitted if the species can still be identified, but you cannot leave remnants of cleaning ashore. Underwater ecological reserves have been established at Scammon's Lagoon, Pulmo Reef and the harbor at Cabo San Lucas. Mexican sportfishing regulations are enforced, and game wardens are afield. In addition, military personnel sometimes check licenses and the contents of coolers.

In February 1991, the Mexico Department of Fisheries adopted new regulations governing sportfishing. The basic aspects of the regulations described in the two previous paragraphs appear to still be in effect, but certain other provisions involving limitations on the use of live bait, changes in bag and possession limits, a prohibition on filleting catches aboard boats and others are new and controversial. In the past fishermen under the age of sixteen were not required to have a license, but under the new regulations this is not mentioned. Confused and poorly translated, the regulations were apparently developed without public input in Mexico or the U.S. and they caused a hue and cry, especially in the San Diego long-range sportfishing community. These things happen frequently in Mexico, and in the past clarifications, retractions and modifications were made and the problems usually disappeared. It is essential that anyone planning a fishing trip to Baja obtain a current copy of the regulations along with his license and read it carefully.

There are U. S. regulations concerning importation of fish taken in Mexico. The Lacey Act authorizes U. S. border officers to enforce Mexican licensing and possession limits. Canadian citizens returning to Canada by way of the U.S. must conform to this U.S. law. A declaration must be filled out at the port of entry, and you must have a Mexican fishing license. The Mexican possession limit is the maximum that may be imported. An entry-dated tourist card, receipts or other satisfactory proof of the time spent in Mexico must be available to import fish in excess of the daily limit.

In recent years sportfishermen have reported that U.S. Customs agents have been enforcing a fifty-pound limit of fish, in spite of the fact that Mexican possession limits are based on the number of fish caught, not their weight. The reason for this is apparently that commercial fish imports are manifested according to weight, and a considerable amount of paperwork is required. Because of this, some unscrupulous importers have attempted to pass off commercial fish as sport-caught, even producing sportfishing licenses. So, if the border officer wants to weigh your fillets, it is because the amount you are attempting to import is so large as to cause suspicion that it is in fact commercial, rather than sport-caught, fish. What if you buy fish for personal use? "Purchased fish for personal use is allowed under the same restrictions as fish caught by an individual."

Obtaining natural baits

Natural bait, especially live or fresh-dead, often takes more fish than artificials, but since it is rarely for sale except in resort areas you will have to catch it yourself. "Reasonable amounts" of bait fish can be taken. Almost any kind of small fish makes good live bait, including herring, Pacific mackerel, sierra, ballyhoo and goatfish. Mackerel-like fish form dense schools and can be spotted with a fish-finder and taken with Lucky Joes, Handy-Dandys, mackerel snatchers, flies or small chunks of bait. Many are attracted by light, so fish at night and hang a Coleman lantern over the side, or better yet, use a floating light working off a storage battery, similar to Fisherman's Paradise floating fish light, item number 1323028. If they will not bite, cast a snag line with a half-dozen treble hooks and a three-ounce torpedo sinker through the school. Ladyfish, excellent gamefish in their own right, and other small species can be caught with feathers, chrome spoons or flies.

There are useful baits besides fish, including sand flea, crab, mussel, clam, lobster, limpet, sea worm and abalone. Shrimpers are often seen at anchor along the western shores of the Cortez, and it is possible to buy whole shrimp or heads. A few cans of inexpensive shrimp pieces or abalone bought locally are a useful backup. It would be well, of course, to bring a supply of natural baits from home. If your RV has a refrigerator, packages of frozen mackerel, anchovy and squid will undoubtedly come in handy.

Fishing from small boats

Rather than chartering or hiring a local boat, many people prefer to bring a cartopper, an inflatable or a trailerboat, and the following chapter discusses the ins and outs of bringing your own boat. If you don't have a boat or choose to leave it home, there are two basic types of boats available in Baja—*pangas* and fishing cruisers. A *panga* is an open skiff, usually of fiberglass, often twenty-two feet in length, powered by an outboard engine of about forty horsepower. Widely used for commercial fishing on both coasts, they are normally hired on a daily or hourly basis with a skipper-guide, and can comfortably fish three or four anglers. They are inexpensive,

Reeve makes a slight miscalculation as to the state of the waves while surf fishing.

John Anglin wings out bait at Conejo.

Shorecasting

The beaches and rocky points along Baja's 1,980 miles of coastline are its least-known and most under-utilized fishery. These offer outstanding fishing for everyone from surf fishermen casting into crashing waves with highly specialized twelve-foot poles, to children with light spinning outfits dropping chunks of clam into rocky holes. A large number of species are available, including corbina, corvina, croaker, surfperch, ladyfish, flatfish, opaleye, cabezon and ocean whitefish. The great sweep of Pacific beaches between El Rosario and Guerrero Negro, and between Bahías Tortugas and Magdalena, especially the outer beaches of the islands forming the latter bay, are usually deserted and frequently offer outstanding surf fishing. Some beaches north of Guerrero Negro even yield such unlikely species as white sea bass and halibut. A few other Pacific locations in Baja Norte have good roads and see fair numbers of fishermen, including Eréndira and San Quintín.

a quarter or a third the daily cost of a cruiser, and fast and maneuverable, permitting access to rocky areas and shallow reefs. However, they have no accommodations beyond bench seats, no head and no protection from the sun, although a few are starting to sport Bimini tops.

Cruisers come in a wide variety of sizes and types and are more expensive than *pangas*, but usually offer live bait tanks, fighting chairs, a cabin and a head, and they can travel farther and can keep fishing in heavier weather than *pangas*.

There are many independent organizations scattered in strategic locations that can supply *pangas* or cruisers, including Alfredo's Sport Fishing and Arturo's Sports Fishing Fleet in Loreto, Dorado Velez Fleet in La Paz, and Finisterra Tortuga Sportfishing Fleet, Fleet Solmar and Pisces Fleet in Cabo San Lucas. In addition, some hotels and resorts located between Mulegé and Cabo San Lucas have their own fleets. *Panga* fleets can also be located in the beach/waterfront area of almost any town catering to sportfishermen and in commercial fishing settlements, although those in the latter locations are sometimes hard at work and not available. Raul Perez and Alberto Lucero offer *panga* fishing trips in the Bahía de los Angeles and Bahía San Francisquito areas, respectively. Appendix A provides information on all the organizations and individuals specifically mentioned above, as well as many hotels and resorts.

Practices vary from place to place, so make sure you clearly understand what will and will not be provided in the way of tackle, bait, food and drink, when to arrive in the morning, how long you will be out, and the price.

We told Mike that it was unlikely he would catch a grouper in the shallow sandy-bottomed flats off our camp on Bahía Concepcíon— they just don't hang around such environments.

The coast between San José del Cabo and La Paz offers some of the most unusual and exciting shore fishing in the world, especially for roosterfish at Punta Pescadero and Punta Arena Sur. Ray Cannon's famous "Tuna Canyon" is located four miles south of Punta Pescadero, where a submarine canyon runs in close to the beach, providing a year-round population of yellowfin tuna that can occasionally be caught from shore. A similar situation occurs at Bahía Frailes, where a submarine canyon approaching the beach allows shorecasters to catch yellowfin and even marlin. An isolated population of white sea bass lives in the upper Cortez, and they can be taken by casting from rocky points. Most yellowtail are caught from boats, and while they are not commonly thought of as an onshore species, they also feed in shallow water and even in the surf zone—although they don't stay any longer than necessary. When they drive a school of bait into shallow water it can be a real melee and they will savagely attack anything offered. Don't expect to catch many yellowtail this way, for they fight hard, and by the time you beach the first fish the bite is usually over.

Getting "unskunked"

Mythology to the contrary, there are times and places where it is difficult to catch fish in Baja, and some fishermen return home skunked. You rarely hear about them, but it happens; who can admit spending an entire vacation in fabled Baja without catching a single fish? There are two solid reasons why some people join this silent minority: a failure to experiment and an unwillingness to change location. Some people have a favorite method of fishing and either have strong fixed ideas about how to go about it, or no ideas at all. They arrive, fish from dawn to dusk, and return home in total humiliation. If they are willing to talk about it at all, you will probably hear the excuse, "They were not biting. We tried everything, we flung everything in the tackle box at them, but nothing worked." Check closer and you will almost certainly find, far from trying "everything," that they limited their fishing technique, to say, slow surface trolling past two or three rocky points on one island off one village. At no time did they experiment with natural baits, change depth, try fast trolling, jigging or shorecasting or buy a few artificial baits not already in their tackle box, and they didn't even bother to check out an island a few miles away or consider moving to an entirely new location.

Real estate salesmen like to joke that the three most important factors in successfully selling a house are "location, location, location," but for Baja fishermen, success comes from "variety, variety, variety." No place on earth provides more species of fish, or more habitats and more conditions of temperature, depth and current in so compact and accessible an area as Baja, and the key to getting "unskunked" is being willing and able to change and experiment. Bring all four rigs recommended above and a wide variety of natural and artificial baits and terminal tackle. Ask around to find out what fish are biting and what baits and lures have been successful. If artificials don't work, try natural baits, and vice versa. Experiment with different depths. Downriggers and paravanes are not widely used in Baja waters, but they greatly expand the depths, temperatures and habitats that can be exploited. Try bottom fishing in 400 or even 600 feet of water,

where the habitat and the species are entirely different. If trolling off rocky points doesn't work, troll off sandy points, or offshore. If trolling doesn't work, try jigging or shorecasting or drifting a live bait. Try night fishing—some species that are seemingly absent appear magically after dark and feed actively. Any skin diver can tell you that fish are unevenly distributed, and large areas have low populations, either seasonally or permanently, so if nothing else works, move on.

Freshwater fishing

Believe it or not, there is a limited amount of freshwater fishing in Baja. A number of small streams in and around Parque Nacional Sierra San Pedro Martír, including the Río San Rafael near Mike's Sky Ranch and the streams in Arroyos la Zanja and San Antonio, contain trout to fourteen inches. Rancho San José offers pack trips to the last two locations. Mexican fishing licenses are good for both fresh and salt water, but there are closed seasons on trout. Laguna Salada once had a thriving fishery for largemouth bass, catfish and less familiar fish like tilapia, and in the winter of 1986 net fishermen brought in a black crappie that would have sorely pressed the current world's record of four pounds, eight ounces. However, the level of the lake is controlled by the flows in the Río Colorado, and recent drought in the South-

Tom Selman prepares for the next day's action on the *Royal Polaris*.

west reduced the lake to a fraction of its size in 1986, destroying the fishery.

Long-range fishing

In addition to small-boat fishing and shorecasting, there is another major category of Baja fishing: long-range. Through the years a growing and evermore elaborate fleet of sportfishing vessels has been carrying fishermen south from San Diego and Ensenada to enjoy some of the most exciting fishing the world has to offer. These trips usually take one of three basic forms: mini-, midi-, and maxi-long-range trips, differing in their length, places fished and species of fish encountered. The definitions are not precise, but mini-trips usually last between two and five days and range between 75 and 350 miles south of the border, fishing Islas San Martín, San Jerónimo, Cedros and Guadalupe, the San Benitos and a number of coastal locations. A wide variety of species is caught, including yellowtail, yellowfin tuna, ocean whitefish, ling, barracuda, bonito, calico bass, and black sea bass. Midi-trips vary between six and ten days and range south to Bahía Magdalena, Rocas Alijos, and various seamounts and banks, as well as stopping at the locations visited on mini-trips. Since

they encounter warmer water, midi-trips often produce species not usually seen on mini-trips, such as wahoo and dolphin, and occasional marlin, as well as yellowtail, black sea bass, ocean whitefish, bonito and barracuda. Maxi-trips take fourteen to seventeen days and usually concentrate on the Islas Revillagigedo, located 250 miles south of the Cape, and places en route like Rocas Alijos, the quarry often being wahoo, dolphin and yellowfin tuna.

There is a fairly well-established annual cycle in the schedule of the boats. May through July is often devoted to midi-trips, June through September to mini-trips for albacore, late August to mid-December to mini- and midi-trips, and mid-December through June to maxi- and midi-trips for the larger boats, mini- and midi-trips for the smaller ones. Per-day costs range between $150 and $180, a few to over $200. These prices are bargains since they include meals, accommodations, bait, transportation, refrigerated holds for fish, crew services and some of the best fishing in the world.

Four of the most prominent organizations offering long-range trips from San Diego are H & M Landing, Fisherman's Landing, Point Loma Sportfishing Association and Lee Palm Sportfishers. Out of Ensenada, Gordo's Sportfishing makes

Our catch of 47 yellowtail, 169 wahoo, 48 yellowfin tuna, 138 grouper, 4 dolphin and 1 marlin was hoisted out of the refrigerated hold of the *Royal Polaris* just before we returned to San Diego.

mini-trips to San Martín, and Ensenada Clipper Fleet offers mini-trips to Islas San Jerónimo and San Martín. Tony Reyes Fishing Tours also offers six-day trips from San Felipe to the Midriff, as well as trips out of La Paz, these ranging south to the Bancos Gorda and north of Mulegé. The San Diego and Ensenada fleets also have day trips on an open-boat or charter basis, as does Fritz's Landing Boat House in Ensenada.

Boats in the sportfishing fleet, Mexican and U.S., are modern, safe, well-equipped and crewed by experienced professionals. Boats based in Mexico are usually not as palatial or modern as those out of San Diego, but they are closer to the action and less expensive. Upon request, all fleet offices will send brochures describing schedules, rates, reservation procedures, and suggestions on tackle—see Appendix A.

Hotels, resorts, package trips and yacht charters

Many Baja hotels and resorts cater to fishermen and hold tournaments and clinics, and some have their own cruiser fleets. A few, such as Rancho Buena Vista, have held an international reputation for world-class fishing for many years. Most of the agencies specializing in Baja California travel listed on page 81 offer fishing package trips, as well as more generalized services such as hotel, resort and airline reservations. Fishing International specializes in worldwide package fishing trips, and has a variety of Baja offerings. A few organizations specialize in specific locations; Bob Butler Baja Fishing offers package trips to the La Paz area, and La Baja Experience Club maintains a fly-in camp near Abreojos. Cortez Yacht Charters and Frazer Charters, Inc. represent a large assortment of sportfishing yachts and can provide charter trips to almost anywhere in Baja waters you could wish to visit, including such hot-spots as Isla Cerralvo, East Cape, Cabo San Lucas and Bahía Magdalena.

Obtaining real-time information

What's biting? The question is a natural one for anyone about to expend a considerable amount of time and money on a Baja fishing trip, but unfortunately there are few catch reports in the newspapers, and advice from returning friends is often too old to be meaningful. However, readers studying Appendix A will note that all the *panga* and cruiser fleets listed have local Baja telephone numbers, as do many of the hotels, resorts, RV parks and organizations offering package trips. All of the long-range fleets, of course, have telephones. While the objectivity of the information received may be a bit suspect, it should be useful if filtered through a series of specific questions, such as "Exactly how many marlin were caught yesterday?," and "Tell me again: you say it was a 100 POUND yellowtail? Are you sure it wasn't 100 ounces?"

Fishing for the future

Mexico has aggressively expanded commercial fishing in Baja waters in recent years, permitting major increases in local gill-netting, and purse-seining for species like anchovy for reduction to fish meal, and even allowing Japanese long-liners to take massive numbers of billfish. (In 1991 Mexico announced that long-lining had been banned to protect the sportfishing industry.) While this was going on, the Trans-peninsular Highway was completed, air transportation was improved and a number of hotels were built, bringing in new

hordes of sportfishermen. All this has placed stress on the fisheries, and there is no doubt that the fabulous fishing in Baja is declining and will continue to do so in coming years. Visiting fisherman can do little about laws that permit this decline, but they can help in a number of very direct and important ways.

"Catch-and-release" has been promoted in recent years as a way to allow people to experience the fun of fishing without damaging the biota. Since released fish are never seen again, the fisherman assumes that all is well. However, Bill Johnston, owner-skipper of the dive boats *Bottom Scratcher* and *Sand Dollar*, says his divers find dead fish littering the bottom after sportfishing boats have been in an area at the Coronados. There is much that individual fishermen—you—can do to reduce this waste.

If you intend to consume any of your catch, keep all fish of legal species caught, regardless of their small size; there are no current minimum size limits for any species in Baja waters. When you have enough for a meal or have reached the bag limit, either quit fishing or practice catch-and-release; Mexico places no restrictions on catch-and-release. However, you can't just jerk the fish off the hook, throw it back and expect it to survive. Unless special precautions are taken, fish often succumb to shock, disorientation, suffocation, internal damage or wounds. Fishermen go to great lengths to learn how to catch fish, but few know anything about how to let them go! Blued, unplated long-shank iron hooks can be removed easily, and salt water and fish juices will eventually rust them away if the line breaks. Never use treble hooks, or hooks made from stainless steel. Consider using barbless hooks, or crimping down barbs with a pair of pliers. When a fish comes alongside keep it upright and try to get the hook out while it is in the water and can breathe. A fish hung vertically can sustain internal injuries, so don't hoist it out of the water if you can avoid it. A fish's slimy coating protects it from bacteria, and fatal infections can occur if this is damaged, so try to get the fish off the hook without touching it. If you must bring a fish aboard use wet hands and grasp it by the lower lip or behind the gill plates, or ahead of the tail fin if it is toothy. Grasp a billfish in the obvious location. A net removes slime, and a gaff is almost always fatal. If the fish is deeply hooked, simply cut the line as close to the hook as possible. Bleeding fish are probably going to die, especially if their gills are involved, so keep such fish for food.

Ultralight tackle is seen as another way to protect the fishery, and it appears to work—the fisherman is often unable and unwilling to take more in a day than the proverbial one. I have set several world IGFA ultralight fishing records with two- and four-pound test line, each requiring almost two hours to get the fish in, and both the fish and the fisherman were completely "spent." I once fought a fish for nine hours on eight-pound test and didn't recover for two days (it got away). However, special precautions are essential here too. Use barbless or blued, un-plated hooks—the chance of breaking a line is high, and the fish may be "wearing" the hook for a long time if you use stainless barbed hooks. Since the fish will be in a state of complete exhaustion and vulnerable to predators, try to keep it under control next to the boat as gently and as long as possible while it recovers.

The largest individuals of most species are often females

with high reproductive value, so let the big ones go. Large fish are probably going to be wasted anyway, since they cannot be consumed immediately and it is difficult or impossible to keep one under refrigeration until you get home. Besides, big fish don't taste any better than little ones! There is a lot of ego involved in dragging home a huge trophy, and letting one go may be about as popular as *coitus interruptus*, but it helps greatly, for the opposite reason.

Bottom fishermen often crank up their catch from great depths, their eyes bulging and stomachs protruding from their mouths. This is no place for catch-and-release, for the fish will almost certainly never make it back to the bottom, but if you decide to release such fish, there is a right way to do it. All of the above ideas about hooks and release techniques apply, and in addition the fisherman should be prepared with a number 14 hypodermic needle, available from farm and ranch supply stores. Lay a pectoral fin back against the fish's body, and with the point of the needle remove a scale from the body at the tip of the fin. Slowly insert the needle through the skin and abdominal wall. When the needle penetrates the gas bladder, air will rush out the end of the needle, telling you that it has penetrated far enough. Compress the sides of the fish until they appear normal or concave, pull out the needle and return the fish to the water. The fish will probably swim rapidly to the bottom, but if it doesn't a few prods from the blunt end of a gaff or net handle should send it on its way. This method works on almost any species of "bottomfish," regardless of size. No vital organs are harmed, and the chance of infection is slight if you keep the needle clean and store it in a vial of alcohol. Thus, for a dollar's worth of equipment and thirty seconds of effort you can greatly reduce this unnecessary loss of fish, and who knows: perhaps the fish will eventually grow to monstrous proportions and fall for your bait a second time.

Selfish and unthinking gringos have brought canning equipment to Baja in hopes of capitalizing on fishing bonanzas, and a magazine article even advocated hauling in an electric freezer and a generator in the back of a pickup. These are rotten ideas. They are probably illegal, since they make it impossible to verify limits and species, and will almost certainly result in exceeding possession limits. A number of years ago a group had messy and protracted problems with local officials at Bahía de los Angeles over a canning operation. Since it focuses on the production of food and is essentially commercial in nature, such conduct is inconsistent with the ethics of sportsmanship and the terms of your Mexican fishing license. In addition, it promotes terrible public relations with the locals. How would you feel if a group of Mexicans set up a canning plant on your beach?

Fishermen occasionally catch sea birds, most often pelicans and boobies. If this happens do not cut the line, for the part still attached to the bird may become fouled in vegetation, rocks or driftwood, and the bird will die of starvation. Slowly reel the bird in and get it under control by grasping the bill and one wing, near its base. A cloth put over the bird's head will help calm it down. A landing net can be used to help restrain the bird or bring it aboard a boat. Beware: a bird may defend itself by pecking, sometimes at eyes. Find the hook and push the barb through the skin, cut the barb off and back the hook out, just as you would with a person who has been hooked. Good judgment is required if the hook is in a joint or near an eye or other vulnerable area, and it may be better to leave the hook alone and simply cut the line as close to the eye of the hook as possible. If the bird has swallowed the hook and it is not visible, cut the line at its bill. Inspect the bird carefully and remove all fishing line from it before letting it go. Look closely; it is often hard to see mono among the feathers.

****

THE WORLD'S WORST FISHERMAN. Fishing tales are inevitably about the man who caught the biggest and the most, but I once had the opportunity to fish with The World's Worst Fisherman. This short biography is authorized, but by mutual agreement I will simply refer to him as Mr. Worst. Mrs. Worst told me that her husband "had always wanted to go fishing, but never had the time," which meant that he had been a busy fellow, for he was forty-five. After a month of planning we finally embarked on a trip to a secret location in the Cortez which was always teeming with big yellowtail. In the first ten minutes of the first day, I hooked a beauty, then my brother got a bigger one, then I got one, then my brother, then I, then my brother, while Worst got nothing. This was also the pattern for the second day, broken only when I would get two or three in a row, followed by my brother. Worst's morale was high at the campfire that night, for no reason other than he still had five days to connect. By the third night, however, his lower lip was protruding a bit, so we decided to figure out the reason for his bad luck. The next morning we identified the problem—although it wasn't simple bad luck. If yellowtail could be seen chasing forage at the surface, Worst's lure would come up covered with scratches from bouncing along the bottom. If they were near the bottom, his bait was skipping across the waves. Rather than trolling just in back of the wake, he would be back either ten feet or 300 yards. If an examination of stomach contents showed the yellowtail were after squid, Worst would bend on a gaudy green Rapala. We discussed this with him, but got no signal that he understood. On the fifth day he continued, his technique unmodified and his stringer empty, and by the last day Worst seemed destined to break some sort of yellowtail non-record. Finally, with only one hour left, he let it all hang out. "You guys are doing something," he informed us, and threw down his rod and pouted. We finally persuaded him to try again, with our coaching. We selected a lure of the exact right size, type and hue. I adjusted the throttle to the exact speed required, and told him to start letting out line. Finally, when the lure was in the right spot just beyond the wake I told him to flip the clutch lever on his reel. At that exact instant a bruiser of a yellowtail grabbed the lure and headed for parts unknown. His reel smoking, Worst finally turned the fish and gained some line, then he lost all of that and more. Back and forth the battle raged, until the fish was finally brought to gaff. Did this ease Worst's frustrations? No, for this certainly proved that we had been "doing something" all along—if we could turn on the fishing just like that, we could certainly turn it off. On the way home, though, he could finally joke about his "bad luck" and we started to plan a book about his fishing techniques, which we would sell worldwide through animal-rights organizations and vegetarian societies.

****

CHAPTER 4
WIND, WATER AND WAVES

Unless your interests are strictly land-locked, you will probably want to bring a boat to Baja. Although there are many *pangas* for hire throughout Baja Norte and Baja Sur, and a number of cruiser fleets are available in Baja Sur, they are not always to be found when and where you need them. Besides, many fishermen, divers, campers and explorers find that piloting their own boat is part of the fun. In addition, the Cortez has some of the finest cruising waters in the world, and while yachts are available for charter, it is difficult or impossible to obtain a small sailboat or outboard in Baja for this purpose.

There have been many fine boating adventures in Baja waters. One of the earliest extensive trailerboat cruises occurred in 1960, when Spencer Murray and Ralph Poole brought their twenty-two-foot lapstrake to San Felipe and cruised to Bahía Gonzaga, Bahía de los Angeles, Santa Rosalía and Loreto, crossed the Cortez to Topolobambo and recrossed to La Paz. After visiting the Cape, they left the boat in La Paz and flew back to the United States. A number of months later it was returned to Ensenada aboard a Mexican freighter. Since then outboard cruisers as small as seventeen feet have crossed from Guaymas to Mulegé without incident, and even cartoppers have made lengthy trips in the Midriff region. I have crossed the Cortez twice in a fifteen-foot aluminum boat, not a recommended activity unless a left-sided tilt to the adventure/safety scale is acceptable to you.

A few small-boat adventures have involved both the Pacific and the Cortez. In 1980 Joe Seidenthal piloted an open twenty-two-foot Paceño outboard, the "*panga*" seen throughout Baja, from San Felipe to San Diego, and in 1983 David Steed carried things a step farther when he "circumnavigated" Baja. Aboard a fifteen-foot inflatable powered by a fifty-horse engine, he voyaged from San Diego around the Cape to the mouth of the Río Colorado in four months. A friend with a trailer picked him up in San Felipe and drove to Ensenada, from where Steed launched and completed the run to San Diego.

The fun has not been limited to powerboats. Many small sailboats have cruised the Midriff and sailed the length of the Cortez, and a number of sailing dinghys have made the Loreto-to-La Paz run. The premiere small-boat sailing voyage in Baja waters is the Hobie Cat trip made by Jeff Hardgrave, Eric Guenther and Dan Mangus. After ten months of preparation, they sailed from San Diego on June 25, 1980, Jeff on a Hobie 18, the other two on 16s, their trampoline bags packed with a vast array of supplies and equipment. Not everything they needed could be carried, so they were supported by two road crews carrying fresh food, water, cold beer and other emergency supplies. Uncooperative winds and all-pervasive dampness plagued the first week, but the first real problems occurred during the week beginning July 4, a trying period during which Dan's boat flipped and turtled, Eric pitchpoled, Dan pitchpoled and was dismasted, and Eric disappeared overnight. Finally safely ashore, they made repairs, but the wind was so fierce that Eric's boat blew over while on the beach with nothing up but a bare pole. At Malarrimo, rudder and sail problems, coupled with fog, caused them to sail too far west, and they landed in a rocky area, resulting in assorted gashes in the fiberglass, two broken end-caps and two sheared rudder pins. After they rounded Punta Eugenia, the wind died and a fog built up, forcing them to anchor out overnight.

But things were not all wet bodies, broken parts and contrary winds. There were grand days when fine breezes filled multicolored sails and had the three sailors traped out, speeding south in brilliant sun, three abreast, with an escort of porpoises at their bows. There were campfires and song writing, hot chocolate and tuna-noodle casseroles, and even a bath in a hot spring. Mexicans greeted them with interest and cooperation and filled them with beer, lobsters and oysters. Their arrival at Bahía Asunción caused a sensation, and they were quickly surrounded by a hundred friendly people, mostly curious kids.

Disaster struck at El Conejo, when Jeff pitchpoled backward while leaving the beach. The boat was a mass of fractured fiberglass, broken aluminum and torn sails, and the trip was over for him, only 50 miles short of their goal. Fortunately he did not sustain a scratch. Dan and Eric continued on the next day. Sailing through the night with a full moon, they rounded Cabo Falso and arrived at Cabo San

Lucas at three in the morning of July 25, greeted by two barking dogs. Their magnificent voyage was over, 1,000 miles, thirty days, five capsizes, two dismastings, one wrecked boat and twenty-three rudder pins later.

Favorite cruising grounds

Among the most interesting and adventurous Baja small-boat cruises is the "Stepping-Stones Cruise" through the Midriff to Bahía Kino, Sonora, described in Chapter 11, the "Coasting to Loreto" route from Mulegé to Loreto, and the "Island-Hopping" and "Coasting to La Paz" routes between Loreto and La Paz, described in Chapter 13. Many cruises start at San Felipe, which is close to the border and has over-the-beach launch facilities. Cruises from there can be as long or as short as desired; Puertecitos is only forty-six miles, Bahía Gonzaga thirty-nine more and Bahía de los Angeles seventy-five more. Boaters wanting a pleasant, undemanding trip often gunkhole around Isla Espíritu Santo or Islas Carmen and Danzante for a week or two. Lengthy cruises along the Pacific coast like that taken by the Hobie sailors are rarely undertaken, due to logistics and weather problems, although it is great fun to explore vast Bahía Magdalena, and larger rigs can head for Banco Thetis for marlin and wahoo. Trailerboaters occasionally launch at San Quintín and spend time at Isla San Martín, diving and fishing around Johnston's Seamount and Roca Ben and exploring the lava tubes on the island.

New roads and improvements to existing roads have opened up great adventures for small-boat sailors, especially the roads to Bahías Tortugas and Asunción. In the past, this stretch of coast was very difficult to get to with anything short of an oceangoing yacht, but now it is possible to haul in cartoppers and inflatables with only modest vehicles, and although there are no paved ramps and over-the-beach launches are necessary, adventurous trailerboat sailors can make the trip without undue difficulty. Best of all, the fine fishing and diving at the Islas San Benito and Isla Cedros are now within the range of small-boaters. The San Evaristo road makes it possible to dive the wall at Isla las Ánimas Sur and the caves of Isla San Diego out of an inflatable or a cartopper, and the road south from Bahía de los Angeles to Bahía San Francisquito makes it easier to get to the Midriff region.

Portable boats

The ultimate boat for fishing, diving and short-range cruising and for exploring Baja's inshore waters may be the largest aluminum boat you can carry on the roof of your vehicle, probably a fifteen-footer if you have a full-size pickup or van. A fifteen-footer can be launched and beached almost anywhere, and can be taken far off-road to remote locations,

Catamarans clutter the beach as the Hobie adventurers take a break from the rigors of the sea.

DAN MANGUS

JEFF HARDGRAVE

Dan takes a big one leaving Todos Santos.

lateral area make this a marginal proposition, and they are best carried upside down on the top of a low utility trailer. Several men can manhandle the boat onto the trailer, which can also carry engines, fuel, tackle, ice chests and other gear. Such a rig will require more manpower and fuel, and much off-road mobility is lost, but it will provide greater range, safety and load-carrying ability than a smaller boat.

The qualities of inflatables make them useful for Baja adventuring: they are light and portable and their low free-board, stability and load-carrying ability make them especially attractive to divers. In heavy weather, an inflatable is far safer than an open aluminum boat. While driving off-road, an inflatable in the back of a pickup will be a lot less hassle than a boat on top. On the negative side, they tend to be wet, take more engine horsepower, use more fuel, have relatively little load volume, and are vulnerable to hooks, knives and fish spines, and attaching downriggers, rod holders and transducers can be a problem. In addition, they take valuable cargo space; an aluminum boat on the roof takes less usable space than an inflatable in a trunk.

Trailerboats

A wide variety of boats have been successfully trailered to Baja, ranging from miserable 1950s fiberglass runabouts with imitation Cadillac tailfins to the latest in Boston Whalers and Farallons, but no one type or make is clearly best for all situations and interests. Among small sailboats, Westwight Potters, Hobies, Dovekies, Drascombe Luggers and Ventures are frequently seen. Sail or power, the choice depends on how and where you plan to use it, seaworthiness, personal preference and pocketbook. While the comfort, safety and range of large trailerable "yachts" are desirable, they are hard to handle on the Transpeninsular and difficult to launch in most locations, and obtaining a supply of gasoline can be a real problem in some areas. There is no sharp limit, but it is probably unwise to trail boats over twenty-four feet or any keel sailboat to Baja.

Chapter 6 has information on preparing trailers and towing under Baja conditions, and many paved ramps are identified in Chapters 9 through 16. Some ramps leave much to be

near-impossibilities with even the smallest trailerboats. In an emergency, a person of average strength can launch and retrieve it alone once the engine and equipment are removed, by "walking" it—lifting one end and carrying it in an arc, then the other, etc. Best of all, the mechanical, insurance and hassle problems associated with trailers are avoided. An engine as small as fifteen horsepower, weighing less than eighty pounds, will keep it on a plane with several campers, divers or fishermen and their gear aboard and provide adequate range and safety. A bit more horsepower is helpful, but engines over twenty horsepower are ordinarily too heavy for one person to carry across a rough beach and install on a boat. As pointed out in Chapter 2, traditional twelve-foot aluminum boats are too small for most Baja activities.

Recreation Industries Co. makes loaders that allow carrying a boat on the top of various types of vehicles, including large motorhomes, cab-over campers and pickups towing fifth-wheel trailers. A bow line and extra tie-downs are necessary to resist lateral and vertical loads caused by crosswinds and wind-blast from eighteen-wheelers on the narrow Transpeninsular. These are also necessary when traveling off-road to resist bouncing and swaying. Loader supports should be checked frequently, especially if they connect to rain gutters.

Another nice rig, on a larger scale, is a seventeen- or eighteen-foot aluminum boat. At 350 pounds or more, these have been used as cartoppers, but their weight, size and large

John Anglin put the last of our fresh water to good use before we left Juanico for Loreto.

desired; the concrete generally ends too soon, and waves undermine the outer end, providing a big surprise as you back the trailer out. Some are in areas with great tidal ranges, making it possible to launch only at high tide. Others are in exposed locations, where it is difficult to launch and retrieve when a sea is running, making guideboards a real asset. There are, of course, many rock, hard clay or sand areas where boats can be launched, too many to list. However, some are in important locations that have no other launch facilities, and hence are identified in later chapters.

Permits and insurance

The Mexico Department of Fisheries requires that boats brought into Mexico by road or sea that are to be used for sportfishing have a boat permit. In practice this means that all boats, except perhaps kayaks and other very small craft, should have a permit. The reason for this is that enforcement personnel rarely, if ever, encounter anyone in Baja with a boat who claims to have no plans to fish. If you are the "first," the subsequent explanations may go on for an hour, and you may be suspected of being simple-minded; who else would come to Baja with a boat and not plan to fish? Permits can be obtained from the Department and from Mexico West and Baja Outfitters, both at their offices and by mail. As required for vehicles and trailers, you must provide your registration papers and a notarized letter from any lienholders giving you permission to bring the boat into Mexico. The details of this requirement and procedures for getting permits have been in a state of flux, so telephone to get current information well before you plan to depart. When you validate your tourist card

upon entry into Baja, the fact you are bringing a boat is recorded on your card, and the boat can stay as long as you can. If you plan to enter mainland Mexico it is essential that you check in advance with a Mexican consulate for additional requirements that may be in effect concerning temporary import permits (not required in Baja).

In the past, if you had to leave Mexico without your boat, it was necessary to place it in bond. However, a new law has established "licensed marinas," which can take custody of it for periods of up to five years, at the discretion of the marina operator. To do this the owner must have a tourist card, passport and proof of ownership, and must appear at the marina at least once a year thereafter, leaving a copy of a current tourist card as proof of this visit. Licensed marinas can also take custody of boats not physically present in the marina, and custody of boats brought in by road.

If you enter Mexico by sea, even in a kayak, you must comply with immigration, customs and Captain of the Port (COTP) procedures for yachts; consult with a yacht agent or refer to a yachting guide. The locations of COTP offices are noted in Chapters 9 through 16. Once in Mexico and traveling by sea, there are procedures established for checking in and out of the various COTP jurisdictions. The COTPs seem to have little interest in boats brought in by road. However, because of increased anti-drug-smuggling activities by Mexican authorities, the chances of being asked for COTP paperwork by naval or law-enforcement personnel are higher than in the past. If you bring a boat into Mexico by road and plan a lengthy trip, say from San Felipe to La Paz, it would be wise to check into the COTP office nearest the launch point

Reeve Peterson and Rob Watson found an inflatable to be the ideal dive boat while looking for the wreck of the tanker *Swift Eagle* at the Islas San Benito.

to get the latest information, especially if your boat is the kind that may attract interest, say a large cruiser with big engines, radar and lots of antennas. Licensed marinas are authorized to give port clearances to their clients for trips of up to seventy-two hours in local waters and to issue clearances for departures and arrivals within Mexico.

The insurance situation has similarly improved. Marine insurance written by U.S. companies is often expensive and has all sorts of exclusions and limitations, and U.S. adjusters are unable to work in Mexico. International Gateway Insurance Brokers now offers standard Lloyd's of London Hull and Liability (called P&I—Protection and Indemnity) contracts that include passenger liability coverage (but not hired crew). Medical payment coverage is also available. Coverage extends to all Mexican territorial waters, and boats under twenty-eight feet and/or $40,000 in value are covered for physical damage while being towed by a non-commercial vehicle on the roads and highways of Mexico. Short-term policies and higher P&I limits are available. Hull age, boating experience and extinguisher credits are available on Hull coverage for larger boats. These policies have no seasonal limits and there are no crew requirements on larger boats.

Marinas, fuel, oil, parts and service

Yachtsmen will find the situation much better than a few years ago. After endless talk and a few false starts there is finally a modern marina in Ensenada, Baja Naval, and more are planned. La Paz has two fine facilities, Marina de La Paz and Marina Palmira. These three licensed facilities offer virtually everything you would find in a U.S. marina, from floating docks with power and water to parts and repair service. Even Santa Rosalía now has a small marina, although its facilities are more limited. Descriptions will be found in later chapters, and the addresses and telephone numbers of the first three are listed in Appendix A. A large complex that includes a marina has been planned for Puerto Escondido, but construction has slowed to a halt.

In other locations don't expect to cruise into a full-service marina, pull up to a fuel dock, find a business catering to yachtsmen and maintaining normal business practices, fill up and be gone. There are fueling facilities at some commercial fishing docks, but your boat may be an intrusion and a disruption. Most of your fuel is going to come from ordinary PEMEX stations, and if you are on a cruise or are otherwise unable to take the boat to the fuel, you must be prepared to bring the fuel to the boat with numerous large cans. Although plugs seem to foul earlier, low-octane PEMEX products do not otherwise bother most outboard engines, but if you have a problem, switch fuels, try an additive or retard the spark. Fuel purchased from an individual, a cannery, or a boat yard is not price-controlled, and you will be charged what the traffic will bear. Two-cycle outboard oil can be hard to find, so carry an extra six-pack.

Parts and service for Evinrude and Johnson outboards are available in Ensenada, San Felipe, Mulegé and La Paz, and there is a Mercury dealer in Ensenada. Mariner dealers are found in Ensenada, Ciudad Constitución and La Paz. Yamaha dealers are located in Ensenada and La Paz. These dealers cater to local fishermen and divers, and parts for very small and very large engines are usually not in stock. In addition, some engines sold in Mexico may be "international" models, whose parts are not interchangeable with those of the same make and size sold in the U.S. There are a few independent repair shops shown on the city maps in Chapters 9 through 16. Parts are not available for inboard/outboards. Automotive parts may fit and seem to work well, but they can be dangerous in marine service. A shop service manual and parts list will greatly simplify handling engine problems. There are marine supply stores in Ensenada and La Paz, described in the text and shown on the city maps.

Beach launching

It is not necessary to carry inflatables and cartoppers across beaches. Recreation Industries makes soft-terrain beach wheels that attach to the transom and allow boats to cross sand and gravel beaches with little effort.

A trailerboat can be launched over a soft beach even with an ordinary two-wheel-drive vehicle, entailing no risk of getting stuck and no undue strain on you, your boat or your vehicle. Before you head south, cut a set of eight two-by-two-foot sand mats from a sheet of three-quarter inch plywood, and get a long length of nylon line, half-inch for small boats, larger if necessary (the boat's anchor line may do). Select a beach that has a smooth, moderate slope all the way to the water. Move the boat on the trailer so that the tongue weight is almost zero. If you can't do this by hand, tie the back of the boat to a tree or large rock and pull ahead very slowly, keeping a snubbing line on the front of the boat if the trailer has rollers. Tie the boat firmly to the trailer to keep if from moving and back the trailer onto the beginning of the beach slope, running each of its wheels onto sand mats before the tow vehicle's rear wheels are in danger of losing traction. Put a sand mat under the tongue wheel if necessary. Block the trailer wheels so they can't roll, detach the tow vehicle, tie the nylon line to the trailer, and loop it around the hitch ball twice and over itself several times. Pull slack out of the line and, holding firmly to the loose end, unblock the wheels and allow gravity to pull the trailer down the beach, making a road with the mats to keep the wheels out of the sand. If the boat and trailer are heavy and you are uncertain whether you can restrain them by snubbing on the hitch ball, pull the tow vehicle forward after blocking the trailer wheels, tie the line to the tow vehicle, unblock the trailer wheels and slowly back down. Before the tow vehicle's wheels are in danger of losing traction, block the trailer wheels, detach the rope from the tow vehicle and move it forward; then repeat the cycle.

The critical part starts once the trailer wheels are in the water, since the sand mats will be harder to place under the wheels and the bottom slope may be too little to allow gravity to move the trailer. If you can't manhandle it out to the point the boat will float, detach the line from the trailer, run it through a pulley or clevis on the boat's anchor, dig the anchor into the bottom in deeper water, tie one end of the line to the front of the trailer and the other to the tow vehicle and drive slowly ahead. In retrieving the trailer, the operation is similar; just remember to position the boat so there is almost no tongue weight.

Equipment and seamanship

Every powerboat should be equipped with a small outboard capable of being started manually and steered independently, and sailboats should have an auxiliary engine. The sun can be fierce and a Bimini top is a real asset. Since waves are often in one direction and wind in another, a flopper-stopper and a stern anchor are handy if you plan to sleep aboard. Local boats have rough sides and no rub-rail padding, so bring fenders if you intend to dicker for fish or shrimp. The best bailing equipment is a sturdy bucket. Tie it to the boat so it will not be lost if you swamp. Due to the lack of swell in the Cortez, the disturbances and foam that mark rocks and shoals are often absent, and a depth finder is essential for larger boats. In the Midriff and the upper Cortez, tides and tidal currents will probably be greater than anything you have ever experienced outside of Alaska, so bring tide tables and use them to plan the voyage.

Make sure you know how far your boat will go on a gallon of gas when the boat is fully laden, and insure that your tanks and metal cans are adequate for the planned trip. Outboards get surprisingly poor mileage; the fifteen-foot, fifteen-horse-power rig recommended above will get only about six nautical miles per gallon when loaded to rated capacity.

To avoid a twice-a-day swim if you don't want to bring your boat ashore each night, bring an anchor, a rode, a buoy, a self-mousing hook, a pulley or metal ring and a long length of half-inch nylon line. Anchor the buoy and tie the metal ring to it. Run the line through the ring, tie it off into a continuous loop and bend on the hook. Clip the hook to the bow-eye of the boat, carry the end of the loop ashore and tie it off. From this point on you never have to get wet; just pull on one side of the loop to move the boat ashore, on the other to get it out to the buoy. This also avoids loss of the boat if the anchor drags.

An aluminum folding chair weighs only about three pounds and contributes greatly to the comfort of a trip if you camp ashore. A propane outfit consisting of a cylinder, safety post, stove and mantle lantern will allow cooking without the need to build fires and will provide light during the long evenings of winter. A double-mantle Coleman lantern burns 1/8 of a pound of propane per hour when set at full brilliance, while one burner on a Coleman stove set at a moderate flame uses 1/3 of a pound per hour. A winter trip typically requires about 3/4 of a pound per day, so five disposable 16.4-ounce cylinders or one five-pound refillable cylinder would be appropriate for a week-long trip. The hoses on most stoves are too short, so bring an extension. The next chapter has additional information on camping and camping equipment that may be useful to small-boaters.

One problem is common to cartoppers and inflatables: keeping things dry. The big bags used by river rafters are light and take a lot of abuse, and the smaller ones used by sea kayakers may be handy. If you can still find them in surplus stores, the large black rubber-coated bags used to pack field telephone equipment work very well. Things like cameras that need protection from bumps as well as moisture can be packed in ammunition cans. A tarpaulin should cover the entire load.

Stay well within the weight and power ratings of your boat. Heavy objects like fuel and water cans should be put in the center, fore and aft as well as athwartships; by keeping the moment of inertia of the boat and its load low, the bow and stern to can rise quickly to the waves. The load must be secured so it can't shift—it may fall to the low side if you roll.

In addition, the center of gravity of the load and the passengers must be adjusted to allow the boat to plane efficiently. Don't compensate for a poorly balanced load by putting an extreme angle on the engine mounting bracket—work to get the balance right. Even a heavily laden boat can broach in a following sea (increase speed down the face of a wave and suddenly turn broadside to the waves), so hold your speed down and drag the bailing bucket if you have to.

To repeat an earlier caveat: *The Baja Adventure Book* should be used as a planning guide. It is not a substitute for the *Sailing Directions* and appropriate nautical charts, so bring a full set. However, since they camp ashore at night and may need to put ashore to avoid heavy weather, sailors of dinghys, Hobies, cartoppers and other very small craft need highly detailed information on coastlines. Due to their small scale and absence of shoreline detail, most marine charts are of little value, and the 1:50,000 scale Mexican topographic maps will be much more useful. See Chapter 8 for further information.

Most sailors recognize the inherent dangers of Baja's Pacific coast and keep their guard up, but the tranquil conditions prevalent in the Cortez can lull you into believing that things are always like that, and tragedies have occurred. In November 1980 a group of twenty-nine young men and eleven staff members from an organization helping troubled teenagers left Guaymas bound for Baja in four converted life boats equipped with sails and oars. A storm hit, "the worst on

Johnny Neptune executes a daring sea rescue off Danzante, *pushing the author's boat back to port, while Will Ashford photographs the exploit.*

record for that area." Three boats arrived safely at Mulegé, but the fourth, with eight people aboard, never made it.

Emergency assistance and communications

Boaters in Mexican waters will not find the extensive communications and rapid response they expect from the Coast Guard in U.S. waters. The Mexican Navy provides search and rescue (SAR) services when vessels or aircraft are available, and COTPs sometimes have boats or can arrange for local assistance. Under a bilateral agreement between the U.S. and Mexico, the U.S. Coast Guard can provide limited SAR coverage off the west coast of Mexico, directed by the Rescue Coordination Center in Long Beach. Surface units, fixed-wing HU-25 aircraft and HH-65 helicopters from San Diego normally can respond to SAR cases as far south as Cedros, and C-130s from Sacramento can operate as far south as Acapulco. Club Deportivo "Bahía Kino" at Bahía Kino, Sonora, at the east edge of the Midriff region, has at its disposal boats, airplanes, four-wheel-drive units, radios and medical personnel and equipment.

The Coast Guard can be contacted on VHF channel 16, often as far south as Ensenada. Many other organizations guard VHF channel 16, including Mexican government coastal radio stations at Ensenada, La Paz, Guaymas and Mazatlan, COTP offices, offices and vessels of the Mexican Ferry System, commercial shipping, Mexican naval vessels and bases, and some marinas. Some operators speak English, although not necessarily fluently. Club Deportivo "Kino Bay" guards CB channel 4 and VHF channel 16. Many other organizations and individuals guard CB channels; see page 87.

Clubs, charters and commercial trips

The Vagabundos del Mar Boat and Travel Club makes frequent trailerboat journeys to the Cortez. The membership fee is modest, and the club publishes a newsletter with all manner of information of interest to trailerboaters and RVers. Most boats are powerboats, but sailboaters are welcome.

Cortez Yacht Charters, Ocean Voyages, The Moorings, and Fraser Charters, Inc., can provide a variety of yacht charters in Baja waters, and the Baja Beach & Tennis Club just west of Maneadero has local sailing trips. The NOLS offers sailing as a part of its "Semester in Mexico" course. Oceanic Society Expeditions has a natural history/camping/sailing trip in the Cortez. A number of hotels, resorts and other organizations rent Hobies or other small sailing craft, including the Baja Beach & Tennis Club, the Estero Beach Hotel, just to the south of Ensenada, the Hotel Stouffer Presidente in Loreto, and Hotel Las Arenas, Hotel Punta Pescadero, Cabo Acuadeportes and Pisces Water Sport Center in the Cape region. Raul Perez and Alberto Lucero offer guided *panga* trips out of Bahía de los Angeles and

The heavy tides encountered in the upper Cortez can be used to simplify engine and boat maintenance and to allow the loading of fuel and equipment with a minimum of hassle.

Bahía San Francisquito, respectively. The mailing addresses of most of these organizations and individuals will be found in Appendix A.

****

FOR WANT OF A PIN THE BOAT WAS (ALMOST) LOST. We had heard that large groupers inhabit the waters around Isla Alcatraz in Bahía Kino, so Reeve and I decided to dive the area. We made camp on the shore northwest of town, launched our twelve-foot cartopper and loaded spearguns, underwater cameras and dive gear. It was a long run to the island, about seven miles, but the water was calm and we made excellent time. Anchored on the south side of the island, we suited up and hit the water. Grouper are very spooky fish, and hunting them proved to be great fun. The visibility was only six feet, which was about the range of our guns, so intense concentration and stealth were necessary. Their lateral lines told the fish of our presence far sooner than our eyes told us of theirs, and the first evidence we had that one was nearby was usually a loud "thump" and a swirl of silt as the fish spooked. Driven by curiosity, one would occasionally stay an extra second or two to see what was happening, and we got a few shots. It was nerve-wracking, each shot requiring instant reflexes and near-perfect aim, but we finally managed to bag two barbecue-size fish.

We were getting into the boat when we noticed whitecaps rolling around the east and west points of the island; a heavy wind had sprung up from the northwest. We started the engine and pulled the anchor, but just after I engaged the shift lever

A small problem at sea; *Andale's* main backwinded and the boom broke at the preventer. Clockwise from the bottom: Paul Payne, Gerry Fulmer and the author's brother Reeve clear the wreckage.

and twisted the throttle the engine raced wildly—the shear pin had broken. We had three extra pins taped to the handle of the motor and I had tools in my underwater camera box, but replacing the pin was a bit tricky in the small and tippy boat. I had to unclamp the engine from the transom, lift it into the boat, remove the propeller, put in a new pin, replace the propeller and clamp the engine back on the transom. After the repair the engine behaved normally, but as we came out of the lee of the island things looked bad; a heavy sea was up and the bay was a mass of whitecaps. Our small boat would be sorely challenged, but we would be safe if the engine kept working and we kept the bow into the waves. Several hundred yards from the island the engine again raced wildly; the new shear pin had broken. We quickly dropped the anchor before the boat had a chance to swing broadside to the waves. It was hairy removing the engine in the wildly pitching boat, but we finally got underway.

About four miles from camp the pin broke again. This time we were in big trouble, for the water was too deep to anchor. We swung broadside and began to roll heavily and take on green water, but a hastily improvised sea anchor consisting of a bucket on a rope finally swung us back perpendicular to the waves. Since our trip back to camp was parallel to the shore we were only a mile or two away from land. We rejected the idea of rowing for shore, since we would be broadside to the waves and might roll over or swamp, and the surf on the beach looked bad. Besides, it would be a long walk back to camp carrying our gear, if any of it survived the ride through the surf. We were in no great physical danger since we were in wet suits and had masks and fins close at hand—the real danger was the loss of our cameras, guns, boat and motor.

In a great spray of wind-driven water I unclamped the engine and started to lift it, when a large wave hit, throwing me against the gunnel. I almost went over the side, motor and all, but Reeve grabbed me and I managed to get my footing. We installed the last pin, started the motor, shifted into gear—and the pin broke almost instantly. Several times the bow of the boat did not rise quickly enough into the ever-growing waves, and the bilges were soon awash in six inches of water. As Reeve frantically bailed I searched for something to serve as a shear pin, and finally found a set of five small jewelers screwdrivers in my camera box. Using a pair of sidecutting pliers, I nipped the hardened steel shaft of one of them and bent it back and forth until it broke. The diameter of the impromptu shear pin was too small, but it lasted about a mile. The second screwdriver broke immediately, but the third, fourth and last one got us to within 500 yards of camp. What now? The wind was blowing us rapidly away from the shore, far faster than we could hope to row. It then dawned on us that when a shear pin breaks, it breaks into three pieces, one long and two short, and that the broken remains of some of the pins were still in the bilges. After a mad scramble on our knees, we removed the propeller and installed two of the long pieces in the propeller shaft, providing new shear surfaces. It worked! We started the engine, held our breaths and rode the crest of a breaker to land triumphantly on the beach in front of our camp. An examination of the engine revealed that a defect in the shifting mechanism was causing the engine to slam out and into gear, breaking the pins.

****

CHAPTER 5

GOING SELF-PROPELLED

Since it carries virtually all road traffic south of Ensenada, the Transpeninsular Highway has greatly influenced the public image of Baja. To most, the scenes passing outside the car window are the only Baja: mile after mile of asphalt road winding across scrubby desert and through desolate canyons, interrupted only by occasional villages, gas stations and glimpses of the sea. The traveler's focus of attention is usually on reaching the next air-conditioned oasis, avoiding contact with everything in between as much as possible. Propose a bicycle or backpacking trip to someone and you are apt to be greeted with a snort and an incredulous, "Whataya, crazy or somethin?" Baja California is certainly the last place where anyone of sound mind would voluntarily forsake the advantages of the internal combustion engine for a trip propelled by human muscle. Right?

Wrong! Despite the common impression, Baja is a joy for adventurous bicyclists, backpackers, hikers, climbers and kayakers. Bicyclists can watch whales mating, visit an Indian art site, challenge a roadrunner to a race, explore a cave, camp on a pristine beach and catch a fish for supper, all during a single trip. Backpackers, climbers and hikers can find another Baja, one not served by roads and thus rarely visited, of high mountains, plunging canyons, pines and oaks, flowing water and emerald pools. Kayakers can revel among remote islands and deserted beaches along the western shore of the Cortez, an area that seems destined to become one of the more popular sea kayaking areas in North America.

Not everyone will appreciate Baja; it may be a paradise, but certainly not the Moslem version. Most self-propelled trips in Baja are made in winter, which is the "off" season for vigorous physical activity for many people, so they will have lots of sore muscles until the kinks get worked out. And once self-propelled in a remote area for the first time, some people experience an uncomfortable psychological shock, a reaction to the utter openness of the empty desert. Accustomed to conditions in the United States, where towns are rarely more than ten or twenty miles apart, some people find Baja's vast empty stretches threatening; they seem to doubt their ability to survive, self-contained and alone, no matter how well-prepared and well-tuned their bodies and their equipment. Some

begin to refer to tiny *ranchos* as "towns" and small settlements as "cities," perhaps a manifestation of a subconscious wish. A few people begin to press for a return to a more crowded, familiar and thus comfortable environment, constantly suggesting that the group get up early, ride late or skip siesta time so that they can "get somewhere." Most people adjust within a few days, and learn to slow down, accept and enjoy. A few don't.

Clothing and camping equipment

True to its image, Baja is often warm or hot, but there are great variations in temperature, and it can occasionally get downright cold, even in summer. The existence of this variation, together with the need for ventilation and sun protection, should form the basis for planning clothing and bedding. Clothes should be loose fitting, light in weight and made of cotton, with long sleeves and legs to prevent sunburn. Bathing suits, shorts and G-strings lead to burns, dehydration, abrasion in case of falls, and unwelcome attention. A sweater and a jacket will be appreciated, and since the windchill law has not been repealed, the jacket ought to have a tightly-woven outer fabric. It is usually unnecessary to bring a lot of extra clothing along simply to stay clean, for even though water is scarce, there are opportunities to wash clothes. Winter hikers and climbers should be prepared for frost in the Sierra de Juárez and Sierra de la Victoria, and snow and hard freezes in the upper reaches of the Sierra San Pedro Mártir.

Light-colored, broad-brimmed straw hats are very inexpensive in Baja and provide the best sun protection and ventilation. Backpackers may want to pin up the back brim to prevent it from rubbing on their packs, and kayakers should glue styrofoam into the crown, since some straw hats sink. Don't forget your sun glasses, and a Swiss Army knife—the kind with tweezers. Everything must be clean, presentable and in good repair; look like a bum in Baja and you will be treated like a bum.

A 2-pound down bag or a 2 1/2- or 3-pound polyester bag should keep most people comfortable most of the year. Bags should have full-length zippers for heat control. A bag liner will facilitate cleanliness and can be used alone on hot nights.

Although bulkier, some people prefer a sheet and several blankets, since they allow comfort all the way from hot nights (nothing or just the sheet) to cool (everything) to cold (everything plus heavy clothing). Bag or blankets, your sleeping gear should be carried in a waterproof cover, since heavy dew is common on the Pacific side and rain is possible. Since ground temperatures also range from hot to cold, the thermal insulation provided by a foam pad makes it preferable to an air mattress. Bring lots of patches if you use an air mattress. Since they do no absorb sweat, plastic and rubber air mattresses become uncomfortable in hot weather, so a cotton sheet will be appreciated.

Most people bring a small, self-supporting tent. It must be designed to allow plenty of ventilation. A poncho is useful, serving as raingear, groundcloth, tent, table cloth, sun shade, kayak sail and extra insulation on cold nights. Scorpions have a tendency to avoid plastic, so people sleeping out in the open should use a plastic ground cloth.

Everyone likes an occasional evening campfire, and burnable materials like wood and cactus and agave debris are usually not hard to find, but for a variety of reasons a stove is the preferable way to cook. Scorpions love to hide in such fuel materials, and most stings occur while people are making and maintaining fires, often when they have their minds on cooking. Use a cheap pair of leather gloves to handle firewood, and never stack it in your arms or allow it to touch the rest of your body. I have always followed these precautions and have never been stung, but one evening a friend told me it seemed that I was over-reacting to the threat of scorpions—he didn't worry about them and had never been stung. Not five minutes later he was returning to the campfire with an armload of agave when a big one nailed him. Scouting up fire materials every time you want a cup of coffee can become a pain on physically demanding trips. Some hard-working bicyclists don't bother to cook, since meals can be purchased from hotels and cafés along the Transpeninsular, and the weather is often so warm that frequent hot meals are not missed. In any event, if you camp near settled areas, it may not be possible to find adequate materials for a fire and you will need a stove anyway.

This cartoon from an 1868 article by J. Ross Browne portrays a typical impression of Baja backpacking.

Gasoline is the only liquid fuel universally available in Baja, so multi-fuel stoves from MSR and Optimus are good choices. (See page 83 for more information on gasoline). Kerosene is difficult to find, and butane cartridges are very rare. Hardware and supply stores sometimes carry Coleman fuel, although you may not recognize it because it is often sold in a cylindrical container rather than the familiar rectangular can, and if you ask you may get a blank look—the locals pronounce it co-LEE-man, with the stress on the second syllable. Because of the extreme temperature differences, fuel is best carried in a metal container with a tight top.

Food and water

A self-propelled trip in Baja does not necessarily mean poor food and discomfort. In fact, with adequate planning it can be quite the opposite. My son Mike and I were to provide a sag wagon for a group of off-road bikers making a trip to Bahía Tortugas and Punta Abreojos a few years ago, but we were delayed and did not catch up with them until they had been underway about a week. The contrast was priceless: Mike and I, in our new one-ton four-wheel-drive pickup, equipped with air conditioning, stereo and deep-pile upholstery, had been underway three days and were tired, dirty and cranky, having been living on Pringles and Coke. The bicyclists, underway for a week, were clean, fresh and cheerful, and had been dining on fresh fish and scallops smothered in garlic and butter sauce. It all depends on how you go about it.

Supplies are apt to be less of a problem in Baja than in similarly remote parts of the U.S. Stores are found in many villages, and locally produced staple foods such as *tortillas*, fruit, eggs and fish are often of good quality and quite inexpensive. A special treat is ranch eggs, produced by hens who have to scratch for a living, a world apart from U.S.-style production-line eggs. When you pedal, paddle or walk up to a tiny *rancho* or fishing camp in need of a meal you will probably be greeted courteously and offered beans, eggs and *tortillas* at a low price. Fishermen sometimes have lobsters too small to be legally sold, and may offer you a mess of them, pan-fried and delicious. Foraging can produce clams and mussels—an army could not starve at the south end of Bahía Concepción—and a fishing kit with a handline, hooks and a few sinkers weighs and costs almost nothing. Ranches and fish camps are not evenly spaced, and may be abandoned or in use only seasonally, and fish don't always bite, so this is apt to be a take-it-while-you-can-get-it proposition. For variety, flexibility and insurance, bring a supply of lightweight foods not available in Baja, including freeze-dried meals, dried fruits, gorp, dried soups and granola bars. Keep your food tightly bundled up—gulls, mice, rats and coyotes like many of the same foods you do.

Active people may require up to a gallon of drinking water a day on warm days and up to two gallons under really hot conditions. In extremely difficult conditions, like the backpacking route from the La Milla campground to the mouth of Cañon Tajo, it can even be higher (fortunately this particular route has water). Although kayakers may be able to bum safe water from passing yachts, and bicyclists from RVs, most will soon be dependent on untreated local water. During their 1975 Cape-to-the-border backpacking trip, Alan Ehrgott and John Cox were forced at one point to drink dark-brown water

Ted Robinson and Wayne Campbell backpack through Parque Nacional Sierra San Pedro Mártir on a brisk spring morning.

so full of tiny beetles that they had to use their teeth as strainers. Don't depend solely on the opinion of locals as to water quality, since they are used to it and will truthfully answer that the water is safe—for them. However, if they say the water is bad, BELIEVE IT. If you must obtain water from a *rancho*, view it with suspicion, and if you don't see a well or windmill on the premises, crank up the anxiety level one notch. The basic rule is to treat all local water, no matter how clean and sparkling it looks. Five minutes of vigorous boiling will kill most disease-causing microorganisms, but getting every last one of them of them takes at least thirty minutes. Devices that use microfilters or silver-based chemicals work well, but are not available in Baja, so bring your own. If you don't have such equipment and don't want to take the time and the fuel to boil water, treat it with purification tablets purchased before you leave home. Although having no factual basis for it, I have reservations about disinfecting water with chlorine bleach or iodine manufactured in Mexico.

Favorite bicycle routes

The ultimate Baja skinny-wheel adventure is the 926-mile tour from Tecate to La Paz, or to Cabo San Lucas, 1,060 miles. Taking three weeks or so, most trips start in Tecate to avoid the hassle and traffic in Tijuana. Many have made the trip, including a few coming from as far away as Switzerland and New Zealand. The first to make the trip were six people in the HEMISTOUR group, who started out from Alaska, bound for Patagonia. In February 1973 they crossed the border at Mexicali and took the unpaved road south of San Felipe, reaching the then-still-unpaved Transpeninsular north of Punta Prieta. They hit pavement at Guerrero Negro and continued on to La Paz. Two eventually made it to Patagonia. Age seems to be no barrier; in 1975 Claire Harvey made it to La Paz at sixty-six, and in 1982 Phil Martin at seventy-three.

There are shorter alternatives. The Mexican bus systems or an airline can be used to get to jumping-off points in Baja or to bypass areas of limited interest. Some bikers find they enjoy Baja Sur the most and go by bus to San Ignacio or Santa Rosalía or fly to Loreto, the most northerly town in Baja Sur with an international airport, and bike south from there. Still another variation is to bike south to Santa Rosalía or La Paz, cross the Cortez by ferry and return home through Sonora— although the road north has headwinds and lots of traffic. If you like prime desert, the Transpeninsular between El Rosario and Bahía de los Angeles is the best in Baja.

Loop trips starting and ending in the same location are of special interest to Baja bicyclists. The only good paved loop trip is from La Paz to Cabo San Lucas on the Transpeninsular, and then north on Route 19 through Todos Santos back to La Paz, a moderate ride of 226 miles, taking six or seven days and visiting some of the nicest towns in Baja. The other major possibility is to follow Routes 2, 3 and 5 around the northern part of the peninsula, although this is a somewhat lackluster journey in places. A number of loop trips of interest to off-road bicyclists are described starting on page 51.

Bikes and equipment

The Transpeninsular has been conquered by a wide assortment of bikes, ranging from exotic racing machines to Channell Wasson's 1920s-era Westfield three-speed, purchased from a thrift shop for three dollars, and even a unicycle. However, the choice of a bike is of major importance, for a fine piece of machinery well-adapted to Baja conditions adds greatly to the fun. The roads tend to be rough, the distances long and the weight to be carried heavy, so a sturdy, easy-riding touring or off-road bike is a better choice than a stiff and fragile racing bike. A viscous-gel saddle, low gears, cantilever or roller-cam brakes, platform pedals and a thumb shifter are assets on any Baja trip.

A compass and a cyclometer will help you locate many attractions noted in this book. If you will be traveling off-road you will need topos—see page 80. A kickstand is a welcome addition, since your panniers may become a home for scorpions if you lay your bike on the ground; try to find the kind that holds the bike upright. Bike locks and chains are a judgment call; in areas south of the border cities crime is rare, a lock doesn't protect your gear, and other than tall cactuses

To reach an isolated beach, Lee and Elaine Waters had to ford a stretch of salty tidal water.

BONNIE WONG

and boojums there sometimes isn't much to lock your bike to. A set of front and rear panniers of at least 2,000-cubic-inch capacity and a seat bag should carry all your food, water, clothing, equipment and camping gear, and a handlebar bag is handy for wallets, cameras and maps. Keep them low to promote stability. Most bicyclists find day-packs too warm for comfort. Racks are a source of problems, and steel is best, if only because Mexican welders can repair steel but rarely aluminum. The best way to carry water is in bladder bags in the front panniers.

Baja has a wealth of rocks, loose gravel, ruts and cracks waiting to pitch you on your head, so a hard-shell helmet designed for biking is a necessity. Get the kind with a sun visor. The Transpeninsular is narrow and you must avoid drifting left when turning your head to look back, so get a rearview mirror that attaches to your helmet or glasses. Since bikers are not common and are thus unexpected, you should maintain high visibility with a bike flag and a safety vest. A bike flag is not a toy; nothing reveals the presence of a biker more quickly and surely than a shocking-pink bike flag darting back and forth on top of a flexible mast.

Preparation, parts and repairs

Baja's long distances and rough roads require that a bike be specially prepared. Screws and nuts worked loose by vibration are a constant problem, so use lock washers everywhere and squirt on the Locktite liberally. Service all bearings, including bottom bracket and pedals, tighten the headset, replace worn brake blocks, brake cables and shifter mechanisms, true the wheels and tighten the spokes. If you are breaking spokes in the U.S. you will break more in Baja. Tires must be new or near-new, with a thorn-resistant strip between each tire and its tube. The rolling resistance of heavy-duty tires and tubes is high, but most people find their much lower rate of flats and failures to be a good trade-off. Remove any fenders—you won't need them. Individuals should carry a basic tool kit, chain repair links and tool, a few spare spokes and tire repair equipment. A few small hoseclamps, some boot material to repair gashes and sidewall cuts, a roll of wire and some duct tape may be appreciated later. A group of worriers can split up the weight and carry a freewheel assembly, front and rear derailleurs, bottom bracket assembly, crankarms and chain rings.

If you start with a well-prepared bike, things can still go wrong, but probably not as often as many people might imagine. My friend Bonnie Wong has led many Baja trips, but she and her fellow bikers have encountered only one broken spoke, one freewheel problem, one broken seat post and one pretzeled wheel, which gave out under a particularly heavy rider on an off-road trip. The record for persistence

A cactus-garden picnic along the Transpeninsular Highway.

BONNIE WONG

seems to have been won by Channell Wasson during his 1981 trip from Ensenada to La Paz aboard the old Westfield. He had to have his bottom bracket welded in Guerrero Negro, and several days later a new tire gave out, permanently. Since a replacement could not be found, he paid eight dollars to a boy for the wheel off his bike. Coming down the grade into Santa Rosalía his coaster brake burned out. He eventually made it to La Paz.

Chapters 9 through 16 identify many bike shops known to be in operation in areas south of the border cities shortly before publication. It is often easier to find a bike shop than an automobile repair shop, but don't expect too much; these shops carry parts for bikes owned by the local people, and you won't find, for instance, a Campagnolo bottom bracket tool. The most common wheels on local bikes are 26 x 1 3/8 and 27 x 1 1/4, and tires, tubes and spokes for these sizes are fairly easy to find. Tires for off-road bikes are hard to find in the sizes used by adults, although 26 x 2.125s are encountered occasionally. The mechanics in these shops are not factory trained, but they have a good deal of experience in solving problems, and many can weld and braze. Some general stores and hardware stores carry common parts.

Underway

Early morning and late afternoon are best for riding because of the climate. Never ride at night, for bike lights are notoriously poor and Baja drivers are not expecting bikers. There are not many trees available and most cacti are too skinny to provide usable shade, so many bikers have taken a siesta in the shade of a dry culvert. Thirty-five to 45 miles a day is a good pace for beginners on the Transpeninsular. More experienced bikers may cover 50 or 60, and a few have made 130.

Drainage is usually poor at dips and at the bottom of grades, causing sand and gravel to collect and making coasting at high speed dangerous. The greatest moving hazards are not eighteen-wheelers, but big motorhomes driven by gringos, who often have little experience with their big toys and are accustomed to wide roads and shoulders. With mirrors projecting out like antlers, these giant rigs occupy the entire lane, and many drivers will try to pass in the same lane even though the other is unoccupied. Some Mexican truckers are distinctly more courteous and will usually pass in the opposite lane if they can. Many large trucks are equipped with muffler cutouts, warning you of their presence miles away.

Most flat tires are caused by cactus thorns. Big ones can be seen and pulled out, but the little ones escape detection and keep pushing through the casing, causing repeated flats. Most thorns are picked up on unpaved areas, so experienced Baja bikers carry their bikes from the pavement to campsites. Ho-ho, you say! Is this like a Boy Scout snipe hunt, something to humiliate the new guys, getting them to carry their bikes around under the hot sun like a bunch of dummies? No, it's for real, and people who do this have far fewer flats than those who stand and smirk.

Chapters 9 through 16 describe all paved highways and all important unpaved roads in Baja, as well as many obscure by-ways. Information of interest to bikers is provided, such as important grades, bicycle shops, places to eat and obtain food and water, etc. In areas where they are easy to find, no specific information on campsites is necessary, but along roads with extensive fencing and agricultural areas, such as Route 3 southeast of Ensenada, many places to stop are identified. In some cases these are modest indeed, often little more than a way to get off the road. With their slow speed, eagle eyes and ability to get their bikes into areas inaccessible even to four-wheelers, bicyclists will discover many more places and should have less trouble finding a place to stop than any other type of traveler; no Baja biker has ever had to pedal all night for want of a campsite.

Hitchhiking and commercial transportation

Like bikers everywhere, those in Baja occasionally have a lazy day and hitchhike a lap or two. The locals are often friendly and curious about bicyclists. Most are willing to provide a free ride, and many a biker has made a lap in the back of a rickety stake truck jammed between a goat, a bale of hay and Grandpa. Tinker and Brian Rovira were once offered a ride in the back of a water department truck and got more than they bargained for. A large section of corrugated metal culvert almost crowded them out, but when the driver stopped and pulled off the cover, it proved to be full of lobsters and scallops, packed in ice. Some were already cooked, so the group broke out fresh limes and had an impromptu feast.

Trips on the Transpeninsular are one-way for virtually

Cycling in cactus country can pose a few problems.

BONNIE WONG

everyone, most bikers pedaling south with the prevailing winds and returning home by plane, bus or private vehicle. Bicyclists often have little trouble hitching rides home on pickups or RVs. Yachtsmen at La Paz or Cabo San Lucas about to depart for the United States are often in need of crew, and space may be found for a bike. There is another attractive alternative. Baja California Tours, Inc. offers a series of bus tours throughout Baja, described on page 83. Large busses are used on some trips, including the ones to the Cape, and the company is willing to bring along bikers and bicycles. Also, the Cape trip is one-way for most passengers, who fly back, and the company will provide bikers transportation back to the U.S. on the otherwise empty busses. A bicyclist thus can take a fine guided tour one way and bike home, or do the biking first and return by bus. The company will also let bikers get on and off at intermediate stops.

Drivers for the Mexican bus companies are usually willing to take bicycles in the luggage compartment on a space-available basis, but may ask you to remove wheels and handlebars. To preserve your chrome and paint it would be well to have several large plastic garbage bags and some duct tape available. If you are with a large group there may be problems, for drivers sometimes won't take more than two or three bikes. Airlines flying between U.S. and Tijuana airports and airports farther south in Baja will carry bicycles, but their policies differ concerning extra cost, whether a box is required and whether they supply it. A given airline may have different requirements depending on whether you are flying to or from Baja. Their policies change from time to time, so get current information and make sure you understand the situation before you depart. Bicyclists can use the ferry system with no problems beyond those experienced by everyone else.

Off-road bicycling

In recent years groups of off-road bicyclists have opened a new spectrum of adventure in Baja, topped by a twenty-five-day trip from La Rumorosa to La Paz led by Bonnie Wong that included 600 off-road miles. On earlier trips her groups have conquered the road south of San Felipe past Bahía Gonzaga to the Transpeninsular; the road south from Bahía de los Angeles to Bahía San Francisquito and then southwest over La Cuesta de la Ley to El Arco and south to the highway; and the road from San Ignacio past Laguna San Ignacio to La Purísima, the Comondús, San Javier and Loreto. Her groups have also visited Cueva Palmarito, a rock-art treasure located north of San Ignacio. These are remarkable accomplishments involving some of the most remote areas left in Baja.

Tinker and Brian Rovira had a surprise of a different kind on one of these trips. They were pedalling down a slope when Tinker saw a huge rattlesnake crossing the road ahead. It was too late to brake or swerve, and with her feet almost at shoulder level and "yelling bloody thunder" (Brian's terminology), she ran over it. Shaken and fearful of finding an angry rattler intertwined among her spokes, she jumped off and waited while Brian inspected. The snake escaped to an uncertain fate.

Off-road bicyclists often feel the trip is over when they hit pavement, but a variety of excellent trips is possible if they can relax their standards a little. The following paragraphs list four loop trips combining on- and off-pavement riding. All starting points have bus service, two have air service, and if you drive to the point of beginning, you should have little trouble finding a place to leave your vehicle. All have water and some food available en route, although not necessarily at convenient intervals, and all have been successfully traveled by bicyclists. The direction (clockwise, counterclockwise) has been chosen to have shakedowns occur in settled areas, to take advantage of prevailing winds, and to avoid long, steep upgrades where possible, although there are conflicts in some cases.

Laguna Hanson Loop Trip: El Cóndor, Laguna Hanson, El Coyote, KM 98 on Route 2, El Cóndor, covering 110 miles off-road, 9 miles on pavement. This easy-to-moderate, five- or six-day trip, passing through pine forests and meadows and encountering many *ranchos* along the way, involves few navigation, logistic or road problems and is the best Baja route for novices.

Vizcaíno Loop Trip: Vizcaíno, Bahía Tortugas, Rancho San Andrés, Bahía Asunción, Punta Abreojos, KM 98 on the Transpeninsular, Vizcaíno, covering 276 miles off-road, 40 miles on pavement. This trip is easy but long, requiring ten to twelve days. Most of the road is graded and fairly level, but there are stretches of washboard. The scenery is not always inspiring, but there are many fine deserted beaches.

Mountain Villages Loop Trip: Loreto, KM 118, San Javier, San José de Comondú, San Miguel de Comondú, La Purísima, KM 60, Loreto, covering 115 miles off-road, 38 miles on pavement. This trip is moderate to difficult and requires about seven days. The climb to San Javier is lengthy and steep, and some later stretches are remote and involve walking, but the towns and the terrain are unique.

Tinker Rovira and Bill Gibson head up one of the "Terrible Three," the steepest and roughest grades in all of Baja.

BONNIE WONG

Cape Coast Loop Trip: La Paz, Las Cuevas, La Rivera, Cabo Pulmo, Cabo Frailes, San José del Cabo, Cabo San Lucas, Todos Santos, La Paz, covering 70 miles off-road, 185 miles on pavement. This trip is easy, requiring seven to eight days. The dirt section is graded, with no major hills. Although most of it is on pavement, this is the most interesting and varied of all the loop trips, including three of Baja's liveliest tourist towns, magnificent deserted beaches on both the Cortez and Pacific sides, and excellent off-the-beach diving on Baja's only coral reef. A mask, snorkel and fins weigh only six pounds, but if this is too heavy to bring along you should have little trouble borrowing them when you get to the reef. Several variations of this trip are possible; bikers could fly into Los Cabos International Airport instead of La Paz, and the Transpeninsular could be substituted for either the Pacific or Cortez segments.

In addition, there are loop trips recommended to four-wheelers in Chapter 6 that may be of interest to the more experienced, determined and physically able off-road bicyclists. Chapters 9 through 16 contain detailed information on all the loop trips and many other routes.

Many of the ideas on equipment, preparation and so forth presented above for skinny-wheelers apply off-road as well. Often the most difficult and important aspect of Baja off-road biking is navigation, and a compass and accurate maps are

The start of the Rosarito-to-Ensenada Fun Ride.

essential. A cyclometer is also a necessity, since speed can be difficult to judge and there are often no kilometer posts to help you gauge distance. Compared to off-roading in the U.S., Baja roads are generally worse, and your daily mileage will be less. The road rating scheme for off-road motor vehicles described on page 1 is of limited use to bicyclists, who can go anywhere a four-wheel-drive can go and more.

Trips and rentals

Touring Exchange, Bob Wagner and Backroads Bicycle Touring have bicycle trips with experienced leaders. Most offer trips to La Paz or the Cape, some accompanied by a sag wagon. A few Touring Exchange trips travel to some of the most interesting and remote places in Baja, and one combines bicycling with sea kayaking. Baja Expeditions has mountain-bike trips in the Cape region and in the Sierra de Juárez in Baja Norte. Baja Surf Club offers mountain-bike package trips out of Rancho Leonero in East Cape, featuring local exploring, an optional guided overnight ride across the Sierra de la Victoria on the Naranjas Road accompanied by a sag wagon, instruction and clinics, plus diving, fishing, waterskiing and swimming at the resort ranch, and boardsailing at its center at the Hotel Palmas de Cortez just to the north. Vela Highwind Center has mountain bikes and clinics at its boardsailing operation at the Hotel Playa Hermosa at East Cape, and the Hotel La Arenas to the north has mountain bikes available. Excursions Extraordinaires offers day-use rental bikes at its boardsailing center at Hotel Punta Chivato. Mr.

ANN KENDELLEN

Bill's Boardsailing Adventures has mountain bikes for the use of guests at its villa at East Cape.

Other biking attractions

Monday International Sports, Inc. and Bicycling West sponsor a number of bicycle fun rides, relays, triathlons and similar events in Baja. The fun rides are especially popular and often involve more people as participants, crew and spectators than the widely publicized Baja 1000 auto race.

Backpacking, hiking and climbing

There is a simple way to tell if you are a true desert rat: simply make a list of your ten favorite Baja locations, and then go back and see how many are associated with water. The chances are that you will fail the test miserably, and that most or all of them are "water places." You won't be alone, for in addition to obvious physiological needs, we all have strong psychological attachments to water. For either or both reasons, Baja's arid climate renders much of the peninsula of limited interest to most backpackers and hikers. Few will choose to follow Alan Ehrgott and John Cox, who worked for three months caching food and water at seventy-five mile intervals before their 110-day Cape-to-the-border backpack-

ing trip.

However, accidents of geology and meteorology have provided a number of places with permanent surface water, allowing lengthy and enjoyable visits. Chapters 9 through 16 describe backpacking adventures in Parque Nacional Sierra San Pedro Mártir, Cañons Tajo and Guadalupe in the Sierra de Juárez escarpment, Cañon del Diablo in the Sierra San Pedro Mártir escarpment, Cañons San Dionisio and San Bernardo in the Sierra de la Victoria, and to La Laguna, a mountain meadow in the Victorias. In addition, two short backpacking trips to waterless locations are included, Mina Santa Marta and the Columbia site.

Also described are a number of "day hikes," short ventures to interesting locations, starting and ending in the same place, including the tip of the Punta Banda peninsula, the Islas de Todos Santos, Isla San Martín, Isla San Jerónimo, Isla Partida Sur, "Manila Palm Oasis," the Gran Cañon on Isla Cedros, the La Milla-Cañon Tajo overlook, the "Bell Dome" route into Cañon Tajo, Cueva Palmarito, the Puerto Balandra-to-Bahía Salinas hike on Isla Carmen, Playa Independence, Parque Nacional Constitución de 1857, Parque Nacional Sierra San Pedro Mártir, El Volcán, Tinaja de Yubay and Mike's Sky Ranch, the last four of which have permanent

Celia Keisling, Jim Clark and Bruce Barrus explore a pool in Cañon San Bernardo.

WILL WATERMAN

surface water.

Baja has some excellent climbs, the most popular being the challenging class 3 climb on Picacho del Diablo, at 10,154 feet Baja's highest mountain. Cerro Salsipuedes, Picacho San Lázaro and Cerro Zacatosa in the Sierra de la Victoria and El Pilón de Parras near Loreto are less demanding class 3 climbs. Tres Vírgenes volcano is a class 2 or 3 climb, while Teta de la India, Pico Banda and the volcano on Isla San Martín are easy class 1 or 2. (Class 1 is ordinary walking. Class 2 is scrambling, sometimes requiring that hands be used. Suitable boots or shoes are needed, but special knowledge and equipment are not necessary. Class 3 is at the limit of climbing without specialized equipment, although boots are required and a rope may be useful for handling packs. Some specialized knowledge is helpful.)

The number of technical climbing areas (class 4, where ropes are used for safety purposes, and class 5, where they are used to support climbers, specialized knowledge and equipment being essential for both) in Baja is limited, but one area provides outstanding conditions. Located on the Juárez escarpment east of the road from Route 2 to Laguna Hanson, it is jealously guarded by San Diego climbers through a conspiracy of silence and hence is largely unknown to "outsiders." The centerpiece of the area is "El Trono Blanco," a 1,600-foot big wall. The approach will put off the belay-from-the-bumper-crowd, but more energetic climbers should not miss this magnificent wall. There are literally hundreds of other climbs in the area, including at least twenty involving upper-class 5 moves. Technical climbs in other regions include the rock face at El Pilón de Parras and Cerro Blanco in the Victorias. Technical climbing in a very unusual setting is possible on Los Frailes at Cabo San Lucas.

In addition to the hikes and climbs described in *The Baja Adventure Book*, the other major canyons in the Juárez escarpment, such as El Carrizo, La Mora and El Palomar, and canyons in the San Pedro Mártir escarpment like La Pro-

Wayne Campbell scouts Picacho del Diablo from a pinnacle on the escarpment of the San Pedro Mártir plateau.

NOLS instructor Jim Clark introduces his students to the realities of the Sierra de la Victoria.

videncia and others to the south, also have year-round water and fine areas for backpack trips and day hikes.

The equipment and techniques required in Baja are no different from those for warm, arid and remote regions elsewhere. You may get away with using running shoes for short forays, but for longer ventures boots are necessary. Avoid extremes; neither lightweights with nylon uppers nor heavyweight clunkers are necessary or desirable. The best boot is a matter of preference, but many desert backpackers, hikers and climbers prefer a medium-weight boot with Vibram lug soles, full-grain uppers and a reinforced toe cap. They should not be of insulated or waterproof construction, and waterproofing compounds should not be applied, for the chances of getting them wet is low and sweat must be free to dissipate. Boots lined with Gore-Tex offer no advantage in desert hiking.

No trails are maintained for recreational use anywhere in Baja, even in the national parks, and there are no signs or route markers, although the more popular ones may be marked by "ducks," small piles of stones or other physical means of showing the route. It is easy to get lost, so carry a compass and a topographic map and leave your itinerary with family or friends. There are a few rangers, but the chance of encountering one in a time of need is remote. In fact, most areas are so little used that it is unusual to meet anyone once off the roads. Although permanent water is available in some places, it is not necessarily where you want it, so you must carry a sizable amount and be prepared to alter your route and your plans if necessary. Chapter 8 describes the topographic maps produced by the Mexican Government.

Most backpackers, hikers and climbers recognize the dangers inherent in a hot, arid climate, but cold and snow can be problems too. The Sierra de San Pedro Mártir can accumulate up to eight feet of snow, and the Ensenada rescue squad has been called out a number of times. In 1987 nine teen-agers on a late-April camping excursion at elevation 4,200 feet in the Sierra de Juárez were reported missing when five feet of snow fell. A comic-opera rescue attempt resulted when helicopters, ham radio operators, the State Judicial Police, forest rangers, rescue squad contingents from Ensenada, San Felipe and Mexicali, the Mexican Army, several ranchers, a detachment of "commandos" and numerous cousins and uncles mostly got in each other's way. However, six days later a convoy of farm tractors, military vehicles and four-wheel-drives, led by a bulldozer, broke through the snow to find the boys holed up in a cabin, out of food and firewood. Given hot showers and filled with *tortillas*, tuna casserole and hot chocolate (they were too young for tequila), everyone survived, although three of the boys sustained frostbite.

The Spring session of the NOLS "Semester in Baja" includes a course in technical rock climbing. The American Alpine Institute offers rock-climbing instruction on Los Frailes at Cabo San Lucas, ranging from an introductory course through 5.10.

Sea kayaking

The kayak route from San Felipe to La Paz is, of course, the ultimate kayak trip, but it is difficult even out of proportion to its 583-mile length, taking as long as a month, even including a few grueling 40-mile days. The 75-mile coast between Bahía Gonzaga and Bahía de los Angeles is one of the most remote in the Cortez, long stretches of bluff making it difficult to land in some places. The 149-mile coast from Bahía de los Angeles to Santa Rosalía is largely uninhabited except in the Bahía San Francisquito area, although there are an increasing number of temporary fish camps, and unlike on the Escondido to La Paz coast, there is little yacht traffic. In 1985 a would-be San Felipe-to-La Paz kayaker got as far as Bahía San Francisquito, spent an hour at the resort bar, hitchhiked out to the Transpeninsular, and to date has never returned to claim his kayak. A far better choice would be to launch at Mulegé instead of San Felipe, thus shortening the route, avoiding most of the problems areas and yet still hitting the high spots.

The Seri Indians used their kayak-like reed boats to cross the Cortez following the "Stepping-Stones" route discussed in Chapter 11. In 1933 Dana and Ginger Lamb crossed the Cortez from the vicinity of Santa Rosalía as part of their epic San Diego-to-Panama trip. In more recent years a number of kayakers have crossed the Cortez by similar routes, but because of the distances and heavy currents involved it will remain a trip for experts.

You don't have to be a forty-miles-a-day, open-water kayaker to enjoy the Cortez. The two most popular kayak routes in the Cortez, the "Coasting to La Paz" route from Escondido to La Paz and the "Coasting to Loreto" route from Mulegé to Loreto, are both well within the ability of most kayakers and are described in Chapter 13. These are favored not only because of their fine scenery, abundant wildlife and

lack of civilization, but also because they are the right distance apart for two- or one-week trips, about 135 and 85 miles respectively. In addition, they start and end at sizable towns on the Transpeninsular, making it possible for those on one-way trips to hitchhike or take the bus back to pick up vehicles. Those with only short vacations can shorten the latter trip by launching at San Sebastián.

Bahía de los Angeles is an increasingly popular kayaking area. There are many islands to explore and sandy campsites, and its relatively compact area makes it a fine place for a slow-bell kayak/camping trip. More ambitious kayakers can head to Puerto Don Juan and south along the coast to Bahía las Ánimas, a round trip taking a week or so, or head north to Isla Coronado. Those with the requisite open-water experience can head out to Guardian Angel. Watch out for winter winds and be prepared to wait them out if necessary.

Bahía Concepción is calm and scenic and is a great place to practice paddling, self-righting and self-rescue procedures. Once you have these down pat, you can head for the open Cortez to try out your skills in waves. Kayakers like to launch at Puerto Escondido and head south along the coast past Isla Danzante for Bahía Agua Verde. The deeply indented western sides of Islas Espíritu Santo and Partida Sur north of La Paz have many fine sand beaches, making them popular destinations for novice kayakers and those interested in leisurely kayak/camping. Boats can be hired in La Paz to carry kayaks and gear to the islands if the five-mile crossing of Canal San Lorenzo is deemed unwise.

A lengthy trip along Baja's Pacific coast can be recommended only to intrepid kayakers, for tales of being overpow-

Hazel Wolf was eighty-one when she made her second trip to Isla Espíritu Santo.

RON YARNELL

ered by currents and wind, getting lost in fog and pitchpoling are the central themes of many of the accounts of kayak trips down this coast. While skill, practice and planning can greatly reduce the risk, even experts have serious problems here. In spite of this, there are still some excellent locations. Bahía Magdalena is a popular destination, where kayakers can seek out gray whales and explore the mangrove-lined waterways, moving camp only when the mood strikes. Although not often visited by kayakers, the coastline north of Santa Rosalillita has much to recommend it, including secluded beaches, plenty of firewood and excellent fishing and foraging. The coast along the southwest shore of the Punta Banda peninsula from La Bufadora is pleasant and undemanding, an ideal place for a first ocean trip, and a trip out to the Islas de Todos Santos can be made once the basics are mastered.

Equipment and preparation

Most Baja kayakers prefer a rigid boat, with high hull volume, a narrow curved bow, a straight stem, little rocker and a foot-operated rudder. The same basic equipment and provisions normally used on any kayak voyage are required, except that more water and reserve food should be taken. Although most routes pass towns and settlements and kayakers often encounter anchored yachts where water can be obtained, a hand-held reverse osmosis watermaker will provide freedom from worrying about water safety and supply, and from carrying excess weight and volume. Down bags are a poor choice for a kayak trip even in sunny Baja. A kayaker's tent should have fine mesh screening, for Cortez routes pass

through prime *jejene* territory. (A *jejene* is a blood-thirsty insect found in salt marshes, mangroves and decaying seaweed; see the stories beginning on pages 140 and 196.) Should you ding or crack your fiberglass kayak beyond the capabilities of your repair kit, materials may not be far away, since most Baja *pangas* are fiberglass and fishermen often have fabric, resin and activator.

Because of their small scale and absence of shoreline detail, most marine charts are of little value to Baja kayakers, and 1:50,000-scale Mexican topographic maps are required. Swift tidal currents of the upper- and mid-Cortez make tide tables essential. See Chapter 8 for information on topos and tide tables. Kayakers will profit by re-reading the sections of the previous chapter regarding paperwork, safety and emergency assistance. Remember, kayakers, all over-the-water distances in this book are expressed in nautical miles. Appendix B provides the conversion factors for nautical miles and kilometers.

Underway

The most favored months for Cortez kayaking are November through April, when the weather is cool. North-to-south trips with the prevailing winds recommended to bicyclists favor kayakers as well. Wind-driven waves in the Cortez can be sizable, but the short fetch allows little swell to build up, and waves usually die down quickly when the wind stops. The absence of large swells means that landings usually can be made without great difficulty. Each day's schedule should be planned with the tide tables in hand. Winds often spring

Kayakers take impromptu advantage of the wind.

WILL WATERMAN

up in mid-day in the Cortez, so an early start is necessary. Ten miles a day is a good average, twenty too much for most people. Beaches given a place name on the topos are often good places to stop for the night. (Mexican fishermen don't stop at a poor campsite often enough to have a name become widely accepted.)

Baja kayakers must be prepared to wait out weather. The number of days for the Mulegé-to-Loreto and Escondido-to-La Paz trips noted above, seven and fourteen respectively, are generally adequate for experienced kayakers in light weather, but a reserve of four or five days' extra food and water should be maintained. Equipped with tide tables, a skilled and flexible Baja kayaker can turn the tide into a friend rather than an enemy; if you are headed north from Bahía de los Angeles to Puerto Refugio, pick a flood; if you are making the Mulegé-to-Loreto run, take advantage of the ebb. Despite its normally placid appearance, the Cortez can change quickly and it deserves respect. In 1978 two groups of inexperienced kayakers were on a trip south along the Cortez coast headed for Loreto. The water was glassy as they started off one morning, but the wind soon came up and one group turned back. The other group of nine pressed on and were trying to round Punta Púlpito when one kayak capsized. Others tried to raft up and help right it and bail it out, but they soon swamped as well. After spending more than twelve hours in the water, suffering from hypothermia and exhaustion, six of the nine made it to shore.

The fun of Baja kayaking is not just in plying the waters. Fishing with a hand line or a short pole can provide fine meals

Kayakers load up for the long drive home.

and great sport. A mask, snorkel and fins can provide marvelous sightseeing, as well as allow you to forage for scallops and clams. The silence and the unobtrusiveness of a kayak make it possible to get close to whales and sea lions without alarm. Only a kayaker, away from civilization's mechanical sounds, can appreciate the intensity of the sound of a huge whale spouting a few yards away. Sea lions frequently doze with a flipper sticking straight up in the air, and a kayaker can paddle close and slip into the water with mask and fins for a better look. Be warned—when they awake to discover you alongside, sea lions can take off in such a fright that you may be left swimming in very polluted water.

Some areas are so remote that animals there have little fear of humans. One paddler in Bahía Magdalena recently had a visit from a small seal, which slid up on the deck of his kayak and looked him over for fifteen minutes. During a kayak trip to Magdalena, Lolly Flowers awoke to find a coyote tugging at her hair. It let go when she yelled, but far from being intimidated, it sniffed around for a while, grabbed a sweater and took off for the sand dunes. A few days later a stowaway was discovered in her kayak, a fat rodent of a species know to locals by the all-purpose name "*rata*." He avoided capture by scurrying into the bow of her kayak while they were ashore, but during the paddle he would suddenly appear. Manuel, as he was named, became something of a pet, but after several days he disappeared. Someone later saw an osprey lifting off the beach with a furry brown cargo and it soon became apparent that Manuel had hitched his last ride.

Baja sea kayaking is rapidly increasing in popularity, and there is a rich offering of trips and courses. Baja Expeditions has a trip to Espíritu Santo and Partida Sur, and a Bahía

Lolly Flowers and Manuel.

Magdalena trip to see the whales and wildlife. Wilderness: Alaska/Mexico has a nine-day trip between the vicinity of Caleta San Juanico and Loreto, a Bahía Magdalena kayaking/whale-watching venture, and a trip out to Isla Espíritu Santo. NOLS offers a three-week Baja kayaking course stressing paddling techniques, ocean safety and hazard evaluation and navigation. Their seventy-eight day "Semester in Mexico" combines sea kayaking, backpacking and sailing; the Spring session includes whale-watching at Bahía Magdalena, the Fall session technical rock climbing. For those past their prime, a "25 And Over" sea kayaking course is available. Southwest Sea Kayaks offers lectures and clinics on Baja kayaking at its San Diego headquarters, and a number of trips; current (1991) offerings include a trip north along the coast from Santa Rosalillita, another out to Isla San Martín after launching in Bahía San Quintín, and one out to Guardian Angel from Bahía de los Angeles. Short trips and instruction are also offered at La Bufadora. Paddling South offers a number of kayak trips in the area between Mulegé and La Paz, including one with instruction in wilderness medicine, and another combining kayaking with a mule trip. Touring Exchange offers a biking/kayaking trip in the Bahía de los Angeles area. Outback Expeditions has a trip in Bahía Concepción and along the "outer coast." Sea Trek Ocean Kayaking Center trips explore the area surrounding Caleta San Juanico. Southwest Sea Kayaks has rental kayaks that can be taken into Baja, and Excursions Extraordinaires offers kayak rentals for day-use at its boardsailing center at the Hotel Punta Chivato.

****

A DESERT ENCOUNTER. During their length-of-Baja bicycle trip Bonnie Wong and her female companions were crossing Laguna Diablo, a desolate dry lake near San Felipe, when two male motorcycle racers roared up out of the mirages in a huge cloud of dust. Very macho, they were dressed from top to bottom in magnificent leathers, topped off with giant helmets, goggles and heavy boots armored with shining studs, and plastic vests providing protection against rocks thrown up by the motorcycle ahead. Their machines gleamed of chromium, and most exterior surfaces not chromed were emblazoned with oil company slogans. Sweltering in the midday sun, they could only manage to stammer a shocked, "Are you ladies lost?" Bonnie explained that they had left from Tecate, had pedaled through the Sierra de Juárez and were headed for San Felipe, where they would take the "back road" through Puertecitos and Bahía Gonzaga, joining the Transpeninsular north of Punta Prieta. At San Ignacio they planned to head south past Laguna San Ignacio, hitting pavement again at Villa Insurgentes, and then ride on to La Paz. At first there was no reaction, but as the magnitude of the adventure sank in, the two motorcyclists finally erupted in a torrent of warnings about the difficulties that lay ahead and heated questions as to how the ladies intended to survive the savage desert. Their concern was well meant, but the absurdity of the scene was priceless, and the "lost" bicyclists laughed for days.

****

CHAPTER 6
WHEELIN' IT

At the height of the winter season over half the traffic on the Transpeninsular Highway carries U.S. or Canadian plates, and 80% of these are motorhomes, trailers, pickup campers or vans. During a two-week vacation you might encounter people from forty states and five Canadian provinces. They are a diverse lot: a British Columbia logger, a senior citizen from New Jersey, youthful surfers from Santa Cruz, a teacher from Illinois, a Saskatchewan wheat farmer, an Amish family towing their tent trailer through Ensenada, the bearded men in severe black coats and flat-brimmed hats, the women in frocks and bonnets. A few come from afar: a cook from Australia, a roofer from Tonga, a postman from Sweden. Their rigs are equally diverse, ranging from a ratty VW camper showing every one of its quarter of a million miles to a gleaming new Blue Bird land yacht sporting a satellite dish and a gold Cadillac dinghy and showing every one of its quarter of a million dollars. Many are visiting Baja for the first time, but it is not unusual to meet people on their tenth or even twentieth trip. One crusty old codger told me he was "wheelin' it" in Baja for the twenty-fourth time.

An RV trip to Baja has many attractions, and there is something for almost everyone. To some people the RV is simply a means of transportation and a place to stay while pursuing other activities. A fisherman can park for weeks on a beautiful sand beach near Cabo San Lucas, the water offshore being one of the world's great marlin fisheries, while a skin diver can drive a sizable rig to Pulmo Reef, one of the few coral reefs on the west coast of North America. A whale-watcher can spend time at Scammon's Lagoon or even Laguna San Ignacio, the winter home of the friendly whales. To others, who simply want to find a felicitous RV park and settle down for a relaxing vacation at San Felipe, Bahía de los Angeles, Mulegé, La Paz or the Cape, the trip itself is the adventure. The weather is usually fine and living is inexpensive: local staple foods are cheap, some RV parks charge as little as three or four dollars a night and there are innumerable beaches, coves and clearings that cost nothing. The crowd at TRIPUI RV Park will appeal to the most gregarious, and loners will appreciate hundreds of miles of remote beaches that rarely see a human being. You can learn something of the ways of a foreign culture in exotic Comondú, or stick with your own kind at Posada Don Diego, as you choose.

Equipment and preparation

A Baja RV trip requires better preparation than one in the U.S. or Canada, for there are no RV supply stores or mechanics specializing in RV repairs. Trailer wheel bearings are generally standard automotive parts, and may be available in Baja auto parts stores, but if your rig requires special bearings it would be well to bring a bearing and seal assembly, grease and a cap, which is often lost when a bearing fails. Non-automotive RV parts and tires are essentially unavailable, although Marina de La Paz carries an inventory of seals, bearings, hubs, spindles, springs, couplers, V-blocks and rollers, roller shafts, balls, lights, U-bolts and other parts, most of it oriented toward boat trailers but possibly useful on other types as well. You might find gas regulators in general and hardware stores, and water pumps and other useful gadgets in the marine stores in Ensenada and La Paz. Many RV problems involve tires and springs, reflecting the excessive weight and speed to which they are often subjected, and the rough roads. Tires should start in excellent condition, and spares should be carried for both vehicle and trailer.

Because of the warm climate, transmission coolers are even more important on large rigs than they are north of the border. Narrow, rough roads and frequent crosswinds make a load-leveling hitch and a sway-control device necessary on all but the smaller trailers. Since shoulders are rare and the side of the road is often rough, skid wheels are needed on rigs with long overhangs. If your trailer has poor ground clearance, see whether the springs are above or below the axle. If they are below, you may be able to gain three or four inches of frame clearance and get additional spring travel by having a mechanic reinstall them above the axle. (This won't help clearance below the axle, of course.) Discuss this with the trailer manufacturer first.

Leveling jacks or a supply of wood blocks will be needed. Bring extra lengths of water and sewer hose and an electrical extension cord, since water, electric and sewer connections in many parks are on the "wrong" side or are otherwise distant. Thirty-amp service is not too common, so a 30-20 amp conversion plug is essential. A few parks still use ungrounded outlets, so a "cheater" plug is also needed. Bring holding-tank chemicals, for you will not find them in Baja. More than one person has found to his sorrow that the lug wrench from his tow vehicle would not fit the trailer, or that his scissors jack had inadequate capacity for a large trailer.

Some parks in remote areas do not have full hookups, and problems with water and electrical systems are common at almost all, so you should be equipped to operate self-contained for at least short periods of time. Unless you plan to stop only at RV parks with electrical hookups or have a generator, you may wish to leave 110-volt appliances home. Broadcast TV is very limited south of the border cities, although a few RV parks now have satellite systems.

Underway

Speeds over forty-five are too fast everywhere, and twenty is sometimes excessive. The Transpeninsular has been kept in better condition than in previous years, but potholes can quickly develop, and fate seems to have placed them at points where it is too late to slow down by the time you see them,

especially if you are towing a less-than-nimble big trailer rig. If you are taking even a few heavy blows from potholes, you are driving too fast and are risking loss of control, blowouts and broken springs.

A checkoff list will help you make sure that drawers and cabinets are locked and equipment properly stowed. Before starting each day inspect the hitch and check all tires with an air gauge, or whack them with a hammer, trucker style. To avoid loss of a wheel or enlargement of lug holes, especially in aluminum wheels, check all nuts once a week. There are no serious height limitations on the Transpeninsular, the lowest known hazard being a conveyer belt in Santa Rosalía on the right side going south, which dips down to thirteen feet ten inches. Butane is widely used for domestic purposes in Baja. In most large towns cylinders can be filled at established butane yards, and village stores can sometimes provide gravity fills. Butane is in short supply in some areas, so fill before you need it. Butane and propane are similar enough to be interchangeable in some applications—read your instruction book.

Many RV parks are described in Chapters 9 through 16. Expect change and occasional problems; parks open and

RV life in Baja is full of problems.

close, electricity and water can fail, the more popular parks may be full, and some are reserved largely for permanent occupants. Parking is available on thousands of beaches and flat spots along the road, but most of these are described in later chapters only if they are in strategic locations.

Extended self-contained operation

Most rigs can manage self-contained operation for three or four days, but comfortable living conditions can be maintained for longer periods if extra equipment and supplies are brought along. There are three primary problems to deal with: water, sewage and electricity.

Unless there is a local source, potable water is likely to be the factor that limits the time you can operate self-contained. Consumption can be greatly reduced by using paper plates and visiting the wilds for calls of nature. If you have the proper soap it is possible to wash pots and pans and take baths in seawater (see Chapter 8). If local water comes from wells or other unpressurized sources, a large plastic jug with a spout or a funnel may be needed for filling tanks. If you introduce untreated water into your tanks, you should treat all of it that is used for drinking and cooking from that point on, and when you return home the system must be chlorinated.

You will need a shovel. From both the ecological and the social standpoints, the best place to dump sewage is at a dump station. However, if the circumstances are such that you must do it elsewhere, gopher holes should be dug for black water. This is ordinarily not a big chore, since soft ground is easily found. Before you depart fill it in, tamp it down and return the area to its prior condition. Gray water can be dumped in a gravel or sand area away from the road and settled areas without lasting harm.

Few things are more depressing than to be without electric lights and heat during the long, cold nights of winter. If you drive regularly, your alternator will probably keep the batteries charged, but if you stop for long periods you will need a generator. If your rig does not have one built in, a portable such as a Honda EX650 will provide all the AC and DC power needed. You can minimize the hours of operation of such a dual-voltage generator by running it at night, operating the RV on 110 volts while the DC system charges the batteries. If your RV does not have cooking or lighting facilities the portable outfit described in Chapter 4 may be useful. Gas is not likely to be a major problem if you start with full tanks and hold heater operation to a minimum. Shut off all pilot lights, and operate the water heater only when needed.

Organized trips and caravans

Some RVers choose to join an organized trip or caravan, and it is not uncommon to see a caravan with a million dollars worth of Southwinds, Winnebagos and Airstreams pull into a Baja RV park. The Vagabundos del Mar Boat and Travel Club sponsors many RV trips. Airstream, Good Sam Club, Point South R.V. Tours, Inc. and Tracks to Adventure operate Baja RV caravans, often accompanied by a wagonmaster, a mechanic and a tailgunner. El Monte RV Center and Cruise America rent RVs and will allow them to be taken into Mexico.

If you don't have your own RV or would like to leave the driving to others, Baja Discovery offers a number of van trips,

visiting Ensenada, Tecate and the Baja Norte wine country, a "cross-peninsular" trip to Ensenada and San Felipe, a trip up into Parque Sierra San Pedro Mártir and to Tecate and Ensenada, and a trip the length of the Transpeninsular. Baja California Tours, Inc. offers guided motorcoach tours to Tijuana, Ensenada and San Felipe, a "Coast-to-Coast" special, and a tour stopping at San Quintín, San Ignacio, Loreto, La Paz and Cabo San Lucas.

Boat, motorcycle and utility trailers

Problems with small trailers are fairly common in Baja, but virtually all can be avoided. Tires thirteen inches and smaller are not advisable, for they are easily damaged and replacements will not be found in Baja tire shops. I once blew out a 5x13 on my boat trailer, and after two days of searching finally found a cracked and worn-out tire of the same size on a wheelbarrow in Guerrero Negro. Its owner knew he had a corner on the market and quoted an astronomical price, but the next day I was surprised to find a large automotive wheel with the same bolt pattern in the Parador Punta Prieta junk yard. The tire was flat and unrepairable, but my boat was light and didn't squeeze the carcass completely down, so I bought it and limped the 750 miles back to San Francisco with a thirty-degree list, the object of much levity from passing motorists.

The general rule in Baja is to avoid loading small trailers beyond half of rated capacity. This may be impossible with boat and motorcycle trailers, which are inherently loaded close to their maximum. Avoid putting containers of fuel and water and heavy coolers in boats carried on trailers; if you must do so, put them directly over the axle. Due to gravel and tar thrown up from the road, trailers should have fenders.

Off-road driving

Except perhaps for fishing, nothing has played more of a part in the lore of Baja California than off-road driving. In 1918 there were twenty-four cars in Santa Rosalía, and three in Mulegé. By the 1920s auto travel from San Diego to the onyx mine at El Mármol had become fairly routine. However, little or nothing was done by the Mexican government to upgrade the roads from the needs of mules and burros to those of the new gasoline-powered vehicles, and passage remained problematical.

A cactus collector once set out on a trip in a Model T Ford truck, accompanied by a fox terrier. The roads were so terrible that he had the misfortune of tipping over sideways, twice. Blessed with foresight, he had included a railroad tie, a shovel and a block and tackle among his equipment. After each upset, he climbed out, dusted off the dog and himself, dug a hole and buried the railroad tie standing upright, rigged the block and tackle between the truck and the tie and started pulling!

Erle Stanley Gardner told of a man named Outdoor Franklin who drove from Tijuana to Santa Rosalía in the mid-1920s, supposedly the first ever to make the trip by car. In 1926-27 the government finally appropriated 3,500 pesos to extend the automobile trail south from El Mármol to San Ignacio. By 1928 automobiles could get to Mulegé, and soon a twice-monthly stage ran between Tijuana and Santa Rosalía. The Automobile Club of Southern California sent an expedition

A trailer rig unloads from a Cortez ferry.

led by Phillip Townsend Hanna as far south as Mulegé that year, resulting in the first accurate road map of the peninsula. Completion of the "missing link" south of Mulegé in 1930 provided a road from Tijuana to Cabo San Lucas, one of the longest roads in Mexico.

By the late 1940s travel by sportsmen and adventurers down the peninsula in pickups and war surplus Jeeps was becoming common, although it never seemed so to the drivers, and tales of broken axles, of hours spent digging out of sandy washes and of days spent traveling a dozen miles filled their books and articles. Even as late as the 1960s things could still be tough. During a 1967 trip to La Paz, Willis Tilton had to deal with over forty mechanical problems with his Jeep pickup, including broken main driveshaft and bent front driveshaft; cracked exhaust manifold; broken transfer case; front drive-line support, front spring main leaf, front differential and starter failures; gas tank punctures; flat tires; and broken headlights. He made it.

Paving of the Transpeninsular was completed in 1973, but a vast system of unpaved roads still covers much of Baja. Although some have felt the bite of a bulldozer, most remain

as the laws of physics intended. To offset this, there have been improvements in trucks, tires and equipment, and the expansion of the paved-road system has greatly reduced the mileages involved in "rough-stuff" trips. In the days before the Transpeninsular everything was rough between distant north and south roadheads, but now you can cruise on pavement or an improved road until close to your destination, only then turning off. Today most off-road trips accumulate only a few hundred miles, often much less. Rugged four-wheel-drive trucks were once the kings of Baja roads, but ordinary pickups and vans are now encountered in even the most remote locations. Well prepared, properly equipped and driven with care, a standard two-wheel-drive pickup or van will take you to almost every location discussed in *The Baja Adventure Book*.

The term "off-road" is misleading, for other than driving on beaches, dry lakes and similar special situations, there is no "off-road" driving in Baja, nor should there be. Driving across untracked desert creates environmental havoc, tearing up slow-growing desert vegetation and leaving scars that endure for generations. Such driving is almost always unnecessary, since unpaved roads will usually be found to take you anywhere you want to go. In addition, it can often result in severe tire damage within a few miles, and even the fabled Baja 1,000 racers wouldn't go a mile if the race were truly off-road. Thus, although the term "off-road" is used throughout this book, keep in mind that what is meant is off-pavement driving.

Tools, spare parts and preparation

The most common problems off-road are the same ones encountered in driving anywhere: flat tires, overheating, failure to start, getting locked out and running out of gas, plus ones that can be attributed to extreme conditions, such as bent tie rods, punctured gas tanks, drive-line damage and getting stuck. Every vehicle venturing into Baja should carry a good spare tire, lug wrench, jack, flashlight, double-bitted screwdriver, medium Crescent wrench, pliers, fan belts, air gauge, water, fuel filters, spare keys in a magnet box, extra fuses and emergency flares. Also, carry a small plastic drop cloth or a dish towel. This should be placed under the scene of all repairs—nothing can be more maddening than a search for a small part in the sand. Vehicles engaged in extensive driving on unimproved roads should also carry a large Crescent wrench, side-cutting pliers, a set of socket and open-end wrenches of conventional or metric sizes as appropriate for the vehicle, duct tape, a set of slot and Phillips screwdrivers of various sizes, a ball-peen hammer, medium-size Channelock pliers, automotive and utility wire, jumper cables (especially if you have an automatic transmission), syphon hose, tow line, shovel, jack pad, sand mats, extra gasoline and engine oil, suitable amounts of food and water, a compass and appropriate maps, tire repair equipment and a Loctite Instant Gas Tank Repair Patch, repair part 12020. Although they are not often viewed as off-road equipment, every person along should have a pair of shoes or boots suitable for long-distance walking; bathroom thongs are the wrong footwear for hiking out to get help.

Cheap jacks that come with new vehicles are unsatisfactory off-road; their lifting height is too limited, as is their capacity. John Anglin and I got stuck once near Bahía Asunción and used a scissors jack to get sand mats under the wheels, forgetting there was a great deal of weight in the van. Without warning the jack screw stripped through its threaded pivot. A fraction of a second before it collapsed, John decided that he really ought to get his arm out from beneath the van, and that tiny lead time averted disaster. A serious off-roader ought to have two jacks, a hydraulic jack of at least three tons capacity and a Hi-Lift. The latter is a heavy-duty bumper jack of about 7,000 pounds capacity and a lift height of about thirty-six inches. A jack pad a foot square cut from three-quarter-inch plywood can be useful, since jacks usually just push down into soft ground, and flat stones can be hard to find.

A set of the sand mats described in Chapter 4 will allow you to cross soft ground. Their sizable area will support a vehicle on almost any kind of ground, their width keeps them from twisting, and they store compactly. Put one under each wheel and use the others to make a "road" as the vehicle pulls forward. You can save a great deal of effort if you use them before you start to bog down.

Traditional five-gallon metal GI cans are the safest way to carry spare gasoline. Plastic jugs can puncture or chafe while being bounced around, they melt quickly if subjected to fire, and their caps almost inevitably leak. The standard flexible GI can spout may be too big in diameter to fit the gas-tank opening on vehicles using unleaded fuel, so you might need a funnel. A surprising amount of grit can be thrown up into the engine compartment, especially if the vehicle scrapes the crown of the road while you are moving, so every vehicle should have an air filter. I have found pebbles as big as robin's eggs in the air cleaner of my van. Batteries are a common source of problems on Baja trips, especially off-road, where the banging around causes sediments to drift down to the bottom of the case, resulting in internal shorts in older batteries. Replace the battery if you are having symptoms, and make sure it is held firmly in its mount.

Much of the specialized equipment hawked in the off-road magazines is of little practical value in Baja. "Auxiliary light bars" with four big quartz/halogen bulbs, with enough luminous power to spot the zeppelins over London, are heavily advertised. However, off-road driving at night is ill-advised for safety reasons, and is almost never necessary. In any event, such lights are needed less off-road than in any other type of driving. What good are lights capable of lighting up the desert five miles away when you are creeping along at ten or fifteen miles an hour, and generally can't see more than several dozen yards ahead because of the twists and turns? Winches are handy at rare intervals, but most end up as expensive substitutes for tow cables when rescuing other

Repairing a broken spring on our bike/boat trailer.

drivers. If you find a winch is frequently necessary, you are probably looking for trouble, don't recognize it when you see it, or lack off-road driving skills. How did the road become a road if every vehicle required a winch? Many of the "roll bars" seen on off-road vehicles are not structurally adequate to provide significant protection, and are sold only to enhance appearance. If you doubt this, try asking a dealer or manufacturer for a warranty of structural integrity.

All loose equipment should be wedged or tied in place to avoid chafing and banging. Think small; I once put a lead fishing weight and a tube of fishing-reel lubricant together in a tackle box, resulting in a thin gray covering of oil over everything in the box, and a quart of olive oil once got together with ten pounds of flour, producing a mess of instant pasta. The large rear door found on some campers can be forced open by shifting cargo when climbing hills, so lash it closed.

Learn something about your vehicle. What is its range with all fuel aboard? Scramble underneath and identify all vulnerable parts, such as differentials, oil pan, fuel tanks, tie rods, etc., and measure the road clearance of each of them. Find a rock with a diameter equal to the least clearance, put it in front of the vehicle and learn what it looks like from the driver's seat. If you can't find a rock use a grapefruit or a watermelon.

Tires

Heavy advertising might lead you to believe that "Baja rated" eight- or ten-ply tires with an aggressive tread design and deeply molded white letters proclaiming a macho brand name are necessary for off-road driving. During 90,000 miles of driving in Baja and 35,000 miles getting there, using both two- and four-wheel-drive vehicles, I tried a variety of tires and kept records on tire mileage, cause of failure, etc. Other than unpatchable sidewall punctures in three radial tires that had to be tubed, I did not have a single failure that could be directly attributed to off-road driving. All others were heat failures, the result of driving at high speeds in hot weather under heavy loads on the California freeways getting to the border, and more slowly on the rough Transpeninsular. Radials gave the best performance, the next best being ordinary four- or six-ply bias-ply tires. Substantially the worst were "Baja-rated heavy-duty" tires, none of which got even close to full tread wear. The frequency of flat tires was about the same for all types, although the "Baja" types seemed to have

Kenneth Brown, superintendent in the onyx quarry at El Mármol, figures out his next move during a 1920 flood.

fewer, simply because they rarely lasted long enough for their tread to wear thin. I was unable to detect the slightest difference in off-road performance, such as the ability to climb hills, lug through sand or deal with rock.

What does this mean to you? If you are a typical Baja driver, with a pickup or a van loaded with people, food and sporting goods, who plans to head for Baja, drive off-road to a favorite campsite and do some local exploring, ordinary radial or bias-ply skins of good quality and adequate load rating with plenty of tread left are probably optimal. Tires of extreme diameter and width provide greater ground clearance and may help on soft ground by increasing the size of the tire footprint, but they add to unsprung weight and inherently lower gear ratios, possibly taking the engine out of its optimum torque range. Aggressive tread designs are noisy on pavement and cause steering and braking difficulties. Radials provide better gas mileage, longer tread life and better flotation than bias-ply, and although their first cost may be higher, total cost per mile is often much lower.

Tire repair

Tire problems are normally limited to simple punctures, and today's tires have far fewer flats than the tires old-time Baja drivers used to complain about. It is not necessary to carry more than one spare unless unusual conditions will be encountered, assuming the ones in use are in good shape. The spare should not be a treadless wreck. Sub-size "temporary" spares are miserable, but you may not be able to bring a decent one due to space limitations in the cubbyholes where they are designed to fit. Liquid preparations sold to eliminate flat tires do not work well; at best they only slow down a leak, leaving a terrible mess when it comes time to patch the tire. The best flat preventer is lots of tread.

There are two basic types of flats, the "good" kind and the "bad" kind. No flat is enjoyable, and the "good" kind is good only in the sense that the other is much harder to deal with. The "good" kind is a puncture through the tread of a tubeless tire. With both radial and bias ply, these can be dealt with without removing the tire from the rim, dismounting the wheel from the vehicle or even jacking up the vehicle. Pump up the tire and spray the stem, tread and sidewall with water and a little detergent from a bottle brought for that purpose, moving the vehicle forward as necessary. Even a slow leak should be obvious, and with luck it will be in the tread, not the sidewall. When the leak is located, pull out the offending nail or cactus spine and plug the leak with a push-through patch, following the directions on the patch kit, pump up the tire and away you go—ten minutes max!

Push-through patches come in various forms. Small kits with a simple insertion tool and a half-dozen patches are available in any parts store. These are inexpensive, but the patches tend to work loose, and sometimes will not seal at all. NAPA auto parts stores carry a specialized insertion tool, lubricant and higher quality patches. A Safety Seal kit is probably what your local repair shop uses, and although it is more expensive, the repairs are permanent and damage to the carcass of the tire is less likely. Always wear safety glasses when installing push-through patches.

The "bad" kind of flat involves a sidewall puncture, or any puncture in a tube tire. The sidewalls of modern tires, espe-

Soft ground provides Victor Cook with healthy outdoor exercise during a mineral collecting trip into Arroyo del Boleo.

cially radials, are thin, and agave spines seem custom-designed by the Devil to puncture tires in this vulnerable location. A push-through patch can be used in an emergency, but they may not seal properly, and the flexing of the sidewall may open up a hole before you get very far. Even if it works, the tire should be limited to off-road use until a proper repair can be made: no high-speed driving. If you get a sidewall puncture, put on the spare and hope that you will make it to a tire repair shop before the next flat. It may not even be necessary to put on the spare, since almost all sidewall punctures are caused by agave spines, and these sometimes leak very slowly, often taking a day or more to get near "the bottom." If the leak is slow enough, just pump up the tire to rated pressure and continue on until until you can get to a tire repair shop, stopping occasionally to add air. Once you get to a shop, the proprietor will probably advise an innertube, although some install a special 6" tire patch (tire patches are not the same thing as innertube patches). Shops in Mexico often use "hot" (vulcanizing) innertube patches on tubeless tires, but these usually peel away before long.

If you are among the unlucky few who have to repair a sidewall puncture, or any flat in a tube-type tire, out in the desert, expect a struggle. Pump up the tire, find the leak with a spray bottle and mark its location on the tire and the location of the tire with respect to the rim with a piece of tape or a pencil. Breaking the beads loose is the first problem, for they are usually frozen on the rim. Deflate the tire completely, place it under the vehicle, put the jack on the sidewall, and break the beads loose by jacking against the weight of the vehicle. Pull the tire off the rim with a tire tool or jack handle. If the tire has an innertube, install a tube patch; for tubeless tires either install an innertube or use a tire patch, the special large size. This will require a NAPA 710-1062 6" by 6" tire patch, a can of NAPA 765-1197 cement and a stitching tool, NAPA 710-1179. (This large patch is also useful in the rare event of a sidewall or tread cut.) If the tire is tubeless, the second major problem will then be encountered, seating the beads when the tire is remounted. If your air pump can't put out enough volume to seat them, wrap a length of rope around the circumference of the tread, tie a knot, insert a jack handle under the rope and start twisting, compressing the tire (this is called a Spanish windlass).

A serious off-roader's tire repair kit ought to include a tire pump, an innertube, tube patches if you use tubes, a push-through patch kit for tubeless, the items noted above, a spray bottle filled with water and detergent, a tire iron or other means of getting the tire off the rim, and a length of line, as well as a jack and a lug wrench. The most useful type of air pump is a hose that screws into a sparkplug hole, NAPA 90-366. This nifty gadget has a sixteen-foot hose and a built-in pressure gauge, produces up to 130 psi and can fill a tire in a minute and a half with no effort on your part. The air pumped has no gasoline or oil fumes and the pressure is easily controllable, making it good for tires, inflatable boats, air mattresses and rubber ducks. Tiny electrically operated pumps cost twice as much, tend to be unreliable and take almost forever to pump up a tire.

Despite all the advice in the previous paragraphs, you should not get overly concerned about flats—well prepared, yes, paranoid, no. Today most tires are tubeless and sidewall punctures are not common on pavement, so most flats will be ten-minute problems. In many years of off-road driving in Baja, I have averaged only one flat per 600 miles, have had only four occasions on which it was essential to demount a tire from a rim off-road, and have had only three sidewall punctures where installation of an innertube was eventually necessary. As an experiment I recently fixed a sidewall puncture with an innertube hot patch, and as of press time it was still holding air after 6,000 miles.

Off-road driving techniques

In rough conditions, slow is good; you will not be breaking axles, spindles or springs, banging passengers around or losing control. In fact, almost all off-road damage results from excessive speed. A careful driver will go up to twenty-five miles an hour on the best stretches of unimproved road, and down to a crawl on the worst, but over the long run will average about twelve miles an hour. Always wear seat belts, and keep them tight; hitting the ceiling can do serious damage to your head. In brushy areas mirrors should be folded back, and arms kept inside.

Grades over about 15% begin to spell trouble for heavily

In one of his foul tempers, Reeve does a little impromptu road work while the author supervises from the comfort of the air-conditioned cab.

loaded standard pickups and vans with small engines and three-speed transmissions. The classic boo-boo is to drive down into a steep arroyo and find that the opposite grade is too steep to ascend, then to try to go back and find the slope you went down is also too steep, especially if the arroyo bottom is soft or rough. Experienced drivers can eyeball such situations well, but if you have any doubts it pays to carry a small clinometer and measure steep grades before you attempt to drive them in a standard vehicle. If the problem is simply a poor power-to-weight ratio, you may have to unload and carry your goodies up the hill, a method Reeve and I used many years ago to conquer the "Terrible Three" south of Puertecitos in our overloaded VW van.

Washboard is encountered on unpaved roads in arid regions throughout the world, and Baja is no exception. The ride can be made more comfortable by letting air out of the tires to perhaps half normal pressure—the engine-driven tire pump noted above is useful when it comes time to fill them up again—but nothing lower, since beads may come loose or casings may move on the rims, tearing off innertube valve stems. Driving at a suitable speed also helps; it's a matter of harmonics, and if you drive very slowly or very fast you will avoid the maddening hammer. However, driving fast can be dangerous, for you can quickly lose steering control, and brakes lose their effectiveness, especially on curves.

Watch for mischief done by vibration. I drove a four-wheel-drive Dodge pickup more than 8,000 miles off-road on my last trip to Baja before the first edition of this book went to press and had a number of problems. Three tiny screws in my underwater light meter backed out, leaving part of the mechanism loose. Eight bolts holding the camper shell to the truck, all lock-washered, vibrated loose, almost depositing it on the side of the road before I discovered what was happening. The constant jiggling caused the steel striker plate on the rear door lock of the shell to saw almost through the brass bolt, twice. Finally, one day I heard an explosion and saw smoke pouring out of the back. Fortunately, just weeks before, I had decided to replace three five-gallon plastic gas cans with metal GI cans. I had to reach through the flames to jerk them out, singeing my arms, but I managed to put out the fire. The jostling had apparently caused a box of old-fashioned farmer's matches to ignite. The explosion was a can of overheated beans.

A great deal of off-road driving was also necessary for this second edition, and there was still a lot to learn. Our Toyota 4x4 was new, "right out of the box," and on the first day of off-roading Reeve and I were headed into "Mission Impossible" (Misión Santa María). We got as far as the truck could go, and I had to turn around in a space only a foot wider than the truck was long, and managed to squash an agave. You guessed it; the result was one of the infamous sidewall-punctures-in-a-radial-tire, on a tire with just over 2,000 miles on it. The lesson? Don't run over agaves. We then noticed that one of the hubcaps was missing, the expensive kind found on mag wheels, and we were unable to find it on the way out to the pavement. Lesson? Remove your hubcaps before doing any off-roading. The leak was slow, and by pumping up the tire occasionally we postponed the day of reckoning until we were camped on the beach at Playa Bufeo. Mellow from cold Dos Equis and freshly speared halibut cooked in tempura, we

began to remove the wheel. The first lug nut came off only with great reluctance, making squealing sounds, and the second and third were so tight that the nuts got hot from friction. The next two were not even finger-tight, and the last one would not even budge. I put my full weight on the wrench and nothing happened, so we lengthened its lever arm with a piece of pipe, and still the nut would not move. What a predicament—how do you deal with a such a flat when you can't even get the wheel off? Finally, with both of us using our full weight—generating perhaps 800 foot-pounds of torque—the stud finally sheared off. Apparently a mechanic at the Toyota dealership had decided to play a joke with his air wrench. The lesson? Make sure your wheel nuts are torqued properly and will come off readily.

We had loaded a large chunk of ice into our cooler, and all was well for a few days, until it had melted to half its original size. During a particularly rough trip up a dry arroyo, the chunk was thrown back and forth and acted like a battering ram, mashing cups of yogurt, a package of weenies, a carton of milk, a stick of salami and just about everything else into a unappetizing pulp. Lesson? Each day brace the ice with cans or bottles so it can't gain any kinetic energy. Finally, the water we saw coming out of the bottom of the truck was not melt-water from the cooler; it was the last of our drinking water coming from a split seam in a plastic jug. Lesson? Keep your jugs from banging around, just like the ice.

Road problems come in two extremes: soft ground and rough, hard ground. Weight is one of the most important controllable variables in driving on soft ground, and the less you carry the better you will fare. It helps to reduce tire pressure, since this increases the area of the tire in contact with the ground. Knowing how much power to use and how long to use it is the key to driving on soft ground. Use too much power and you will be banging and slamming; too little and you simply can't keep moving. Drive at moderate speed in the highest gear in which you can sustain progress, with a smooth, steady throttle. Avoid stopping if you can. If you must stop, get out and dig away the ridges that build up in front of the tires; even small ones may keep you from getting rolling again. If you get stuck on a beach, use a bucket to wet the sand around the wheels and make a track ahead. Don't try to return to harder ground by running perpendicular to the contour line, but drive at an angle of twenty degrees to it.

If you have four-wheel-drive, stay in compound low and drive in higher gears, rather than in high range and lower gears, allowing you to downshift almost instantly to "stump-pulling" gear if you start to bog down. Avoid the temptation to keep your foot on the accelerator when progress has come to a halt, especially with two-wheel-drive, for the powered wheels will dig in, making it harder to get out, and grit may be driven through universal joint seals if they touch ground, causing a mysterious failure months later. A little digging early on saves a lot later, and with sand mats, a Hi-Lift and a shovel, you should be able to work your way out of some pretty hairy situations. A Hi-Lift can walk a vehicle sideways; jack up one end and push the vehicle sideways, toppling the jack, then jack up the other end, push it sideways, etc. This procedure can be dangerous and is not recommended by the jack manufacturer. Backing out of a hole is frequently best, but the passage of wheels sometimes breaks up the structure of packed sand and fine gravel, turning it into thousands of tiny ball bearings. When pulling out, make sure the front wheels are pointed straight ahead, or else they may simply skitter along half-sideways, wasting a great deal of power.

Surface hardness is not necessarily a good measure of "sinkability," especially on sand and dry lake beds. A crust can form which seems solid when you walk on it, and appears to support the vehicle at first. I once drove out on a beach that had a rock-hard surface. I got fifty yards into it when there was a crunching sound and down she went. Nothing I could do with a Hi-Lift could get the van to stay on top of the crust, and I had neglected to bring sand mats, so I finally had to hire a local with a long rope to pull me out. One early traveler parked for the night on the hard surface of dry Laguna Chapala, only to find the next morning that his vehicle had broken through the crust and was slowly sinking into the bottomless muck below.

Few problems with sand turn out to be serious, since firm ground is rarely far away, but with mud and water things can be very different—see the stories on pages 70 and 120. No one wants to move every time there is a little sprinkle, but if it rains steadily or hard, consider moving to pavement or at least to an improved gravel road. If you must drive through a flooded stream or dip in the road, find out how deep the water is first. On many roads vertical rulers have been installed to show the depth of the water. If it is deep but otherwise driveable, remove the fan belt, which throws water over the engine, and put a Baggie over the distributor, which is vulnerable. Drive slowly, maintaining a constant speed. If you are pulling a trailer beware of water approaching spindle-deep; the inner hub seal on some rigs is not completely waterproof because a nasty little gadget called a "Z-ring" has been inserted between the spindle and the seal, apparently to avoid the cost of machining a smooth surface on the spindle. I once crossed a knee-deep stream a half-dozen times pulling a sixteen-footer and got about a half-mile down the pavement when huge clouds of black smoke appeared in the rearview mirror. Water had gotten past the Z-ring and wiped out bearings, races, electric brakes and the seal, requiring a trip back to San Diego while the rig stood on the side of the Transpeninsular for two days.

Problems encountered on rock may result in damage to tie

We crossed a meandering stream thirty-four times on the round trip to La Bocana.

rods, oil pans, differentials and suspension, which is much more serious than just the hassle of digging out of a soft spot. Most problems can be avoided by holding speed down and mentally "driving ahead," planning your route farther in advance than you normally do. Sometimes you might have to get out and move loose rock or fill in a hole, and a few minutes of labor can save endless problems later. If you have any doubts have someone walk ahead and look things over. Avoid getting high-centered on the crown of the road, don't let large rocks pass under the vehicle, and don't hit big holes with brakes locked, for the stress on the suspension and rolling gear becomes terrific.

Sand or pebbles on top of rock can mean trouble, since the material can act like ball bearings, reducing traction. If the road tilts to one side, this can be downright dangerous, and on numerous occasions I have found myself skittering sideways to seeming disaster. Pebbles can also cause a loss of steering control, and several times my four-wheel-drive has decided to go where it wants, regardless of the commands conveyed to it with the steering wheel. If you get stuck in an area with pebbles or cobble, beware. I once was pushing on the back of a van, when it started to get some traction. As it pulled away a rock the size of a baseball was ejected backwards by one wheel, striking me forcibly in the chest. Stones can be ejected from the front wheels if the vehicle has front-wheel or four-wheel drive, and remember, the front wheels can turn more than thirty degrees from the axis of the vehicle, throwing stones out to the side.

Favorite off-road runs

Chapter 5 describes four loop trips for off-road bicyclists, including the Laguna Hanson, Vizcaíno, Mountain Villages and Cape Coast Loop Trips. All of these also make fine trips by off-road vehicle. The Two Parks Loop Trip, described below, is too long for all but the most intrepid bicyclists, but for off-road drivers it is in many respects the ultimate off-road trip in Baja, since it has everything: both national parks, long easy stretches to relax on, a few short, difficult places to test yourself and your machine, empty beaches, the ocean and the mountains.

Two Parks Loop Trip: El Cóndor, Laguna Hanson, KM 55+ on Route 3 to KM 138, Mike's Sky Ranch, Mile 29.7 on the Observatory Road, Parque Sierra San Pedro Mártir, KM 140+ on the Transpeninsular, Colonet, Johnson Ranch, Eréndira, Punta Cabras, KM 23 on the Santo Tomás-Punta San José Road, Santo Tomás, Uruapan, Ojos Negros, El Coyote, KM 98 on Route 2 and back to El Cóndor, covering 306 miles off-road, 76 miles on pavement.

The following route provides a long and challenging trip passing through some of the most interesting places Baja has to offer:

El Cóndor, Laguna Hanson, KM 55+ on Route 3 to KM 164+, across Laguna Diablo to San Felipe, Puertecitos, KM 229+ on the Transpeninsular, Bahía de los Angeles, Bahía San Francisquito, El Arco, Vizcaíno, then follow the route of the Vizcaíno Loop Trip to KM 98, San Ignacio, Laguna San Ignacio, La Purísima, the Comondús, San Javier and Loreto, covering 970 miles

off-road, 110 on pavement, one way.

Trailering and RV-ing off-road

RV trips on unimproved roads require careful thought. Excessive width, height and length, long overhangs, low power-to-weight ratios and limited maneuverability may make the probability of damage and excessive hassle unacceptably high. Some rigs simply are not up to heavy pounding; joints will begin to work loose, causing leaks, and vegetation along the road will scratch that new airbrush mural of the Last Supper of which you are so proud. In addition, getting stuck in a big RV is a much more serious proposition than in an ordinary vehicle. Even turning around may be impossible, a problem more serious than many imagine—try backing a trailer several miles.

In spite of this, improvements to some unpaved roads make it possible for small-to moderate-sized rigs to get to locations previously unreachable, including the road from Vizcaíno to Bahía Tortugas and Bahía Asunción, La Rivera past Pulmo Reef to San José del Cabo, the Bahía San Carlos road, Bahía de los Angeles to Bahía San Francisquito, La Paz north of San Juan de la Costa, and others. Bob and Bonnie Rauch have made a number of such off-road trips in their twenty-foot Champion motorhome. Powered by a 318 Dodge and equipped with oversized tires, duals in the rear, this rig has taken them to Bahía Tortugas, Malarrimo (via the route from the west), Puerto Chale, San Juan de la Costa, the Comondús and San Sebastián. Although a heavy jolt once lifted the front wheels eighteen inches off the road, the only damage incurred was a shock-absorber bracket sheared off and some deep scrapes on the bottom. Chapters 9 through 16 identify a number of unpaved roads that may be suitable for such trips, but the final judgment lies with the driver.

Towing small utility, motorcycle or boat trailers on unimproved roads can be risky, since their high crown may damage low axles. I once bent the axle on a motorcycle trailer, but managed to shackle a chain to each end and bend it straight again with a Hi-Lift. On another trip a spring broke and it looked like we were in trouble—how do you fix a spring or get a replacement in the geographic center of the Baja boondocks?—but we made a temporary repair by removing a U-bolt from a bracket holding the winch and using it to shackle the axle to the frame. Horizontal and vertical forces caused by bumps and potholes are considerable, and the resulting strain on tie-downs and their attachment points can be enough to break the tie-down or bend boat, bike or trailer parts. More than once I have looked in the rearview mirror to see a motorcycle fallen over, and once to see my partner's Trail 90 dragging behind us. Firm tension must be maintained on tie-downs, so use adequate line and trucker's hitches, or better yet use nylon strap and a lever device, or a small strap winch made by Aeroquip. There must be a large area of contact between boat and trailer or you will experience fiberglass cracks and other damage. Fenders often flap like bird wings on washboard sections and finally break off due to metal fatigue. They should not be removed, since gravel and sand will eventually erode that shiny gel-coat and chrome, and there seems to be no solution other than to insure that the brackets that hold them are sturdy and to inspect them frequently.

Motorcycling

Baja has been conquered by everything from humble Vespas to grand Gold Wings, and every ride has his own opinion on the ideal Baja bike. In general, though, a rider touring Baja on the paved road system but planning off-road forays will be happiest with a four-stroke machine of moderate weight, with a 250-350 cc engine and a range of at least 200 miles. Two-stroke enduro machines also work well, but motocross bikes, due to their small tank sizes and difficult-to-use power curve, leave something to be desired.

Tool and parts kits on most bikes are inadequate, and plugs, points, condensers, chain lube, a spare tube (two if the tires are of different sizes), tire repair kit, air pump and tow rope should be carried. The pump that comes with a Motobecane moped works well; carry it in a plastic bag to keep grit out. All this will probably not fit in the bike's tool kit, so make a cylindrical container out of plastic drainage pipe and hold it on with bungee cord. Tube liners help reduce the number of flats. Plastic hand guards will keep thorns and cactus spines away from vulnerable hands. All Mexican dogs hate all bikers, and a can of Halt carried on a handlebar clip may save tooth marks on your boots or worse. Wire a spare ignition key in a hidden location. A small plastic painter's drop cloth spread under the bike will avoid the loss of small parts of repairs are necessary. Switch to conventional oil or bring what you need, since synthetic oil is not available in Baja. If you don't already have a washable air filter, get one.

Bikes should be serviced and brought up to top condition before heading south. A bike breakdown in the desert can be a far more serious proposition than one in a truck, so file a "flight plan," and carry adequate food and water. The uniform of the day should be a brain bucket, eye protection, gloves and boots suitable for hiking. Use sunblock cream and lip glop generously. In dusty conditions check the oil level, wash the air cleaner, and lube and adjust the chain every day. Engine oil is a major factor affecting the life of a bike engine, and in dusty conditions a change every 200 miles would not be excessive.

The section on camping in Chapter 5 generally applies to motorcyclists as well. There are few motorcycle repair shops in Baja, but their parts selection is poor, and the brands they handle are often unfamiliar; see Chapters 9 through 16. Mike's Sky Ranch is the only resort in Baja catering largely to off-road drivers and motorcyclists.

****

CAMPFIRE STORIES. No aspect of the lore and legend of Baja California generates more fun at campfire gatherings than tales of what goes wrong when driving off-road in the desert. Here is a sample of what you might hear over the crackling of a Baja campfire and the pop of freshly opened cervezas.

Backing-down is not a skill ordinarily associated with off-road driving, but it can be vital. Mike and I were driving north of the "low road" between Cadajé and Laguna San Ignacio. Consisting of just a single pair of wheel tracks, it crossed many miles of mud flats. It seemed firm enough to drive on, but when we stopped and tested the sides of the road we went in over our boot tops in gooey mud just two feet off the wheel tracks. Driving carefully, we seemed to be in the

"middle of nowhere"—nothing was visible but mud and sky—when a truck appeared on the horizon. I slowed down and stopped, but the other driver aggressively kept coming until his bumper was only inches from ours. Three Mexicans, very large and rough-looking and not exactly exuding empathy and good humor, got out and in unison suggested in unmistakable terms that it was going to be us who pulled off to the side of the road. We could see tequila bottles on the floor of the cab and a shotgun in a rack in the rear window and quickly began to appreciate their logic; after all, it was their country. Our wheels got no more than six inches off the tracks when they started to sink into the mud, and we barely managed to pull back. The three men were becoming impatient, perhaps anxious to see the tip of our aerial disappear into the muck, and we had to do something, fast. We couldn't go around, over or under them, and that left only one direction. I shifted into reverse and started down the narrow wheel tracks, using the rearview mirror to steer. Steering with a mirror is confusing—every turn of the steering wheel must be the opposite of what the mirror suggests—and after a dozen close calls, I found I had to twist myself around to actually see where I was driving. Finally, after almost an hour, we came to a place where I could safely get out of the way, and the truck pulled away in a cloud of blue smoke and a shower of beer cans. When I tried to drive normally, I found I had a "crick" in my neck, which I couldn't straighten out for several days.

That wasn't the end of the mud problems. Reeve and I had parked our van near Puerto Chale while on a wreck dive near Punta Tosca, and when we returned a week later we found it perched on an island, surrounded by acres of mud caused by a series of high tides. Lacking traction and four-wheel drive, only kinetic energy would save us from an enforced month-long camp-out, so it was "pedal-to-the-metal" while we were still on firm ground. In a great spray we hit the liquid mud, our rear wheels throwing up roostertails, swerved back and forth, totally out of control and unable to see through the windshield but headed, we thought, in approximately the right direction, hit a rise, bounded four feet into the air and skidded to a stop in front of the astonished other half of our party, who had slowly crossed to dry land earlier in their fat-wheel 4x4, calm, clean and unconcerned.

Small pickups are light and agile and do well off-road, but their low clearance sometimes produces startling results. Victor Cook and I were bouncing down a rocky road, checking out mineral collecting sites. I had just finished commenting on how well his Toyota was handling the terrain when there was a loud crunch and we saw something lying in the road behind us. It proved to be the left front torsion bar, torn off the truck by a rock. It was badly bent, but spare Toyota torsion bars are hard to come by fifty miles from the nearest pavement, so we decided to try to forge it back into shape. We turned up the regulator on our propane stove, heated the bar, and with a sledge used for cracking mineral samples and a rock for an anvil, I hammered the bent part back into shape. Miraculously, it fit perfectly on the first try. We smugly thought that our ingenuity had overcome a once-in-a-million fluke, but two days later there was another crunch. This time the right torsion bar had been ripped off, giving us a second chance to perfect our newly acquired blacksmithing skills.

*A number of years ago, Mike and I were creeping along
the Puertecitos-Bahía Gonzaga road in a brand-new pickup,
our first experience with four-wheel-drive. Some improvements had been made to the road, but the going was
rough, and we were bottoming out and doing some wheel-
spinning, but we were conquering the "Terrible Three," the
three worst grades on the worst road in Baja, with yawning
chasms and grades of 32%. Rusted wrecks along the way
provided mute testimony as to the struggles of less skillful
travelers, and I began to fantasize that we were going to be
the first, well almost the first, to make it unscathed. "Skill and
the right hardware," I though, "that's what it takes, lots of
skill and the right hardware!" I began to imagine myself as
a great Baja 1000 off-road driver and started humming the
Marlboro song—dada da dittie da dada—when we encountered a truck coming the other way. Without stopping, the
driver shouted, "Heard about the Honda ahead?" I didn't
know what he was talking about and kept humming and
dreaming. Perhaps I would enter next year's 1000! I could
see myself sitting in an Ensenada bar, calmly waiting until
the second-place car finally crossed the finish line. The next
driver to pass asked the same question, but I kept humming,
only not so loudly. We could see Bahía Gonzaga ahead, when
we overtook something that didn't belong there, a tiny and
rather ancient Honda sedan. The driver had never been to
Baja before, had never been off the pavement and his car was
loaded to the roof line with luggage and camping equipment,
but there he was, having conquered the worst Baja had to
offer and still rolling! I stopped humming, my great Dodge
and dreams of off-road glory humbled forever.*

****

CHAPTER 7
EXTRA ADDED ATTRACTIONS

Surfing adventures

Baja is the last frontier of California surfing, the last place where you can escape the crowding and the confrontation that have marred the scene in Southern California for many years. There are two basic surfing regions. The first, between Tijuana and Ensenada, is essentially an extension of Southern California conditions. The weather, water, beach litter and most of the people are the same, and San Miguel is as well-known to generations of Southern California surfers as Rincon. Tame and familiar stuff, but fun, friendly and dependable.

The second region, the 1,032-mile coastline from Ensenada to the Cape, has almost every conceivable kind of surfing condition. Prevailing winter northwesterlies produce a succession of highly reliable point breaks on the many capes dangling south from the Pacific coast like icicles. Stretches of beach sweeping between them may work well only a few days or weeks a year, but so many miles are involved, with so many combinations of exposure, bottom terrain, beach curvature and angle to the swell, that there is usually little difficulty in finding something that is working well. With the coming of summer, south winds and waves from tropical storms produce a far greater variety of conditions and enough lefts to keep an army of goofy-foots happy, and opening up locations that work best in south waves like Isla Natividad and the Cape. Individual surfers have favorite seasons, but there is really no best time of year—the big southern boomers of summer may be more fun, but they tend to be less consistent than the waves of fall and winter.

Any list of the top surfing locations on the coast from Ensenada to the Cape would include Puntas San José, San Telmo ("Quatro Casas"), San Jacinto ("Freighters"), Baja, San Carlos, Santa Rosalillita, Abreojos, Pequeña and San Juanico, plus El Conejo. Reliable breaks, with easy access and good camping, all can be reached with two-wheel-drive vehicles. In addition, there are two fine island sites, "El Martillo" and Natividad, both objects of a great deal of current interest. Surfers are a tight-lipped lot when it comes to recently "discovered" locations, and a magazine article raving about El Martillo's "good juicy all around high perfor-

mance wave[s] with ... nice steep takeoff[s]" failed to inform readers where the place is located (the Islas de Todos Santos near Ensenada). El Martillo often has ten- or twelve-foot faces when surfers at San Miguel, only seven miles away, are sitting in their pickups wishing. The islands can be reached easily by boats launched at Ensenada or Punta Banda. Surfers without their own can rent *pangas* or charter one of the Gordo's Sportfishing fleet boats.

Natividad is more difficult to reach, but it's worth it; there are those who claim that "Open Doors," the break on its east end, is the best beach break on the west coast of North America. Scorpio Surfing Tours offers fly-in package trips to Natividad between late June and September. The island is only five miles off the village of Punta Eugenia, which has good road access and *pangas* available for hire. However, Natividad is primarily a summer site, dependent on big south waves that often wipe out the landings at Punta Eugenia and the island. These and many other surf sites are described in later chapters.

Surfers are among the great storytellers of our times, and their legends have given the region south of Ensenada a lurid reputation. These run the full gamut from the usual *bandido* roadblock, iguana-up-the-pant-leg and flash-flood-washes-away-tent-with-people-in-it stories to imaginative creations about the killer whale that chased a surfer through the waves and floundered in the shallows as the wave receded, and the surfer who tried to outrun a pack of sea snakes. The weavers of most of these tales would probably refuse a polygraph test, but there is no doubt that a trip to these distant regions is a very different proposition than a day trip to San Miguel. There are no hotels or RV camps in the better locations, and a few may require an off-road vehicle. There are no Coast Guard stations your buddies can call when a rip carries you out to sea, and medical attention for bumps, bangs and sea urchin stabs can be a day away. There is an extensive lobster fishery along Baja's Pacific coast, and pots are sometimes anchored in or drift into surfing areas, their buoy lines waiting to ensnare surfboard leashes. Despite these difficulties, the southern region offers fine surfing under a variety of adventurous conditions, and the lack of a crowd allows working on form and technique without the constant distraction of watching for collisions.

As with any trip to Baja, preparation is everything. Surfers planning to camp should study Chapter 5, and Chapter 6 will be of interest to those traveling in RVs and off-road. There are surf shops in Playas de Rosarito and Ensenada. In the Cape region rental boards are available at Victor's Aquatics at the Hotel Posada Real Cabo, and a shop at Costa Azul, located just west of San José del Cabo at KM 28+, has surfboard rentals, sales and accessories.

Extrapolating Southern California wave reports as far south as Ensenada is not too risky, but obtaining reliable information on surf conditions farther south is essentially impossible. Wave-Trak offers a recorded telephone surfer's wave report that includes Baja, but the farther south the less specific the information. Although some useful information might be available about Baja Norte on NOAA's 162.4 megahertz short-wave weather report, no AM/FM broadcast band radio reports are available, and other than hotels in the Cape region there is nowhere you can telephone to, even if you happen to speak Spanish. Word-of-mouth testimonials from returning surfers are almost always too old to have any real value, so the best thing you can do is watch weather maps for cold fronts moving southeast in winter and for tropical storms in summer. The difficulty in obtaining current information, plus the time that will elapse before you arrive on the scene, make a surfing trip to the southern region a go-and-hope proposition. If things don't stack up once you arrive, move to a new location and keep trying. There is so much diversity in Baja surf conditions that it pays to drive rather than wait.

Boardsailing

The number of boardsailors visiting Baja has increased by a factor of ten in recent years. Baja has finally been "discovered," and for good reason, for there is everything anyone could want, ranging from mill ponds to rolling ocean swells, from gentle zephyrs to boom-bending blasts, and vast rideable areas that never see more than a board or two at a time. The orientation of both coasts is roughly northwest-southeast, and since prevailing winds are northwest along the Pacific coast and north in the Cortez, fine, reliable, side-shore conditions are frequently encountered.

Along the Pacific coast, K 38+ ("El Portal") is an old favorite with boardsailors, but it is getting too popular with

Willy Morris rides a frothy face at "Open Doors,"Isla Natividad.

PHOTOGRAPH BY FLAME

their surfer brethren. Bahías San Quintín, Magdalena and Almejas provide long rides in good winds, with no ocean swells. Bahía Santa María (the "outer bay" at San Quintín) sometimes has a refracted swell and there are ocean swells at the point, but the winds are good and there are fine sand beaches. Bahía Santa Rosalillita, also a favorite with surfers, often has strong, reliable winds, giving it a reputation as something of a "jock" area. One boardsailor recently spent six weeks there, and was skunked only two days. Waves range from the calm of the bay to perfect sets of big waves off the point, providing a fine place for intermediate sailors making the transition to waves. Bahía Tortugas is not often visited by boardsailors, but is free of ocean swell and frequently has heavy winds, and you can't get carried too far if you have trouble with waterstarts and tacking. Punta Abreojos is very windy, and the heavy June thermals that are the bane of local fishermen are a joy to boardsailors. El Conejo, too, is a favorite with heavy-weather sailors. There are, of course, many small "secret" locations, small bays and coves offering fine sailing, but by and large most other Pacific coast locations are for experts only, due to large swells, tidal currents and fog.

At the Cape, Playa el Médano at Cabo San Lucas and the small coves to the east attract novice and intermediate boardsailors. Cabo San Lucas is generally out of the area affected by the heavy north winds that funnel down the Cortez in winter, but southern fronts provide fine onshore and cross-onshore conditions in summer. With a body of warm water and a major land area to the east, an ocean to the south and mountains and an ocean to the west, East Cape gets brisk, dependable winds between mid-November and mid-March, making it the most popular boardsailing location in Baja, the Cabo Pulmo and Bahía las Palmas areas being favorite places.

There are breaks for surfers of almost every experience level: Mike catches a good one on his Boogie Board at Cieto Lindo.

There are also fine beaches and good boardsailing around Cabo Frailes, Punta Arena Sur, Punta Colorada and Punta Arena de la Ventana, but the Canal de Cerralvo offshore of the last point is largely for experts, with heavy currents that change direction and velocity with the tides. During warm months a strong afternoon breeze of almost clock-like regularity blows at La Paz, providing fine conditions, especially at Balandra.

Loreto has good winds and general side-shore conditions. Placid Bahía Concepción is the ideal spot for beginners, for the wind often funnels down the bay, resulting in side-shore conditions in many locations. The shape and orientation of the spit at Requesón allow novices to find good conditions with wind from almost any direction. Santispac is fun and compact, but the surrounding hills keep the winds down. At the north end of the bay, Punta Arena often has the heaviest winds, since the surrounding land is low. Low Punta Chivato north of Mulegé sticks out well into the Cortez, freeing it from the influence of the higher topography to the west and providing the best in speed sailing conditions during the north winds of winter.

Bahía de los Angeles is the eastern end of the famous "Baja Shuttle." In winter the bay has frequent katabatic (gravity) winds, but no swell builds up since they come from the north and the west. When the winds are up, boardsailors try speed sailing, and when it's calmer they play and explore the many islands. When a Pacific front approaches, they pack up and head west for Santa Rosalillita, only seventy-four miles away, to take advantage of the wind and the waves. When the front dies, everyone rushes back to Bahía de los Angeles. Since the two types of wind have separate causes, one or the other is often at work, providing almost continual boardsailing action in a variety of conditions.

Like their surfer cousins, Pacific-side wave sailors should watch the weather maps for fronts in winter and for tropical storms in summer. Speed sailors should look for a stagnant high over Southern California, hopefully with another high to the east, good indicators that strong north winds are blowing down the Cortez. Local thermals and gravity winds cannot be identified from weather maps, of course.

Make sure your equipment is in top shape and bring essential spare parts and plenty of sail tape. Baja Surf Club, headquartered in the winter at the Hotel Palmas de Cortez at East Cape, seems to be the only place in Baja regularly offering sailboard parts and repairs, although other hotel and resort shops might help you if they can. Due to the wide variety of conditions, it will pay to bring both a short and a long board and a full quiver of sails. A kayak paddle can turn your board into a vessel for exploring on no-wind days.

Baja's remote conditions require additional attention to safety matters. Rig a leash between mast and board in case the universal breaks or pulls out of the mast foot, and let someone know where you are. A wetsuit is a necessity on both coasts because of windchill—if it isn't blowing you won't be out there. Watch for changes in wind direction, especially if you are riding a short board and/or aren't big on tacking, and for increases in velocity—if winds get up too much, head for camp. Unless you like being stranded miles from camp don't stray too far, certainly in areas with heavy currents, for Baja winds, especially in the Cortez, can drop to nothing in minutes. Boardsailors construct elaborate arguments for not wearing life jackets: they are not needed, sailboards can't sink and they "always" stop when a rider falls off, there is no place to stow a jacket, you can't swim well in a jacket and the best place to be in the surf is often five or ten feet down. These arguments have a certain validity, but all are based on conditions "back home," where there is safety in numbers—if you get in trouble there is always someone around to help. However, few boardsailors have any experience out on the water alone, really alone, so think it out—what will YOU do to stay afloat if you are injured and no one is around? The same thing holds for helmets—you may be the biggest thing around in hot-dogging and wave sailing circles back home, but what will YOU do if your mast decides to bend itself double over your skull?

There are an ever-increasing number of boardsailing operations in Baja, currently (1991) including Excursions Extraordinaires at the Hotel Punta Chivato north of Mulegé, Baja Surf Club at the Hotel Palmas de Cortez, Vela Highwind Center at the Hotel Playa Hermosa, and Mr. Bill's Boardsailing Adventures at East Cape, all offering package trips. Rental boards are available at the Estero Beach Hotel and the Baja Beach & Tennis Club south of Ensenada, Fantasia

Destinations at the Stouffer Presidente Hotel just south of Loreto, the La Concha Beach Resort at La Paz, and the Hotel Las Arenas, Cabo Acuadeportes (two locations) and Pisces Water Sport Center in the Cape region. Green Tortoise bus trips have an optional boardsailing program.

Rock-art treasures

At more than a hundred sites scattered from the U.S. border to the Cape, explorers, miners, ranchers and archaeologists have discovered that early Indian tribes had graced the barren peninsula with art treasures ranging from simple petroglyphs pecked on exposed rocks to enormous murals painted on cave walls. The most spectacular lie in the southern Sierra de San Francisco and the northern end of the Sierra de Guadalupe, an area bisected by the Transpeninsular Highway near San Ignacio. Often painted on the back of rock shelters, the murals depict figures of humans and animals painted life size or larger. They can extend hundreds of feet in length and to heights of thirty feet, a scale so grand that local legends insist the artists were giants.

The murals were executed in a flat wash technique in red, black, white and, occasionally, yellow, using mineral pigments and brushes made from short pieces of agave or milk-

Windsurfer Keir Becker takes a big one at K 38.

Ron Smith and Robert Connick discuss the fine points of a mural at Gardner Cave.

weed fiber. They generally depict humans, deer, mountain sheep and rabbits, but also may include mountain lions, birds, fish, sea mammals, raccoons and rats, frequently rendered near life size, in a realistic but static style. Many human and some animal figures are "bicolor:" a figure was divided in half and each half painted a different color, usually black and red. Another important characteristic is "overpainting:" the artist painted new images over those painted at an earlier time. The effect can be startling, a cacophony of animal and human figures with no apparent order or logic. In addition to representational paintings, there are many examples of abstract art, often taking the form of curvilinear figures or "checkerboards," intersecting lines forming squares filled with colors.

The few artifacts found at the sites around San Ignacio indicate that the murals were painted by Cochimí Indians between the mid-14th and early-16th centuries. Scattered descriptions occur in writings of the Jesuit missionaries, and in 1883 Herman Ten Kate, a Dutch physician, published an account of his archaeological activities in Baja that mentioned a few sites. Leon Diguet, a French chemist at the mines in Santa Rosalía, published a paper in 1895 describing many sites.

However, it took mystery writer Erle Stanley Gardner to bring the art to public attention and generate the great interest that it now enjoys. Having heard rumors about a site north of San Ignacio, he assembled two expeditions in 1962 and found a number of art sites, including the crown jewel of Baja Indian art, known as Gardner Gave or Cueva Pintada. The local people, of course, knew about most of them all along.

Burro trips to see Gardner Cave and the other sites in the area can be arranged in the village of San Francisco, north of San Ignacio. Cueva Palmarito, also north of San Ignacio, can be approached within several miles by vehicle and hence can be visited in the course of a day. Guides can be obtained at nearby Rancho Santa Martha. Guided trips to Palmarito and other sites can be arranged in San Ignacio. Viajes Mario's in Guerrero Negro also offers two-day guided trips to the areas around San Francisco. Las Pintas, a minor site near El Rosario, can be visited by off-road vehicle.

Some art sites are accessible to casual travelers. The "Playhouse Cave" near Cataviña is an easy fifteen-minute hike from the Transpeninsular. Cueva Ratón, a site near San Francisco, can be visited by auto, requiring only a two-minute hike. Gruta San Borjitas, north of Mulegé, is considered a major site and is only a fifteen-minute hike from a roadhead, and it may be possible to arrange guided trips at one of the hotels in town. The "Unhappy Coyote"in the Bahía Concepción area is just a fifteen-minute walk off the pavement. Raul Perez offers bus trips to see Cochimí art sites in the Bahía de los Angeles area, and Green Tortoise bus trips stop at some minor sites. Museums in Mexicali, Bahía de los Angeles, La Paz and Todos Santos have artifacts and photographs. A burro trip to the great mural sites in Cañon San Pablo is described at the end of Chapter 12.

You are well advised not to attempt a "freelance" trip. Most sites are remote, and problems in learning their location, arranging for guides, burros and equipment, compounded by language barriers, are formidable and costly. In addition, laws resulting from severe damage by unthinking tourists and pothunters restrict many activities. In 1977 an article appeared in a backpacking magazine about a trip to an art site. The people were described as intelligent and caring, but the article went on to describe how they despoiled the site by removing artifacts. Even professional anthropologists can be guilty. I once conducted an "FBI style" search of a nasty trash pile at one site and found the name and address of a prominent anthropologist on a number of magazine wrappers and letters.

Shelling

Baja's diverse underwater habitats, especially in the Cortez, produce an astounding variety of mollusks, and many beaches and flats are so remote that their conchological treasures lie undisturbed, providing fine collecting opportunities. Many of the more prominent sites are identified in Chapters 9 through 16.

There are some opportunities to purchase shells. Palomar Market in Santo Tomás sells a variety of native shells, as do shops in Ensenada and La Paz. There are also less conventional ways to purchase them. An abalone fishery exists along the Pacific coast, and divers will give you specimens of black, red, green, corrugated and "blue" abalone (apparently a hybrid), as well as other creatures encountered during their travels along the bottom. Divers take vast quantities of sea urchins, whose sex organs are flown to Japan to be sold fresh at high prices, and a fine "basket" should not be too difficult to obtain. In addition, local fishermen harvest pismos, scallops, *chocolate* and butter clams, several species of cockle, owl limpets, rock oysters and mussels, and wavy turbans are

Suzy, Georgia and Judy search for sea buttons on the beach at Isla San Francisco in the Cortez.

taken for bait. Commercial divers land near the old salt pier in Guerrero Negro and may have shells for sale at low prices, most notably lion's paw. Scallop divers around Bahía Concepción usually have a variety of shells available. Shrimp trawlers working the Cortez bring up loads of live mollusks and often have specimens. The museum at Bahía de los Angeles has an extensive collection of local shells.

Mineral collecting

Jesuit Father Johan Jakob Baegert, who served in Baja in the mid-1700s, found the main ingredients of the peninsula to be largely " . . . petrified sea shells, mountains . . . of flint, . . . wacke stones held together by a mortar-like substance, . . . smooth polished stones . . . and . . . a mixture . . . which [defies] identification and can only be classified as pieces of California." Baegert's description didn't deter too many prospectors and for over 400 years men have searched the arid peninsula for economic minerals, primarily gold and silver. However, remarkably little is known of Baja's potential for amateur mineral collecting. The geological knowledge of early prospectors was generally limited to locating gold or silver and getting it out of the ground, and papers in the recent professional geological literature are devoted to economic or descriptive geology, rarely touching on subjects of direct interest to collectors. Until completion of the Transpeninsular, large areas of Baja were accessible only at the cost of a great deal of time and money, which relatively few collectors were able to afford. Even today little has been published, and much of Baja remains unknown to collectors.

There are only about 250 known mines and mineral sites in Baja's 53,280 square miles, an amazingly small number for an area so large. When the sites are plotted on a map, three things become apparent: most sites are in Baja Norte, enormous "blank spots" exist without a single site, and the locations of non-economic mineral sites are strongly correlated with accessibility; few are far from roads. The cause of this uneven distribution could be that Mother Nature was stingy with Baja California and decided to locate most of her meager allocation in northern areas and near roads to insure that collectors could get to them easily, but the more likely reason is that many sites remain undetected or unreported.

Collectors thus have choices ranging between two extremes: confining their collecting activities to areas of proven mineralization or heading for unknown country. Six areas have extensive mineralization: (1) a broad band extending south from the border through La Rumorosa, El Alamo and San Vicente, including areas west of Parque Nacional Sierra San Pedro Mártir; (2) areas on both sides of the Transpeninsular between El Rosario and Rosarito; (3) the area around El Arco; (4) the Santa Rosalía area, where almost sixty minerals have been found; (5) the Concepción peninsula; and (6) around El Triunfo, where thirty-five have been identified. The major areas with few or no sites are located: (1) in the interior east of the Transpeninsular between the latitudes of Camalú and of El Rosario; (2) in Pacific coastal and interior areas from the latitude of Santa Rosalía to that of Loreto; and (3) the entire peninsula south of the latitude of Loreto, with some exceptions like El Triunfo, magnesite deposits on Isla Santa Margarita and phosphate deposits on the coast between Loreto and La Paz. There are a number of known but almost unexplored sites, including the "Columbia" area southwest of Cataviña.

Chapters 9 through 16 identify many mineral sites, some prominent and even world-famous, others minor. Although of little direct interest, the latter have been included to help

A specific gravity of 58? Don Nelson and Jim Smallwood find something amusing about Jim's analysis of a mineral sample.

Don Nelson and Jim Smallwood examine strange, dust-covered speleothems in "Cueva Tres Pisos," the Three Story Cave.

readers identify general areas of mineralization. The Mexican government produces topographic maps which show many mines, plus a series of geologic maps—see Chapter 8.

People living in the old mining areas south of La Rumorosa occasionally have specimens for sale, primarily epidote. Small-scale miners, especially those working around El Alamo, sell raw gold at market prices. In 1983 an American was able to purchase an unusual and beautiful half-ounce gold nugget from an Alamo miner. Miners at El Arco sell copper-bearing minerals, and people living around El Aserradero south of Laguna Hanson often have specimens. The Palomar Market in Santo Tomás sometimes has samples of selenite and actinolite. The museum in Bahía de los Angeles has mining and mineral displays.

Cave exploring

Sometimes those "pieces of California" have big holes between them. Other than a sentence here and there in the scientific literature, generally related to the life and times of the resident bats, my efforts in the library to learn of the existence of caves in Baja proved fruitless. However, after asking every bartender, butcher, cab driver, waiter, Captain of the Port, rancher, shepherd, goat driver, fisherman and sea urchin diver within earshot, and passing out hundreds of handbills in Spanish, I came up with a fair number, which are described in later chapters. Solution, lava-tube and sea caves are included. Several caves have been omitted to avoid disruption of their bat colonies. All are modest, but are offered as proof that caves do exist in Baja. Some of the natural history cruises down the Pacific coast mentioned in Chapter 1 stop at Isla San Martín to see the lava tubes.

****

TRAPPED! I wanted photos of sally lightfoot crabs, so I decided to enter a small sea cave south of Bahía San Francisquito in my aluminum cartop boat. I cut the engine and rowed into the entrance, but soon the channel was barely wider than the boat and the ceiling became so low that I had to kneel. With my mind in neutral, I pressed on, propelling the boat by pushing an oar against the sides of the cave, my strobe illuminating the scene at intervals in brilliant white light. The channel turned several times and soon it was pitch-black. The water had been calm, but without warning there was a heavy surge, perhaps from the wake of a passing vessel, and the boat was rammed through the rapidly narrowing channel, slamming and screeching against the rough rock. When it finally came to a halt, the boat was firmly wedged in place and the flat ceiling had dipped so low that the top of the outboard engine was almost touching rock. Pushing on the sides of the cave would not budge the boat an inch. Trapped, but not for long, I thought! Kneeling in front of the engine was awkward, but I managed to pull the starter and it coughed into life. I shifted into reverse and raced the throttle, but nothing happened, except that I was enveloped in clouds of acrid smoke. Gagging and gasping for breath, I hit the stop button.

I sat in the darkness for a while, deciding what to do. If I could not break free I was going to have to abandon ship, but I could not quite squeeze over the transom because the engine and several rod holders were blocking the way. What would happen if the tide came in—would it fill the cave? I could see myself, nose pressed against the ceiling, sucking in the last small bubble. It might be possible to get over the bow, but I would have to free-dive under the boat in the pitch-darkness, swim to the entrance, where there were only sheer bluffs for hundreds of yards on either side, and hike for many miles to find help. I cursed myself over and over; what a dummy! What a dummy! How could I have let this happen? I had no water and no food except for a fish that had been baking in the bilges all day, and no shoes other than a pair of wet-suit booties, and I had told nobody where I was going. Later, I don't know how long, I was lying on my back, sick from the smoke, shivering, hungry and cursing, when another idea popped into my head. I lay on my back, put my feet against the ceiling and gave a heave with all the strength of my legs and back. Instantly the boat broke loose, and a few minutes later I was bobbing up and down off the entrance to the cave in the rose-colored twilight.

****

CHAPTER 8
A BAJA SURVIVAL KIT

Uninformed Americans are sometimes reluctant to travel in Baja, fearing the legendary "Mexican roadblock," hassles with police demanding *mordida* for inadvertent infractions of unfamiliar laws, and bouts of Montezuma's Revenge. However, in my thirty-four trips to Baja by land, sea and air, some more than four months long, Montezuma got even only once, I paid only one bribe—a Tijuana traffic cop assured me that he would take the money and pay the fine for me—and other than several swift maneuvers at PEMEX stations, never to my knowledge have I been cheated; if it happened it was done so skillfully I never knew it. Once I had to leave a van in Baja for three months while I returned home. Although it was jammed with outboard motors, SCUBA gear, a hooka compressor, cameras, camping equipment and tools, I returned to find it intact, not so much as a dust mote disturbed. Try that in your home town!

Only once have I been aware of being deliberately misled—three young Mexicans in a pickup told me that I absolutely must not turn right at the next dirt road if I wanted to find Gruta San Borjitas. Fortunately they were such unpracticed liars that their intentions were obvious. By far the most dangerous and disagreeable part of my travels to Baja has been driving through Los Angeles on the way to the border, and the worst drinking water I ever had to endure in Baja was some I filled my tanks with while in San Diego.

Still, Mexico is a very foreign country; the language, money, customs, laws and regulations are distinctly different, and traveling there is not like traveling in Canada. In fact, the cultural and economic factors that separate the U.S. and Mexico may be among the greatest found between adjacent countries anywhere in the world. There is a great deal to know, and the following "survival kit" of facts, opinions and ideas is intended to promote a pleasant Baja adventure.

Tourist cards

U.S. citizens must have a tourist permit (everyone calls them tourist "cards," for reasons obscured by the mists of time) in order to stay more than seventy-two hours in border areas, or to travel south of Maneadero or San Felipe. Enforcement is spotty and erratic, but possession of one may help you avoid problems later, especially if you decide to cross to the mainland.

There are two types of cards. A single-entry card is good for one visit of up to 180 days—the exact length will be determined by the Mexican immigration official who validates the card. If you get less than the full 180 days, you can ask for a longer period at the time the card is validated, or at any *Migracíon* (immigration) office in Mexico at a later date. The second type, multiple-entry, allows any number of visits during its 180-day period. Both types can be obtained at the Mexican Consulate General, Mexican Consulates or Mexican Government Tourism Offices, and single-entry cards can also be obtained from some airlines, insurance companies and travel agencies, and from *Migracíon* offices. Obtaining a card before crossing the border will save hassle and time, especially on holidays and weekends. There is no charge for either type, but you must show proof of U.S. citizenship, such as a valid passport or certified birth certificate. Armed-forces IDs are sometimes rejected. Naturalized U.S. citizens can use a valid U.S. passport, a Certificate of Naturalization or a Certificate of Citizenship. The cards must be used within 90 days of issue, and the document used to prove citizenship must be carried while you are in Mexico.

Having a card in your possession is not enough—you must also have the card validated at a *Migracíon* office in Mexico. This sounds easier than it is. The offices at the ports of entry into Baja described in this book—Tijuana, Otay Mesa, Tecate and Mexicali—are often busy and parking is hard to find, especially at Tijuana and Mexicali. There is an office in Playas de Rosarito, but it is somewhat out of the way for those heading south. The office in Ensenada is conveniently located, but it is often unexpectedly closed during business hours. The office at Maneadero is permanently closed, and if you pass this point without possessing a validated card you are technically breaking the law. What to do? Try to have your card validated as early in your trip as possible. If you have made a reasonable effort and yet arrive at Maneadero with the card still not validated, go on and try at the La Pinta Hotel or the *Migracíon* office in Guerrero Negro. To the south offices will be found at ferry terminals, international airports and in the larger towns where it may be possible to validate cards—see the index. If you are headed for areas south of San Felipe you should have your card validated before you arrive there—the *Migración* office in San Felipe is currently (mid-1991) closed and there is no way to validate a card.

Technically, you must return your single-entry card at the border when you depart Mexico, but few people actually do so, and border officials might be suspicious if you tried. This is the big problem with multiple-entry cards—there is no parking provided for this purpose at the border stations, and yet you must "check-out" properly if you intend to return without a hassle. Also, multiple-entry cards may be a source of complications if you attempt to validate them anywhere except at the border crossings.

In addition to a tourist card, a person under eighteen traveling without both parents present must have a notarized letter granting permission to travel in Mexico. It must be signed by both parents if the minor is traveling alone, or by the parent not present if traveling with just one. If the child's parents are separated or divorced, the parent having custody must sign the letter, which must be accompanied by the separation or divorce papers. If one parent is dead, the living parent must sign the letter, which must be accompanied by the death certificate. If both parents are dead, the child's guardian must sign, and the letter must be accompanied by the guardianship papers. These requirements are rarely enforced in Baja.

Canadians

The rules described above for U.S. tourists generally apply to Canadians as well. A valid passport or birth certificate is required to get a tourist card. A Canadian consulate is located in Tijuana—see the map on page 91, and Appendix A. Because of unfamiliarity with the currency and a lack of information as to the current exchange rate, Canadian dollars and travelers checks are not readily accepted in Mexico, and problems are sometimes encountered even in Southern California. Canadians should change their money into U.S. dollars at the U.S.-Canadian border and into pesos at the U.S.-Mexican border. Because of the automatic conversion on billing or because the locals don't know the difference, Canadian credit cards seem to be as acceptable as U.S. cards. The Canadian Department of External Affairs publishes a useful booklet, "Bon Voyage, But . . . ," describing visas, medical matters, import controls, consular matters, foreign laws, money and many other subjects.

Pets

To take a dog or cat into Mexico you must obtain a rabies vaccination certificate and an Official Interstate and International Health Certificate for Dogs and Cats (Form 77-043) signed by a vet, and have both approved by a Mexican consul. In practice, these requirements are often ignored in Baja. To get back into the U.S. dogs and cats must be free of evidence of diseases communicable to man when examined at the port of entry. Dogs, but not cats, must be vaccinated against rabies at least thirty days prior to entry, and a valid rabies certificate must be available. If a certificate is not available or the thirty-day period has not elapsed, the dog can still be admitted with some hassle; information can be obtained at the border.

Dogs like to go to Baja too; Soni the surfing Shorthair grabs a nice right at "Zippers."

U.S. Customs has a booklet available, "Pets, Wildlife," describing regulations on dogs, cats, birds, monkeys and other pets and wildlife.

Canned dog food is available in many stores in Baja Norte. Cat food is hard to find south of the border cities, but inexpensive canned tuna and mackerel are readily available. In Baja Sur both canned and dried dog and cat foods are usually easy to find in the large towns. Cat litter is hard to find everywhere. Although most are involved in large-animal practice, there are many vets and a number of veterinary pharmacies.

Maps, guides, tide tables, satellite images and aerial photographs

Mexico publishes a wide variety of topographic, geological, soil, aeronautical, weather and tourist maps, aerial photos and LANDSAT images. There are gaps in coverage and place names are often missing or applied to the wrong locations. They are generally accurate in their physical representations, although some "phantom" islands are shown, those northwest of the south tip of Guardian Angel Island, for instance. Although catalogs list them as available, the Mexican government has never gotten around to actually printing topos for many large Pacific and Cortez islands, and even when smaller islands are within the geographic coverage of given maps, they are often not shown—map G12A68, San Nicolás, for instance, does not show Isla Ildefonso. Most were developed years ago and do not show recent road construction. Beware of searching for roads that a map labels "*en construcción*" (in construction)—they are often planned but rarely built. The

United States, Great Britain and Mexico publish nautical charts of Baja's Pacific waters and the Sea of Cortez. Charts published by Mexico are usually copies of U.S. charts, although a few are original and useful.

The Map Centre, Inc. sells a vast array of Baja nautical charts, topographic maps, books and other products by mail. The Defense Mapping Agency handles mail-order sales of U. S. nautical charts, tide tables, sailing directions and other publications. Many are also available from authorized DMA sales agents. Cruising Charts sells cruising guides for Bahía de los Angeles, Puerto Refugio and the Midriff region, as well as large-scale strip charts for Puerto Peñasco, Bahía Kino and San Carlos on the eastern side of the Cortez, plus a cruising guide to San Carlos. Agencia Ajorna in Ensenada and La Paz and Agencia Aboroa in La Paz sell U.S. and Mexican nautical charts. Desert Enterprises sells copies of a number of historic maps of Baja California.

Tide Tables for the West Coast of North and South America, published by NOAA, has tidal stations for Ensenada, San Carlos, La Paz, the entrance to the Río Colorado, plus Tepoca Bay, Puerto Peñasco, Guaymas, Topolobampo and Mazatlan. Cruising Charts publishes tables for the Cortez, with stations at La Paz, Loreto, Santa Rosalía and Bahía de los Angeles, plus Puerto Peñasco, Bahía Kino and San Carlos. The University of Arizona publishes tables for the northern Cortez. The Earth Observation Satellite Company handles LANDSAT imagery, and Compania Mexicana Aerofoto sells aerial photos and controlled mosaics.

Compasses

Many descriptions of the locations of shipwrecks, geological features, dive sites, "fishing holes," etc. in later chapters depend on compass cross bearings. To be able to take full advantage of this information, the reader should obtain a bearing compass. An ordinary backpacker's compass, which utilizes a needle to indicate north-south, is not well adapted to taking bearings (a few models have a mirror that allows reasonably accurate bearings). A bearing compass has a sighting mechanism and a circular compass card with degrees marked on its periphery, allowing accurate readings. Coghlan's lensatic engineer compass, stock number 8164, available at many outdoor stores and large drug chains for about $10, is suitable.

Off-road drivers should obtain an auto compass. Make sure it is of the "compensating" type, allowing the compass to be adjusted for the deviation caused by the magnetic influence of the vehicle. Non-compensating compasses are subject to deviation in excess of thirty degrees, often making them worse than useless. Airguide stock number 1699, found in many auto supply stores, is a compensating type, costs less than $10 and can be attached with double-faced tape to the windshield, where deviation is normally at a minimum.

Mexico West

Mexico West Travel Club, Inc., publishes a monthly newsletter, *Mexico West*, which contains eight pages of articles, news stories and travel tips on Baja California and mainland Mexico's west coast. In addition, the club offers tourist cards, fishing licenses, boat permits, books and a travel information service, plus member discounts on insurance, hotels, restau-

rants, auto and RV rentals, RV parks, expeditions, diving and sportfishing. The savings on the first trip should more than pay the annual membership fee.

Travel agents

Almost any travel agent can provide information and reservations for the larger hotels and resorts in Baja. However, there are a number who specialize to some degree in Baja and have more detailed personal knowledge and better sources of local information. These include Baja Hotel Reservations, Baja Safari, Mexico Resorts International, Pan-American Hotels International, Inc., and Sun Tours. Some organizations organize and promote specialized package trips, which have been described in previous chapters. There are also agencies in the larger towns and even one in Guerrero Negro, Viajes Mario's. Information is also available from the Mexican Government Tourism Office, the State Secretaries of Tourism of Baja California [Norte] and of Baja California Sur, and the Tijuana Tourism and Conventions Bureau. See Appendix A for addresses and telephone numbers.

Money and credit cards

Although U.S. dollars are accepted almost anywhere, the Mexican national currency is pesos, and that is what the locals use and understand. If you use dollars, businessmen outside of the major tourist towns may not know the current exchange rate and will protect themselves by requiring an unfavorable exchange rate. If the person is dishonest, the transaction provides opportunities for flim-flam. Most money problems can be avoided by a simple expedient: convert some of your money to pesos. The decimal system is used and is easy to understand, and since almost all businesses make change in pesos anyway, you would soon be dealing with an impossible mix of pesos and dollars whether you liked it or not. If this makes you uncomfortable, use a small calculator to figure the dollar equivalent of each purchase. The conversion can be made at numerous *casas de cambio* (money changing businesses) at most tourist towns and all border crossings, and at banks throughout Baja.

While most money-changing businesses seem honest, it pays to ask for a calculator tape of the transaction and study it closely before slipping your money through the window. A few businesses, hoping you will not notice, may try to figure a "commission" into the transaction, something not announced in the advertising of their buy and sell conversion rates. This is sometimes as much as an outrageous 10%, so ask first, and if any commission is charged take your business elsewhere. You can convert pesos back to dollars when you return. There is competition, so shop around for the best rates. Hotels and airports offer the worst rates.

In 1875 a peso was worth almost exactly a dollar, but since then it has continued an irregular but precipitous slide to its mid-1991 level of about 3,500 to the dollar. It seems in danger of dropping even more, so don't convert large amounts into pesos or plan to hold them for long periods. Get your pesos in small denominations, for many businesses and gas stations can't make change even for 10,000 peso notes. The handiest are the 5,000 peso bills. Mexican coins are almost worthless; one day I rewarded a small volunteer windshield washer at a PEMEX station with a large handful of coins. I thought I was being generous, but got a very sour look.

It is difficult to cash personal checks in Baja, so the remainder of what you expect to spend should be converted to small-denomination traveler's checks from large, well-recognized institutions such as Bank of America or American Express. Many tourist establishments will honor major credit cards, but don't plan to use them in smaller towns or at businesses catering to the local people.

Mail

Outside the larger towns, the post office is often in a small store, a tiny sign sometimes proclaiming "*Correo*," sometimes not. If you can't find it ask; everyone knows. Postage is very inexpensive. Hours of post office operation are erratic, and service ranges from mediocre to bad. When addressing letters and packages, print clearly and avoid using middle names and initials. Delivery times to the U.S. range as follows: from Ensenada five days; La Paz, Bahía de los Angeles and Loreto six; El Rosario eight; Bahía Asunción, Cabo San Lucas and Bahía Tortugas ten; Mulegé, Isla Cedros and Guerrero Negro thirteen. If you are writing to someone in a small Mexican town and don't know his street address, use the address "*Domicilio Conocido*" (location of home known) and it will often get there. Send a general-delivery letter in care of "*Lista de Correos*." When the letter arrives, the postmaster will add the name of the addressee to an alphabetic list posted in the office. The addressee must present identification, and picking up mail for another person can be difficult, even if you have a note authorizing you to do so. If it is not claimed within a set time, officially ten days, it is returned to the sender. There is a mail-forwarding system, but making it work is almost impossible.

Telephone and telegraph

The telephone system in Baja provides rather low quality service, by U.S. standards anyway. Delays, poor sound quality and other problems are common, and during periods of high traffic the number of lines across the border can't handle it all and "busy" signals are often encountered. However, automatic direct-dial equipment is being installed, additional areas are getting service, existing towns and cities are getting their own area codes and the system is slowly being modernized. The Mexican government announced recently that the system will be privatized, which should result in further improvements.

Most of the Mexican businesses and organizations listed in Appendix A have the new direct dial numbers, making a call from the U.S. rather simple. Only AT&T has lines into Baja, and if you subscribe to Sprint or MCI things occasionally go wrong when you access AT&T. However, making a call from one Baja location to another or to the U.S. may not be quite so easy. Although public telephone service is absent in small villages along the Transpeninsular, many have at least one official telephone, often located in the *Delegación Municipal* building (the equivalent of city hall), which might be made available in an emergency. There are special *larga distancia* (long distance) stations scattered in the larger towns and villages, staffed with an operator and often located in pharmacies or other businesses—look for the sign. Go in armed with a piece of paper listing the city, state, country, area code and number you are calling and your name. Local calls are cheap, but long distance charges, aided by surcharges and a substantial tax, can be impressive. Calls from Baja hotels are often relatively easy, although time consuming; you just give the required information to the hotel operator and she works at it until success or failure is achieved. My last call home from Baja to the U.S. before this book went to press was made from a tourist hotel in La Paz with the aid of an English-speaking operator during low-rate hours. It took one hour and twenty minutes to finally get through and the call cost almost $18.00 for fifteen minutes.

Telegrams can be sent to and from over forty locations in Baja, including all the larger cities and many villages, right down to small places like Bahía Tortugas, Puerto Lopéz Mateos, Punta Abreojos, Isla Cedros, La Purísima and the Comondús. Western Union can handle telegraphic money orders to all these locations.

Public transportation

International airports are located at Tijuana, Mexicali, Loreto, La Paz and San José del Cabo. At present (1991) Aero California, Aeromexico, Alaska and Mexicana offer flights between the U.S. and Baja, and all but Alaska have flights within Mexico. Aerolineas California Pacifico, S.A. offers flights between Guerrero Negro, Cedros and Bahía Tortugas. Charter air service is available from Mustang Aviation in San Diego, and at the international airports and some local airports in Baja, including Ensenada, Guerrero Negro and Santa Rosalía. The DC-3 chartered by Excursions Extraordinaires for its boardsailing package trips to Punta Chivato is available to other passengers as well.

Soc. Coop. de Producción Pesquera flies multi-engine cargo planes from Ensenada to Isla Cedros and Bahía Tortugas. Dubbed the "Cannery Airline," it permits private passengers, opening great opportunities. Someone needing to return to the U.S. from one of these remote locations to see a doctor or get parts can fly to Ensenada, take a bus to the border, have access to the full facilities of San Diego, and be able to return in as little as three days. Currently there are flights on Wednesdays and Saturdays, departing about 9 a.m. from the airport at El Ciprés, south of Ensenada. Reservations and information can be obtained by telephone. Delays and interruptions to service are frequent, but fares are low.

The Mexican Ferry System operates between Santa Rosalía and Guaymas, between La Paz and Topolobampo, and between La Paz and Mazatlan. The system is ill-managed and inefficient, information is difficult to obtain and the reservation system is unreliable. The system is now run by a private company, and although increases in the quality of service have been promised, to date the only noticeable effect has been an increase in prices. However, prices are still not all that high, especially for foot passengers, the people are friendly and the trip can be an interesting experience. The ferries can take RVs of any size, and bicycles and motorcycles are no problem. Accommodations range from inexpensive salon class, where you get a reclining chair, to private suites with bathroom and shower.

A 300-passenger 32-knot catamaran, the *Baja Express*, now provides passenger service between La Paz and Topolobampo. Reservations and information are available from Sun Tours. It may be possible to bring bicycles—discuss this with Sun Tours before getting too deep into your plans.

A number of Mexican bus companies operate in Baja California, several of which run between Tijuana and La Paz. A trip on one of these can be an unusual and inexpensive adventure, and bicyclists sometimes use them to great advantage. Information on schedules, routes and terminal locations can be obtained from the tourist offices listed in Appendix A. Baja California Tours, Inc. offers bus trips throughout Baja and will allow passengers to join or leave the trips at scheduled stops.

U.S. automobile rental companies vary in their regulations on bringing their cars into Mexico. Most prohibit it altogether, but a few—Dollar, for instance—will allow them to be taken into Baja as far south as Ensenada. Most of the tourist hotels have a rental agency in the lobby or can otherwise arrange rentals, and all the international airports have rental desks. Taxis are available in all large cities and in some of the smaller ones like Loreto.

Vehicle regulations and insurance

Your U.S. or Canadian driver's license is valid for driving your own vehicle or a rental vehicle. You must have valid original registrations or notarized bills of sale for all vehicles, driven, towed or carried, and for trailers and boats. If there is a lien on any of these, or if any are borrowed, you must have a notarized letter from the lienholder or owner authorizing you to drive it in Mexico, who will probably require proof of insurance. You cannot lend, rent or sell your vehicle to a Mexican. If you bring a vehicle to Mexico, it must depart with you when you leave. If it is wrecked or stolen, or if you must leave Mexico temporarily without it, you must contact the nearest office of the *Registro Federal de Vehiculos*. These are elusive, tending to open, close and move without notice; ask the local civil authorities about their locations. Check with nearby RV parks—a few are authorized to take custody of such vehicles.

Temporary import permits for vehicles are not required in Baja as they are on the mainland, but if you take the ferry to the mainland they are available at ferry offices. There are several important complications involved in obtaining these permits. For instance, only one permit will be issued per person. If you are alone and have your motorcycle aboard your pickup, you have a problem. The number of permits issued is also limited to the number of licensed drivers. Those anticipating taking the ferry from Baja to the mainland should obtain current information from a Mexican Consulate or Tourism Office concerning the requirements for temporary import permits.

Mexico does not require vehicle insurance, but it would be most unwise to drive without it. Mexican law treats accidents seriously, and they may be considered a criminal as well as a civil matter. If you have an accident, police will determine whether you are responsible. You will usually be free to leave in a few hours if you are not at fault, or the next day if written statements are necessary. If you are at fault, your vehicle may be impounded and you will be charged and brought before a judge. You may be held until judgments against you are satisfied, and a Mexican insurance policy is a swift way of proving financial responsibility and reducing red tape. Although some U.S. and Canadian policies may partially cover your vehicle for physical damage while in Mexico, the Mexican government does not recognize U.S. or Canadian insurance as valid in Mexico.

In general, Mexican policies can be written to provide the same basic coverages available in the U.S.: collision, upset and glass breakage, fire and total theft, property damage, civil liability and medical payments. Liability coverage can be obtained alone. Unfortunately uninsured motorist coverage is not available. According to one company, 92% of Mexican drivers do not carry auto insurance, so if you are in an accident and the other party is at fault, you almost certainly will never collect a dime. Motorcycles can be insured only for public liability and property damage. Theft coverage provides only for total theft, not pilferage of contents. Some companies offer coverage for fines, legal costs and bond costs. Damage to the underparts of a vehicle caused by driving on poor roads is not covered. You may invalidate coverage if you are drunk or under the influence of drugs, if you are unlicensed, or if you permit an unlicensed driver to drive. If you are towing a trailer, it must be insured along with the tow vehicle. The same rule applies to campers and boats. Under such coverage a boat is insured only while being towed or attached to the insured tow vehicle, not while being launched or afloat. Some policies contain geographic limits within Mexico, so make sure you know what they are.

Policies for one day or more are available at many insurance offices in the U.S. near all border crossings, some having drive-up service open seven days a week. You must present your registration or notarized affidavit and driver's license. Rates are based on the value and type of vehicle and are regulated by the Mexican government, but companies vary widely in services provided, availability of adjusters and so forth. Rates may seem high, but remember that they are the same for all drivers, regardless of age or driving record.

There are less-expensive alternatives. International Gateway Insurance Brokers offers annual policies that require no reporting of entry to and exits from Mexico. The break-even point for an annual policy can be as low as fifteen days compared to the daily policies described above, so substantial savings are possible. A multiple-entry policy with a reporting provision is also available; just before you cross the border you call them or send a card, and when you return, notify them again. You will be charged only for time spent in Mexico. They also offer a "Tour Aid" that is similar to U.S. motor club benefits, including travel accident protection, legal services, road service and towing reimbursement, parts service, hospital emergency deposit and emergency cash. Adjusters are available throughout Mexico, claims are handled at their U.S. office and paid in dollars, and discounts are available to members of Mexico West.

A tear-out application for Mexican automobile insurance offered by International Gateway Insurance Brokers will be found at the end of this book. Persons using this application will receive a discount in the form of a waiver of the $10.00 ClubMex membership.

Fuel, parts, service and repairs

Petroleum products are sold by PEMEX, a government monopoly. In the U.S., oil companies may have service stations on all four corners of an intersection, each competing vigorously by offering clean restrooms, computer-assisted tune ups, parts and repair services, as well as gas and oil. Operating under monopoly conditions, PEMEX does not find it necessary to work so hard. Stations rarely offer more than gas and oil and a small selection of filters, additives, fan belts and minor parts. Multi-grade oils and oils of 30 weight and less are hard to find. Encountering an operational restroom is a cause for surprise, and one both clean and operational a cause for unrestrained joy. PEMEX does not take plastic, so payment must be in cash. Dollars are usually accepted, but expect to get a low exchange rate. Stations are rarely open all night and they offer no mechanical services; they are gas stations, not service stations—if you need mechanical assistance you go to a *mechánico*. You will probably have to check your own oil and tire pressure, and many stations do not have an air compressor. If you run out of gas do not expect to find a container to borrow at the station.

Mexican gasoline comes in two basic grades, Nova and Magnasin. Coming from a blue pump, Nova is leaded and officially 80 octane. At about $1.00 a gallon (1991), it is the fuel of the masses. Magnasin, officially lead-free and 87 octane and dispensed from a green pump, is the fuel of tourists, costing about $1.35 a gallon. Silver-colored pumps labeled "Extra" will be seen occasionally. This is a lead-free, higher-octane fuel in the process of being phased out. It seems indistinguishable from Magnasin. Because local demand for expensive Magnasin is low, it is frequently unavailable in the boondocks. Magnasin pumps have been installed at the La Pinta hotels at San Quintín, Cataviña, Guerrero Negro and San Ignacio. They are available to all travelers, not just hotel guests.

Mexicans chuckled when Chevy tried to market a car called "Nova" ("no-go" in Spanish). Did PEMEX know something when they gave the same name to their gasoline? Is there hidden meaning in the name of the new gas, Magnasin? The actual octanes of Magnasin and of Nova are considerably lower than advertised, leading to pinging problems in some engines. "Octane boosting" additives are available on both sides of the border. I have never found one that made the slightest improvement, although some people report success with JB Gas Treatment and Moroso. It will be necessary to set back the ignition timing if these don't work; see your maintenance manual or consult a mechanic. It would be well to discuss this with a dealer if your vehicle has oxygen sensors or computerized controls. A retarded spark reduces mileage by 10-20%, so reset it to factory specifications when you return. If you have dual fuel tanks just fill one with high-octane fuel before you leave the U.S. and use the other for the local product. If you encounter pinging while pulling your trailer up a long grade on a hot day just switch tanks. In hot weather engines will sometimes "diesel" (continue to run when the ignition is turned off). This is damaging and should be stopped immediately. With a stick shift just put the transmission in gear, press on the brake and let out the clutch. With an automatic transmission it is more difficult, but try turning the key on, pressing on the brake, shifting into reverse and then turning the key off.

Diesel fuel can be easier to find than in the United States. If the local PEMEX does not have it, find out where large commercial fishing boats are fueled, or ask at the local cannery. You will need a funnel, since the nozzle used for boats is too large for vehicles. PEMEX stations do not carry LPG, but butane is the domestic fuel of choice and is sold by yards, stores and bulk trucks. It is inadvisable to drive LPG vehicles into Baja. It is not uncommon to find two dozen cars and trucks lined up early in the morning, some with a dozen or more twenty-five gallon cylinders to fill. The line does not always get shorter as the day wears on, and spot shortages are common. It's one thing to have to wait in line once a month to fill the cylinders for your trailer, another if it's every day or so to keep you engine humming along. Mechanics and parts for LPG vehicles are not available in Baja.

Chapters 9 through 16 identify all PEMEX stations known to be in operation in Baja south of the border cities. In the larger towns and cities their locations are shown on the maps. The text identifies the others and the types of fuel normally available as M (Magnasin), N (Nova) and D (diesel). Since Extra is being phased out in favor of its clone Magnasin, high-octane unleaded fuel will be identified simply as "M." Remember that spot shortages are common, especially of Magnasin. Butane yards are also identified.

Most mechanical problems are minor, and if you carry a good spare tire, lug wrench, jack, flashlight, double-bitted screwdriver, medium Crescent wrench, pliers, fan belts, air gauge, water, fuel filters, spare keys in a magnet box, extra fuses and emergency flares you will be able to handle most of them. Off-road drivers require the additional parts and equipment outlined in Chapter 6. You may encounter dirty fuel occasionally, especially if it comes from drums at remote locations, and Baja travelers should be prepared to recognize and replace clogged fuel filters. Symptoms are ominous: the engine often starts readily, but when you apply the accelerator you are greeted with bucking, kicking, backfiring and a lack of power. Changing a filter is a simple matter, but if you don't recognize symptoms or don't have a wrench and a spare filter and know how to install it, a clogged filter can become a major problem. New tires are difficult to purchase outside of the major cities, but many *llanterias* (tire shops) sell used tires at very low prices, some in fairly good condition. Batteries are available in most parts stores and in some PEMEX stations, but you may have difficulty in locating a battery with side terminals, marine batteries or deep-cycle RV batteries.

Tijuana, Mexicali, Ensenada, Ciudad Constitución, La Paz and San José del Cabo have U.S.-style automobile dealerships. Most towns and some smaller settlements have a mechanic, but he is sometimes not in business full-time and may not even have a sign posted. While these mechanics often show great ingenuity, parts may take a week or more to get, and they can do little with electronic ignition, smog-control or fuel-injector problems. They do not have machine-shop equipment needed for turning down brake drums and discs, planing down warped heads or facing off flywheels. Work on automatic transmissions must be scrupulously clean, an impossibility in most locations. Parts stores tend to be small with incomplete inventories, but they can usually obtain what you need if you can wait. Specialized parts for four-wheel drive and all parts for off-brand vehicles may be hard to get, as may those for diesel and LPG vehicles. Chapters 9 through 16 list many parts stores and mechanics.

Local motoring traditions

Mexicans have driving habits that are distinctly different from those of Americans and Canadians. They often use the left-turn signal for highly ambiguous purposes, such as signaling a left turn to indicate that it is safe for you to pass. Intended as a courtesy, this signal can be dangerous. I have seen this signal from a vehicle moving at highway speed and have started to pass it, only to have the vehicle swerve into a left turn, its brake lights out of operation. In periods of reduced visibility, truckers often signal a left turn to oncoming traffic to mark the left margin of their rig, since their clearance lights are usually burned out. I once had an oncoming trucker signal a left during a rainstorm, only to have him suddenly swerve left in front of me, leaving me shaken and angry in the ditch. Both the "safe-to-pass" and "left-side" signals should be greeted with great suspicion—don't leave the driving to others.

Some locals are poor drivers, with no training and little experience, and their vehicles are often in bad condition, with poor brakes, worse tires and headlights missing or out of adjustment—although Baja's increasing prosperity is making these less common each year. Their low beams are frequently burned out, and in approach situations they will sometimes turn off their lights in an effort to avoid blinding you, a startling courtesy. What appeared to be an approaching motorcycle once blinded me with his high beam. When he switched to low beam, he suddenly seemed to swerve across the road. To avoid a head-on crash I swerved right and thumped across the desert for fifty yards. I was cursing all the world's motorcyclists as he sped away, until I saw a pair of tail lights and realized what had happened; it was a pickup with burned-out right low-beam and left high-beam lights.

Not rain, nor darkness, nor heavy traffic, nor fatigue, nor worn tires, not even monstrous potholes slow Mexican truck-

The road department has been busy and chuckholes like this five-incher being measured by John Anglin are not as common as they used to be on the Transpeninsular.

ers in keeping their appointed rounds, and the resulting wreckage can be seen scattered along the Transpeninsular. Some big rigs sport muffler cutouts. Ostensibly installed to save fuel, their real purpose is to terrorize. Many trucks are graced by hand-lettered slogans, including the Spanish versions of such familiar American standards as "King of the Road," "Passing Side-Suicide" and, yes, even "Death Before Dishonor." Most convey mere bravado, but one should elicit deep respect, a skull and cross bones with "*Precaución: Benzedrinos*" lettered on each side. Believe it.

It is becoming increasingly common to encounter military checkpoints. No "probable cause" is required for a search of your vehicle, and the personnel are usually military, not police, with sub-machine guns close at hand. This is very threatening to people from countries like the U.S., where military personnel are normally prohibited from enforcing civil law. The purpose is, of course, the control of drug trafficking, so if it happens to you remember that we, the United States, have laid heavy pressure on Mexico to do just this.

Driving the Transpeninsular

Paved road systems have existed in the northern part of Baja Norte and the southern part of Baja Sur for many years, but it was not until 1973 that the Transpeninsular Highway was finally completed. The only paved road extending the length of the peninsula, the Transpeninsular was built to modest engineering specifications. It is narrower than its U.S. counterparts, shoulders are often nonexistent, striping and safety signs are normally absent, and culverting and drainage are poor. The sub-base is inadequate and the paving thin, often as little as a half-inch thick, and heavy traffic quickly produces a moonscape of potholes. However, in recent years the government has made an effort to upgrade the highway. Concrete bridges have been completed at a number of stream crossings that used to cause trouble after rains, parts of the highway are even beginning to sport center lines and warning signs, and road crews are doing a better job of keeping ahead of the potholes. In recent years RV drivers arriving on the ferry from Guaymas have been complaining about the roads in Sonora and loudly wishing they were as good as in Baja! Things still go wrong; in late 1990 storms washed out six short stretches of the Transpeninsular near Loreto, and six months later not a shovel or a pick had been lifted to make repairs.

There are two basic safety rules on the Transpeninsular: never speed and never drive at night. In level country forty-five miles an hour is the highest speed than can be sustained safely under the best of conditions, and in hilly terrain the safe speed may be less than twenty. Much of Baja is open, unfenced rangeland, and cattle, burros and goats wander onto the highway. At night a black cow may be draped over the hood before your foot can reach the brake pedal. The short days of winter require that additional driving time be scheduled; a border-to-the-Cape trip takes three full days in winter if driving is limited to daylight hours and safe speeds. A table of distances between points on the Transpeninsular will be found in Appendix B.

Do not depend on finding gasoline at every station along the Transpeninsular, especially on long holidays and during winter. The PEMEX stations at Cataviña, Parador Punta

Prieta and Villa Jesús María are remote from shipping terminals, and tank trucks are sometimes delayed by mechanical, weather or road problems. Some stations depend on locally generated electricity, often produced by tiny gasoline-driven generators, and if these will not run there is no way to operate the pumps. A pump failure recently put the station at Cataviña out of operation for two months. If one station can't pump gas, those on either side quickly run out and problems spread like falling dominoes. The basic rule for drivers in this notorious "gas gap" is to top off before your tank is half-empty.

Speaking Spanish

An inability to speak Spanish is apt to be far less of a problem than many people imagine. English and Spanish share a Latin root and have many words in common. Many locals have been to the United States or have dealt with Americans for years and hence speak a bit of English. You may occasionally have to resort to nonverbal communication; if you don't know the word for a physical object, draw a picture; if you need a spare part, bring the broken one. In the El Rosario supermarket Rob Watson and I wanted to buy some honey, but could not find it. Neither of us could remember the word, and we did not have a dictionary, so Rob tried to act out what we wanted. Fluttering his hands at his shoulders and skipping down the aisles on tiptoes emitting loud buzzes, he stuck his face into a display of plastic flowers. At first there were dumfounded looks, but with a roar of laughter everyone got the idea at the same time, and there was a rush to show us where the *miel de abeja* was to be found. An American lady once tried to use this method to explain to a La Paz pharmacist that she needed a box of suppositories. There was a great deal of confusion at first over exactly what was required, but the correct message was finally understood.

Getting into and out of trouble

Most legal rights enjoyed in the United States are also found in Mexico, and foreigners (you) have virtually the same rights as citizens, but there are important procedural differences. If you need help, there is a U.S. Consulate General in Tijuana, and Don Johnson, owner of the Hotel Serenidad in Mulegé, is a Consular Agent. The U.S. State Department maintains a Citizen's Emergency Center in Washington, D.C., which can be reached by telephone. Both the State of Baja California [Norte] and the State of Baja California Sur have established offices to provide free legal assistance to tourists, the Attorney General for the Protection of Tourists (Procuraduria de Protección al Turista), with offices in Tijuana, Mexicali, Ensenada, San Felipe and La Paz. In the towns and villages, civil authority is exercised by the "*delegado*," an elected official who can be found at the *Delegación Municipal* or *Subdelegación* building. In remote areas a local citizen may be appointed similar duties. The most common causes of jail sentences and/or deportation are possession of recreational drugs, problems resulting from alcohol consumption and working without a permit. Public drunkenness is against the law in Mexico. Leave your stash and your nose candy at home—offenders found guilty of possessing more than a token amount of any narcotic substance, including marijuana and cocaine, are subject to a minimum sentence of ten years, and it is not uncommon for persons charged with

drug offenses to be detained for up to a year before a verdict is reached.

If you need physical assistance, help can come from a number of sources. There are teams providing ambulance, paramedical, off-road and mountain search and rescue and similar services, located in Tijuana, Mexicali and Ensenada, with smaller organizations in a number of towns and villages. These can be contacted through local civil and military authorities. The famous Green Angel patrol operates over most paved roads in Baja. It consists of green pickups, each normally crewed by two men, one of whom hopefully is proficient in English. They can assist with minor repairs, provide small parts, sell gas and oil at cost, and arrange for towing and repairs. Although some routes are patrolled twice a day in mainland Mexico, in Baja it is more often once a day and sometimes not even that. Air-Evac International, Inc. and Critical Air Medicine specialize in transporting critically ill and injured patients by aircraft, and operate throughout Baja. Marine emergencies are discussed in Chapter 4.

Prior to 1976 American and Mexican ambulances were not allowed to cross each other's border to pick up or deliver patients, and communications difficulties and other problems hindered medical care and transportation. In that year the Binational Emergency Medical Care Committee was formed, which developed and sponsored an agreement between the two countries concerning the transportation of patients. Today the Committee has a two-member bilingual staff responding to requests for emergency services and information from both sides of the border. In addition, the Committee provides first aid, search and rescue, Emergency Technician

Most of the time you are out of luck if the electricity fails, but sometimes local ingenuity can solve the problem.

and CPR training to personnel in the U.S. and Mexico, and conducts seminars on trauma care, legal matters and other subjects. Should you have a problem, or wish to donate time or money, the Committee can be contacted at the address or 24-hour hot-line in Appendix A.

Radio communications

CB radio is monitored by boaters, RV drivers and organizations such as the Green Angels, various rescue teams, and CB clubs in Ensenada and La Paz. Many local citizens use it as a substitute for a telephone system. There is little agreement as to the proper channel for emergency communications. As in the U.S., channel 9 is the most frequently monitored, but some organizations monitor channel 1, 3, 4, 7, 10 or 16, so if you can't raise someone on channel 9, try others, and if you are listening for others needing help, use your scanner.

As of January 1, 1991, permits for CB radios were no longer required for U.S. and Canadian citizens. However, the regulations concerning permits seem to change weekly, and if you plan to bring a CB call a consulate beforehand and get the latest information. The State of Baja California [Norte] maintains the Rural Radio Telephone Net, providing emergency radio communications between many stations in Baja Norte. Marine communications are discussed in Chapter 4.

Staying clean

Laundromats can be found from the border to Colonia Guerrero (at Posada Don Diego RV Park) and from Mulegé to the Cape. In between you may be able to find a traditional Mexican washerwoman, and some hotels, motels and RV establishments provide laundry service if you are a guest. If you can't find one, borrow an old sailor's trick: put your laundry in a five gallon bucket with a tight fitting lid, fill it three-quarters full with water, add soap, put on the lid and put it in your vehicle or boat. Baja's rough roads or choppy seas should have it clean in a few hours. Vel, a solid detergent bar widely available in Baja, washes human bodies satisfactorily in saltwater, but to avoid a sticky film, don't air-dry yourself; use a towel. Joy dishwashing detergent has long been the standard among yachtsmen for washing dishes in saltwater.

Staying well

Diarrhea is the most talked about medical problem among travelers in Mexico, and the conventional wisdom is well taken; don't drink untreated water; avoid greasy, highly seasoned or unaccustomed foods; wash, peel and/or cook all fresh food; and take care in selecting restaurants. In Baja there should be few problems in obtaining sanitary drinking water. All major cities and most larger villages have installed modern systems, and residents of San Diego visiting Mulegé, for instance, sometimes complain that they can't get water that good back home. Some of the remote villages, including Abreojos and Bahía Asunción, have desalinization plants that probably turn out better water than anything you drink at home. In addition, clean, inexpensive bottled water is available in virtually all food stores in Baja. It is thus possible to completely avoid water problems with little expense or trouble by simply using bottled water for drinking and food preparation, and reserving untreated local water for washing

Hmmmmmmmm; let me think about that for a minute.

and flushing. Chapter 5 has information on treating local water if this becomes necessary.

If you get diarrhea and there are no unusual symptoms, use fluid replacement, rest and diet control. Drink plenty of fruit juices and pure water. Milk and diuretics like coffee, tea and alcohol should be avoided, and the diet should be bland and non-greasy. Pepto-Bismol is widely available in Baja, and its active ingredient, bismuth subsalicylate, has been shown to be effective in preventing and treating mild diarrhea. Imodium A-D is highly effective and is available in some Baja pharmacies, the tablet form being preferable for travelers.

Sunblock lotions of number fifteen or higher are essential, at least for light-skinned people. If you start using a sunscreen, keep using it, for it offers no residual protection and your skin will not have had a chance to acclimate. I have a light complexion, and it used to seem that I could even get "moon-burned," but with modern sunblocks I can now make a two-week trip to Baja and return home only slightly pink. Lips are highly susceptible to burning and resultant lip cancer, but effective lip balms containing sunblocks are available. If you do get burned, get out of the sun and apply cold, wet dressings or a commercial burn preparation. To avoid infection do not break blisters, but instead let them dry up naturally. We had a good home remedy for sunburn when I was a boy—vinegar. It stung like crazy for several minutes and we smelled like tossed salads for the rest of the day, but it quickly reduced the pain, reduced blistering and speeded recovery.

There are numerous local physicians and dentists, many of whom speak some English, many hospitals and clinics can be found in settled areas, and some of the small villages have a Red Cross station, a few of them equipped with ambulances manned by enthusiastic drivers. Rob Watson once cracked up his trail bike while speeding down a beach near Colonet—witnesses said both he and the bike flew ten feet into the air after he hit a hole, but the bike unfortunately came down second and landed on top of him. I drove him into town to get stitched up, and the ambulance drivers quickly loaded him up and with siren blaring and lights flashing roared down the road to the clinic—two hundred yards away, the most exciting event in Colonet in six months.

A prescription is not needed for many common drugs, and in rural areas the people often rely on the pharmacist for medical advice. Occasionally one of the locals will assume medical duties. Papa Diaz of Bahía de los Angeles (now deceased) estimated that he had removed over a thousand fish hooks from the extremities of visiting fishermen. I once happened to be in his office when a man came in with a large hook deeply embedded in a finger. With confidence and skill gained over many years, Papa sat him down, cleaned the site, gave him a shot of Xylocane, pushed the hook through until the barb was exposed, clipped it off, backed the shank out and dressed the wound. No physician could have done it more skillfully.

Bringing things back

Upon returning from Mexico, you are currently (1991) allowed a maximum of $400 in duty-free personal and household goods, including one liter of alcoholic beverage, 100 cigars and 200 cigarettes. About 2,800 other kinds of items may also be duty-free; write to the U.S. Customs Service for a "General System of Preferences" leaflet.

The Endangered Species Act, the Lacey Act, the CITES Treaty, the Marine Mammal Protection Act and other laws, treaties and regulations limit the import of some animals, plants and the products made from them. Many kinds of fruits, vegetables, plants, plant products, soils, meats, meat products, hard corals, birds, feathers, reptiles, snails and other live animals and animal products are restricted. Virtually all live birds originating in Mexico are prohibited. As noted in Chapter 3, the amount of fresh fish and other seafood brought into the U.S. must conform to Mexican possession limits. Common items purchased or found in Baja that are illegal to import into the U.S. include sea-turtle products such as cosmetics containing turtle oil, whale bones, teeth and baleen, and some species of cacti. Narcotics and controlled drugs are prohibited. If you use a prescription drug that contains a narcotic or a habit-forming drug, get a note from your doctor or a copy of the prescription, and keep the drug in its original container. You should contact the U.S. Fish and Wildlife Service or U.S. Customs Service before bringing back items made from ivory, animal skins, or fur. Customs has a useful booklet, "Know Before You Go," that contains detailed information on restricted or prohibited articles, currency, medicines, narcotics, alcohol, tobacco, perfume, agricultural items, pets, declarations, exemptions, residency requirements, duty, duty-free items, shipment and storage.

Both the U.S. and Mexico are signatories to a United Nations convention which makes it illegal to remove from Mexico or import into the United States certain cultural property. In addition U.S. Customs enforces the Convention on Cultural Property Act. The provisions of these are complex, but basically what they boil down to is that if you intend to bring back something that is old or unusual, outside the realm of ordinary tourist items, it would be well to discuss it with U.S. Customs first.

Canadians driving through the U.S. must conform to U.S. customs regulations, and must also meet the letter of Canadian law when they return home. A pamphlet, "Don't Bring it Back," publication 5054E, describing various prohibited, restricted and conditional items, is available from Agriculture Canada.

Survive the savage desert?

The early sportsmen and adventurers who visited Baja were concerned with finding ways to survive the "savage" desert, but today the problem is the reverse. Slowly in most places, and not so slowly in others, Baja is showing increasing signs of the stresses of civilization.

One of the major problems involves the disposal of trash. Cans, bottles and other trash disfigure arid landscapes for years and perhaps "forever." Plastic products are being recognized as particularly dangerous to wildlife. Surveys have shown that plastic items account for half of the man-made products on the ocean's surface, and sandwich bags, styrofoam cups and pellets, six-pack yokes, picnic utensils and bottles are being found on even the most remote beaches of the world. Some scientists believe that these are an even greater source of mortality among marine animals than the highly publicized oil spills and heavy metals. Discarded fishing nets, monofilament line and six-pack yokes are especially dangerous to fish, seabirds and marine mammals, who often die when they become entangled in them. Some species of turtles are attracted by plastic bags, which look like the jellyfish they eat. Birds have been found with pens, toy soldiers, poker chips and fishing bobbers in their stomachs. Several years ago yachties headed for Cabo San Lucas spotted a sea bird with its head rammed through the side of a large plastic jug; apparently the bird thought the jug was prey of some sort and dove on it head first! With the aid of scissors the jug was cut off and the bird flew away.

The best policy for short visits is a conscientious effort to bring back home everything—every wrapper, every can, every pull tab, every inch of discarded fishing line. Many Baja

This fellow almost strangled in a net until we rescued him.

ROB WATSON

kayakers and bicyclists, despite their extremely limited space and ability to carry weight, seem to be able to leave immaculate campsites, with nothing to mark their passage but foot prints and tire prints. Some other Baja travelers with far more ability to carry out their trash are real slobs—it sometimes seems that the bigger the RV the more trash that is dumped. The observation that Mexicans are often the worst offenders may be correct, but it is certainly no excuse.

If the length of the visit is such that it is not possible to bring back everything, trash should be collected until it can be disposed of at a proper dump site. However, you should not get rid of everything indiscriminately. Baja dumps are informal affairs, and trash and garbage are never bulldozed under, so items that may blow around, like Frito bags and Twinkie wrappers, should be saved and burned at the evening campfire. If you need to wrap food for storage, use plastic wrap rather than aluminum foil, and burn it when done. Aluminum foil is also used in juice cartons and food containers, so if you burn them, pull the foil out of the ashes the next morning and discard it properly. Avoid having your engine or transmission oil changed while in Baja, for used oil is inevitably dumped behind the shop. If it must be done, do it yourself, funnel the used oil into a suitable container and bring it home.

Instead of limiting yourself to maintaining the status quo, why not try to make things better and clean up a campsite when you arrive? Collect all plastic, paper, cardboard, rubber, cloth, rope, fishing line, nets and man-made wooden objects and burn them. If you can haul out non-burnable objects to a proper disposal site, do so. Set a goal—how about a "125%" policy; 100% of your trash and 25% more of that left by the inconsiderate oaf ahead of you? If you can't, but are in a coastal area and have a boat or kayak, place steel cans in the fire to burn off paper labels and corrosion coatings. Collect these cans and other metallic items from the fire debris, gather all aluminum cans, glass containers and other items, and sink them in very deep water. Since aluminum foil might be carried back to the beaches by currents, haul it out with your own trash. The result of perhaps an hour's work will be an immaculate campsite you can enjoy for the remainder of your stay. If you are on a ten-day trip this will involve less than 0.5% of your time, a small price to pay for the sense of accomplishment it will bring. In addition, those who follow may be more likely to leave the campsite clean for your next visit.

There is another major problem: the human brain has a hard-wired set of criteria for campsites, and a small number of places end up getting the majority of use. As time passes, human wastes and toilet paper collect behind every rock and bush within walking distance, and because of the arid climate stay there for a long time. In coastal areas, there is a very simple and effective way to avoid contributing to the mess: use the ocean for your bathroom. This requires some psychological adjustment, but it can be done in complete privacy and cleanliness. Maintain personal hygiene in the European manner rather than by using toilet paper. If you are inland select a sandy area and follow the example of your cat.

Don't break in virgin territory. Avoid driving off the paved and unpaved road system, for vegetation crushed under wheels may show no new growth for years, and wheel tracks

This boy could not speak a word of English, but he was able to make his intentions clear—he was going to carry Jim Smallwood's pack all the way up Cañon San Bernardo.

can remain visible for generations. Ruts provide a channel for erosion, and visitors returning after a number of years often find a small canyon where they expected to find a road to the beach. When camping, use existing campsites and fire locations. If you must build a fire in a virgin location, the best place is at the bottom of an arroyo or on a beach below the high tide line, where the ashes will be carried off and dissipated. When hiking stay on established trails. If you go ashore on a small island, confine your visit to beaches and avoid hiking inland. For biogeographic reasons, the rarest flora and fauna are often found on the smallest islands, especially in upland areas, and many Baja islands, especially those in the Cortez, are home to some of the rarest living things on earth.

Chapter 1 has suggestions for safely viewing birds, whales and pinnipeds, and Chapter 3 describes practices that can increase the survival rate of fish and birds that have been hooked and released.

****

MECHANICAL MARVELS. *Groggy from the long drive home from Loreto, I did not realize at first that the pickup ahead of me was not moving. I came to my senses at the last moment and screeched to a stop in a shower of dust and gravel, inches from its bumper. Two anxious young Mexicans scrambled from underneath the truck and dusted themselves off. Embarrassed, I got out, apologized and offered to help with the repairs they were making. With obvious pride, they refused, announcing that they were mechanics. Judging by the condition of their vehicle, that seemed to be a dubious claim. Although its original heritage was Ford, circa 1954, it was now the bastard son of a dozen parents. Parts of the body had been appropriated from a rusted wreck of unknown vintage and summarily bolted on. The steering wheel was so large that it almost touched the windshield, the only intact piece of glass aboard. All other windows, all the lights, even the face of the speedometer, were shattered. The engine was leaking oil and emitting little gurgles of steam. The upholstery appeared to have been savaged by army ants, and the right front tire, considerably larger than the others, pointed to starboard, obviously far out of alignment. Both bumpers and the right front fender had either disintegrated or been appropriated for more important uses. If these fellows were mechanics, I thought, I was Fred C. Dobbs.*

The truck would not shift into second gear—a clevis had fallen off the transmission and was nowhere to be found. Within twenty minutes they had fashioned a replacement from a piece of scrap metal, using a rock for a hammer. They got in and tried to start the engine, only to find that the battery was almost dead. Laughing and cursing, they quickly diagnosed the problem; the generator was not charging. With no test equipment more complicated than a piece of wire, they found that the source of the problem was the voltage regulator. They removed the cover and bent several electrical contacts with a pair of pliers. We rigged jumper cables from my battery, and the truck started immediately. Having little faith in their repair, I expected it to stop when I removed the cables. Grinning when I was proved wrong, they handed me a cold grape Fanta and pulled away in an eye-watering cloud of purple smoke.

I never expected to see them again, but as I approached El Rosario the battered truck was parked by the side of the road and my two friends flagged me down. They said their fuel pump was broken and asked if I had a piece of tubing eight or ten feet long. I didn't see the connection, but I dug through my junk box and found an old piece of outboard fuel line. They lashed a plastic jug full of gas to the roof of the truck, ran the fuel line from the jug down through a glass-less window and a hole in the firewall into the engine compartment. After sucking on the line to create a syphon, they connected the end of it to the carburetor. The inside diameter of the line was too large, but they made a clamp by twisting a bit of wire. To my surprise the engine came to life immediately, and they started across the dry river bed. I expected to see them again at any moment, but as the miles passed I came to realize that I had finally met two of that legendary but dying breed: honest-to-goodness, real live do-anything-with-nothing Baja mechanics. Rather than a rolling comic opera, their hurdy-gurdy wreck of a truck was a monument to great mechanical skill and ingenuity. I never saw them again, but remain confident that they safely reached their destination: Sacramento.

****

CHAPTER 9
TIJUANA TO SAN QUINTÍN

On the U.S.-Mexican border at the San Ysidro crossing

The border crossing at San Ysidro is open twenty-four hours a day. (The Otay Mesa crossing to the east is open from 6 a.m. to 10 p.m. daily.) Tourist cards can be obtained and validated at the *Migración* office (1), located in a building on the right immediately across the border. Unfortunately, parking is very difficult to find. Tijuana is a major city, and there are many hotels, restaurants, theaters, night clubs and other facilities catering to tourists, and virtually any product or service you can think of is available, including a few your mother would not approve of. Information can be obtained at

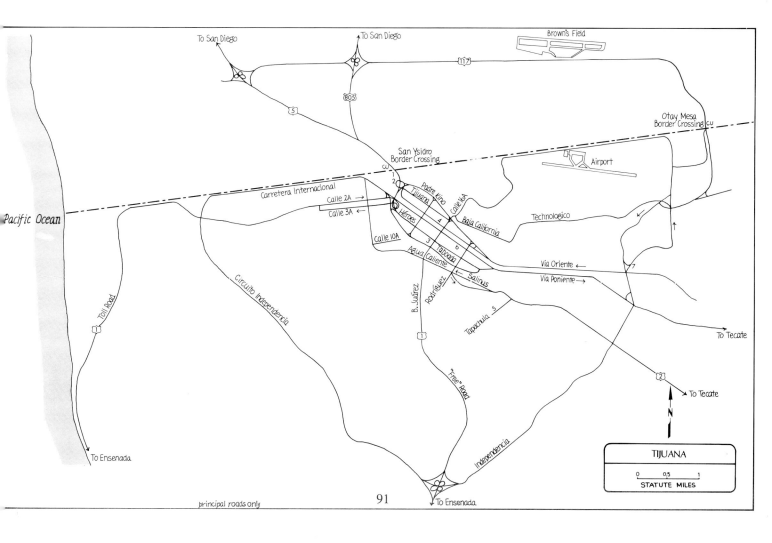

principal roads only

91

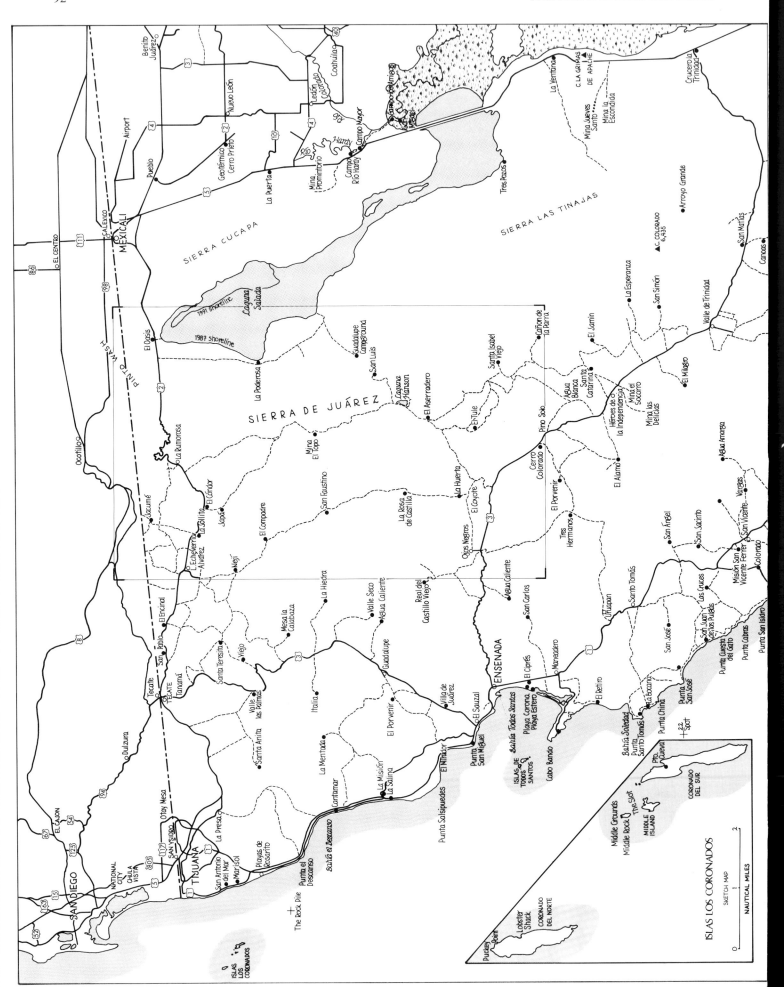

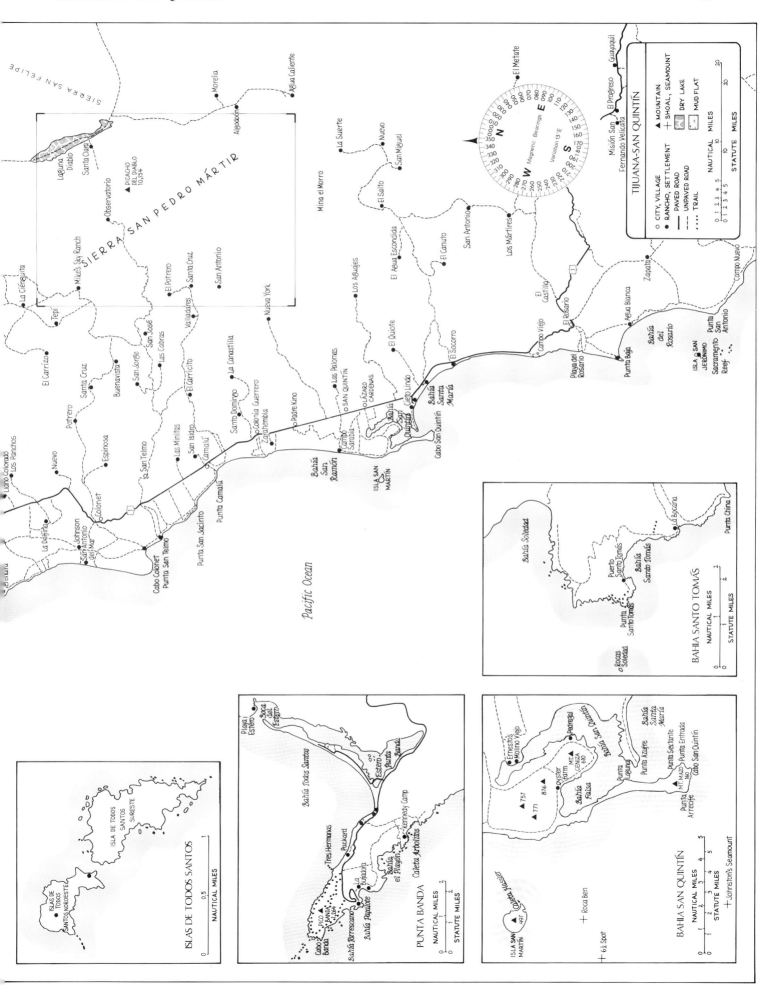

SIERRA SAN FELIPE

Laguna Diablo
Santa Clara

Morelia
Algodón
Agua Caliente

PICACHO DEL DIABLO
10,154

Observatorio

SIERRA SAN PEDRO MÁRTIR

Mike's Sky Ranch

La Ciénaga
Tepi

El Carrizo

El Potrero
Santa Cruz
Santa Cruz
San Antonio

Nueva York

El Metate
El Progreso
Guayaquil

Misión San Fernando Velicatá
El Campo Nuevo

Zapata

TIJUANA-SAN QUINTÍN

○ CITY, VILLAGE
● RANCHO, SETTLEMENT
▲ MOUNTAIN
+ SHOAL, SEAMOUNT
PAVED ROAD
UNPAVED ROAD
····· TRAIL
DRY LAKE
MUD FLAT

Magnetic Bearings
Variation 13°E

NAUTICAL MILES
STATUTE MILES

La Suerte
Nuevo
San Miguel
Mina el Morro
El Salto
El Agua Escondida
Los Aguajes
El Canuto
San Antonio
Los Mártires

Santa Cruz
San José
San Jorge
Buenavista
Las Cabras

Valladares
El Carricito
El Carricito
Santa Domingo
La Canastilla

Las Palomas
El Quiote
SAN QUINTÍN
LÁZARO CÁRDENAS
Cielito Lindo
El Socorro

El Rosario
Campo Viejo
Agua Blanca
Punta Baja
Playa del Rosario

Bahía del Rosario

Punta San Antonio

ISLA SAN JERÓNIMO
Sacramento Reef

Potrero
Espinosa

La Delfina
Johnson
San Antonio del Mar

Llano Colorado
Los Panchos
Nuevo

Colonet
Cabo Colonet
Punta San Telmo

Las Minitas
San Isidro
Camalú

Punta Camalú
Punta San Jacinto

Santa Domingo
Colonia Guerrero
Zanzembla

Padre Kino

Bahía San Ramón

ISLA SAN MARTÍN

Campo Sarabia

Bahía San Quintín

Cabo San Quintín

Bahía Santa María

El Castillo

Pacific Ocean

Bahía Soledad

Puerto Santo Tomás
Bahía Santo Tomás

Punta Santo Tomás

La Bocana
Punta China

Rocas Soledad

BAHIA SANTO TOMÁS

NAUTICAL MILES
STATUTE MILES

Playa Estero
Roca del Estero

Estero

Punta Banda

Bahía Todos Santos

Kennedy Camp

Tres Hermanos
Packard

Bufadora
Bahía el Playón
Caleta Arbolitos

Cabo Banda
PICO BANDA
Bahía Barrescoso
Bahía Papalote

PUNTA BANDA

NAUTICAL MILES
STATUTE MILES

ISLA DE TODOS SANTOS
SURESTE

ISLAS DE TODOS
SANTOS NOROESTE

ISLAS DE TODOS SANTOS

NAUTICAL MILES

Ernesto's Molino Viejo
Peñasco

MT. CENIZA 610

Bahía Santa María

Bahía San Quintín

ISLA SAN MARTÍN
497
Caleta Hassler

757
771
876

Oyster Farm

Punta Azufre
MT. MAZO 160

Punta Sextante
Punta Entrada

Punta Laguna

Cabo San Quintín

Bahía Falsa

Punta Arrecife

+ Roca Ben
+ Johnston's Seamount
+ 6¼ Spot

BAHIA SAN QUINTÍN

NAUTICAL MILES
STATUTE MILES

the Tijuana Tourism and Conventions Bureau offices at the border (2), in town (3) and in San Diego. The State Secretary of Tourism and the Attorney General for the Protection of Tourists have offices in the Centro de Gobierno (4). The Consulate General of the United States is located in Colonia Hipódromo (5). There is also a Canadian Consulate (6).

Motorists heading south should take the Ensenada Toll Road. The traffic pattern immediately south of the border crossing requires quick wits, since you must get in the correct lane on very short notice. Look for signs saying "Ensenada-Cuota." After a dizzying counterclockwise overpass, you should end up going west on Carretera Internacional, paralleling the border fence. After the road climbs a hill and swings south, go right (west) at the first major interchange and you will soon be on the toll road.

Bicyclists should cross the border at Tecate, although the Otay Mesa crossing is convenient for those heading for the Tijuana airport or central bus station (7). The crossing at San Ysidro is difficult to approach without riding on freeways, and once across the border the bicyclist is plunged into the midst of the most reckless drivers and most sign-less streets on the continent. The Toll Road is closed to bicyclists and it will be necessary to pedal through the heart of Tijuana to the "free road" (old Highway 1). It's a strange way to start a bicycle trip, but if you must cross at San Ysidro, consider walking your bike through the pedestrian crossing and taking a cab to the southern outskirts of town—many are available just south of the border crossing. If you can't afford the cab fare and must cross at Tijuana, use the Otay Mesa crossing and head for Av. Independencia and its junction with old Highway 1, missing a great deal of the heavy traffic, maybe. Once out of town, the "free road" is a fair-to-good two-lane road, crossing rolling hills until it reaches the coast near Playas de Rosarito, sixteen miles from the border crossing. It then heads inland near La Misión, ending near El Sauzal in forty more miles, with occasional places along the way to obtain food and drink and spend the night.

On the Ensenada Toll Road

KM	LOCATION
9+	Toll booth, information, restrooms, food, drink. The islands to the west are the Coronados.

THE ISLAS LOS CORONADOS

More people fish and dive at the Coronados, located eight miles offshore, than any other location in Baja, and so many dive boats, sportfishing vessels and yachts are present that the place often looks like an American lake. In spite of this, fishing and diving are excellent, perhaps because the islands are closed to commercial fishing. Many fishermen pursue yellowtail between April and October, but many other species are taken in season, including bonito, barracuda, various species of rockfish and a few white sea bass. Productive fishing locations include the "Middle Grounds" north of Middle Rock, "Eighty-Five Foot Reef" ("Jack-Ass Rock Ledge") 3/4 mile east of the lighthouse on the south tip of Coronado del Sur, and "The Rockpile," seven miles, 131° from the same point. In calm weather fishermen cast lures in

to big calico bass along the western shores of Coronado del Sur. There is also excellent fishing on the "Tijuana Flats," a triangular area between the border, Playas de Rosarito and the Coronados. Work the drop-offs and holes where fish congregate, drifting an anchovy, mackerel, squid or octopus on the bottom.

Thousands of novice divers have made their first open-water check-out on the east side of Coronado del Norte at a place known as the "Lobster Shack," the shack there having succumbed to the elements a few years ago. The western side of the island has fine spearfishing, but is exposed to ocean swells. A sea cave cuts across the south tip of Coronado del Norte. "The Slot" between the two middle islands is one of the best dive locations in the vicinity. A reef extending north from Coronado del Sur has rich sea life, including unusual invertebrates like white sea urchin and chestnut cowrie. Eighty-Five Foot Reef has good spearfishing, but because of its depth it is for advanced divers only. "Five Minute Kelp," just south of Coronado del Sur, also has fine diving and fishing.

Over 160 species of birds have been observed at the islands, and over 30 species are thought to have nested on them. Today only western gulls, and to a lesser extent brown pelicans, nest in significant numbers, the others having been decimated by egg collectors, feral and domestic animals and pesticides. Unfortunately, a few goats continue to wreck havoc on Coronado del Sur. The islands are a bird sanctuary and landings are not permitted. There is a sea-lion colony on the western side of Coronado del Norte, and harbor seals can be seen hauled out in several locations, along with an occasional elephant seal.

Most vessels anchor in the lee of Coronado del Sur, which is well protected from the prevailing winds, although it is little more than an open roadstead. While it is very small, Puerto Cueva on Coronado del Sur offers some protection, as does "Moonlight Cove" on the east side of Middle Island. The concrete foundations seen at Puerto Cueva were once part of the "Coronado Yacht Club," a casino and hideaway for San Diego sinners in the 1930s. The next anchorages to the south are Ensenada and the Islas de Todos Santos. (A small commercial harbor is located at El Sauzal.)

On the Ensenada Toll Road at KM 9+

22	**San Antonio del Mar**. KOA campground with full hookups, ice, restrooms and showers.
25	Oasis Club de Playa. Easily the finest RV park in Baja, with full hookups, restaurants, restrooms, showers, beach, beach break, *palapas*, swimming pools, tennis, volleyball, jacuzzi, sauna, gym, game room, laundry, mini-market. No on-the-ground sleeping or tents allowed (tent trailers OK).
29+	**Playas de Rosarito**. The fast-growing small city of Rosarito is tourist-oriented, with a wide range of hotels, motels, RV parks, restaurants, stores and services, most of them found along the main street. Information can be obtained from the State Secretary of Tourism office next to the police station. A *Migración* office is located in the same building. There is a surf shop in town, and a long beach break.

Fine fishing is encountered one mile offshore, where a sixty-to-eighty-foot drop-off parallels the beach. Jasper is found on the beaches and calcite in nearby hills.

35   Exit to "free road" several hundred yards north of KM marker.

SIDETRIP ON THE "FREE ROAD"

The coast from Rosarito to a point about eight miles south of Cantamar has long been famed for surfing. However, access to some of the sites favored by prior generations is becoming difficult due to the construction of private resorts and communities. K 35, K 55, and K 58+ (Rancho Alasitos), all popular in the past, are now virtually inaccessible. Still, there are some good sites left, well worth trying. The KM markers on the "free road" do not match those on the nearby toll road, so "K" will be used to avoid confusion.

K 38+ (once "Santa Martha," but now "El Portal" to the younger generation), with short lefts and longer rights on the reef off the point, does well on most swells and now seems to be the most popular surfing area north of San Miguel. The best boardsailing conditions here occur during frontal wind conditions, although there is a fairly reliable local thermal. Parking is normally adequate, but camping is spartan, the beaches are rocky and the breaks are often crowded.

Cantamar at K 47 has a PEMEX (MN), stores, doctor, dentist, auto parts, tire repair, pharmacy, bakery and a restaurant. K 48 ("Cantamar Dunes") has a beach break, and the rolling dunes are a favorite with off-road and ATV drivers. K 52 is an area of rocky headlands, with interesting tide pools and primitive camping. The beach break at K 59+ (La Fonda), reached by a road just south of the Hotel La Misión, is confused and sometimes mushy but often has the largest waves in the vicinity. There is a rough road down the cliffs to a wide sand beach. The toll road can be reached a hundred yards south of La Fonda.

Back on the Ensenada Toll Road just north of KM 35

35   Toll booth.
53   **Cantamar**. Already described.
69   Parking, sand beach, beach break.
72   Baja Ensenada RV and Beach Club. Large, modern RV park, with full hookups, restrooms, showers, restaurant, lounge, clubhouse, laundry, store, sauna, swimming pool, jacuzzi, tennis, volleyball, sand beach, beach break with quirky sandbars.
73   **La Salina**. Camping, RV parking, beach break.
83   "Cueva Huevos."

****

CUEVA HUEVOS. It sounded intriguing; a cave north of Ensenada that swooped down from a plateau to end in the ocean. Based on a short description from a man who claimed to have entered it many years earlier, Reeve and I decided to find it, using our highly scientific, time-tested, state-of-the-art method: asking the natives. We hit the jackpot the first day. In our poor Spanish we announced to a man in a pickup that

Fancy footwork at K 37.

we were cave explorers, traveling all over Baja hunting for caves, and asked whether he knew of any in Arroyo Cantamar. He looked puzzled for a moment, but his face soon brightened and he announced in Spanish, "Yes, there are many in this area; many, perhaps more than anywhere else in Baja." Our spirits soared—we were about to come up with a major geological discovery! He was obviously pleased at having helped us, and he continued. Pointing to a small rancho, he said, "Yes, there are some over there, and over there, and there, and there!" We asked about their size and he proudly announced that they were all uniformly large. We marveled at our luck; we had found the most knowledgeable man in all of Baja on our first try! With no prompting he continued, "Yes, we have the finest chickens in Mexico." Confused by his sudden change of direction, we prodded him on, hoping he would return to the subject of caves. With excited jabs, he pointed at each ranch and exclaimed, "There, and there and there! More caves!" It seemed that every tiny rancho within sight had been built adjacent to a fine cave. "Yes, fine chickens and many, many big caves." We wondered if the locals could be using the caves for hen houses.

In a flash our dreams of speleological glory evaporated as we realized we had been asking about cuevas *(caves) and his replies concerned* huevos *(eggs). Our strangely accented Spanish had apparently caused him to believe that we were "egg explorers," driven by a bizarre fetish that caused us to wander ceaselessly throughout the length and breadth of Baja intent on studying the eggs of each region. Once this problem in semantics was cleared up, we found that he knew nothing about caves, in Baja or anywhere else.*

Disappointed but firm in our resolve, we worked our way south, stopping at ranches and asking small boys. As time passed the locals became less and less certain that absolutely no caves were to be found, and soon we started to get a few vague positive responses—the farther south the more positive. We stopped at a road repair camp and were directed to a man who worked as a collector at a toll booth. This man was certain he had been in a cave long ago, but when we followed his directions we found nothing. We returned to see if he could take us there. He could not, but Rafael Aguilera of EL Sauzal could.

Just before dark we arrived at what appeared to be an ordinary hole in the ground. Reeve and I chimneyed down to seventy feet before it leveled out. The air was saturated with water, our camera fogged up, and it became difficult to breathe. We followed a flat, sandy-bottomed corridor, passing through chambers with ceilings twenty-five feet high. Large boulders lay about, their upper surfaces matching the ceiling configuration, causing a degree of apprehension. We finally came to an abrupt halt at the foot of a cliff. We could see a tunnel eight feet above us, but when Reeve climbed up, he found it became very narrow and he was unable to see how far it extended. An acute case of "yellow fever" overtook us and we turned back—after all, we owed it to science; if we never returned to the surface the world would be denied knowledge of what we had discovered.

Was this the cave that swooped to the sea? We do not know. Sand and silt may have filled parts of it, perhaps due to changes in hydrology when the nearby Toll Road was constructed. Ripples in the sandy floor were a sign of flowing water, and they continued right to the barrier that had stopped our progress. All that water has to go somewhere, and a dedicated caver willing to tunnel through sand below the foot of the cliff might be able to locate chambers farther downstream. We found indications of other underground structures nearby, and there appeared to be a collapse near the entrance. Experienced cavers may find that this area is riddled with caves, and that one does indeed lead to the sea.

Very small, Cueva Huevos is the most accessible cave in Baja. Simply drive north on the Ensenada Toll Road 0.1 mile past the KM 83 marker. The entrance can be found in a flat area 100 yards east of this point.

****

KM	LOCATION
84	**El Mirador Viewpoint**. Spectacular views of the coastline. Gray whales occasionally come close enough to be seen with binoculars.
94	**Playa Saladmando**. Cobble beach, very modest camping and RV parking, small rigs only. One-lane dirt road, 26% upgrade coming out.
94+	The wreck of the Mexican destroyer *California*, run aground in 1972 while on a cadet training cruise, can be seen in shallow water just off the shore. Several of the crew provided insights into the causes of the disaster: "She goes now to God because this thing that has happened to her is a thing of God," stated one young man, confident that it was not a "thing" of the navigator. With rigorous logic, another stated that "the water kept running in faster than we could pump it out."
99	Toll booth. San Miguel Village RV Park just to the south has water and electric hookups, beach camping, showers, restrooms and a restaurant. This is probably the most popular surfing area in Baja, with a classic right point break that handles almost any

Reeve ropes down into "Cueva Huevos."

wave well. Parking is plentiful, access is easy, and the breaks sometimes crowded. The upper beach is sand, the lower cobble.

100+	PEMEX (MN).
101+	Route 3 to Tecate.
103	PEMEX (MN).
103+	Anzuleos Universales, a fishing tackle shop with an assortment of rods, reels, line and terminal tackle, plus clams, squid, anchovies and advice. 106 Butane plant.
107+	Junction. If you plan to just pass through Ensenada en route to points south, avoid taking the left fork, contrary to what the signs say. The easiest route through town is described at the end of the following section on Ensenada.
112	**Ensenada**.

ENSENADA

Long an Indian camp and the site of a large ranch during the early 1800s, Ensenada began to develop in 1870 with the gold rush at Real del Castillo. Hotels, gambling halls and restaurants were built, and the new boom town was soon filled with adventurers. Many people were from north of the border, and restaurants served imported ham and eggs at $2.50 a plate. The mines did not prosper, and after the Mexican Revolution in 1910 the town faded into a small fishing village. However, it started to grow again in the 1930s, due to improved port facilities and increasing tourism.

Today Ensenada is a small modern city, with busy waterfront industries, hotels, restaurants, tourist attractions and many facilities and services. Ensenada is advancing economically, and there is a good deal of new home construction and a new U.S.-style shopping center with shops and a supermar-

ENSENADA

0   0.25
STATUTE MILES

N

Bahía Todos Santos

ket, Misión Centro Commercial (1). The numerous accommodations include the Hotel Villa Marina (2), the Hotel Misión Santa Isabel (3), the Corona Hotel (4) and the Cortez Motor Hotel (5). The Campo Playa RV Park (6) has full hookups, restrooms and showers. Restaurants offer almost any kind of food one could desire, ranging from the lofty Gallic cuisine of El Rey Del Sol (7) through excellent middle-class American-style burgers at Cha Cha (8) to the proletarian Italian pizza of La Fabula, next door to the Corona Hotel. You might even find traditional Mexican food at some establishments.

There is a lot to do, see and buy. Many shops and souvenir stands are located along Av. Lopéz Mateos, and Bodegas de Santo Tomás Winery (9) offers guided tours Tuesday through Saturday at 11 a.m., 1 p.m. and 3 p.m., and Sundays at 11 a.m. and 1 p.m., with samplings of wines, breads and cheeses. Don't miss the fish market (10), as much a social institution on weekends and holidays as a place to buy and sell fish, with noisy *mariachi* bands, street vendors hawking everything imaginable, and throngs of people munching on piscatorial treats best left undescribed. Hussong's Cantina (11) has become something of a cult since it opened in 1892. The attraction can't be the decor—yellowed cartoons and hundreds of business cards tacked to peeling walls looming over battered furniture sitting on sawdust-covered floors. It can't be the beer or the booze, which are standard issue. No, the attraction seems to be the sociology of its American patrons,

who come to see and be seen doing a lot of things no one would think of doing at home. The State Secretary of Tourism office (12) can provide information on many other attractions and accommodations. The office of the Attorney General for the Protection of Tourists is located in the same building.

Fishing is declining due to heavy commercial netting, but it is often better than in much of Southern California. There are three primary fisheries: bottom species among the rocks at the end of the Punta Banda peninsula, ling cod and various bottom fish in the cool water immediately west of the Islas de Todos Santos, and albacore twenty-five miles or so west of Ensenada during July and August. In addition, Ensenada party boats often venture out to other locations along the coast, often in pursuit of prized yellowtail.

Ensenada has a number of sportfishing boats, everything from miserable skiffs up to the new *Executive Clipper*, which offer trips ranging in length from a few hours up to mini-trips that go as far south as Islas San Martín and San Jerónimo. A trip on an Ensenada party boat is great fun. The crews engage in theatrics, cries of "Yellowtail!" greeting every hookup, regardless of species, and multiple hookups rating a Mexican battle cry. The largest operations are Fritz's Landing Boat House, Gordo's Sportfishing, and the Ensenada Clipper Fleet, which have offices in the sportfishing dock area (13) providing tickets, tackle sales, rental equipment, bait and highly optimistic predictions. Nearby Gordo's Smokeshop has facilities for cleaning, smoking, canning and freezing your catch.

A perfectly normal Monday afternoon at Hussong's Cantina, just one of about 4,680 Mondays since it opened.

Most day trips head for Punta Banda, the Islas de Todos Santos or Punta San Miguel. The Clipper Fleet also offers whale-watching excursions with a bilingual guide. There are many *pangas* available, and their enterprising skippers make Ensenada the easiest place in the world to rent a boat, or to phrase it another way, they make Ensenada the hardest place in the world to avoid renting a boat—they won't take no for an answer. To get rid of one young pest, I told him that I had cancer and was going to die by 2 p.m. He didn't blink an eye, pointing out that half-day boats were available.

There are currently no good locations in Ensenada to launch a trailerboat—the ramp at Gordo's and one just to the north are becoming almost inaccessible due to construction and heavy traffic in the area, and parking is almost non-existent. However, there are ramps along the Punta Banda peninsula to the south, described later. If you get back to Ensenada you may be able to buy live bait from barges anchored in the harbor, although the commercial boats get first call. Frozen bait is usually available at fleet offices. Sales, parts and service for Evinrude outboards and marine supplies, charts and equipment can be found at Agencia Ajorna (14). Johnson outboard motor sales and service are available at Equipos TerraMar (15), Industria Mexicana de Equipo Marino (16) is a Yamaha dealer, Motores de Baja California (17) handles Mercury and Promarina (18) handles Mariner. Another Evinrude dealer is located on the Transpeninsular south of the main part of town.

Diving in the immediate vicinity of Ensenada is poor, and most divers head for Punta Banda or Todos Santos. There are at least a dozen wrecks in the vicinity of Ensenada, none of great interest. Almar Dive Shop (19) does not have a SCUBA compressor or offer rentals, but it does sell wet suits, fins, masks, spearguns and regulators, and a wide variety of small, hard-to-find parts such as O-rings, spear points and rubber mouth-pieces, and regulator repairs are available. El Yaqui Dive Shop is located south of town on the Transpeninsular. Calmarinos (20) manufactures and sells wet suits, gloves, boots and hoods, and also sells fins and other accessories.

San Miguel Surf Shop (21) sells boards and equipment, makes repairs and has rental boards. Baja Surf Center (22) rents, sells and repairs boards and sells wet suits, clothing and accessories. Boats can be chartered at the waterfront for surfing trips to El Martillo. A group of surfers could have great fun by chartering one of the larger sportfishing boats for the day.

The harbor is fairly close to an all-weather anchorage, although it is still uncomfortably open to the south. Locals in *pangas* meet visiting boats, offering to rent moorings and sell fuel and water. Ensenada has long suffered from a lack of marina facilities, but this is being remedied. Baja Naval (23) has floating docks with twenty-four slips from thirty-three to eighty feet, water and 30/50 amp electrical service, a Travelift, boatyard services such as carpentry, fiberglass repair, mechanical overhauls, welding, electronic repairs, topside and bottom painting, and more. Fueling is still by drums (mid-1991), but permanent facilities are being installed. Baja Naval is a licensed marina, providing custody and clearance services. The marina monitors VHF 16 and 77. Reservations are necessary. There are many plans afoot and new construction is underway in the waterfront area; future generations of

yachties may be pleased.

Ensenada is a port of entry, with a COTP (24), customs (25) and immigration (26). The *Migración* office is conveniently located for persons heading south and wishing to obtain tourist cards, but it is sometimes closed unexpectedly during normal business hours. There are Ford (27), Dodge/Chrysler (28) and Chevrolet (29) dealers in town. A Volkswagen dealer is located on Av. Gral. Clark Flores (the northwest extension of Calle 10, off the map). A Nissan dealer can be found on the Transpeninsular just south of town. The office of the Soc. Coop. de Producción Pesquera (which operates the Cannery Airline) is located on Av. Ryerson (30). There is also an office at El Ciprés airport, south of town.

Travelers passing through Ensenada can avoid some hassle by taking the route along the waterfront, rather than the posted route through the center of town. At the junction at KM 107+ take the right fork and continue south along the coast until the highway curves left (northeast) in the vicinity of the shipyards, the highway there becoming Av. Azueta. Pass over a series of speed bumps, and curve right (southeast) at the stoplight onto Blvd. Cardenas, just before the PEMEX. Continue on Cardenas until you must turn left (northeast) onto Calle Sangines. Continue a half-mile, to where a right (southeast) turn at the stoplight will put you back on the Transpeninsular.

ISLAS DE TODOS SANTOS

Mother Nature used different specifications for each of these two islands: the northwest one is flat and relatively featureless, the southeast one rugged and much higher. Although the islands are frequently visited by party boats and commercial fishermen, fishing can be good for yellowtail and bottom species. It is still possible to catch large fish, and a few years ago a 260-pound black sea bass was taken west of the northwest island. As is common on most Pacific islands, divers often visit the eastern sides due to calm and protected conditions, but the turbulent western sides have the most prolific underwater life. Visibilities are generally good because of the distance from the coast. Although at least six wrecks have occurred around the islands, none is of significant interest to divers.

The southeast island is the more interesting, and is visited frequently by yachtsmen, boaters and kayakers. A series of small coves on the eastern side provide anchorages, and several pebble beaches permit landings. Kayakers usually camp on a large flat area over the northernmost cove. The shore is rocky, but there is normally little surge. During periods of extreme tides, kayaks should be carried to the top of the bluff. Hikes are pleasant, and in spring there are masses of wildflowers. A number of birds nest on the island, including western gull, brown pelican, double-crested and Brandt's cormorants, great blue heron, osprey and black oystercatcher, and many migratory species are also seen. A species of cinnamon-colored rabbit can be spotted from 200 yards away, apparently defying the laws of natural selection.

Tide pool exploring is excellent around the south end, and a seven-room sea cave can be found. Just to the east at a higher elevation is an egg-shaped relic sea cave. A modest cave system is located 300 yards, 220° from the second cove from the north on the east side. The four-foot-square entrance to one cave is partly obscured by brush at the foot of a north-facing bluff. There is an incipient collapse at the entrance, two more a few yards inside and a large one in the main chamber. The floor sounds hollow and shakes when struck, so digging might reveal additional chambers. The cave opens on the other side of the bluff into dense brush and boulders. A dozen yards west is a squeeze leading to another cave, which also shows collapse signs. The system is small, and the largest cave is saved from being a grotto (caves go to total darkness, grottos don't) only by a right-angle turn, and then only at high noon, but as is so often true in caving, the mystery of the site is the real attraction: if the geology of the island permits these obvious caves, can there be more?

There are two lighthouses on the northwest island, one active, the other abandoned. The point break southwest of the lighthouses, christened "El Martillo" (The Hammer) by surfers, is both the most talked-about and the least-visited major surfing site between Tijuana and Ensenada. In the northwest swells of winter big rollers from deep water immediately offshore wrap around the rocky peninsula jutting from shore, producing big, booming rights. In the summer southern swells produce lefts almost their equal. Flexibility in tactics is essential, as the break can be erratic. Sneaker waves are common, so be careful where you operate your boat. The topography of the area produces odd wave patterns, and it is not unusual to encounter point breaks on the north end of the southeast island at the same time these big rights are coming in. Southwestern swells produce long rides in the channel between the

Suzy Peterson emerges from the depths of the small cave on Todos Santos, which we named "Cuevacitas Suzy" to commemorate her speleological accomplishment.

two islands, and if conditions are exactly right, waves reflecting off the shores of both islands combine into monumental proportions. Your dainty little tri-fin is likely to be maxed out in this area; think big.

There are lighthouse and naval personnel stationed on the northwest island and a small fish camp. A permit to land on the island is required from the naval commander in Ensenada. The channel between the islands is very shallow and must be avoided by all but the smallest boats. Bahía Santo Tomás is the next satisfactory anchorage south, although Punta Banda can provide marginal protection.

On the Transpeninsular Highway at Ensenada

Reset odometer at the intersection of Sangines and Reforma (Route 1). This is KM 7 for this section of the Transpeninsular, but since many KM markers are missing, miles will be used until Maneadero.

MILE	LOCATION
0.5	Boat dealer, Evinrude sales, parts and service.
0.6	El Yaqui Dive Shop, in a shopping center at the northeast corner of this intersection, has sales, rentals, service and air.
1.3	Nissan dealer.
2.8	PEMEX (MN).
3.6	El Ciprés airport, departure point for Cannery Airline flights to Isla Cedros and Bahía Tortugas. The office is 100 yards south of the control tower. A large ice plant is across the highway from the airport entrance.
4.7	Road west to beach resorts (signed). At Mile 0.8 turn right (020°) for Playa Corona (Corona Beach), left (200°) for Playa Estero (Estero Beach). Corona Beach has a small store, beach camping and RV parking sites. Estero Beach is an elaborate resort with a hotel, RV park with full hookups, restrooms, showers, restaurant, boardsailing, Hobies, jet skis and several paved launch ramps leading into Estero Punta Banda. Halibut, spotfin croaker, sharks and other fish are taken in the estero. At high tide in calm weather, boats can run the channel into Bahía Todos Santos, but it would be well to discuss this with local residents first, since channels and conditions change frequently. The outer beaches have unpredictable beach breaks.
8.6	**Maneadero.** PEMEX (three stations, MN at all, D at two), stores, groceries, meat and vegetable markets, tires, bakery, medical, dental, pharmacy, veterinarian, bank, post office, telegraph, auto parts, mechanics, motel, chapter of Alcoholics Anonymous. The sign nailed to the butcher-shop wall advertising a doctor's office requires some deep thought. Junction with road west to Punta Banda.

SIDETRIP TO PUNTA BANDA

The Punta Banda peninsula is one of the most popular diving and fishing locations in Baja Norte. The KM markers are absent in many places, so miles will be used.

6.4   Paved road northeast to Baja Beach & Tennis Club (signed). Although the club is private, its dive shop, fishing trips and sailboat cruises are open to the public, and jet skis, sailboards and Hobies are for rent. The dive shop offers rentals of SCUBA equipment, wet suits, fins, etc. An underwater video camera is available to those who can convince the manager they are qualified to use it. Trips are offered to the Islas de Todos Santos. Shell collecting and spearfishing are not normally permitted on trips unless a boat is chartered specifically for these purposes.

7.6   La Jolla Beach Camp. RV sites with water hookups, showers, restrooms, tennis, horseshoes, ice, mechanic, pebble beach. The concrete launch ramp requires calm water and high tide and is getting rough. Villarino Camp next door has some full hookups, showers, toilets, a small store, post office, cafe, block ice, pebble beach. Rental boats and bait can be obtained along the beach to the west. A geologic fault, Falla Agua Blanca, dives into the sea here, and divers can see gas discharges and hot-water springs along a cleft parallel to shore in thirty feet of water.

8.0   Road south (signed "Colonel Esteban Cantú") to Caleta Arbolitos and Bahía el Playon, popular dive sites. The road can handle sedans, but in spite of the signs proclaiming an RV park, do not attempt this with a trailer or a large RV. Go left at Mile 0.6 for Arbolitos, right for Kennedy's lobster camp and El Playon. If you go right you will soon encounter a second fork at a concrete block shed; turn left for Kennedy's (very rough), right for El Playon. The coast in this area is rugged and very beautiful, and you will have to clamber down cliffs to get to cobble beaches. A davit at Kennedy's can be used with a line to lower small boats to the beach. The underwater life is typical Southern Californian, with kelp, lings, rock cod, lobsters, anemones and sea urchins. The area is well picked over, but good spearfishing and scallops can be found to the southeast. Visibility averages twenty to thirty feet, but it can get as low as eight and as high as forty-five. An underwater arch can be found southeast of the two largest islets

The start of the Baja Triathlon at La Jolla Beach Camp.

in Arbolitos, and friendly sea lions may follow you through it. There are a number of sea caves, arches and blowholes along the coast to the southeast, and a cave near a prominent bird rock a mile from Arbolitos has an open top that can be entered in calm weather.

8.7 Concrete launch ramp into Bahía Todos Santos, exposed and usually covered with pebbles, although small boats can be launched in calm weather. Masses of fossilized clams can be seen frozen in the cliffs and scattered among the cobblestones. Thriving seventy million years ago, the species was peculiar, for a clam anyway: its two shells were not mirror images.

10.0 Sedan road west to Rancho Packard, which has camping and RV parking. After following a steep road to the beach, divers will find a sloping rock-and-cobble bottom. Conditions are modest, but they improve closer to the point. There is a small wreck 024° from the green-roofed ranch building in thirty-two feet of water.

11.1 Class 1 trail to the top of 1,264-foot Pico Banda, with spectacular views of the peninsula, the Islas de Todos Santos and Ensenada. An interesting four-mile loop hike starts by following a trail northwest around the mountain, then paralleling the coastline on top of vertical sea cliffs to the end of the peninsula, where hematite, gypsum and copper deposits have been reported. There are great views of the surf pounding the many tiny islets and pinnacles extending toward the Islas de Todos Santos. The trail then circles back along the southern shore of the peninsula past fine sea caves (to be described shortly), returning to the paved road at Mile 11.5.

13.0 **La Bufadora**.

LA BUFADORA, BAHÍA PAPALOTE AND THE TIP OF THE PENINSULA

Located on the shore of Bahía Papalote, the settlement of La Bufadora has restaurants, small tourist businesses, campgrounds, RV sites (no hookups) and restrooms. The settlement gets its name from a sea spout that sometimes jets a plume of water a hundred feet high. The road to the sea spout is crowded with taco stands and souvenir shops. La Bufadora Dive offers air, limited equipment rentals, boat rentals, a house sleeping up to twenty, day trips and highly unpredictable days and hours of operation. The cement launch ramp near the dive shop is steep and ends on a pebble beach, making it unsuitable for launching trailerboats, although it is handy for cartoppers and inflatables. Be careful of sneaker waves and surge from refracted swell. The anchorages here and at Bahía el Playon to the southeast are open and surgy. The first satisfactory anchorage to the south is Bahía Santo Tomás.

Kayakers will find the southern shore of Punta Banda to be a very pleasant location for a leisurely two-day trip—the scenery is spectacular, the weather normally sunny, and the coast usually in the lee, and there are many small beaches that permit secluded camping. This "mini trip" is perhaps the least demanding and most pleasant one available in Baja, an excellent first trip for beginners. If you get up enough gumption, you can crank out to the Islas de Todos Santos, about seven miles from La Bufadora. There are no really good places to land on the way, the channel has strong currents and there is boat traffic.

"Cueva de los Tunels Paralelos," one of the finest and most accessible sea caves in Baja, is located about a mile northwest, its various chambers, tunnels and arms extending a total of 300 yards. One narrow chamber extends 80 yards in an almost straight line, and ceiling heights range up to 20 feet. There are many intriguing features, including a natural bridge, arches, an "almost connection," where two chambers fall short of connecting by only a yard or so, and entrances scattered in unnoticed places. Another nearby sea cave, "Cuarto Con Muchas Ventanas la Mar," is quite different. Instead of having long narrow chambers, it is as wide as it is deep, and half of its area is awash at low tide. Not exceptionally large, Paralelos has 8,000 square feet under the drip line, and Cuarto 6,200. They can be reached by boat from La Bufadora or by the trail from Mile 11.5. More sea caves can be found along the north coast of the peninsula.

Bahía Papalote is one the better dive sites in Baja, having both close road access and easy beach entries, with mixed bottoms and large areas covered with kelp. Sandy areas are rich in gastropods. A spring area can be found at seventy to ninety feet, venting hot water and gas. Diving along the coast to Cabo Banda is excellent, kelp and sea life becoming denser with each mile. At least four vessels and two multi-engine aircraft have been lost nearby, but the only wreck of interest to divers may be the old steam auxiliary sailing vessel *Santo Tomás*, which sank in 1946. The exact location of the wreck is not known, but old-timers who lived in the area at the time say it sank southeast of Cabo Banda. The end of the peninsula is easily the most interesting dive site in the Ensenada area, with dozens of small islets, craggy pinnacles and rock walls covered with colorful anemones, sponges, algae and hydrocorals. There are many caves and crevices harboring lobsters, which shoot out like Roman candles when they feel trapped. This area is for advanced divers only, for heavy currents can change velocity and direction in minutes.

The California Current produces upwellings of cold water off Bahía Papalote and Cabo Banda, and fishermen will encounter numerous species of bottomfish, often in water less than sixty fathoms. Shorecasters willing to do some hiking will find dozens of small coves and beaches along the trail past the sea caves to the point. Shops near the sea spout often sell natural baits.

Back on the Transpeninsular Highway at Maneadero, KM 21

You should have a validated tourist card to proceed south of Maneadero. The stoplight in this vicinity marks the end of "civilization" as we know it; the next one is almost 700 miles to the south.

KM	LOCATION
25	Gentle up- and downgrades to KM 43.
41+	A park immediately on the left (northeast) has spreading oaks, a pavilion, fireplaces, camping and

RV parking. Road northeast to Uruapan, continuing on to Route 3.

43   Grades increase to KM 45 as the highway crosses a ridge.

45   Hang on! A branch of the Falla Agua Blanca crosses the road here.

47+   Road west (signed) to La Bocana and Puerto Santo Tomás.

SIDETRIP TO PUERTO SANTO TOMÁS

The two-lane graded road is capable of handling moderate RVs and trailers, the steepest grade being a modest 12%. Set odometer. Fine shaded campsites will be found about Mile 4.3. Just beyond this point a Y will be encountered: take the right (285°) fork to remain on the new graded road, take the left (260°) fork to follow the old road along the Río Santo Tomás with its many shaded campsites—the two routes join again at Mile 5.3. At Mile 12.7 a pickup road can be seen winding up the hills to the south, passing the vicinity of the old Ink and Marguerita mines and reaching the coast in the vicinity of Punta San José in eight miles. At Mile 15.2 a road runs south to Punta China, a heavily mineralized area where chalcopyrite, epidote, calcite and prehnite have been found, along with an abundance of fossils. The shoreline one mile southeast of Punta China is riddled with interesting caves. The Puerto Santo Tomás road reaches La Bocana at Mile 16.7, which has a store, camping, RV parking, rental cabins, a beach, and right point, beach and reef breaks. The road then swings north after climbing a short slope. Note the road meandering into the hills at Mile 19.0, and arrive at Puerto Santo Tomás at Mile 19.4. *Pangas* can be rented, and a concrete launch ramp (requiring high tides and calm conditions) is available. The anchorage provides protection from all but south weather, although dense kelp can be a problem. Landings can be made in the lee of the point. To the south, Puntas San José, Cabras and San Isidro provide marginal anchorages. Cabo Colonet is better, but Isla San Martín is far preferable if heavy weather is expected.

Punta Santo Tomás diverts the California Current and creates a circular countercurrent, pulling up cool bottom water containing nutrients and producing a rich underwater environment and limited visibilities in the bay. In spite of local commercial fishing activity, Bahía Santo Tomás has the first relatively unspoiled fishing encountered south of the border, and the vast underwater plain offshore can provide a fine mixed bag of ling cod, calico bass, ocean whitefish, yellowtail, barracuda, bonito and several species of rock fish and flatfish. Excellent fishing is found in a "hole" due west of an abandoned concrete building foundation on a finger-like point a mile north of Punta Santo Tomás, where sonar indicates a steep-sided depression at 150 feet. Boats from San Diego take yellowfin and albacore fifteen miles offshore, and local boats fish the "22 Spot," 5 1/2 miles, 189° from the point. Surfers will find a fair beach break at the bottom of the cliffs in the bay.

Rocas Soledad, 1 1/4 miles west of the point, has sheer walls, caves, crevices, pinnacles, abundant wildlife and excellent visibility, making it the premier dive site between Punta Banda and San Martín. The deep blue of surrounding depths, red urchins, yellow and red encrusting sponges and the largest specimens of Pacific green anemone on the Pacific coast, with discs that can expand to fourteen inches, provide a field day for photographers. Because of their coating of orange-hued encrusting sponge, it is easy to spot large rock scallops, and abalone hide in deep crevices. Schools of ocean whitefish and sheephead often approach within photographic range. A 500-pound anchor will be found nearby. Depths of over 100 feet prevail close to the rocks, but a shelf extending 40-150 yards south makes it possible to anchor in 40-70 feet.

A trail heads west and then north from the settlement, passing a number of sea caves and a massive rock arch. Camping in almost total solitude can be found on Bahía Soledad's south shore, accessible by the road going north from Mile 19.0. The road gets no maintenance, and with loose rock, ruts and slopes to 21%, it is for pickups or better.

A prominent sea cave on the western end of this shore shows evidence of a large hidden chamber; heavy surf results in booming repercussions as air and water are expelled from the chamber, producing a violent horizontal geyser hitting the opposite wall. The bay is large and shallow, with depths of twenty to sixty feet, bottoms being boulders, shelf rock and sand. Visibility in the northern and central parts of the bay tends to be poor, but currents occasionally clear the south end, and visibilities of forty feet or more can be encountered. Thick kelp beds harbor opaleye, kelp bass and dense schools of fry, and the beaches along the eastern margin of the bay offer outstanding corbina fishing almost year-round. The bay is too open and exposed for anchoring in anything short of a flat calm, although it should be useful in south weather. Several small vessels and a plane have been lost in the bay, their locations unknown.

Back on the Transpeninsular Highway at KM 47+

51   **Santo Tomás.** PEMEX (MN), motel, restaurant, groceries, ice, medical, post office, tire repair, ruins of outbuildings of Dominican Misíon Santo Tomás (1791-1849). Believe it or not, this was once the capital of the northern territory of Baja California. El Palomar Trailer Park has full hookups, restrooms, showers, recreational facilities, barbecues and camping in the olive groves. Palomar Market has local shells for sale and is one of the few businesses in Baja regularly offering mineral specimens, primarily selenite and actinolite.

SIDETRIP TO PUNTA SAN JOSÉ AND PUNTA SAN ISIDRO

Two-tenths of a mile southeast of the PEMEX, turn south and 200 yards later turn right (200°) onto the graded road seen winding up the hills. At KM 23 a sedan road (signed) heads south to Punta Cabras. Turn northwest at the junction at KM 30. A road west of the ranch at KM 38 connects with the Puerto Santo Tomás road mentioned earlier. Arrive at the lighthouse at Punta San José at KM 41. There are fine reef and right point breaks and plenty of room; the Fifth Army could surf here and no one need get burned. The cliffs are high, but a bulldozed ramp makes it easy to carry boards to

What? You guys want to hear *La Cucaracha* again? Musician Jim Smallwood and singer Pancho Cuosino do not seem too pleased with the latest request.

the beach. The surf and the sloping volcanic shelf-rock beaches make it a poor place to launch a boat, and diving is always bad for the same reasons plus zero visibility. The lee of the point provides a marginal anchorage, completely open to west and south weather. Dense kelp also may be a problem.

Ammonites can be seen frozen in the sedimentary cliffs throughout the area. An interesting scavenger and fossil beach is found below the first arroyo north of the lighthouse, but access is a problem, since it is not possible to follow the beach north around the point. An impromptu ladder down the cliff has been constructed from junk, but it doesn't look too sturdy, and chubby visitors should consider bringing their own knotted rope.

To get to Punta Cabras and Punta San Isidro, go back to the junction at KM 23, reset your odometer and take the sedan road south. (The old coast road south from the junction at KM 30 reaches Rancho San Juan de las Pulgas in three miles, where a difficult stream crossing may cause problems for those not in four-wheel-drives.) At Mile 7.7 arrive at Punta Cuesta del Gato. A Japanese vessel, *Tampico Maru*, was wrecked south of the point in 1957. It remained intact for a number of years, and the turn of its bilges was a prime habitat for abalone. Recently, however, the locals have been salvaging its metal and little remains. The coast to the north and south is broken by a series of volcanic points, where spectacular blowholes expel great jets of water, and many small coves and beaches provide fine camping and shorecasting. A sandy cove at Mile 8.3 has easy access and occasionally has excellent reef breaks. Punta Cabras at Mile 10.8 provides a marginal anchorage in prevailing weather and has a very small but sandy landing place. At Mile 14.8 encounter Punta San Isidro with good beach and reef breaks. The lee of the point is a suitable anchorage only in the best of conditions. The next anchorage south is Cabo Colonet. At Mile 16.6 arrive at Castro's Fishing Place, described in the next section.

Back on the Transpeninsular Highway at KM 51

58	Moderate upgrades to KM 63+, then mostly downgrades to San Vicente.
78+	Paved road south to Eréndira (signed).

SIDETRIP TO ERÉNDIRA AND PUNTA SAN ISIDRO

Set odometer. There is a PEMEX (MND), small stores, groceries and a cafe in Eréndira at Mile 10.7. At Mile 11.0, the pickup road to Colonet, a key part of the Two Parks Loop Trip, can be seen crossing the river bed to the south. The road swings north at Mile 11.6, reaching Castro's Fishing Place at Mile 12.6, which has fishing boats and cabins with bunk beds, two-burner stoves and refrigerators for rent (bring your own sleeping bags and utensils). Small boats can be launched at the landing. The locals launch boats to twenty-four feet down the steep dirt ramp using Castro's rusty tractor. Fishing is for a mixed bag on local reefs and offshore to ten miles. Shorecasters find opaleye, cabezon, sheephead and calico bass close to the landing. Copper and iron mines are located nearby.

Back on the Transpeninsular Highway at KM 78+

88+	Sedan road southwest (signed) to ruins of Dominican Misíon San Vicente Ferrer (1780-1833). There are important copper and iron deposits in the area, and in 1915 a geologist estimated that a hematite deposit 2 1/2 miles from the mission contained five million tons.
90	**San Vicente.** PEMEX (two, MND in one, N in the other), modest motel, stores, groceries, auto parts, bakery, medical, dental, pharmacy, liquor, cafes, post office, fruit and meat markets, ice, hardware, public showers, welder and tire repair. Bicyclists should top off with water before heading south.

****

"CUEVA TRES PISOS." The rumor was interesting: after entering the cave above a stony beach, you could follow its spiraling path up to an entrance near the rim of a mesa several hundred feet above the ocean—but no one was certain where it was. After losing a day to false leads, we stopped to ask directions from a group of Mexicans who were roasting mussels and playing guitars on a beach south of Eréndira. They never heard of the cave, but invited us to sample a batch of fresh homemade "red-eye." Encouraged by Jim Smallwood's guitar, the party continued on into the afternoon and loud choruses of "La Cucaracha" soon could be heard rising above the booming surf. As darkness fell so did many of the singers, and we found several of our new friends spread-eagled face down in sticky ice plant. By nine the fire was dead and all that could be heard was loud snoring and the surf.

Jim, Don Nelson and I quietly stole out of camp at first light the next day and hiked south in hopes of finding the cave. Many waterspouts and blowholes shot into the air, one so enormous we christened it "La Ducha de la Reina." As we *rounded a rocky shoulder we knew immediately we had found our cave. From a diameter of perhaps ninety feet, the funnel-shaped entrance quickly narrowed down to six feet. After following a narrow tunnel into total darkness, we entered a chamber twenty feet high and thirty wide. It continued up for a hundred feet and, as expected, opened into sunlight. A few bats hung upside down, their retinas reflecting an ominous pink color. A chimney spiraled upward in fits and starts, perhaps to another entrance.*

We climbed down a steeply pitched tunnel that narrowed to a crawl. On the other side we found increasing signs of speleothems and came on a series of squat columns formed by fusion of stalactites and stalagmites. Large crystals and wide bands of mineralization graced the chamber walls. Wiggling through a squeeze, Don thought he heard a whisper of air rising from the silty soil and became aware of an extremely faint and low pitched booming noise—waves—which did not seem to be coming from the entrance, but rather from the floor of the squeeze. As we approached the entrance, Jim stepped into a soft spot and fell into the ground up to his calf, and the ground trembled so much we pulled him out and fled for safety outside. The soft spot was an incipient collapse and our cave was certainly underlain by other chambers.

The entrance to another cave was discovered at a lower elevation eighty yards to the south, and we found that it curved directly under the first cave. We did not explore it fully, but it is possible that a connection exists between the two levels. This still would not explain the wave noises, for even this cave was substantially above sea level. Directly in front of the first entrance the sea had cut a tall, narrow channel in a rocky cliff. The angle did not permit us to see into it very far, but judging by the large amount of water that flowed out on the ebb of each wave, there seemed to be a large tidal sea cave running directly under us. With Don belaying, Jim rappelled down over the crashing surf and was able to see into a cave running far into the mesa; our cave had three levels, not two. We wanted to explore the sea cave, but the surf and a rising tide made it dangerous.

To visit the cave, turn southwest in San Vicente just south of the post office. Set odometer. At Mile 0.3 turn half-left (240°) at the intersection, swing south at Mile 0.7 and turn right (265°) at Mile 4.5, signed "Playas Lopéz Rayon." Encounter the Eréndira-Colonet coast road at Mile 12.9 but continue straight ahead, reaching the coast at Mile 14.4. Turn left (205°) and drive to the end of the road at Mile 14.7. Hike southeast along the coast, arriving at a sand beach at Minute 30. (Four-wheel-drives can get to this beach by turning southeast on the Eréndira-Colonet coast road at Mile 12.9 and then turning toward the coast at the sideroad 0.6 mile from the intersection.) Fifty yards up the arroyo, a trail winds up the cliffs south of the beach. The entrance to the cave will be found after fifteen more minutes of hiking.

****

Back on the Transpeninsular Highway in San Vicente

KM	LOCATION
91	Gentle rolling hills to KM 108, then moderate up- and downgrades to KM 117. Bicyclists often must fight headwinds into Colonet.
126	PEMEX (N), auto parts, telephone.
126+	Graded road west (signed) to San Antonio del Mar, seven miles, suitable for RVs and trailers. Set odometer. At Mile 4.5 a road is encountered running north past Rancho Johnson to Eréndira, part of the Two Parks Loop Trip; continue straight ahead for the beach. At the beach there is camping, RV parking (no hookups), beachcombing and a beach break, but watch for rocks on the bottom. Surrounding dunes are popular with off-road drivers. Many people return year after year for the excellent surf fishing.
127	**Colonet.** Groceries, medical, pharmacy, stores, bakery, meat markets, cafes, tires, bus stop, mail. There are good reef breaks on big waves. Shore casting is good for croakers and surfperch, but bottom fishing is often poor. At least a dozen wrecks have occurred nearby, including a twin-engine plane, but diving is poor due to almost-zero visibility. Cabo Colonet's lee provides good protection from prevailing weather, although it can be windy and surgy. The next anchorage to the south is San Martín.

With Don Nelson on belay, Jim Smallwood investigates the tidal sea cave.

140+   Road east (signed "Observatorio") to Parque Nacional Sierra San Pedro Mártir.

SIDETRIP TO PARQUE NACIONAL SIERRA SAN PEDRO MÁRTIR AND PICACHO DEL DIABLO

High in the mountains to the east is a wonderful but little-used national park, the finest in Baja. You will travel at least 125 miles before you return, so make sure you have adequate gasoline. The road is normally well-maintained and can handle sedans. Set odometer. At Mile 5.7 pass through the village of San Telmo, and at Mile 11.4 through a settlement where groceries and sodas can be purchased. At Mile 29.7 a road signed "Rancho El Coyote" goes north to Mike's Sky Ranch. (If you decide to take this road look before you leap—a description will be found on page 245.) A right turn at Mile 30.1 (signed) will take you to historic Rancho San José. Founded in 1907 by the Meling family, this 10,000-acre cattle ranch has guest facilities and offers horseback riding, swimming and hiking, plus mule trips to the high country. At Mile 41.2 park and hike 200 yards north to Mina Socorro. Harry Johnson, father of one of the founders of Rancho San José, made a gold strike here before the turn of the century. Just as he finished constructing a ditch to bring in water from distant Arroyo San Rafael for placer mining, the Mexican Revolution and new riparian laws brought operations to a halt. The buildings have been dismantled, but aqueducts, holding ponds and an assortment of junk can still be seen. Pegmatites have been reported several miles south, yielding tourmaline. At Mile 45.3 a pipe sticks out of the bank, its waters allegedly good to drink. A concrete horse trough just downhill provides a great place to take a bath.

Jesuit Father Baegert complained, "There is no semblance of a forest in [Baja] California, there is also no trace of a meadow or of a green turf," but as you drive upward you will pass through a fascinating biological transition that will prove him wrong on all counts. Leaving the familiar chaparral of the lower regions, you will first enter a pinyon-juniper zone, with pinyon pines, junipers and oaks, then a zone where the dominant trees are Coulter, Jeffrey, lodgepole and sugar pine, incense cedar, white fir and quaking aspen. The rare San Pedro Mártir cypress, endemic to this area, is found in a few isolated locations, the largest known individual having a circumference of fifteen feet. As expected, the bird species change with increasing altitude. Birds found in the lower reaches include pygmy nuthatch, pine siskin, red crossbill, mountain quail and violet-green swallow. Although the upper mountain reaches approximate a Canadian boreal forest, the avian species there include those normally found at somewhat lower elevations, such as western bluebird, pinyon jay, black-tailed gnatcatcher, wrentit and house finch, along with birds more typical of high mountain areas such as Cassin's finch, dark-eyed junco and mountain chickadee.

Your arrival at the park entrance at Mile 47.4 may be something of an occasion; during a February 1991 visit my wife Judy and I seemed to be the only visitors in the entire 170,000-acre park. Camping is permitted, but there are few formal facilities. Firearms, motorcycles and off-road driving are prohibited, and fires must be confined to the concrete fireplaces available in some of the campsites. Since much of the park is above 6,000 feet, temperatures average fifteen degrees cooler than surrounding lowlands. Hard freezes are common in winter, and snow sometimes blankets higher elevations. The sky is usually bright blue, and at night starlight can be so bright it produces shadows, and you can sometimes see a brilliant line of light creep along tree trunks during moonrise. Best of all, you are almost certain to have the silence needed to enjoy this majesty, with no RV generators or rock music to be heard and no rotten kids to distract you, unless you bring your own.

Reset odometer at the park entrance. At Mile 8.2 a road heads south to La Tasajera meadow, and at Mile 9.2 the road passes Vallecitos meadow, with a number of pleasant campsites. At Mile 9.9 a road heads southeast to the place where the approach to Picacho del Diablo begins. At Mile 10.5 a road heads north through a fire fighting camp, ending in about three miles near Cerro Venado Blanco. At Mile 12.2 a gate may prevent further travel by vehicle. Park and hike up the road, where a number of dome-topped buildings will be encountered which house astronomical telescopes, the largest an eighty-four-inch reflector. No scheduled public tours are offered, but supervisory personnel may be willing to show you around. Views of the lowlands and the Sea of Cortez to the east are wonderful.

The park offers fine hiking and backpacking. A number of meadows will be found scattered south of the road connected by a web of cattle trails. Some are large, occupying several square miles, including Vallecitos, La Encantada, La Grulla and Santa Rosa. Some have permanent, year-round water, including La Corona, Santo Tomás, La Encantada and La Grulla, while El Alcatraz and Santa Rosa usually have water in the spring months. La Grulla often has a running stream and marshy ponds. Vallecitos is frequently dry, but the arroyos to the east draining toward the meadow sometimes have water. Four arroyos draining to the west have year-round streams: San Rafael, La Tasajera, La Zanja and San Antonio. The arroyo at Misíon San Pedro Mártir almost always has water. The accompanying map also shows many small springs, which may or may not have water.

The trails shown on the map have never been surveyed and their locations are approximations only. Most are pleasant and undemanding, passing through open, park-like country with little or no brush-busting needed and little change in elevation. Other trails undoubtedly exist. A thirty-mile loop trip from Vallecitos to La Encantada and La Grulla and back to Vallecitos visits three of the largest meadows, and a sidetrip could be made to climb Cerro Botella Azul. A round trip from La Grulla to El Alcatraz and Misíon San Pedro Mártir and back would add about twenty-two miles, passing from the pines into the lower chaparral country to the south. The mission, in a narrow and very lonely valley, was founded by the Dominicans in 1794 and operated until about 1806. Little but foundations remains.

Since there are no signs marking the correct trails, it is easy to become confused, and you must carry a compass and topo at all times. Picacho can be seen from many high points, forming a useful landmark. If you become lost, head directly for the Observatory Road; going in any other direction might result in difficulties. Inform someone of your intended route and do not expect to be rescued by rangers or passersby. The

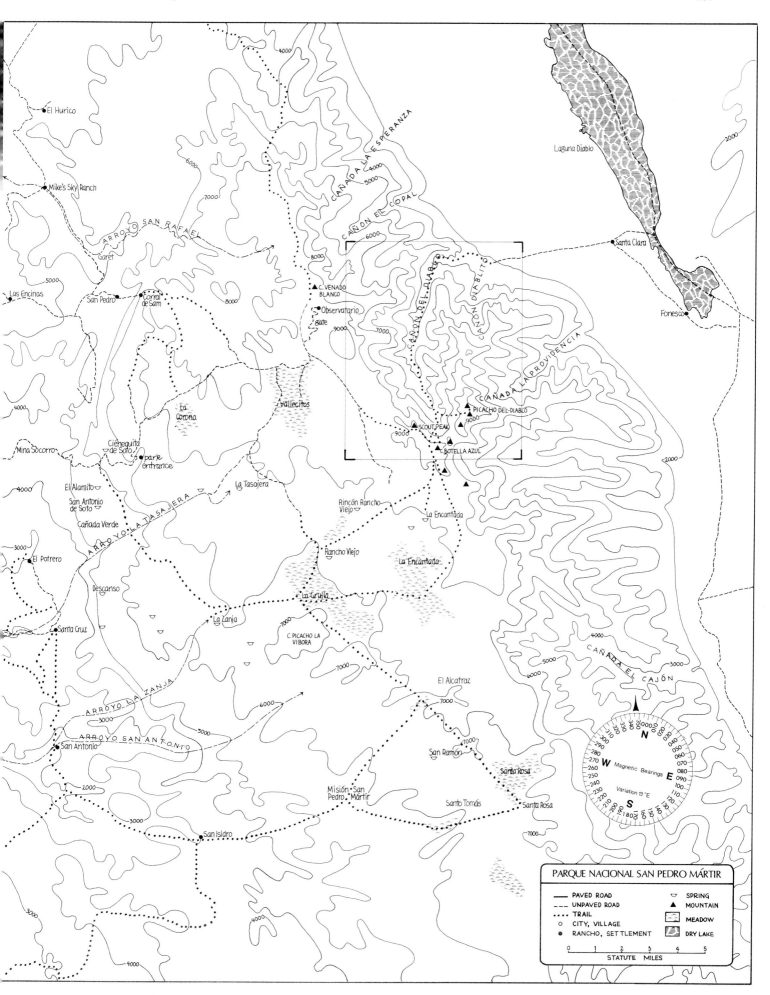

El Hurico

Mike's Sky Ranch

ARROYO SAN RAFAEL

Garet

Las Encinas

San Pedro

Corral de Sam

La Corona

Vallecitos

Cieneguita de Soto

park entrance

Mina Socorro

El Alamito

San Antonio de Soto

Cañada Verde

ARROYO LA TASAJERA

La Tasajera

El Potrero

Descanso

Santa Cruz

La Zanja

ARROYO LA ZANJA

ARROYO SAN ANTONIO

San Antonio

Misión San Pedro Mártir

San Isidro

CAÑADA LA ESPERANZA

CAÑON EL COPAL

C. VENADO BLANCO

Observatorio

gate

CAÑON DEL DIABLO

CAÑON DIABLITO

CAÑADA LA PROVIDENCIA

PICACHO DEL DIABLO

SCOUT PEAK

BOTELLA AZUL

Rincón Rancho Viejo

La Encantada

Rancho Viejo

La Encantada

La Grulla

C. PICACHO LA VIBORA

El Alcatraz

San Ramón

Santa Rosa

Santo Tomás

Santa Rosa

Laguna Diablo

Santa Clara

Fonesco

CAÑADA EL CAJÓN

Magnetic Bearings

Variation 13°E

PARQUE NACIONAL SAN PEDRO MÁRTIR

—— PAVED ROAD

--- UNPAVED ROAD

•••• TRAIL

○ CITY, VILLAGE

● RANCHO, SETTLEMENT

▽ SPRING

▲ MOUNTAIN

▨ MEADOW

▨ DRY LAKE

0 1 2 3 4 5
STATUTE MILES

best time for a trip is late spring; it is still cool, nature is in bloom, there is plenty of water and the fire danger is low.

A pickup road leads south from Mile 8.2 to the vicinity of La Tasajera meadow, passing through some of the finest country in the park; other than the road, a cow or two, a possible vapor trail in the sky and, of course, you and your vehicle, this is what Mother Nature intended. Set odometer. At Mile 2.8 the road drops into an arroyo and begins a 23% upgrade in rough stuff, returning to meadowland at Mile 3.4. At Mile 6.8 take the right (180°) fork. At Mile 7.2 there is a short, rough upgrade of 27% and then immediate steep downgrades as the road enters a deep canyon. Although the road continues several more miles, in early 1991 it was not safely passable beyond this point due to steep grades, deep ruts and soft sand, even by four-wheel-drive.

Three of the year-round streams mentioned earlier—San Rafael, La Zanja and San Antonio—have a surprise: trout. The climate would seem too hot and the flows of water too low to support them, but there are indeed trout, a few running to fourteen inches. A heat-tolerant species closely related to rainbow, they were identified by naturalist E.W. Nelson in 1905. Originally found only in Arroyo San Antonio, they were transported by mule-back into the other streams in the 1930s. In 1937 some were taken to a hatchery in Redlands, CA in an attempt to determine if they could be established in the U.S., where their ability to withstand heat could be valuable. However, the hatchery and all its fish were wiped out in a flood the next year. Another attempt at a hatchery in Oregon failed when a frog climbed into a pipe and the pond drained. The easiest place to fish for them is in the Río San Rafael near Mike's Sky Ranch, described in Chapter 16. La Zanja and San Antonio are a little tough to get to in the park, but fishermen might use the road to La Tasajera just described to get within an eight-mile hike of the upper reaches of Zanja. Another route is by way of a short road heading south from the Observatory Road several miles southwest of the park

The west face of Picacho del Diablo from the escarpment of the San Pedro Martír plateau.

entrance. This leads to a small meadow, from which a foot trail drops into a canyon and then crosses Arroyo Tasajera to Zanja, eight miles from the trailhead. Rancho San José offers pack trips to the streams from mid-May to mid-October.

Climbing Picacho del Diablo

Picacho is the highest mountain in Baja California, rising to 10,154 and 10,152 feet. A massive, nearly bare double peak of pale granodiorite, it rises from the escarpment that borders the San Pedro Mártir plateau on the east. From October to May the peak is sometimes covered with snow, and because it can be seen from over seventy-five miles away, it presents a strange spectacle to travelers driving south from torrid Mexicali. The peak was first climbed in 1911, and many hundreds have succeeded since then. However, Picacho should not be taken lightly, for the climb can be arduous, and novice route-finders may become confused since during the ascent you cannot see the peak until you are almost on top. In 1967 two climbers became lost for a month and narrowly escaped death due to exposure and starvation. The same year a climber had a heart attack and died during an ascent. His friends buried him in a branch of "Slot Wash" and continued on, recording the event in the summit register. Despite these caveats it is an interesting class 3 climb within the ability of most persons in good physical condition. Limited technical gear may be welcome if you wish to take one of the more difficult approaches or to traverse between the two summits.

A sedan road leads southeast (125°) from Mile 9.9, past Vallecitos meadow. Reset odometer. Look for a concrete block shed at Mile 0.4. About 80 yards past the shed you will encounter a Y; take the left (080°) fork. At Mile 2.1 pass between two pines close to the road, the left one having a large scar due to missing bark. In about 200 more yards pass a large aspen on the left, very close to the road. At Mile 2.25 arrive at the parking place. There is little else to distinguish this spot, so make sure you have followed the preceding directions exactly—if the road starts to climb and rough stuff is encountered, you have gone too far (the road continues about four more miles to a beautiful pine-rimmed meadow). Park, set your altimeter to 8,130 feet and start hiking southeast up the arroyo, following its meanders. Except for a few short detours, the route follows the arroyo all the way to the eastern rim of the plateau, most of it well ducked.

At Minute 30 the route leaves the arroyo and turns north at a large cairn to avoid dense brush. At Minute 45 you will be back in the arroyo, near a large grove of dense aspen at elevation 8,330. (A trail leads a half-mile north from the aspens to the rim of the escarpment, where there is a great view of Cañon del Diablo to the north.) Ducks are scarce until the other side of the grove. Skirt the south margin of the aspens, hiking east to a low saddle. Sight 022° and note "Scout Peak," a striking orange-colored knob, rising 300-400 feet above the surrounding terrain. Cross the saddle, drop into the arroyo at elevation 8,450 and continue east on the south side of the arroyo, which is again well ducked. At Minute 75 arrive at a point south of Scout Peak. This knob should be climbed to get the lay of the land and bearings for the next part of the route. Mineral collectors may find a garnet- and tourmaline-bearing pegmatite in the vicinity, a chunk of which is in use as a summit cairn.

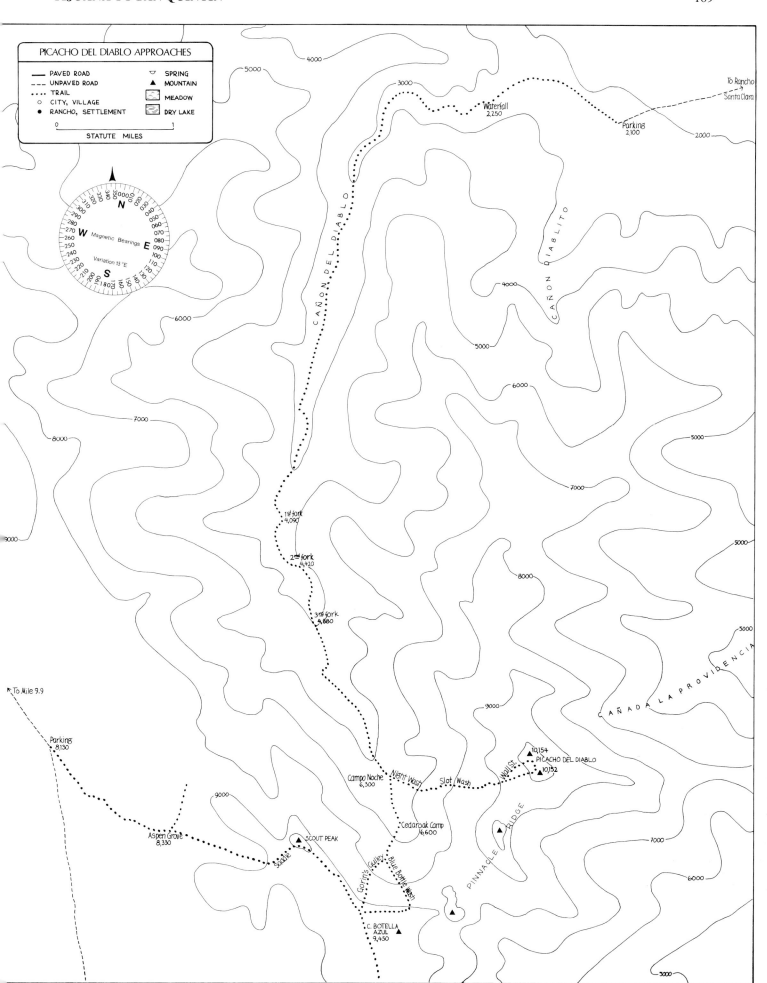

PICACHO DEL DIABLO APPROACHES

—— PAVED ROAD	▽ SPRING
– – – UNPAVED ROAD	▲ MOUNTAIN
···· TRAIL	MEADOW
○ CITY, VILLAGE	DRY LAKE
● RANCHO, SETTLEMENT	

STATUTE MILES

Magnetic Bearings

Variation 13°E

Waterfall
2,250

Parking
2,100

To Rancho
Santa Clara

CAÑON DEL DIABLO

CAÑON DIABLITO

CAÑADA LA PROVIDENCIA

1st fork
4,090

2nd fork
4,420

3rd fork
4,880

To Mile 9.9

Parking
8,130

Aspen Grove
8,330

Saddle

SCOUT PEAK

Gorin's Gulley

Blue Bottle Wash

Campo Noche
6,300

Night Wash

Slot Wash

Nail St.

10,154
PICACHO DEL DIABLO
10,152

Cedaroak Camp
6,600

PINNACLE RIDGE

C. BOTELLA
AZUL
9,450

Picacho's north peak bears 057° from Scout Peak. A series of bare white peaks runs south from Picacho, swerving west to a rounded, brown, tree-covered 9,450-foot peak, bearing 123°, known as Cerro Botella Azul, which sits on the rim of the escarpment. This crescent-shaped ridge, known as "Pinnacle Ridge," is a difficult and waterless technical route to Picacho. Look for "Blue Bottle Wash," a major wash strewn with white boulders northeast of Botella Azul, the contact face between brown and white granites and the easiest descent into Cañon del Diablo. The wash is reached by contouring south and then east toward Botella Azul, starting the descent when approaching its north side. The descent is straightforward with the exception of several detours around waterfalls, ending several hundred yards south of "Cedaroak Camp." Climbers with a hunger for problems may prefer a trying, time-consuming and extremely steep route known as "Gorin's Gully." It is difficult to see from Scout Peak, but the top can be located northwest of Botella Azul. A rope and a few nuts and carabiners will be required, since several places require a series of ten-to-thirty-foot pitches of class 5 downclimbing.

Cedaroak Camp will be reached at Minute 315, elevation 6,600 feet. Floods have knocked down many of the cedars, making camping difficult, so boulderhop downstream until you reach "Campo Noche," a large campsite at 6,300 feet. A nice swimming hole will be found nearby.

Start the ascent of Picacho by climbing east up "Night Wash," a large, shallow gully intersecting the main canyon at Campo Noche. Night Wash is well ducked to a headwall at

Wayne Campbell rappels past an obstacle in "Gorin's Gully."

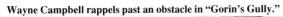

Ted Robertson takes a break near the summit.

elevation 7,400, from where the route contours left over a small ridge and drops into huge Slot Wash. Water is often found in Slot Wash. Slot Wash is bisected at elevation 8,200 by a granite knob. Take the left fork, and immediately past the knob climb 30 feet up the left side of the wash to a shoulder. A ducked route leads along this shoulder to a steep 200-foot class 3 friction slab at 9,000 feet. At the top of the slab turn north and climb a ducked trail that switchbacks up a brushy slope. After 250 vertical feet, "Wall Street," a narrow passage between steep granite walls, will be reached. Keep climbing, and at 10,154 feet you will have conquered Picacho's north summit. On clear days views are magnificent: to the east lie the lowlands, the sparkling Cortez and mainland Mexico, 140 miles away; to the west lies the Pacific.

The traverse to the south summit encounters a difficult pinnacle en route, although exhaustive route-finding can keep it down to a highly marginal class 3. In common with many granite peaks, Picacho has numerous knobs, chicken heads and solution pockets along the traverse. Slot Wash can be reached by dropping directly down from the south summit. Allow eight to ten hours for the ascent from and return to Campo Noche. The round trip from the parking area will take a minimum of three days. Spring is the best time to make the climb, while there is plenty of daylight and water, and the weather is still cool.

Mexican topographic maps San Rafael H11B45 and Santa Cruz H11B55 are generally correct except for nomenclature. The mouth of a small canyon 3/4 mile northwest of the mouth of Cañon del Diablo is incorrectly labeled "Cañada el Diablito," while the real Cañon Diablito is not labeled.

"Cañada la Providencia," shown east of the observatory is actually Cañon del Diablo, while a canyon farther east also labeled "Cañada la Providencia" is in fact correct. The "Picaho [sic] el Diablo" shown due east of the observatory is not the "right" one, while the real Picacho is not labeled. Cerro Botella Azul is not identified, and a peak a mile southeast is incorrectly named "Cerros la Botella Azul," and a "C. Pico del Diablo" is shown another 1/2 mile southeast. An approach from the mouth of Cañon del Diablo is described in Chapter 16. Centra Publications offers an excellent topographic map that shows this and other routes to Picacho, as well as other climbs and hikes in the park and surrounding areas.

Back on the Transpeninsular Highway at KM 140+

KM	LOCATION
142	Road west to Punta San Telmo, with several spots difficult for sedans. The turn is hard to find because of missing KM markers, but it is located 3/4 mile south of the Parque road. Set odometer. Turn north at Mile 4.8, and arrive at the point at Mile 6.7. Known to surfers as "Quatro Casas," this place has fine right point and reef breaks. Low cliffs at the point are no problem, and the beaches are pebble and sand with some shelf rock. Mushy beach breaks are found to the south along the sedan road to Punta San Jacinto.
146	Sodas, snacks, pharmacy, mail, mechanic, bus stop.
150	Sedan road west (signed) to Punta San Jacinto, six miles. The wreck of the coastal freighter *Isla del Carmen*, driven ashore in 1981, lies near the point. Known as "Freighters" to surfers, even though there is only one, this place has excellent right point

The Mexican coastal freighter *Isla del Carmen*, stranded five miles north of Camalú in 1982.

breaks on large swells, some a mile from shore. The road south to Camalú can handle sedans.

157+	**Camalú.** PEMEX (ND), stores, groceries, fruit and meat markets, cafes, auto parts, mechanic, tires, bus station, telephone, mail, medical, dentist, pharmacy. Turn southwest at the PEMEX for the beach, which has good right point and reef breaks. Sportfishermen are rare, but a beach launch is possible, *pangas* are for hire, and thresher sharks and a wide variety of pelagic and bottomfish are taken offshore. Punta Camalú is not too popular with boardsailors, but occasionally good conditions coincide, so it's worth a stop to check it out. Diving is poor.
169	Sedan road east (signed) to ruins of Dominican Misíon Santo Domingo (1775-1839), five miles. Set odometer. History indicates that the good padres said mass in caves at Mile 4.0. If so, it must have been a chummy affair, for the dozen or so grottos are very small. The bluff above the mission is a source of garnets.
171+	**Colonia Guerrero.** Stores, restaurants, groceries, fruit and meat markets, bank, mail, motel, auto parts, tires, bakery, ice, liquor, telephone, telegraph, medical, dental, pharmacy, showers.
172+	Butane plant, road west to Mesón de Don Pepe and Posada Don Diego, which are RV parks, each having full hookups, restrooms, showers and restaurant. Don Diego has laundry machines, the last until Mulegé, and a dump station. The beach several miles west has a long beach break and lots of pismos. As for the strange placement of that telephone pole on the highway, the specifications said to put it there, so who's to argue?
188	**San Quintín.** Spread along the highway between KM 188 and KM 195, the San Quintín/Lazaro Cardenas area has a wide variety of businesses and services, including PEMEX (two, one with MND, the other MN), medical, dental, pharmacy, veterinarian, meat, fish and fruit markets, groceries, *tortilla* factory, bakery, auto parts, mechanics, welding, tires, motel, cafes, bus station, bicycle shops, hardware, liquor, showers, bank, taxis, telephone, telegraph, mail, cinema, ice plant and even a Chinese restaurant. Information can be obtained at the Motel Chavez. The area is growing rapidly; there are computer and video stores, and a rush hour seems to be developing.

SIDETRIP TO BAHÍA SAN QUINTÍN AND ISLA SAN MARTÍN

Bahía San Quintín is one of the major geological features of Baja's west coast. Five basalt craters mark its location from many miles away (the sixth crater is San Martín). Shallow mud flats that cover most of the bay are nurseries for hordes of fish, mollusks and crustaceans, and eel grass attracts large numbers of brant and as many as twenty species of ducks and other geese each winter. Many other species like the place as well, and the bay and surrounding land areas are probably endowed with more bird species than any other location in

JOHN ANGLIN

Will a quarter-inch wet suit keep a horde of angry bees from stinging the author as he smokes out their hive for some breakfast honey?

Baja.

A complete check list might contain well over a hundred species, but some of the more interesting or uncommon (in Baja) birds include red-throated and common loons, western grebe, laysan albatross, snowy egret, little blue and tri-color herons, reddish egret, black-crowned night heron, greater white-fronted, snow and Canada geese, green-winged teal, northern pintail, blue-winged and cinnamon teals, American wigeon, greater scaup, white-winged scooter, common gold-eneye, bufflehead, red-breasted merganser, ruddy duck, black-shouldered kite, northern harrier, Cooper's hawk, ferruginous hawk, golden eagle, merlin, sora, semipalmated plover, American avocet, greater yellowlegs, spotted sandpiper, whimbrel, dunlin, Wilson's phalalope, parasitic jaeger, ring-billed gull, Caspian and least terns, black skimmer, common barn, burrowing and short-eared owls, black swift, Anna's hummingbird and tri-colored blackbird.

The Pacific coast west of San Quintín has sandy beaches alternating with dark volcanic points, with excellent surf fishing and good beach breaks. For a short tour of the area, turn west at the south end of the military base in town, follow the graded road past Pedregal, wind south of Mt. Ceniza, swing past the oyster farm (buy some!) and arrive at the beach at KM 19. The road to this point can handle RVs and trailers, but the coastal road to the north deteriorates quickly. The local cooperative has blocked access south to the San Quintín peninsula.

The Bahía San Quintín area is becoming popular with boardsailors, since it offers just about every condition anyone could want, from flat calm inside the bay to long, open Pacific beaches with long waves and good wind, to big refracted

rollers wrapping around the point. To take full advantage of this, the well-equipped sailor will head for this area with both a wave and a slalom board. Beginners who have not got their tacking and waterstarts down pat should be aware that a current often sweeps south along the open Pacific beaches.

Around 1885 the California Development Company sold tracts of land around San Quintín for wheat farming, built a flour mill and started construction of a railroad to Ensenada, but the scheme quickly failed due to inadequate rainfall. A huge steam engine from the mill can be seen at the Molino Viejo (Old Mill) Motel at the head of the bay, along with the remains of the railway causeway. The skeleton of a pier lies several miles south of the motel. Molino Viejo offers rooms, some with kitchenettes, guides, a nineteen-foot Bayliner and a large skiff, and good advice based on many years of experience in the area. Bring your own food, tackle, frozen squid and anchovies, plus a flashlight (electricity off late at night). Reservations are suggested. Ernesto's Resort Motel next door has cabins, some with kitchens, and food service for guests. Campo de Lorenzo, just to the north, has RV sites with full hookups (electricity evenings only), restrooms, showers, boat rental, guide service, and boat and trailer storage. To get to the area turn west at KM 3 south of San Quintín and follow the signs. The road is suitable for moderate RVs and trailers, but may become a problem in wet weather.

San Quintín is the first place south of the border combining both unspoiled fishing and a launch ramp capable of handling sizable boats. No local party- or charter-boat operations are in regular business, but *pangas* can be rented. Other than clam, mussel and cut fish, no bait is for sale locally, so bring frozen squid or anchovy. The ramp at Molino Viejo is hard-packed sand, and doesn't look like much, but boats to twenty-eight feet have used it successfully at high tide. The only other area with road access and deep water close to shore is southeast of the oyster farm in Bahía Falsa, a useful spot for cartoppers, since there are many areas to camp in nearby. Channels running south from Molino Viejo and Bahía Falsa join south of Ceniza to form a Y, then continue on to Punta Azufre. Although these channels have as little as six feet of water at low tide and are poorly marked, small boats should have no undue difficulty in navigating them if depth finders are used to stay in the channel and speed is held down.

Fishing in the "inner bay" north of Punta Azufre is largely for flatfish, although bottomfish are found in deeper areas near the entrance. Diving in the inner bay is poor for obvious reasons, but the ferry *Morena*, lying in shallow water northwest of the sandspit at Punta Sextante, provides an unusual dive. The last sidewheeler built in California (1920) and the last steam ferry on San Diego Bay, she was brought to San Quintín for use as a cannery hulk shortly after the Second World War, but she soon sank. When not completely sanded in, sections of the hull are home to huge lobsters (the locals do not set traps due to the current), and giant black sea bass appear out of the haze like darkroom images. The dive is strictly a slack-water proposition, and visibilities are normally less than six feet due to the silt stirred up by heavy currents.

All-weather anchorages can be found in any of the deeper areas of the inner bay, and the lee north of Punta Entrada is useful in prevailing winds. Breakers and strong rips occur east of Punta Entrada, and the bar here has as little as six feet of water at low tide, with sandbars often exposed. Surfing is good over the bar, with a fast inside break, but you need a boat to get there. The "outer bay," Bahía Santa María, provides good protection from prevailing weather, although refracted swells can be sizable. The next good anchorage south is Punta Baja. Fishing off Cabo San Quintín can be excellent for a mixed bag of bottom and pelagic fish.

San Martín and the seamounts and shallow areas to its south are among the best offshore fishing and diving locations between San Diego and the Islas San Benito. It is possible to visit the area by trailerboat and even cartopper in good weather if normal safety precautions are observed, the island being a twenty-mile run from Molino Viejo. Choose your weather and tides carefully and while in the "inner bay" stay in the channel; for some boaters the run is an easy romp of several hours, others complain of weed-choked props, heavy tidal rips, and huge waves at the point, and then a long run against heavy wind and waves.

Johnston's Seamount, known to local fishermen as the "240 Spot," is located six miles, 240°, from Cabo San Quintín. When you are over the site, Mt. Mazo will bear 052° and the peak on San Martín 340°. Named for Bill Johnston, owner-skipper of the San Diego-based dive boats *Sand Dollar* and *Bottom Scratcher*, it has two peaks, one of which rises to within 10 feet of the surface, the other to within 55. It is a renowned location for underwater photography. The most unusual feature here and at Roca Ben to the north is the world-class giant mussels which thrive on their southern sides down to 80 feet. Normally found intertidally, dense beds of individuals averaging nine inches have been seen, the record just under ten. In 1964 the 257-ton steel tuna fishing vessel *Mary S.* struck the seamount. She has been examined by insurance-company divers, but since she lies in 220 feet of water she is too deep for sports divers. The seamount has hordes of yellowtail and bottomfish, a few marlin in the warm months and, sometimes, yellowfin.

Dave Buller kicks out to the end of the old pier in Bahía San Quintín.

Roca Ben, 2 1/2 miles south of San Martín, is a rocky pinnacle rising to within 12 feet of the surface at low tide. Roca Ben is one of the most colorful dive sites on Baja's Pacific coast. The scenery is magnificent, the deep blue of surrounding depths contrasting with bright green grass, red sea stars and blue stony hydrocoral studding sheer volcanic walls. Large lobsters, mussels, scallops and abalone abound, including huge threaded abalone. Visibilities average 50 feet and sometimes go to 80, and full wet suits are required. The area is frequented by bonito and a variety of bottomfish, including ling cod to thirty pounds. At low tide Roca Ben can be found easily, since surf and boils often mark its location. However, at other times it can be elusive and a compass fix may be helpful; when you are over the site, Mt. Mazo will bear 110° and the peak on San Martín 346°. Great care must be exercised while diving and fishing in the vicinity. In 1987 the charter fishing vessel *Fish 'N Fool* out of San Diego was overwhelmed by a huge breaker near Roca Ben and sank with the loss of ten lives. Do not approach the area unless it is flat calm, and stand off at least a half-hour to determine if there are any "sneaker" waves coming in. The swells were only 3 or 4 feet when the vessel went down, but the breaker was reported as being 20 feet high. The vessel is now in 165 feet of water, an unsafe depth for sports divers.

Because it is several hundred yards in diameter, a shallow spot known as the "6 1/2 Spot" to long-range fishermen, two miles southwest of Roca Ben, is easy to locate with a depth finder. Bearings to the landmarks just cited are 099° and 010°, least depth forty feet, visibility fifty to seventy feet. However, instead of having soaring walls and jagged pinnacles, the area is flatter and less scenic than Roca Ben. Yellowtail are the primary quarry between late summer and December, when fish migrating along the 100-fathom curve move in to forage. Ling, ocean whitefish and calico bass are also caught. Dirty water and rapid changes in water temperature can quickly end the bite, but this instability can cause conditions to change for the better too, and over the long run the area is quite dependable. Long-range boats out of San Diego make frequent trips in season. Yellowfin tuna are often found fifteen miles west in August and September.

San Martín is volcanic, its crater rising to 497 feet. Caleta Hassler, formed by a low, rocky peninsula jutting toward the east, is the first good anchorage south of Ensenada. An aquaculture operation is getting in the way, but anchoring conditions are excellent, especially during south and west weather, although northwest swells can refract enough to make it uncomfortable. If this occurs, a move south of the rock wall may help. In spite of Hassler's good reputation, at least eight yachts and small vessels have been lost there, so keep a sharp watch.

If they are not biting at the seamounts, the areas around the island often produce lots of whitefish, lings and barracuda. Sandy bottoms in Caleta Hassler have flatfish and unusually large kelp bass. Although frequently ignored, calico fishing can be excellent, and twenty to thirty hookups a day on bonito are possible. Water condition at San Martín is a good barometer for fishermen and divers headed south to Sacramento Reef; if the water is clear at San Martín, it is likely to be clear at the reef.

The island is also a fine dive site, having spider crabs two

Exploring one of the great lava tubes on San Martín; clockwise from the upper left, Jeffrey Smith, Don Nelson, Victor Cook, Rich Kremer and John Williams.

feet in diameter and diverse and abundant nudibranchs in Caleta Hassler. The south coast has extensive kelp beds, and the jumbled rock bottom drops quickly to 20 feet offshore, then slopes to 100 feet within 200-300 yards. Outer coasts are exposed to full ocean swells and have good populations of fish and lobsters among rocky shelves and caves. A number of wrecks have occurred around the island, but none are of significant interest to divers.

San Martín has the only lava-tube caves known in Baja. Dozens of tubes are too small to explore, but there are three major systems. The most accessible can be found by climbing from Caleta Hassler toward the crater. At the first plateau, maneuver so the end of the natural breakwater bears 068° and look for a large collapse. Similar tubes can be found on the north and west slopes. They range up to twenty-five feet in diameter, but their length has not been determined. Scrambling through them is reminiscent of the movie *Fantastic Journey*; the smoothly turning and twisting tubes seem like the bloodless arteries of a giant. Be careful; during their epic

kayak voyage in 1933 Dana and Ginger Lamb were almost trapped in the system on the western slope. Divers should keep an eye open for underwater entrances to the lava tubes.

A faint class 2 trail leads to the summit. Near the top look for a large area of jumbled rock, the collapse of a large cave. The western slope has a trail to an old lighthouse. A steady procession of gray whales can be seen passing to seaward in winter, often just outside the surf line. Another trail leads from Caleta Hassler along the eastern shore to the north coast, where sea lions and elephant seals haul out. Harbor seals can be seen in the small lagoon on the south shore, and a number of species of birds nest on the island. The island has excellent wildflowers in the spring. Waves on the outer coast are often large and well-shaped, but due to difficult access, steep rocky beaches, cliffs and thick kelp beds, surfing is poor.

Back on the Transpeninsular Highway in San Quintín

196/0	Start a new KM numbering sequence.
11	Road west (signed) to Cielito Lindo RV Park, the La Pinta Hotel and fine beaches, three miles. The La Pinta has rooms, restaurant, bar, tennis, horseback riding and a magnificent beach. A PEMEX on the way has Nova only, but the hotel has a Magnasin pump. The wreck of the ex-U.S. subchaser *Scandia* lies off the hotel. Cielito Lindo has a motel, restaurant/cantina and RV sites with operational restrooms maybe, showers not likely and water and electricity hookups almost never. The beach break is good on south swells, and excellent surf fishing for barred surfperch is found south to El Socorro. A road heads northwest from the RV sites along the beach to within several hundred yards of Punta Azufre, and a party of fishermen, surfers or divers could haul in a cartopper or an inflatable, camp on beaches and work the Cabo San Quintín area two miles away. The road becomes very soft near the point. Speedsailing conditions are excellent—boardsailor Frank Hewitt made a broad reach from Punta Azufre to the hotel that averaged thirty knots.
15+	Sedan road west (signed) to Honey's Trailer Park, with some water and sewer hookups, showers, restrooms, dump station, camping and a fine beach.
23+	Sportfishing and diving boats for rent, guides.
24	**El Socorro**. Beaches, camping, RV parking, reef breaks. A road leads northeast about thirty miles to the Mina El Morro gold and copper area, where small pegmatite veins with deep emerald-green sphene containing chromium have been reported. The shoreline south from El Socorro for about thirteen miles has good surfing, offering shore and reef breaks. A number of dirt roads approach the water, allowing solitary camping. However, sleeping on the ground leaves a lot to be desired; the soil is very fine silt, and a windy night and a heavy dew leave a terrible mess the next morning.
37	The wreck of a large multi-engine aircraft lies in sixty feet west of this point, but it is hard to find due to a dearth of good landmarks and a featureless

bottom; ask local divers. The area is loaded with big lobsters.

39   The hills to the east are topped by a weather-resistant Pliocene deposit containing abundant giant barnacles, pismo clams and sand dollars.

41   Moderate upgrades until KM 51+, then a 14% downgrade to El Rosario, KM 56.

****

A CONSTITUTIONAL MATTER. People vary greatly in their tolerance for heat. Will Ashford, Mike and I once drove off-road to a rock-art site, accompanied by Saturñino Diaz, a Mexican gentleman of considerable years. The temperature was at least 90 °, and as luck would have it our van went down to the axles in deep sand. We started to dig it out, and within minutes Will, Mike and I were bathed in sweat and feeling faint. Saturñino, dressed in red longjohns and a quilted coat, kept working, showing no signs of stress. After a rest in the shade of a palo verde we tried it again, and had to quit within minutes, to the barely concealed contempt of our new friend. Finally we remembered our cooler of cold sodas, but a thorn bush prevented us from getting the side door of the van open, and there was no other way to get to it. Using our Hi-Lift, we jacked up the back of the van and gave it a push, causing the jack to tip over and moving the van sideways a foot or so. We then jacked up the front of the van and again pushed it sideways. After thirty of the most awful minutes we had ever experienced, we had moved the van three feet and were gulping down cold Cokes. Saturñino said he didn't need a drink and kept working. An hour later we broke free to harder ground, the three of us faint, sick and almost prostrated by the heat. As we headed back to his ranch Saturñino tried a Coke, but when we arrived an hour later it was still half-full.

****

CHAPTER 10

EL ROSARIO TO BAHÍA DE LOS ANGELES

On the Transpeninsular Highway north of El Rosario

KM	LOCATION
56	**El Rosario.** PEMEX (two, one with MN, one with N), cafe, stores, restaurants, medical, bakery, meat market, tires, auto parts, motels, Pesca office. The Cafe Espinosa was the last outpost of civilization in the days before the Transpeninsular was completed, and virtually all travelers stopped in to get information, a lobster taco and one last cold beer before starting out across the wilderness ahead. The supermarket sells groceries, produce (generally of poor quality), meat, ice, Coleman fuel, beer, liquor, limited hardware items and—get it while it lasts—Sloane's Liniment. A fish inspection station is often in operation on the Transpeninsular in the northeastern part of town.

SIDETRIP TO THE PETRIFIED FOREST AND PLAYA DEL ROSARIO

The Transpeninsular makes a 90° turn northeast in El Rosario. At this point turn southwest onto a pickup road, set odometer, and just short of Mile 0.1 take the right (260°) fork. At Mile 0.9 encounter a Y. The left (210°) fork leads to a fish-packing plant which has a diver's decompression chamber. Take the right (270°) fork. At Mile 1.3 encounter a bluff; take the right (290°) fork. The road soon passes through Baja's "Petrified Forest," a geologically old region of eroded washes and gullies, where branches and entire tree trunks of fossilized conifers and palms can be seen. In the 1960s, the fossil bones of a large duckbilled dinosaur that roamed the saltwater marshes seventy-nine million years ago were discovered here, as well as amphibians, lizards, snakes, crocodiles, turtles and several mammals. A terrestrial bird the size of a robin from this location has been termed one of the most

important discoveries in avian paleontology in this century. Arrive at the cobble beach at Mile 4.5, which yields petrified wood and dinosaur bones, red jasper and jasp-agate, some showing red plume and orbicular patterns against a background of white and black agate.

SIDETRIP TO PUNTA BAJA AND BAHÍA DEL ROSARIO

Starting in El Rosario, turn southwest, but take the left (164°) fork just before Mile 0.1 and cross the river at Mile 0.9. This crossing is flat and sandy and is usually no problem, and from this point on the road can handle RVs. Take the right (230°) fork at Mile 1.0, and at Mile 1.5 look on the right for the ruins of Dominican Misíon El Rosario (in operation 1774-1832, but these buildings date from 1802). At Mile 2.5 come to a fork and continue straight ahead (245°). Turn left (160°) at the fork at Mile 2.9, signed "Punta Baja," and arrive at the settlement at Punta Baja at Mile 10.3. Bottom fishing in Bahía del Rosario is excellent, and spearfishermen will find many spots within free-diving range, visibility normally being fifteen to twenty-five feet. Cartoppers can be launched off the beach, and *pangas* are for hire, but trailerboats cannot be launched here. Boats heading for Isla San Jerónimo and Sacramento Reef can avoid the kelp that clogs the bay by staying well offshore. The anchorage off the settlement is satisfactory, although refracted swell is often present. The first anchorage to the south is at Jerónimo. Beach diving is poor throughout the bay, but you might try the lee of the point. On the right waves, thin-walled tubes wrap around the point, providing excellent surfing.

The coast between the mouth of the river and the point has been the scene of a number of wrecks, the largest being the wooden screw steamer *Union*, which hit a reef in calm weather early in the morning of July 5, 1851. The crew and passengers got ashore safely, together with $270,000 in gold coin. When the passengers returned to San Diego the story

116

came out: the crew had celebrated the Fourth of July so enthusiastically that the helmsman was unable to steer. In the early 1960s an old Mexican lady told my friend Harry Wham that she remembered stories from her childhood about the wreck of a vessel named "Hunion" on the beach in "Ensenada Bapoor." Harry's Spanish was not too good, but the wreck was apparently the "Union" in "Steam Cove" (*vapor* is Spanish for steam), and he located large amounts of rusted machinery, visible only at extremely low tides, and a campsite littered with period bottles and chinaware. Gold and silver coins still wash up occasionally, probably from baggage left aboard.

Alcohol figured prominently in another wreck, but this time it was the rescuers, not the crew, who had hangovers; in 1978 the vessel *Noroeste* went ashore with a cargo of 1,000 cases of Tecate, leading to a legendary week-long toot in the tiny settlement.

The small fishing camp of Agua Blanca can be reached by taking the left (228°) fork at Mile 2.5. Although it is more exposed than Punta Baja, the flat sand beach is an excellent place to launch a cartopper for diving and fishing in the bay. *Pangas* may be available for hire. Pick your weather carefully, for boats have overturned in the surf. The route to Jerónimo and Sacramento Reef crosses great fields of kelp. Nearby beaches provide outstanding beachcasting for spotfin and yellowfin croaker, to the point that you may not be able to eat them all.

Isla San Jerónimo

Ten miles south of Punta Baja, Jerónimo (San Geronimo) has a fair anchorage off the settlement near the southwest point. The island has been disparaged as a "barren pile of bird lime," but you can land at the village, hike to the lighthouse to see its antique acetylene equipment, and visit the sea lions and the shearwaters and other birds at the north end. If you see something that looks like a gray snake with prominent black stripes, it is probably not a snake at all, but the Geronimo Island legless lizard, endemic to the island. In addition, the island is home to the side-blotched lizard, the western patch-nosed lizard and the endemic white-footed mouse *Peromyscus maniculatus geronimensis*. The remains of the U.S. tuna clipper *Western Sky*, wrecked about thirty years ago, lie on the west side. According to local legend, survivors didn't even get their feet wet, since it was rammed into a narrow cove hardly wider than the vessel itself. Diving around the south end is excellent, and a fine reef extends southwest almost a half-mile. Sea lions inhabiting the inner reef are friendly and put on a great ballet. The vessel *Linda* sank here in 1949 while at anchor. The Mexican fishing vessel *Resolute* lies in sixty feet off the north coast, but is difficult to dive due to dense kelp and heavy surge. The first useful anchorage to the south is Bahía San Carlos, but beware, infamous Sacramento Reef is on an almost direct line between the two.

Sacramento Reef

Centered three miles southeast of the island, Arrecife Sacramento (Sacramento Reef) has been described as a "seething cauldron of Hell." Since its shallow reaches are exposed to ocean swells, the reef is nothing but white water in anything short of a flat calm. Many vessels have been wrecked, often while blindly coasting north along the twenty-fathom curve. Though a place of danger and death to ships and sailors, it pulsates with underwater life, and biologists have termed it a "biological miracle." The most outstanding feature is the dense growth of surf grass, with blades up to twelve feet long, forming homes for great numbers of horn sharks. Gray sponges reach huge proportions, and growths of bryozoans are the heaviest on the Pacific coast. Big black sea bass and large lobsters are common, especially on the eastern margins of the reef. In recent years the visibility has decreased on the reef, possibly caused by runoff from increased farming along the coast to the north. Only time will tell what effect this will have on dive conditions and the underwater life.

The name of the reef comes from the big sidewheel steamer *Sacramento*. Carrying a treasure of gold and silver bullion and coins, she was steaming up the coast in December 1872 when her deck officer smelled kelp. It was too late to do anything, and the ship crashed on the reef. The passengers and crew made it safely to Jerónimo and were rescued. The wreck was visible for many years, and as late as 1932 her huge paddle shaft could be seen sticking out of the sea. In the 1950s and 60s Harry Wham, Leonard Bern and others dove the wreck and found onyx doorknobs, china and silverware, coins, brass valves, large vases, sailor's buttons and bottles. The gold? Newspapers of the day claimed every penny of the treasure was recovered, variously reported as between $335,000 and $2,000,000, but shipping and insurance companies had a strong self-interest in issuing such proclamations. Today authorities differ, but local sea-urchin divers may reluctantly show Polaroid photos of small bars, which

Reeve hits the water at Sacramento Reef, assisted by hose tender Rob Watson.

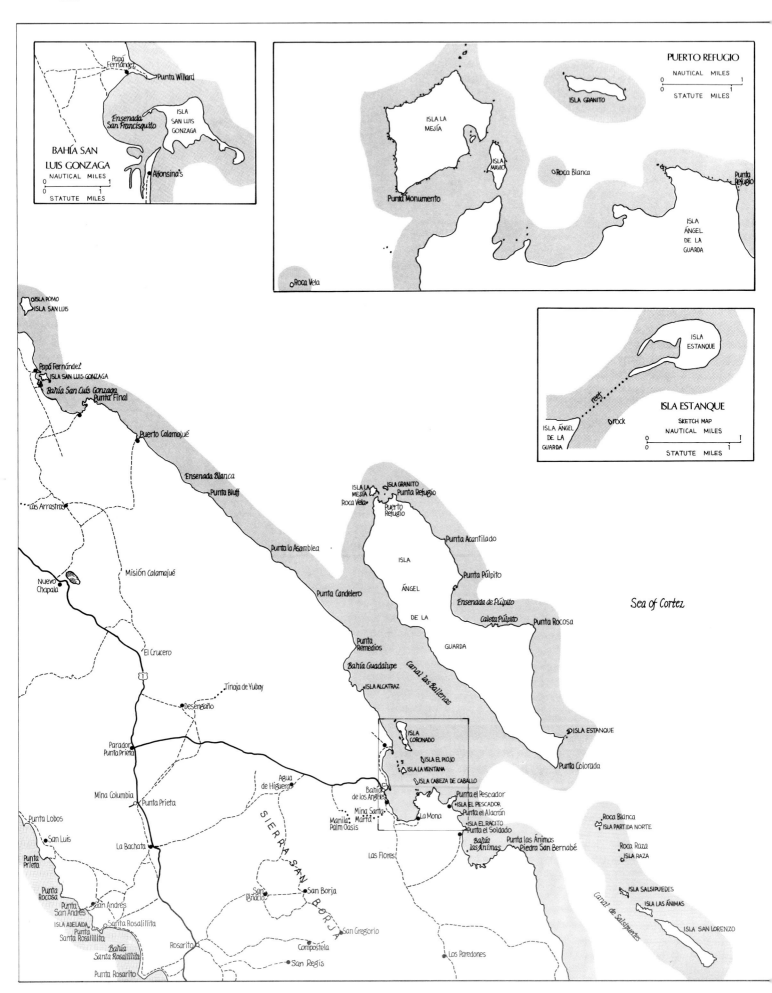

Papá Fernández
Punta Wilkard

ISLA
SAN LUIS
GONZAGA

Ensenada
San Francisquito

BAHÍA SAN
LUIS GONZAGA

NAUTICAL MILES
0   1
STATUTE MILES
0   1

Alfonsina's

PUERTO REFUGIO

NAUTICAL MILES
0   1
STATUTE MILES

ISLA GRANITO

ISLA LA
MEJÍA

ISLA
MAVIO

Roca Blanca

Punta
Refugio

Punta Monumento

ISLA
ÁNGEL
DE LA
GUARDA

Roca Vela

ISLA POMO
ISLA SAN LUIS

ISLA
ESTANQUE

ISLA ESTANQUE

SKETCH MAP
NAUTICAL MILES
0   1
STATUTE MILES
0   1

reef

ISLA ÁNGEL
DE LA
GUARDA

rock

Papá Fernández
ISLA SAN LUIS GONZAGA
Bahía San Luís Gonzaga
Punta Final

Puerto Calamajué

Ensenada Blanca
Punta Bluff

Las Arrastras

Punta la Asamblea

ISLA LA
MEJÍA
Roca Vela

ISLA GRANITO
Punta Refugio

Puerto
Refugio

Punta Acantilado

Nuevo
Chapala

Misión Calamajué

Punta Candelero

ISLA

ÁNGEL

Punta Púlpito

Ensenada de Púlpito

Caleta Púlpito   Punta Rocosa

Sea of Cortez

DE LA

El Crucero

Punta
Remedios

GUARDA

Canal las Ballenas

11

Tinaja de Yubay

Bahía Guadalupe

Desengaño

ISLA ALCATRAZ

Parador
Punta Prieta

ISLA
CORONADO

Agua
de Higuera

ISLA ESTANQUE

Punta Colorada

Mina Columbia

Punta Prieta

ISLA EL PIOJO
ISLA LA VENTANA

ISLA CABEZA DE CABALLO

Punta Lobos

Bahía
de los Ángeles

Punta el Pescador
ISLA EL PESCADOR
Punta el Alacrán

Roca Blanca
ISLA PARTIDA NORTE

San Luis

Mina Santa
Marta

ISLA
Manila Marta
Palm Oasis

La Mona

ISLA EL RACITO
Punta el Soldado

Roca Raza

Punta
Prieta

La Bachata

Punta las Ánimas
Bahía
las Ánimas   Piedra San Bernabé

ISLA RAZA

Punta
Rocosa

SIERRA SAN BORJA

Las Flores

Punta
San Andrés   San Andrés

San
Ignacio   San Borja

ISLA SALSIPUEDES

ISLA ADELAIDA
Punta
Santa Rosalillita

Santa Rosalillita

ISLA LAS ÁNIMAS

Rosarito

San Gregorio

Canal de Salsipuedes

Bahía
Santa Rosalillita

Compostela

Los Paredones

ISLA SAN LORENZO

Punta Rosarito

San Regis

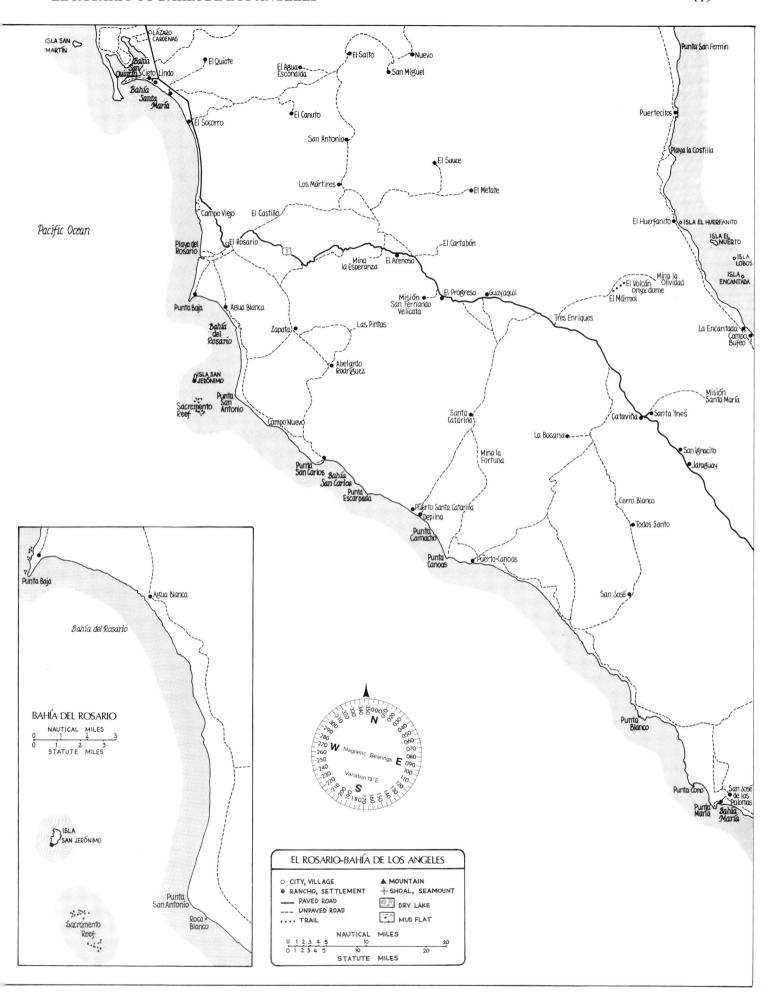

ISLA SAN MARTÍN

LÁZARO CARDENAS

Punta San Fermin

El Quiote

El Salto

Nuevo

Bahía San Quintín

Cielo Lindo

El Agua Escondida

San Miguel

Bahía Santa María

El Socorro

El Canuto

Puertecitos

San Antonio

Playa la Costilla

El Sauce

Los Mártires

El Metate

Pacific Ocean

Campo Viejo

El Castillo

El Huerfanito

ISLA EL HUERFANITO

Playa del Rosario

El Rosario

El Cartabón

ISLA EL MUERTO

ISLA LOBOS

Mina la Esperanza

El Arenoso

Punta Baja

Agua Blanca

El Progreso

Guayaquil

Misión San Fernando Velicata

El Volcán onyx dome

Mina la Olividad

El Mármol

ISLA ENCANTADA

Bahía del Rosario

Zapata

Las Pintas

Tres Enriques

La Encantada

Campo Bufeo

ISLA SAN JERÓNIMO

Abelardo Rodríguez

Misión Santa María

Sacramento Reef

Punta San Antonio

Santa Ynés

Cataviña

Campo Nuevo

Santa Catarina

La Bocana

San Ignacito

Jaraguay

Mina la Fortuna

Punta San Carlos

Bahía San Carlos

Cerro Blanco

Punta Escarpada

Puerto Santa Catarina

Depilna

Todos Santo

Punta Camacho

Punta Canoas

Puerto-Canoas

San José

BAHÍA DEL ROSARIO

Punta Baja

Agua Bianca

Bahía del Rosario

BAHÍA DEL ROSARIO

NAUTICAL MILES
0   1   2   3
0   1   2   3
STATUTE MILES

N
NW NE
W   E
SW SE
S

Magnetic Bearings

Variation 13°E

Punta Blanco

ISLA SAN JERÓNIMO

Punta Cono

San José de las Palomas

Punta María

Bahía María

Punta San Antonio

Roca Bianco

Sacramento Reef

EL ROSARIO–BAHÍA DE LOS ANGELES

○ CITY, VILLAGE
● RANCHO, SETTLEMENT
— PAVED ROAD
-- UNPAVED ROAD
···· TRAIL

▲ MOUNTAIN
+ SHOAL, SEAMOUNT
▤ DRY LAKE
▦ MUD FLAT

NAUTICAL MILES
0 1 2 3 4 5   10   20
0 1 2 3 4 5   10   20
STATUTE MILES

Even boojums fall in love.

they claim to be gold taken from the wreck of the "*muy rico yate*" *Goodwill*, lost in 1969. However, the location they describe is that of the *Sacramento*, and they seem to know nothing about how the reef got its name.

Chart 21041 correctly shows a line of small islets along the south margin of the reef. The *Sacramento* is located south of the easternmost islets in this line. If you can't find it, ask one of the locals to take you to "Roca Timon." The wreck is scattered over a large area and is hard to see due to heavy growths of plants and animals. Storms sometimes rearrange things and remove growths, making things easier to identify for a while. Huge timbers are partly buried in sand, and small artifacts lie about the bottom. Her tremendous cylinder, boilers and walking beam must be out there somewhere.

The 161-foot schooner *Goodwill* is another fine dive. She is located in the northwest reaches of the reef, near the islets shown on 21041. An attempt to recover her bronze towing bitts a number of years ago caused excited rumors about Jesuit church bells to sweep through downtown El Rosario. The wreck shown on 21041 is apparently the U.S. tuna clipper *Countess*, lost in 1949. The site is marked by a large propeller and a monel shaft, so there should be no confusion with the *Sacramento*. There are many other wrecks, and divers often have a hard time figuring out where one wreck ends and another begins.

Diveable areas of the reef cover about two square miles. It is not safe to dive or fish if swells exceed two or three feet, even if you can launch safely off the beach at Punta Baja or

Agua Blanca. Fishing and diving boats out of San Diego occasionally visit the reef.

****

A VOYAGE IN A SEA OF MUD. Too much rain is more often a problem in the desert than too little. My partner Rob Watson and I once drove our van to Agua Blanca, planning to scout new fishing and diving sites. After several days of exploring Bahía El Rosario and a visit to Jerónimo, we returned, loaded our equipment in the van and hoisted the boat onto its roof. It was starting to rain lightly, so we took a skinny-dip in the ocean, using the rain to rinse off the soap and several weeks of accumulated grime. Several locals were standing around laughing, we thought, at our soapy behinds. We looked around and noticed that there wasn't a single pickup left where there had been a dozen when we arrived. Although puzzled, we took our time, and it was raining hard by the time we finally pulled out and headed back for El Rosario. We soon understood why the pickups were gone and what had been so funny to our onlookers—we were in big trouble. The first hundred yards of the road up from the beach was running with liquid mud. Fortunately it was not yet very deep, and our spinning wheels would finally dig down to dry soil. In little jerks and starts we made it to the crest of the ridge behind the camp.

The countryside ahead of us was a sea of gooey mud, and the nearest pavement was a dozen miles away. Huge clods attached themselves to the wheels until they could hardly turn, and it became almost impossible to steer. We caught up with several Mexicans who had also not left soon enough, and felt a certain solace that at least we were not the only dummies. Everyone got behind a stuck pickup and pushed, but the mud was so slippery that our boots skidded backwards and we fell into the morass. A four-wheel-drive came along, only barely able to make headway. The driver attempted to pull us out of a mud-hole with his winch, but it just dragged his vehicle forward. We tried to jack up the van with our Hi-Lift to put on chains, but it just pumped down into the mud. We didn't have a jack pad or flat piece of wood, and there were no stones about, so we sacrificed the lid to our lobster pot. We finally got the chains on, and they seemed to help us pull out of the goo, but they soon broke and wrapped tightly around the axle. We flipped a coin to see who was going to visit the black purgatory under the van, and I lost. One chain was so tight I had to hacksaw it off.

Just as everyone was becoming resigned to an involuntary week of rest and contemplation, we had an idea. The worst mud seemed to be where earlier drivers had churned everything up, and the soil off the side of the road appeared to be firmer, so I pulled over and immediately got better traction. We were building up a little speed when an agave blocked the way. We could not risk stopping, and with a lurch and a bound the van passed over it. With tires spinning wildly we slowly made a traverse up the side of a canyon. The van started to skid sideways, but we made the crest and finally got to a reasonably firm road and eventually made it to El Rosario.

As we pulled up to the supermarket, with every surface— human and mechanical—covered with mud, we were greeted with catcalls and whistles from the crowd of loafers who had assembled earlier for such purposes. When we came out of

Will Ashford makes a wax rubbing of a petroglyph.

Beneath the surface of every dirty, smelly, grizzled Baja desert rat is a suave, sophisticated man-about-town; all it takes is a horse trough, a razor and plenty of soap to let it show through.

High adventure; Mike, Reeve and I ferry a pair of Hondas from Puerto Lopéz Mateos out to Isla Magdalena to explore the beaches for shipwrecks and treasures.

Jim Smallwood and John Williams survey Cañon Tajo from a ridge east of La Milla.

Not everyone averages twelve miles an hour; a Baja 1000 racer slides into an unmarked turn.

Reeve finds something amusing about Rob Watson's sextant technique while off Punta Juanico.

A cooperative manta takes Marilyn Danielson and a pair of remoras for a ride.

Bikers swing past a tranquil lagoon on the shores of the Cortez.

Jim Skotchdepole enjoys Bahía Concepción.

Ensenada's Cuerpo Rescate rescue squad highlines an injured man across a rain-swollen arroyo.

A mast-top camera provides a view of Jay Laswell in the midst of a jibe.

Oscar Villavicencio told us that the Indians who once lived near Rancho el Progreso had a sense of humor—and he took us to the proof!

A fire and a bowl of turkey tetrazini warm up Wayne Campbell and Ted Robertson at a chilly camp at the 6,600-foot level in Cañon del Diablo.

Fishing action off Rocas Alijos, 175 miles west of Bahía Magdalena.

Lolly Flowers, Christy Crahan and Linda Redman explore the Victorias, the only sign of "civilization" being a jet trail in the sky.

Recreating an ancient scene, Dee Bray drinks from a tiny trickle of water in the shade of Cueva Flechas, a rock-art site north of San Ignacio.

the store with a big supply of soap, towels and alcoholic fortification, there was another torrent of derision—we had two flat tires. The agave we ran over had extracted its revenge.

****

Back on the Transpeninsular Highway in El Rosario

Until this point, the Transpeninsular has passed through areas that have had substantial populations and paved roads for many years, but the "real" Baja begins here: unfenced ranges, lonely ranches and miles of almost uninhabited desert. The PEMEX stations at Cataviña, Parador Punta Prieta and Villa Jesús María (73, 139 and 198 miles from El Rosario, respectively) sometimes do not have gas, so top off in El Rosario and fill again at every opportunity. The next supermarket is in Guerrero Negro, so get your supplies while you can. Bicyclists will find the highway between El Rosario and Cataviña the most challenging on the entire Transpeninsular, with rolling hills requiring hundreds of gear changes. They will also find that locating a flat campsite away from traffic noise can be difficult in places. Travelers headed "south" early in the day should beware—since the highway runs generally east and southeast for many miles, a blinding sun hovering over the road ahead increases the danger of an already difficult stretch of highway.

KM	LOCATION
71	The strange plants north of the road are boojums (cirio). They defy precise description, for the simple reason that analogies fail; there is nothing else like them, although "huge, skinny, upside-down carrots" comes fairly close. Found only from the southern end of the Sierra San Pedro Mártir south to the Tres Virgenes area, on Guardian Angel Island and in a small area in Sonora, boojums reach sixty feet, and are often crowned with a cluster of spindly branches at the top. Some assume grotesque shapes, sometimes bending down to touch the ground in a living arch, and a boojum forest has been compared to "a convention of drunken skywriters." They have no edible fruit and make poor firewood, thus serving no purpose of man other than to amuse and amaze.
76	The plants on the south side of the road that look like giant green porcupines are a species of agave. They grow slowly for many years, and then suddenly put up a towering stalk covered with yellow flowers, after which they die, a habit leading to the name "century plant." Some species are used in making tequila and mescal.
77+	Road south (signed "Abelardo L. Rodríguez") to Bahía San Carlos.

SIDETRIP ON THE BAHÍA SAN CARLOS ROAD

Set odometer. A fascinating jumble of rocks named Las Pintas exists east from the road at Mile 11.6. Drive 0.1 mile past the corral and turn northeast on the faint wheel tracks. Follow them nine miles until they end in a wide arroyo marked by a grove of dátilillos (which resemble Joshua trees).

Mike takes a badly needed shower in the waterfall at Las Pintas.

Las Pintas, not quite visible, is 200 yards upstream. The road to this point can be negotiated by pickups with difficulty, but only four-wheel-drives should attempt to drive directly to the site due to very soft ground. Oyster shells, ammonites and trilobites by the million can be seen frozen in various stages of petrifaction at the site, and a stream magically appears from the dry sands of the plateau above and shoots through the air into a sandy-bottomed grotto, a nifty spot for a shower. It then passes through a long, water-carved cleft to disappear into the desert below. To top it off, Indians have graced the place with petroglyphs and small paintings.

Water seeping through fossil beds for millions of years has produced striking orange and white stains and a number of grottos, some of them hollowed-out rocks reminiscent of gigantic sugar Easter eggs. One grotto, formed by an enormous flat-bottomed boulder resting on five stone feet, has a sandy floor—a cool and inviting spot. Graced by total silence and a wealth of natural history, the place is a great spot for loafing and dreaming.

Continuing on the road to San Carlos, cross Cañon San Fernando at Mile 18.3, and at Mile 38.0 turn east at the intersection to go to the fishing village, west to Punta San

Carlos. In the past, the road to the San Carlos area was often one of the better long, unpaved roads in Baja Norte, being well-graded and having only three 14-18% grades, all relatively short and smooth. While it should be possible to make the drive with a tent or utility trailer or small RV, it would be inadvisable to bring a trailerboat. Cartop and inflatable boats can be launched with few problems. Divers and fishermen will find a large kelp bed and scattered pinnacles southwest of the point, almost virgin territory. In 1920 the vessel *Newark* sank near the point with a cargo of the sublime and the ridiculous—onyx and guano. Surfers like the reef and right point breaks, and many boardsailors make the trek to enjoy good winds and everything from calm inside the bay to waves at the point. The sea caves to the north are worth a visit, and the locals report a large fossil deposit northeast of the village. The anchorage provides satisfactory shelter in moderate prevailing weather, but is swept by heavy swells at times. The lees of a series of points along the coast to the southeast—Escarpada, Canoas, Blanco, Cono, María and Santa Rosalillita—provide anchorages with modest protection, the last often being the best. Little more than open roadsteads, all are subject to south weather and tend to be uncomfortable. Boats coasting south generally start a "shortcut" at San Carlos and head directly for Isla Cedros, avoiding these relatively poor anchorages and cutting down the distance.

Back on the Transpeninsular Highway at KM 77+

92	The large, solitary cactus standing north of the road is a cardón. Found only in Baja from approximately this latitude to the Cape and in a small area in Sonora, these giants may have twenty or more branches and approach fifty feet in height. Perfumed flowers appear in the spring, but the fruit is poor.
99	Pickup road south to Mina la Esperanza, four miles, yielding fair-to-good turquoise. A road north signed "R. Los Mártires" leads to several open-pit copper mines where chrysocolla, malachite and azurite have been found.
101+	**El Arenoso.** Mina Ursula, to the south, is believed to contain a million tons of hematite.
104	Tiny cafe. The road tends to level out at this point to gentle grades.
104+	The low shrubs with dagger-like leaves on the north side of the highway are dátil, a species of yucca. Up to fifteen feet high and having a woody trunk, normally unbranched, and leaves twelve-to-nineteen inches long, they are common in Baja Norte. Dátil can easily be confused with dátilillo, another common yucca, which will be seen along the highway at KM 232+, another seven-nine miles ahead. Having seen both, you should have little difficulty distinguishing them.
110	Specimens of malachite have been found nearby.
114	Road southwest (signed) to Misíon San Fernando Velicatá, three miles. In 1769 Franciscan Father Junipero Serra, now a candidate for sainthood despite the fate of his Baja flock and their culture, founded a mission on this site, the name being a

Hispanicized version of *Guiricata*, name of the local Indian tribe. Cliffs to the west were quarried to supply stone for an aqueduct. The area is rich in copper and iron, and a half-dozen mines with grand names like Copper Queen and Julius Caesar were established in the early 1900s. Hematite, malachite, chalcopyrite, chalcanthite, bornite and cuprite can be found nearby.

116+	**Rancho El Progreso.** Food and drink.
127+	**Guayaquil.** Groceries. Road southeast (signed) to Puerto Santa Catarina.

SIDETRIP TO CATARINA

This road is suitable for pickups, with a few grades to 19%. Set odometer. Pass a ranch at Mile 19.1, and take the right (227°) fork at Mile 21.2. As you bump and bang down this road, reflect on the fact that it was the main route from the onyx mines at El Mármol to the beach at Catarina, and wagons loaded with huge pieces of the stone routinely made the trip, later being replaced by trucks with solid rubber tires (more on El Mármol later). One of the world's finest deposits of fossil ammonites is located at Mile 33.4. Extinct for seventy million years, these cephalopods have only one modern counterpart, the chambered nautilus. Resembling huge snails and ranging in size from softballs to beach balls, their fossilized remains litter the walls and bottom of the ravine, especially after a hurricane has washed away large amounts of soil. A fossilized ammonite can be seen at the museum at Bahía de los Angeles. Fist-sized specimens of jasper have been found on the beach at Mile 40.1, some with plume-like formations in several shades of red and a background of red and white jasp-agate, others with concentric circles of black and red on a white agate background. These beauties are hard and unfractured, and cut into fine cabochons. The wrecks of several vessels can be found on the beach. The vessel *Boxer* sank here in the 1920s with 500 tons of onyx aboard.

A sideroad leads south from the fork at Mile 21.2 to Punta Canoas. Mineral collectors have found malachite at Mina la Fortuna, five miles from the fork. Canoas is regarded as only a fair anchorage. Fishermen report the sunken wreck of an old sailing vessel just north of the point.

Back on the Transpeninsular Highway at KM 127+

143	**Rancho Tres Enriques.** Food and drink.
144	Road northeast (signed) to El Mármol.

SIDETRIP TO EL MÁRMOL AND EL VOLCÁN

Turn northeast on a gravel road capable of handling sedans. Set odometer. Just past a corral and windmill at Mile 0.9, take the right (045°) fork and arrive at the site at Mile 9.0. About 1900, Southwest Onyx and Marble, an American company still in business in San Diego, began operations; wells were dug, and homes, a store and a jail were built. Later a schoolhouse was constructed with onyx walls thirty inches thick, the only one in the world.

Quarried from a deposit 3,000 by 1,200 feet in area and about 40 feet thick, El Mármol onyx was prized for its beautiful veins and subtle shades of brown, tan, red and yellow. Using wagons and later trucks, it was transported to Catarina. The ruts they left were filled with onyx chips and rolled with a water-filled barrel pulled by a burro, producing another El Camino Real of sorts. At Catarina the blocks were lightered out to ships from a wooden dock, which carried them to the United States, where craftsmen fashioned products ranging from ink pots, doorknobs and gearshift knobs to the exteriors and interiors of banks, churches and mansions. A specially selected slab was carved into a bathtub for actress Theda Bara.

Known as Brown's Camp, after the superintendent and his son, who would be superintendent after his father, the busy village grew to several hundred people. Well known to travelers, it was the last source of fuel, water and supplies for almost 300 miles south, and in 1928 Phillip Townsend Hanna compared its strategic importance to Baja travelers to that of Khartoum to travelers between Cairo and the Cape of Good Hope. In its time El Mármol provided a major part of the world's supply of onyx, but with the advent of plastics and inexpensive building materials, demand fell off and by 1958 the miners and their families had drifted off. El Mármol no longer rings to the sound of air drills, although trucks still come occasionally to haul away stone quarried years ago to be cut into souvenirs and knicknacks.

Today a certain sadness prevails. The homes have fallen down, their lumber has been salvaged, and the famous schoolhouse is slowly succumbing to the elements, its walls cracking and shifting badly. A few people still remember the past; many of the tombstones in the cemetery are graced with plastic flowers. Old-timers tell of a rare hail storm that caused blocks of quarried onyx to ring like a carillon, and of a cavity that was exposed when a block of onyx was cut—the dazzling, crystal-lined prison and palace of a tiny frog.

Mineral collectors will find all the onyx they could ever want, and lesser amounts of mossy jasper and moss agate. A four-wheel-drive road running south offers collecting opportunities. Standing at the schoolhouse sight 129° and note the road climbing a hill near the horizon. Look for a pegmatite dike at Mile 2.0, and modest amounts of agate at Mile 4.0. Minerals have been found on flat-topped ridges to the south, primarily agate, augite and andesite. To the the east of these ridges is a high basalt-capped mesa nearly a mile in diameter, higher than anything in the vicinity, where large olivine crystals have been collected.

A hike up nearby Arroyo el Volcán is of interest, for there you can visualize the process by which onyx is formed and, if you are lucky, possibly see the only geyser in Baja. A half-dozen bubbling springs deposit thin layers of fresh onyx over a quarter-acre or so. The clear water tastes acidic and faintly sweet. About once a month the geyser shoots up a sixty-foot plume of gas and water for several minutes. Immediately south of the springs a dome of onyx has grown to about thirty feet high, causing the tiny spring at its top to reach higher and higher. A hundred yards south, a beautiful layer of striped onyx has been exposed by erosion. Using dry-washing methods, miners used to obtain considerable amounts of gold in the jagged peaks nearby. Good-quality sphene crystals have been found at the mouth of the arroyo near the shores of the Cortez, but since the igneous rocks there are barren, it seems that the sphene must have washed down from somewhere nearby.

To visit the El Volcán onyx dome area sight 040° from the schoolhouse and note a single-lane sedan road in the distance. Set odometer. At Mile 4.0 the road crosses the arroyo; the spot will be obvious. Park and hike up the arroyo about fifteen minutes. Those with pickups can continue on the road past Arroyo El Volcán. At Mile 7.0 the road passes through areas of heavy mineralization and numerous mining claims. It ends at Mile 10.3 at the La Olividad barite mine, with magnificent views of the Cortez.

Back on the Transpeninsular Highway at KM 144

KM   *LOCATION*
146   The strange plants with many whip-like branches on both sides of the highway are ocotillos. A common desert plant, they are seen as far south as Bahía Concepción. Often leafless and seemingly dead, these spartan, no-nonsense plants quickly sprout small green leaves and unexpectedly beautiful mustard-red flowers after a rain. The world record seems to be held by a specimen with forty-eight whips at

Huge blocks of onyx at El Mármol. There's a boy in there somewhere.

As I pressed the shutter I hoped for a truly spectacular photograph of Victor Cook drinking from the El Volcán geyser, but I had no luck—it erupts only once a month.

the bottom of the Cuesta de la Ley on the El Arco-Bahía San Francisquito road.

157   Entering prime desert scenery, with jumbled boulders, stately cardóns and forests of boojums.

160   Modest campsites on both sides of the road.

163   Road south to Cerro Blanco, signed "Faro San José."

SIDETRIP FOR LOVERS OF PINES, REDWOODS AND COOL FOGS

If the fine country around KM 157 has failed to improve your opinion of desert scenery, a sidetrip to Cerro Blanco is in order. Turn south at KM 163 onto a pickup road and set odometer. Stay left (183°) at the fork past the windmill at Mile 8.8, and left (150°) again at the fork at Mile 10.2. Until this point things have been rather ordinary, the environment being altered by grazing cattle and the side of the road littered with empties discarded by fishermen headed for Canoas. However, after a short but bumpy 36% grade to the top of a ridge, there is little to mark the hand of man other than the road itself. The vegetation becomes dense and lush, with yellow, red, purple, blue and lavender flowers, elegant palo verde, and slopes covered with boojums and cardóns. One old cardón has lost all its major vertical branches, and in its struggle to survive has sent its only remaining branch sideways, the branch's weight carrying it to the ground. New growth sprouting vertically now gives this long, gnarled appendage the appearance of a rain-forest nurse log. Six species of cactus share a twenty-yard circle, one with vicious three-inch spines, wisely chosen by hummingbirds for their nesting sites.

The road drops into a deep, shaded canyon and crosses and recrosses a reed-filled marsh surrounded with palms, home to a hundred-thousand frogs and a million tadpoles. There is often flowing water in the marsh, which looks clear and clean. Quail and rabbit seem to be everywhere, and shy deer, never

forgetting, even here, peek out of dense thickets. At Mile 17.4 the road climbs out of the canyon and things slowly revert to the ordinary. Reality finally returns beginning at Mile 21.7, with several automobile carcasses, a deserted ranch and finally, at Mile 22.5, the old Cerro Blanco onyx quarry and its clutter of battered machinery and discarded oil cans.

There is another attraction in the area, made known by space-age technology. During a 1981 flight, astronauts aboard the shuttle *Columbia* used an infared radiometer to locate an area three miles in diameter about five miles west of the quarry, having iron oxide minerals, kaolinite and possibly alunite in its surface materials. Geologists later found gold and silver, and molybdenum, copper, lead and zinc-bearing minerals as well. There are no roads into the area, but mineral collectors could make an adventurous two-day backpacking venture into almost virgin territory. The terrain is fairly steep, but careful route-finding with a topographic map in hand should hold problems to a minimum.

Back on the Transpeninsular Highway at KM 163

171+   A small stream crosses the highway, watering a few graceful palms, a great stop for lunch. If you need a bath or a good campsite, sandy areas and deep emerald-colored pools (wet years) can be found about a half-mile upstream. An interesting and easily accessible display of Indian art can be found in a small grotto near here. Red, yellow and black paintings scattered about its walls and ceiling include abstract designs, humans and a stylized sun. The bicolor tradition is evident on several figures. The grotto is so small that only a few people can crowd in. In fact, it is on such a small scale and the art so simple that one cannot help imagining that it was a playhouse for Cochimí children—hence its unofficial name, the "Playhouse Cave." Look for dark stains on the ceiling from ancient campfires. The exterior of the site has been vandalized by Mexicans armed with spray cans, but the art was not damaged. The grotto is easy to locate; park on the north side of the highway and sight 359°. The grotto is located among the largest boulders forming the skyline.

172   The "fat" trees next to the road are copalquín, or elephant trees, members of the sumac family. Endemic to Baja and widespread, they seem to prosper in poor conditions, sometimes becoming great prostrate giants on desolate lava beds where nothing else grows. They bear two colors of flowers, some white with touches of pink, others pink to light red. Note that the compound leaves are small, that the branchlets are gray, and that balls of parasitic orange dodder grow on many individuals; these observations will be needed to distinguish copalquín from an almost identical species that will be described shortly.

174+   **Cataviña.** PEMEX (MN, D improbable), cafes, grocery, tires. The Hotel La Pinta has rooms, restaurant, bar, pool, tennis court, horseback riding and local hikes, as well as a Magnasin pump. The RV park has full hookups, restrooms and showers, although things almost never work. The park has been landscaped with desert plants, including copalquín, just described. However, if you look closely you will note that some of the "fat trees" in the park are not copalquín; a few have red-brown branchlets, and their compound leaves are much smaller. These are torote, also called elephant trees. Despite being almost indistinguishable at first glance and having an overlapping range, they are not even in the same family as copalquín; they belong to the torchwood family. Dodder does not seem to grow on torote. These specimens are transplanted, but the two species can be seen growing side by side in the wild in many locations in this region, including along the road to the beginning of the Manila Palm Oasis hike near Bahía de los Angeles.

176 Paved road northeast (signed) to Rancho Santa Ynés, 0.7 mile. Rooms, bunk beds, showers, hot food and cold beer are available, making it a favorite with motorcyclists, bicyclists and campers.

SIDETRIP TO "MISSION IMPOSSIBLE"

A four-wheel-drive road runs from Rancho Santa Ynés across a boulder-strewn desert and sandy arroyos to Misión Santa María. Founded in 1767, the mission was abandoned two years later when the Jesuits were expelled by royal decree. Graced with plenty of water, the site has many stately palms and pools, and the thousands of frogs never object to a few skinny-dippers. Some adobe walls still stand, and it is not hard to trace out how the Jesuits and their converts struggled to bring "civilization" to this remote region. There is another attraction—the road is one of Baja's worst, so much so that the mission has been dubbed "Mission Impossible." Set aside three hours for the driving portion of the trip in to the mission. Yes, that's correct, three hours; driving faster than four or five miles an hour will endanger your vehicle and perhaps its occupants.

Start in front of the two large boulders forming the entrance to the restaurant/bunkhouse complex. Set odometer and drive north, make a right (060°) turn in about 100 yards, and another right (140°) in about 200 more yards to get around a fenced corral/storage yard. The road then curves left (060°) and crosses a sandy arroyo. Take the right (050°) fork at Mile 0.7 and the left (030°) at Mile 0.8. At this point you should begin climbing a sandy ridge, and since there are no crossroads from this point on (as of 1991), you can't get lost. At Mile 1.7 you will encounter a difficult arroyo crossing, with deep holes, loose rock and an upgrade of 14%. Walk this first—if you are not absolutely sure you can cross this arroyo with no difficulty, turn back while you can. If your vehicle makes this one, you should be able to drive within walking distance of the mission. The road continues, crossing a number of arroyos and a long stretch of fairly flat desert. At Mile 9.7 the Cortez can be seen ahead; the prominent point in the distance is Punta Final. At Mile 12 enter a steep downgrade, with loose rock making it difficult to avoid slipping sideways. At Mile 12.4 stop and note the palm grove ahead—the mission site lies ahead twice the distance to the palm grove. This point is the limit most vehicles can go without undue risk.

Stop here and walk to the mission, which will take about forty minutes, one way. If you insist on tempting fate by driving, walk the route first; just ahead lie a number of extremely bad downgrades, with loose rock, huge holes and bad ruts. You might get in safely, but getting out might be something else again.

Back on the Transpeninsular Highway at KM 176

The highway southeast from this point has long, gentle grades, mostly up, until KM 192, then traverses generally level dry-lake country with only occasional grades to KM 25, south of Parador Punta Prieta.

187 **Rancho San Ignacito**. Food and drink.

192+ **Rancho Jaraguay** (signed). There are several gold mines in the vicinity.

205 Mother Nature stockpiled a large supply of boulders here to spread over the desert as she did around Cataviña, but the job was never finished.

229+ Road northeast (signed) to Puerto Calamajué, Bahía San Luis Gonzaga, Puertecitos and San Felipe. See Chapter 16 for a description.

230+ **Rancho Nuevo Chapala**. Food and drink. Laguna Chapala, to the northeast, is dry for years at a time, and its hard, flat surface, marred only by deep polygonal cracks and a thick layer of dust, was a welcome relief for drivers before the Transpeninsular was opened, permitting high speeds and easy driving, if only for a few miles. However, it has no

As dusk falls, a Baja 1000 biker races south.

outlet, so when rain finally came a lake formed that could be three miles in length and a yard deep. As the water dried, mud of unimaginable depths formed. Nothing, neither man nor beast nor vehicle, could conquer the mud, and travelers had to pick their way around the rocky margin of the lake, at the cost of many shredded tires.

232+   The trees on the southwest side of the road with dagger-like leaves resembling the Joshua tree of the United States are dátilillos. Growing from this region to the Cape, they are often cut into fence posts, many of which take root and produce a living fence. They are very common, sometimes forming great open "forests," especially along the El Arco-San Francisquito road. They can be confused with dátil, noted at KM 104+, but dátilillos are generally much taller and may have branches extending anywhere from the trunk, and dátil leaves are shorter, being six to fourteen inches long.

239   Crest of a ridge, magnificent desert views ahead.

280   **Parador Punta Prieta**. The PEMEX (M) here is in a key location, but it has the worst record for reliability on the entire Transpeninsular. The cafeteria may be open, there is a small cafe, and the junk yard across the highway is a good source of parts. Mechanical repairs and towing service may be available. The RV park is not in operation, but you might be able to park for the night. Road east to Bahía de los Angeles.

SIDETRIP TO BAHÍA DE LOS ANGELES

11+   Road north to Tinaja de Yubay.

Mike studiously avoids looking at a broken beam above him while climbing out of Mina Luz de Mexico, east of Desengaño.

SIDETRIP TO TINAJA DE YUBAY

Known since ancient times, Yubay has played an important part in Baja history. Because it was the only permanent, year-round water hole for many miles, most travelers passing through the region stopped here, including such historical figures as Link, Consag, Crespi and Serra, and modern adventurers Arthur North and Harry Crosby. Although its drainage is only several hundred acres, impervious rock and the shade from surrounding bluffs insure that the forty-by-twenty-foot pond rarely drops below its normal five-foot depth. The place is beautiful, with white sand and emerald waters surrounded by steep granite walls, and a visit makes an interesting day hike. Since rains sweep the site clean, swimming is fine. Although early travelers complained that it was hard to find, you should have no difficulty. Turn north 0.2 mile east of the KM 11 marker onto a pickup road and set odometer. Take the right (010°) fork at Mile 3.5 and continue north. At Mile 6.0 go east on a little-used sandy road, which ends at a turn-around spot at Mile 8.4. At this point observe the large stony massif to the northeast, capped with a thin, dark horizontal stratum. Yubay is located up an arroyo in the massif, bearing 035°. A round-trip hike takes two hours plus exploring and swimming time.

In early 1991 hikers found Yubay filled in and showing only a few small pools. Apparently heavy rains had carried large quantities of sand into the pool. Based on hundreds of years of recorded history, Mother Nature should soon return it to its former glory.

The area is heavily mineralized, and collectors have found pink and green tourmaline. Mina Desengaño, northwest of the fork at Mile 3.5, was a thriving enterprise in the 1930s, planes flying in monthly to carry out gold.

Back on the highway to Bahía de los Angeles at KM 11+

21   Elephant tree forest.
44   Pickup road south (signed) to Misíon San Borja.

SIDETRIP TO MISÍON SAN BORJA

Set odometer. Take the right (245°) fork at Mile 2.1 and the left (180°) fork at Mile 4.0. The area is mineralized; note the quartz pavement at Mile 4.7 and the broad band of quartz on the hill at Mile 12.8. Deer, coyote and many species of birds inhabit this area. Take the left (165°) fork at Mile 15.0 and arrive at the mission at Mile 22.4. Driven at safe speeds, this will take about three hours. The handsome stone church, built by the Dominicans in 1801 of stone quarried in the surrounding cliffs and remaining in use until 1818, is the first well-preserved mission building south of the border. Treasure hunters have damaged its walls looking for hidden gold, and its two bells have been stolen (a cow bell now takes their place). A hot spring and a cold spring are located a five-minute hike, 155° from the mission, an old kiln can be seen near the graveyards, and stone aqueducts are visible in the orchards. A few people still live in the vicinity, so respect their privacy and avoid walking in the gardens. The church is still in use, and you may be asked for a small donation.

Back on the highway to Bahía de los Angeles at KM 44

49	Boojum forest.
51+	Road south.

SIDETRIP TO "MANILA PALM OASIS"

An interesting day hike can be made to a palm oasis in the mountains west of Bahía de los Angeles. Four-tenths of a mile east of the KM 51 marker, turn south on a dirt pickup road and set odometer. At Mile 2.1 a torote and a copalquín grow side-by-side. At Mile 2.3 the road turns into a sandy wash and gets too soft for two-wheel-drive vehicles. As you approach Mile 2.7 the road will run directly toward what appears to be a low, rounded hill, but what is actually the end of a ridge, where the trail begins. Hike left (southeast) up the sandy arroyo, which becomes steeper and more rocky and meanders wildly, doubling back on itself many times like a gigantic water slide. Arrive at the lower end of the oasis at Minute 120.

Back on the highway to Bahía de los Angeles at KM 51+

52+	Beautiful vistas of the Cortez.
65	**Bahía de los Angeles**.

BAHÍA DE LOS ANGELES

In the days before the Transpeninsular, no place symbolized American images of Baja California better than Bahía de los Angeles. After three or four long, hard days in a four-wheel-drive truck, jolting across hundreds of miles of terribly rough road, a brilliant sapphire-blue bay studded with brown islands suddenly appeared over the last rise, everything tinted slightly mauve by the mysterious Cortez haze. A tiny outpost of civilization could be found at the foot of the mountain, where friendly fishermen lived in palm-thatched adobe homes, everything and everyone dominated by the desert wilderness on one side, the incredible blue bay on the other. Mama and Papa Diaz provided accommodations, food, gasoline, cold beer and advice to sturdy four-wheelers and occasional pilots from the north, all of whom loved the place for its solitude, inaccessibility, pristine beauty and fine fishing.

The completion of the Transpeninsular brought change; the village slowly grew, a small semipermanent community of Americans was established, fishing declined a bit and litter became a problem. The once virtually deserted shoreline north and south of town is slowly filling up with homes, shanties and "permanent" trailer sites. However, the village and its surrounding bay are still as unspoiled as any place in Baja that can be reached by paved road. In keeping with its old image, the town is friendly, unpretentious and a bit rough around the edges. Sadly, Papa died recently. There seems little danger the town will go through a rowdy and boisterous phase like San Felipe, since it is too far from the border to encourage visits by the drink-raise-hell-and-go-home-Sunday crowd. It isn't paradise, for summers can be extremely hot, and in winter gravity winds funnel down from the canyons to the west at fifty miles an hour for as long as a week, turning inflatable boats into zeppelins and confining RVers to canasta. In any event, a visit to Bahía de los Angeles is always one of the high points of any trip to Baja.

Casa Diaz (1) and Villa Vita (2) have rooms for rent. With a restaurant, a bar and a pool, the latter is a close approximation to a U.S. motel, although its maintenance ranges from fair to poor, depending on the unpredictable whims of the management. Villa Vita's RV park (across the street) is also frequently in poor condition, with a dump station and possible electric and water hookups. Guillermo's (3) has full hookups, showers and restrooms, often in bad repair, and a restaurant; Casa Diaz full hookups, showers and restrooms. Town electric and water utilities tend to be unreliable. Self-contained RVs can park on the beach north to Punta la Gringa, but be careful of tidal flooding in lower areas; I stepped out of my trailer door one morning into the Cortez! I finally located my motorcycle when I saw a handlebar sticking out of the water. The PEMEX (N) frequently runs out—in early 1991 the town was without fuel for three weeks—so buy gas before you need it. Despite the sign on the highway leading into town, Magnasin is not currently (1991) offered. Diesel is sometimes available at a garage (4) near Casa Diaz. This garage also makes mechanical and welding repairs. There is no butane yard, but some of the stores offer gravity fills—ask around. There are no customs, immigration or COTP offices. Postal matters are handled informally; outgoing mail is left at the PEMEX and it collects until someone goes to the U.S. Incoming mail is handled by the grocery store at the south end of town—see the map. With permission of Casa Diaz, incoming mail can be received through their post office box in Ensenada. There are no auto parts or hardware stores, laundromats or commercial transportation. Some of the businesses in town keep siesta hours from one to three in the afternoon.

Raul Perez, a local resident, has a twenty-six foot *panga* in which he takes groups on natural-history, camping, fishing, diving and exploring trips throughout the area. From March through early June he takes birding groups to Isla Raza to see the elegant and royal terns, and Heerman's and yellow-legged gulls (more on Raza in the next chapter). In addition, he has a sixteen-passenger bus for trips to see the local Cochimí art, available as road conditions permit. He speaks excellent English and has a thorough knowledge of the local flora and fauna. The location of his home is shown on the map (5) and his address is listed in Appendix A.

Since 1974 Glendale Community College has sponsored the Baja California Field Studies Program at Bahía de los Angeles. From a single class in marine ecology, the program has expanded to include courses in marine biology, marine ecology, marine invertebrates, geology, natural history, and the geography and history of Baja California, as well as in student leadership, first aid, philosophy, physical education, Spanish, English, psychology and other subjects. From a field station (6) known as "Estación del Mar Cortes," the program exposes students to the area's natural beauty and rich and complex ecosystem; biology and ecology students are often out in the bay or exploring nearby islands. The Spanish classes provide a unique experience in Mexican culture; students go into town and regularly interact with the local

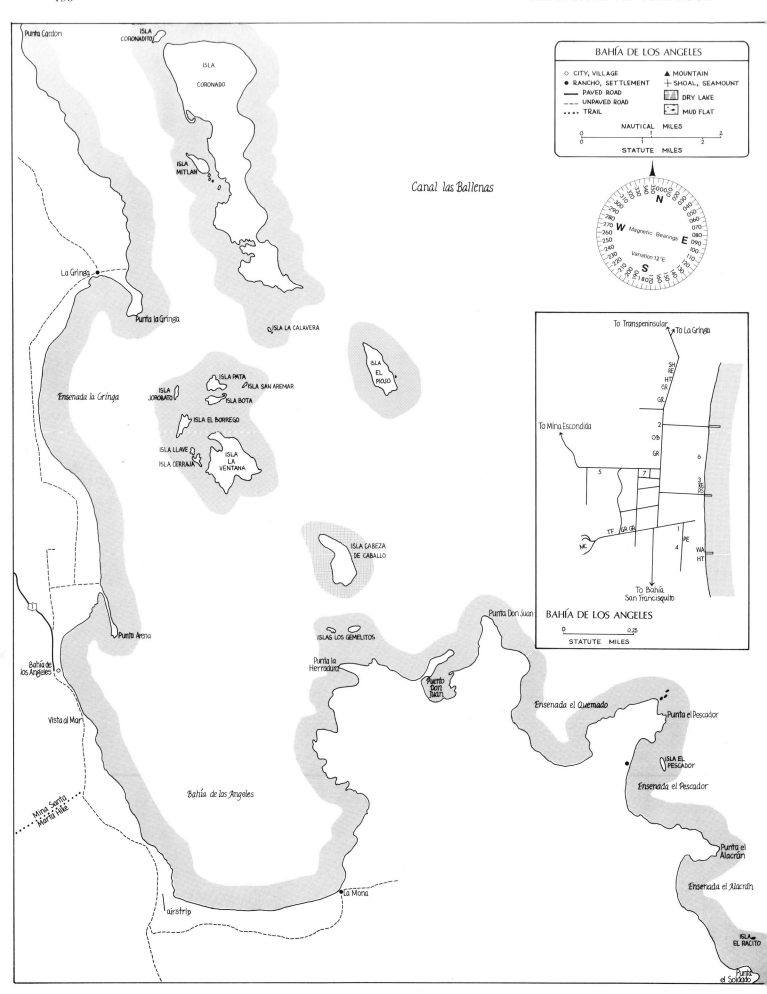

Punta Cardon

ISLA
CORONADITO

ISLA
CORONADO

ISLA
MITLAN

Canal las Ballenas

BAHÍA DE LOS ANGELES

○ CITY, VILLAGE   ▲ MOUNTAIN
● RANCHO, SETTLEMENT   ┼ SHOAL, SEAMOUNT
— PAVED ROAD   DRY LAKE
--- UNPAVED ROAD
···· TRAIL   MUD FLAT

NAUTICAL   MILES

STATUTE   MILES

N
W   Magnetic Bearings   E
Variation 12°E
S

La Gringa

Punta la Gringa

○ ISLA LA CALAVERA

ISLA
EL
PIOJO

Ensenada la Gringa

ISLA PATA
ISLA SAN AREMAR
ISLA
JOROBATO   ISLA BOTA

ISLA EL BORREGO

ISLA LLAVE   ISLA
ISLA CERRAJA   LA
                    VENTANA

To Transpeninsular
To La Gringa

SH
RE
HT
GR

GR

To Mina Escondida   2
OB
GR   6

5   7

3
RE
PS

TF GR GR   1
MC   4   PE
                             WA
                             HT

To Bahía
San Francisquito

BAHÍA DE LOS ANGELES

STATUTE   MILES

ISLA CABEZA
DE CABALLO

Punta Arena

Punta Don Juan

ISLAS LOS GEMELITOS

Punta la
Herradura

Puerto
Don
Juan

Ensenada el Quemado

Punta el Pescador

Bahía de
los Angeles ○

Vista al Mar

ISLA EL
PESCADOR

Ensenada el Pescador

Bahía de los Angeles

Mina Santa
Marta Hike

Punta el
Alacrán

Ensenada el Alacrán

● La Mona

airstrip

ISLA
EL RACITO

Punta
el Soldado

people, and part of the final exam consists of staging theater skits in Spanish in the town plaza. Course offerings change from year to year, and current information can be obtained from program coordinator José Mercadé at the college address listed in Appendix A. The classes are open to all applicants, not just Glendale students.

A fine museum has been constructed with contributions of money, materials, artifacts and volunteer labor, and land donated by the local *ejido*. The Museo de Naturaleza y Cultura (7) is open afternoons and has many fine displays, including geological samples, shells, fossil ammonites, Cochimí art and artifacts, and displays depicting life on rural ranches, and a replica of a mine shaft complete with railroad, ore cart and hanging buckets. The skeleton of a young gray whale hangs from the ceiling. Ore samples from local mines are given away, and books and T-shirts are sold to support the museum. A slide show on local fish, birds, turtles and history is presented twice a month. Don't miss this unusual and interesting museum!

The bay is known primarily for yellowtail from late April or early May through October, and dolphin, sierra and yellowfin tuna are also present in the hottest months, white sea bass a bit earlier. There are many other species, and the fishery resembles Southern California, with ocean whitefish, several kinds of rockfish and even sheephead around, the leopard grouper and pargo found elsewhere in the Cortez being uncommon. The result is perhaps the most mixed of "mixed bags" available in Baja, and it is not uncommon to encounter twenty and even thirty species during a week's fishing vacation. Big fish still inhabit the area; in 1988 Rafael Cuevas caught a 430-pound black sea bass on 80-pound-test line. Although good catches are possible throughout the year, the cold months tend to be spotty. *Pangas* and guides can be arranged at Guillermo's and Casa Diaz, as well as through Raul Perez. Live bait is not available for sale, but can be taken with Lucky Joes or snagged with treble hooks near Punta Arena or several miles to the south of the point.

The bay provides good jigging and trolling, especially around the islands. The most productive locations include the east coast of Isla Coronado and the reefs off its north and southeast points, and east of Isla Cabeza de Caballo. The deep water of Canal las Ballenas yields rockfish, various basses and ocean whitefish, but because of its swift currents fishing ventures must be planned around the tide tables. Shorecasting with cut bait produces sand bass, triggerfish, guitarfish and rays. In spring the shoreline from Punta Arena north to La Gringa is a good place for yellowfin croaker, and halibut to fifteen pounds are taken in the inner harbor. Shorecasting equipment is an asset, for it may be the only technique possible during windy periods. Incidentally, when asking a local fishing guide to take you to Coronado, San Aremar or El Borrego, you may get a blank look—departing from their official names, local usage has identified these islands as Smith, Rasita and Flecha, respectively.

Whale- and bird-watchers can remain engrossed for days or weeks on end. More than a dozen species of whales and dolphins have been seen in the Canal, including blue, finback, gray, Bryde's, Minke, humpback, pilot, sperm, pygmy sperm, killer and false killer whales, and bottlenose and common dolphins. Bryde's whales are the most common, more so than fin whales, for which they are often mistaken. Bryde's whales are seen most frequently in winter, especially January, when they feed on large squid. Fin whales cruise the Bahía de los Angeles area and the Midriff region year-round, peaking in the Canal in spring and summer. Sperm whales are less common, and are seen most frequently in February. One party recently had the good fortune to see a baby blue, apparently only just weaned. Grays are encountered only rarely. Dolphins put on a great show for almost any passing boat and sometimes break into organized groups in Puerto Don Juan, apparently herding forage fish.

At least fifty species of birds are seen around the bay and its islands, including yellow-legged gulls, a Cortez "almost endemic," and such expected species as pelicans and pink-footed and sooty shearwaters, and various terns, petrels, cormorants, boobies and other sea and wading birds. The less-expected include Pacific loon, redhead, common goldeneye, red-breasted merganser, south polar skua, Clark's nuthatch, American robin and scarlet tanager. There are nesting ospreys on Islas la Ventana, Coronado and El Pescador, a pelican colony on Isla el Piojo, and a frigatebird resting site on the southeast point of Coronado.

Although the area has been popular with divers for many years, the dive shop that was once here has closed, and divers must therefore go self-contained. The channel between Coronado and Isla Mitlan offers good snorkeling, and Isla Coronadito has good spearfishing. The east coast of Coronado has fine diving, especially about one-third of the way south from the north cape, where rocks and boulders form caves and small crevices. Many species of fish will be encountered, including Gulf opaleye, browncheek blennies, triplefins, finescale triggerfish and Cortez damselfish, as well as sea fans and soft corals. Spearfishermen should find good populations of yellowtail and Gulf grouper. An excellent reef continues from the southeastern tip of the island. The east coast of Piojo is known for its colorful nudibranchs. I once made fifty free-dives to thirty-five feet to photograph one of these purple and gold-lamé beauties and didn't recover from aching Eustachian tubes and palpitating sinuses for three days. Many octopus live in holes in rocky and gravel areas throughout the bay. Although beach diving is generally poor, the reefs north of La Gringa have brilliantly colored sea fans and encrusting sponges, the latter in a dozen hues.

The fifty-foot wooden fishing vessel *Marcelo* ran onto the reef between Ventana and Cabeza de Caballo in 1983, and her wreck now makes a fine dive site. Lying approximately four hundred yards southeast of the prominent "window" landmark on Ventana, the reef is about a hundred yards long. A half-dozen shallow rock pinnacles are barely covered at moderate tides, so take care approaching the site. The bulk of the wreck is about twenty feet from the southeastern pinnacle in ten to fifty feet of water. Deeper sections of the reef have the most colorful sea life in the bay, and a proposal has been made to make it a national marine park. Local divers report a large wreck in deep water southwest of Ventana. About 1981, a fishing boat burned and sank off the east side of Isla el Racito, a low, rocky islet 700 yards north of Punta el Soldado, and the wreck presents one of the finest displays of plant and animal life in the Cortez, a great attraction for underwater photographers. It lies in ten to sixteen feet of water about a hundred feet off the east side, midway between the north and south points.

There are concrete launch ramps at Villa Vita, Guillermo's and Casa Diaz, all with parking available. The best anchorage is inside Punta Arena, or near La Gringa. When these get too choppy or dusty, boaters like to move to Don Juan. This almost-landlocked, all-weather cove is a popular jumping-off point for boaters headed for the Midriff region, described in the next chapter. A fine sea cave is reported in the vicinity; when anchored in the cove, go ashore where the spit forming the north shore joins the "mainland." Hike north across the spit to the bay and then southwest along the shore, and the cave will be found just above sea level. Boats coasting south from Don Juan will encounter open anchorages at Ensenada el Pescador, Ensenada el Alacrán and Bahía las Ánimas, located six, eight and fifteen miles from Don Juan. The first two provide protection from north and west winds, the last from all but north, and their sandy beaches permit easy landings. Because Isla el Pescador (Isla Rocallosa) is a sensitive bird breeding area, no one should go ashore on the island from February through June. A tourist camp has been constructed on the shore of the bay opposite the island. There are no good anchorages along the forty-four-mile coast from Ánimas south to Bahía San Francisquito, but the following chapter describes anchorages at the offshore islands.

Even a Trail 90 can't conquer everything.

The area is prime territory for small-boat and kayak sailors. Three basic choices are available, in ascending order of effort: stay close, go south to Ánimas, or head for Guardian Angel. Ventana has a good campsite on its northwest side in a small cove with a sand-and-gravel beach. A trail leads to the peak on the island. The cut between Islas Pata and Bota is well-protected and there is a beach of crushed shell on Pata. Piojo has a good sand beach at its south end, although it smells of guano and its name might cause concern (a *piojo* is a louse). Coronado, especially, has good campsites, one east of the tidal spit on the southwest side of the volcano, another opposite Isla Mitlan, and a third on the sandy beaches of the cove on the east side that almost splits the island in two. The last is good if the weather is unsettled, since an easy portage can be made to the opposite cove, allowing you to "switch sides" if the wind comes up. However, tie down your kayak if you are camping in this spot, for several have been carried away by the wind.

A more demanding trip can be made by journeying east out of the bay and then southeast down the coast to Ánimas. Since it can be reached by road, a relaxing one-way trip of only twenty-one miles or a round-trip of forty-two is possible. The sand beaches at Don Juan, and Ensenada el Quemado (just north of Punta el Pescador), Ensenada el Pescador and Ensenada el Alacrán provide good camping. Ánimas has a number of good campsites, especially in a tiny cove near Punta las Ánimas, and offers good local exploring and snorkeling in the mangrove areas. Kayakers and small-boat sailors are not likely to find any regular source of water along this stretch of coast, although the number of temporary fish camps seems to be increasing each year, and there is a tourist camp at Pescador.

The most venturesome may wish to head from La Gringa past ten miles of alternating rocky bluffs and small pebble beaches to the deserted white sand beaches of Bahía Guadalupe (Bahía de los Remidios). The beach near Punta Remidios is protected by the low, rocky point. Guardian Angel, only seven miles northeast, is described in a later section. The current in the Canal can be heavy, and as noted earlier, and winds can be fierce, so take off at first light and keep a "weather eye." Try to use a flood tide to help push you toward Puerto Refugio, the prime destination on the island. Mexican 1:50,000 topos H12C42, Campo Juárez, and H12C52, Bahía de los Angeles, provide details from Remidios to the western side of Ánimas. Mexican 1:50,000 topos of the island are not available, but 1:250,000 topo H12-7, Isla Ángel de la Guarda, provides some detail.

Boardsailors also have many choices. Many just like to explore the islands. Some enjoy getting someone drive them to La Gringa and making a downwind run to play in the islands, returning directly to town. Still others like to take advantage of every opportunity; when the famous winds are blowing they try speed sailing, when it's calmer they play around the islands, and if it stops they head for Santa Rosalillita. Most avoid the southern part of the bay, since winds are cut off by the surrounding topography and tend to be gusty and erratic.

Collectors will find copper minerals at Mina El Toro north of La Gringa, reached by taking a pickup road seven miles north from the vicinity of the fishing cooperative. The volcano on Coronado should provide igneous specimens. "Desert rose," a microscopically crystallized variety of chalcedony quartz, can be found at a site across the bay. Heading south on the "main drag" in town, turn right (210°) at the white concrete-block fence marking the Casa Diaz complex, and then make the first left (135°) and set your odometer. Signs along this part of the bay indicate that the beaches are marine mammal haul-out sites and that trespass and camping are prohibited. The real objects of concern here are nesting migratory birds and turtles, and the signs must be heeded. Turn east at Mile 4.4. The road follows the curve of the bay, eventually turning north near the end of an abandoned landing strip. Adjacent to the first group of buildings in the American-owned settlement known as La Mona, north of the end of the airstrip, turn east on the first road encountered. Follow the road to its end; the sites are located in ravines to the north and east.

Popular shelling sites are found along the beach at low tide from Punta Arena to La Gringa. Net fishermen frequently snag unusual specimens in deep water, especially beautiful hard corals and occasional specimens of black coral, which are approaching the northern end of their range, judging by their size. The museum has a shell collection of 500 local species.

The two-day trip to Mina Santa Marta is the most interesting backpacking venture in the area. The mine was one of the great engineering schemes in Baja in the late 1800s. Ore was transported from the mine across a deep canyon by an overhead bucket-and-cable system and dumped into narrow-gauge railroad cars, which carried it to an incline railway with two pairs of rails. The weight of the descending cart would pull an empty one up the incline. At the bottom, the ore was again dumped into rail cars and towed by a small steam locomotive to a stamping mill on the edge of the bay. A round-trip hike to the mine takes two days, with no water at any point. Drive south from town on the road described above, and at Mile 2.0 turn west at the town dump and park (not a very auspicious place to begin). Hike west for several minutes to where you encounter the lower railroad grade running southwest. You will see stone work, rock fills and cuts at the beginning of the steep incline railway, and a pack-animal trail with many switchbacks paralleling it. The route turns west up a very steep section, and at Minute 210 you will come out on a fairly level ridge. Look west and note the large notches carved into the head of the ridge on the canyon's western side. The cable-and-bucket system ran from the mine, passed over two large wheels sitting in these notches and crossed the canyon. The upper railroad grade continues west, following the contour line into the canyon, where a great deal of stone work was necessary to provide a level grade. The trail heads up from the level spot, follows a small gully northwest, and then runs along the ridge in a series of switchbacks. Desert bighorn have been seen in this area. The trail then turns west, and you should arrive at the mine at Minute 390.

Farther to the south, the Las Flores area is worth a visit. First worked around 1890, Mina San Juan, located in the mountains about eleven miles south of town, was large and profitable, yielding $2 million in silver until production ended with the Mexican Revolution. Ore was carried from the mine by a narrow-gauge railroad to an overhead bucket-and-cable system, which led to another railroad, ending at a smelter at Las Flores. A tiny, almost toy-like locomotive used on the "San Juan-Las Flores Railroad" is on display in the town park.

To visit Las Flores drive south from town on the road described earlier to Mile 9.4. A smelter and boiler lie on the west side of the road. The buildings and machinery were salvaged long ago, but the stone vault used to store the silver still stands, its walls three feet thick. Old bricks that lined the smelter can be found occasionally, some having the inscription "Laclede, St. Louis." One had the date "1826" cast in its side. Small ceramic cups used as molds to form ingots also can be seen. Many artifacts from Las Flores are on display at the museum.

The road through Las Flores continues on to Bahía San Francisquito, eighty-two miles (from town). This road has been graded and improved, making it possible to bring in moderate RVs and trailerboats, and although it is badly washboarded, it is a far better way to get to the bay than that through El Arco.

The big island off Bahía de los Angeles to the northeast is Guardian Angel, forty-six miles long. Once a part of the peninsula and now moved thirty miles south by tectonic forces, the island is the result of sea floor spreading about a million years ago, its rocks being of Miocene volcanic and Pliocene sedimentary origin. The geology is colorful, some areas graced with broad layers of gray, white, pink, green and red. Old reports indicate silver has been found, and rumors persist that mineral collectors have found geodes from an unknown source. In spite of being mountainous and second

John Anglin never stays lost for long.

in land area in the Cortez only to Isla Tiburón, it has no permanent surface water, although a few sparse palms indicate underground water.

Although there are historical records and archaeological evidence of temporary fishing and sea-lion-hunting camps, the island has never been permanently inhabited. Other than three rough airstrips cleared at Puerto Refugio, west of Punta Rocosa and on the east side about one-third of the way up from the south tip at an old scallop camp, a small population of feral cats left by fishermen years ago, and one foreign weed, the island and its flora and fauna are in virtually pristine condition. Seemingly barren from a distance, it supports moderate numbers of agave, cacti, cardón, elephant trees (both kinds—torote and copalquín) and, on the high peaks at the north end, boojum. In all, 199 species of vascular plants, 15 reptiles and amphibians, and 3 small land mammals have been recorded.

Bird-watchers might add great blue heron, reddish and snowy egrets, osprey, ring-billed gull, lesser scaup, surf scooter, snowy plover, belted kingfisher, American oystercatcher, burrowing and great horned owls, kestrel, prairie falcon, red-tailed hawk, sage thrasher, Say's phoebe, Hutton's and gray vireos, vermilion flycatcher, Chipping, Lincoln's, Brewer's, Savannah and white-crowned sparrows, phainopepla, lark bunting, Wilson's, MacGillivray's, Nashville, yellow-rumped and orange-crowned warblers, green-tailed towhee, rufous hummingbird, hermit thrush and Bewick wren to their check lists, as well as the usual sea birds. The yellow-legged gull nests on the island.

The most scenic and interesting area is Puerto Refugio at the north end, the first good anchorage southeast of Bahía Gonzaga. It is satisfactory in weather from all directions, but you may have to move around to stay out of the chop. Landings can be made in a number of small coves along Refugio's southern shore, and sandy beaches provide excellent camping. Each of its islands has a distinct character. Granito (Isla Alcatraz) has sea lions, brown pelicans and oystercatchers, and divers will find a reef extending from its northwestern tip. Mejía is known for lizards, giant cardón and nesting osprey, with a reef extending north. Tiny Roca Blanca has sheer dropoffs onto sand bottoms. Brant's cormorants have been known to nest on Roca Vela, two miles southwest of Mejía. Many kinds of gamefish visit the area, and enormous pileups of yellowtail have been reported. The bay is so unusual and interesting that it is a favorite destination for boaters out of Bahía de los Angeles, in spite of the fact it is a forty-mile run, partly because of the whales that may be encountered in the Canal.

Sea caves are reported on Guardian Angel's east side. An anchorage protected from south and west weather is available in Caleta Púlpito. An open anchorage sheltered from prevailing winds can be made south of Punta Rocosa. The deep reefs off the point are noted for big groupers and fine SCUBA diving. Kayakers and small-boat sailors should use care in the vicinity of Rocosa; when the prevailing north winds that "bounce" off the northwest-southeast range of mountains oppose a flood tide the area turns into a maelstrom of white water.

Isla Estanque (Isla la Víbora), a small island near the southern end on the east side, contains an almost landlocked saltwater pond. It makes an excellent all-weather anchorage for shallow-draft boats and has the added attraction of a strange underwater garden. Algae thrive at certain times of the year, and a dive will reveal a world of muted, almost formless brown shapes. A strange stillness prevails; gamefish do not enter the pond, and what animal life there is moves slowly—it is a noncompetitive world in slow motion. The lack of bright color, especially green, brings on a somber mood and reminds one of Cousteau's television program about Lake Titicaca, without the frogs. Don't try to enter the pond from the south, since a reef extends across from the big island. Round the island counterclockwise and enter the pond from the east, parallel to and north of the reef. The pond goes to four fathoms, but we once scraped over the rocky entrance in a sloop drawing seven feet. Bats inhabit much of Baja, and you may see a special kind near Estanque and south to Isla San José, one that lives on seafood. Watch for ghostly forms skimming over the waves at dusk, catching small fish with their claws.

The south end of Guardian Angel provides fine camping, but there is something you must know: the bats don't eat bugs. Reeve, John Anglin and I ran our grossly overloaded fifteen-foot cartopper out to the sandy beaches there one year. The days were glorious—fine weather and great spearfishing for flatfish, sometimes in water only four or five feet deep—but the first night was sheer hell. Any thesaurus can provide scores of adjectives that come close—fiendish, ferocious and frightful are a few—but nothing in English is completely up to the task of describing the *jejenes*. They crawled up our noses and ears and we soon had trickles of blood running down our necks. The wind came up the second night and they disappeared, so over the campfire we composed a ditty—inspired, I think, by Janice Joplin—"Please God, if you'll keep it blowin' from this point hence, I'll give up gettin' the Mercedes Benz." Divine intervention didn't work, and on the third evening Reeve let out a few favorite curses and stalked out of camp into the darkness up the canyon with his bedroll under his arm. Fifteen minutes later he was back with good news—there were no *jejenes* a hundred feet higher than our camp. He had found the secret, and we slept through the night from then on.

Three days later we were headed southeast for Isla Partida Norte when our prayers were answered, too late and too well—a fierce north wind came up and the boat swamped and sank. After a few anxious minutes it popped to the surface, minus its cargo. The flotation was not adequate to get the gunnels high enough above the waves to allow bailing, so we the emptied two outboard gas tanks and used the anchor line to make a sling between them, lifting the boat. At this point the wind dropped to a flat calm, and after bailing the boat out we paddled back to Guardian Angel with swim fins. It was several hours until we managed to attract a passing boat, but fortunately our cooler had bobbed to the surface with its vital cargo of beer, so we had a few cool ones as we contemplated our latest lesson in small-boat seamanship.

On the Transpeninsular Highway at Parador Punta Prieta

KM	LOCATION
280/0	Start new KM numbering sequence.
13	**Punta Prieta**. Groceries. Fossilized mammal bones fifty-seven million years old have been found near here, including a hyracotherium, a horse the size of a dog. Arsenopyrite, hematite, gold and silver and large, well-formed quartz crystals occur at Mina Columbia, 7 1/2 miles west.
24+	**Rancho la Bachata**. Restaurant. A great deal of low-grade calcite is found nearby, but large, clear two-inch crystals have been dug up 1/2 mile south of the ranch buildings.
25	Gentle to moderate rolling hills to KM 75.
38+	Sedan road west (signed) to Santa Rosalillita.

SIDETRIP TO SANTA ROSALILLITA AND SURROUNDING AREAS

This area is a favorite with surfers and boardsailors. Set odometer. Note the sideroad at Mile 8.1 (but don't turn), and arrive at the beach at Mile 9.6. The road is capable of handling RVs, with one 13% grade, and there is plenty of camping and parking along the beach and in the dunes north of the point. Shallow Bahía Santa Rosalillita is a satisfactory anchorage in prevailing seas, the best between Bahía San Carlos and Cedros. Limited supplies of gasoline and water may be available in the village. The area is rarely visited by sportfishermen or divers.

Boardsailors like the bay for its strong and reliable afternoon winds, large area and range of wave sizes, from calm inside to sizable at the point. Many boardsailors rate "Sandy Point" as the best wave-sailing beach in Baja. The right point break here is reputedly the longest in Baja, some surfers claiming rides of more than a mile. During frontal conditions an endless succession of perfectly formed four-to-eight-foot waves often sweep around the point. However, storms sometimes rearrange bottom contours and move the bar, resulting in rides that fall short of the glowing reports. If this happens, salvation may not be far away. Punta Rosarito to the south is a "magnet for waves," with a reef break good on almost any swell. There are three more surfing areas to the north, with configurations similar to Santa Rosalillita: Punta San Andrés, Punta Prieta (not to be confused with the town of the same name on the Transpeninsular) and Punta María, each a rocky point forming a small bay open to the south. These five places—Rosarito, Rosalillita, San Andrés, Punta Prieta and Punta María—are sufficiently different from one another that if the surf is not good in one place, it usually is at one of the others, making this one of the most reliable surfing and wave-sailing areas in Baja.

Although the coastline north from Santa Rosalillita to Punta María is not often visited by kayakers, it has the makings for a fine trip: easy access by road, plenty of scenery, excellent snorkeling, fishing and foraging, numerous small coves, good campsites with a minimum of litter and ordinarily plenty of wood for evening campfire gatherings. A round-trip involves only about fifty-two miles, making it a pleasant and undemanding five-day trip.

A graded road running to the northwest has improved access to these areas, and the wide, white-sand beaches and uncrowded camping along the coast are worth a trip to see even if you are not a surfer. Other than an occasional ranch and several small fish camps, the area is uninhabited, and the beaches and many campsites are almost free of litter. To get to the new road, return to the sideroad at Mile 8.1, reset odometer and turn northwest (320°) on a graded road, signed "San José de las Palomas." At Mile 4.0 turn left (180°) onto a sedan road, pass Rancho San Andrés, and arrive at an intersection within 1 1/2 miles. Continue straight ahead (230°) between the cliffs (if the weather is wet, take the right fork, 280°). The road will cross mud flats, swing north and arrive at the cove in another 1 1/2 miles. This area, known to surfers as "Alejandro's," has good camping, easy access to the sand beach and a well-shaped but short right point break.

To continue on to Punta Prieta (Punta Negra), return to Mile 4.0 and continue west (280°) until Mile 15.5, where a sharp left turn (160°) onto a pickup road will take you to the beach in a little over two miles. There are a wide sand beach, excellent camping, and reef and beach breaks. Anchorage conditions are poor. Continuing on from Mile 15.5, the improved road ends at Mile 20, and the roads beyond require pickups. The surfing potential at Punta Lobos at Mile 22.4 appears low, but there is good camping, and a four-wheel-drive road through deep sand reaches a fine sandy cove to the west.

At Mile 27.6 take the left (275°) fork, and steer for the arroyo dead ahead. The road will climb the arroyo, swing north, then west and then south, arriving in about four miles at the north coast of Bahía María in the vicinity of a small fish camp. A fine sand cove is located west of the camp. The bay has excellent boardsailing, and the point has right point and reef breaks, and good skin diving. However, the point is 3/4 mile west of the campsite. The locals recommend driving on the beach for 1/3 mile, to where a road can be seen climbing a hill, ending very close to the point. Calculate the tide first and remember that the AAA tow truck is a long way off. The anchorage here is shallow and open, often with refracted swell and surge.

****

GHOST STORY. I was the last to arrive back at camp after a day of exploring Playa María on trail bikes. I had discovered pieces of firewood buried behind the first line of dunes, and it had taken me an hour to pry them loose and drag them back behind my bike. High spirits prevailed, encouraged by glorious weather, good friends and a lobster dinner. We started a fire, but as the flames spread a sudden change in mood struck all of us simultaneously. For no apparent reason the usual happy chatter was absent, and even the normal Honda versus Kawasaki disputes faded into an uneasy silence. As the embers died we fell into a fitful sleep.

Dawn provided no release from our mood. Hoping to obtain more firewood, we returned to the dune with shovels and an ax, and a little digging revealed the source of the wood to be a shipwreck. Large gray timbers soon appeared, embedded with bronze and wrought iron spikes. Hundreds of bronze sheathing nails still protruded from her planking. She was a total wreck and nothing could be determined of her size or shape. Finally we brushed off a timber and found a name burned or scraped into a plank: Jenny Thelin. *We had burned a part of Wolf Larson's ship,* Ghost*!*

The ninety-one-foot schooner Jennie Thelin *was constructed in 1869 near Santa Cruz, CA. Until her stranding at Playa María in 1912, she had a rowdy career involving poaching and transportation of illegal immigrants, with occasional periods spent carrying lumber and guano, and her loss was possibly an insurance fraud. Such infamy could not go unrecognized, and Jack London used the* Thelin *as the model for the* Ghost *in his novel* The Sea Wolf. *The* Thelin's *captain, Alexander McLean, inspired the Wolf Larson character, played by Edward G. Robinson in the 1941 movie.*

The battered bones of the famous ship lying at our feet caused a sense of awe among us. Never destined to take her place in a maritime museum, she will continue to disintegrate until no trace remains. No matter; we would have no hand in dismantling her. We mounted our bikes and rode off, never to disturb her again.

****

The schooner ***Jennie Thelin.***

CHAPTER 11
THE MIDRIFF REGION

The "Midriff" region of the central Cortez contains about fifty-five islands, islets and pinnacles, the major islands being Guardian Angel, Partida Norte, Raza, Salsipuedes, las Ánimas Norte, San Lorenzo, San Esteban, Turners, Tiburón, Patos and San Pedro Martír. (To promote a smoother and more useful flow of information, Guardian Angel was described in the previous chapter.) Remote and unspoiled, all are uninhabited except for fishermen and guano collectors living in temporary camps, plus game wardens, and there are only occasional visitors. The Cortez is less than sixty miles wide at this point and enormous tidal currents race by, forming giant whirlpools and pulling up nutrients from deep waters, which support vast quantities of plankton. These in turn provide food for animals higher in the food chain, and the area is alive with birds and marine mammals, especially dolphins. Fin and Bryde's whales are seen year-round, and blue whales visit the area from late winter to late spring. Gamefish, primarily yellowtail, grouper, cabrilla, and white and black sea bass, are abundant and provide one of the least-stressed fisheries in the Cortez. In warm months yellowfin, marlin and dolphin migrate into the area.

The "Stepping-Stones" Cruise

The waters of the Midriff offer some of the world's finest small-boat cruising. Although there are no all-weather anchorages, a boat crossing from Bahía de los Angeles to Bahía Kino in Sonora never needs to be more than seven miles from land, and some shelter from weather from almost any direction can be found. There are no marinas, parts stores or villages, and little chance of help from passing vessels in case of emergency. Writers pursuing literary effect have given the area an aura of danger and mystery. Ray Cannon's description of a crossing was titled a "Voyage of Terror," due to a storm he encountered. Actually, the weather is normally tranquil, and a well-equipped and seaworthy cruiser, a small sailboat or even a cartopper operated in a conservative manner, can make the voyage safely. I have explored much of the area and crossed the Cortez twice in a fifteen-foot cartop outboard. However, this is not to say that it is always tranquil. Southern *chubascos* can reach the Midriff from mid-May to mid-No-

vember, peaking in August and September, and abnormal water temperatures occasionally cause them to form in other months. During the fall and winter months, passing cold fronts and stagnant high-pressure areas in the southwestern U.S. can cause wipeout conditions in the Midriff, and it is not unheard of for kayakers and small-boaters to have to "hole-up" for a week. There are no reliable weather reports available, and every traveler must have adequate food and water and avoid the temptation to travel if there are any doubts; keep a "weather eye" at all times. If you get into trouble remember that Club Deportivo "Bahía Kino" monitors CB channel 4 and VHF channel 16.

The nearest paved launch ramps in Baja are at Bahía de los Angeles. Many people launching there spend the first night at Puerto Don Juan, sorting out gear and getting things shipshape before starting the crossing the next morning. An alternative is to drive the road from Bahía de los Angeles to Bahía San Francisquito, where trailerboats can be launched over the beach. Inflatables and cartoppers also can be launched, and the resort may have SCUBA air. You could, of course, start in Kino.

Twenty-three miles from Don Juan is Partida Norte (Isla Cardinosa), the first in a chain of islands running southeast to San Lorenzo. The island has an anchorage in a small bay on the northwestern side, and another off a sand beach on the southeastern side. The island has the largest concentrations of petrels in the Cortez. The *jejenes* can be fierce, so be prepared to move. Fishing is best north of the island, and south half-way to Raza. Diving is excellent, especially around Roca Blanca, 1,200 yards north.

Your first impression of Raza, five miles from Partida Norte, is apt to be "ho-hum." Only 150 acres in area and less than a hundred feet high, with sparse vegetation and abundant guano, it seems to be just another tiny, lifeless, rocky island. Not so, for Raza is the scene of a spectacular pageant of conflict, disaster, death and renewal. In March or April vast numbers of Heermann's gulls arrive and begin to scratch out nesting sites. Since every square foot of available land is occupied by these noisy, aggressive birds, it would seem foolhardy for another species to attempt a beachhead. How-

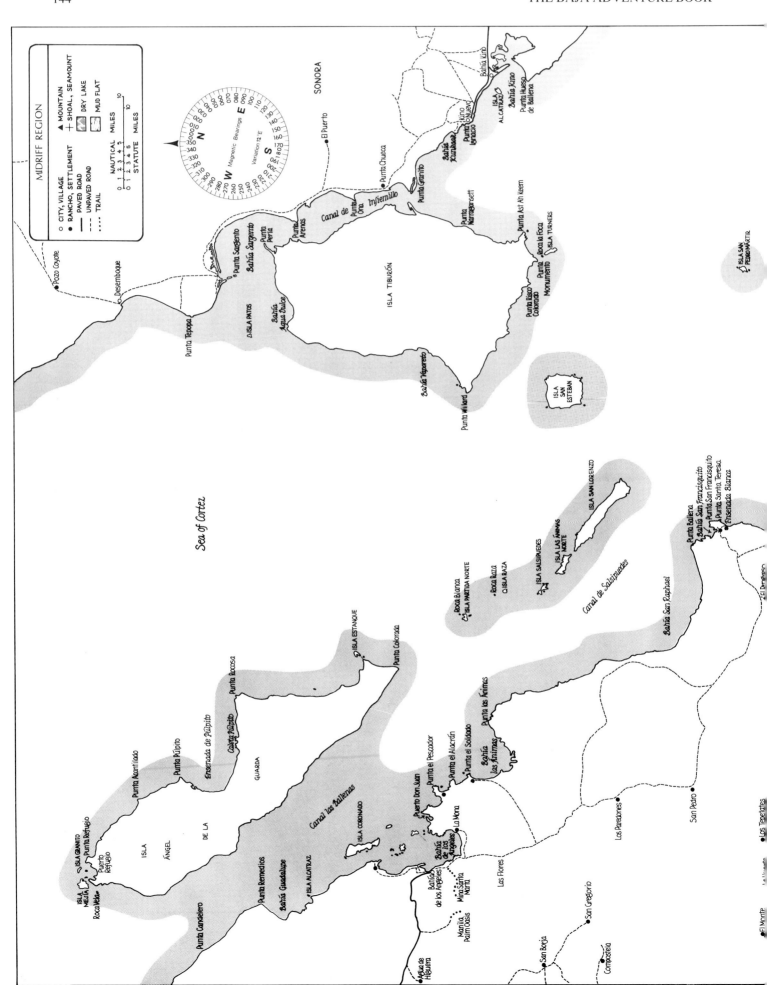

ever, elegant terns and, to a lesser extent, royal terns soon begin to arrive with high strategyand nesting on their minds. Several hundred thousand birds may be on the island at one time.

After walking about for a while, preening themselves with an air of massive indifference, one night the terns suddenly fly into a dense formation, alight in a predetermined location and force the gulls away. By dawn they have assumed a circular defensive formation thirty or forty feet in diameter surrounded by outraged gulls. You could say the gulls were "terned out," but they soon counterattack, strutting about, engaging in rowdy behavior and pecking open freshly laid eggs. By evening many terns have been frightened off and the circle has shrunk by half, but during the night the missing terns return and the circle widens. As days pass, some eggs hatch and a few chicks manage to survive the seesaw battle, enough to insure a stable population.

Besides the Heerman's gulls and the two species of terns, Caraveri's murrelet has been known to nest on Raza. The island is also visited by other species: eared grebe, great egret, greater yellowlegs, wandering tattler, spotted sandpiper, whimbrel, sanderling, least sandpiper, yellow-legged gull and pomarine jaeger have all been seen.

In addition to this natural spectacle, Raza offers a man-made mystery. Piles of stone, some as high as five feet, are scattered throughout the island. Aerial photographs show an amazing 1,100. Theories differ on their purpose and origin. Some people claim the piles were made by egg gatherers, who

discovered that by piling up stones the tern-versus-gull land grab could be eased and egg production increased. Others insist they were constructed by guano collectors who cleared the area to facilitate deposition and collection of valuable fertilizer. Some say Seri Indians from Tiburón used Raza as a burial ground and the piles are monuments. A Seri once told me this was not true, that Raza was used as a penal colony, where prisoners stacked rocks to hold up canvas sun shades. A few claim that there *are* graves on the island, but for guano collectors who expired due to the hot sun and the stench.

Indians collected eggs on Raza for centuries, doing little permanent damage, but by the early 1900s the copper mines at Santa Rosalía developed and the hungry miners had to be fed. Raiders measured the freshness of eggs by their specific gravity; fresh eggs sank in a bucket of water, old ones floated. If there were too many old ones they simply smashed every egg in sight, and the bereaved parents would promptly lay replacements. By the 1960s outboard motors had greatly increased the efficiency of the operation, causing a drastic decline in bird populations, so in 1964 President Lopéz Mateos declared the island a wildlife preserve. Although closed to casual visitors, the "big picture" of the annual nesting spectacle can be seen from a boat. Wardens on the island may provide an escorted tour if you can attract their attention from the lagoon and determine the current regulations before going ashore. Raul Perez provides *panga* trips to the island from Bahía de los Angeles (see page 135).

Raza has a fair anchorage on the south side, but Partida

The mysterious stone "monuments" on Raza.

Norte and Salsipuedes are close and provide more secure conditions. Diving around Raza is good, but not up to the standards of the other islands, although Roca Raza, one mile north, is excellent. Local divers have attempted to locate the end of a huge metal chain found off the northeast tip, but it is so long the water becomes too deep for their hookas.

Salsipuedes, four miles from Raza, is 1 1/2 miles long and is almost pinched in half two-thirds of the way south, forming two coves, one opening north, one south, and both providing good anchorage. Fishing is best on the northeast side, where the bottom is steep and has numerous ledges and small caves harboring black sea bass. Fishing is also excellent for yellowtail, cabrilla and sierra. Diving is good almost anywhere, especially at the pinnacles off the northwest end and on the south reef.

Las Ánimas Norte (Isla San Lorenzo Norte), a little over a mile from Salsipuedes, has several small anchorages, one on the northeastern side, the other at the south end. The east end is known for large grouper and black sea bass in water to 500 feet, and feeding frenzies of yellowtail sometimes cover three or four acres. Diving is good, but the island should not be confused with Isla las Ánimas Sur several hundred miles south.

San Lorenzo, the southernmost island in the chain, is separated by a narrow channel from las Ánimas Norte and is high and steep, with a few narrow gravel beaches. Two small coves on the southwestern side provide anchorages with marginal protection from prevailing winds. Small sand beaches will be found on the western coast three miles from the northwest end and at the southeast tip. Although the island appears to be barren, zalate (wild fig), elephant trees and copal flourish in the canyons. San Lorenzo, las Ánimas Norte and Salsipuedes collectively have the world's largest colony of nesting brown pelicans. Although the yellow-legged gull tends to nest alone or in small groups, the largest number of nests in the world is found on the island. The bottom drops to 2,000 feet within 1/2 mile of shore. Fishing is usually best on the northeast side and to the south.

The Canal de Salsipuedes between the chain of islands and the Baja coast is deep, running to over 800 fathoms in places, and swift tidal currents form huge whirlpools. In the early 1700s, Jesuit Father Juan de Ugarte tried to sail his sloop up the channel, but had to give up after twenty days of continuous effort. Modern sailors and kayakers are apt to be equally frustrated unless their schedules are timed to the tides.

San Esteban is sixteen miles east of the north tip of Salsipuedes and can be seen easily, since it rises to 1,771 feet. Its coast consists primarily of sea cliffs, except for a large gravel beach on the east side. Boats can anchor off the southwest spit. Diving is excellent, especially on the reef extending 1/2 mile off the northeast tip, although there are reports of aggressive sharks. Yellowtail fishing is fine all around the island, including the reef just mentioned. Few thrills in fishing can equal letting down a bait into a horde of silvery shapes streaking erratically through the clear blue water of this reef.

Esteban was formed of volcanic rock extruded as a result of sea-floor spreading during the Pliocene epoch. Being somewhat more remote than most of the larger Cortez islands and about midway between the Baja peninsula and the main-

land, it has the distinctive flora and fauna that might be expected. Birds include house finch, blue-gray gnat catcher, kestrel, shrike, osprey, burrowing owl, verdin and ash-throated flycatcher, as well as an endemic race of black-throated sparrow, *Amphispiza bilineata cana*, and the curved-billed thrasher subspecies *Toxostoma curvirostre insularum*, found only on Esteban and Tiburón. Migrants and wintering birds include Swainson's thrush, vermilion flycatcher, Cassin's kingbird, Hutton's and gray vireos, Bullock's oriole, rufous and Allen's hummingbirds, western flycatcher, hermit thrush, yellow-rumped, orange-crowned, black-throated gray, MacGillvray's and Wilson's warblers, green-tailed towhee, black-headed grosbeak, and four sparrows—white-crowned, Brewer's, Lincoln's and chipping. In addition, there are 117 species of vascular plants, 5 of which are endemic to the island, 8 amphibians and reptiles, 4 of which are endemic, the gigantic blotched chuckwalla *Sauromalus varius* and the small rattlesnake *Crotalus molossus* being the most distinctive.

Although Esteban has no permanent potable water, bands of Seri Indians used to maintain camps on the island, traveling there from the mainland and Tiburón in their reed boats. Other than one endemic species of white-footed mouse, the island has no land mammals, and the Seri diet was mainly sea lion, fish, shell fish, chuckwalla and edible native plants. The San Esteban people were known as great gamblers, and they sometimes engaged in games where the stakes were life and death. Seri legend indicates that the men would challenge each other to a game of "chicken." Climbing to the top of a steep gravel slope that ended at the edge of a cliff high over a rocky beach, each would take his turn sliding down the slope in a large turtle shell. At the last possible moment before plunging over the cliff, each would leap out, and whoever came the closest to the edge was the winner. If someone misjudged his timing and went sailing over the edge, the first man to yell "Your wife is mine" obtained the right to marry the widow-to-be, even if he already had a wife. The cliff can

Lloyd Rice and Jim Purvis fill a goody bag off Tiburón.

be seen on the east side of the island, a short distance north of the main canyon.

I have camped on Esteban, equipped with several large coolers full of ice, vegetables, fresh milk, meat and vast quantities of beer, a nylon canopy to keep the sun off, a radio to keep me entertained, a sleeping bag and an air mattress to allow me to sleep comfortably and an aluminum boat driven by an outboard engine to take me anywhere I wished to go with little effort. I found the experience rather demanding and knew I would be dead in two days should I be deprived of my comforts. One can only marvel at the remarkably hardy people who once lived out their lives on this tiny scrap of rock and appreciate the unique culture that made it possible. Seri legend indicates that in the 1800s Mexican troops rounded up and deported the entire population of the island.

****

A SHARP PROBLEM AT HAND. Reeve, Dick Mandich and I had risen before dawn, anticipating another tussle with the big yellowtails off our camp on Esteban. Cold "C" rations were quickly washed down with cans of Coke, and as the sun rose we were trolling through the calm waters. The horizon revealed nothing, not a panga, *not a shrimper, and there wasn't even a vapor trail in the sky—we seemed to be the only people on earth. The yellowtail were temporarily absent so we decided to jig for some bottom dwellers. I snapped on a large metal jig, dropped it to the bottom and commenced pumping the rod. Several fish fell for our inducements and were hoisted to the surface, their eyes bulging. Unhooking a fish, I looked away as I dropped it in the cooler. I felt something odd and when I looked back I found that a very large and stout treble hook had rammed into my thumb just below the nail. Reeve reacted with sympathy pains and Dick seemed a little pale, but everyone soon calmed down. Recalling our Red Cross first aid classes we decided not to try to back the hook out—the large barb would drag a considerable amount of flesh with it—so I pushed the hook point the rest of the way through the thumb. The old fly-fisherman's trick of wrapping a piece of line around the shank under the barb would not work; the ball of line would have been almost a half-inch in diameter. Reeve dug through the tackle box and found a large pair of side-cutting pliers which should have made short work of the hook, but try as he might, he could do no more than put several small dents in the tempered metal.*

The situation began to look serious. I had gotten a tetanus shot recently, was losing only a small amount of blood and was feeling no intense pain, but I obviously could not go around for the remaining ten days of our trip with a large lure dangling from my thumb. The nearest permanent settlements were Kino, thirty-five miles to the east and Bahía de los Angeles fifty-five miles to the northwest, long trips in a fifteen-foot aluminum cartop boat. As we motored back to camp Reeve remembered that we had a tool kit with a hacksaw and a pair of ViseGrip pliers. Dick calmly squeezed the ViseGrips until he had the shank of the hook in an iron grip. With Dick bracing the pliers on a large rock, Reeve began sawing off the protruding end, producing the same effect as a thousand fingernails dragging across a hundred blackboards. After ten minutes the blade broke, with only half the diameter cut. We had no spares, so Reeve gripped a section

of the broken blade in a rag and kept sawing. The blade sections kept breaking until all of them were too small to hold. Remembering that it was very hard, Reeve took another pair of pliers and started to bend the hook back and forth at the cut. After a few minutes the metal finally fatigued and broke, and I applied a little iodine and slowly backed out the shank of the hook. Ten minutes later a dressing had been applied and we were speeding away from camp in pursuit of the yellowtail. The wound healed uneventfully.

****

From San Esteban, boaters usually head for Isla Turners (Isla Dátil) off the southern tip of Tiburón, thirteen miles east. Turners is high and rocky, but landings are possible on pebble beaches on the east and west sides. Although exposed, anchorages can be made on mixed bottoms. The Ensenada Chamber of Commerce likes to tout that city as the "Yellowtail Capital of the World." Not so! The title belongs to a small wash rock just west of the north tip of Turners. Spearfishing is excellent, especially around Roca la Foca (Isla Cholludo), between Turners and Tiburón.

With an area of 385 square miles, Tiburón is the largest island in Mexico, extending 33 miles north-south and 18 east-west. Good anchorages can be found between Punta Monumento and Punta Risco Colorado, in a bight north of Punta Ast Ah Keem ("Dog Bay"), and at Bahía Agua Dulce. Fishing is good all around the island, especially along the northwest coast and at the south tip. Spearfishing can be world-class; Don Barthman's 550-pound jewfish came from Tiburón waters. Tiburón is closed to outsiders. Persons wishing to land on the island must request permission from the chief of the Seri tribe through the Instituto Nacional Indigenista, which is listed in Appendix A. No one at the Instituto is currently (1991) fluent in English.

The channel between the island and mainland Sonora is shallow, with shifting sandbars and currents so swift that it is known as Canal de Infiernillo (Channel of Little Hell). Fishing in the Canal can be good all year for cabrilla, corvina, sierra, pargo, grouper, halibut, and sea bass to forty pounds, and shelling and clamming are excellent. With due care for the currents, especially at the north and south entrances, the Canal can be safely navigated by cartoppers, and there is a fair amount of traffic from local divers and fishermen who might be able to render assistance if things go wrong. The Seri have a boat ramp near Punta Chueca, and offer *pangas* and guide services, as well as ironwood carvings, baskets and other art. The Seri have their own feelings about being photographed, and it is customary to ask permission and make a monetary offer first.

During a trip many years ago Reeve, Dick Mandich and I were sentenced to an involuntary stay on Tiburón during a period of bad weather, but our supply of beer and ice finally failed us and we decided that the time for our departure was at hand, "weather eye" or not. Reeve volunteered to shuttle the equipment across the Canal in our cartopper, and even to this day—twenty years later—the memory is chilling; the forty-knot winds from the north rammed against a heavy tidal current running the other way, and every square foot of the Canal was lashed to a froth. Reeve disappeared into the melee within seconds, only to reappear airborne every minute or two. They were not waves in the conventional sense; churned into monumental proportions by the opposing forces of wind and tidal current, they reflected back off points and shores and combined into freakish sharp-pointed peaks that seemed to violate the laws of physics, only to have their tops ripped off by the wind. Ominously, Reeve did not appear for several minutes, but finally through the binoculars we could see the boat leap above the spray, going sideways, only to disappear again. Ten minutes passed, then twenty, and after an hour we thought he was a goner, when the bow of the trusty Gregor nosed through the waves to slide up on the beach in front of us, its skipper having the biggest grin even seen by man. We all made it back safely, but when I returned home I found we had drowned! It seems that a camper who had seen us depart ten days earlier had decided that no one could possibly have survived all that weather and had telephoned my wife to report the tragic event, after calling the California Highway Patrol with the license number of our van.

Not all mariners are so lucky and the Canal is alleged to be the scene of many shipwrecks, some carrying treasure. Chico Romero, a famous Seri Indian leader, now dead, told my friend Tom Crutchfield that Spanish sailing vessels com-

Cardón poke out of a bountiful supply of fertilizer on San Pedro Mártir.

ing up the Sonora coast in periods of strong southwest winds would be driven helplessly into the Canal. Having limited speed and poor tacking ability, they were swept north by the current and eventually went aground. The tribe would then kill survivors and strip the copper sheathing off the hulls to make arrowheads. There may be some truth to this, for several collections of Seri artifacts include arrowheads made from copper sheet. During a trip in the Canal in the 1960s, Tom's boat was disabled and he drifted over two wrecks in four fathoms north of Punta Chueca. The Seri knew of the wrecks and later told him that their ancestors had followed their "usual" procedure with the survivors. Some treasure hunters believe that gold removed from Mexico City before its capture by Hernan Cortés was aboard a schooner later wrecked in the Canal.

The Canal de Infiernillo is also the scene of a strange natural phenomenon. In the winter green turtles partially bury themselves in the mud and sand, and begin a dormant period that may last for up to three months. Situated about ten to fifteen feet apart, they lose weight and accumulate thick coats of algae on their shells. They rarely surface for air, and no one has found out how they manage to survive for so long without oxygen. The Seri hunted for them with long spears at low tide, limiting the take to their immediate needs. However, in the late 1950s commercial fishermen joined in the slaughter, with the usual devastating outcome. In 1990 President Salinas declared a total and permanent ban on turtle hunting in Mexico, insuring that the turtles can slumber in peace.

Several books on shipwrecks indicate that a Dutch frigate named *Draecke* foundered June 12, 1689 in ten fathoms one mile off the south tip of Tiburón with $1 million in gold and silver bullion, specie and pearls. No historical records of such a ship seem to exist, and except for two hints, *Draecke* appears to be a figment of someone's imagination. First, Seri oral history says that about the year 1900 children in foraging parties found Dutch coins on a beach between Punta Risco Colorado and Punta Monumento. No one seems to know whether this is authentic oral history or a modern extension of a fairy tale told to the Seri by outsiders.

The second hint is a stunner—Seri scallop divers have found a wreck in this vicinity. As this edition of *The Baja Adventure Book* went to press the details had not been confirmed and I have not yet been able to dive on the wreck. However, this is what is known thus far: the wreck was found in 125 feet of water in a small cove just west of Punta Risco Colorado. It is reportedly large, "possibly 150 feet" (almost certainly an exaggeration). The "casting" of the hull is clearly visible, probably rock ballast, debris and a coating of caliche. Some solid wood still exists in the transom and outboard rudder, and short stubs of its three masts can still be seen, at least two feet in diameter. Two sabers, each about two feet long, were found sticking into a mast. A large wooden gear lies nearby, and possible debris from the steering wheel is visible. Only time will tell whether this is the long-lost *Draecke*.

Two more attractions

Two more islands attract boaters having adequate time and range, Patos and San Pedro Martír. Patos, north of Tiburón, is not known for ducks, as its name implies, but for pelicans;

its population in 1966 was estimated to be between 50,000 and 100,000 of the birds. The island has a thick coating of guano, and in the mid-1800s great sailing ships came to load the rich fertilizer. To boost production the island was cleared of vegetation and Peruvian guanay birds were introduced. The guanay died out and the big ships are gone, but today a few men continue to haul away the smelly material in *pangas*. The sandy-bottomed southern anchorage is excellent, but fishing is not exceptional and there is little to see except birds, rock and guano. Diving is only fair, although there are a few wrecks, including a large wooden wreck 130 yards west of the southwestern point, and another one 500 yards southeast of the island. There is, however, a great attraction in the south anchorage.

In 1858 the full-rigged ship *John Elliott Thayer* burned at anchor while loading guano at Patos, the victim of arson by a disgruntled crew member. Seri oral history indicates that many years ago the tribe supplied meat, fish, water and firewood to large sailing ships at Patos, and that one of them burned and sank. Ramona Blanco, a Seri woman now dead, could remember its masts sticking out of the water at the turn of the century. In 1982 I located the *Thayer* and found her to be a dandy wreck; huge wooden timbers and thick planking still formed the recognizable outline of a sailing ship. The site was littered with debris, obviously of mid-19th century American origin, including many types of glass bottles, silverware, three types of ceramic plates, bronze spikes and copper sheathing, a huge iron capstan, anchors, an iron object that was perhaps a gaff-jaw, a large metallic ring, brass sailor buttons and iron harpoons.

About 1964 an American treasure hunter recovered a dozen gold coins from a wreck in the vicinity, apparently Lima Mint 1780 Charles III eight-escudo coins. He obtained permits from the Mexican government enabling him to explore the wreck, but various problems arose and he was not able to continue. He later turned over his information to CEDAM, the Mexican/American diving archaeology organization, stating that his research in a mission archive in Mexico City had revealed that the gold had come from one of three Spanish ships wrecked in 1780, carrying ten million similar coins. Making no effort to verify the story, in spite of obvious inconsistencies, and aware that the *Thayer* would have to have miraculously landed on top of the "treasure ship" in a manner similar to the movie *The Deep* (I told them so), CEDAM nevertheless announced an expedition. Gathering in Hermosillo in June 1983, unwary members traveled to Desemboque, on the Sonora coast north of Patos, to begin diving operations. You guessed it: the alleged treasure ship proved to be the *Thayer*. How could Lima Mint Charles III eight-escudo coins dated 1780 come to be aboard a U.S. sailing vessel sunk in 1858? Easy; by an act of Congress this coin was legal tender in the United States for many years, and it was often carried by ships to pay locals suspicious of paper money, in this case the Seri who brought water and firewood. How could CEDAM swallow a whopper about a Spanish treasure ship carrying the greatest treasure in world history, hook, line and sinker, with no effort at verification, even after they had been warned? No one knows.

A full-rigged ship *John Elliott Thayer*.

COURTESY PEABODY MUSEUM OF SALEM

Ten million gold coins or not, the *Thayer* is a fine dive. She is located 320° from the aids-to-navigation light on Patos, 283° from a rocky outcrop forming its southwest cape, and 053° from the left tangent of a small island south of Punta Sargento. Depth averages forty-five feet and currents can be swift; during the CEDAM clown-show one diver was swept away and almost drowned, and Lloyd Rice and I were at the limits of our endurance as we arrived back at the boat with the sodden diver in tow. On exceptional days visibility can approach sixty feet, and she can be seen from the surface. And who knows, could Captain Pousland have anticipated paying more than ninety-six escudos to the Seri?

You might have some difficulty in developing enthusiasm for a remote, smelly, noisy chunk of guano-covered volcanic rock jutting out of a cold sea swept by heavy currents, and you would not be alone, for San Pedro Mártir is among the least-visited islands in the Cortez. Upon closer inspection, you will find it to be a beautiful and wonderful place, pulsing with life. About one square mile in area and a thousand feet high, it is located twenty miles south of Turners. Since the island is surrounded by deep water and subject to heavy currents, tidal mixing causes plankton to thrive, and they support an extensive food chain. The island is home to myriad sea birds, primarily blue-footed and brown boobies, frigates,

A proud boobie father shows off his babies.

brown pelicans, cormorants, red-billed tropicbirds and yellow-legged gulls. Birds of prey include red-tailed hawks, peregrine falcons, kestrels and great horned owls. Say's phoebe, Allen's hummingbird, western flycatcher, yellow-rumped and Wilson's warblers, and Brewer's, Lincoln's and white-crowned sparrows often visit.

Blue-footed boobies are the most numerous birds. Their comical and not-too-bright appearance and demeanor are responsible for the name, which comes from the Spanish *bobo*, meaning clown or dunce. They are, however, skilled flyers and plunge divers, and groups of blue-footed boobies sometimes make synchronized dives when they see food near the surface. Unlike most diving birds, they seize prey from below and swallow before reaching the surface. Boobies examine trolled lures intently and sometimes make the wrong decision, to the consternation of fisherman. In pairing off for mating purposes, boobies go through an elaborate courtship ritual. After a period of waddling, goose-stepping and showing off its bright blue feet, a bird of either sex may "skypoint," stretching its neck, bill and tail feathers vertically and canting its wings. Skypointing is accompanied by honks if the bird is a female, whistles if a male. Ceremonies after mating are limited to "foot-showing" when the male lands near the nesting site. Two or three eggs are laid on bare ground. Plunge diving is difficult to learn, and young birds receive food from their parents long after they have learned to fly at seven or eight months. The easiest way to tell male from female is to look at their eyes; a female's black pupil appears to be larger than a male's. Actually they are the same size, but females have a ring of black pigment around the iris.

Red-billed tropicbirds, which look like large white terns with two long sweeping tail feathers and red beaks, also breed on the island. They too are plunge divers, feeding on fish and squid. Although not gregarious, they can be seen nesting together on cliffs, their shrill cries cutting the air.

Since rainfall averages only three inches a year, guano collects year after year, giving the island the appearance of an iceberg. Protruding through the deep white riches is a forest of dwarf cardón cactus and lesser numbers of chollas, zalates and a mallow having seasonal orange flowers. In fact, twenty-four types of higher plants have adapted to the exotic high-nitrogen, low-rainfall environment. Two species of lizard, both found nowhere else on earth, scurry over the white surface. They are bold and even show a streak of curiosity—a number of them watched intently and moved closer to get a better view as I changed film in my camera. No land mammals have been found except introduced rats. In the 1880s more than 135 Yaqui Indians and their families lived on the island, mining guano for an American company, a remarkable, and perhaps unique, setting for a human settlement.

Due to a steep and rocky bottom, boaters may encounter some difficulty anchoring. Given suitable winds, the anchorage of choice is a small sandy area off the eastern side. The place can be noisy, for numerous sea lions inhabit small ledges and contribute their barking to the fearful din of the birds. The best place to land is in a tiny cove on the east side. A series of fine sea caves invites examination with an inflatable dinghy. Diving areas are limited, since depths in excess of 200 feet are encountered within a dozen yards around much of the island, although a sizable area with depths of 20 to 60 feet is located around two islets at the south end. Visibility is usually 30 to 60 feet, and the bottom is jumbled cobble, boulders and shelf rock. Another small dive site can be found along the western shore. I have always found a full wet suit to be needed, but there are reports of warm-water Moorish idols and garden eels. Large numbers of heavy-duty gamefish will be encountered.

Schools of crazed yellowtail so large that estimates were phrased in terms of acreage have been seen around the island. Bottom fishing is excellent, and commercial hand-line boats come from La Paz to work the area. Try fishing in 200-250 feet of water several hundred yards south of the island and off its northeast side. The western side drops steeply and has a series of ledges and caves loaded with grouper. Typical catches include yellowtail, bonito, cabrilla, black sea bass, white sea bass, and yellowfin, and dolphin "pile-ups" have been reported, but most anglers come for big grouper. Catches are seasonal, with March and April tops for white and black sea bass and cabrilla, May through July for yellowtail, and August to October for grouper, dolphin and yellowfin.

People on the Stepping-Stones Cruise often head for Bahía Kino to refuel and resupply or to pull their boats out, making it a one-way trip. Small vessels can anchor in the bay at Kino, but many shoals and only marginal protection make it a tenuous location. The best small-boat anchorage in the winter is in Old Kino, also used by a number of shrimpers. In south winds boats can find shelter in the lee of Punta San Nicholas (Kino Point). Although there are no marinas in the area yet, four launch ramps are available. Club Deportivo "Bahía Kino" operates an all-tides ramp, available for a small fee, and has a clubhouse with a meeting hall, library, barbecue, arts-and-crafts center, and cooking and recreation facilities, and the club offers group insurance for boats and vehicles, fishing licenses, boat permits, mailbox and other services, as well as the search-and-rescue service noted earlier. The small, tourist-oriented town has hotels, a number of RV parks, stores, restaurants, a health clinic, telephones and limited mechanical services. The Kino Bay RV Park has 200 sites with full hookups, laundry, showers and ice. The restaurant across the street has excellent American and Mexican food. No marine parts or supplies are available, but gas, diesel, four-and two-cycle oils, additives, belts, batteries and accessories can be obtained at the PEMEX (MND). Near the PEMEX are a tire repair shop, a beer store and ice. There is also a mechanic, Manuel Monue, who speaks English and has a supply of parts. Hermosillo, a major city, is two hours away on a paved road.

****

CANNIBALS! The hair on the back of their necks rose at the mention of the word, and the darkness beyond the circle of light from our campfire on Tiburón intensified, I hoped, the mood of fear. Reeve and Dick Mandich listened intently as I continued with my repertory of Seri Indian stories.

The accounts of Cabeza de Vaca in 1536, Padre Gilg in 1692 and R.W.H. Hardy in 1829 revealed that a "primitive" tribe lived on Tiburón and on a narrow strip of coast between today's Desemboque and Guaymas. By the mid-19th century Mexican cattle ranches began to appear in their arid territory, made possible by the construction of deep wells. The Seri

resented the intrusion and considered cows, horses and burros fair game. Conflict soon broke out, and the following years were bad ones for the Seri, as constant warfare and epidemic diseases caused a drastic decline in their numbers. No one could find anything good to say about them, and stories of unrestrained violence and even cannibalism began to circulate. A weaver of tales named J. Bulwer Clayton published a newspaper account claiming that in 1867 he had been shipwrecked on Tiburón and every survivor had been killed and eaten but him, and that he had been spared only because he had been emaciated by scurvy. He said his captors decided that he would be more appetizing if he were healthier, and started to cure him with herbs. "Probably the only man who ever put his foot on Tiburón Island and lived to tell about it," Clayton reported that after being held for eighteen months he escaped to Sonora on the back of a turtle.

Magazines and newspapers liked to publish such stories well into the 1930s. Most were either outright fabrications like Clayton's or simply rank speculation about travelers who had disappeared, but all were given a degree of credibility by a few real incidents. In 1893 two treasure hunters disappeared, and although their bodies were never found (or perhaps because they were never found), it was reported that the Seri had mashed them to a pulp with stones and eaten them. In 1896 a newspaper reporter was stoned to death after landing on Tiburón, his companion narrowly escaping. Captain George Porter, who had participated in several of the earliest natural-history expeditions to Lower California, sailed his junk to Tiburón in the summer of 1897 to collect sea shells and curios. When he failed to return, Mexican soldiers searched the island and found a shoe, the remains of a large campfire and the junk's stern plank. Although there were no signs of a struggle and no human bones gnawed clean, it was assumed that Porter and his crewman had been barbecued over the coals of their own boat.

Anthropologists have shown that the Seri were in fact a remarkable people. Living in a harsh and demanding environment, they were great hunters and sailors, voyaging throughout the Cortez in reed boats, and had achieved considerable artistic skill with finely woven baskets and thin, hard pottery. While there was undoubtedly violence, I knew there was never a shred of reliable evidence that anything unusual had ever ended up in Seri cooking pots, but I wasn't about to ruin the spell by telling Reeve and Dick. The night had grown even darker, and the world seemed to end outside the circle of our campfire, so I began another story.

It seems that in 1904 two Yaqui bandits had been causing trouble in Sonora, but pursuing soldiers finally caused them to flee to Tiburón. Governor Izabal sent a message to the Seris, "Bring in the Yaquis with their hands tied to a pole and you will receive a reward." However, the Seri did not speak Spanish and the messenger was forced to communicate in sign language. The Seris got the idea, or most of it anyway. In due time they appeared to collect their reward, carrying a pole to which two pairs of Yaqui hands were tied. The incident was reported in National Geographic *and the Guaymas newspapers.*

I was silently congratulating myself for reducing my audience to a quivering, jelly-like state of fear when we heard the faint whisper of an outboard motor. Our eyes strained to adjust to the darkness and we could finally make out the slim shape of a panga. *It stopped just off our camp and for no apparent reason the two men in the boat sat watching us for perhaps an hour, not moving a muscle. Reeve and Dick sat equally motionless, hoping that the men were not Seris planning their menu, and even I became apprehensive. Finally, the motor started and they slowly disappeared. The mood didn't seem ripe for more cannibal stories, so we inflated our air mattresses and settled down for the night. No one said a thing, but each knew the others were lying awake, listening for the sound of knives being sharpened and the clank of pots. We had just dozed off when there was a pistol shot and a scream, and someone raced across the campsite. Leaping out of our sleeping bags, Dick and I prepared to defend ourselves from attack, stark naked and shivering in the cold. Reeve was screaming for help, but as I gathered my wits I realized they weren't screams—he was laughing, howls of laughter, at Dick and me! A resinous knot in the fire had exploded, waking Reeve, who saw a coyote stealing food from our packs, so he had yelled and thrown a stick.*

After the uproar died down we knew there was to be no sleep that night, so we stoked up the fire and I started another story. It seems that a party of four American gold prospectors led by Tom Grindell disappeared in Seri country in 1905, so his brother went to find out what happened, and. . .

****

CHAPTER 12

GUERRERO NEGRO TO SAN IGNACIO

On the Transpeninsular Highway at KM 38+ south of Punta Prieta

KM	LOCATION
52	**Rosarito.** Groceries, cafes, tire repair. El Marmolito onyx quarry can be reached by driving southeast on the "old," unpaved Transpeninsular and taking the left (066°) fork at Mile 7.4. Although virtually unknown to fishermen, the beaches from Punta Rosarito and south to Guerrero Negro are among the finest surf fishing locations in Baja. The prime quarry is migratory white sea bass, taken with heavy surf rigs between March and May, although a few are taken as early as January and as late as June. Look for steep drop-offs with sand and cobble bottoms just offshore, and fling out a squid. Throughout the year you might also find yellowfin croakers in the surf line, and barred surfperch a bit farther out. Halibut, although not often considered a surf fish, are also frequently taken here.

THE LOST CAVE OF EL ZALATE

In his 1895 paper on Indian rock art, Leon Diguet indicated that a site named The Cave of El Zalate was located "near the 29° [parallel of latitude], about fifteen leagues from Calamahi [Calmallí] near the road from Calamahi to San Borga [Misión San Borja]." Zalate has never been re-located, and its elusiveness may be caused by varying definitions of a league. In English-speaking countries, a league was 3.0 miles, the old Spanish league used in California was 2.63 miles and the French league (Diguet was French) was 2.5 miles, so the cave could thus be 45, 39 or 37 miles northwest of Calmallí. None of these seems likely, since they place the cave very close to or even north of Misión San Borja. However, in 1910 Arthur North provided a more likely definition: a "Mexican league"

was the distance you could ride a mule in an hour, about 2 miles. Since Diguet had no accurate way of measuring distances, this may be the definition he used, and the cave may thus be only 30 miles from Calmallí. In Diguet's day two Calmallís existed, the mining camp where gold was discovered in 1882, and Calmallí Viejo, 10 miles north. El Camino Real, the "Royal Road" linking the Jesuit missions, ran from Misión Santa Gertrudis northwest past Calmallí Viejo to Misión San Borja and was still in use in the late 1800s. Since maps of the day show no other road in the vicinity, Diguet may have simply followed El Camino Real. These speculations place Zalate about 7 miles east of Rancho San Regis, a visiting station of Misión San Borja.

The Cochimí Indians of the area were like anyone else; they appreciated well-watered sites with shelter and plenty of food. Zalate is thus not likely to be found on featureless open desert—the place will almost certainly be "somewhere." If the appropriate small-scale topographic map (Isla San Esteban H12-10, 1:250,000) is laid out and the route of El Camino Real plotted, fifteen "Mexican leagues," or thirty miles, will indeed take the rider to "somewhere," deep (1,350 feet) and spectacular Arroyo Paraíso. In 1974 Harry Crosby described a descent into awe-inspiring drop-offs, sheer faces, impassable palisades and the necessity to build a trail with stones to allow the passage of pack animals. In 1975 he described the arroyo as "a place of trees, water, and huge blocks of granite," with sandy flats and a pool "thick with rushes." Cochimí did inhabit the arroyo, and a painting of a deer and a few other simple figures were found.

Nothing more is known about the cave (probably a grotto or an overhang), nor about the art itself, since Diguet described nothing more than its location. Rancho San Regis still exists, and can be reached by driving southeast from Rosarito on the old, unpaved Transpeninsular, turning northeast at Mile 6.3, and arriving at Mile 19.3. There may or may not be a beautiful zalate (wild fig tree) marking the mouth of the cave; they are short-lived. See page 191 for a description of

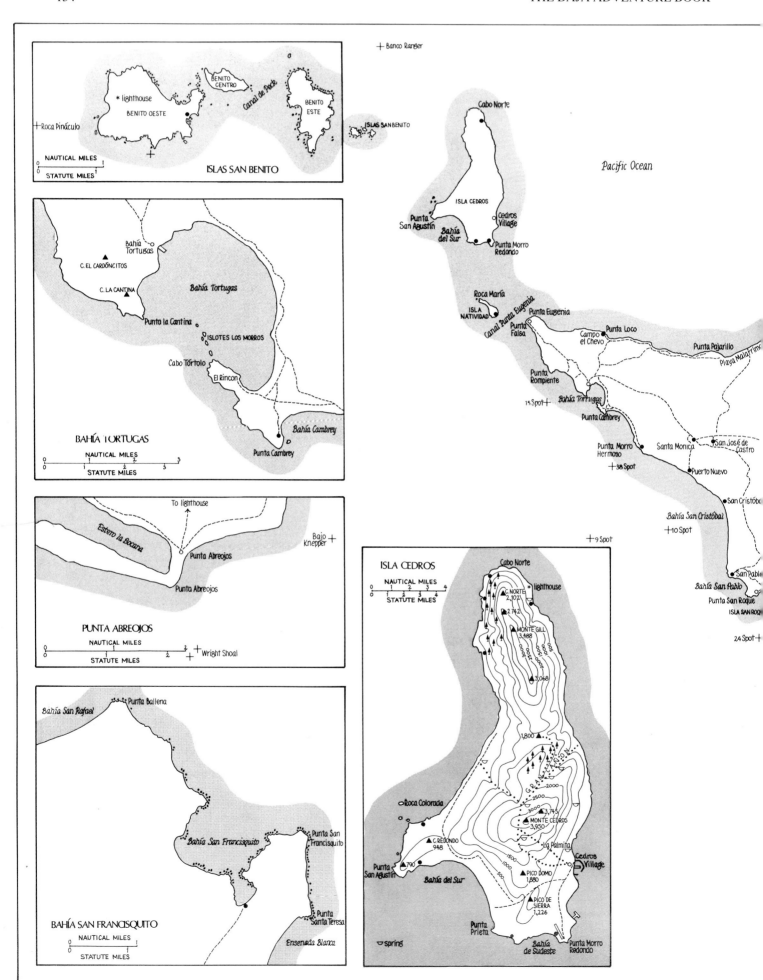

+ Banco Ranger

ISLAS SAN BENITO

+ Roca Pináculo

BENITO OESTE
* lighthouse
BENITO CENTRO
Canal de Pecte
BENITO ESTE

ISLAS SAN BENITO

NAUTICAL MILES
STATUTE MILES

Pacific Ocean

Cabo Norte

ISLA CEDROS

Punta San Agustín
Bahía del Sur
Cedros Village
Punta Morro Redondo

BAHÍA TORTUGAS

Bahía Tortugas
C. EL CARDÓNCITOS
C. LA CANTINA
Bahía Tortugas
Punta la Cantina
ISLOTES LOS MORROS
Cabo Tórtolo
El Rincon
Bahía Cambrey
Punta Cambrey

NAUTICAL MILES
STATUTE MILES

Roca María
ISLA NATIVIDAD
Canal Punta Eugenia
Punta Falsa
Punta Eugenia
Campo el Chevo
Punta Loco
Punta Pajarillo
Playa Malarrim

Punta Rompiente
Bahía Tortugas
15 Spot +
Punta Cambrey
Punta Morro Hermoso
Santa Monica
San José de Castro
38 Spot +
Puerto Nuevo
San Cristóbal
Bahía San Cristóbal
10 Spot +

To lighthouse

Estero la Bocana
Bajo Knepper +
Punta Abreojos
Punta Abreojos

PUNTA ABREOJOS

NAUTICAL MILES
STATUTE MILES
+ Wright Shoal

9 Spot +

ISLA CEDROS

NAUTICAL MILES
STATUTE MILES

Cabo Norte
lighthouse
C. NORTE 2,101
2,742
MONTE GILL 3,488
3,068
1,800

Roca Colorada
2000
2500
3,745
MONTE CEDROS 3,950
C. REDONDO 948
La Palmita
Cedros Village
Punta San Agustín
790
Bahía del Sur
PICO DOMO 1,880
PICO DE SIERRA 1,226

San Pablo
Bahía San Pablo
Punta San Roque
ISLA SAN ROQUE
24 Spot +

BAHÍA SAN RAFAEL
Punta Ballena
Bahía San Rafael

Bahía San Francisquito
Punta San Francisquito

Punta Santa Teresa

BAHÍA SAN FRANCISQUITO
NAUTICAL MILES
STATUTE MILES

Ensenada Blanca

spring
Punta Prieta
Bahía de Sudeste
Punta Morro Redondo

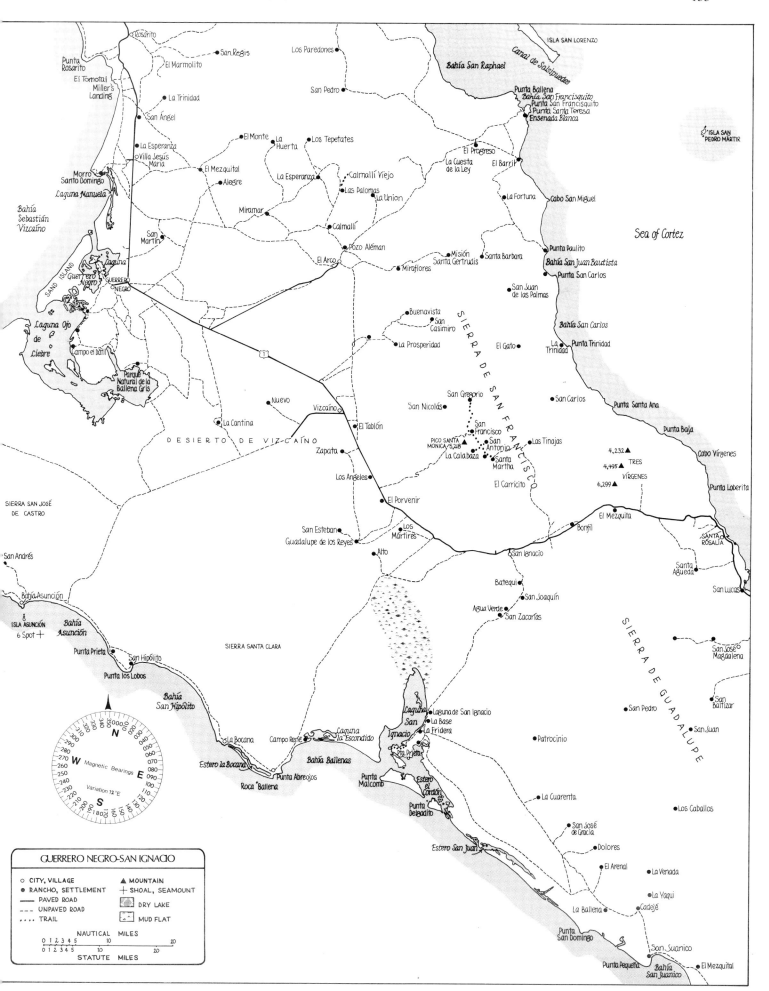

156   THE BAJA ADVENTURE BOOK

a zalate and page 221 for a photo.

On the Transpeninsular Highway at Rosarito, KM 52

68   Road west to El Tomatal (signed), 3.1 miles, which
     has a palm-shaded campsite not too far from the
     beach. The large island visible in the distance is
     Cedros.
73   A sedan road goes west 0.1 mile south of the KM
     marker to Miller's Landing, three miles. This wind-
     blown spot was the shipment point for onyx from El
     Marmolito, and chunks can still be found scattered
     over the cobble beach. There is excellent surf fishing
     at times and reliable reef breaks, although the ride is
     not too long.
75   The highway crosses plains until a few miles west
     of San Ignacio, and the scenery is flat, featureless,
     boring and often windswept.
90   **Rancho La Esperanza.** Food and drink.
95   **Villa Jesús María.** PEMEX (MND), cafes, grocer-
     ies, medical, mechanic, tire repairs.
96   Road west (signed) to Morro Santo Domingo
     (Morro Laguna).

SIDETRIP TO MORRO SANTO DOMINGO

Although it has excellent fishing and is close to the Transpeninsular, the Morro Santo Domingo-Laguna Manuela (Estero Santo Domingo) area is little known to most gringo
visitors. Set odometer. Follow the paved road to Mile 0.9, turn
southwest, and arrive at the beach at Mile 7.0. The graded
sand-and-gravel road can handle RVs and trailers, but it is
often washboarded. This desolate spot was once served by
regular steamship service to San Diego! In the heyday of the
gold mines in the Calmallí and Alemán areas in the 1800s,
the steamer deposited supplies on the beach, which then were
hauled to the mines on mule-back, the steamer heading back
with the gold. Although the lee of Morro Santo Domingo
makes a fair anchorage, boats coasting north or south rarely

**We tried to reassemble a whale found near Miller's Landing, but
there were vital parts missing and we never did get it working again.**

use it, since it is far off the normal Isla Cedros-points-north-
or-south route. The vessel *Alice* foundered here in 1925, but
don't plan to salvage her cargo, for it was ice.

Camping is usually good, but the shoreline sometimes
changes, leaving little room on the beach, especially during
periods of high tide. Take care that you do not camp in a tidal
area. Small boats can enter and leave the lagoon through the
north entrance, but the south entrance is often unsafe due to
heavy surf. Launching directly into the lagoon is difficult
because of soft ground and the many *pangas* lined up along
the inside beach, and it may be best to use the beach south
and east of the fish camp and run the boat through the north
entrance into the lagoon.

The lagoon extends south about nine miles or so, and is
very shallow and often choked with eel grass, its bottom being
mixed mud and sand. Surge created by tides and winds may
leave a boat anchored in three or four feet of water high and
dry thirty minutes later. These conditions make the lagoon a
biological "factory," and the place seems fin-to-fin with
yellowfin croaker, corvina, corbina, halibut and various
basses, especially in its southern reaches. For those with a
boat, the southern end of the lagoon is one of the finest
fisheries in Baja.

In suitable weather, the ocean coves south of Morro Santo
Domingo offer outstanding fishing for corbina, yellowfin
croaker and halibut, especially in the summer, and white sea
bass, giant sea bass, yellowtail, ocean whitefish and grouper
are also taken. Always guard against sneaker waves and
heavy tidal currents in this vicinity.

Just south of the concrete buildings at Mile 7.0 a road
winds west along the bluffs, passing a series of beautiful
sandy coves. A 25% grade and deep sand will cause problems
for two-wheel-drives. As noted earlier, the coves along this
shore offer outstanding fishing, and it's usually no problem
to scramble down the cliffs with a surf rod in hand. Northwest
swells march past the point like soldiers, and surfers will find
a long ride, although fairly deep water immediately offshore
keeps things a little mushy. There is good camping on the
bluff near the lighthouse. Surf fishermen with a four-wheel-
drive with flotation tires or plenty of people to push should
drive about a mile north of the concrete building, where a very
poor road will be found running west. In about two miles this
road arrives at a hard-packed beach on the outer coast. Turn
south at this point and drive a half-mile. A series of small
coves from here to about 3/4 mile south are home to hordes
of very unsophisticated halibut, croaker and corvina.

Back on the Transpeninsular Highway at KM 96

121+ The magnificent dunes a few miles to the west are
      spread over sixteen square miles.
128   Latitude 28° north, separating the states of Baja
      Norte and Baja Sur. A time zone change occurs here;
      Baja Sur is one hour ahead of Baja Norte. A La Pinta
      Hotel and the Benito Juárez RV Park are located
      here. The hotel has rooms, a restaurant, a bar and a
      Magnasin pump, and it may be possible to transact
      tourist-card matters here. The RV park has full
      hookups, showers and toilets, but things rarely work.
      The birds nesting on the signposts are ospreys.

These magnificent fish-eating hawks have taken to nesting on man-made structures throughout the Guerrero Negro area, often favoring high-tension poles. Their nests are an eclectic mixture of twigs, seaweed, fish nets, tapes from cassette cartridges, rope, surprisingly large pieces of driftwood, fish and bird skeletons, and Bimbo bread wrappers. This point is also KM 221 for the beginning of a new KM sequence.

220   Agricultural inspection station for north-bound vehicles.

218   Butane yard.

217   **Guerrero Negro junction**. If you are heading north it is advisable to gas up in town and at Parador Punta Prieta, Cataviña and El Rosario, as gas supplies are not always reliable.

SIDETRIP TO GUERRERO NEGRO

Guerrero Negro's odd name came from the whaling bark *Black Warrior*, wrecked at the entrance to Laguna Ojo de Liebre (Scammon's Lagoon) in 1858. She had loaded so much whale oil after a season of hunting that she was unable to sail through the entrance and went aground while being towed by whaling boats. The name is also odd for a ship; *Black Warrior* is said to have received it because she had once been engaged in trade with Zanzibar. Today, almost all yachts coasting north or south avoid Laguna Guerrero Negro because changes have occurred in the pattern of commercial shipping and dredging. Older charts and pilots are out of date and reliable information is next to impossible to get. Guerrero Negro, the first large town south of San Quintín, has many supplies and services, including PEMEX (two, one with MND, the other MN), motels, restaurants, liquor, bank, taxis, tires, mechanics, auto parts, groceries, fruit and meat markets, ice, bakeries, post office, laundry service, *tortilla* factory, telephone, telegraph, COTP, immigration, Pesca office, medical, dental and pharmacies. The *Migración* office is near the Banamex building. Showers are available at the Dunas Motel. The La Ballena supermarket, 200 yards west of the El Morro Hotel, sometimes has excellent produce, something of a rarity in this part of the world. Good seafood dinners and local information can be obtained at the Malarrimo Restaurant. The restaurant also has an RV park with electric and water hook-ups, showers, restrooms and rooms to rent. Leaving at 10 a.m., Aerolineas California Pacifico, S.A. flies to Cedros and Bahía Tortugas every day except Wednesday and Saturday, and has charter aircraft.

Guerrero Negro is often dismissed as a company town with little beyond logistics to interest visitors, but in fact there are things to see and do. The warm climate, steady breezes, many square miles of flat, low-lying desert and close proximity to the ocean make the area an ideal location for solar production of salt. Exportadora de Sal, S.A. (ESSA) operates over 300 square miles of diked ponds south of town and around Scammon's, producing five million tons a year. Shipped in barges to Cedros, it is loaded into bulk carrier ships for shipment to mainland Mexico, Japan, Canada and the United States. The company currently (1991) offers tours Mondays, Wednesdays and Fridays. The schedule changes, so check

The steep slopes and soft sand of the dunes near Guerrero Negro make you feel like flying.

well in advance at their offices near the western end of the business district. A travel agency, Viajes Mario's, offers salt company tours, trips to Parque Natural de la Ballena Gris to see the whales, and two-day Indian art trips to the Sierra de San Francisco, as well as fishing trips, hotel reservations, airline tickets and charter flights to Cedros and elsewhere. The office is located in a small building with a white sign set back from the "main drag" in town, fifty yards east of and on the opposite side of the street from the first PEMEX encountered when driving into town. Its mailing address and telephone number are listed in Appendix A.

The old salt-loading pier at Puerto Viejo on Laguna Guerrero Negro attracts many visitors. A small number of RVers and tenters even make this their Baja destination and stay for weeks at a time in spite of its lack of facilities. It is found by turning west at the ESSA offices and driving seven miles. The marshes en route are a bird refuge, and a dozen or more species of gull, duck, heron and other wading birds may be seen. Gray whales occasionally come close to the pier, an unusual situation; where else can you sit in your trailer and watch a whale swim by? Mario Rueda offers three-hour whale-watching trips in the vicinity aboard a thirty-five-foot barge, leaving daily from the salt pier during February and March. Information can be obtained at the La Pinta Hotel or Malarrimo Restaurant, and reservations for group trips can be made by writing to his post office box. Fishing off the pier produces enough cabrilla, sargo and other species to keep things interesting. Mullet for bait can be snagged with treble hooks, and small boats can be launched off a sandy area near the pier. Local scallop divers often return to the dock with interesting shells.

THE MYSTERY OF CONSAG'S WRECK

Almost two-and-a half-centuries ago a mysterious ship-wreck was found on a remote Baja beach and then virtually forgotten. In recent years an incredible find by a party of beachcombers and a lucky series of events have allowed me to weave together a possible explanation as to the identity, location and circumstances of the wreck.

During a journey in Baja in 1751, Father Fernando Consag encountered a "tongue of sand" that stretched out toward the Pacific. A party of his men set out to explore it and returned two days later with a soup bowl, a cup, a China plate and a quantity of white wax they had taken from a shipwreck found at the water's edge. The site was littered with baskets of goods similar to what they had brought back, and with large platters and vases, and hammered lead and bronze objects. Consag's diary does not provide an adequate map, and most of the place names he used can no longer be identified. However, his description of the "tongue of sand" is unmistakable—it was obviously "Sand Island," visible from the old salt pier at Puerto Viejo.

While doing library research for the first edition of this book, I came across an article by Midge Hamshaw in which she told of a 1962 beachcombing trip to Sand Island in a Second World War "duck" amphibious jeep. Midge, her husband Wes and their friend Scotty Johnson found a jackpot of modern flotsam, but one item in a photograph attracted my attention, a very unusual clay "urn." It hit me like a lightning bolt—could the urn be an artifact from Consag's wreck? With great good fortune, I was able to locate Midge and Wes. From photographs I took, the Smithsonian Institution was able to determine that the urn was salt-glazed stoneware of German

A treasure of Pacific flotsam collected by Midge and Wes Hamshaw (left) and Scotty Johnson (right) during a 1962 trip to the island across from the salt pier. The urn Wes is holding was manufactured in Germany between 1690 and 1710!

MIDGE HAMSHAW

origin, manufactured for the foreign trade between 1690 and 1710 in the Westervald region of the Rhineland. The date, locations, descriptions, geography, everything I knew about the matter, were consistent—Wes, Midge and Scotty had possibly found a remarkable historical artifact from Consag's wreck!

Assuming it was part of the ship's cargo, the urn and the date of Consag's visit place the wreck between 1690 and 1751. Consag's men described the wreck as old, for iron objects and nails fell into dust when they were touched, and since the urns were not manufactured after 1715 and were somewhat fragile, the earlier years of this range of dates seem more likely. As there were few other ships in this region between these dates, one obvious possibility is that Consag's wreck was a Manila galleon, one of the "black ships" of *Shogun* television fame. These ships sailed between the west coast of Mexico and the Far East between 1565 and 1815. Poor construction, bad navigation, storms, lightning, scurvy, starvation, fire, careless loading and rotten timbers caused the loss of thirty ships, thousands of lives and 60 million pesos in property. The goods found by Consag's men were consistent with a such a vessel en route to Mexico, and one possibility is that the wreck is the *San Francisco Xavier*, which disappeared after leaving Manila in 1705.

Further research produced a scientific study of carbon-14 dating of sea shells found inland along the same beach. This provided more clues; the beach is advancing, and if the wreck was at the water's edge in 1751, it should now be a hundred yards inland. Remarkably, Wes recalls that the urn was found in the first line of dunes about that distance from the beach! As to the lateral position of the wreck along the beach, little is known, for Consag's account does not contain enough information, and Wes cannot remember exactly where they found the urn (more than twenty-five years had passed).

There is another odd twist to the story. Why did Consag's men find no items of great value—where was the treasure? The Manila ships carried jewelry, devotional pieces, sword hilts, ornaments made of gold and ivory, gold bells, coins, gems and at least one "pearle as big as a dove egge," plus such exotic items as artificial noses and alligator teeth capped with gold. The local Indians probably did not haul these things away. Archaeologists have not found such objects at Indian sites anywhere in Baja, and in any event a pot, a knife, an ax or even a nail would be of infinitely more value to people at the cultural level of the local Indians than, say, a crown. There is, however, a logical explanation as to what happened to the treasure, provided by a "tall tale" known to the people of Guerrero Negro.

Dutch pirates aboard a schooner working the west coast of Mexico about this time supposedly quarreled and began to kill each other, until only one was left alive, the large African helmsman. Unable to manage the ship alone, he ran it ashore on a beach in Bahía Vizcaíno. Since he could not fit all of the ship's treasure into his wooden sea chest, he donned dozens of rings, crowns and ornaments. Heavily armed, he started across the salt flats, dragging his chest. He soon died of thirst and his skeleton, picked clean by the birds, disappeared into the salt, along with the treasure.

The tale has a certain validity for the local people. Every-one knows that gold flakes can be found on any beach in the vicinity (actually iron pyrites). Also, there is the odd name of the nearby lagoon: Guerrero Negro. Skeptics claim that in the 1950s the gringo manager of the salt works made up the tale, keeping his men digging full-speed by offering "finders-keepers," but others say that it had "always" been known to the local people.

This tale has appeared in the literature of Baja a number of times, but whether it still motivates the workers of Guerrero Negro is doubtful. Still, could it have a factual basis; could the ship have been Consag's wreck? Is it possible that someone from the ship actually carried the treasure away? Since no one associated with the wreck survived, the details of the story—the men were Dutch pirates and had quarreled, the only survivor was an African helmsman—could be known to no one, and are probably embellishments added by later storytellers. However, could the core of it—a ship was wrecked and one man survived, only to die crossing the salt flats carrying a treasure—be an authentic example of oral history, passed down from eyewitnesses through generations of Indians? The tale would also explain why no human bones were reported by Consag's men; all the crew but one were killed at sea and presumably dumped over the side, and the last man alive walked away from the ship.

The operator of a big ESSA scraper may someday set his blade a little too deep and provide the motivation for archaeologists to finally solve the mystery. It will be interesting to find out if the "finders-keepers" offer is still good. Please don't grab your metal detector and head for Sand Island—if Consag's wreck is indeed a Manila galleon, or any wreck that old for that matter, Mexican law allows only professionals working under permits to disturb it.

OFFSHORE ISLANDS

Because of its two peaks, one 3,950 feet, the other 3,488, Isla Cedros can be seen easily from Guerrero Negro in clear weather, a distance of sixty-one miles. Not often visited by outsiders except for long-range fishing vessels and passing yachts, the island offers good fishing and diving and some unusual hiking. The island is served by the Cannery Airline with flights from Ensenada, and flights from Guerrero Negro can be arranged. Cedros is only thirteen miles from Punta Eugenia, and it should be possible to launch small boats there or hire a *panga*. By way of Isla Natividad, you never need get more than five miles from land. Since the run from Bahía Tortugas to the village on Cedros is only thirty-five miles, the graded road from Vizcaíno also opens up the region to trailerboats (more on this later). Small-boat adventures in this area are for experienced sailors with seaworthy boats only, for fog and wind are common.

Since the island has abundant food and water, Cedros once had a sizable Indian population, estimated at between 500 and 1,000. In 1539, Francisco de Ulloa "discovered" the island, but the Cochimí inhabitants greeted him with stones and clubs, to which he replied with dogs and crossbow bolts. In 1602 Sebastián Vizcaíno found that local attitudes toward strangers had not changed. However in 1732 Jesuit Father Sigismundo Taraval managed to get in a few words before the clubs and stones started, and the Indians were so im-

We didn't find any of the five anchors that Francisco Ulloa lost off the water hole at La Palmita in 1539, but we did find why he may have lost them; boulders that look like huge popcorn balls lie scattered over the sand bottom chafed through his lines.

pressed with his sweet talk about souls, saviors and salvation that they agreed to leave the island almost en masse and settle around Misión San Ignacio. The few who remained died of smallpox, leaving the island uninhabited for the first time in 2,000 years. Yankees and Russians after seals and sea otters often visited the island in the late 1700s, and in the mid-1800s Chinese and Japanese divers came to take abalone. In 1920 a cannery was built, first specializing in abalone, later in sardines. A lobster fishery became important, the live catch being flown to Ensenada. In the 1960s the island became an important trans-shipment point for the salt produced at Guerrero Negro.

Today the sizable village on the island has a cannery, COTP, customs, immigration, stores, *cantinas*, cafes, gasoline, diesel, water, a hotel of sorts, a little produce, postal and telegraph offices and a decompression chamber. A new commercial harbor has been constructed at the village. An airstrip and salt shipment facilities are located at the south end of the island. The primary anchorages are off the village, in Bahía del Sur, and several miles south of the navigation light near the north end. The first anchorage south is Natividad, but Bahía Tortugas is highly preferable.

While this is not virgin territory, fishing is good anywhere on the west side and around the southeast cape for yellowtail, kelp bass and barracuda. Long-range sportfishing boats out of San Diego occasionally fish the area. Good diving is found at the north point of the island and around the south end, especially in Bahía del Sur. Although at least twenty-five vessels have gone to the bottom near Cedros, they are either in deep water or on the beach, and the area is not known for wreck diving. A dive on a Cannery Airline plane that crashed into the ocean off the end of the airstrip can be thought-provoking, especially if you plan to leave the island by plane.

Many thousands of years ago Cedros' climate was wetter than today. As it became dryer its forest of pines died out, except for two small stands, which today depend on moisture from fogs to survive. Early Spanish explorers thought them to be cedars and hence gave the island its name. The cool shade and the smell and rustle of pine needles provide an unusual Baja experience. A trail leads to them from the village, but the most interesting and direct access is found by hiking southwest from the mouth of the Gran Cañon, on the eastern side of the island seven miles north of the village. The canyon can be identified by watching for the first small grove of pines visible on the crest of the mountains as you travel by boat north from the village. When this grove is due west you are off the Gran Cañon.

Watch for deer as you hike; an extremely rare subspecies of mule deer found only here still holds out against local poachers. Keeping the pines in view, hike southwest up the main wash. Soon the walls of an arroyo will block the views of the pines, but at Minute 60 they will reappear dead ahead. Stop and make a mental note of the scene at the crest at 252°; the "trail" reaches the crest at this point. Keep hiking up the canyon, and at Minute 80 a prominent fortress-like hill with a number of small caves will be seen on the right side of the canyon, blocking the pines. Just beyond the base of this hill an arroyo will be seen bearing 240°. Hike up this arroyo until Minute 100 and locate a rocky hill 60 feet high with a sharp, cone-shaped tip; it's hard to miss. Pass this to your left, and at Minute 105 the arroyo will divide into two branches. Stop and relocate the spot where the trail reaches the top, now bearing 282°. The right-hand branch of the arroyo is the correct one, but do not enter it yet. Rather, hike up the ridge separating the two branches, bearing 262°, for two reasons: a high and almost impassable rock cliff blocks the right arroyo 200 yards up, and the ridge has a stand of magnificent desert

Reeve inches his way up a rock wall on the way to the pine forest.

Reeve finally gets some use out of his high-school geometry course; the pine was fifty-eight feet high.

plants you will not want to miss. Agave and gnarled shrubs cling to this wind-whipped ridge of sand and rock dust in a seemingly impossible environment. Continue up the spine of the ridge until it levels out, then swing into the correct (right) arroyo and continue climbing. It will get steep, but good hand and foot holds can be found. At one point it will be necessary to scale a 20-foot cliff, but this should cause few problems. The last 50 yards to the crest will require scrambling up a slope of loose rock and sand on all fours, and you should arrive at the crest at Minute 140, altitude 1,500 feet. The pine forest runs along the rim of the canyon and down the slopes to the northwest toward the incoming fog, many trees 40 and 50 feet high, some festooned with gray moss. A faint trail follows the ridge, so old that parts of it are worn into the rock, providing grand vistas of the coast and the ocean to the west. Forest fires have decimated a few areas.

A stone shanty supposedly constructed by 19th century sea-otter hunters can be found in Gran Cañon by returning to the fortress-shaped rock and continuing up the canyon (southwest) for a mile. When you arrive back at the beach at the end of the day, tired, hot and sweaty, reflect on the fact that the Indians used to fell the pines with crude tools and drag them to the beach to construct rafts.

Mineral collectors should explore slopes of the Gran Cañon south of the otter shack for chromite in yellowish-brown serpentine country rock. A gold-and-copper mine will be found west of the navigation light at the north end of the island, yielding pyrite and minor amounts of chalcopyrite, bornite, covellite and copper carbonate. There are also reports of manganese minerals. The second grove of pines is located in this vicinity.

Nature-watchers will find much of interest. Goats, cats, dogs and burros have been released on the island, but their influence on the ecology has not been as drastic as on some other Baja islands, perhaps because miners and fishermen often hunted them for food, and possibly because the goats and burros had to compete with the already established deer. Native mammals include the Cedros wood rat and the Cedros pocket mouse, both endemic, while the Cedros brush rabbit and the Cedros white-footed mouse are endemic sub-species. There are seven lizard species and five snakes, the Cedros leopard lizard, Cedros alligator lizard, Cedros horned lizard and Cedros rattlesnake being endemic to the island. Many bird species are present, but only the Cedros Island wren is endemic. Cedros is also home to a population of Pacific tree frogs, seemingly out of place in the arid climate.

The waters around the three Islas San Benito—Este (East), Oeste (West) and Centro (Central)—sixteen miles west of Cedros, are the most consistent yellowtail fishery on the west coast of North America. They lie near the 100-fathom migratory path and are far enough offshore that they are not plagued with dirty water as is Isla San Martín. The best locations are north of Benito Central, north and east of Benito East, southwest of Benito West, and at Roca Pináculo, just under a mile west of Benito West. Fishing for large kelp bass is also good around all the islands.

Excellent visibility, extensive kelp fields and many reefs and pinnacles provide the best cool-water diving in Baja, rivaled only by Sacramento Reef and the seamounts south of San Martín, and the best white sea bass and yellowtail spearfishing on the Pacific coast. Not a common fish, whites can be found hanging around the outer fringes of the kelp canopy, especially around the south tip of Benito East and along its west coast, and along the north side of Benito West.

After diving the kelp canopy south of the two western islands, Rob Watson marveled at the enormous number of yellowtail. We pooh-poohed him, saying what he saw were bass with yellow tails, but he persisted. After thirty seconds in the water we too became believers; incredible numbers of yellowtail, the correct kind, live under the kelp. The dense canopy is a problem for rod-and-reelers, but provides heart-stopping action for spearfishermen. Big, big, bugs abound. With outstanding spearfishing for yellowtail, Roca Pináculo is an exciting open-water dive. "Yellowtail Alley" between Benito East and the small islet to the north is another fine spearfishing site. Yellowtail are often too swift to permit a shot—by the time your safety is off, they are long gone. However, they are also curious, so take out your diver's knife and tap loudly on the barrel of your speargun. The noise will often cause them to return. Nature-watchers will like a pinnacle southeast of the navigation light on the south side of

Bernie Eskesen investigates the huge anchor off Benito West.

SUE DIPPOLD

Benito West. When over the site the light will bear 312°, the south tip of Benito East 076°.

Benito West offers several good wreck dives. Just before the newly constructed lighthouse was scheduled to begin operation in 1934, the U.S. tanker *Swift Eagle* went ashore almost at its foot. She lies in shallow water, her bow section rising to within six feet of the surface. The stern is somewhat deeper, but in one place you can stand on a bitt with your head above water. Although her stern is badly damaged, the bow sections are fairly intact. Hull plating is missing in many places, exposing ribs and allowing entry into the hull. Capstans, hausepipes, ports, valves, piping, pumps, anchors, engine blocks and lengths of chain can be seen. To dive the wreck, go by outboard or inflatable to the north side of Benito West; larger vessels cannot approach the wreck safely. Look for the lighthouse and turn toward shore when it bears 175°. A second wreck, the Mexican super-seiner *Tecapah*, run ashore about 1988, lies in the large cove on the west side of the island, southwest of the lighthouse. The lighthouse keeper attributes the wreck to the fact the helmsman was "asleep at the wheel," and the velocity of the encounter was such that she lies in very shallow water.

At least a dozen other wrecks have occurred nearby, but only a few have diving potential. Two are located on the southeast side of Benito East: *Souster*, a tuna boat, and *San Juanico*. Locals say they barbecued survivors from the latter vessel—the cattle she was carrying, that is. Metal wreckage of one wreck can be seen in a cove 1/2 mile north of the south point, the other lies 100 yards north—it is not certain which is which. In the 1970s the tuna vessel *Paramount* sank north of Benito Central. A fisherman I met off the Benitos claimed to have seen her go down, and he drew a map placing her about about 1/2 mile off the beach, but the truth is that this is pure guesswork, and given the Mexican love for exaggeration, she may be much closer. Other locals also place her 1/2 mile north, but state she is in 100 to 150 fathoms. This cannot be correct since the 100-fathom line is not reached until two miles north. She may be in relatively shallow water and is potentially a fine dive site, but there are no reports that she has been located. A ten dollar bill waved around the village ought to produce a flood of information, some good, some bad. A twenty ought to produce an eyewitness—the wreck is not too old—who should be able to put you very close.

A huge anchor can be found in 50 feet on a sand bottom 200 feet off the southeast point of Benito West. Locals say it was lost by the U.S. vessel *Tatuche* in 1943. When you are over the anchor the north peak on Benito East will bear 056°, the south end of Benito East 090° and the cross on top of the hill south of the village on Benito West 293°.

A number of bird species nest on the islands, including black, least and Leach's storm petrels. Beachcombers may find objects of interest in a number of locations. The wreck of the wooden tuna clipper *Southern Pacific* is scattered along the north shore of Benito West, due north of the settlement. Wrecked in 1971, she was equipped with a seaplane. Her engines, a shaft and a five-foot propeller lie in three fathoms. Benito Central's north coast is strewn with all manner of flotsam. An enormous colony of sea lions lives on the island, some so friendly and curious they inhibit spearfishing; you can't shoo them off. A large number of elephant seals inhabit

Benito East. Local divers give them healthy respect and stay well clear if they see them in the water. Sea caves are found on Benito East.

Good anchorages are found off the settlement on Benito West and off the south side of the island, but kelp can be dense. No regular source of gas or supplies will be found at the settlement, although emergency assistance might be obtained. Long-range fishing and diving vessels out of San Diego visit, as do some natural-history cruises. Small boats can make the voyage from Cedros, but the route is exposed to ocean waves and currents. There is a good deal of coming and going of *pangas* between Cedros and the settlement, and it should not be difficult to obtain a ride or hire a boat. Take care; in 1951 an abalone boat turned over en route to Cedros, drowning twenty-three people.

Back on the Transpeninsular Highway at Guerrero Negro junction, KM 217

KM	LOCATION
208	Sedan road to south (signed "Laguna Ojo de Liebre") to Parque Natural de la Ballena Gris, seventeen miles.

SIDETRIP TO SCAMMON'S LAGOON

The road crosses a number of salt flats and is badly washboarded, but it can handle moderate RVs. This whale-watching site on Scammon's is both a disappointment and a joy. The whales are normally far from shore and binoculars are necessary to see any detail, but on a broader scale how many places in the world can you drive to in an ordinary sedan and see three or four whales breaching or spy-hopping simultaneously? Local entrepreneurs sometimes offer whale-watching trips from the park and from the fish camp a mile east. The park is an underwater ecological reserve. A deposit of fossilized shark teeth can be found mixed in the surface gravel northwest of the park.

Most visitors are so entranced by the whales that they do not recognize that the lagoon, with its shallow waters, extensive mud flats and marshes and rich production of fish, mollusks, worms and other creatures, is prime avian territory. Given its biological and geographical similarity to nearby Laguna San Ignacio, it might be expected that check lists for the lagoon would approach 100 species, but for unknown reasons less than half that appears more realistic, and the species composition differs noticeably. The more interesting and unusual (for Baja) birds include horned grebe, American white pelican, snowy and reddish egrets, little blue and tricolored herons, northern pintail, northern shoveler, gadwal, American wigeon, redhead, common goldeneye, bufflehead, ruddy duck, bald eagle, clapper rail, lesser yellowlegs, red knot, glaucous gull, Caspian and least terns, short-eared owl, marsh wren and green-tailed towhee.

A very rare creature used to live in the area. Years ago an old man in Guerrero Negro told me about a species of jack-rabbit, known locally as *orejas de vela* (sail-ears), that lived along the eastern margin of the lagoon. When the breezes came from the west in the morning they found they could use their big ears to sail deep into the desert to forage. When the

Elephant seals like to throw gravel on their backs, perhaps to keep the flies off or for the cooling effect. These females live on Benito East.

breeze from the east began in the evening they could then sail back to drink at a place known as *Fuente de Liebre* (Jack Rabbit Spring). Those with the largest ears prospered, and as the years passed the species kept evolving ever-larger ears. However, fishermen in Bahía Vizcaíno began to find them in the stomachs of sharks, and the scenario was obvious: while sailing back to the spring in the evenings they had forgotten to furl their ears in time and were blown into the bay, only to be eaten by hungry sharks. By now so many have been eaten that the species may be extinct, leaving only jacks with regular ears.

****

THE MUD FLAT STORY. Occasionally even the most modest of vehicles can triumph over the fancy four-wheelers, at least for a while. My partner John Anglin and I were skirting the east end of Scammon's in my Chevy van, trying a shortcut from Guerrero Negro to the road to Tortugas. As night fell the wheel track we were following disappeared and it became necessary to steer by compass. To liven things up I put on a Vivaldi tape, and John found a bottle of tequila in a duffel bag. The terrain was so smooth and flat we seemed to be flying, and I found I could drive forty and even fifty miles an hour. This was the way Baja ought to be: no banging and bumping, no clouds of dust, no hot sun! We discovered the secret of drinking tequila; just learn to accept the fact that it tastes like turpentine, and after that it's not too bad. We were thoroughly enjoying ourselves, but finally we picked up the Tortugas road and were soon creeping down a steep, rough grade in a series of hairpin turns toward Malarrimo. Arriving at the beach just as the fifth straight rendition of Four Seasons finished, we bedded down for the night, very mellow and ready for sleep.

We awoke the next morning to find three men standing over us, a Jeep and a Power Wagon parked nearby. "How did you get that thing here?" they wanted to know, pointing to the van. I responded that I had driven it. They then wanted to know our route, which I described. As I confirmed that it was indeed a perfectly ordinary battered 250-cube, three-speed Chevy van with a fifteen-foot boat on top and a moun-

tain of gear in back, a look of disdain came over their faces, and one of them said, "No way, man." We insisted; the van was right in front of them, wasn't it, and there were no parachutes lying about, were there? Finally one of them blurted out, "You guys claim to have crossed the mud flats in that piece of junk?" Not comprehending his meaning, I replied, "Mud flats? What mud flats?" Only then did we look at the van; an inches-thick layer of gray mud covered the sides, sagging and folding to give it the appearance of a stuffed elephant mounted on little wheels. Apparently we had crossed an extensive mud flat without realizing it during party time the night before, our high velocity saving us from disappearing into the awful ooze. John spoke up instantly. "Mud flats? What mud flats?" he repeated, following it with a knowing chuckle; he wasn't about to let these four-wheel guys with their chrome-plated roll bars, fat tires and tuck-and-roll upholstery put us down. I caught on, adding with a scoff, "It was nothing. We could hardy tell we were crossing them," without stating the reason why.

We were making progress, for their disdain was obviously melting. "Wow! That's hard to believe. It takes a big four-wheel rig with flotation tires to get through gook like that. You actually made it in that thing without sinking up to your keesters?" Continuing our minimalist approach, we flatly denied that our accomplishment was anything out of the ordinary, subtly implying that only less-than-skilled drivers needed to rely on the advantages of four-wheel-drive, to the obvious discomfort of our audience. We were making rapid progress, for now we had their rapt attention. I discussed several theories on soft-ground driving, not mentioning their recent origin, and John told of the times we had come to the aid of other drivers, creating the impression that some of them might even have been four-wheelers, simply by leaving it unsaid.

Finally, they respectfully thanked us for sharing our knowledge, strode over to their vehicles and started to drive off—and we had the exquisite pleasure of seeing the Jeep sink to the axles in soft sand. Struggling to hold back the roars of laughter trying to escape, we stoically watched as they rigged a winch line from the Power Wagon, our undeserved triumph complete, if short-lived. Our comeuppance came after breakfast, when we loaded up and started out across the sand, getting perhaps fifty yards before we too sank to the axles.

****

On the Transpeninsular Highway at KM 208

189+   Road northeast (signed) to El Arco and Bahía San Francisquito.

SIDETRIP TO EL ARCO AND BAHÍA SAN FRANCISQUITO

Although the graded road south from Bahía de los Angeles is now the preferred route to Bahía San Francisquito, this road through El Arco passes through one of the more heavily mineralized areas in Baja, and it may be useful for making loop trips. The road into El Arco was once paved, but maintenance was ignored from the start and it is now a moonscape of potholes. In a thousand years anthropologists may be poking about trying to figure out why a road was built and then immediately allowed to fall into ruin. Sandy trails on each side of the pavement provide good driving.

Set odometer. At Mile 25.4 arrive at El Arco. In 1882 extensive placers eventually producing over \$3 million in gold were discovered at nearby Calmallí. Gold was discovered later at El Arco, and in the 1920s a thousand miners were at work. Today copper and gold mining continues sporadically at a low level. Hopes are high for newly discovered deposits, but little seems to change from year to year. Semi-employed miners sometimes offer samples of quartz, hematite, turquoise, chrysocolla and malachite. Pseudomorphs of pyrites in scattered crystals have been found nearby.

To continue on, locate the *Delegación Municipal* building, identified by its twin radio towers, at Mile 25.8. Pass this on your left, continue straight ahead (335°) and immediately drop into an arroyo, staying right (020°) at the intersection at Mile 25.9. Arrive at Pozo Alemán at Mile 27.9, a collection of ramshackle buildings with a total population of two. At the cemetery take the left (045°) fork. Continue straight ahead (045°) at the fork at Mile 35.8, pass through a great dátilillo forest beginning at Mile 50.8, and arrive at the beginning of La Cuesta de la Ley at Mile 54.7. "The Slope That Rules" has been tamed by bulldozers, and today sedans can normally make it with some difficulty, but even in years past it was overrated; with its one mile of grades, the steepest only 27%, it was no challenge to the "Terrible Three" south of Puertecitos. At Mile 62.5 arrive at Rancho el Progreso, turn left (330°) and join the Bahía de los Angeles-Bahía San Francisquito road at Mile 63.2. Turn left (070°) at the fork at Mile 72.6 and arrive at the inner harbor of Bahía San Francisquito at Mile 74.2.

This harbor is the only all-weather anchorage between Puerto Don Juan and Santa Rosalía. Trailerboats as large as twenty-two feet have been brought over the road from Bahía de los Angeles and launched here across the gently sloping sand beach. There is relatively little pressure from sport or commercial fishermen, and sea bass and groupers get very, very large. There is an excellent seasonal fishery for yellowtail, which pass the area heading south in early November, returning north in late May and early June. One of the most productive fishing areas is Bahía San Rafael, beginning five miles to the northwest of Punta San Francisquito. Whales often are seen in Canal de Salsipuedes. Diving is good off Punta San Francisquito, but is better around Isla San Lorenzo.

Alberto Lucero, a local resident, offers fishing, diving, camping and natural-history trips throughout the area and to the islands in the Midriff from November through April. In addition he and his wife Deborah sell hand-painted clothing, desert art and gourmet Baja cuisine, and he is a welder. Nova is usually available and possibly Magnasin. They have a home on the inner bay and monitor VHF channel 16, "Blue Fox." Reservations and information can be obtained by writing to the address listed in Appendix A. Allow a month for a response.

Ensenada Blanca, in the lee of Punta Santa Teresa, four miles "clockwise" from the inner bay, provides good protection from prevailing weather. Punta San Francisquito Resort, on the sandy shore of the bay, has rental cabins, meals and a SCUBA compressor. *Pangas* and guides are available, and

Nova is usually for sale. Shelling in the area is good, primarily for murex, olive, cowrie and pearl oyster. The anchorage off Rancho el Barril, eight miles south, is nothing but an open roadstead. It is a long, desolate seventy-four miles from El Barril to Santa Rosalía, with only a few points providing even marginal protection, the best of which is Cabo San Miguel, and only a few fish camps or ranches.

Back on the Transpeninsular Highway at KM 189+

144   **Vizcaíno.** PEMEX (MND), motel, restaurant, groceries, auto parts, tires, stores, ice, bakery, pharmacy. The attendants at the PEMEX are magicians, so watch closely.

THE VIZCAÍNO LOOP TRIP

One of longest and most interesting off-road trips in Baja crosses the Desierto de Vizcaíno to Bahía Tortugas, heads south through Bahía Asunción to Punta Abreojos and returns to the Transpeninsular in the vicinity of San Ignacio. The attraction is not the scenery, for most of the trip is across flat coastal plains, but rather the remoteness and grand scale of the desert. Once you near the ocean the reward is more than sixty miles of the most deserted and pristine beaches in North America, plus fine diving and fishing. With luck, you might see an antelope, one of Baja's rarest animals (only about ninety are still left). The Vizcaíno is not a prime birding area, with relatively low numbers and no species unique to it, but sightings might include sage sparrow, the uncommon LeConte's thrasher and endemic gray thrasher, as well as birds typically found throughout Baja in similar habitats.

Large areas inside this great loop are covered with a rare type of dune. Called "transverse dunes," they form when winds blow steadily in one direction, causing the surface to look like huge plowed furrows in a farmer's field. Similar dunes have been observed in northern Australia. The central Vizcaíno is among the most inaccessible wildernesses left on the peninsula. However, change is coming; the major roads have been graded and water and power lines have been extended to the coast. It is now feasible to make the trip in sizable RVs, and adventurous trailerboaters equipped for over-the-beach launches have access to Isla Natividad, Cedros and the Benitos, and to the south, Asunción and Abreojos.

The road to Tortugas is often rough and washboarded, so plan on at least a six hour journey. Gas and supplies may or may not be available in Tortugas, Asunción and the other villages along the way, so make sure you are topped off. Set odometer. Bicyclists may be able to leave their vehicles at the restaurant at Mile 0.8. The pavement, much of it in poor repair, ends at Mile 18. At Mile 46.2 encounter a graded road south, ending on the coast road east of Asunción. Watch for outcroppings of magnesite around Mile 55.0 (there are working mines in the vicinity). The road north to legendary Playa Malarrimo is found at Mile 72.4.

SIDETRIP TO PLAYA MALARRIMO

Long the most famous beachcombing area in Baja, this beach has yielded U.S. Navy mops and firefighting foam containers, human bodies, palm and redwood logs, hatch covers, enormous numbers of light bulbs and Twinkies wrappers, airplane wings, shipwrecks—both in their entirety and in thousands of various parts—prized Japanese glass fishing floats and a twelve-foot torpedo emitting buzzing noises. A statistical analysis of the huge crop of cans and bottles would reveal that humans drink a great deal of alcohol, cover their food with layers of catsup and are deeply concerned about underarm odor. While you are searching, try to figure out why empty catsup bottles are almost always capped, while alcohol bottles are generally open. The beach is slowly advancing, so it might pay to explore areas as far as 500 yards inland. Shell collectors will find dozens of species, many specimens beach-worn, a few fresh. Spend the night; there's usually lots of firewood.

The road north from Mile 72.4 is hard to spot; if you miss it keep going until you see the sign for Rancho San José de Castro, and go back (east) 0.4 mile. The twenty-six mile road, with an 18% grade in one stretch, is for pickups or four-wheel-drives only. Because of deep sand those in two-wheel-drive pickups should stop a half-mile short of the beach and walk in; if you can see the water you are already in trouble. An easier approach from the vicinity of Bahía Tortugas is described in the next section.

Back on the Vizcaíno-Bahía Tortugas road at Mile 72.4

At Mile 72.8, a short road runs south to Rancho San José de Castro, a possible source of water and meals. At Mile 75.6 note the intersection with the old road to Asunción (more on this later). Bahía Tortugas (Puerto San Bartolomé) at Mile 107.3 is the finest all-weather anchorage between San Diego and Bahía Magdalena. The sizable town has groceries, hotel and rooms, restaurants, liquor, taxis, medical, pharmacy, *pangas* for hire, Pesca office, mechanics, auto parts, tires, telegraph, bank, PEMEX (N only, diesel at the pier) and ice at the packing plant. The cannery has a decompression chamber. No COTP is assigned, but naval personnel may ask to see vessel papers. Tickets and information on the Cannery Airline can be obtained at a two-story house with a big satellite dish at 20 de Noviembre Number 4 several blocks north of the cannery. The airport is a mile north of town.

There are no organized RV parks, but camping is possible at many sandy locations around the bay. A favorite place with many visitors is Bahía Cambrey (described shortly). Boats can be launched over a sand beach west of the pier in town, at a number of locations along the eastern margin of the bay, or over a hard sand and gravel beach near the fishing camp at its southwest end. Fishing in the bay is difficult in some areas due to beds of weed, but outstanding fishing for sand bass, kelp bass and ocean whitefish is found outside between Cabo Tórtolo and Punta Cambrey (Punta Thurloe). The main channel out of the bay, about a mile wide and marked by light-houses on its north and south margins, offers excellent fishing for bonito, yellowtail, barracuda and dolphin in season, out to about four miles. There is good offshore fishing at the "15 Spot," six miles, 248° from Punta la Cantina (Punta Sargazo); at "38 Spot," twelve miles, 150°; at "9 Spot," twenty-two miles, 176°; and at "10 Spot," twenty-five miles, 138°. Hand-liners working from *pangas* account for part of the commercial catch in the area, and they need bait, so gillnets are maintained along the south shore of the bay. This bait is sometimes sold from a boat anchored off the village and might be available—ask at the beach.

Gray whales come close to shore, occasionally entering kelp beds. A friend and I were fishing near Punta Cambrey when a gray plowed through the kelp like a gigantic bulldozer not five yards away, apparently oblivious of our presence. At least four fishing vessels have sunk in the bay, but the only known diveable wreck is in sixty feet of water, 2/3 mile southeast of Punta la Cantina. Divers almost acquired a magnificent wreck when the Japanese armored cruiser *Asama* hit a rock at the mouth of the bay while on a First World War patrol, ripping a fifteen-foot gash in her hull. "Unfortunately," she was refloated three months later and made it back to Japan.

The road to the village near Punta Eugenia is normally passable by passenger cars. Reset your odometer, drive north from the Kaluha cantina and follow the signs starting near the airport, arriving at Mile 16.5. Small boats can be launched inside the natural breakwater, and *pangas* are for hire. There is no good place to launch trailerboats. A building in the village houses an inoperative decompression chamber. Due to low visibilities, diving is poor in the immediate vicinity of the village.

Natividad lies five miles west. Although it is within easy range of a boat launched from Eugenia or Bahía Tortugas, few sport divers or fishermen come to the island. Scorpio Surfing Tours has a camp on the island, with rooms, showers and an outhouse, and it offers trips from late June through September, with transportation by chartered multi-engine aircraft. The primary break is "Open Doors," a sand-bottom beach break on the east side of the island, off the end of the airstrip. Big swells from July to September bring extraordinary surf, with almost every wave producing stand-up tubes and great rights and lefts. It is only a short paddle to the lineup, and the bottom is free of obstructions. In winter, northwest swells can wrap around the point into the teeth of the wind, providing fine conditions free of chop. With hollow faces to fifteen feet, "Siren Bay" on the southwest side of the island about a mile southeast of the north cape works well in winter. Getting to this site takes about forty-five minutes in a boat from the village. Described as "gnarly," it is not for novice surfers, since there is no way to escape except back the way you came, and a broken leash means a lost board and a long swim. A third major break, "Frijole Bowl," a reef break off the south point, has occasionally seen faces over twenty feet during winter, no place for beginners.

The anchorage off the village at the south end is open and subject to refracted swell, and can be very windy. No regular source of fuel or supplies will be found. A decompression chamber is located in the village. In 1909 the brig *Blakely* was lost along the southeast shore. In addition, villagers report two vessels in about fifty feet a hundred yards off the west end of the landing. Chart 21011 shows a wreck on the southwest side.

Back in the vicinity of Bahía Tortugas, a road runs north and then east along the coast to the Malarrimo area. It can be found by driving east on the main road 1.8 miles east from the "Bahía Tortugas" road sign on the eastern outskirts of town. This road gets occasional maintenance and is less susceptible to washouts than the road described earlier. Bob and Bonnie Rauch have successfully made the run in a twenty-foot Champion motorhome.

Just 2.1 miles from the sign, a sedan road turns south and winds along the eastern shore of the bay. The sandy shores here provide good camping and a place to launch boats. At Mile 11.0 the road ends at Bahía Cambrey (Thurloe Bay). The sandy bottom of the bay is home to astronomical numbers of pismo clams. Stretching east and then south for five miles or more, the beds are so dense that the mere act of anchoring can uproot a dinner-load. Shellers will find specimens of a dozen or more species on the beach, most sea-worn, a few fresh. Vehicles can get near the beach and small boats can be launched, but a rocky berm makes it difficult to launch trailerboats. The bay provides an open anchorage, the next anchorages to the south being Bahías San Pablo, San Roque, Asunción, San Hipólito and Ballenas.

To continue the Vizcaíno Loop Trip, return to Mile 46.2 or Mile 75.6 on the Vizcaíno-Bahía Tortugas road to reach Asunción. Both routes are normally satisfactory, but only the one from Mile 46.2 is capable of handling motorhomes and trailers. There are virtually no ranches along either route once past the Santa Monica-Rancho San José de Castro area, although enough water for a bath might be found at deserted Rancho San Andrés. Asunción, ninety miles from Tortugas via Mile 46.2, sixty-five via Mile 75.6, has a health clinic, pharmacy, mail, telegraph, Pesca office, groceries, desalinization plant and rooms for rent. There is no PEMEX, but several locals sell Nova from drums. Diesel might be available at the cannery in an emergency.

After climbing down low cliffs, surfers will find good reef breaks at the point. Boats can be launched over the beach in town and at a steep unpaved area 1/4 mile inside the point. Anchorages off the village and at Isla Asunción are satisfactory in prevailing seas. Fishing is excellent on reefs around the island and directly offshore, at "24 Spot," six miles, 245° from the south tip of Isla Asunción, and at "6 Spot," three miles, 120° from the same place.

Diving near town is limited, but the island has excellent spearfishing. I once fired up my hooka and made a dive off the island. When I reached the bottom, stood up and looked around, I was stunned to see a dozen, twenty—no forty—lobsters within the range of visibility. Had they chosen to act collectively the outcome would have been quite different. Three large U.S. fishing vessels have been wrecked near the island.

A rich deposit of fossilized shark teeth can be found by hiking from the north end of town on course 343°, aiming for the area between a large red-colored tableland and a row of hills. At Minute 75 you should arrive in a deep and distinctive canyon with a fair amount of tan, chalk-like deposits. Lying in the gravel, the teeth range in size from 1/4 inch to an inch or more. Also to be seen are assortments of fossilized scallops, whelks, clams and sand dollars.

San Roque village can be reached by locating the SSA Centro de Salud health clinic in Asunción and driving 9.6 miles north on a sedan road (muddy after rains). Boats can be launched over the sandy beach, and *pangas* are for hire. The anchorage is only fair. Although seldom visited by boaters, Bahía San Pablo to the north offers a deep but otherwise good anchorage. Long-range boats from San Diego sometimes fish San Pablo.

Good fishing for yellowtail and bottomfish is found northwest of Isla San Roque. Due to a small navigational error on August 8, 1921, Captain J. C. Zastrow provided future skin divers with an interesting wreck off the island. The steamer *San José* can be found south of its southeast tip, her booms, winches, plates and ribs scattered over a wide area at depths up to thirty feet. Another wreck lies on a sand bottom east of the island. Originally about seventy feet long, she lies in forty feet of water. When you are over the wreck, the aid-to-navigation tower on the island will bear 230°, and the central and largest islet among the small group to the southeast 126°. Large numbers of kelp bass and sand bass frequent the area, and the bugs get so big you can eat their legs like king crab.

The coast between Bahía Cambrey and Bahía San Pablo is penetrated by only a few poor roads, but many roads reach the beaches from San Roque south. This stretch is a surf fisherman's paradise, perhaps the least stressed and most productive beach fishery in Baja. The beaches between San Roque and Asunción have superb beachcasting for corbina, and the rays of the setting sun passing through the waves often reveal hordes of fish searching for food, a stirring sight to anyone, fisherman or not.

Continuing on the Vizcaíno Loop Trip, reset odometer and drive east from Asunción along miles of beautiful sand beach. At Mile 19.6 take the left (100°) fork. (The right fork leads to the tiny settlements of Punta Prieta and San Hipólito.) Bahía San Hipólito has a large anchorage which is satisfactory in prevailing seas, and a good reef break. The rocky beaches around Mile 43.5 are a favorite with shorecasters, small bits of clam often producing large numbers of yellowfin croakers and sand bass.

The small town of La Bocana, at Mile 49.0, has grocery stores, tires, restaurant, health clinic, pharmacy, telegraph, mail and a desalinization plant. There is no PEMEX, but Nova is sold from drums, and diesel may be available at the packing plant. Boats can be launched over the low sand beach south of the packing plant. The entrance to Estero la Bocana is shallow, allowing only the smallest boats to anchor. Large numbers of cabrilla, croaker, corvina, corbina, shark and halibut are taken inside the estero, and although there is an active commercial *panga* fleet, dolphin, yellowtail, and black and white sea bass are still numerous offshore.

The road to Abreojos passes close to the estero, offering numerous chances to launch small boats. Abreojos, at Mile 60.0, has very limited groceries, Pesca office, telephone, telegraph, ice, tires, health clinic, restaurant and a desalinization plant. No PEMEX again, but locals sell Nova and possibly Magnasin out of drums. The anchorage east of the point is marginally satisfactory, being open to the south, with refracted swell and lots of wind. A number of vessels have been lost due to confusion around the many offshore reefs and pinnacles; they didn't name it "Open-Your-Eyes" for nothing. The point has a fantastic right break in good swells—some fans claim it is the best right point break in Baja. Abreojos is well-known and much discussed among several generations of boardsailors, who capitalize on passing fronts, especially from March to May or June. Fishing is excellent, and shorecasters take corvina, corbina and croakers. Wright Shoal, a mile southeast of Punta Abreojos, and Roca Ballena, four miles west, produce white seabass and yellowtail, and a dozen grouper and black sea bass approaching fifty pounds would not be too much to hope for during a single trip. Cartop and inflatable boats can be launched northeast of town.

Sailors heading south from Abreojos will find that tidal currents, shoals and shifting sand bars make the entrance to Laguna San Ignacio dangerous, and the first good anchorages south of Abreojos are large, shallow Bahía San Juanico and Bahía Santa María.

Leaving Abreojos, reset odometer. At Mile 6.1, a road east will be noted leading along a sandy peninsula forming the western margin of shallow Laguna la Escondido (Estero de Coyote), which offers excellent fishing for spotted bass, grouper, corvina, halibut, sierra, barracuda and maybe, just maybe, snook. Much of the inside of the estero is lined with mangrove, so see page 200 for some fishing hints. The deep area just inside the entrance can be fantastic, as close to fool-proof fishing as can be found in Baja. The estero is very shallow and turns into mud flats in periods of very low tides—check your tide book before coming and avoid low periods. Various basses, croaker and grouper are taken in the channel leading to the ocean. White water is often present on a sandy reef directly south of the channel entrance, and boaters launching inside the estero must use great caution when heading for Wright Shoal or Roca Ballena, even in periods of relative calm. Boaters have made it safely around the white water area by heading south out of the channel for 1/2 mile until the beach breakers are cleared, then turning east and running a mile or so until the white water area is bypassed. Better yet, watch for local *panga* fishermen heading out and follow them.

Camping is possible at many places along the peninsula and near the entrance to the estuary—a fee may be charged. Campo Rene will be encountered partway to the entrance. Campers are welcome, and cartoppers, inflatables and small trailerboats can be launched in the estuary. La Baja Experi-

Reeve, Rob and I almost exploded from eating too many lobsters.

ence Club leases property here and has a rustic camp with sleeping tents, a large dining tent and showers, with power provided by an electrical generator. Fly-in package tours and rental tackle are available.

The road northeast from Abreojos to the Transpeninsular is graded but is sometimes badly washboarded. At Mile 54.3 the Transpeninsular is reached at KM 98.

Back on the Transpeninsular Highway at Vizcaíno, KM 144

118   Road northeast to San Francisco (signed).

SIDETRIP TO THE SIERRA DE SAN FRANCISCO

This sidetrip will take you to some of the most spectacular mountain scenery in Baja, with the added attraction of its finest rock-art site closely accessible by car. The new road has no grades over 14% and while it can handle small motorhomes, there are sharp switchbacks and few places in which to turn around. At least six hours should be allowed for the trip. Set odometer. After crossing flat desert for six miles, the road switches back a number of times to the top of a narrow ridge, climbing toward massive Pico Santa Monica, at 5,218 feet the highest point in the Sierra de San Francisco. There are deep canyons on each side, and although the road closely approaches their edges, it pays to stop occasionally and do some hiking to actually look over the edge.

After passing several small ranches, the road swings around the upper reaches of Cañon San Pablo at Mile 20.0. One of the most magnificent canyons in Baja—on a par with, but very different from, Cañon Tajo far to the north—this narrow, thousand-foot-deep, palm-lined gorge is the location of Gardner Cave, the crown jewel of Baja rock art, as well as several other fine sites. With its treasures of man-made and natural art, the entire area should be made into a national park (more on the canyon at the end of this chapter). At Mile 21.0 arrive at the site of Cueva Ratón (signed). While not of the caliber of the sites farther downstream, this site has a 30-foot-wide mural showing figures of humans, deer, lions, mountain sheep and other animals, with examples of the bicolor and overpainting traditions. All visitors to the site must have a guide, obtained at the village of San Francisco at Mile 22.5. The local policeman keeps a sharp eye. Arrangements can be made in the village for three-day burro trips to see Gardner Cave.

Since you were probably intent on the scenery ahead on the way up, the trip back to the Transpeninsular will be an all-but-new treat: canyon walls resembling a vast book with pages fifty feet thick, and vistas of the head of Laguna San Ignacio and the Sierra Santa Clara, over forty miles away.

Back on the Transpeninsular Highway at KM 118

98   Road southwest (signed) to Abreojos (already described). Modest cafe.
90   Rolling hills with gentle to moderate grades until KM 17+.
85   Halfway point between Tijuana and Cabo San Lucas.

Bernie Eskesen and Ruben Villa Carmona sort through shark teeth.

77+   Agricultural inspection for north-bound vehicles.
73+   **San Ignacio junction**.

SIDETRIP TO SAN IGNACIO

The scenery on the Transpeninsular for more than a hundred miles has been flat, featureless and boring, and an arrival at San Ignacio, with its ponds and large groves of palms, is one of Baja's most pleasant surprises. A Jesuit mission was founded in 1728, and a massive stone church with walls four feet thick was completed fifty-eight years later by the Dominicans. Spring water was distributed through the town by a system of stone-lined channels and octagonal cisterns that still can be seen. A wide variety of fruits was grown at one time, but date palms now dominate everything. Some grape vines were planted so long ago that they now assume tree-like proportions. In 1928 Phillip Townsend Hanna worried that the introduction of electricity and cinema would be the "ruination of one of the most engaging spots conceivable," but these evils have had little influence, and the village remains amiable, low pressure and much like it was in the past. A great deal of story telling, loafing and surreptitious drinking goes on under the massive Indian laurel trees in the town square, and a visit to the church and a walk through the village can occupy several hours.

Sales and services available include PEMEX (MND), tires, mechanics, stores, restaurants, bank, health clinic, pharmacy, taxi, telephone, telegraph, mail, meat market, groceries, ice, RV parks and motel. The La Pinta Hotel offers rooms, restaurant, bar, volleyball, a pool and a Magnasin pump. Potable water can be obtained from spigots in the square. The trailer park behind the PEMEX theoretically has full hookups, restrooms and showers, but things rarely work. La Candelaria Trailer Park (signed), 1 1/4 miles into town from the highway, has no facilities, but it is located in the palms and is clean and quiet. The kids can watch for turtles in the pools, and the nightly frog chorus is the best in Baja. The access road may be a little tight for large rigs. It may be possible to make arrangements to visit Cueva Palmarito in the Rancho Santa Martha area and other rock-art sites to the north; ask at the La Posada Hotel, south of the square a few blocks. See page 177

Mike snorkels with a baby.

for a bit of the history of the family that owns this hotel.

SIDETRIP TO LAGUNA SAN IGNACIO

Laguna San Ignacio is one of the world's major gray whale breeding grounds, and one of the few places where friendly whale behavior has been observed. The road from San Ignacio has been graded and improved, and sedans and small motorhomes can make the trip. However, be warned—the road is narrow, making it difficult to pass approaching vehicles, and sections of the road have world-class washboard. The drive takes three hours one-way.

Starting in town on the south side of the square, set odometer and drive east, turn right (170°) at Mile 0.3 and left (090°) at the large satellite dish at Mile 0.5. The road will quickly climb a hill, swing right and head south. Half a dozen ranches will be passed in the first fifteen miles, and you will encounter the fish camps of Laguna de San Ignacio, La Base and La Fridera at Miles 36.0, 37.0 and 40.0, respectively. The scenery and camping opportunities nearby are not inspiring, mostly desert scrub, mangroves and extensive mud flats, and there are no whales to be seen at first, but your disappointment should be short-lived. Six miles southwest of La Fridera is Punta Prieta, a low-lying point with a rocky margin jutting into the lagoon. The waters surrounding this point and south to the entrance of the lagoon are the winter home of the friendly whales. Due to mud and tidal flats it might not be possible to drive all the way to Punta Prieta, but you should be able to get within walking distance, and a tent camp can be set up on the point if you want to stay overnight.

The scene offshore in winter is magnificent. Grays look awkward because of their immense size, but they are in fact extremely graceful and have a repertory of movements requiring great agility. They often spy-hop and appear to be scanning the horizon. The motive is probably just what it seems to be: they want a better view. Many whales will be seen breaching, leaping completely or almost all the way out of water and landing with tremendous splashes, sometimes two or three times in a row, the leaps about fifteen seconds apart. They may do this to dislodge parasites, but some people believe it is a demonstration of their immense power, or perhaps a whale sport or even just for the fun of it. Adults and babies often "corkscrew," rolling over again and again as they move through the water.

This grand ballet is presented far closer to shore than the one at Parque Natural de la Ballena Gris near Guerrero Negro, so binoculars will reveal small details. The whales soon become aware of your presence, and a few may come closer and spy-hop to get a better look at the curious creatures watching them. Between the loud "whooooosh" of breathing whales and the yipping of coyotes, campers sometimes have trouble sleeping. Fishermen from the camps are often willing to take you in their boats into the midst of all this cetacean activity. The whales seem unconcerned by the presence of boats, allowing you to get close to see mothers nursing their babies, mating activity and the whole repertory of whale ballet.

The motivations of whales can never be known, and some people insist that grays are not "friendly" but merely curious. However, based on our experiences during a visit to the lagoon, Mike and I decided they are indeed friendly. Together with two young men we met, we hired a fisherman to take us to Punta Prieta. There were dozens of whales nearby, and when we stopped the boat a cow and a calf immediately changed course and headed directly toward us. We were soon the recipients of nuzzles and nudges from a twenty-five ton mother and her two-ton calf, both intent on being scratched and petted. After they had spent forty-five minutes with us we moved to another area, only to quickly gain the attentions of another pair, and later in the day, a third. As we leaned over the side, each of the three mothers repeatedly swam under her baby and pushed it to the surface, as if urging it to get a better look. Both the mothers and the babies were very playful, and as the babies grew more familiar with us they became bolder, one even becoming rambunctious. The mothers occasionally swished their great flukes under our boat, bouncing it on huge boils of water. One mother rolled on her side and repeatedly vented spray and smelly breath directly at me as I took photographs, too often to be mere chance.

Another mother even played a joke on Steve Prasser. He was sitting with his rear hanging over the side of the boat, when she let out a great blast of bubbles directly beneath him. Mike, then thirteen years old, had the wonderful experience of snorkeling for a short time with a mother and baby. You take your chances when you dive here—whales generally accept humans above the water as friendly, but not so often below the surface.

Like Parque Natural de la Ballena Gris, the whale show rarely gives visitors time to recognize that the lagoon and surrounding areas are prime birding territory. A complete check list might approach a hundred species, but the more interesting and uncommon (in Baja) include common loon, horned grebe, northern fulmar, American white pelican, pelagic cormorant, great, reddish and snowy egrets, little blue and tricolored herons, black-crowned and yellow-crowned night-herons, greater white-fronted goose, northern pintail, American wigeon, redhead, ring-necked duck, greater scaup, white-winged scooter, common goldeneye, bufflehead, common and red-breasted mergansers, ruddy duck, northern harrier, merlin, semipalmated plover, American avocet, greater yellowlegs, red knot, dunlin, pomarine and parasitic jaegers, Thayer's gull, rhinoceros auklet, short-eared owl, rufous hummingbird, black phoebe, LeConte's thrasher and America redstart.

The regional map for this chapter shows two roads heading southeast from an intersection near La Fridera, the "high road" and the "low road." The intersection can be found as follows: from the center of La Base camp drive south on a sandy, one-lane road, staying left at the forks at Miles 0.5, 0.8 and 1.4. Encounter the intersection at Mile 3.0. For the "high road" turn left (102°), for the "low road" continue straight ahead (174°) and make the first left (110°). From this point on, the map is a vast simplification, for there are dozens of impromptu roads; when one becomes too muddy the locals find another way and a new road develops. Accurate maps and road directions are thus impossible, and the trip requires a compass, patience and plenty of time. Pickups or four-wheel-drives are advisable on either route.

The "high road" winds past coastal mesas and arroyos and is rough and slow. The "low road" across the mud flats is fast and smooth, but after rains or extreme high tides it can be impassable. Do not stray off the wheel tracks, even in dry weather, for a bottomless pit of gooey mud lies on either side. If you encounter an approaching vehicle on the mud flats, do not pull over to allow it to pass; one vehicle should back down to firm ground. Approximately fifty-six miles from La Base by either road the pleasant settlement of Cadajé is reached, and nine more miles will take you to San Juanico, located at the head of beautiful Bahía San Juanico. The tiny village has a PEMEX (N), several small stores and a restaurant specializing in fried lobster. The head of Bahía San Juanico provides an excellent anchorage, although surf may discourage landings.

The highly regarded point breaks at nearby Punta Pequeña are best on south summer swells. Nineteen miles southeast of San Juanico, just before the road crosses Arroyo San Gregorio, there is a right (195°) turn, signed "La Bocana," that leads nine miles to Punta San Juanico; avoid turns until in the vicinity of the point. Although less consistent than Pequeña, Juanico also has excellent surfing, especially in southwest to northwest swells. Several intermittent streams empty into the nearby estero, causing sanding and frequent changes in bottom contours, and surfers often find conditions changing day by day. These conditions often make the bay in the lee of the point a poor place to anchor.

Approximately twenty-five miles southeast of San Juanico there is an important intersection where you can continue south, arriving at Villa Insurgentes in sixty-eight more miles, or turn northeast through La Purísima and San Isidoro, joining the Transpeninsular at KM 60 (see the map on page 175). This latter road is part of the Mountain Villages Loop Trip, described in the next chapter.

Back on the Transpeninsular Highway at KM 73+

59+   Pickup road north (signed) to Rancho Santa Martha.

SIDETRIP TO THE RANCHO SANTA MARTHA AREA

Set odometer. Swing left (330°) off the graded road at Mile 1.0, and arrive at Rancho el Carricito at Mile 11.3. The road makes an abrupt right (100°) turn at the ranch and then swings north again. The scenery grows more beautiful as you gain altitude, with twisted volcanic shapes and fantastic horizons. Arrive at the ranch at Mile 28.3. Guides can be obtained for a hike to see the rock art at nearby Cueva Palmarito. The two-hour hike is a small price to pay; a great mural is worked across the back wall of a rock shelter 150 feet long and 40 feet high, with figures of red deer, a black mountain lion and other animals. Over a dozen human figures are shown, many in headdress, some in the bicolor tradition, others in vertical stripes. The ranch can provide horses or burros for those unable or unwilling to hike.

Back on the Transpeninsular Highway at KM 59+

53   **Ejido Bonfil**. Cafes, groceries, mechanic, tire repair.
41   Parking for the Tres Vírgenes climb.

SIDETRIP TO THE TRES VÍRGENES

The Tres Vírgenes are the most recently active volcanos on the peninsula, Father Consag's diaries describing an eruption that occurred in 1746. In 1857 large volumes of steam were reported, and recent climbers have reported gas and vapor from fissures near the summit. Due to the cactus and the dense brush on the approach and its 6,299-foot altitude, a climb of the southernmost peak represents a major challenge. It appears best to simply park at KM 41 and start hiking. Altitude at the parking spot is 1,600 feet and the straight-line distance to the summit is four miles. It is a fairly strenuous

A most unlikely setting; amid drizzle and swirling clouds, Jim Smallwood heads up one of the Tres Vírgenes.

DON NELSON

class 2 and 3 climb with a good deal of traversing. Two full days should be set aside for the round trip, allowing some exploring time. The crater is a smoothly rounded bowl, providing flat spots for camping, and the view from the rim is spectacular. No water will be found on the climb.

Mineral collectors may find much of interest. In 1792 naturalist José Longinos reported that the area was a source of red, yellow and black ocher pigments used by Cochimí Indians in their grand rock paintings throughout central Baja. He also found a wide variety of minerals, including jasper, sardonyx, a number of types of chalcedony and spars, sulfur deposits and even marble. Modern mineral collectors have found zeolites such as scolecite and heulandite. Sulfur deposits also have been located in surrounding areas, mainly in the valley between the two northernmost peaks and in a valley four miles northwest of the north peak. A road running north at KM 32 should shorten the amount of hiking necessary to get to these places. Construction of a geothermal project is underway eleven miles north on this road.

Back on the Transpeninsular Highway at KM 41

35   Eight percent downgrade to KM 31.

****

A TRIP TO CAÑON SAN PABLO. Although we arrived at Rancho Santa Martha tired from the long drive from Los Angeles, we were excited about the prospect of a burro trip into Cañon San Pablo to see the great Cochimí rock-art murals. Everything was ready, and our guides, Ignacio and Guadalupe Arce, quickly set about loading a mountain of equipment on the sad-eyed burros. Within an hour we were aboard our mounts and following a trail toward a distant ridge. Most of our group were city-bred and only two or three had ridden before, a fact well known to the burros, who managed a delicate balance between resignation and rebellion, depending on who was aboard. At first the scenery seemed dull, just cactus, scrub and rock, but we were rapidly gaining altitude. Someone finally looked back and we realized that we had been passing through some fine country, a valley of small green and rose hills rimmed by blue mountains.

The trail became steeper, and we were finally forced to dismount and were soon scrambling on all fours. Each burro was extremely careful where he stepped. If a front hoof successfully found a flat spot on the trail, the little burro brain would direct the rear hoof on the same side to the same spot. If a stone rolled or the burro stumbled, the rear hoof would try a different spot. The pack burros made the last fifty yards to the pass in a series of lunges, their loads swinging precariously, and we entered a broad valley with vistas of the brilliant blue Cortez.

Our first camp was nothing more than a clearing among the thorns, with no water or food for the burros other than cactus lopped off with machetes. Free of their loads, they were soon lying upside down, rolling and kicking in a dust hole like frisky dogs. After a fine supper and a dreamless sleep under a canopy of stars, we awoke and began what became our morning routine: build a fire, make coffee and apply a blanket and saddle to each burro, drink more coffee and pack

duffel, eat breakfast and tighten cinches, drink more coffee and load the burros, drink more coffee and start out. Any deviation from this routine upset the burros for the rest of the day.

We found that a definite social order existed among the burros; they had well-developed ideas of who should be first in line, who should be second and so on, and no burro violated that order without fear of retaliatory action by his fellows. These ideas often conflicted with those of the riders, but the burros always won in the long run. We also found that they were very knowledgeable about the route we were following. Using reins, verbal supplications and body-English, we attempted to turn them toward the route we had chosen when we encountered forks, and they frequently resisted and went their own way. We soon observed that they were almost always correct; with their native ability and years of experience they knew better than we which way was best, and we gave up trying to steer. My burro, though, always wanted to turn to the left. Since he had a snow-white mane and had tried to bite the leader burro, I made a political statement by naming him O'Neill. We had a similar lack of success in regulating their speed, which was ahead slow, but both cowboys were able to motivate their mules enough to achieve a full gallop. Their secret proved to be the threat of the spur, and we could see the mules roll their wide-set eyes back, watching for the least movement of the cowboy's heels. There were no marks on their flanks, but the cowboys explained that it is not the rowel that provides the motivation but the noise created by steel jingles hanging from each spur. Pavlov had a point.

Our fascinations were not merely visual. Every day was a concert of a thousand sounds, some soothing and pleasant, others rough and abrasive. Wind and bird songs provided a backdrop for the constant chatter of the riders. Our passage across the desert produced the sound of rolling stones kicked loose, of thorns scraping across leather chaps, and of machetes cutting brush. The cowboys added to the wonderful din with their singing and whistling and piercing screeches,

Burros carry a party of explorers up a steep trail toward the great Cochimí murals in Cañon San Pablo.

created by pulling a leaf between their fingers. They continually made supervisory noises to the burros, including clucks, sucks, growls, shouts, cries, threats, curses, the crack of whips and the whack of open hands on saddles. The burros added to it all, providing the noise of hooves striking ground, metal shoes scraping rock, whinnies, groans, he-haws, teeth clamping on bits, stomach noises and—there's no really polite word—farts.

We came to a tiny ranch with a thatched roof, surrounded by citrus trees and covered with cascades of magenta bougainvillaea so bright they seemed to glow from within. The following day we arrived at the village of San Francisco, visited by Erle Stanley Gardner during his expeditions in 1962 (the village can now be reached by road). As we began the steep descent into Cañon San Pablo we entered a different world of palms and pools. Thousand-foot-high walls shaded the bottom of the canyon a good part of the day, a welcome relief from the glare of the high country. How different from the cactus, dry rock and open vistas we had passed through earlier!

It grew late and we made camp and swam in emerald pools. Our burros loved the place and broke out in a comical chorus of he-haws that went on most of the night and remained funny until ten. Guadalupe had a good knowledge of local herbs and potions, and he treated everyone to a tea reputed to have aphrodisiac properties, a fact he casually mentioned as the last swallow went down. Fortunately for the collective dignity of our group, it didn't work. The fire was almost dead when both cowboys suddenly became alert, although no sight or sound was detectable to us city folks. Running in a crouch, Guadalupe grabbed a .22 rifle from a scabbard and fired at an unseen target across the camp. Rushing over, he reached into a brush pile and triumphantly hoisted a mortally wounded ring-tail cat, a beautiful creature that looks like a skinny raccoon with a long striped tail. Oblivious to his horror-stricken audience, Guadalupe an-

A cacophony of figures at Gardner Cave.

nounced with a golden-toothed grin that ring-tails carry cattle diseases, a fact possibly new to veterinary medicine.

The next day we finally had a chance to see what we had come for, Gardner Cave. After a short hike, we scrambled up a rugged slope to a long, overhung rock shelter. We had seen photographs of the Grand Mural, but they did not evoke a sense of the immediacy and power of the real thing. As we huffed and puffed up the slope, we looked up and there it was—incredible, dramatic, stunning. How could untutored Indians, using simple materials, have created such a scene? Spread along the back of a shallow overhang was a mural hundreds of feet long of larger-than-life deer, mountain sheep, men, fish and birds, rendered in black and red. Although painted over five hundred years ago, most were bright and well preserved, thanks to the resistant qualities of the rock and the protection of the overhang.

Most Cochimí stylistic conventions could be seen: overpainting, bicolor figures, the outline-and-wash technique. By the standards of a Vermeer the figures were crude, with no fine brush strokes and no subtle shadings of color, but there was no mistaking what the artists hoped to depict: it was power—power over animals, power over men, and power over nature. We spent hours in front of them, and as time passed we found the artist's spell growing on us. Familiarity with this art did not breed contempt; unlike the insipid droolings of a Jackson Pollock painting, the more we saw, the more we appreciated what we were seeing.

Gardner is only one of many art sites in the area, but it drew us back again and again, and we photographed every detail, from every conceivable angle. Days passed and too soon we were aboard our trusty steeds heading back to Santa Martha. As the miles dragged on, they grew tired and cranky, but as we topped the last pass they could see the ranch in the valley, and they suddenly came to life. Instead of a steady, listless plodding, a definite liveliness appeared. As we approached level ground, they abandoned all thoughts of pro-

Ignacio and Guadalupe load a patient burro.

priety and considerations of social order, and began a pell-mell rush for home. Not that they were galloping, mind you, but compared to the standards of the previous week it seemed as if rustlers at work during the night had substituted unbreakable stallions for our docile donkeys. What had taken hours a week ago now flew by in minutes. O'Neill in his haste brushed me against a thorn tree, inflicting a hundred punctures on my thin gringo skin. With a total lack of dignity, I came thundering up to the ranch and suffered a final humiliation. As I reined O'Neill to a halt and started to swing out of the saddle, the cinch let go and I crashed to the ground at the feet of a laughing eight-year-old.

****

Ron Smith photographs a herd of deer painted over five hundred years ago.

CHAPTER 13
SANTA ROSALÍA TO LORETO

On the Transpeninsular Highway near the Tres Vírgenes

KM	LOCATION
17+	Begin a 16% downgrade to KM 13+, then moderate up- and downgrades until reaching the shores of the Cortez at KM 7+.
13+	Mina Lucifer. Turn southwest, drive one mile. The mine was noted for pyrolusite, and specimens of chrysocolla and red jasper with manganese swirls also have been found. Old maps show other mines north of the highway.
12	A massive hill containing gypsum was bisected during highway construction, providing the most accessible mineral-collecting site in Baja, with selenite crystals and sheets, as well as the satin spar variety, some having encrustations of malachite.
11+	Butane yard.
7+	Specimens of palm root petrified by red jasper have been found in arroyos to the north.
6	Isla Tortugas, twenty-three miles east, is the tip of a 6,000-foot Holocene volcano rising from 5,000-foot-deep water. Because it has no good anchorages it it not often visited by sportfishermen, but it sometimes has the best grouper fishing in the Cortez. Described as "barren and useless" by passing yachtsmen, the island is in fact unexpectedly rich in flora and fauna, with seventy-nine species of vascular plants, relatively large populations of lizards and rattlesnakes (one species being endemic), and even an endemic mouse. Small fumaroles indicate the volcano is still active.
5+	Mouth of Arroyo de Soledad and Arroyo del Boleo.

SIDETRIP TO ARROYO DE SOLEDAD AND ARROYO DEL BOLEO

Set odometer. Drive west to the fork at Mile 0.1; go left (250°) for Arroyo de Soledad, right (280°) for Arroyo del Boleo. The roads extend four or five miles into each canyon, passing dozens of old mines, where rare minerals have been found, including crednerite, phosgenite and remingtonite. Mina Amelia, at Mile 3.7 up Soledad, has yielded cumengite, pseudoboleite and boleite. The first two are found only here, and boleite at only three other locations in the world. The mine was exhausted long ago and parts of its shaft have caved in, but in the mid-1970s it was reopened to obtain these minerals. It might be possible to extract samples from the tailings, but I found an easier way: I simply bummed some from an employee at the old mining company office in Santa Rosalía, who had a drawer-full.

Back on the Transpeninsular Highway at KM 5+

2	Mouth of Arroyo del Purgatorio, site of a major copper strike in 1868 and now a mineral collecting area.
0	**Santa Rosalía.**

BAJA'S COPPER TOWN

Erle Stanley Gardner, in one of his books on Baja, wrote, "Once more I resolved never again to try for detailed information in advance of a trip of exploration. Once let a place get the reputation of being unbeautiful and it's hard indeed to approach it impartially." This seems to apply specifically to Santa Rosalía, for it *is* unbeautiful, and travel writers have hence given it short shrift. Superficially, the place is gritty and unattractive, an almost comically ugly smelter dominating everything. The town has a distinctly non-Mexican character, with straight streets and buildings constructed of milled lumber instead of crooked lanes and adobe, and in lieu of an historic stone mission, its church is made of cast iron. In spite of this, it is an interesting place, and contrary to Gardner's idea, the key to appreciating Santa Rosalía is understanding its unusual history.

In 1868 José Rosa Villavicencio discovered some odd blue-and-green deposits northeast of his ranch, which proved to be a type of high-grade copper carbonate and oxides known

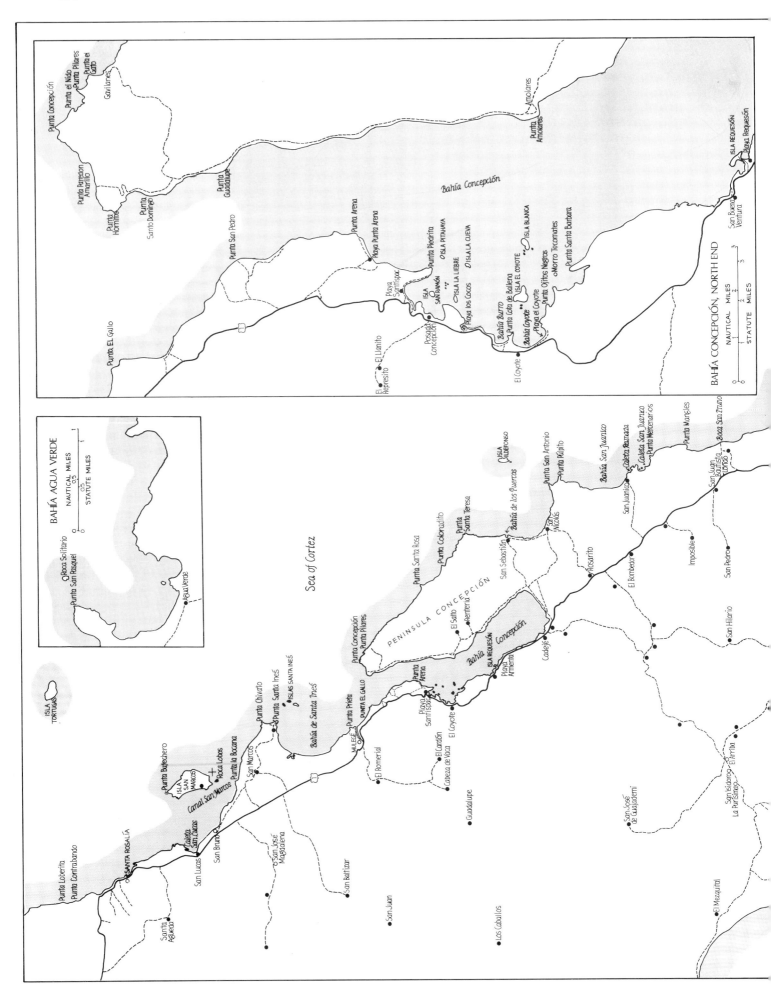

BAHÍA CONCEPCIÓN, NORTH END

NAUTICAL MILES

STATUTE MILES

BAHÍA AGUA VERDE

NAUTICAL MILES

STATUTE MILES

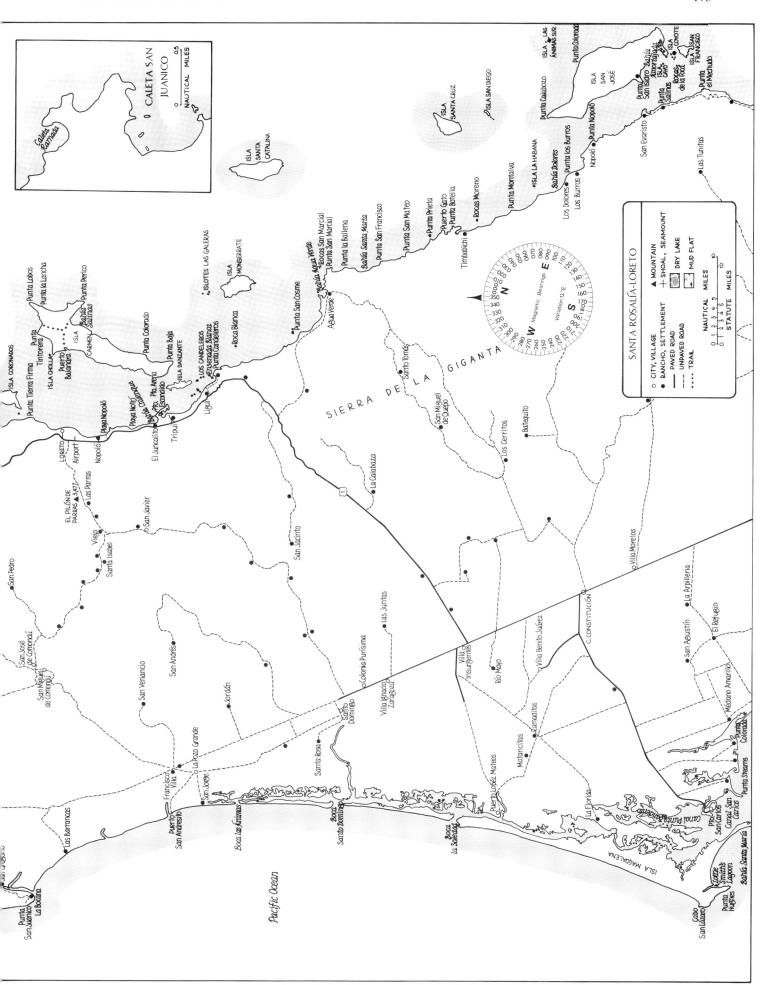

Caleta Ramada

ISLA SANTA CATALINA

ISLA SANTA CRUZ

Isla San Diego

ISLAS LAS ÁNIMAS SUR

Punta Colorado

Bahía Amortajada

ISLA CAYO

Punta San Isidoro

ISLA CORONADO

ROCAS de la POZA

ISLA SAN FRANCISCO

COYOTE

Punta el Mechudo

Punta Calaboso

ISLA SAN JOSÉ

Punta Salinas

San Evaristo

Las Tunitas

Punta los Burros

Punta Nopoló

Isla La Habana

Bahía Dolores

Los Dolores

Los Burros

Nopoló

Punta Montalva

Rocas Moreno

Punta Prieta

Puerto Gato

Punta Botella

Timbabichi

ISLOTES LAS GALERAS

ISLA MONSERRATE

Bahía Agua Verde

Bocas San Marcial

Punta San Marcial

Punta la Ballena

Bahía Santa Marta

Punta San Francisco

Punta San Mateo

Punta San Cosme

Roca Blanca

Agua Verde

Santo Tomás

SIERRA DE LA GIGANTA

San Miguel de Quepo

Los Cerritos

Batequito

Villa Morelos

La Arpillería

El Refugio

Punta Lobos

Punta la Lancha

Punta Perico

Punta Tierra Firma

Punta Tintorera

Bahía Salinas

ISLA CARMEN

Punta Colorado

Punta Baja

Puerto Balandra

ISLA CHOLLA

ISLA DANZANTE

LOS CANDELEROS

Ensenada Blanca

Punta Candeleros

Pto. Arena

Bahía Chileno

Pto. Escondido

Ligüí

Tripui

El Juncalito

LORETO

Airport

Nopoló

Playa Nopoló

EL PILÓN DE PARRAS ▲ 3477

Las Parras

Viejo

Santa Isabel

San Javier

San Pedro

San José de Comondú

San Miguel de Comondú

La Calabaza

San Jacinto

San Andrés

San Venancio

Jordán

Colonia Purísima

Villa Ignacio Zaragoza

Las Juntas

Río Mayo

Villa Insurgentes

Villa Benito Juárez

C. CONSTITUCIÓN

San Agustín

Médano Amarillo

Santo Domingo

Santa Rosa

Francisco Villa

La Paz Grande

San Jorge

Puerto San Andresito

Boca Las Ánimas

Boca Santo Domingo

Boca la Soledad

Puerto López Mateos

Matancitas

Ramaditas

La Florida

CANAL Punta Entrada

Pto. San Carlos

Canal San Carlos

Punta Colorado

Punta Belcher

Punta Stearns

ISLA MAGDALENA

Lottie Smith's Lagoon

Punta Hughes

Bahía Santa María

Cabo San Lázaro

Las Barrancas

Punta San Juanico

La Bocana

Pacific Ocean

SANTA ROSALÍA-LORETO

○ CITY, VILLAGE   ▲ MOUNTAIN
● RANCHO, SETTLEMENT   ✛ SHOAL, SEAMOUNT
━━━ PAVED ROAD   ⬚ DRY LAKE
━ ━ UNPAVED ROAD   ⬚ MUD FLAT
······ TRAIL

NAUTICAL   MILES
0   1 2 3 4 5   10
0   1 2 3 4 5   10
STATUTE   MILES

Magnetic Bearings

Variation 12°E

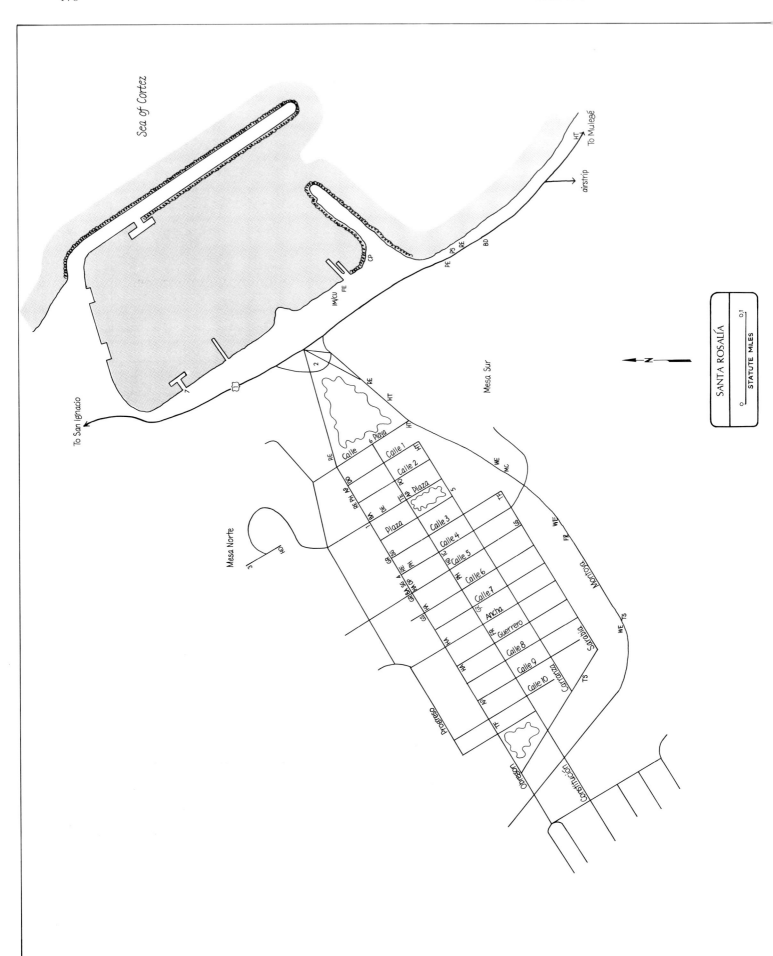

as "boleos" due to their ball-like shape. He decided to take immediate advantage of his good luck and sold his mineral rights for sixteen pesos. A copper mine under German management operated until 1885, when a French company, Compagnie du Boleo, was formed. A mining railroad and piers were built, and equipment for a smelter was transported in square-rigged sailing ships from Europe around Cape Horn. The town was laid out on classic company-town lines: straight streets and virtually identical wooden buildings with corrugated iron roofs, their walls painted in horizontal green and white stripes. Society was highly segregated; French mining company officials lived on Mesa Norte, Mexican government officials and soldiers dwelt on less-desirable Mesa Sur and the masses sweltered in the arroyo below.

Soot and gas from the smelter made the town almost uninhabitable, and there seemed to be only two choices: move the smelter or move the town. Instead, engineers worked out a unique solution; a tall stack was constructed a half-mile away and connected to the smelter by a huge horizontal duct. In 1897 a church (1) constructed from prefabricated cast-iron sections was erected. Designed by Alexandre Gustave Eiffel, of tower fame, it is certainly the most unusual church in Baja.

By the turn of the century Santa Rosalía was a major world copper producer, and a parade of square-rigged ships carrying European coke to the smelter sailed up the Cortez. Sailors speaking a dozen tongues walked the streets, seeking the same types of entertainment and social services demanded by sailors everywhere. Well-known to sailors, Santa Rosalía was never a favorite port. There was no harbor at the time and no stevedoring services, so the crew of each ship had to undertake the hot, heavy and dirty task of lightering coke ashore, a chore that sometimes took several months. The heat was fierce and other than one brothel and several bars and restaurants there was little to occupy their off hours, and the jail was frequently filled to overflowing. Rather than face Santa Rosalía many sailors tried to desert. One who was successful was a German sailor on the bark *Reinbek*, Frank Fischer. After a fist fight with the first mate and a short stay in jail Fischer started hiking to the northwest until he came to the village of San Ignacio. Here he established himself as its blacksmith, becoming well known to generations of early Baja travelers suffering from broken springs and axles and inoperative engines. His descendants still operate the La Posada Hotel in San Ignacio.

British owners, anticipating that the opening of the Panama Canal in 1914 would be unfavorable to sailing ships, began selling off their square-riggers, and the German flag became an increasingly common sight in Santa Rosalía. However, on August 1, 1914, Germany invaded Belgium. Three days later England declared war on Germany, and a dozen of the big German square-riggers were interned by Mexico and spent the duration of the war swinging at anchor off the town. Idle German sailors, unable to stand the heat and boredom, deserted and spread out over Mexico, some en route to the

Santa Rosalía in the days of the great sailing ships.

COURTESY ENRIQUE PATRON LARA

U.S., some trying to get back to Germany, others settling temporarily or permanently in Mexico, becoming cotton pickers, farmers, prospectors, sailmakers, teachers, circus workers, watchmen and longshoremen. One even joined the U.S. Army.

After the war production continued and almost 375 miles of tunnels were eventually dug, forming a vast underground network, and more than 18 miles of narrow gauge railroad track were in use. The mines were hot, dangerous and dirty places, where "men's hearts and bodies wilt almost as rapidly as a bride's corsage," as Phillip Townsend Hanna put it. By the 1920s ore became scarce, but small-scale operators continued work by removing the pillars of ore left to support ceilings in the old shafts—the mining equivalent of a logger cutting off the branch on which he is sitting.

The mines and the smelter are now closed, ending this unique chapter in Baja history. A restored locomotive (2) can be seen in the park, and a display of railroad equipment is located on the beach north of town. The beautifully restored Hotel Frances (3), with its wide verandas and polished wood floors, is certainly the most unusual hotel in Baja. Smells from the old bakery (4) on Avenida Obregon from square-rigger days still make it hard to walk by without stopping. Little remains of French culture; *coq au vin* is still on some menus, but it always turns out to be something totally foreign to the mother country, and the question *"Parlez vous francais aqui?"* will be greeted with blank looks.

Old photographs hanging in the Palacio Municipal (5) and the Biblioteca Publica (6) show that little has changed physically in the town since the days of the French. However, there have been noticeable social changes in recent years. There seems to be more hustle and bustle, with increasing traffic requiring numerous one-way streets and even a few traffic lights. Urban shuttle-busses now ply the town, mobile taco stands constructed from the rear half of discarded pickup trucks inhibit the flow of traffic, low-riders prowl with boomboxes proclaiming the macho status of their drivers, and a disco shop forces its own ideas about music on all within earshot. All this increased activity seems to be producing less wealth—the stocks of food and goods at the CONASUPER and several other stores have dwindled greatly, and the Hotel Frances is now (mid-1991) closed. Even so, the town has a distinct charm and a unique history shared by no other in Baja, and a visitor will be well rewarded.

Ferries bound for Guaymas leave from the terminal. There are no RV facilities in town, but trailer parks are located at KM 193 and 182 to the south. It is highly inadvisable to take large motorhomes or trailers into the central part of town. There is no paved boat ramp, but small boats can be launched across the beach at San Lucas Trailer Park at KM 182, and large trailerboats can be launched at Mulegé. Santa Rosalía is a port of entry, and there are COTP, immigration and customs offices. Marina Santa Rosalía (7) has been constructed in the harbor, providing a dozen modern slips, each with water and electricity. There is no fueling facility at the marina, but boaters can haul it from the PEMEX, just 500 yards to the southeast. The next satisfactory anchorage to the south is Caleta San Lucas, nine miles.

Divers will find little of interest. Although there have been five major shipwrecks in the area (full-rigged British iron ship

Selene, 1890, U.S. wooden bark *Arcturus*, 1895, U.S. barkentine *Modoc*, 1896, Compagnie du Boleo iron steamer *Korrigan*, 1907, and the German bark *Wandsbek*, still at anchor after internment, 1923), all the remains were used in breakwater construction, salvaged for scrap or, in one case, converted to a warehouse. A few rusty plates from the *Selene* can still be seen on the rocky beach a hundred yards north of the Restaurant Selene in the waterfront area.

Captain of the Port Rafael Elizondo, known and respected by generations of American yachtsmen, tells of a sea cave in Santa Rosalía. When he was a boy he and his friends would swipe a watermelon, and to avoid detection they would dive through the underwater entrance of the cave into an air-filled chamber. Gloating, the boys would sit on the tiny beach and eat the melon in the dim blue light. The cave is located 0.2 mile south of the COTP office.

There is only one PEMEX (MND) in town, and in recent years travelers have found it advisable to keep all vehicle and trailer windows and doors locked or attended at all times, to insure that the gas pump reading is zeroed before filling begins, to know approximately how much fuel will be needed to fill the tanks and the price per liter, and to have a calculator ready to insure that all mathematical calculations of volume and price are on the up-and-up. Also, make sure that your gas comes out of the same pump used by the locals.

On the Transpeninsular Highway at Santa Rosalía

0/197   Start new KM numbering sequence.

193   RV park, full hookups, restrooms, showers, restaurant, bar.

189+   Place where litterbugs, despoilers of archaeological sites and those exceeding bag limits may end up.

182   **San Lucas**. Shallow Caleta San Lucas has excellent fishing for snapper, grouper and halibut. A deep hole at the entrance has immense numbers of bass, and outside lurk leopard grouper, shortfin corvina, sierra, barracuda, yellowtail, gulf grouper, skipjack, pargo, roosterfish, amberjack, snapper, dolphin and a dozen or so other species. The best fishing is within a five-mile radius from the entrance, and that's a lot of territory! This area is near the juncture of the northern Cortez, with its cool waters, and the more tropical southern Cortez, and migrant species and year-round residents from both are often present, so good catches are possible all year long, usually becoming outstanding between May and October. A prime fishing area is a half-mile off a solitary hill at the northern end of the rocky arm forming the eastern side of the cove—you can't miss the hill. A wreck near the entrance offers good snorkeling. Mangroves at the north end are home to many birds. San Lucas Trailer Park near the north end has *panga* rentals, toilets, showers, *palapas* and a restaurant, but no hookups. The potable water is of doubtful quality. The best launching location is at the RV park, since most other beaches turn into mud flats at low tide. A narrow channel running roughly due south from the park winds through the shallows to

the entrance. The cove is a good all-weather anchorage for shallow-draft boats. The next anchorages are at the south end of Isla San Marcos, eight miles, and at Punta Santa Inés, twenty miles.

180 Road east to public beach and campsites among the palms.

176 Isla San Marcos, five miles to the northeast, was once the bed of an ancient lake. In it, vast amounts of gypsum precipitated out, and the island is now the site of a large mine. Huge amounts of gypsum are shipped to the U.S. and other countries to make drywall. The north point has excellent fishing for yellowtail, barracuda and grouper, while the south end has some of the best tide pools in the Cortez. The anchorage at the south end of the island has good protection from north weather. Sand and cobble bottoms and rocky reefs are found from San Marcos south 3/4 mile to Roca Lobos. This diversity of habitat produces fish to match, and it is not uncommon to catch two dozen species in a day. Launch at Mulegé or Caleta San Lucas, but if you want to save running time camp on Lobos. The waters surrounding the tiny island are loaded with yellowtail, barracuda and snapper, and divers will find foraging excellent. A three-fathom reef, located one mile, 060° from Lobos, has produced groupers to a hundred pounds.

157 Road southwest to Rancho de San Baltizar, seventeen miles.

SIDETRIP TO GRUTA SAN BORJITAS

Gruta San Borjitas is among the best known and most studied Cochimí rock-art sites in Baja. Known in the Mission Era, it was visited and photographed by Leon Diguet. Due to the number and quality of its figures and the fact that it is both well preserved and closely approachable by vehicle, it is the subject of continuing interest today. The grotto is on Rancho de San Baltizar, which is private property, but guided trips can be arranged in Mulegé; inquire at the Las Casitas or Vista Hermosa Hotels (9 and 10 on the Mulegé city map).

Back on the Transpeninsular Highway at KM 157

156 Road northeast (signed "Punta Chivato") to Punta Santa Inés, fourteen miles.

SIDETRIP TO PUNTAS SANTA INÉS AND CHIVATO

For many miles to the north, most RV facilities have been places to stay overnight en route to other places, but the Santa Inés/Chivato area is a place to stay and play. Although washboarded, the graded sand road can handle any RV. With its sparkling beaches and good fishing, diving, shelling and boardsailing, it is the Baja destination for many RVers and campers. Potable water, showers, toilets and a dump station are available at the RV park, and camping is permitted near the point. Garbage is collected regularly, but there are no hookups. Hotel Punta Chivato, located west of the point, has rooms with showers, dining room, bar, pool, gift shop and

Gruta San Borjitas. The gentleman is José Eduardo Lopéz, our guide.

beach, plus fishing boats and guides. At high tide trailerboats to twenty-eight feet have been launched here. The old paved ramp is scheduled to be replaced in the near future. The best anchorages are in the lee of the point and west of the hotel. The next anchorage is the estero at Mulegé, ten miles south. Since the estero is limited to small boats, larger craft should head for Santispac, inside Bahía Concepción.

Shore fishing can be good, especially for yellowtail near the aid-to-navigation light tower on Punta Santa Inés. Ladyfish action can be found in the hot months by casting small chrome spoons, feather jigs or soft plastic lures from the shore with light spinning gear at dawn or dusk. Tuna, billfish and dolphin are offshore in the warm months and close-in there are reefs everywhere with lesser species. Seven miles, 040° from Inéz the water begins to get very deep, in excess of 400 fathoms, and yellowfin tuna are often present in the summer months. The wreck of a private plane can be found in three fathoms 1/2 mile southwest of the hotel. A good diving reef extends east from Punta Santa Inés. A shipwreck can be found in the cove south of Punta Chivato, name and date unknown. The locals report that a large sailboat sank north of Punta Chivato in 1981. Mexican divers have found gold coins the diameter of a silver dollar but twice as thick, in a small bay northwest of Punta Chivato with the intriguing name of "Caleta Muertos." Shelling is outstanding, especially at "Shell Beach," which is the western curve of the shore as it begins to swing south; the shallow bay must be wall-to-wall mollusks. Roosterfish are sometimes taken along this beach.

Boardsailors will find excellent winds in the December through February season. The bay off the hotel offers speed sailing in flat conditions, with winds accelerated by the venturi effect of the hills to the north, and reaches are measured in miles. Beginners will not be left out; although the winds are usually brisk by mid-morning, they tend to be light earlier, and the south beach is sandy and the bottom shallow. Punta Chivato's north shore provides advanced sailors with a sandy launch, waves and strong side-onshore winds. Excursions Extraordinaires offers package tours to Chivato, flying from Tijuana or San Diego by DC-3. The flight is available to anyone, not just sailors. Since the airstrip is close to the hotel, you can be sailing the afternoon of your departure. A support boat is on the water full-time and will tow boards back to the beach if need be. Instruction is available, and if you tire of sailing, mountain bikes, snorkeling equipment and sea kayaks are available. Rental boards and instruction are available to walk-ins, and kayaks and mountain bikes can be rented for day use.

The Islas Santa Inés, especially the southernmost island, are good for yellowtail, snapper, pargo and amberjack. The Mexican fishing vessel *Britania*, lost in 1980, lies 150 feet east and 300-400 feet south of the northern tip of the south island in 5-15 feet of water. The historic schooner *Abel Miranda* lies somewhere in the vicinity. Built in 1859, she was the oldest vessel in the Mexican merchant-marine register and the last merchant sail in the Cortez when she was lost in 1957. According to Socorro Real Rocha, the captain's sister, she sank near the south island.

Back on the Transpeninsular Highway at KM 156

143   Moderate up- and downgrades into Mulegé.
136+   Road west to ice plant; follow the power lines 0.6 mile.
136   Auto parts store has Evinrude parts and service.
135+   **Mulegé**.

BAJA'S TROPICAL VILLAGE

Although well north of the Tropic of Cancer, Mulegé is Baja's stereotypical tropical village, with thousands of graceful palms, thatched roofs and masses of bougainvillaea, an unexpected green oasis in a drab brown desert. The Jesuits founded a mission here in 1705 at the site of an old Indian settlement, and in 1719 the sailing vessel *El Triunfo de la Cruz* was launched, built of wood cut in the mountains. Misión Santa Rosalía de Mulegé (1) was completed in 1766, but a *chubasco* almost wiped out the settlement four years later. U.S. troops occupied it for one day in 1847 in the Battle

Sorting and drying the Mulegé date harvest.

of Mulegé. The mission was abandoned in 1828, but the building has been restored. During the *chubasco* of September 9, 1959, nearby arroyos carried as much as sixty feet of water, and boulders twelve feet in diameter were swept away.

The celebrated Mulegé Territorial Prison (2) provided a unique chapter in the annals of penology. At dawn each day two soldiers would hike up from their barracks, one carrying a conch shell, the other a massive brass key. Upon reaching the prison one would blow a signal while the other opened the massive gate and let the prisoners out! At six in the evening the gate clanked shut to the sound of the conch and prisoners lost their freedom until dawn. Plans to remodel the prison into a museum have been postponed year after year.

Despite its ups and downs, Mulegé is now fairly prosperous and manages to maintain a languid, slow-bell approach to life that attracts many repeat visitors; few Americans and Canadians encountered in the streets have been to Mulegé only once. It is the first town south of Ensenada where tourism is a major industry, and there are many shops, grocery stores, restaurants and hotels, and a laundromat, the first since Posada Don Diego. Jorge del Río RV Park (3), Huerta Saucedo RV Park (4), Río Oasis RV Park (5), Poncho's RV Park (6) and Villa María Isabel RV Park (7) all have full hookups, showers and restrooms. Jorge's is often filled with permanents. Villa María Isabel also has an American-style bakery. Storage space for vehicles and boats can be obtained at some of the parks. Camping and RV parking are permitted on the public beach at El Sombrerito and on the beach south of the "river" entrance.

The Hotel Serenidad (8) on the shore of the "river" has rooms with showers, cottages, pool, airstrip, bar and a dining room, the scene of famed Mexican fiesta banquets on Wednesdays and pig roast buffets on Saturdays. The Hotel Las Casitas (9) has rooms with showers, a dining room, fishing trips and local excursions. The Vista Hermosa Hotel (10) has rooms with baths, pool, dining room and bar and a great view of the Cortez. Due to its narrow streets, motorhomes and vehicles towing trailers or boats should avoid using the PEMEX in town, heading instead to the one at KM 130+ just to the south. There is no tourism office. Don Johnson, owner of the Serenidad, is a U.S. Consular Agent and has an office in town (11, second floor).

Beach diving near Mulegé is not exceptional and most divers head for Bahía Concepción, Punta Concepción or the "outer" coast of Peninsula Concepción. Locals report a large wrecked sailboat in four fathoms 150 yards southeast of Punta el Gallo, located three miles southeast of the mouth of the estero. Mulegé Divers (12) has SCUBA and snorkeling excursions, air, and limited sales and rentals. SCUBA qualification and resort courses are available, but not full certification. The shop currently (1991) operates a custom twenty-foot boat with twin engines. No spearfishing is permitted on trips, but one-of-a-kind shelling is allowed.

There have been reports of a dozen different minerals from mines in the area, mostly copper-bearing, but the reports are too vague to be useful in relocating the sites. The beautiful spiny oyster is found along the coast south of town.

Few people come to easygoing Mulegé to expend a lot of energy, but joggers are often seen on the roads along either side of the estero, and you can climb the stairs to the aid-to-

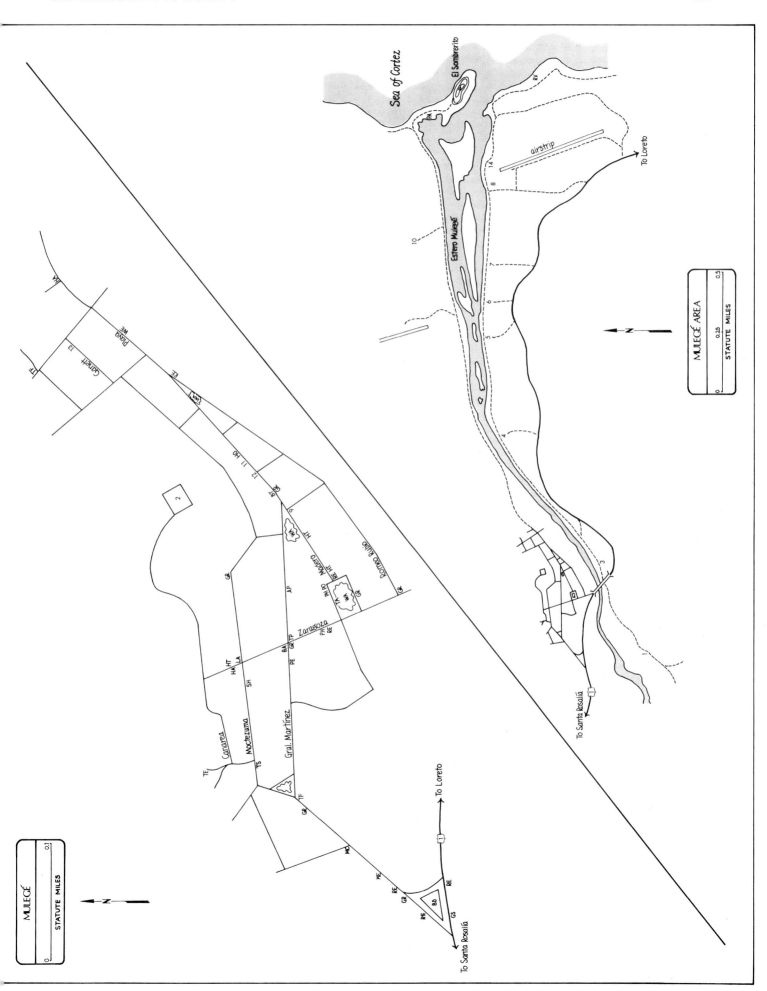

navigation tower on top of El Sombrerito to see the sights.

Mulegé claims to have the only navigable river in Baja, but it is actually a saltwater estero reaching the bridge, where it meets a small stream of fresh water coming over a dam. Shallow-draft boats can anchor in the mouth of the estero, but it has many shoals and is best entered at high tide. The "outside" anchorage north of El Sombrerito is unprotected. The next good anchorage south is Santispac in Bahía Concepción, or Bahía de los Puercos on the "outside coast" of Peninsula Concepción. There is a COTP office in town (13), but no customs or immigration. The Villa María Isabel, Huerta Saucedo and Río Oasis RV parks have concrete ramps, as does Fisherman's Landing (14), and a beach launch can be made at El Sombrerito. All require medium or high tide.

Ray Cannon's story of a titanic struggle with a snook established Mulegé as *the* place in Baja to try for snook, but Ray never succeeded in actually catching a Mulegé snook and neither have many others. Yellowtail, roosters and a dozen other varieties can be taken by shorecasters off the beaches on either side of the mouth of the estero, especially from early fall to midwinter. Fishermen with boats usually concentrate their efforts on yellowtail, amberjack, pargo and grouper at Punta Hornitos, Punta Concepción, Punta el Gato and the "outer coast." Farther out in the Cortez yellowfin tuna, dolphin, marlin and sails are found in the hot months. Boats and guides can be arranged at Villa María Isabel, at most of the hotels and at the landing near El Sombrerito. Live bait may be available between April and June.

SIDETRIP ALONG THE COAST TO LORETO

The eighty-four mile "Coasting to Loreto" kayak and small-boat trip from Mulegé to Loreto is one of the most beautiful and enjoyable in Baja. The shoreline is generally steep and rocky, cliffs and bluffs alternating with pebble and cobble beaches. Except between Rancho San Nicolás and Punta San Antonio, there are few sand beaches. Some landings are steep and exposed, making them difficult in anything short of a flat calm. As fate would have it, the best camping spots are often less than or more than a kayaker's normal ten-to-twenty mile daily run apart, and trips require flexibility and careful planning. Water can normally be obtained at the ranches at San Sebastián, San Nicolás and San Juanico, and yachts are frequently found at anchor at Caleta San Juanico. Vehicles and trailers can be left at any of the RV parks along the "river" or in the vicinity of Fisherman's Landing in Mulegé. The appropriate 1:50,000 topos are Mulegé G12A57, San Nicolás G12A68, Santa Rosa G12A78 and Loreto G12A88.

The crossing of the mouth of the bay is best made by way of Punta el Gallo to Punta Hornitos, a distance of six miles. The beach south of the aid-to-navigation tower at Hornitos is shelf rock giving away to sand, and is often used by kayakers and small-boat sailors as their first overnight stop. Shelling along the beach is excellent, and the point has good diving and fishing. The anchorage is well-protected from all but westerly and southerly winds.

The five-mile coastline from Hornitos around Punta Concepción to Gavilanes is mostly low cliffs alternating with

pebble and cobble beaches. Gavilanes, marked by a number of concrete building foundations and mining excavations, has an exposed pebble and cobble beach. The mine was once a prominent source of manganese, but it has not operated since the Second World War. Look for numerous thin veins of pyrolusite an inch wide spaced at intervals of ten to fifteen feet, and small deposits of vanadinite, quartz, limonite, dolomite, calcite, aragonite and manganiferous travertine. Manganese cobbles can be found on the beaches. The waters to the east offer good fishing, and divers will find numerous small reefs and large boulders on a sandy bottom.

The coast south to San Sebastián is generally rocky cliffs, although there are a number of narrow pebble and cobble beaches in the mouths of arroyos. The first sizable flat area is seven miles south of Gavilanes, marked by the stone foundation of a building. The lee of Punta Santa Rosa, 2 1/2 more miles, provides very marginal protection and a pebble beach. Punta Coloradito (Punta Colorado), four miles from Punta Santa Rosa, can be recognized by its bands of rust and yellow. The first sand beaches south of Punta Concepción are found three miles southeast of Coloradito. However, the first really good sandy campsite is found at the head of a tiny bay immediately northwest of Punta Santa Teresa. The bay is too shallow for anything but kayaks and small boats, but it does provide a marginal lee which facilitates landings.

Punta Santa Teresa, five miles from Coloradito, is rocky and has poor anchorage and landing conditions. The five-mile coast from Teresa to San Sebastián is primarily cliffs alternating with steep pebble beaches. San Sebastián provides an

The hand-laid rock pavement on the old road south of Mulegé sees little traffic today.

idea of what things were like in Baja in the "old days" before the Transpeninsular was completed. Isolated and still relatively unknown, it has no tourist facilities, stores or launch ramp, just a few ranch buildings, pigs, goats and chickens, a pebble beach and shaded campsites—although you might be able to hire a *panga*. The cove in front of the settlement, known as Bahía de los Puercos, is a Baja rarity—a snorkeling site with excellent beach access, protected waters and unspoiled conditions, with huge morays, groupers, parrot fish and possibly a dozen other species. A large variety of shells can be found, including coffeebean, several species of *Thais* and unusually large tent olives. In April or May roosterfish show up, and in the hot months dolphins. Yellowtail migrate past the area in November and June, and grouper, bonito and barracuda stay all year. The cove provides a good anchorage, protected from all but east winds.

Isla Ildefonso, about nine miles offshore (charts differ, some placing it closer), has no beaches, although it is possible to land in tiny coves in calm weather. Anchorage conditions are poor. Since it is free of land predators, several dozen species of birds live on, nest on or pass by the island, including brown and blue-footed boobies, Heermann's and western gulls, murrelet, belted kingfisher, sparrow hawk, peregrine falcon, burrowing owl, osprey, house finch, ladderback woodpecker, rock wren, white-crowned sparrow, lark bunting, orange-crowned warbler, raven, brown pelican and great blue heron. The Cortez endemic fish-eating bat is also present. The tide pools are among the best in the Cortez. The reefs at the north and south points are the best dive locations, their great pinnacles and walls being covered with sessile marine life. Green and jewel morays are common, and jawfish can be seen peeking out of their burrows. There are large populations of lobsters, one of the rare places where all three varieties—California, pinto and slipper—can be found in close proximity. Black coral can be seen in deep water off the island. Bonito, grouper, snapper and cabrilla are taken year-round. In warm months trolling feathers work well for dolphins in the deep water to the east. One June a friend was snorkeling off the island with a pole spear when he came face-to-face with a large sailfish. Eyeing each other warily, each saw that the other was equally well-armed and they mutually decided to back off and swim away.

The coast immediately south of San Sebastián is cliffs, but the terrain gradually becomes lower, giving way to sloping plains. There are a ranch and a sand beach at San Nicolás, five miles from San Sebastián. The coast east of San Nicolás is sand-and-pebble beaches backed by low dunes, all very exposed to prevailing winds. The lee of low Punta San Antonio, five miles east of San Nicolás, provides modest protection and a sand beach. Punta Púlpito, two more miles, is a rocky massif visible for many miles. However, it is an indifferent anchorage subject to surge. Camping is poor, since the beach is almost entirely steep cobbles, with only a small sandy area. The water off the point is deep and cold, and big gamefish sweeping in provide exciting fishing and diving. The climb to Púlpito's 500-foot summit offers spectacular views.

The shoreline between Púlpito and Caleta Ramada (Ensenada Puerto Almeja) is largely cliffs with narrow pebble beaches, although sand beaches are encountered in the vicinity of Rancho San Juanico. The ranch is up the arroyo, unseen

from the beach. Ramada, 9 1/2 miles from Púlpito, is open to the north and has a sand beach at its south end. A small sand beach on its east side gets some shelter from prevailing seas and may be useful to kayakers and small-boaters, although Caleta San Juanico (Ensenada San Basilio) is much preferable.

Caleta San Juanico, two miles from Ramada, is one of the best anchorages in the Cortez, providing protection from all but southeast weather, and it is not uncommon to see as many as a dozen yachts at anchor. Juanico has clean sand beaches and good camping; hiking in the surrounding canyons and hills is interesting, and shelling is excellent. The cape forming the east side of the anchorage provides a small cove, containing a campsite with a sand beach. A rocky hill provides shade from the sun in the afternoon, and a thatch-roofed shelter fends it off the rest of the time. At times the population of small fish in the cove is so dense that there seem to be more fish than water, and squadrons of pelicans put on the best diving show in the Cortez just yards off the camp. Snorkeling is excellent, with clear, calm water and dozens of species to observe. Attempts made to improve the road from the Transpeninsular to serene and unspoiled Juanico have so far been defeated by the rains. Let us hope that the rains continue, since the objective is the construction of an RV camp and tourist facilities. Juanico, as it is, is unique; RV camps aren't.

The eight-mile coast from Juanico to Punta Mangles is high, with only a few cobble beaches in front of steep cliffs. Mangles is a fair anchorage in north weather, although it can be surgy. Camping ashore is only fair, with a sand-and-gravel beach in front of a stagnant mangrove lagoon. The coastline lowers south of Mangles, giving way to low plains and sandy beaches near San Bruno, four miles. The coast south of San Bruno quickly becomes steep again, with only a few cobble-and-pebble beaches until Punta Tierra Firma, where it becomes lower again, with long stretches of low cliffs and pebble beaches until Loreto. Camping along this stretch of coast is generally poor, so boaters and kayakers often stop at Isla Coronados, nine miles south of San Bruno. The sand bottoms on either side of the spit sticking out to the southwest of the island provide good anchorages in almost any weather, and there is excellent camping. Loreto is five miles south of the island.

Back on the Transpeninsular Highway at KM 135+

130+   PEMEX (MND). Plans call for a store, laundromat, restaurant, showers and other facilities here.

130   Some of the most dramatic scenery in all of Baja lies along the west shore of Bahía Concepción from this point south, with unexpected panoramas of brilliant blue coves, brown islands and white sand beaches. The shallow bay is the largest protected body of water in the Cortez, and water temperatures in summer can rise to over ninety degrees. The water stays warm throughout the rest of the year, making it a fine place to swim, water ski and sail dinghies, Hobies and sailboards during a winter vacation. Winds often spring up in the afternoon, so divers and fishermen can plan an early day, sailors a late day. There are no marinas and only one paved launch ramp, al-

though sizable trailerboats have been launched across the sand beaches at Santispac and Posada Concepción. Serious fishermen tend to avoid the bay, but it can yield pan-sized sierra and cabrilla for the kids, with an occasional surprise like a barracuda, pargo or snapper to keep things interesting.

126 Gentle-to-moderate up- and downgrades with stretches of level road until KM 98, south of Loreto. Note the microwave tower ahead. A rocky cove between two cliffs on the beach east and a little south of the tower is a reported source of "moonstones," two-inch translucent-to-milky chalcedony nodules with color inclusions of red, orange and yellow. It can be reached safely only by boat. The jumbled boulder bottom in this vicinity has excellent fishing for pargo, cabrilla, snapper, corvina and heavy-duty grouper.

121 The fishing vessel *Bonito* sank in three fathoms, 3,000 yards off Punta San Pedro in 1963.

118+ Sedan road south (signed) to Playa Punta Arena, 2.3 miles, which has a public beach and a boat launch over soft sand, but no facilities. Boardsailors like the wide range of conditions, from waves east of the point to calm inside. The land is low, so the winds are often the heaviest in the bay. Try a downwind run south through the islands to Playa Requesón, nine miles.

114+ **Playa Santispac** (signed). Public beach, pit toilets, showers, cafe, restaurant with a bakery. Truckers sometimes sell block ice, and fishermen often hawk shrimp and scallops. The beach is jammed on holidays, with dozens of jet-skiers and waterskiers tearing around offshore. Hills break up the breezes, but many boardsailors and Hobie sailors visit the place anyway. The anchorage is popular, and excellent snorkeling can be found among the islands. The old wooden shrimper *San Gabriel*, home to hordes of small fish, lies in three fathoms 250 feet northeast of Isla Pitahaya. (There are differences in the names applied to the islands in the bay by various charts.)

113+ Beach camping, access a bit difficult.

112 **Posada Concepción**. RV park with full hookups, showers, restrooms and tennis (most sites are occupied by permanents).

111 **Playa los Cocos** (signed). Public beach, no facilities. The area is popular with boardsailors, although the surrounding hills tend to keep things gusty and unpredictable.

109 **Bahía Burro**. Public beach, *palapas* and trash barrels, anchorage. An airplane wreck lies 200 yards off the south point in two fathoms.

108 **El Coyote**. Restaurant, El Coyote RV Park, no facilities. Isla Blanca has the best diving in the area, with lots of marine life and caves on the southwest side.

107+ Sedan road (signed) to Playa el Coyote. Locals take their children on picnics here and look for a pirate ship supposedly wrecked somewhere to the south. Fishing is often good along the rocky beaches and cliffs from here south to El Requesón, primarily for

cabrilla, pargo and snapper, plus an occasional barracuda.

106 Site of "The Unhappy Coyote." One of the most engaging examples of Indian rock art in Baja, this painting is of a lop-eared coyote, his mouth open and tail sticking straight astern, his back humped up and his left front paw swollen. At first glance this simple portrait, mottled and a bit indistinct due to aging, hardly seems to rate a second glance, but it seems to grow on most people, at least those with some imagination. The Cochimí artist not only created a coyote but even managed to convey something of its physical and mental state—he is obviously hassled and dejected, perhaps due to a thorn in his paw. In addition to the coyote there are over a dozen other painted figures including seven fish, a man and something that looks like a very pregnant pussycat. The Unhappy Coyote can be visited by stopping at KM 106. At the marker sight 101° and note the three small rock shelters. Do this quickly and watch for traffic—the shoulder is narrow. Drive one-quarter mile north and park on the east side of the road. The shelters can then be reached by hiking about 400 yards south along the old unpaved highway.

94+ Public beach, RV parking, restaurant, *palapas*, concrete launch ramp, usable only at high water.

92+ **Playa Requesón** (signed). Beach, camping, pit toi-

Sailboarding action at Bahía Concepción.

lets, anchorage for small boats. The configuration of this area allows novice boardsailors to find side-shore conditions no matter which way the wind blows. A wreck dating from about 1940 lies four miles southeast, its top six feet from the surface. The plants that look like they are standing on stilts at the edge of the water are mangrove. Forming dense thickets in saline locations avoided by other vegetation, they serve important ecological functions. Their roots offer shelter to hordes of fry and other small creatures and tend to trap particles, causing the mud flats to extend, in turn providing homes for countless worms and mollusks. Their branches and leaves attract many species of birds, whose droppings enrich the environment below. Several species are found along peninsula shores from Bahía las Ánimas south in the Cortez and in many lagoons on the Pacific side, as well as on some Cortez islands from Isla Coronado south. The greatest mangrove lagoon in the Cortez is located at Bahía Amortajada on Isla San José.

90+   **Playa Armenta** (signed). Public beach, no facilities. Fishing camps along the beach to the south often have scallops for sale.

81   The area on the west side of the road has some plants common to similar habitats throughout much of Baja. The trees with green trunks are palo verde; those with white trunks are palo blanco; those having slender, leathery leaves with rolled margins, two-to-five inches long, are palo San Juan; and the straggling, almost shapeless, trees with sharp thorns that resemble cat's claws are palo fierro. Despite sharing the common name "palo" and having overlapping ranges, they are not closely related. Palo fierro, also known as ironwood because of its dense wood, was widely used for carvings and tool handles, while palo verde bark was once popular for tanning leather, so much so that both species became rare in parts of their ranges. The distinctive "bearded" cactus is garambullo, found widely in lower elevations throughout much of the peninsula.

76+   Road east to Peninsula Concepción and San Sebastián.

SIDETRIP TO PENINSULA CONCEPCIÓN AND SAN SEBASTIÁN

A road runs east and then north to the vicinity of Punta Hornitos. The shores on the east side of the bay are less indented by bays and less scenic than those on the the west side, but there are many fine sand-and-pebble beaches, and good camping, exploring, shelling, mineral collecting, fishing and diving are to be found. Best of all, the crowds encountered at Santispac and other west-side locations during holidays are absent—in fact, most campsites are usually deserted. The road crosses coastal plains and there are no major grades, although several arroyos and places where the road follows the upper margins of pebble beaches may cause problems for sedans. At KM 76+ turn east, set odometer and pass an abandoned RV park at Mile 0.5. Shells to be found at

the south end include *Dosinia ponderosa, Oliva spicata, Murex elenesis, Strombus gracilior*, variegated auger and giant egg cockle. In addition, enormous numbers of *chocolate* clams live in the sandy shallows along this stretch of beach. Divers will find them in as little as three feet of water. Don't bother looking for a vent hole—the really big vents are giant egg cockles— but rather for a small, suspicious-looking indentation in the sand. Just plow your thumb through the loose sand. *Chocolates* have a smooth, vitreous, light brown shell.

At Mile 5.5 take the left (020°) fork, and at Mile 5.6 take the left (345°) fork. Note the second fork well; it may be important later. The wreck of a wooden sailboat lies in shallow water west of this point. The sandy arroyo at Mile 6.1 is the severest test of vehicles for the next fourteen miles. Watch for frigate birds sitting on tall cactus, quail and several species of hawks. There are many campsites with pebble, shell and sand beaches along the road, and the shallow waters offshore are loaded with clams. At Mile 15.2 a road leads east to Rancho Renteria; continue straight ahead. Take the left (350°) fork at Mile 17.1; the right leads to Rancho el Salto. Punta Amolares at Mile 20.0 has excellent shelling. There is an onyx deposit in Cañon Amolares, 2 1/4 miles, 059° from the point. Poor road conditions will probably keep sedans from going much farther north. Quartz, calcite and barite are found in the mouth of Arroyo Minitas de Guadalupe, passed at Mile 27.3. The beaches from here to Punta Hornitos are prime shelling areas.

At Mile 30.5 arrive at an important intersection. The left (290°) fork leads about two more miles to the vicinity of Punta Hornitos. The right (110°) fork goes east up an arroyo through highly mineralized areas, the earth bright with shades of tan, mustard and rose. At Mile 34.7 the road ends at Gavilanes, described earlier. Most of the building foundations are in the next cove to the north.

To drive to San Sebastián, drive to Mile 5.6, take the 045° fork and arrive at the beach in nine miles. The road is unimproved, but there are no major grades or soft spots, and sizable motorhomes and trailers have made the trip, including, believe it or not, a fifth-wheeler that arrived minus a lot of plumbing. It should be possible to tow in small trailerboats, but the pebble beach is fairly steep, so launching might be difficult.

Back on the Transpeninsular Highway at KM 76+

60   Road southwest (signed) to San Isidoro and La Purísima. This road is part of the Mountain Villages Loop Trip, described beginning on page 188.

0   **Loreto junction.**

SIDETRIP TO LORETO AND ISLA CARMEN

Unlike its neighbors to the north, Loreto is neither a mining town nor a sleepy tropical village, and it has an identity all its own. Founded by Jesuit Father Juan María Salvatierra in 1697, it was the first permanent Spanish settlement in the Californias, serving as a political capital, a military center and a base for Jesuit operations. A shipyard and a school to teach

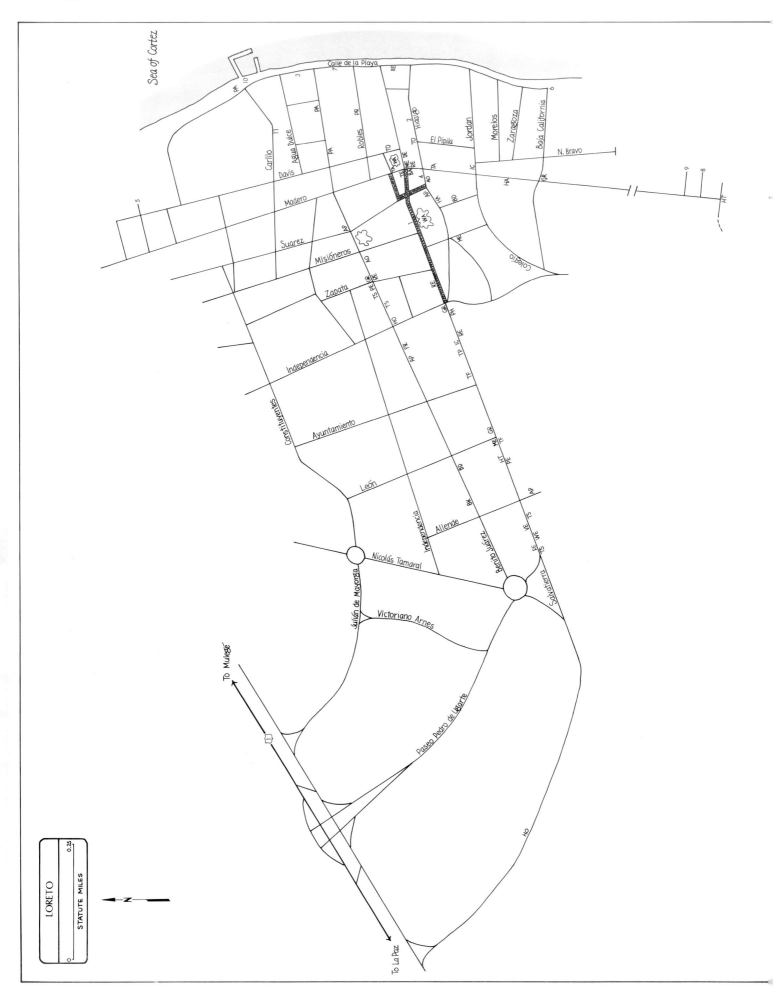

LORETO

STATUTE MILES

0   0.25

Sea of Cortez

Calle de la Playa

Carillo
Agua Dulce
Davis
Madero
Suarez
Misióneros
Zapata
Independencia
Ayuntamiento
León
Constituyentes

Robles
El Pipila
Jordan
Morelos
Zaragoza
Baja California
N. Bravo

Allende
Independencia
Benito Juárez
Salvatierra

Nicolás Tamaral

Julián de Mayorga
Victoriano Arnes

Paseo Pedro de Ugarte

To Mulegé

To La Paz

Indians to handle sailing vessels were established. The mission building was completed in 1752, and the town seemed to be thriving. However, a series of misfortunes occurred: a hurricane ravaged the town in 1829, the capital was moved to La Paz in 1830, and in 1877 a severe earthquake struck, badly damaging many buildings, including the mission church. Coupled with an inadequate economic base, these disasters caused Loreto to decline into a backwater for more than three-quarters of a century.

The town has prospered in recent years, due in part to the new hotel complex at Nopoló. An international airport south of town brings in planeloads of tourists, part of Salvatierra Street has been turned into a shopping mall, shuttle buses cruise the streets, many new homes are under construction and some of the streets are being paved. At times it seems that every second vehicle is a dump truck. Loreto's prosperity has deep roots, and stores catering to the local people sell everything from color TVs to gas ranges. Would Father Salvatierra believe all this?

The town has a wide variety of sales, services and attractions; see the accompanying map. The old mission church (1), still in use and incongruously part of the shopping mall, has been renovated several times, funded in part by 500,000 pesos won by its priest in the national lottery a number of years ago, and there is an interesting museum next door.

Loreto has long catered to sportfishermen, offering hot action for almost all the species of fish that fishermen come to Baja to pursue. The Flying Sportsman's Lodge, now closed, was one of the original fly-in fishing resorts in Baja, operating its own DC-3. As the town changed, so did the fishermen; rather than a relatively small number of dedicated fisherman, new facilities have brought in large numbers of tourists, to whom fishing may be an incidental pleasure, to be squeezed in between a day on the tennis courts and a day in the pool. Their sheer numbers, together with increased commercial netting, have resulted in a decline in the fishery. A few years ago many would-be fishermen at a beachfront hotel watched in horror as a commercial boat netted a reported ten metric tons of fish directly off the hotel. The new complex to be constructed at Puerto Escondido, with its hundreds of boat slips, and the "fisherman's pier" planned for the Nopoló area will certainly accelerate this trend.

In spite of it all, there are still plenty of fish—the netters proved that—and it's the trend more than the actual numbers of fish taken that is the worry. Many people still find excellent fishing, especially those with a boat big enough to get well out into the Cortez. The action is quite seasonal, with the warm months best. In July the area east of Isla Carmen outside the 100-fathom line, reached about two miles east of both Punta Lobos and Punta Baja, provides some of the hottest dolphin action in Baja. Dolphins are not often caught by casting off a beach, but it happens near the navigation light at Punta Arena on Carmen. Other good dolphin areas include the south tips of both Carmen and Danzante. The waters between Islas Coronados and Carmen sometimes have excellent runs of yellowtail. Other favorite offshore fishing spots include the areas south and east of Coronados, the water off Punta Lobos, and the deep water between Loreto and Carmen. The beaches north of Loreto occasionally have roosters in the spring, and yellowtails from December to April.

Pangas can be rented at offices on the beach in the north part of town, and *pangas* and cruisers are available at Arturo's Sports Fishing Fleet (2) and Alfredo's Sport Fishing (3). Deportes Blazer (4) sells fishing tackle. There is a Pesca office on the outskirts of town; from Loreto junction, drive south on the Transpeninsular 0.1 mile and watch for a sign on the southeast side of the highway.

Most divers head for Coronados or Carmen, although divers with fast boats often choose Islas Danzante, Monserrate and Santa Catalina, Los Candeleros or the Bahía Agua

Bob Jackson's grouper was taken off Loreto.

LLOYD WHITENECK

Verde area. Diving conditions at these places will be described in later sections. Deportes Blazer has air, limited sales and rentals. The shop operates several fast dive boats and has a supply of hard-to-find gadgets like wishbones, sling rings, speargun points and snorkel tabs. In addition, there is a dive shop at the Stouffer Presidente Hotel at Nopoló.

The La Pinta Hotel (5) has rooms, a restaurant/bar and a pool. The Hotel Oasis (6) has rooms, bar, tennis courts, pool and gift shop. The Hotel Misión de Loreto (7) has rooms and a pool. Loremar RV Park (8) has a beach, pull-through spaces, full hookups, tenting spaces, laundry service, restrooms and showers, and offers fishing, diving and sightseeing trips. There is no ramp, but Loremar has a launch vehicle that can handle sizable boats. Las Palmas RV Resort (9) has a beach, full hookups, laundry and a launch ramp, normally covered with sand. Alfredo's Sport Fishing also offers car rentals, excursions, hotel reservations and tourist information.

Small boats can be launched at Loremar, or over the sand beach at the north end of town, large trailerboats at Puerto Escondido, fifteen miles south. During periods of north weather, Carmen's chain of mountains—some in excess of 1,500 feet, extending over its entire twenty-mile length—plus its northeast-southwest orientation, tends to funnel heavy winds past Loreto, and with lots of fetch and plenty of wind the channel is often choppy. Skippers of small boats, especially cartoppers, should give careful thought about trips to Carmen; a safer choice would be Danzante. The anchorage off Loreto is nothing more than an open roadstead, so plan to bring your boat ashore each night. A small-boat harbor (10) and a concrete launch ramp were under construction in early 1991. The first good anchorage south is Escondido. There is a COTP (11) in town, and customs and immigration at the airport.

The waters around Carmen are among the best in the area for finding blue and fin whales, and the waters to the south have blue, fin, Minke and Bryde's whales. Carmen has two good anchorages, Puerto Balandra on the west side and Bahía Salinas on the east. An old miner's map shows numerous copper claims near a landing spot 1 1/2 miles north of Balandra. Composed of marine sedimentary and Holocene volcanic rock, Carmen is the site of a large volcano, its crater the source of exceptionally pure salt. The salt operation is now closed, but about 40,000 tons a year used to be shipped from the pier in Bahía Salinas. The 120-foot vessel *Engenada* sank in 1981 and can be found 1/2 mile directly off the salt pier in the bay. Many years ago salt was carried by burros from Salinas to Balandra, and a hike on the trail might provide mineral-collecting opportunities. Divers will find *chocolate* clams abundant on shallow sandy bottoms off the western shores. The best diving and spearfishing are off the north end and along the east coast. Also, a reef about 1,500 yards south of the south tip of Carmen comes to within a dozen feet of the surface and offers outstanding snorkeling. The water is alive with fry and tiny mysids, and large barracuda, leopard groupers, barred pargo and dog snappers are common, along with king angels and several species of grunts.

There are at least nine sea caves on the north shore near Punta Lobos and on the west side south of Isla Cholla, the longest stretching more than 150 feet. All except one are in a limestone cliff, bordering on a fine sand beach. The last one,

near the point, is in volcanic rock and has a 30-foot underwater passage to another entrance, transited by free-diver Dave Bunnell in 1984. At least two others have extensive air chambers, as evidenced by large volumes of air expelled during periods of heavy surge.

Back on the Transpeninsular Highway at Loreto junction

0/120	Start new KM numbering sequence.
118	Road west (signed) to San Javier.

THE MOUNTAIN VILLAGES LOOP TRIP

This trip passes through fine mountain scenery and visits a number of interesting villages, the first of which, San Javier, has the finest Jesuit mission church in Baja. Although the road to San Javier is rough and has grades to 14%, sedans make the trip, and the hotels in Loreto can arrange van trips. Those continuing on to the other villages will need a pickup or four-wheel-drive. In 1990 storms damaged the roads badly and it may be a considerable time until they are completely repaired. This loop trip is a favorite with off-road bicyclists, but due to steep grades some walking will be necessary, and brakes should be in top condition. There are ranches along the way where extra water may be obtained, but since these sources are not totally dependable, the amount carried by bicyclists needs to be adequate to get from village to village. The road between San Javier and San José de Comondú carries little traffic.

Set odometer. Starting at Mile 1.4, commence moderate up- and downgrades, soon followed by a steady climb. Water may appear in canyon bottoms starting about Mile 8.7, sooner if the weather has been wet, and it might be possible to find a swimming hole. As the road switches back and forth the scenery becomes more spectacular, with zalates (wild fig trees) clinging to almost vertical canyon walls and palms lining the bottom of the canyon.

El Pilón de Parras, a huge pyramid of rock next to the road, is an excellent climb. A number of approaches are available, starting at about Mile 11.1. Its summit is at 3,477 feet, and since the altitude of the road at its closest approach is 1,330 feet the total climb is over 2,100 feet. The climb is class 3, with a good deal of traversing necessary to avoid technical sections. It is strenuous, and a long day should be planned, but the views of the deeply eroded Sierra de la Giganta and the blue waters of the Cortez are smashing. Rock climbers will find a technical climb on a sheer rock face at Mile 11.6. After a fifty-minute class 2 and 3 approach, the face will be encountered at elevation 2,100 feet. About three pitches in length, it is crossed by a large diagonal crack, and the closer you get the more impressive it looks. The rock is strong and there is plenty of placement. Once above the approach, the climb is lower- to upper-class 5.

At Mile 11.9 encounter Rancho las Parras, with a stone chapel, small dam and citrus and olive trees. At Mile 13.0 the road reaches the summit at 1,700 feet, offering fine views of the canyon below and of the Cortez. Occasional small streams and ponds may be found from here to San Javier. Pass Rancho Viejo at Mile 16.6, and at Mile 18.0 note the road to the right

(295°); you will need it later.

Arrive at San Javier at Mile 22.1. In 1699 Jesuit Father Francisco Píccolo founded a mission at Rancho Viejo, but in 1707 the site of the present village was developed as a garden and visiting station by Father Ugarte, and in 1720 the mission was moved there. In 1744 the stone church was started, taking fourteen years to complete. The golden altar and its paintings were carried by burro and ship from Mexico City. The care-taker lives five doors to the north and will show you the antique vestments and let you climb to the tower, which has three bells, two dated 1761, one 1803. The church is still in use, and on December 2 and 3 of each year the almost-deserted village is filled with people from surrounding ranches, there to celebrate Saint Javier's birthday.

Tiny stores sell very limited groceries and cold sodas. Drinking water can be obtained from spigots along the divided parkway serving in lieu of the traditional plaza. Several women will prepare meals, and you can buy oranges from children.

To continue on the trip, return to the intersection at Mile 18.0, reset your odometer and turn left (295°). The road will immediately swing right along the old route of the Loreto-San Javier road. At Mile 0.4 turn left (020°) at a concrete marker. The rough road has seen some improvements like culverts and concrete causeways, but many have been swept away by floods. At Mile 9.5 start a major upgrade, two miles of loose rock, bumps and slopes up to 21%. Bicyclists will walk this one.

Good campsites are difficult to find at the top of the mesa, as almost everything is cobbles and boulders, so start looking early. There are great views of the canyons to the west, making the area a fine sunset spot. At Mile 13.3 start a mile of switchbacks, loose rock and downgrades of 23% into a canyon. A cold six-pack goes to the first person who can explain the purpose of the strange stone structure at Mile 15.4. The rough road levels out a bit, with no major grades until Mile 19.7, where a mile of 19% upgrades is begun, and Mile 24.7, where a mile of 21% downgrades ends at the village of San José de Comondú.

San José de Comondú and its twin village San Miguel de Comondú, two miles away, occupy the bottom of a fertile, well-watered canyon, and the drop from the harsh, sun-drenched lava mesa into these villages is one of the most startling imaginable. Suddenly you enter a cool sea of green, so dense with oranges, sugar cane, figs, corn, grapes, palms, bougainvillaea and a dozen other flowering plants that there doesn't seem room for the people. Most of the buildings are traditional adobe, and except for the electric lines, vehicles and a TV satellite dish, it could be a scene from the previous century.

A small plaza is encountered immediately upon entering San José. The stone building is a missionary house from Misión Comondu, the bell in front dating from 1708 (the church was torn down). Water can be obtained from spigots in the plaza, and a store sells food and drink and Nova from drums. The post and telegraph offices are located a little farther on. A third of a mile from the plaza there is a road right (335°); take note but continue straight ahead. Two-and-one-quarter miles from the plaza, turn right (253°), cross the canyon bottom and enter San Miguel de Comondú. Despite

Jim Smallwood top-roping on the rock face at El Pilón, camera-shy Don Nelson unseen.

its appearance, San Miguel is the older village, established in 1714 by Father Ugarte to supply food for Misión San Javier. Look for antique sugar-cane presses, operated by burros walking in circles. There are mail and telegraph offices, cold beer, drinking water from spigots, and Nova from drums at the store. There are no cafes or lodgings in either village, but you can ask around about home-cooked meals and a place to stay. There is a health clinic in San José.

To continue on the trip, return to the intersection noted previously, reset your odometer and turn left (335°) through a corridor of palms, encountering an 18% upgrade on the other side of the canyon. At Mile 0.75 take the left (335°) fork and pass a cemetery on the right. Once on top of the mesa, the road improves, but there are many gentle-to-moderate grades. Campsites are hard to find, so start looking early. The great Arroyo de la Purísima can soon be seen ahead, and the road begins to descend. Note the road going right (010°) at Mile 18.8; you may need it later. At Mile 19.7 you will arrive at El Arriba, a small community of palm-thatched homes and citrus groves. An aqueduct cut through stone cliffs and crossing fields parallels the palm-lined road for miles. San Isidoro, with a general store, cold beer, water from spigots, food stores, pharmacy, telegraph and a modest motel, is reached at Mile 21.2.

There are great views of the village and the surrounding

palm groves and ponds at Mile 22.7. At first glance El Pilón, the massive rock formation towering over the village, might look like a volcano, but it was actually formed because a cap of weather-resistant rock shielded it while the rest of the valley eroded away. A local climber fell from the top some years ago, and a cross was erected there in his honor. La Purísima is reached at Mile 23.3, with a food store, cold beer, water from spigots, ice plant, auto parts, doctor, dentist, meat market, clothing/shoe store, telegraph and post offices and a general store selling Nova and diesel from barrels. There is no cafe in either village, but if you need a meal it should not be too hard to find someone willing to cook one. The road continues about five miles southwest down the canyon to an important intersection, from where you can go north to San Ignacio, or south to Villa Insurgentes. You may see sizable travel trailers in the village; the locals bring them north from Villa Insurgentes, since the road is much better than any other approach to La Purísima.

To return to the Transpeninsular, go back to the intersection at Mile 18.8, reset your odometer and turn left (010°). The road has been improved, with some grading and culverting, but is less scenic and interesting than earlier parts of the trip. At Mile 21.6 go straight ahead, arriving at KM 60 on the Transpeninsular at Mile 33.0.

Back on the Transpeninsular Highway at KM 118

117 Road east (signed) to Loreto International Airport.

111 **Nopoló.** A sedan road runs east (signed) to the FONATUR tourist complex and the Stouffer Presidente Hotel. The hotel offers rooms and suites, restaurants, bars, pools, shops, laundry service, local tours, and travel and car-rental agencies. A tennis center is nearby. Fantasia Destinations, based at the hotel, offers SCUBA air, rental equipment, diving trips, a resort diving course and a PADI open-water course. No spearfishing or shell collecting is permitted on dive-shop trips. They also offer fishing trips, waterskiing and instruction, and rentals of sailboards, Mini-fish, Sunfish and Hobies. February is the big wind month.

107+ They don't rival the Golden Gate, but the only two suspension bridges in Baja can be seen here.

103 **Playa Notrí** (signed). Public beach, no facilities.

El Pilón and the countryside near La Purísima.

The beach is a source of several species of cowrie shells.
98   The road levels out until KM 83.
97+   Road east (signed) to El Juncalito.

SIDETRIP TO EL JUNCALITO

This palm-lined little cove is a favorite with many travelers, offering camping, *palapas*, trash cans and a nice beach. The road in can handle almost any RV. A small fee is charged. Launching cartoppers and inflatables over the sandy beach is easy. There is fine shorecasting in Bahía Chuenque for yellowtail along the south shore from December to April, and jack crevalle and roosters are taken in the spring. Divers will find good foraging for purple-lips among large rocks below the cliffs outside the cove to the south, also the habitat of many sizable snapper, grouper, pargo and cabrilla. The cove is a fair anchorage in all but north or northeast weather.

The strikingly beautiful tree on the beach with creamy-yellow bark and bright-green deciduous leaves is a zalate, or wild fig. Found from San Ignacio south, zalates often choose exposed locations where no other large trees are able to survive, sometimes clinging to sheer cliff faces, their root systems taking advantage of every available crack. The tree can be seen from the highway at KM 99, but a better (and safer) look can be obtained by driving to the shore and heading north around the curve of the bay past the small rocky headland. While zalates are fairly common, this will be your only chance to see a mature tree close to the Transpeninsular until south of La Paz.

An old man from Juncalito tells a tale so implausible as to virtually guarantee its authenticity—no one would have made it up. It seems that about 1951 an American man and his wife flew two "B-24 bombers" from Los Angeles with a cargo of tomato crates, hoping to unload in La Paz and return with a cargo of tomatoes. However, a rare fog blanketed La Paz and they turned back and attempted an emergency landing at Loreto. The woman's plane ran out of fuel and crashed in the bay off the old man's house, killing her. Tomato crates continued to wash ashore for weeks.

Implausible or not, divers will find the wreckage of a large twin-engine plane in the exact spot described by the old man. It lies in twenty-two feet of water on a gently sloping cobble bottom seventy-five yards south of Isla Chuenque, the only island in the bay. When you are over the wreck the central peak on the island will bear 342°. The two large air-cooled radial engines are easy to locate, each with fourteen cylinders. The area is littered with large quantities of aluminum wing sections, ribs, sheet and structural parts, stainless hose, plastic sheet from the windows and the landing gear. Based on the engines (Wrights), the plane was probably a DC-3, the standard civil transport of the era.

Back on the Transpeninsular Highway at KM 97+

94+   Road east (signed) to Puerto Escondido.

SIDETRIP TO TRIPUI, PUERTO ESCONDIDO AND ISLA DANZANTE

The TRIPUI RV Park complex, 1/2 mile east of the highway, has full hookups, restrooms, showers, laundromat, restaurant, store, pool, sports facilities and vehicle storage. Two-thirds of the RV spaces are now (1991) occupied by permanents, leaving about thirty for passersby, as well as a small motel.

Puerto Escondido is the finest all-weather anchorage for larger boats in the Cortez, completely surrounded by land except for its sixty-five-foot wide, nine-foot-deep (at high tide) channel. Tidal current flows through this channel at up to four knots. A concrete launch ramp is available inside the harbor entrance, suitable for even large trailerboats—inquire at TRIPUI as to the rules and fees. Construction has been underway for about five years on a major development of the area, which may some day provide a yacht club, markets, sports club, beach, condominiums, residential subdivisions and other facilities. In early 1991 construction was at a standstill, but rumors persist that things are to get going again. The Moorings has an office at the waterfront and offers yacht charters. Yachts may still anchor in the harbor and trailerboats can be launched, but RVs may no longer be parked in the area. There is a part-time COTP office nearby; the main office is in Loreto. Dinghy and boardsailors will find calm and safe conditions inside the bay.

The outer harbor area, known as the "Waiting Room," is also a good anchorage. Divers will see garden eels and might be able to ride whale sharks, which occasionally visit the area. In 1932 the 101-ton yacht *Aimee* burned and sank here. Several massive black coral trees can be seen in deep water off Punta Coyote, the easternmost extension of the peninsula forming the bay. Divers report that dense schools of yellowtail inhabit this area year-round at depths of 100-120 feet, a fact not known to many visiting fishermen.

The island three miles to the southeast is Isla Danzante. There is an excellent anchorage in a cove on its west shore near the north tip, often used by antisocial boaters wishing to escape crowded Escondido. There is a good deal of commercial netting, but fine fishing is still available, the productive locations including the reefs and small islands from Danzante south to Punta Candeleros and the water outside the 100-fathom line five miles east of Danzante.

Diving is best on Danzante's east side and on the reef at the south cape, where garden eels have been seen in the sand at sixty-five feet, and black coral in deeper water. The south cape is also excellent for fishing and spearfishing, with barracuda, yellowtail, leopard grouper and snappers. Fishing and diving are good near a rock visible from the surface four miles, 072° from the south cape of Danzante. When you are over the site the south cape will bear 252°, Punta Perico on Carmen 011°. A large bank offering excellent bottom fishing and diving is located three miles, 086° from the south cape of Danzante. With a least depth of thirty-six feet, it can sometimes be seen from the surface.

****

AN EPISTLE ON EVINRUDE. We were heading back to camp after a day of diving, when the engine suddenly acted up. The symptoms were puzzling; it would start and run momentarily, backfire and then quit, with gas spraying out of the air intake. It obviously could not be fixed in situ *and it was not until after midnight that we got back with the aid of another boat. With abundant advice from an audience of several locals from the nearby settlement, I tore the engine apart the next morning and found that one of the four leaf valves had broken. These consisted of flat metal springs fastened at one end to a metal plate, each covering a hole in the plate. This assembly allowed the air-fuel mixture to pass from the carburetor into the crankcase, but not the other way. My audience soon grew to five, and they began to offer their best advice: drive the 150 miles to the nearest dealer, order the part and pick it up two weeks later.*

Since I couldn't wait, I had to devise a repair. I cut two pieces of sheet aluminum slightly larger than the hole in the metal plate behind the broken leaf, and fastened them together with a small machine screw. By blocking the hole I hoped that the three remaining valves would allow the engine to operate satisfactorily. As I worked in the hot sun my audience grew to seven, all of whom soon started shuffling about and making clucking noises—sure signs, I feared, of disapproval. Finally, one of them could restrain himself no longer; "It would never work, never," he said, to the obvious approval of the crowd.

The repair completed, I reassembled the engine and carried it down to the boat, accompanied by a group of jeering children. I got no help from my critics, none of whom wanted to be associated with such an obviously futile endeavor. With every eye on me I squeezed the fuel bulb, gave the starter a yank, and the engine roared to life—the first time, as best I can remember, that it had ever started on the first pull. Unfortunately, the engine was in gear—the interlock that normally stopped it from starting while in gear was not adjusted properly—and the sudden acceleration threw me backward and I lost my footing. Draped across the engine on my stomach, feet up, nose almost in the water, it took me half a minute to regain my balance. As the boat sped away I finally looked back; the beach was deserted, my critics apparently having decided that the pain of being wrong was greater than their amusement at my predicament.

The spectacle did not end without comment, however; my fellow divers had arrived back in camp from a supply run to town at just the right moment. Around the campfire that night my valve-repair triumph was forgotten and the central topics of conversation were endless commentary on how silly I looked draped over the engine, countless recreations of the event, and abundant speculation as to how far the boat would have gotten before running out of gas had I been pitched into the water.

****

Back on the Transpeninsular Highway at KM 94+

Although mostly just steep cobble, the beaches from here south to Ensenada Blanca are a favorite with pickup-campers and those with small trailers and motorhomes, as well as bicyclists, and many fishermen prefer them to any other in the Loreto area. There are a number of faint, almost unnoticeable trails that lead to the beach, permitting camping with some degree of privacy and ready access to Danzante and the other islands. Diving around the small islets just offshore is excellent.

KM	LOCATION
94+	Opposite the road to Escondido, a sedan road heads southwest 0.7 mile to the mouth of Cañon Tabor, a fine hiking location. At one point there is a huge boulder wedged in the narrow canyon, making it necessary to scoot under it and then climb a notched log. There are palms and surface water in some places. Bighorn sheep have been seen in the canyon.
84+	**Rancho Ligui.** A sedan road (signed) heads east to a public beach, no facilities. One-half mile from the highway a sedan road heads right (110°) to Ensenada Blanca. Several spur roads along the way lead to seaside campsites, one with a fine sand beach. Ensenada Blanca is shallow but well protected from all but north winds. The beaches are sand and silt, with some rocky areas. The tiny settlement has a small store. The road continues around the curve of the bay.
83	Seven percent upgrades and many switchbacks to KM 77, then ups-and-downs to KM 45.
63+	Road southeast (signed) to Bahía Agua Verde, twenty-four miles. This steep but graded and sometimes maintained road descends through hairpin turns to a beach opposite two small islands on the shores of the Cortez. The scenery alone is worth the trip. The beaches are mostly steep cobble, although short stretches of sand can be found close to Agua Verde. Although the road closely parallels the water, sideroads leading to the beaches are limited, making it difficult to find a place to camp. The road is important in that it opens the Agua Verde area to fishermen and divers having cartoppers and inflatables, who would otherwise have to run over twenty miles from the beaches near Danzante. In addition, Isla Monserrate is only eight miles away and Isla Santa Catalina fifteen. Agua Verde and the islands are described in the next section.
60+	Road south (signed "Rancho Huatamote") to a clearing with some camping sites and a bit of shade.
45	On top of a mesa, mostly gentle downgrades or level from here to KM 123, south of Ciudad Constitución. Headwinds are frequent in the afternoon.
17	PEMEX (MND), ice, sodas and food.
0	**Villa Insurgentes.**

SIDETRIPS SOUTH ALONG THE COAST TO LA PAZ

The coast between Loreto and La Paz is one of the most interesting areas in the Cortez. South of Ensenada Blanca roads penetrate in only two places, Bahía Agua Verde and San Evaristo, and the area is unspoiled and almost deserted. The Sierra de la Giganta assume wildly improbable shapes; lopsided domes, fantastic plunging cliffs and strange valleys, all worked in red and purple rock, disproving Jesuit Father

Rob Watson claimed to have seen glowing eyes looking back at him while exploring a sea cave near San Francisquito.

Baegert's claim that there is no scenery to please the eye in Baja California. There is a great deal to do here, including hiking and exploring, nature-watching, fishing, diving for edibles and making friends with manta rays. Some of the islands are home to unusual wildlife, such as black jackrabbits and silent rattlesnakes, and the waters surrounding them are alive with hundreds of species of fish. With adequate planning, drinking water should not be a problem, for there are a number of permanent ranches and settlements along the coast, and two settlements on the islands offshore, and yachts frequent the area. A trip down the coast can assume either of two basic forms: a coastal trip by kayak or small boat, or an offshore island-hopping cruise in a more seaworthy craft.

Coasting to La Paz

Marine charts of this coast are inadequate for kayaking and small-boat cruising, but the following 1:50,000 Mexican topographic charts are useful: Ligui G12C29, San José de la Noria G12C39, Timbabichi G12D31, Los Burros G12D41 and San Pedro de la Presa G12D51-52.

Staying very close to the coast, the distance from Escondido to La Paz is 135 miles. Ensenada Blanca, 7 miles south of Escondido, was described earlier. A small cove several miles south of Punta Candeleros provides a sand beach and a small anchorage, good in all but north weather. The rocky coast gives way to sand near Bahía Agua Verde. Nineteen miles from Ensenada Blanca, Bahía Agua Verde is formed from numerous small coves, one or another of which will provide protection from weather from any direction except northeast. The largest black-coral forest in the Cortez can be

found in 80-150 feet off the rocky pinnacle of Roca Solitario, a 115-foot-high pinnacle at the mouth of the bay. There is a tiny settlement in back of the white sand beaches. The well here has reportedly become saline, so don't plan on getting water. A road, already described, connects with the Transpeninsular at KM 63+. Punta San Marcial, 3 miles from the bay, has a fine sand beach and forms a good anchorage on its south side, protected from north weather. Large catches of yellowtail, dolphins and roosters are common in season, and excellent diving is available on the reef off the south point. A small but interesting sea cave south of the point can be entered by boat.

The coast from Marcial to Puerto Gato is mostly bluffs, with a few sand beaches. Puerto Gato, an open bight north of Punta Botella (Punta San Telmo), fourteen miles from Marcial, is celebrated as the most colorful anchorage in Baja, with a backdrop of rocky layers in red, white and black. Its beautiful sand beaches permit easy landings, but the anchorage is open to the east and can be surgy. Diving on the reef in the southern part of the bay is outstanding. Although there are no deep underwater canyons to draw tuna in as there are at East Cape, they sometimes approach shallow water nearby. Punta Botella, the site of a multimillion-ton deposit of high-grade phosphate with a uranium content, has several sand beaches.

The coast from Puerto Gato to Nopoló is mostly bluffs, with small beaches at the mouths of canyons. Bahía Timbabichi (Bahía San Carlos), an open bight 2 1/2 miles south of Botella, is protected from north weather. Landings can be made on the fine sand beach, and there is a sizable mangrove lagoon worthy of exploration. Several families live nearby and water may be available.

Punta los Burros is located fifteen miles from Timbabichi. North of the point is Rancho los Dolores, which has a sand beach and irrigated gardens of citrus, figs and grapes. Water and fruits in season can be purchased, and it may be possible to obtain fuel in an emergency. The anchorage is poor and usable only in west and south weather. Immediately south of the point is Rancho los Burros, which has an open anchorage and a beach, and may have water. Nopoló, a small settlement with an anchorage open to the east, is 6 1/2 miles from Los

Kayakers explore a remote coast.

WILL WATERMAN

Burros. Pebble beaches here alternate with sand beaches. The villagers are friendly, and gas and water may be available.

The seven-mile coast from Nopoló to Bahía San Evaristo is mostly bluffs, with a few beaches. Evaristo is an excellent all-weather anchorage, and a settlement just to the north has water and possibly emergency gasoline. Fine sand beaches provide many campsites, and snorkeling at the point is excellent, with many small reef fish inhabiting boulders and cobble down to a sand bottom at twenty feet. A night dive will reveal large numbers of an unusual sea cucumber with a wormlike body up to four feet long, uncommon in the Cortez. The following chapter describes the road between Evaristo and La Paz.

A ranch will be found near Punta Arena (Punta Salinas), two miles south of Evaristo. Five miles farther south is a headland of 300-foot cliffs called Punta el Mechudo. There are a number of sand beaches between Evaristo and Mechudo.

Use the regional map in the following chapter for the remainder of the "Coasting to La Paz" trip. Between Mechudo and San Juan de la Costa, twenty-eight miles, there are more beaches and a few small fish camps and ranches. The phosphate-mining town of San Juan de la Costa, a healthy walk from the beach, has a public restaurant and water from spigots. Since the coast south of this point is relatively featureless and uninteresting, and because the town has good road access, kayakers and small-boat sailors may wish to end their trip here rather than going on to La Paz. During periods of calm, stable weather, boaters and experienced kayakers sometimes head from Isla San Francisco directly for Isla Partida Sur, eighteen miles, since Partida Sur and Isla Espíritu

John Anglin pops a purple-lip off Candeleros.

Santo just to the south are two of the nicest camping and loafing islands in the Cortez.

Should you choose to follow the coast, the distance from San Juan de la Costa to the entrance to La Paz harbor at El Mogote is twenty-six miles. There are occasional fish camps and ranches along the beach, with cliffs alternating with pebble beaches and cobble beaches, slowly giving way to sand. There are no good anchorages, and fishing and diving are poor, but the beaches and low points provide good campsites, and it is often possible to scout up driftwood for a fire.

The Island-Hopping Cruise

Those in adequate vessels may wish to island-hop from Escondido to La Paz by way of Islas Danzante, Monserrate, Santa Catalina, Santa Cruz, San Diego, San José, San Francisco, Partida Sur and Espíritu Santo, a trip of about 127 miles. A group of small rocky pinnacles known as Los Candeleros are found 2 miles southeast of Danzante. These are fine deep-dive sites, with plenty of large fish and shellfish. Low-lying Monserrate is 12 miles from Los Candeleros. Its surface looks largely barren, but surrounding waters teem with fish and lobsters. The north end has an anchorage useful in south weather and a sand beach where landings can be made, and reefs off the north points provide fine diving and fishing. In prevailing weather boats can be anchored off the southeast side, although it is very exposed. Islotes las Galeras, a small group of islets two miles north of the island, are seldom visited but have excellent fishing and diving on a jumbled bottom, with numerous rocky ledges.

Eleven miles east of Monserrate is Isla Santa Catalina (Isla Santa Catalan), one of the most famous islands in the Cortez. Home of the "rattle-less" rattlesnake, the island is visited by many natural-history tours. Unlike ordinary rattlesnakes, this small, docile and very rare snake sheds its terminal scale with each molt and thus never develops a rattle. First described in 1953, their days are probably numbered, since feral cats prey on them. A question for visitors to the island: do rattle-less rattlesnakes still shake their tails when disturbed, and if so, why? Another curiosity is an unusually large barrel cactus which often reaches ten feet in height and three feet in diameter, named *Ferocactus diguetii*, after Leon Diguet of rock-art fame who discovered it. Equally strange is the torchwood plant, which bears two distinct types of flowers. Several coves east of the light on the south end provide good anchorages, and landings can be made. Sand beaches are found on the west side. Diving is excellent all around the island, with numerous rock walls, caves and crevices. A mysterious wreck, possibly two, has been reported on the east side near the south end, but no details are available.

Isla Santa Cruz, nineteen miles from Catalina, is steep and barren. Surrounding waters are deep, and the only good anchorage is on the east side, where there is a pebble beach. A sea cave large enough to enter with a boat can be found at the north end of this beach. The best diving and fishing are encountered at the north end, with huge boulders and rocky ledges home to groupers and bottomfish. The southwest reef also offers good fishing and diving.

Isla San Diego, four miles from Santa Cruz, has an anchorage in an open bight on the northwest side. The shoreline is almost entirely steep cliffs, but a landing can be made on the

Our sloop *Azabache* was too large to get in close at Las Ánimas Sur, so Reeve and Mike loaded the hooka in the dinghy.

southwest side. The island has a large population of scorpions, mice and lizards. The southwest reef is an outstanding dive site, with intricate lava formations honeycombed by grottos. An especially fine grotto system can be found in thirty-to-forty feet of water near two pinnacles awash at the end of the reef. Huge groupers and large populations of lobsters are often seen here, along with orange corals and red, gold and white sea fans.

While it is off the direct island-hopping route, fishermen and divers, especially underwater photographers, should visit Isla las Ánimas Sur, nine miles east of Punta Calabozo on Isla San José. Seen from the west, the island resembles a whale chasing a fish, the aid-to-navigation tower on the island being the whale's spout and a small islet being the fish. Ánimas Sur is one of the premiere deep dives in the Cortez, the sheer sides of the island plunging almost vertically to about 300 feet. So steep is the bottom that it is very difficult to anchor safely, although in calm weather small boats may be able to anchor in 80 feet off the south side. The water is deep blue, indicating its depth, and visibilities often exceed 100 feet. Upwellings of cold, nutrient-rich water promote spectacular growths of gorgonians on the steep walls. Because of the variety of micro- and macro-habitats available, few locations in the Cortez have such a range in the size of fish present, from clouds of tiny fry to colorful reef fish to heavy-duty gamefish, including grouper, marlin, dolphin and shark. Watch for rare longnose butterfly fish. There are a number of caves, including one on the east side at 60 feet, which you can enter and chimney up through passages. Although this is SCUBA coun-

try, free-divers might get a shot at large groupers and jacks around the pinnacles on the east side.

Isla San José, seven miles south of Isla San Diego, is the largest island in the chain, about eighteen miles long. The principal island rocks are mixed Miocene volcanic and Pliocene and Pleistocene marine, the island itself the product of fault-block uplift in the Pliocene. With a sizable area and some surface water, the island supports a wide variety of wildlife, including such large mammals as deer, ring-tailed cats and coyotes. Scorpions up to six inches long wait to terrorize campers. There are twenty-one species of reptiles and amphibians, of which one is endemic, and 138 vascular plants, none of which are endemic. The low rate of endemics is due to the close proximity of the peninsula. Birders will be kept busy, with black and western wood phoebes, green-tailed towhee, savannah sparrow, black-headed grosbeak, turkey vulture, red-tailed and peregrine hawks, osprey, kestrel, screech and great horned owls, green and great blue herons, black-crowned night-heron, great, reddish and snowy egrets, white ibis, clapper rail, belted kingfisher and American oystercatcher being present at least part of the year.

The island was home to Pericue Indians until the mid-1700s. Gold, silver, copper, lead and calcite occur on the island. There is good diving off the north tip of the island, where diveable depths extend more than a mile from shore, and at Punta Colorada. A sea cave so large it can be entered with a dinghy will be found near this point. There is relatively little commercial fishing along the east side, so sportfishing and spearfishing are good. A salt works has been in operation at Punta San Isidro (Punta Salinas) on the west shore, and fuel and water sometimes can be obtained at the settlement. The anchorage south of the point is suitable in prevailing weather. Bahía Amortajada, at the south end of the island, provides a good anchorage in south weather, but is completely open to west and northwest winds, and the *jejenes* can be miserable; Lynn and Larry Pardey of *Seraffyn* fame complained about the "flying teeth." West of the bay, the waters around Isla Cayo have good diving, much of it within free-diving range, and sections of it are loaded with shellfish. Garden eels can be seen in sandy areas.

The entrance to a large mangrove lagoon is on the shore of the beach forming the margin of Bahía Amortajada. It is the largest mangrove area in the Cortez, and a dinghy trip is worthwhile. There are many small channels off the main waterway, and once in the mangroves it's a whole new Baja experience. Large numbers of birds inhabit the thickets, including the big and obvious ones like herons, egrets and ibises, and others so small and reclusive you may not be aware of their presence unless you stop the engine and sit quietly for a while. The waters are filled with large numbers of fish, and oysters can be seen clinging to mangrove roots. The visibility is often good, and a snorkeling venture is an experience to remember. Bottoms range from clean sand to the blackest of gooey mud. For the stout-of-heart, a night dive ought to be fantastic!

Between San José and Isla San Francisco is tiny Isla Coyote (Isla Pardito), site of a prosperous fishing settlement, with neat homes and a well-cared-for look. It might be possible to obtain emergency gas and water here. Diving is especially colorful among the rock islets to the west and at the solitary rock to the north, all of which have huge orange and red sea fans and many reef fish.

Isla San Francisco, two miles south of San José, was worked for pearls from the late 1500s to the early 1900s, and between 1881 and 1886 a German operated a one-man gold mine on the island. There are good anchorages on both sides of the spit extending to the south, and in south weather a bay on the northwest end is usually satisfactory. The end of the spit provides good diving with fine visibility in periods of north weather. Watch for garden eels and jawfish on the sandy bottoms. The sand beach on the west side of the spit has good shelling if you like your shells small, including the olive, pearly top, venus, hoof, sea button and bean families, and four or five species of tiny clams. Marine life on the east side is very different, and pearl oysters, nerites, cowries and arks are found on the rocky beach. Quartz pebbles also can be found in quantity. The deep water to the east has good fishing for dolphin and yellowfin tuna in season.

The next island in the chain is Partida Sur, eighteen miles from Isla San Francisco. Because Partida Sur and Espíritu Santo are close to La Paz and because many diving and fishing trips to them begin in that port, they are described in the next chapter.

****

NECESSITY IS THE MOTHER OF INVENTION. We had learned much about botany, ornithology and marine biology during a long day of diving and exploration near Amortajada, but little did we realize as we bedded down for the night that we were about to undergo a required course in entomology! As the moon rose, a primordial urge descended on the resident jejene *population. Blood! Human blood! In seconds the air was full of horrid little black flies. Rather than sticking you with a tube like an honest mosquito seeking a square meal, they are "pool feeders;" using scissor-like mouth parts they slash your skin and greedily lap up the oozing blood. They are found in salt marshes, mangroves and decaying seaweed, the prime locations being the coast south of Puertecitos, Guardian Angel Island, especially the north and south ends, Isla Partida Norte, Isla Turners and, you guessed it, Amortajada. The best defense is avoidance, and moving your camp or boat as little as a mile can put you out of range. An increase in elevation of only a hundred feet also helps; sleep up a canyon, not on the beach.*

We didn't know these things at the time, and desperation drove us to don all available clothing, pull plastic bags over our hands and climb into our sleeping bags, in spite of the warm night. This helped, but many succeeded in finding tunnels and crevices. We wondered if we would be sucked dry, leaving three mummies to be prodded and photographed by passersby. About four in the morning I was forced out of my sleeping bag by a call of nature and was bitten in an extremely sensitive location. My dignity destroyed, I dashed back to the safety of my sleeping bag, my chore unfinished. We lay on our air mattresses stifling in the heat and fighting off swarms of insect invaders, watching the moon travel on its westward journey, inch by inch. Just before dawn an idea hit all three of us simultaneously and there was a rush for our duffel bags. Dawn found three exhausted skin divers asleep on the beach in full wet suits, masks in place and breathing through their snorkels, surrounded by hordes of frustrated insects angrily trying to penetrate the neoprene.

****

The unfortunate photographer was sinking rapidly in the slime and expecting attack by swamp creatures as he took this photograph of Judy, Suzy and Mike exploring the Amortajada lagoon.

CHAPTER 14
BAHÍA MAGDALENA TO LA PAZ

On the Transpeninsular Highway at Villa Insurgentes

KM   LOCATION

0   **Villa Insurgentes**. PEMEX (two, one MND, the other ND), bank, stores, groceries, meat markets, restaurants, beer, *tortilla* factory, ice, auto parts, tire repair, medical, pharmacy, veterinarian, telephone, telegraph and mail. The town of Puerto Lopéz Mateos can be reached by driving northwest through town and taking a left (262°) at Mile 1.4 (signed). The pavement ends at Mile 4.7, and the town is reached at Mile 21.7. Lopéz Mateos has cold beer, meat market, groceries, water spigots in the square, health clinic, pharmacy, Pesca office, long-distance telephone, telegraph and mail. Gasoline is available from drums, and *pangas* can be rented. More on Lopéz Mateos will be found on page 203.

0/236 Start new KM numbering sequence.

221+   Butane yard.

212+   **Ciudad Constitución**. Dozens of wells tapping huge underground aquifers have converted the surrounding areas into Baja's equivalent of Indiana, and the thriving town has the first automobile dealerships (Chevrolet and Nissan) and new-tire dealers since Ensenada. In addition, there are hospitals and doctors, dentists, pharmacies, opticians, veterinarians and a veterinary pharmacy, PEMEX (two, MND in both), mechanics, auto parts, Mariner outboard dealer, airline offices (Aeromexico and Aero California), airport, telegraph, long-distance telephone, post office, department stores, restaurants, meat markets, bakeries, beer, hardware, travel agents, banks, hotels, laundromat, bike shops, sporting goods, an ice plant, 33 Flavors Ice Cream, a yoga parlor and a psychiatrist. The large supermarket in the north end of town on the east side of the Transpeninsular is a close approximation to a U.S.-style store. Campestre La Pila Trailer Park at the south end of town has a dump station, water and electric hookups, pool, tent sites, toilets and showers. Drive south from the downtown area and watch for the large electrical sub-station on the east side of the road. Turn west and watch for signs.

SIDETRIP TO THE BAHÍA MAGDALENA AREA

Commencing at Boca las Ánimas, a series of narrow barrier islands stretches south for over 130 miles. Two of them, Islas Magdalena and Santa Margarita, form Bahía Magdalena and its southern extension, Bahía las Almejas. Although this vast area has a great potential for fishing, diving, kayaking and other activities, it is seldom visited by outsiders. Access and facilities are limited; there is only one paved road to the bay, only one paved launch ramp, and no hotel, resort or fishing operation that caters to sportsmen. Commercial fishermen tell of sixty-pound snook netted in the hundreds of miles of mangrove-lined waterways and small bays, but ordinary techniques common to Baja fishing simply do not work. Storms often cut new channels and silt up old ones, changes which are not reflected on the marine charts. However, unfamiliarity and mystery are the stuff of adventure, and there is a great deal to see and do.

Bay and blue-water fishing

Bahías Magdalena and Almejas are shallow, half their area averaging 60 feet or less, and large areas are exposed at low tide. However, the bay east of the shoreline between Punta Entrada and Puerto Magdalena is fairly deep, some locations being over 140 feet, especially north and east of Punta Belcher. In these areas you can catch cabrilla, grouper, yellowtail and black sea bass. Favorite spots outside the entrance include the area between Punta Magdalena and Morro Howland and off Punta Hughes. Surf fishing can be excellent on the beaches north of Morro Howland. If it's too rough to land, pull up on the protected beach several miles north of Puerto Magdalena on the "inside" and hike over the hills.

Larger boats have access to world-class big-game fishing offshore. The 100-fathom line is nine miles off Punta Entrada, but sailfish and dolphin are caught within five miles, marlin

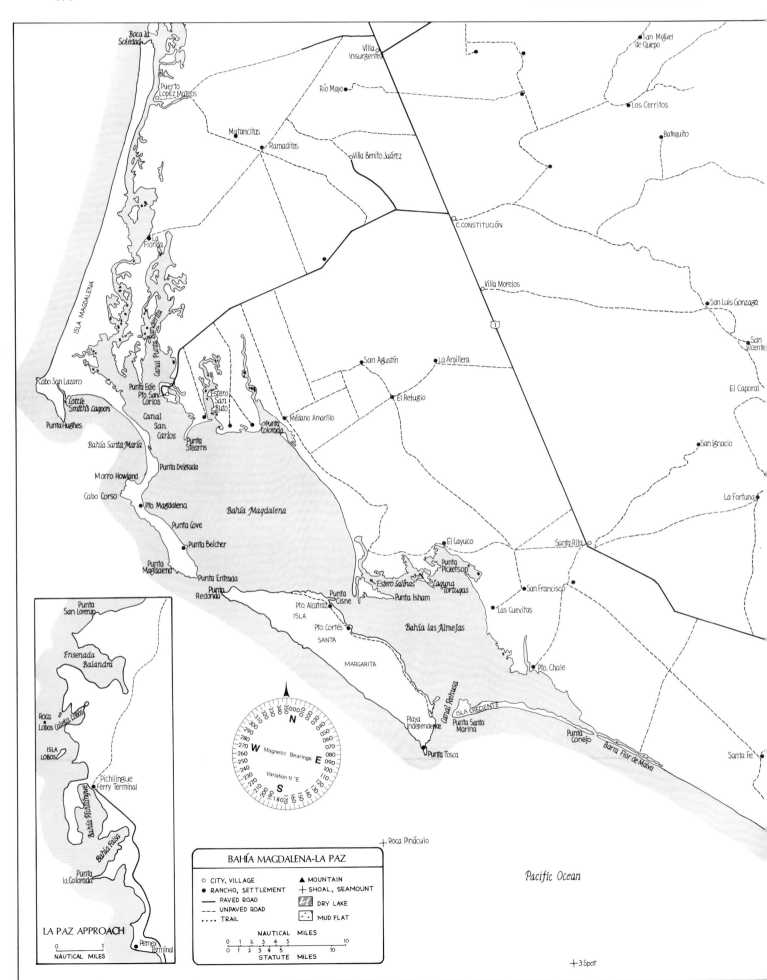

Boca la
Soledad

San Miguel
de Quepo

Villa
Insurgentes

Puerto
López Mateós

Río Mayo

Los Cerritos

Matancitas

Batequito

Ramaditas

Villa Benito Suárez

La
Florida

C. CONSTITUCIÓN

ISLA MAGDALENA

Villa Morelos

San Luis Gonzaga

Canal Punta Banderita

San Agustín

La Arpillera

San
Vicente

Cabo San Lázaro

Punta Edie
Pto. San
Carlos

Estero
San
Buto

El Refugio

El Caporal

Lottie
Smith's Lagoon

Canal
San
Carlos

Médano Amarillo

Punta Hughes

Punta Colorada

Punta Stearns

San Ignacio

Bahía Santa María

Punta Delgada

Morro Howland

San Ignacio

Cabo Corso

Pto. Magdalena

Bahía Magdalena

La Fortuna

Punta Cove

Punta Belcher

El Cayuco

Santa Rita

Punta
Magdalena

Punta Pickerson

Punta Entrada

San Francisco

Punta
Redonda

Punta
Cisne

Estero Salinas

Laguna
Tortugas

Punta Isham

Pto. Alcatraz

ISLA

Las Cuevitas

Pto. Cortés

SANTA

Bahía las Almejas

MARGARITA

Pto. Chale

Canal Rehusa

ISLA CRECIENTE

Playa
Independencia

Punta Santa
Marina

Punta
Conejo

Barra Flor de Malva

Punta Tosca

Santa Fe

Roca Pináculo

Pacific Ocean

LA PAZ APPROACH

Punta
San Lorenzo

Ensenada
Balandra

Roca
Lobos

Caleta Lobos

ISLA
LOBOS

Bahía Pichilingue

Pichilingue
Ferry Terminal

Bahía Falsa

Punta
la Colorada

Pemex
Terminal

N
NW   NE
W   E
SW   SE
S

Magnetic Bearings

Variation 11 °E

BAHÍA MAGDALENA–LA PAZ

○ CITY, VILLAGE
● RANCHO, SETTLEMENT
— PAVED ROAD
--- UNPAVED ROAD
···· TRAIL

▲ MOUNTAIN
+ SHOAL, SEAMOUNT
▦ DRY LAKE
▨ MUD FLAT

NAUTICAL MILES
0 1 2 3 4 5   10

0 1 2 3 4 5   10
STATUTE MILES

+3 Spot

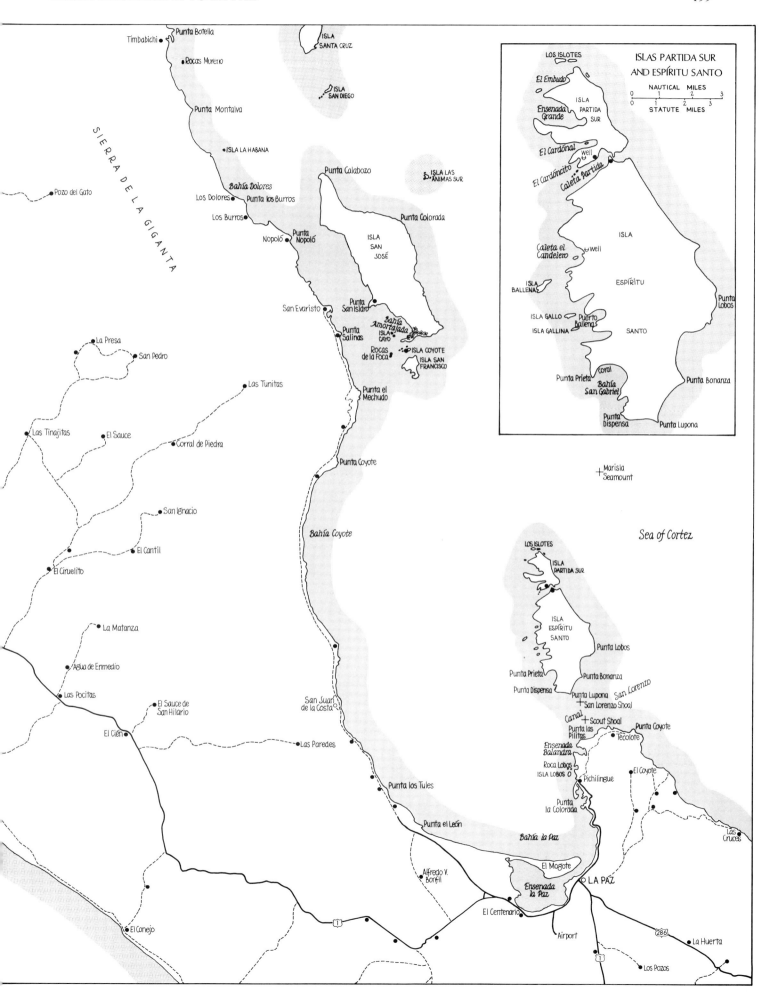

Punta Botella
Timbabichi
Rocas Moreno
ISLA SANTA CRUZ
ISLA SAN DIEGO
Punta Montalva

SIERRA DE LA GIGANTA

ISLA LA HABANA
Punta Calabozo
ISLA LAS ÁNIMAS SUR
Pozo del Gato
Bahía Dolores
Los Dolores
Punta los Burros
Punta Colorada
Los Burros
Punta Nopoló
Nopoló
ISLA SAN JOSÉ
San Evaristo
Punta San Isidro
Bahía Amortajada
La Presa
Punta Salinas
ISLA CAYO
San Pedro
Rocas de la Foca
ISLA COYOTE
ISLA SAN FRANCISCO
Las Tunitas
Punta el Mechudo
Las Tinajitas
El Sauce
Corral de Piedra
San Ignacio
Punta Coyote
El Cantil
Bahía Coyote
El Ciruelito
La Matanza
Agua de Enmedio
Las Pocitas
El Sauce de San Hilario
San Juan de la Costa
El Cién
Las Paredes
Punta los Tules
Punta el León
Alfredo V. Bonfil
El Conejo
El Magote
LA PAZ
Ensenada la Paz
El Centenario
Airport
Los Pozos
La Huerta
Las Cruces
Bahía la Paz
Punta la Colorada
Pichilingue
El Coyote
ISLA LOBOS
Roca Lobos
Ensenada Balandra
Punta las Pilitas
Tecolote
Punta Coyote
Canal
Scout Shoal
San Lorenzo Shoal
San Lorenzo
Punta Lupona
Punta Dispensa
Punta Prieta
Punta Bonanza
Punta Lobos
ISLA ESPÍRITU SANTO
ISLA PARTIDA SUR
LOS ISLOTES
Sea of Cortez
Marisla Seamount

ISLAS PARTIDA SUR AND ESPÍRITU SANTO

NAUTICAL MILES
0   1   2   3
STATUTE MILES
0   1   2   3

LOS ISLOTES
El Embudo
ISLA PARTIDA SUR
Ensenada Grande
El Cardónal
well
El Cardóncito
Caleta Partida
ISLA
Caleta el Candelero
well
ESPÍRITU
ISLA BALLENA
SANTO
ISLA GALLO
Puerto Ballena
ISLA GALLINA
Punta Lobos
Punta Prieta
coral
Bahía San Gabriel
Punta Bonanza
Punta Dispensa
Punta Lupona

preferring it a bit deeper. Banco Thetis, a favorite with long-range boats from San Diego, and known for marlin, yellowfin, wahoo and giant sea bass, is eighteen miles, 290° from Cabo San Lázaro, least reported depth 6 fathoms. Thetis has been fished by trailerboats using the launch ramp at Puerto San Carlos. When water temperatures and wind are favorable, boats often get into boils of wahoo so bold that they will attack baitfish seeking refuge in the shadow of the boat, and thirty fish a day to sixty pounds is possible. Fishermen have been known to complain that they can't get their baits past the marlin to the other species of fish. Another fine location is "6 Spot," sixteen miles, 266° from Punta Hughes. A large rig could make productive daily runs to these locations for as long as fuel permitted, anchoring in the lee of Punta Hughes at night. Live bait is no problem, for mackerel can be caught by the ton near Punta Entrada. For those with adequate range a little-fished 22-fathom spot known as Roca Pináculo, eight miles, 192° from Punta Tosca, offers the same species as Thetis. In addition, "3 Spot," twenty-two miles, 133° from Tosca, offers good fishing. To date no one seems to have mustered the courage, but spearfishermen should note that all but one of these locations are within easy diving depth.

Fishing action at Banco Thetis.

The best months for bay fishing tend to be October, November and December. The offshore locations are best in the summer and fall, although there are reports of good catches as late as early February, depending on water temperatures and currents. Frequent northwest winds and fog may cause problems. It is common to be able to fish only one or two days a week, and wipeouts of two weeks are possible. April, May and June are usually the windiest months, September, October and November the calmest. Alternating shore and sea breezes often push fog back and forth, creating clear and foggy periods sometimes only hours apart. If it's a total wipeout, cheer up; Puerto Escondido is only 109 road miles away and La Paz 166, and the Cortez will probably be calm.

Fishing in a green jungle

A wide variety of fish can be caught in the mangrove areas fringing much of the eastern coastlines of both bays and the inland waterways to the north, including but certainly not limited to cabrilla, corvina, snook, mangrove snapper (red bass), yellowtail and halibut. The variety of fish present is so large that something is usually biting. The best boat is a cartopper or an inflatable, since larger rigs will have trouble with extensive shoals. If you insist on using your big Whaler, make sure you have a length of line and a videocamera—you will be able get some great shots of your crew doing Bogart/Hepburn *African Queen* routines if you stray from the channels. The outside of a bend in a waterway will probably be deep and hold more fish, so anchor on the inside and cast across to the other side, giving you the advantage of playing the fish directly away from the cover. Trolling or casting parallel to the outside perimeter of the mangroves allows you to cover more territory, at the cost of allowing some fish to get into their roots when hooked. If you can't cast to an enticing location, use the current to drift a bait into place. Fish at high water, for at low tide some of the big fish have left for deeper water. An incoming tide is usually better than the outgoing, because the previous low has concentrated fish in deeper spots and the water is clearer. If you are after snook, drift or anchor; they are spooked by even the smallest motors. Watch for large fish working mullet. Rays often can be seen "flapping" on the bottom to dislodge small organisms, and other species rush in to join the feast.

The wreck of the *Independence*

The outer shores of Islas Magdalena and Santa Margarita have been the scene of more major shipwrecks than anywhere else in Baja California. The first was a tragedy, the greatest maritime disaster in Baja history. Early on a February morning in 1853, the 211-foot sidewheel steamer *Independence* rammed a submerged pinnacle north of Punta Tosca with 400 passengers and crew jammed aboard. The situation was deadly, for heavy surf was breaking at the foot of dark perpendicular cliffs and no one would survive if the ship broke up in this location. The captain backed the ship off the pinnacle, turned northwest and slowly ran her along the coast. Steam pressure was falling rapidly, so after 3/4 mile the ship was turned toward a small beach and run aground. Flames roaring out of the furnaces soon touched wood and spread rapidly. Terrified people began to jump overboard and strug-

Salome Hiquera and Reeve Peterson measure the paddlewheel shafts from the *Independence*. Salome is a lighthouse keeper at Punta Tosca.

gle in the sea, clinging to flotsam. A woman attempting to climb overboard snagged her full skirts on a davit and was left swinging until she was consumed by the flames and dropped into the sea. Rather than let their children burn, parents threw them overboard to an almost certain but less painful death by drowning. Swimmers were sucked under when the ship rose and settled in the waves, and others clinging to chicken coops were swept out to sea. On the beach men were seen looting corpses and quarreling over the spoils. About 150 people died and were buried in shallow graves high up on the beach and in the canyon beyond. The survivors were soon rescued by whaling ships at anchor inside the bay.

Over 130 years of surf and storm have not succeeded in erasing all traces of the *Independence*, and a visit to the beach will teach you all you want to know about ghosts. The two ten-inch-diameter iron shafts that carried her paddlewheels lie among the rocks on the beach, and several anchors, a capstan, booms and twisted iron parts can also be seen. Above the beach, numerous shards of pottery and thousands of rusted iron objects lie about, mingled with human bones. Magnetometers have failed to reveal the presence of sizable metal objects outside the surf line, but her huge boilers, massive

walking beam and paddlewheels must be out there somewhere. As with all Baja wrecks, look but don't touch.

"Playa Independence" can be reached in several ways. In Canal Rehusa a sand spit forms a shallow, sandy lagoon three miles north of the lighthouse. An arroyo heading southwest from the south end of this lagoon climbs to a pass and then drops down to the beach, a hike of about three miles one-way. Allow six hours for a round trip, including several hours at the site. In calm weather a boat can be landed on the beach: proceed northwest along the outer coast from Punta Tosca for 2 1/2 miles and look for a sandy beach fronting an arroyo, the first substantial sand beach northwest of the point. A broad stripe of green rock runs diagonally up the hill forming the northwest shoulder of the arroyo.

A nautical comic opera

Seventeen years after the *Independence* disaster, the sidewheel steamer *Golden City*, one of the largest and finest wooden oceangoing ships ever constructed, went aground eleven miles north of Lázaro in a fog. The actions of her captain, crew and passengers provide the great comic opera of Baja shipwrecks. As the lifeboats went over the side, a

The *Golden City* in 1867, three years before her loss on Isla Magdalena.   COURTESY NATIONAL MARITIME MUSEUM

passenger became involved in a shouting match with Captain Comstock and several officers over whether he or the treasure of gold bars should go ashore first. The choice was easy, and they triced him up by tying his hands behind him and connecting the rope to a spar above, leaving him lurching about the heaving deck, standing on tiptoes. Blustering, cursing, waving a saber in one hand and a revolver in the other, the captain began bullying everyone in sight. Once ashore, a number of steerage passengers got into a fight over a cask of liquor that had washed up, which the captain ended by striking one of them in the face with his saber. A cow that swam to the beach was promptly slaughtered and boiled in a huge pot of seawater. At first light the next day it was found that the steamer had broken in half aft of her paddleboxes, discharging a flotsam of 43,000 chests of tea, hundreds of bales of silk, and more liquor. The steerage passengers began drinking and quarreling, and Captain Comstock found it necessary to strike Mr. James Murphy over the head with a pistol and kick him in the face. Drunken passengers continued to stagger around the beach, Mr. Murphy later having a "fit."

Some time later the steamer *Colorado* appeared off the beach. Since the surf was too rough to permit safe embarkation, Captain Comstock asked that the ship anchor in Bahía Santa María. He then assembled the passengers and ordered them to "go down the beach," waving his saber toward the south, swearing and threatening to shoot. With no guidance as to the route to be taken, and without adequate water or food, groups of people started out, a number of old or invalid passengers being carried on litters. One elderly gentleman was carried seated upright in a chair. Everyone finally arrived, safe and reasonably sober. A small lagoon at the north end of the bay was named "Lottie Smith's Lagoon," after the first woman rescued from the ship. The *Colorado* made steam for San Francisco, leaving Captain Comstock, a small crew and a number of volunteer passengers, duly fortified with a large supply of wine, to guard the treasure and baggage. Two days later the unfortunate Mr. Murphy was seen jumping over the rail of the *Colorado*. The ship was stopped, but no sign of him could be found. Captain Comstock and the others were picked up several weeks later by the steamer *Fideliter*, treasure intact and bottles presumably empty.

The most beautiful shipwreck that ever happened

The next wreck was the antithesis of the *Independence* tragedy. At about seven in the morning of April 13, 1909, the lookout on the U.S. cruiser *West Virginia* saw distress signals near Punta Tosca. They proved to be from the 343-foot steel steamer *Indiana*, which had run aground in a fog in calm seas and was resting easily. Because of their shallow draft the naval vessels *Navaho* and *Fortune* were able to come almost alongside, and all passengers and their luggage were taken off without so much as a pair of wet feet. Transferred to the cruiser *California*, they were treated royally as the ship headed for San Francisco. Officers gave up their cabins so the survivors could be comfortable, and the band played on deck each evening. One happy woman wished ". . . Mother had been wrecked with us; she would have enjoyed every hour of it." Another found it ". . . the most beautiful shipwreck that ever happened." Passengers pleaded unsuccessfully with Captain Cottman to slow the *California* down to give them another day, and it was with regret that they finally reached San Francisco, arriving a day earlier than if the *Indiana* had not been wrecked.

Although nothing can be seen of her above water, large sections are still intact and she makes a fine spearfishing site, since the hull is home to many large groupers. She lies on the east side of Punta Tosca 300 yards north of the lighthouse in eighteen to twenty-four feet of water on a sand bottom. There are heavy tidal currents coming from Canal Rehusa, but usually only refracted swell. Visibility averages about ten feet.

A submarine mystery

The U.S. submarine *H-1* was underway in the darkness early on March 12, 1920. Seeing what appeared to be the entrance to Bahía Magdalena, the captain ordered the helmsman to turn northeast. Suddenly a rending shock hit the vessel and she listed violently and began taking water through the conning-tower hatch. Deceived by a long, low stretch of coast opposite Puerto Cortés, with high hills on each side, her captain had run her aground on Santa Margarita. Seawater hitting the batteries caused a dense cloud of chlorine gas and forced the skivvie-clad crew to don life jackets and jump into the huge breakers. The wreck was seen by an accompanying ship and the survivors were picked up the next morning, but four men were dead, including the unfortunate skipper.

The weather remained rough, but crew members from the *U.S.S. Vestal* finally got aboard several days later, and found a profound mystery; someone had looted the boat. Her magnetic compass, gyro repeaters, rifles, pistols, ammunition, bombs and detonators had been stolen. The lock on the safe had been torn off, and her signal books and confidential publications were gone. On March 24 the *H-1* was towed off the beach and it promptly sank. Due to the hazards and expenses involved in refloating her, she was abandoned and stricken from Navy records.

Although pilots have not been able to see the outline of the wreck from the air, there seems to be no further record of her fate, and the Navy Historical Center is of the opinion she was never salvaged. If the sea has not completely destroyed her, she is one of the greatest prizes in Baja diving. Lying on a flat bottom in a precisely known location, she should be relatively easy to locate with a magnetometer. She sank in nine fathoms at 24-24-54 north latitude, 111-50-45 west longitude, 9 3/4 miles northwest of Punta Tosca. On March 24, after the *H-1* sank, the following was recorded in the *Vestal's* log: "Rt. peak

CHARLES VELTON

The U.S.S. *H-1* on the beach at Isla Margarita, 1920.

100° true. Gorge Rock 315° true." The *U.S.S. Brant's* log for March 23 shows her position as "Outer Twin Sisters bearing 119° true, Point Toscok [Tosca] 130° 30 minutes true. . ." Most of these names and locations appear on marine chart 21121, "Rt. peak" apparently being the 1,631-foot peak and "Gorge Rock" one of the rocks at the foot of the white bluff. To convert true bearings to magnetic, subtract eleven degrees to account for local variation.

Four tiny guardians

The next wreck was the 5,643-ton vessel *Colombia*, which went aground at Punta Tosca in a heavy gale on September 13, 1931, carrying 234 passengers and crew, and $850,000 in gold and silver bars. The steamer *San Mateo*, the first vessel to arrive at the scene, found her a total wreck. Lifeboats were scattered over an angry sea, but everyone was rescued without injury. The *Colombia* had survived a series of mishaps since she had been launched in 1915, including a mutiny and being torpedoed once, grounded once and driven ashore twice. This time, however, her luck ran out and she was declared a total wreck and abandoned to her underwriters, with the gold still aboard. Some believed that Mexican law held that a ship was abandoned only when "every living thing" had been removed, and that such a vessel belonged to the first person who got there and established himself in command. Captain Oaks, possibly foreseeing this, had left an alley cat and a mongrel dog on board, and it was found later that passengers had also left two monkeys. There was some doubt whether this quartet met the letter of Mexican law, and even greater doubt as to whether the "lawless ranchers and coast pirates" of the region would honor their presence, so a salvage tug was sent racing to protect the treasure. Boats were reported swarming around the wreck by the night of the 14th, and it seemed only a matter of time until the treasure would be discovered. The tug arrived late in the afternoon of the 15th, and it was found that people had been aboard. However, they were unaware of the treasure, which was now reported in the newspapers to be worth only $185,000. Salvage divers cleared a path to the vaults with dynamite.

Today she lies on a sand bottom in about fifty feet of water, twenty yards east of the last wash rock south of Punta Tosca. Surge and currents can be a problem, but exploring her is great fun, and large jewfish, cabrilla and lobsters abound. The wreck is badly broken up, huge metal plates and ribs lying about. The gold? As was usual in such circumstances, the owners and insurance companies wanted it believed that everything was recovered, and a photo of Miss La Vina Harper sitting on a large stack of gold and silver bars was prominently displayed in the newspapers. However, many believe that a substantial amount was not recovered, and several diving expeditions have been organized over the years. Harry Rieseberg salvaged $2,000 in gold, but a later group, working for almost two months, recovered nothing of value. Who knows, even if there is no gold left perhaps Mrs. Arthur Vaughn's $35,000 necklace still lies on the bottom.

A few more wrecks

The fishing vessels *West Point* and *Liberty Bell* will be found in Bahía Santa María, one mile, 054°, and 1.6 miles, 047°, respectively, from Punta Hughes. The 424-foot Canadian dry cargo ship *Westbank Park* was driven ashore by a storm outside Punta Entrada on October 6, 1945. She was a prominent landmark for a number of years, but she has slowly succumbed, until today only a rusty bow section is visible above water. She can be found by locating a striking lopsided, cone-shaped hill a mile west of Punta Entrada, saved from becoming an island only by a tiny sandspit. The wreck is 200 yards east of this hill. The fishing vessel *Shasta* was lost in 1965 in Canal Rehusa off the west end of Isla Creciente. Loaded with huge lobsters, she was once a popular dive site, but several years ago her mast fell over and she is now difficult to find. If you do locate her watch out for sharks; Dave Buller had to scramble up the mast to escape a mob of them.

Other activities

Fishing, diving and visiting wrecks are not the only activities the area provides. The vast expanse of the bay and its breezes make it an excellent location for boardsailing. The downwind ride from Lopéz Mateos to Puerto Chale is one of the longest protected runs—seventy miles—in Baja. Vast quantities of clams lie scattered all over the bottom of the bay. Gray whales can be seen in winter months, and whale-watchers in a boat anchored inside Punta Entrada are apt to see a magnificent ballet of breaching and spy-hopping. Whales frequently use Boca la Soledad, and up to a hundred of them can be seen cavorting in the narrow channel. *Panga* fishermen at Lopéz Mateos are often willing to take out whale-watchers. Those without a boat can see them from the beaches near town.

An enormous variety of birds inhabits the area, either permanently or seasonally. A complete check list might go to a hundred species, second only to the Bahía San Quintín area in numbers. The two bays, as might be expected, share many species. The more interesting and uncommon (in Baja) species include: common loon, western grebe, wedge-tailed shearwater, American white pelican, great, reddish and snowy egrets, little blue heron, yellow-crowned night-heron, white ibis, green-winged teal, northern pintail, gadwal, American wigeon, canvasback, redhead, bufflehead, red-breasted merganser, bald eagle, sharp-shinned hawk, crested caracara, sora, greater yellowlegs, red knot, dunlin, south polar skua, ring-billed, yellow-legged and glaucous-winged gulls, least tern and common barn owl. Large numbers of brant and other geese and ducks winter on the bay.

Surfers rarely visit the area because of the difficulty in

WILL WATERMAN

Bruce Barrus provides the music while Elizabeth Wolfe and Scott Wright do the paddling on a trip to Bahía Magdalena.

getting to the outer beaches, but Punta Hughes has a long point break on south or west waves. During conditions of south and southwest swells and heavy tides, standing waves build up in Canal Rehusa. The tidal speed closely matches the speed of advancement of the waves, and the resulting "standing waves" provide the most bizarre ride in Baja surfing, the longest, possibly an hour, and the shortest, ending perhaps several hundred yards from the starting point; the water rushes by but the speed of the waves over the ground is almost zero. A bit mushy and difficult to set up perhaps, but a once-in-a-lifetime experience.

A kayak trip to explore the bay and see the birds and whales would be high adventure. Mineral collectors will find magnesite, amphibole asbestos and tremolite on Santa Margarita. The many miles of flat sand beach north of Lázaro contain a jackpot of flotsam, but a motorcycle or an ATV is required to inspect it completely.

Camping in mangrove areas leaves something to be desired, as they can be boggy, buggy and damp, so try the east side of Isla Magdalena, where sandy areas are to be found, or better yet, camp at the *bocas* leading to the ocean north of Lopéz Mateos. Here you have the best of two worlds: clean sand, lots of firewood, ocean surf fishing, with the mangroves close by. Santa Margarita also has many fine sandy beaches. If camping on the "inside," bring a stove, since mangrove wood makes a lot of smelly smoke. A tent will be appreciated unless you like to wake up wet from the dew and covered with wind-blown sand. If you park in the mangrove areas be careful of the tides; we once returned to Puerto Chale from a wreck dive to find our vans on an island, surrounded by

saltwater and gooey mud. Kayakers and small-boaters should use care in the vicinity of Boca la Soledad and the other openings between the barrier islands—strong tidal currents can sweep the unwary out to sea to a certain capsize and an uncertain future in the breakers.

Launching and anchoring

The easiest access to the bay is at Puerto San Carlos, reached by a paved road (signed) going west from Ciudad Constitución. Just north of the bridge at KM 54+ there is a small beach with a marine railway, a concrete dock and a water spigot. It is a good launch area for small trailerboats, but it is used by *panga* fishermen and access may be a problem. At KM 56 there is a public beach with *palapas* and pit toilets. San Carlos, at KM 58, is a deepwater port, with a COTP, customs and immigration. Magnasin, Nova and diesel can be obtained at the PEMEX, and large boats can obtain diesel and water at the pier; see the COTP. The town has a modest motel, Pesca office, ice, water from spigots in the square, beer, groceries, meat market, restaurant, auto parts, hardware, medical clinic, dental, pharmacy, post office, telegraph and long-distance telephone. Regular bus service is available to Ciudad Constitución. A decompression chamber has been delivered to the health clinic, but in late 1990 it was still not operational. There are no RV facilities, but many flat spaces to park in can be found. The Flying Sportsman's Lodge once operated a fishing camp south of town. Although it is now out of operation, you can park for a small fee, and water is available. It is found by driving 0.2 mile, 060° from the PEMEX, then 120° for another 1 1/2 miles, passing the COTP office on the right. Boats as long as twenty-eight feet have been launched from the concrete ramp here, but tides of at least five feet are required, and sandy spots on the road leading to the ramp may be a problem. There are many areas where beach launches can be made. *Pangas* and guides can be hired for fishing, diving, whale watching and transportation to the outlying islands.

The bay and waterways can also be reached by unpaved roads leading to Lopéz Mateos, Puerto Chale and several other points. Small boats can be launched over the beach north of the cannery at Lopéz Mateos and at the settlement at Puerto Chale.

The best anchorages for boats coasting north or south or fishing the offshore banks are at Bahía Santa María, inside Punta Entrada, at Puerto Cortés, around Punta Belcher and off Puerto Magdalena. The anchorage at Punta Tosca is convenient, although surgy and sometimes rough. Good anchorages also can be found almost anywhere between San Carlos and Lopéz Mateos, and boats can use Boca la Soledad to gain access to the ocean in good weather. Canal Rehusa is too shallow for all but the smallest boats, and there are heavy currents and sand bars. The next anchorage south of Punta Tosca is at Cabo San Lucas. It may be possible to obtain limited fuel, water and emergency assistance at the small naval base at Puerto Cortés, at Puerto Alcatraz, and at Puerto Magdalena.

****

A BOATING/BIKING/BEACHCOMBING ADVENTURE. One bright winter day Reeve, Mike and I decided to see what we could find in the way of treasures and wrecked ships on the outer beaches of Isla Magdalena. As we loaded our two motorcycles into our cartop boat, the word spread through Lopéz Mateos, and within minutes we were surrounded by a mob of incredulous schoolboys, each insisting on helping. Hoping that we could land on the crescent of flat beach at Boca la Soledad, we headed north through the calm waterway separating Magdalena and the mainland. Floating very low in the water, we passed a pod of gray whales, which seemed to swim closer to see the unusual sight. Several Mexican fishermen were taken aback at the motorcycle-equipped whale-watchers, and we could see them shaking their heads in wonderment.

Landing with no problems, we pulled the boat high up on

We found this beautiful yacht stranded on Isla Magdalena. It was later salvaged unharmed.

the beach, mounted our bikes, rounded the point and headed south along the magnificent Pacific beach. Within a few miles we found the fantail of a large wooden vessel and then the ribs and timbers of another. Within twenty minutes a beautiful forty-foot sloop appeared ahead, intact, unmarked and ready for sea except for its sails and electronics (don't rush to the scene; it was later salvaged). The next wreck was a Catalina 27 sailboat, inspiring some deep thought by Reeve, who owned an identical boat and had been considering a trip to Baja. An intense feeling of exhilaration prevailed as we sped down the deserted beaches at fifty miles an hour. The breakers put up a low mist which limited our view of the beach ahead to a mile or two, heightening the mystery of the place. Large flocks of sea birds scrambled for a takeoff, accurately bombing us with tokens of their displeasure at being disturbed. Secure in their isolation, dozing seals scarcely knew we were there until we had already passed. Soon, we found a small sloop, and then a capstan and a keelson from a large vessel, and then another unattached fantail and several winches. Five miles north of Lázaro a 450-foot ship lay parallel to the water's edge. She was heavily damaged, but firebricks from her boilers were still lined up in neat rows, some missing sections forming nesting sites for ospreys. Close to Lázaro was the vessel Jupiter, *of similar size and construction. After riding about thirty-eight miles, we arrived at the lighthouse and inspected its extensive collection of flotsam and nautical trash.*

With great anticipation, we set our odometers and headed north for the highlight of the adventure, an attempt to locate the Golden City. *The accounts of the survivors in the newspapers of the day placed the wreck eleven miles north of Lázaro, so we simply headed north along the beach, and when our odometers said eleven, we stopped our bikes and started searching. With almost magical luck, we found her in minutes, just beyond the first line of dunes. Massive timbers sixteen inches square and up to forty feet long lay everywhere, along with thousands of bronze and iron fastenings. Mysterious buried objects lay just below the surface, each having length, width and height, but a consistency of little more than iron-stained sand. Planking that once sheathed the hull was studded with hundreds of small bronze nails that held her copper sheathing. Huge amounts of broken ceramics and glass bottles lay over an area of several acres, perhaps marking the location of the ship's dining and cooking areas. There was no sign of her massive boilers, of her giant steam cylinder, with its eight-foot, nine-inch bore and twelve-foot stroke, nor of her forty-foot paddle wheels. We took nothing except for a small sample of wood, which I later sent to the University of Arizona Dendrochronology (Tree-Ring Analysis) Laboratory. The lab identified the wood as red pine, of East Coast origin, about 1862. Right on, U of A; she was built in New York in 1863!*

By dusk we were back in camp, trying to tell a crowd of Mexican boys about what we had found. To our surprise, some of them knew a little of the history of the "Ciudad de Oro." *Over a campfire they told us tales of other shipwrecks and pirate treasures that lay on the outer beaches, and named several vessels that I had never heard of before, providing reason enough for our next boating/biking/beachcombing adventure.*

****

Back on the Transpeninsular Highway at Ciudad Constitución

Except in its final miles, the highway between Ciudad Constitución and La Paz is the second most boring drive in Baja. Since it is 132 miles long, bicyclists will spend a night on the road, but unfortunately the only campsites to be found are little more than sideroads away from traffic noises.

KM	LOCATION
157	**Santa Rita**. Store, cafe, tires, limited auto parts. Road southwest (signed) to Puerto Chale, fifteen miles.
154	Hematite and malachite are found nearby.
139+	Two-tenths of a mile southeast of the KM marker a dirt road leads south 1/4 mile to several flat desert campsites. They are out of view from the road, but truck noise may be a problem. You take what you get in this area.
130	One hundred yards southeast of the KM marker another dirt road leads south to flat campsites.
127+	Food and drink.
127	Start gentle ups and downs until KM 34, becoming a little steeper as you continue.
114	Small cafe.
112	**Las Pocitas**. Tire repair, medical, mechanic.
110+	Cafe.
100	**El Cién**. Cafe, store, tires, PEMEX (MND).
80	Sedan road southwest (signed) to El Conejo, ten miles. Long a favorite with surfers, Conejo has easy access and excellent lefts and rights on a small rocky point, working well in almost any swell, although best when they are from the northwest. The place is windswept, with frequent cross-onshore winds, making it popular with heavy-weather boardsailors, especially during frontal conditions. In summer it can be a blow-out all day. Be careful of a strong current paralleling the shore and of frequent sneaker waves. Driftwood sometimes can be found for campfires, and there is good surf fishing. Lobsters and oysters may be purchased from the locals. Diving potential is almost zero.
76	Cafe.
55+	Dirt road southwest to campsites. This road, which leads to the Punta Bentonita area, is graded but washboarded. Go right (200°) at the sideroad at Mile 0.8. Don't expect too much here; it's just a few flat places with no scenery to speak of, but at least it's out of sight, road noise should not be a problem and you won't be impeding traffic on the main dirt road. The sideroad continues on a short distance and loops back to the main dirt road, but large rigs may have trouble turning around.
34	Magnificent views of La Paz and Isla Espíritu Santo. General moderate downgrades and then level road into La Paz.
21+	Agricultural inspection station.
17	Paved road northwest, signed "San Juan de la Costa."

SIDETRIP TO SAN EVARISTO

As noted earlier, the highway from Ciudad Constitución is the second dullest section on the Transpeninsular. However, the dullest, between Guerrero Negro and San Ignacio, had a gem waiting near the end (San Ignacio), and this section is no different. The trip to Evaristo is best made early in the morning in clear weather. Turn at the sign, set odometer and drive northwest. The washboard gets bad past the end of the pavement at Mile 14.1, but since the road is graded, sedans and motorhomes can continue. The road follows the shoreline, and there are a number of places to camp. Most beaches are pebble and cobble, but sand will be found at Miles 20.0 and 22.8. At Mile 23.8 take the right (010°) fork (the left fork leads to San Juan de la Costa, a phosphate mining town with a public restaurant and water from spigots).

Mother Nature soon begins the most colorful display of sedimentary showmanship in all of Baja. Some layers of sandstone are graced with easily described colors, such as black, purple, gray and pink, and there are three shades each of green and beige. Others require physical analogy: persimmon, cinnamon, coffee, guacamole, salmon and grape Popsicle. Up close, each color is muted, just touches of pastel in otherwise ordinary rock, but the "big picture," from a distance, is stunning. Erosion has carved strange shapes; there is a turtle with a green shell spotted with brown, and a salmon castle with green battlements.

At Mile 29.0 the road squeezes between the blue Cortez and a cliff of brick-red, green and tan rock, the most colorful half-mile drive in Baja. Past the cliff, add olive drab, burnt umber and salmon-tan to the list of colors. Only pickups and four-wheel-drives should continue beyond Mile 31.2. There is another beautiful display just ahead; the road winds up a huge wedge of rock, and near its top is a castle seemingly molded out of sand, perched on a green cliff plunging into the blue sea. When just past the sand castle, stop and peek over the edge for another visual treat. The road soon winds inland to avoid Punta el Mechudo, with loose rock, switchbacks and grades to 27%. At Mile 33.5 the road gets its turn; ordinary gray to this point, it becomes green, not just faintly green but *green*.The road returns to the coastal plain and to ordinary desert colors at Mile 37.4, and arrives at Evaristo at Mile 45.6, described in the previous chapter.

Back on the Transpeninsular Highway at KM 17

15+	RV park, full hookups, beach.
14+	Oasis Los Apripez Trailer Park. Full hookups, showers, toilets, laundry, restaurant, pool, beach.
11+	PEMEX (MND).
9	Road south (signed) to La Paz International Airport.
6	Junction. Turn south for the Cape region, bypassing downtown La Paz.
5+	The office of the State Secretary of Tourism is located on the south side of the road. The office of the Attorney General for the Protection of Tourists is located in the same building. They share a sub-office downtown in the waterfront area (1).
4+	Casa Blanca Trailer Park. Full hookups, laundry, pool, tennis, showers, restrooms, market, snack bar.
0	**La Paz**.

LA PAZ

In 1533 Hernán Cortés, conqueror of Mexico, sent two ships to explore the west coast of Mexico, looking for a shorter way from New Spain to sources of the spices so highly prized in Europe and, of course, for gold and pearls. The crew of one ship mutinied and sailed into a large bay, where Indians killed most of them when they became too cozy with the local ladies. However, the few survivors told of pearls, and in 1535 Cortés himself founded a colony, which failed in less than two years. In 1596 Sebastián Vizcaíno attempted another colony, which he named La Paz (The Peace), since the Indians were now found to be friendly. However, the stockade and most buildings burned down, and the place was abandoned.

Between 1616 and 1635 explorers carried pearls back to Spain, and La Paz soon became a center for diving activity, Indians performing the dangerous task, of course. In 1683 another colonization expedition tried again, this one led by Jesuit Father Eusebio Kino and accompanied by Admiral Otondo y Antillión and a group of marines. The Indians had changed their minds again, shooting arrows and carrying on, so the admiral invited a group of them to a feast, which ended when he fired a cannonball into their midst.

By 1720 the cannonball had been forgotten, and a Jesuit mission was established by Fathers Jaime Bravo and Juan de Ugarte. However, there were further uprisings, which ended only after epidemics had killed most of the Indians. With few souls left to save, the mission was abandoned in 1749, and it was not until 1811 that a permanent settlement was established. By 1830 the growing village had become the territorial capital. It was captured and held briefly by American forces in 1847 during the war with Mexico, and adventurer William Walker tried to take over the city in 1853 but failed.

Pearls became harder to find, and in 1874 compressed-air diving equipment was introduced. By the early 1900s pearls had become so rare that an oyster-cultivation farm was built, whose rock basins and buildings can still be seen on Isla Espíritu Santo. The scheme didn't work, and the industry went into a steep decline, ending in 1940, when a blight killed off most surviving oysters.

Today the old La Paz of adobe, palm and bougainvillaea is giving way to hustle and bustle and modern construction. The capital and largest city in Baja Sur, La Paz is a center for fishing, agriculture, ranching and transportation, and an important city to foreign visitors. By many measures, the small city is the most pleasant and enjoyable in Baja, and you should allow time for a visit. The weather is fine between November and May, with warm days and balmy nights.

There are many places to stay, in every price range. The Hotel Los Arcos (2), on the Malecón, has rooms, shower baths, pool, coffee shop, dining room, bar, auto rentals and travel agency. Hotel Palmira, at KM 2.5 on the road to Pichilingue, has rooms, showers, pool, tennis, dining room, bar, travel agency, disco and convention facilities. La Concha Beach Resort, at KM 5 on the same road, has rooms, restaurant, bar, pool, snorkeling, SCUBA diving, beach, sailing,

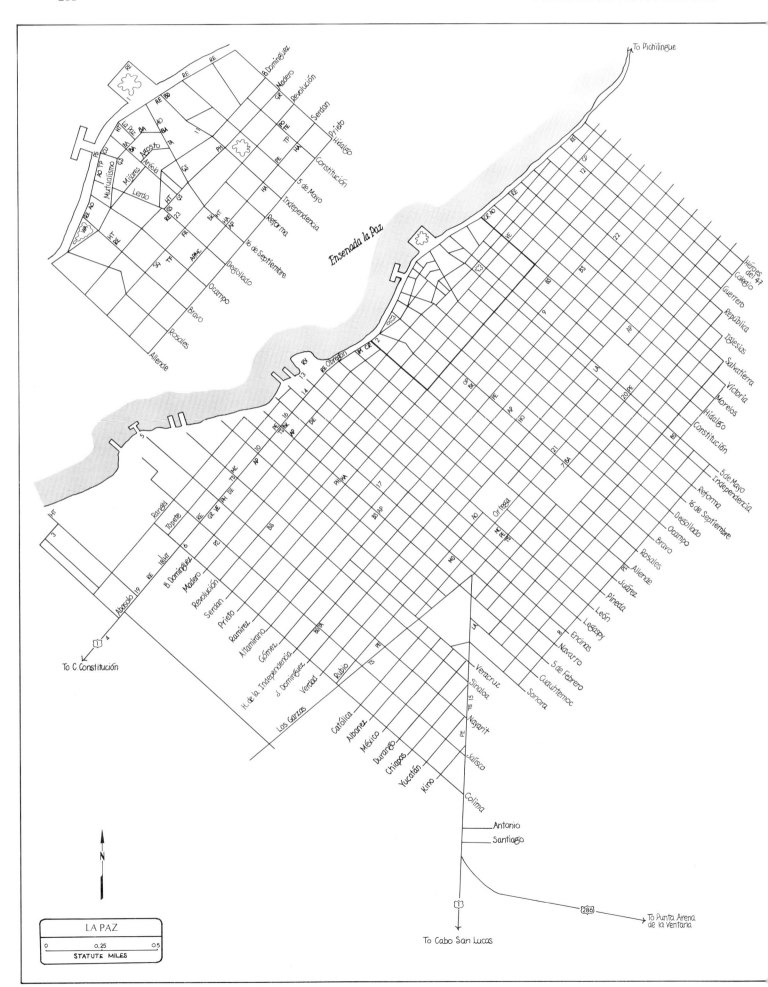

boardsailing, parasailing and excursions. La Paz Trailer Park (3) offers full hookups, showers and toilets, pool, laundry, store and storage. El Cardón Trailer Park (4) has full hookups, showers and toilets, disposal station, laundry and pool. Aquamarina RV Park (5), operated by La Paz Diving Service, has full hookups, restrooms, showers, satellite TV, laundry machines and pool.

Most products and services are available, and many duty-free shops sell imported products. Important to those yearning for the familiar, there are two CCCs (6 and 7), the largest supermarkets in Baja Sur, carrying many U.S. brands. The modern international airport has flights to the U.S. and mainland Mexico, as well as to Cape region locations.

You say you are suffering from the heartbreak of psoriasis and your sciatica is throbbing again? Centro Botanico (8) has an enormous variety of potions, poultices and "natural remedies," any one of which is guaranteed to quickly return anyone to glowing health, no matter what the complaint (nothing in writing, of course). There are so many dark and desiccated apparitions on the shelves that suspicions may soon arise that this in fact is not a medicinal herb shop, but the trophy room of a head-hunting tribe. The accompanying map shows many restaurants, stores and other places that may be of interest. Further information can be obtained from the office of the State Secretary of Tourism.

All manner of traditional tourist activities are available, ranging from tennis to picnics on the beach to trips on glass-bottomed boats to pub-crawling. There are a number of good beaches in town, and Avenue Obregon continues northeast from the downtown area to curve north along the bay past other beaches. All have easy access and good boardsailing, ranging from onshore to side-shore conditions, depending on where you are. November through February often has the heaviest winds. The Museo de Anthropologia (9) has photographs and exhibits on Indian life and rock art, the history of Baja California Sur, and fossil shells. Several shops along Obregon sell a wide variety of shells, some local. Various hornshells, olives, murexes and augers are found in La Paz harbor and north to Tecolote.

The waters north and east of La Paz have long been among the most prominent fishing locations on the continent, and a number of world records for sailfish, roosterfish and amberjack were set there in the 1950s and 60s. The fishery has declined, although there are recent records for yellowtail and black skipjack. The best fishing is now in deep water off the east sides of Islas Espíritu Santo and Partida Sur, primarily for wahoo, yellowfin tuna and dolphins between June and November, and sailfish from August to October. Yellowtail migrate from the upper Cortez and are found in large numbers in winter and early spring off rocky points, reefs and headlands throughout the region.

The Dorado Velez Fleet operates fishing cruisers from twenty-five to thirty-two feet, and fishes Espíritu Santo, Isla Cerralvo and the La Paz area. Information and reservations can be obtained at the fishing desk at the Los Arcos Hotel. Bob Butler Baja Fishing offers package trips to La Paz, fishing the prolific Ensenada los Muertos/Cerralvo area out of pangas launched at Muertos. Reservations can be made at the fishing desk at the Los Arcos or as listed in Appendix A. Information on other fleets and boats is available from any hotel or travel office in La Paz.

Most divers head for Espíritu Santo, Partida Sur, Los Islotes, the wreck of the Salvatierra or Marisla Seamount, which are described in later sections. The best months are generally April through June for spearfishermen, June through October for photographers and nature-watchers. Few people dive the harbor, but the vessel San Lorenzo, which exploded and sank in 1973, will be found off the foot of Av. Jalisco. The boat Don José, operated by Baja Expeditions (10), offers a wide variety of diving and natural-history trips. Marisla, operated by La Paz Diving Service, offers dive expeditions throughout the southern Cortez; she docks at the Aquamarina RV Park. Baja Diving & Service (11) has SCUBA air and full equipment sales and rentals (except cameras). It is also a SCUBAPRO dealer and makes repairs on equipment, including regulators, but excluding spearguns. An International PADI facility, it offers a variety of instruction. Trips are offered to nearby Espíritu Santo and Los Islotes, and the wreck of the Salvatierra and local snorkeling areas, as well as longer trips to Islas San José, San Francisco, Las Ánimas Sur, Cerralvo, San Diego and Santa Cruz. Their boats range from twenty-two-foot pangas to a forty-five-foot platform boat. Baja Sur Internacional (12) has SCUBA air, rentals, service, local trips and guides.

With its fine harbor and many services and attractions ashore, La Paz is a sailor's city, and often over a hundred foreign yachts are swinging at anchor in the bay at the height of the season. The "La Paz Waltz" requires good anchoring equipment and technique because tidal currents of up to six knots swing the anchored boats first one way and then the other. A local summer breeze called the coromuel was supposedly named after the pirate Cromwell when locals observed that he sailed out with the strong breeze that sprung up from the south in the afternoon and arrived back with the northwesterlies the next day. The coromuel is often felt as far north as Evaristo and as far south as Muertos, providing welcome relief from the heat, but plaguing boaters and yachtsmen in exposed anchorages. La Paz is a port of entry, with a COTP, customs and immigration. Cortez Yacht Charters offers cruising and sportfishing out of La Paz, ranging from a single day to as long as desired, in both power and sail—see Appendix A. Inquire at the marinas and the office of the State Secretary of Tourism about other yacht charters.

Marina de La Paz (13) offers the full range of facilities and services you would expect at a marina in the United States, including slips having potable water and electrical service, diesel fueling facilities, maintenance services, mechanical repairs, restrooms, showers, telephone, fax, public VHF radio and, admirably, a used oil disposal facility. Their marine store carries a variety of maintenance materials, parts and accessories with familiar brand names, and an inventory of boat-trailer parts and equipment. Marina Palmira, located at KM 2.5 on the road to Pichilingue, is similarly equipped, with slips having water and electrical service, fueling, telephone, laundry, showers, ice, maintenance, boat storage and a marine store. Both are licensed marinas, providing custody and clearance services. Aquamarina RV Park also has a marina, with docks, moorings and the facilities of the park. There are concrete ramps and parking at all three marinas. The ramp at Pichilingue leads to protected water and has good parking nearby, but the concrete surface is getting a bit rough. There are numerous beaches north of town over which small boats can be launched.

Agencia Ajorna (14) has Johnson sales, marine charts, and parts and service, and there is a Mariner dealer (15). Agencia Abaroa (16) is a well-equipped marine dealer, selling a wide variety of parts and equipment and nautical charts. Dodge (17), Ford (18), Volkswagen (19), Nissan (20) and Chevrolet (21) dealers are in business. The Chevrolet dealer also handles Johnson parts. Moto Servicio Piteco (22) has limited motorcycle parts, service and tires, and there are numerous bicycle shops. Deportes Ortiz (23) is a close approximation to a U.S.-style sporting goods store.

Ferries to Topolobampo and Mazatlan and the Baja Express hydrofoil to Topolobampo operate from the terminal at KM 17. The launch ramp mentioned earlier will be found on the north shore of the cove immediately north of the ferry buildings. The pavement ends here, but a good gravel road, capable of handling any normal vehicle, continues north to popular beaches at Ensenada Balandra and Tecolote, the last-named about seven miles from the ferry area. The beaches at Tecolote are fine sand, and spots for RV parking and camping can be found, but fearsome *jejenes* are sometimes present. Small boats can be launched over the beach, but the place is exposed and waves can make it difficult. Boardsailers will find exposed onshore conditions.

Finally, don't get confused like your author did—there are two "Av. Independencias," meeting at right angles. Yes, it is possible to stand on the corner of Independencia and Independencia! One runs northwest-southeast, the second northeast-southwest. The name of the second is actually "Héroes de la Independencia," but the letters of the first three words on the street signs are small. There are also two "Av. Héroes," Av. Héroes de la Independencia, just mentioned, and Av. Héroes del 47. To top things off, there are three "date" streets, 16 de Septiembre, 5 de Febrero and 5 de Mayo. Careful, now.

SIDETRIP TO ISLAS ESPÍRITU SANTO AND PARTIDA SUR AND MARISLA SEAMOUNT

Three good anchorages, Bahía Pichilingue, Caleta Lobos and Ensenada Balandra, will be found five, eight and ten miles north of the east tip of El Mogote. All are easily accessible by road, and hence fishing is generally poor. Pichilingue is an all-weather harbor and the location of the ferry terminal. The preferred anchorage is off the pier and buildings on the south end of the bay, a U.S. coaling station during the First World War. A large anchor and the wreck of a wood vessel sheathed with copper lie in two fathoms off the pier. Isla Lobos, recognizable by its white coating of guano, and Roca Lobos, a rocky islet to the north, have fair diving. Caleta Lobos, east of Roca Lobos, is open to the southwest, but provides good protection from other directions. Sandy Balandra is scenic, and its beaches are often compared to powdered sugar. Novice boardsailers love the place, but yachties should beware—the bay tends to be shallow, especially in its eastern reaches. The "mushroom" rock seen on postcards is located on the north shore. Although a popular anchorage, it is exposed. Pichilingue beaches leave a lot to be desired as campsites, but kayakers will find clean sand beaches and good camping at both Lobos and Balandra. The first good anchorage along the coast to the south is Muertos, described in the next chapter.

Salvatierra, an ex-U.S. Navy Second World War LST, sank in Canal San Lorenzo in 1976, and is now one of the premiere dive sites in the La Paz area. Colorful photographic subjects abound, including yellowtail surgeonfish, grunts, goatfish, angelfish, morays, rays and several species of large parrot fish. Her propellers and rudders are easily accessible, and large schools of fish hide under her stern, often so dense you literally have to brush them aside to swim through. The ship was carrying a cargo of trucks and trailers and many still can be seen scattered over the sandy bottom.

The wreck is relatively easy to find. There are two aid-to-navigation structures in Canal San Lorenzo: the southernmost, Scout Shoal Light, is a concrete tower, the northernmost, San Lorenzo Shoal Light, a metal pipe structure. The wreck is located about one mile east of the latter structure. When you are over the wreck Scout Shoal Light should bear 206°, San Lorenzo Shoal Light 267°. You can get directly on top of the wreck without the aid of a compass. When in the vicinity of the wreck note the red mound sticking up behind Punta Dispensa on Espíritu Santo, and the two black spots on the ridge line of the point (these spots are not visible past noon). When light barely shows between the right side of the red mound and the left black spot you are on a line of position passing over the wreck. Stay on this line and maneuver until Scout Shoal Light is barely inside the right tangent of the land mass to the south (in the vicinity of Balandra). When this happens you will be over the wreck. If visibility is good, the wreck can be seen from 200 yards away as a large dark patch. Local fishing boats frequent the vicinity. She lies in fifty-seven feet, her highest part rising to within twenty-three feet of the surface. Tidal currents in excess of three knots are possible in the channel, requiring divers and kayakers to plan their activities using the tide tables.

Isla Espíritu Santo

Dramatically and unexpectedly beautiful, with deeply indented coves along its west coast and high bluffs formed from folded strata of pink, red, white, yellow and black, Espíritu Santo is a favorite with divers, sailors and kayakers. There are sand beaches offering fine camping in most of the coves. Kayakers should be able to scrounge drinking water from the numerous yachts normally at anchor, enabling lengthy stays. Water for washing and bathing can be obtained from a well found about about 150 yards up the canyon from the building on the beach at the north end of Caleta el Candelero. The surface of the water in the well is normally about sixteen feet below ground level, so you will need a bucket and a line. The slightly saline water is clean, and might serve as drinking water in an emergency.

Bahía San Gabriel is only a fair anchorage, being a bit too shallow and open to *coromuel* winds. A coral reef covers about a half-acre near its north shore, readily seen due to its dark color. A hike ashore is worthwhile. Stone basins and building foundations of the old oyster farm can be explored along the southeast shore, and millions of fiddler crabs skitter through the mangroves. Birding is excellent, with a full complement of shore birds, including great blue and green herons, snowy egret, osprey and American oystercatcher; raptors such as turkey vulture, red-tailed hawk, kestrel and great horned owl; and such migrant and wintering species as gray flycatcher, Bewick wren, black-headed grosbeak, green-tailed towhee, Savannah sparrow, Brewer's sparrow and lesser goldfinch, plus the usual seabirds. Espíritu Santo is home to one species of ground squirrel, two of mice, one rat, ring-tailed cat and the famous black-tailed jackrabbit. Twenty species of reptiles and amphibians inhabit Espíritu Santo and Partida Sur. Fine shelling can be found near Punta Lupona and Punta Bonanza.

Diving around Islas Gallo and Gallina is poor, but the north side of Isla Ballena has good SCUBA diving and serves as a fair anchorage during *coromuel* winds. Caleta el Candelero is a fair anchorage, also open to the *coromuel*.

Caleta Partida, separating Espíritu Santo and Partida Sur, is the best anchorage in the area, its roughly circular shape giving fair protection from the *coromuel*, and the low spits jutting from each island allowing fresh breezes on hot nights. If you anchor near the northwest shore, the bluffs bring welcome shade in the afternoon. Dinghys and kayaks can transit the shallow channel between the islands. There are several fishing settlements in the vicinity.

Isla Partida Sur

Although very narrow and tending to be hot, El Cardóncito is a fair anchorage, and the surrounding rocks are interesting. The reef extending to the southwest from its mouth is one of the best snorkeling sites in the area. Large groupers inhabit its outer reaches, but they seem thoroughly checked out as to the intent of spearfishermen. A masonry well will be found about 150 yards up the canyon from the small sand beach, its depth and water quality being about the same as those of the well on Espíritu Santo. The trail to the well continues to the top, providing nice views of Caleta Partida. The next cove to the north, El Cardónal, almost cuts the island in half, and the low profile of the land to the east allows breezes. Ensenada Grande has lots of scenery and sandy beaches, although the anchorage is open and often surgy. Just an open roadstead, El Embudo provides protection from south weather. A wreck lies in the cove.

Los Islotes

Los Islotes are islets north of Partida Sur. The surrounding waters have the best diving in the area and are often visited by La Paz dive boats. The greatest attraction is a colony of friendly sea lions, who put on a wonderful show of underwater acrobatics, often doing barrel rolls around divers and indulging in a one-sided game of "chicken"—rushing in and veering off at the last second. The best diving is among the boulders on the north and east sides. In general the site tends to be deep, although there is limited snorkeling close in. Many species of fish can be seen, most notably mantas, sharks, king angelfish and yellowtail surgeonfish, and many octopuses. A reef abounding with gamefish and gorgonians will be found starting 800 yards southwest. SCUBA is required over most of its area.

As mentioned earlier, cruisers out of La Paz fish the deep water east of the islands. The waters on the west side are not exceptional, although numerous willing cabrilla in Caleta Partida make fishing fun for youngsters, and bottom fishing is good from the north point of Ensenada Grande to Los Islotes. Yellowtail are found throughout the area in winter and early spring.

Marisla Seamount

As described in Chapter 2, manta rays and hammerhead sharks have made Marisla Seamount (El Bajo) the most famous dive site in Baja California. In addition, even though it is heavily fished by local hand-liners, there are some very large fish on the seamount. John Riffe tells of a group of divers who came up from their first dive raving about the huge fish. One man, though, complained that he had seen nothing. After his second dive he still had seen nothing, so John followed him down on the third dive. The scene was priceless: the diver was found annoying a tiny moray in a pile of boulders, all the time being observed by a huge jewfish not three feet away.

The seamount is located 8.2 miles, 032° from Los Islotes. When you are over the site the largest of the Islotes will bear 212°, the highest point of Isla San Francisco 287°, and the left tangent of Espíritu Santo 166°. Local commercial fishermen often anchor a buoy on the seamount, and in calm weather fish the area in *pangas*. There are three distinct underwater peaks arrayed along a 300-yard line running 120-300°, the northernmost rising to within eighty-three feet of the surface, the central peak to within fifty-two feet and the southern to within sixty-nine feet. The central peak, with its shallow depths and relatively flat top, is the primary dive site and anchoring location, although the hammerheads seem to prefer the north peak. Note the direction of the current and set up a

We anchored our sloop *Gypsy* in El Cardóncito during a 1982 trip.

Mike frolics with friends at Los Islotes.

drift dive. Garden eels can be observed in sandy areas around the peaks. Marlin, tuna and jacks have been seen around the area.

****

CLOUDBURST. As we headed home we were jabbering happily about our diving trip to the islands north of La Paz, when we found our eyes struggling to focus on the terrain ahead. The familiar desert brush, the sere plains, the dark clouds, all had disappeared into a gray veil—rain! We soon passed into a torrent; it was not mere rain but a cloudburst, and for an instant the front of our VW van was immersed in a waterfall while the rear was dry. We were forced to drive at a crawl, and after a mile or two my brother slammed on the brakes so hard we were thrown against our seatbelts; two figures were standing in the middle of the road. They proved to be that species of young American known to the locals as "heeeepies," *complete with backpacks, bedrolls, combat boots and a drooping cardboard sign announcing their destination, Los Angeles. Impressed with the effectiveness of their hitchhiking technique, we slid the side door open and they jumped in. Although thoroughly soaked and shivering, they were cheerful and began to reiterate their experiences with an astounding variety of tidal waves, earthquakes, typhoons and tornados.*

Villa Insurgentes was awash in two feet of water, and as we turned east toward Loreto we drove up to a number of Mexican drivers sitting in their trucks in front of a large pond extending across the road. Against much generous advice, we started across, assuring them of the invulnerability of German engineering. Exactly at the point of no return the engine gasped, steamed a bit and died. Amid joyous honking from our audience we got out and pushed the van to shallower water ahead. Ten minutes of drying the electric system revived the engine, and we pulled slowly away, our hippie friends displaying a well-known Italian street gesture to our detractors through the rear window.

The rain moderated, but many low spots were deeply flooded and the engine quit three or four more times. At one point a torrent of water slowly pushed the van sideways, the wheels bouncing in tiny hops, but through a small miracle the engine revived itself before we went over the side into a morass of mud. As night fell we began to encounter boulders and rocks which had slid onto the road, forcing us to stop and clear the debris in the light of our headlights. Finally, the long hours and heavy work made sleep essential. The rain had stopped and our headlights illuminated two thatch-roofed palapas, *erected at the bottom of a steep slope. A boulder larger than the span of my arms had rolled down the slope and punched a huge hole through one of them. Too tired to give it much thought, we blew up our air mattresses under the other* palapa *and crashed. After several hours we found we were all still wide awake, waiting for the sound of the next boulder, so we hurriedly packed up and left. Dawn found us grinding past Loreto, a golden sun rising into a clear blue sky.*

****

CHAPTER 15

THE CAPE REGION

On the Transpeninsular Highway at La Paz

The road starts out level, with only minor ups-and-downs until KM 169. Fence-building ranchers are making it increasingly difficult to find good campsites.

KM	LOCATION
0/216	Start new KM numbering sequence.
213	Route BCS 286 to Punta Arena de la Ventana and Ensenada los Muertos.

SIDETRIP TO PUNTA ARENA DE LA VENTANA, ISLA CERRALVO AND ENSENADA LOS MUERTOS

Turn east at KM 213, about 2 1/2 miles south of the waterfront in La Paz. The pavement ends at KM 44 in the town of Los Planes, which has groceries, Nova and diesel from drums, tire repair, medical, dental, pharmacy, meat market, restaurant and water from spigots in the square. The gravel road from this point on is improved and can handle any vehicle. At KM 46+ the road swings north. At KM 54+ take the left (003°) fork, and the left (007°) fork again in 2 1/2 miles (the right at the second fork leads to the Hotel las Arenas, which has rooms with showers, dining room, *pangas* and a cruiser fleet, live bait, rental tackle and snorkeling equipment, as well as such amenities as tennis courts, billiards, a pool and a game room. From January through March boardsailing equipment, Hobies and mountain bikes are available). From the second left fork the beach is another mile, beyond the salt evaporation ponds.

The waters around Punta Arena de la Ventana are the finest roosterfish grounds in the world, and the channel out to Isla Cerralvo has excellent striped marlin, wahoo, sailfish and dolphin, and merely fine amberjack and grouper. Although there are fish to be caught all year, May through October are the best months, peaking in the last two weeks of July and the first two of August. The point is low and flat, with a fine sand beach over which small boats can be launched. The only anchorage, north of the point, is an open roadstead sheltered from south weather. Boardsailors will find exposed onshore

and cross-onshore conditions and good winds. The waters close to the point are shallow out to a thousand yards or so, with rocky fingers crossing sandy areas, but snorkeling is not too exciting, unless you are a spearfisherman. Shelling along the beach can be rewarding, and an exploration with mask and fins will reveal deep, sandy pockets between coral heads which trap many shells. Most are sea-worn, but some are fresh, and it would not be unusual to find twenty species in an hour or two of diving. Unimproved RV parking and camping can be found just west of the navigation tower. A wrecked ship lies at the water's edge to the west.

Cerralvo, six miles north of the point, is the southernmost island in the Cortez and is much larger than it appears from Punta Arena; you are seeing only the south coast. For a number of reasons, both oceanographic and icthyological, many of the fish that migrate in and out of the Cortez pass on each side of the island, often very close to shore. The close-packed schools produce some of the hottest fishing action imaginable, peaking in mid-May and again in October. The fish must be fin-to-fin around Roca Montaña, a pinnacle coming to within a fathom of the surface about 1,200 yards south of Punta Montaña. (The rock got its name when the steamer *Montana* struck it in 1874. "Unfortunately" for divers, it did not sink.) Wahoo are often thick offshore. The bottom is crowded with invertebrates, including crown of thorns, sponges, hydroids, gorgonians, cowries, conches, spindle cones, nudibranchs, lobsters, arrow crabs, urchins, sea stars, brittle stars and several species of coral. There are vast beds of garden eels in sandy areas, and black coral can be seen in deep water. Spearfishing for large gamefish is excellent. A reef about 1 1/2 miles north of Punta Montaña on the east side also has excellent diving.

The west coast of the island is marked by white fossil deposits of oysters, corals, scallops and an echinoid. Two miles north of Punta Sur is the prominent white stripe of such a deposit. The mouth of a canyon lying several hundred yards south of the deposit has pristine and spectacular desert vegetation, largely untouched by domesticated animals. At the north end, a wreck lies 200 yards south of Arrecife de la Foca in seventy feet on a sand bottom, the name "Mazatlan"

ISLA ESPÍRITU
Punta
Prieta
SANTO
Punta Bonanza
Punta
dispensa
Punta Lupona
San Lorenzo
Shoal
Canal San Lorenzo
San Juan
de la Costa
Scout Shoal
Punta Coyote
La Paredes
Ensenada
Balandra
Tecolate
Roca Lobos
El Coyote
ISLA LOBOS
Ferry
Punta los Tules
Punta
la Colorada
Punta el León
Las Cruces
Bahía la Paz
Punta la
Gorda
El Moqote
LA PAZ
Ensenada
la Paz
Alfredo V.
Bonfil
El Centenario
Airport
(286)
La Huerta
Punta
Bentonita
Los Pozos
San Isidro
Guamúchil
San Pedro

ARRECIFE
DE LA FOCA
Punta Norte
Punta
el Limón
Punta el
Mostrador
ISLA
CERRALVO
Canal de Cerralvo
Punta
Sur
Punta Montaña
Roca Montaña
Sea of Cortez
Bahía la Ventana
Punta Arena
de la Ventana
Punta Perico
Ensenada los Muertos
Los
Planes
Bahía los Muertos

Boca de Álamo
El Triunfo
San
Antonio
La Palmillita
Punta Pescadero
El Carrizal
Los Inocentes
San Bartolo
San Quintín
San
Sebastián
Valle Perdido
Bahía las Palmas
Los Barriles
Buenavista
La Ribera
Punta Colorada
San Pedro
El Salto
CAÑON SAN DIONISIO
San
Dionisio
Las Cuevas
Punta Arena Sur
San Juan
del Aserradero
Santiago
El Enchnal
Punta los
Mangles
Pacific Ocean
SIERRA DE LA VICTORIA
Santo Domingo
CAÑON SAN BERNARDO
Agua
Caliente
Cabo
Pulm
Todos
Santos
San Andrés
El Guerigo
Boca de
la Sierra
Miraflores
CAÑON SAN PABLO
El Salto
La Trinidad
Cabo
Fraile
Santa
Fraile
Punta
Lobos
Punta
San Pedro
El Pescadero
El Refugio
Caduaño
La Calabaza
Boca de
Saladc
Punta
Pescadero
Playa
los Cerritos
El Aguaje
Naranjas Road
Palo
Escopeta
Punta
Peruche
Punta
Gasparino
El Saltito
Santa Anita
Las Destiladeras
Plutarco
Elias Calles
Airport
La Fortuna
Cabo
el Cajoncito
San José Viejo
Boca
el Barranca
Candelaria
El Salteador
Santa Rosa
Punta Gorda
Migriño
SAN JOSÉ
DEL CABO
Pueblo la Playa
Banco Golden Gate
Banco Gorda Primero
Banco Gorda
Segundo
San Cristóbal
Palmillas
San
Carlos
Punta Palmilla
Bahía San José del Cabo
Punta
los Arcos
Bahía Chileno
Bahía Santa María
CABO
SAN
LUCAS
Punta Cabeza Ballena
Cabo Falso
Bahía San Lucas
Los Frailes

Banco
San Jaime
95 Spot

The Drop-off

N
000
350 010
340 020
330 030
320 040
310 050
300 060
W 290 070 E
280 080
270 090
260 100
250 110
240 120
230 130
220 140
210 150
200 160
190 170
180
S
Magnetic Bearings
Variation 11°E

showing on her steel stern. This may be *Korrigan IV*, lost in 1966, one of a series of vessels once associated with the copper company in Santa Rosalía. The engine, boilers, propellers and stern section can be seen, and the area is strewn with debris. The area is loaded with large fish. There are no good anchorages at Cerralvo, although boats sometimes use the area off the navigation light at Punta Sur and a small cove at Punta el Limón.

For those with an adequate boat, outstanding fishing can be found east of Cerralvo at "88-Fathom Bank," 15 1/2 miles, 040° from the light at Punta Arena. When over the bank, the north end of Cerralvo will bear 298°, the south end 246°. This bank gets little traffic from La Paz or the hotels at East Cape, and the chances are good that you will be alone. The fish are prolific and unsophisticated—there is a record of a triple hookup on a blue marlin, a striped marlin and a sailfish! If that isn't enough, there are dolphin in the forty-pound class, and wahoo to sixty.

To get to Ensenada los Muertos go back to KM 54+ and take the right (083°) fork, arriving in two miles. This shallow, sandy bay is the only good anchorage between Balandra and Bahía Frailes, forty-eight and fifty-two miles respectively. Diving is only fair, but a huge anchor, metal rails and ore carts will be found scattered over the bottom, mementos of a silver-mining operation in the 1920s. There is RV parking above the beach, but no facilities are available. The beach is soft sand with steep cobbles above it, but local fishermen have cleared paths, and if their boats are not blocking the way it should be possible to launch small trailerboats using sand mats. Cabrilla and pargo are taken in the immediate vicinity, "big fellows" in deeper water. Bob Butler Baja Fishing, based in La Paz, offers *panga* fishing trips out of the bay. Boardsailing conditions are good, with calm water and offshore breezes along most of the shoreline, and waves outside.

Back on the Transpeninsular Highway at KM 213

203   Butane yard.
191   Restaurant.
185   Mexico Route 19 south to Todos Santos.

HIKING AND BACKPACKING ADVENTURES IN THE SIERRA DE LA VICTORIA

The intersection of Route 19 and the Transpeninsular Highway marks the approximate northern limit of the rugged Sierra de la Victoria. This granitic range has a roughly north-south axis, the Pacific slope being much steeper than the Cortez side. Both sides are cut by a series of parallel canyons having an east-west orientation. Four of the six highest peaks in the range are centered about eighteen miles northeast of Todos Santos: 6,855-foot Cerro las Casitas, 6,507-foot Cerro Picacho la Laguna, its companion 6,432-foot Cerro la Aguja, and 6,300-foot Cerro Verde. The other two, 6,264-foot Cerro Salsipuedes and 6,002-foot Cerro Blanco, are in the southern half of the range. So rugged is the terrain that only a few flat areas of any size exist in the entire range, the largest and best-known being La Laguna, a meadow about a mile long and 1/2 mile wide, located at 5,600 feet between Picacho la

Laguna and Cerro las Casitas. Temperatures below freezing are possible, fog and heavy dew are fairly common, and the sound of thunder is frequent. Rainfall is much heavier than in any other part of Baja, up to thirty inches in some micro-climates, most of it occurring between July and November. Small streams and springs can normally be found in the upper regions of virtually all the larger canyons. However, in addition to the seasonal variation, rainfall varies widely from year to year; in 1988 hikers in Cañon San Bernardo found its emerald-colored swimming holes had been reduced to "puddles of cow wee-wee," while in the fall of 1990 backpackers returning from La Laguna were marveling at the "jungle" created by recent heavy rains.

The region is a wilderness much different from anywhere in the United States, a great deal of it highly isolated and inaccessible even by foot due to difficult terrain and dense vegetation. Except in the northernmost part, there is no well-defined crest, and steep canyons make it difficult to hike in a north-south direction. However, a geographic peculiarity makes it possible to hike considerable distances in an east-west direction without undue difficulty: some of the canyons on opposite sides of the Victorias almost meet. Two of these situations provide the primary backpacking routes in the Victorias: from Rancho San Dionisio up Cañon San Dionisio to La Laguna and then to San Juan del Aserradero (La Burrera), fifteen miles; and from Boca de la Sierra up Cañon San Bernardo and then to Santo Domingo, fourteen miles. These routes once had trails used by the locals to visit friends and relatives on opposite sides of the sierra, but with the advent of motor travel they have fallen into disuse and have almost disappeared. However, floods keep canyon bottoms fairly free of brush, and backpackers and hikers will encoun-

Bernie Eskesen checks out an old mining cart at Muertos.

SUE DIPPOLD

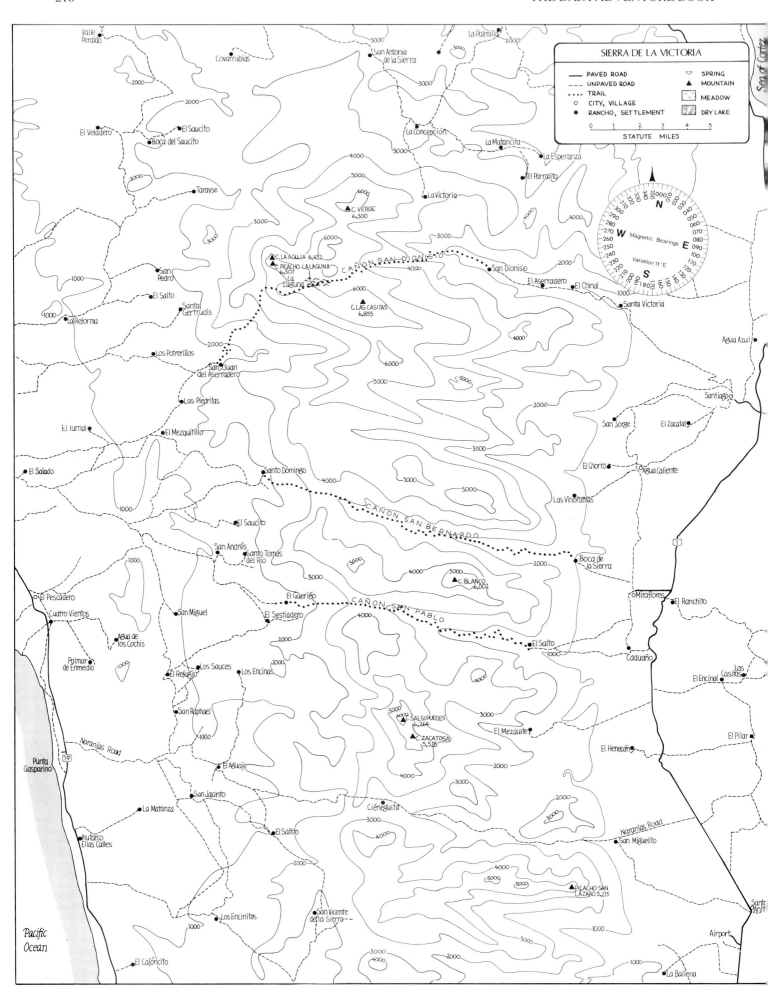

Sea of Cortez

SIERRA DE LA VICTORIA

——— PAVED ROAD	▽ SPRING
- - - UNPAVED ROAD	▲ MOUNTAIN
····· TRAIL	MEADOW
○ CITY, VILLAGE	DRY LAKE
● RANCHO, SETTLEMENT	

0   1   2   3   4   5
STATUTE MILES

Magnetic Bearings

Variation 11°E

Valle Perdido
Covarrubias
San Antonio de la Sierra
La Palmilla
El Veladero
El Saucito
Boca del Saucito
La Concepción
La Matancita
La Esperanza
Tarayse
El Parralito
C. VERDE 6,300
La Victoria
San Pedro
C. LA AGUJA 6,432
C. PICACHO-LA LAGUNA 6,507
La Laguna
CAÑON SAN DIONISIO
San Dionisio
El Aserradero
El Chinal
Santa Victoria
El Salto
Santa Gertrudis
C. LAS CASITAS 6,855
La Reforma
Agua Azul
Los Potrerillos
San Juan del Aserradero
Santiago
Las Piedritas
El Turnal
El Mezquitillo
San Jorge
El Zacatal
El Salado
El Chorro
Agua Caliente
Santo Domingo
Las Vinoramas
CAÑON SAN BERNARDO
El Saucito
San Andrés
Santo Tomás del Río
Boca de la Sierra
C. BLANCO 6,002
El Güerigo
CAÑON SAN PABLO
Miraflores
El Ranchito
El Pescadero
San Miguel
El Sestiadero
El Salto
Caduaño
Cuatro Vientos
Agua de los Cochis
Las Casitas
El Encinal
Palmar de Enmedio
Los Sauces
Los Encinas
El Refugio
San Raphael
C. SALSIPUEDES 6,264
El Mezquite
El Pilar
C. ZACATOSA 5,528
El Henecán
Naranjas Road
19
Punta Gasparino
El Aguaje
San Jacinto
Cieneguita
Naranjas Road
La Matanza
San Miguelito
El Saltito
Plutarco Elías Calles
PICACHO SAN LÁZARO 5,215
Los Encinitas
San Vicente de la Sierra
Santa Anita
Pacific Ocean
El Cajoncito
Airport
La Ballena

ter emerald-green pools, massive rock formations and fine, unspoiled scenery. Six days should be set aside for the Dionisio hike, and five days for San Bernardo. The best time of year is generally November to February, when the wet season is over, water is plentiful and everything is green. Because it is often the best-watered, has the easiest access and is the most suitable for day hikes and short backpacking forays, the San Bernardo route is described beginning on page 222.

La Laguna is a popular destination for backpackers and naturalists. It was once the bed of a lake, but erosion cut through its rim about 1870, leaving a grass-covered meadow. It was used as a potato farm in the heyday of the silver mines at El Triunfo. Two small streams flow through it, one toward the Cortez, the other toward the Pacific. Several rangers watch for fires and tend a small weather station in an old farm building at the upper end of the meadow.

Baja was once cooler and wetter than today. As the climate became hot and dry, the flora and fauna of surrounding lowlands changed dramatically, but in small "island" environments high in the Victorias, especially around La Laguna, a wonderful mix of the rare, the ordinary and the seemingly out-of-place remains. An all-inclusive list would be impossibly long, but you will find pinyon pine, mosses, prickly-pear cactus, jewel lichen, algae, oak, madrono, fern, marigold, monkey flower, evening primrose, willow, rose, geranium, palmita, strawberry, sorrel, wild grape, watercress, deer, coyote, pocket gopher, water beetle, mosquito, band-winged grasshopper, walkingstick, waterstrider, dragonfly, caddisfly, Pacific tree frog and the exotic-looking sotol, with its yucca-like leaves perched on top of a tall, thin trunk. With luck, you might see a mountain lion.

Birders will encounter a mix strange indeed: Cooper's hawk, greater roadrunner, common barn owl, acorn and ladder-backed woodpeckers, red-naped sapsucker, western wood-peewee, willow, western and dusky-capped flycatchers, black phoebe, plain titmouse, bushtit, white-breasted nuthatch, western bluebird, Swanson's thrush, solitary, Hutton's and warbling vireos, Townsend's, black-throated blue and black-throated gray warblers, Louisiana

The meadow at La Laguna.

Joe Farrell leads a group up Cerro Blanco.

WILL WATERMAN

waterthrush, black-headed grosbeak, lazuli bunting, rufous-sided towhee, rufous-crowned sparrow, yellow-eyed junco and Scott's oriole, as well as the endemic Xanthus hummingbird and the uniquely plumaged endemic subspecies San Lucas robin. Sober-faced naturalists can undoubtedly provide very objective explanations for all this diversity, noting La Laguna's high altitude, generous rainfall at high elevations, aridity of the surrounding regions, the influences of the nearby Pacific and Cortez, and its position just north of the Tropic of Cancer, missing being "tropical" by less than four miles. Still, it seems certain that there is at least a bit of magic involved. So unusual is La Laguna that it has been proposed as a national park.

Cirilo Manriquez Trasviña can provide mules and guide service for very inexpensive five-day forays from Rancho San Dionisio into the Victorias to La Laguna. His mailing address and telephone number are in Appendix A, and he can be contacted at a building 100 yards south of the PEMEX station at KM 109. Backpackers may prefer the shorter route, via the trail northeast from San Juan del Aserradero, described later in this chapter, or to make it a one-way trip from either end.

Backpacking outside of the canyons is difficult, often requiring heavy brush-busting and the use of machetes. In 1984 the National Outdoor Leadership School began its three-month-long "Semester in Baja" course with a backpacking trip from Rancho San Pedro to the vicinity of La Ciéneguita on the Naranjas Road. This route follows the north-south axis of the range, rather than the "easy" east-west way, and almost everyone agreed it was the most challenging trip they had ever taken.

There are a number of interesting class 3 climbs in the Victorias, including Cerro Salsipuedes, 5,528-foot Cerro Zacatosa, and 5,215-foot Picacho San Lázaro. The Naranjas Road, the closest approach to all three, is described beginning on page 223. The only good technical climb in the Victorias is Cerro Blanco, accessible from Cañon San Bernardo. Cerro Blanco, Salsipuedes, Zacatosa and San Lázaro are plainly visible from the Transpeninsular, and bearings are provided in later sections, but due to a lack of established trails nothing in the way of specific approach information can be given.

The following topographic maps of 1:50,000 scale are available for the Victorias: San Antonio F12B13, El Rosario F12B23, Las Cuevas F12B24, Todos Santos F12B33, Santiago F12B34, La Candeleria F12B43 and San José del Cabo F12B44.

Backpackers and hikers in the Victorias face challenges, and the area is not likely to appeal to the weak of spine or limb. However, the area is both highly interesting and largely unspoiled, qualities that are becoming very difficult to find in today's world.

On the Transpeninsular Highway at KM 185

169   Rolling hills to KM 103, with moderate grades and numerous blind curves.

164   **El Triunfo**.

SIDETRIP TO EL TRIUNFO

In 1862 the Triunfo Gold and Silver Company began operations and El Triunfo soon had a population of 10,000, the largest mining town in Baja California. Today the town is home to only 500 people and is little more than a collection of time-worn adobe buildings. Nature was generous to collectors at El Triunfo, in variety if not quantity, for in addition to silver and gold, thirty-three other minerals have been found, second only to Santa Rosalía. The simple sulfides and sulfosalts predominate, but carbonates, halides, silicates, oxides and other groups also are represented. Fine garnets to a half-inch in white rock have also been reported. There is a grocery store in town, cold sodas can be purchased and water is available from spigots.

Back on the Transpeninsular Highway at KM 164

156   **San Antonio**. When mining boomed in the region during the mid-1800s, San Antonio and El Triunfo were great rivals, but San Antonio failed to keep up. Today the tables have turned and it is distinctly the more clean, pleasant and prosperous, with a PEMEX (MN), library, stores, groceries, medical, mail, tele-

graph, beer, cold sodas and water from spigots. The architecture of its church, built in 1825 and remodeled a number of years ago, may be the most unusual in Baja, a massive concrete amalgam of the features of a railroad locomotive and a river steamer.

131   A beautiful zalate lives on the rocks on the north side of the road.

128+   **San Bartolo**. Cafe, groceries, fruit, sodas, famous springs of exceptional purity.

110+   Sedan road east to the shores of Bahía las Palmas.

BAHÍA LAS PALMAS

Stretching from Punta Pescadero south to Punta Arena Sur, Bahía las Palmas is world-famous for its gamefish. In one recent year fishermen were complaining that hordes of dolphin and sailfish made it difficult to catch blue marlin! For over ten miles the 100-fathom line averages less than a mile offshore, the closest lengthy approach anywhere in the Cape region, which may account for the fine fishing and many successful resorts. Blue and black marlin and sailfish are taken from May to October, sometimes by astonished fishermen in cartoppers. Roosters are caught year-round, but fishing for them is best from May to October. Yellowtail are best from January to April, and striped marlin, dolphin, tuna, wahoo and lesser fish inhabit the area all year, although the warm months are the most productive and December through March can be slow. Four miles south of Punta Pescadero is the famous Tuna Canyon, where Ray Cannon found depths of 50 fathoms a hundred yards from shore and a year-round population of large yellowfin tuna. Roosters can also be caught from the beach at Tuna Canyon, and at the beach north of Punta Pescadero. Diving is pleasant but not spectacular, with large sandy areas broken by reefs, although gunning for pelagic gamefish should be great.

The bay is the most popular boardsailing location in Baja, with many clean, sandy beaches, pleasant weather, good campsites and winds often in the eighteen to twenty-five knot range between mid-November and mid-March. Sometimes there are good winds two weeks or more on either side, but they tend to be lighter and less consistent. Winds during this period are normally from the north, producing side-shore conditions from Punta Pescadero to the Buena Vista area. The beach from Buena Vista to Punta Colorada is often sandy and the launch easy, but the shoreline has curved eastward to the point that boardsailors may begin to encounter onshore winds. Riders should have previous high wind experience or the ability to learn quickly, and be able to make confident water starts. In most locations there is usually enough chop that uphauling doesn't work out. A number of boardsailing operations are located along the shores of the bay.

There are no protected anchorages from Muertos to Cabo Frailes, the bay being little more than an open roadstead, although Punta Arena Sur can provide marginal protection, and there are no marinas or fuel docks. Although a number of concrete ramps have been built through the years, all have been destroyed by waves or deeply buried by sand. All beach launches open into unprotected waters and can be used only in calm conditions.

SIDETRIP TO BEACH RESORTS AND RV PARKS

A number of resorts and RV parks on the beaches of Bahía las Palmas are reached by driving east on the sedan road at KM 110+. Set odometer. The Hotel Palmas de Cortez at Mile 0.35 has rooms, showers, pool, gift shop, tennis, dining room and bar, and offers cruisers, *pangas* and fishing guides, live and frozen bait, rental tackle and a boat-launching service. Baja Surf Club manages a large boardsailing operation at the hotel, with equipment rentals, parts, repairs and service, instruction and package trips, as well as horseback riding, snorkeling, tennis and racquetball. They have a wind guarantee, and if you can't yet make water starts they will shuttle you back up the beach if need be. The Club also offers mountain-biking vacations out of Rancho Leonero, exploring the area in a series of local rides. Once a week an optional guided ride is offered across the Victorias on the Naranjas Road, with a night of camping on a Pacific beach.

Turn left (000°) at the Palmas, encountering the Hotel Playa Hermosa at Mile 0.45, with rooms, shower baths, bar and dining room, a cruiser and *panga* fleet, live and frozen bait, rental tackle and snorkeling gear. Vela Highwind Center, located at the hotel, has boardsailing package trips, instruction, clinics, high-wind seminars and special events featuring racing, barbecues and margaritas. In addition, they have mountain bikes and clinics on riding technique, snorkeling, fishing, tennis and volleyball.

Martin Verdugo's Trailer Park at Mile 0.5 has full hookups, tent sites, showers, restrooms, a washing machine, restaurant and an over-the-beach launch service for small boats. Playa de Oro RV Resort at Mile 0.9 has full hookups, laundry facilities, ice, showers, restrooms, boat launching, *pangas* and cruisers to thirty-two feet. Playa de Oro is much favored by boardsailors, with clean cross-onshore winds.

The road continues north, passing pebble and cobble beaches. At Mile 8.2 the road deteriorates, with a rough surface and grades to 25%. The road is passable by sedans with difficulty. Hotel Punta Pescadero, located at Mile 9.1, has rooms and villas, dining room, cantina, gift shop, pool, a cruiser and *panga* fleet, live and frozen bait, tackle rentals, snorkeling, a SCUBA compressor and equipment rentals (diving facilities reserved for guests, no regulators available), trail bikes and sailing dinghys, as well as tennis courts, horses, ski boats and other amenities. An excellent diving reef extends right in front of the hotel. The hotel has no facilities for RVs and trailers.

Back on the Transpeninsular Highway at KM 110+

KM	LOCATION
109	PEMEX (MND), groceries. Mr. Bill's Boardsailing Adventures is found by driving east on the graded dirt road across from the PEMEX. The new bed-breakfast-and-lunch villa has four bedrooms. Each bedroom has a private bath, and the living room/dining room and kitchen are shared by all the units. Several hotels that have restaurants and bars are within easy walking distance. The beach is in front

of the villa, everything is pre-rigged and unlimited changes are allowed. Transportation is available to other sailing sites and for downwinders. Mountain bikes are available for the rare non-wind days.

106	Rancho Buena Vista is one of the best-known fishing resorts in Baja with probably more IGFA records than any other place in the world. It offers cottages with baths, pool, tennis courts, dining room, bar, cruisers, rental tackle, live and frozen bait and a sand beach. The resort is closed August 16 through October 9.
105	Hotel Spa Buenavista, which offers rooms and bungalows with baths, pool, mineral baths, tennis, volleyball, horseback riding, dining room, bar, beach, a cruiser and *panga* fleet, live and frozen bait, tackle rental, and snorkeling gear. Boat and trailer storage can be arranged.
103+	La Capilla Trailer Park, which has full hookups, showers, restrooms and a sand beach. Rancho Leonero is also reached from this point. Turn east at KM 103+, set odometer, turn right at Mile 0.6, follow the signs and arrive at the ranch at Mile 4.3. Although the sandy road has some bumpy areas and several 20% grades it is passable by sedans. The ranch has rooms, lounge, dining room, barbecue, volleyball, fishing cruisers and *pangas*, live bait and rental tackle. East Cape Divers at the ranch has two compressors, limited rentals and sales of small items. The shop is available to visitors as well as guests. Spearfishing (no tropical species) and limited shell collecting are permitted. Diving is excellent right in front of the resort, and a boat dive at Pulmo Reef is offered. As noted earlier, Baja Surf Club runs a mountain-biking operation at the ranch.
103	The road levels out, with only occasional arroyo crossings and gentle grades until Cabo San Lucas.
93	**Las Cuevas**. Paved road northeast (signed) to La Rivera.

SIDETRIP ON THE "EAST CAPE COAST ROAD"

Part of the Cape Coast Loop Trip, this road passes Pulmo Reef, one of Baja's great natural wonders, Cabo Frailes, with its spearfishing and unusual beachcasting, some good diving wrecks, and dozens of miles of the finest and most pristine beaches imaginable. Improved and graded, the road from La Rivera can handle sedans and moderate RVs throughout its length, although washboard, washouts and rough sections are common. Spur roads to the beaches have been slow to develop, but campsites can be found at places where the road dips into arroyos near the water and along lengthy stretches of beach approaching San José del Cabo. Bicyclists will find no dependable natural sources of water, but it should be possible to bum a supply at eight or nine small settlements and ranches scattered along the way, as well as from passing RVers and local drivers.

Momentous changes are in store for the area. Road crews have paved the road from the Transpeninsular to La Rivera, and have begun work on a paved road from a point a mile or so southwest of La Rivera that will extend to San José del

Cabo, forever changing this once remote and pristine coast. Surveys are not yet available, so this section of new road is not shown on the accompanying regional map.

Turn northeast at Las Cuevas and arrive at La Rivera at Mile 7.0, which has groceries, tires, restaurants, mail, long-distance telephone, cold sodas and beer. At Mile 7.5 is an intersection. The graded dirt road left (280°) leads 1/2 mile to Corrcaminos Trailer Park. Located in a wonderful old mango orchard (crop ripe for picking in summer), the park has a sand beach, restrooms, showers, dump station, water hookups and tent sites. Electrical hookups should be available soon, and a paved launch ramp is scheduled for the future. Boardsailing is excellent, with good winds and cross-onshore conditions.

Continuing on the East Cape Coast Road trip, turn right (090198) at Mile 7.5, passing a PEMEX (MND) at Mile 8.2. At Mile 8.6 note the road left (045°) to Hotel Punta Colorada, with rooms, shower baths, dining room and bar, as well as cruisers, *pangas*, rental tackle, and live and frozen bait. Boardsailors will find lots of wind and cross-onshore conditions. This is one of the more challenging areas in Baja, and if you are looking for logo waves, this may be the place. A number of sandy shallow bars about 100 yards out have the reputation of being the best place in Baja for wave-jumping.

At Mile 15.2 a sideroad northeast leads to Punta Arena Sur, scene of fine beachcasting for roosters. Shifting sands may require four-wheel drive. Inshore are jack crevalle, sierra and ladyfish, out several miles dolphin, skipjack, yellowfin tuna, sailfish and black, blue and striped marlin in season. The water east of the lighthouse is a top location for high wind and wave boardsailing. The lee of the point is tops for speed sailing, with lots of sand beach and cross-offshore conditions. The bay, known as "Bahía Rincón" to boardsailors, is a good place to practice jibes and water starts.

At Mile 24.6 arrive at Cabo Pulmo. The reefs are something of an oddity, since coral reefs are rare or absent along the western coasts of all the continents. This is not due to cultural bias on the part of the polyps, but to the fact that waters off western coasts tend to be cooler than those off eastern coasts. Because of the earth's rotation and related wind patterns, ocean currents are forced into a clockwise pattern in the northern hemisphere and counter-clockwise in the southern. Thus, on western shores cool water is carried toward the equator, restricting coral growth. Because of this, hard corals have managed to establish sizable reefs in only four locations along the west coast of North America: one in Panama, one in Costa Rica, one on mainland Mexico, and at Pulmo. (There are coral heads and patches in many Cortez locations and a very small reef in Bahía San Gabriel at Isla Espíritu Santo.)

Although they are not quite as colorful as tropical reefs and lack their diversity, the reefs at Pulmo are true coral reefs. Starting near the shore south of Cabo Pulmo and running in a northeasterly direction, broad rows of coral heads of two dominant species continue for 1 1/2 miles, ending in depths of seventy feet. The row pattern is caused by the geology of the area: the corals are cemented to elongated ridges of basaltic rock protruding from the sandy bottom. The astronomical number of nooks, crannies and cavelets formed by the reef are home to large numbers of creatures. Accounting for all these biological marvels would fill the remainder of

this volume, so it will not be attempted; go see for yourself.

Pulmo is one of the most famed diving locations in the Cortez, second only to Marisla Seamount. The water is warm and the visibility is often thirty to fifty feet, occasionally seventy-five. Since the innermost coral heads can be found in only a few feet of water immediately off the beach, neither SCUBA nor a boat is essential. As you enter the water, be ready for a surprise; at some times of the year small *sardinas* are so numerous they may envelop you in a silver cloud, bringing on vertigo. Once, in deeper water, I was approached by a school of goatfish, which turned and began making endless circles, placing me at the center of a living carousel, its leader apparently having come to the conclusion that he was at the end of the procession rather than at its beginning. Certainly, do not miss a night dive. The small white islet at the south end of the bay is also a fine dive site.

Another outstanding dive site lies just offshore, Bajo El Pulmo. With a least depth of thirty-two feet, it is located approximately 2,500 yards, 050° from Cabo Pulmo. A little searching may be necessary, but it should be possible to see it as you approach. With coral heads, deep caves, many species of sea fans, colonies of yellow colonial tulip corals, dog and yellow snappers, grunts, coral and giant hawkfish, bicolor and bumphead parrot fish, sea bass, broomtail grouper and an occasional jewfish, the place is spectacular.

Pulmo is an underwater ecological reserve, and fishing, spearfishing, foraging and shell collecting are not permitted. Camping areas can be found, although it may be necessary to get permission if on private property. Small boats can be launched across the beach, *pangas* are for hire, and there is a small restaurant. Cabo Pulmo Beach Resort offers small rental homes and bungalows with bath and kitchen facilities, and has sailboards, kayaks and an outboard boat available for guests. Pulmo is a poor overnight anchorage, and yachtsmen will be far happier at Bahía Frailes. Avoid anchoring on the reef, for you can cause severe damage to the coral. There is often a good afternoon breeze and the bay is popular with boardsailors. In winter the prevailing north winds often exceed twenty knots, providing excellent cross-shore conditions.

Since the road to Pulmo is normally good, and there is access to the water, it should be possible to bring in a sizable trailerboat and launch using sand mats. Sailfish are numerous in deep water offshore, sometimes producing two or three per boat per day. There are several shipwrecks in the area. In 1941 the old 107-foot steel auxiliary sailing vessel *Colima* sank with a cargo of beer and general merchandise, the cause being " . . . the poor state of the bottom of the ship." Lying in about thirty-five feet of water, what is left is now scattered across a sandy bottom and can sometimes be seen from the surface. To visit her, maneuver until Cabo Pulmo bears 154° and the rounded peak having the greatest apparent height on the western skyline bears 250°, a point about 1 1/4 miles from the cape. The wreck is sometimes hidden by sand.

The large Mexican purse seiner *Vencedor* sank in the vicinity in 1980, and now lies scattered over the bottom. The extensive collection of junk, excellent visibility, bright sand bottom, easy accessibility and almost artistic setting make the *Vencedor* a fine dive site. Start just east of Cabo Pulmo and note the dark, cone-shaped rock at the end of the Cape. When this rock bears 209°, put it astern and proceed on course 029°. Look to the south and locate the rocky massif forming Cabo Frailes. When its central peak bears 174° and the water depth is forty-five feet, you will be very close to the wreck site.

Continuing on the East Cape Coast Road, arrive at Frailes at Mile 29.0. A deep submarine canyon winds into the bay, having depths of over 400 feet within 400 yards of shore, and shorecasters have caught yellowfin tuna and marlin. The closest approach of the canyon to the shore is at that point where the right tangent of Cabo Frailes bears 055°. Spearfishermen with sufficient courage will encounter large gamefish by lying in wait in the deep water along the south margin of the point. Divers have seen sandfalls in the canyon. A fairly secure anchorage can be made south of the point, the next satisfactory anchorage to the south being Cabo San Lucas, forty-five miles. The lee of the point is too well protected from wind to be a good boardsailing site, but by the time it has reached the south end of the bay the wind is strong and steady, providing good speed-sailing conditions. The sandy beaches yield fine paper nautilus. You can't get any farther east on the Baja peninsula than Frailes, and in some respects this marks the southernmost extent of the Cortez—the beaches to the south start to show ocean swell and surf. If north winds start to blow and your engine refuses to run, don't worry—Easter Island is only 3,013 miles south.

Because it is the first place where the sweep of the coast begins to face the south swells of summer, the vicinity of Punta Peruchera (Boca de Tule) at Mile 39.5 is ordinarily the first place in the Cortez where hope begins to stir in the hearts of surfers. The point itself isn't much, but there are a number of reef and beach breaks. These tend to be a bit small and

mushy most of the year, but can assume heroic proportions during the summer hurricane season. At Mile 44.6 you will encounter one of the greatest zalates in Baja, a giant of a tree in a typically nontypical recumbent pose. A steel tuna vessel can be found fifty yards off the beach in about twenty-five feet of water at Rancho las Destiladeras, Mile 47.7. Beach-combers may enjoy investigating a wreck on the beach 300 yards southwest of the above vessel. The wreck of the Mexican freighter *Morelia* can be seen on the beach at Mile 49.9. The U.S. fishing vessel *Waldero*, stranded in 1949, is buried in the dunes 200 yards northeast of the *Morelia*. This general area, known as "Shipwrecks," is highly regarded by boardsailors. Punta Gorda at Mile 54.9 has point and reef breaks, and storms sometimes deposit many shells on the beach. A 165-foot vessel, name and date unknown, is reported in forty-five feet of water off Punta Gorda.

The wreck of a large steel ship is 800 yards off the beach at Mile 59.2. When you are close to the wreck, the lighthouse east of San José del Cabo should bear 255°. Now look for three low hills north of the coast road. When you are facing north, the left one is the most pointed, the right one is slumped over and the center hill is rounded. The peak of the center hill should bear 318°. The left and center hills are obvious from the road. The wreck is in about thirty-five feet of water on a sand bottom and usually can be seen from the surface. Possibly the Greek refrigerator ship *Anastacios*, lost in 1980, she is home to squadrons of fish, some quite sizable.

At Mile 61.2 pass a lighthouse on the left, and at Mile 61.5, shortly after passing a grocery store, go straight (260°) at a fork. A maze of crossroads develops as you approach San José del Cabo, but continue west, steering for the north end of the

The great zalate near Mile 44.6.

large grove of palms surrounding the freshwater estero. At Mile 61.8 pass the road to Pueblo la Playa fishing village, and at Mile 63.1 cross a stream, a great place for a bath if you don't mind eyes. Arrive at the intersection of Av. Benito Juárez and Antonio Mijares at Mile 63.3. Use the city map provided on page 225 to continue.

Back on the Transpeninsular Highway at Las Cuevas, KM 93

84+   Road west to Santiago (signed). PEMEX (MND), groceries, stores, medical, pharmacy, long-distance telephone, mail, telegraph, restaurant, motel, cold beer and sodas, ice, water from spigots, small zoo of local animals. The road to Rancho San Dionisio, jumping-off point for the Cañon San Dionisio-La Laguna backpack/burro trip, is found by turning right (355°) at Mile 1.5, then half-right (320°) at Mile 1.9 and then continuing straight ahead (300°) at the intersection at Mile 2.4. The ranch is reached at Mile 14.4. The road is capable of handling sedans. The mouth of the canyon can be seen at 300° from KM

84+.

81+   Tropic of Cancer.

71   PEMEX (MND). Road west (signed) to Miraflores, which has groceries, stores, medical, dental, cold beer, long-distance telephone, water from spigots, leather shop.

SIDETRIP TO CAÑON SAN BERNARDO

An interesting day hike or backpacking trip can be made up Cañon San Bernardo. Stop and sight 272° from KM 71; the mouth of the canyon can be seen in the distance. If you plan to climb Cerro Blanco, sight 260° and study the domed summit. Turn west on the paved road to Miraflores, at Mile 1.4 enter town, and turn right (345°) at Mile 1.7. At Mile 1.9 go half-left (310°), and at Mile 4.9 arrive at the tiny settlement of Boca de la Sierra. The road can handle sedans.

The approach to the canyon begins on the road several hundred yards southeast of the settlement. A dam in the lower reaches of the canyon provides water to the surrounding farms. Either follow the aqueduct upstream or follow the trail to the west over the hills to the dam. Past the dam the canyon

The south face and summit dome of Cerro Blanco.

soon becomes rugged and beautiful, with massive rock formations and emerald-colored swimming holes, some of which get to thirty feet across and fifteen feet deep. The stream occasionally forms low waterfalls, and there are many fine zalates and palms. Firewood is plentiful and there are numerous places to camp.

Five miles from the dam Cerro Blanco lies two miles south, offering rare technical challenges. Careful scouting will reveal long fingers of bare granite which run from the bottom of the canyon far up the slope, greatly reducing the amount of brush-busting required. Climbs on the south face range from easy class 5 on up, and the summit dome has numerous cracks of varying degrees of difficulty. Continuing up the canyon, you will reach the crest about twelve miles from the dam, at approximately 3,000 feet. West of this point a fairly well-defined cow trail runs down to Santo Domingo and the roadhead. The appropriate topos are Santiago F12B34 and Todos Santos F12B33; if you are not going all the way to Santo Domingo you don't need the second one.

Back on the Transpeninsular Highway at KM 71

| 62 | Clear views of Cerros Zacatosa and Salsipuedes, bearing 254° and 259° respectively, approximately ten miles away. |
| 54 | Naranjas Road (signed). |

SIDETRIP ON THE NARANJAS ROAD

Less energetic explorers can visit the Victorias by vehicle on a road which crosses to the vicinity of Punta Gasparino on the Pacific side. Before you leave the Transpeninsular at KM 54, sight 223°, 273° and 275° to San Lázaro, Zacatosa and Salsipuedes, respectively, and set odometer. The road meanders through brush-covered hills and scenic canyons, with dark emerald ponds shimmering in light-colored rock. There are very few signs of civilization—just a few cows, small flocks of goats and an occasional ranch. Soon after you start, zalate and oak trees will be seen, somehow out of place amid the palms. At Mile 5 San Lázaro lies two miles south. This white granite knob provides a difficult class 3 climb and marvelous views of the sierras and the plains to the south. There are no established trails, so it is a compass-and-bushwhacking proposition until you are high on the slopes. Zacatosa and Salsipuedes lie 3 and 3 1/2 miles north from Mile 14, both difficult class 3.

The crest of the range is reached one mile farther west at about 3,400 feet, from where the Pacific can be seen. The road east of the crest is graded, but to the west it is poor, with switchbacks and slopes to 30%. Turn right (004°) at a small cluster of buildings marked "El Aguaje" at Mile 23.1. The road quickly swings west, and a power line will be seen

Nils Green and Linda Redman survey the Victorias from the summit of Cerro Zacatosa.

WILL WATERMAN

paralleling it almost all the way to Route 19. Take the left (252°) fork at Mile 24.7, and at Mile 30.8 arrive at Route 19.

The Naranjas Road is a civil engineering disaster-in-the-making, with poor culverting and steep, unstabilized grades, so go now before nature makes it impossible.

****

CUTTING IT CLOSE. When the Naranjas Road was still under construction Reeve and I drove up into the Victorias from the Pacific side. Angling up the steep mountain sides, the road continued to narrow until only inches kept us from plunging down extraordinarily steep slopes that continued for hundreds of feet, ending in boulder-strewn creek bottoms. The van was heavily loaded with camping and dive gear, and there was a fifteen-foot boat on the roof, so we frequently smelled burning clutch. We encountered a section blasted through solid rock where the fit was so tight we had to fold in the left outside mirror. The door on that side could not be opened, and the right led to thin air, so if we had had to get out of the van to fix something we would have had to burrow through the equipment in back to get to the rear door. Finally we came to a point where a huge boulder lay six feet away from a rocky cliff. Two Mexican road workers smiled as we pulled up, knowing that we would never be able to squeeze between the cliff and the boulder. They said they were working on the problem, but it was too hot for such heavy labor and they were about to head home for several days of rest. Perhaps the boulder would be out of the way by April.

We didn't like the prospect of backing down the road for perhaps five miles; the slightest inattention, the smallest jerk of the steering wheel, even an untimely hiccup, and we would be history. I got out and spanned the opening between the boulder and the cliff with my arms. No way, it was too narrow! Reeve, not so ready to give up, pulled a length of line off a fishing reel and we measured the width of the inside of the van and compared it to the opening. It still did not look like we could make it; the opening seemed to be exactly the width of the van. We measured again, more carefully this time. The line was stretchy, but there might be perhaps an eighth of an inch of clearance. With big grins, the men assured us that the gap was too narrow, but I pulled ahead, backed down, moved over, pulled ahead, and kept repeating the process with Reeve coaching me until there was equal space on each side of the van. Both outside mirrors were folded back, but it looked like we going to have to unbolt and remove their mounts from the doors.

Luck was with us; as I crept forward each mount passed through small cracks and crevices in the rock. Walking slowly backward in front of the van, Reeve made signs to turn right and then left, but finally his hand went up; the men were right—the van was wider than the gap. Their grins gave way to beaming smiles, and their body-language—legs crossed, leaning jauntily on both picks—signaled certainty and anticipation at the upcoming spectacle. After five more minutes of backing and filling, the van was repositioned slightly and I pulled ahead at a creep. There was a faint sound, like the tearing of a piece of paper, but the van was finally on the other side, much to the disgust of our audience, who suddenly lost interest and got back to work, swinging their picks and studiously looking the other way. Reeve jumped in, and when

we had made it around the next bend we got out and found a shallow scratch on one side of the van extending three or four feet, and a scratch in the protruding bumper on the other. We did not return to congratulate them, but the men had been right—the van was wider than the gap, by the thickness of a layer of paint and a little chrome!

****

Back on the Transpeninsular Highway at KM 54

46+   **Santa Anita**. Groceries.

43+   Los Cabos International Airport.

39+   **San José Viejo**. Groceries, auto parts.

36+   **Santa Rosa**. PEMEX (MND), Volkswagen dealer, car rental, tire repairs, meat market, bike shop, cafe, groceries, pharmacies, liquor.

33   **San José del Cabo**.

SAN JOSÉ DEL CABO

In the late 1600s and the 1700s the Manila galleons stopped at San José del Cabo to obtain water and fresh provisions, en route to Acapulco. A Jesuit mission was founded in 1730, but epidemics quickly killed most of the Indians. In 1822 English sea lord Thomas Cochrane attacked the town, and in 1847 the U.S frigate *Portsmouth* landed a company of marines to occupy the town. Mexican patriots besieged them for several months, almost wiping them out until reinforcements arrived. Today's Avenue Antonio Mijares is named for a Mexican lieutenant killed in an attack. The mission church was destroyed in the battle, and the present one (1) was built in the 1940s.

In recent years there has been a great deal of new construction, including a number of fine hotels and many condominiums, and San José del Cabo is one of the most beautiful towns in Baja. The Stouffer Presidente (2) has rooms and suites, gift shop, dining room, bar, disco, and travel and car rental agencies, plus a beach, pool, horseback riding and tennis. A golf course is nearby. Hotel Posada Real Cabo (3), also on the beach, has rooms and suites with shower baths, pool, tennis, dining room, bar and gift shop. There are many others—see the travel agents listed on page 81.

The mouth of the Río San José is blocked by a wide sandbar most of the year, and there is a large lagoon harboring more than 180 species of birds. The Stouffer has canoes and paddle boats available for birding ventures.

A long stretch of sand beach, known as the Costa Azul, one of the most magnificent in Baja, sweeps past the town, providing fine swimming and loafing. However, the water immediately offshore is very deep, and when swells are present, especially in summer, a booming surf renders water activities difficult. Although some individual combinations of bottom contour and wave direction permit surfing along the Costa Azul, the waves sometimes go from top to bottom in six seconds or less, and most surfers head east for the Punta Gorda or Shipwrecks areas, or for "Zippers," "The Rock," "Old Man" and points west. Victor's Aquatics at the Posada Real rents surfboards.

Fishing trips can be arranged at the Stouffer and Posada

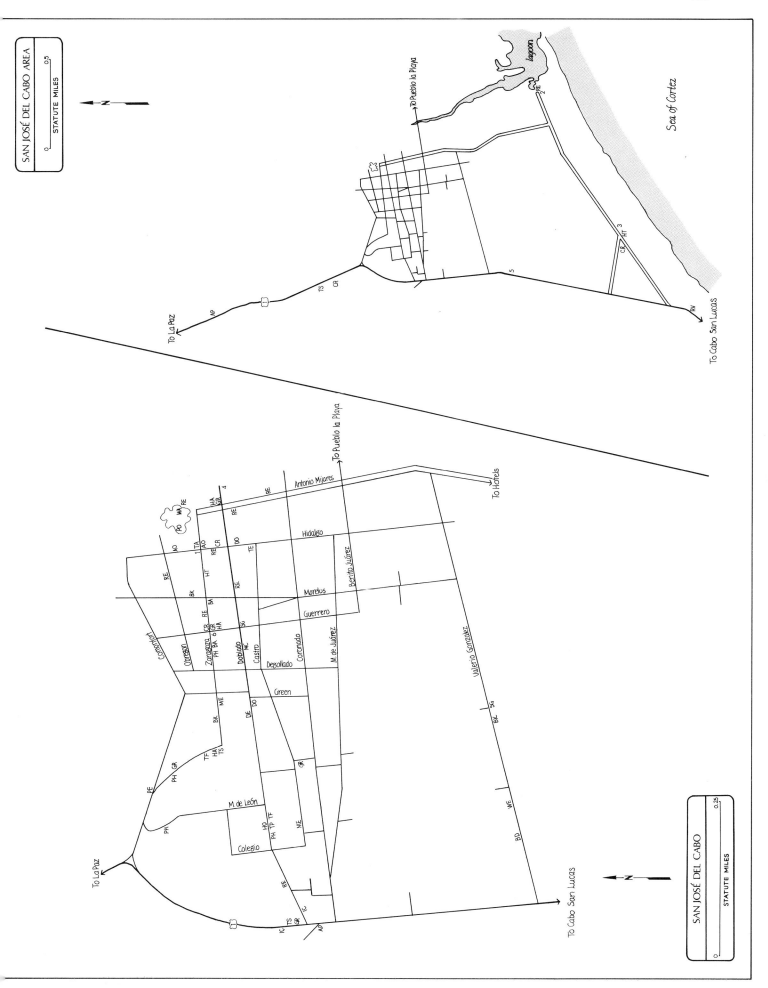

SAN JOSÉ DEL CABO AREA

STATUTE MILES

To La Paz

To Pueblo la Playa

lagoon

Sea of Cortez

To Cabo San Lucas

SAN JOSÉ DEL CABO

STATUTE MILES

To Pueblo la Playa

To Hotels

Antonio Mijares

Hidalgo

Morelos

Guerrero

Benito Juárez

Coronado

Castro

Degollado

Green

M. de Juárez

Valerio González

Obregón

Zaragoza

Doblado

Comonfort

M. de León

Colegio

To La Paz

To Cabo San Lucas

Real. *Pangas* can be hired for fishing and diving trips to the Bancos Gorda at Pueblo la Playa. (Since the only trailerboat launch facilities in the area are at Cabo San Lucas, a description of the Bancos Gorda and other Cape fishing areas will be found later in this chapter.) Victor's Aquatics can also provide sportfishing guides and boats. Although there is no harbor and the anchorage is just an open roadstead, a COTP will be found in town (4), customs and immigration at the airport. There is a Nissan dealer (5), as well as a movie theater (6). Many restaurants and other businesses offering a wide variety of sales and services are shown on the accompanying map.

Early in 1991 tourism officials announced plans to increase the number of hotel rooms in San José del Cabo and Cabo San Lucas and the area in between from 3,000 to 13,000, as well as to increase the number of condominiums, all within five years. Let us hope these plans prove to be fantasy.

Back on the Transpeninsular Highway at KM 33

KM	LOCATION
30	Brisa del Mar Trailer Park and Motel. Rooms, tenting, full hookups, toilets, showers, pool, beach, recreation room, restaurant, bar, laundry.
29	Zippers. Short, fast inside break.
28+	Trailer parking, rooms to rent, surfboard sales, rentals and accessories.
28	The Rock is the middle break, and "Old Man" is the long outside break.
26+	**Playa Palmilla**. Set on 1,000 acres, with 2 1/2 miles of beach, the luxury Hotel Palmilla offers rooms, suites and villas, tennis, golf, fishing, snorkeling and sailing. Dive Palmilla, located at the hotel, has full equipment rentals, PADI certification up to Divemaster and Instructor, air and trips to Pulmo and other local attractions. The shop is open to all. No spearfishing or shelling on trips. The small bay is used as an anchorage but is very exposed. In south swells several point and reef breaks off the hotel provide good surfing; not too reliable, but when they work they really work.
26	Butane plant.
23	Public beach.
19	Public beach.
16	A long stretch of public beach, with entrances 0.2 and 0.5 miles west of the KM marker.
14+	Hotel Cabo San Lucas. Located on 2,500 acres, the luxury hotel has rooms, apartments and villas with baths, dining room, bar, pool, horseback riding, tennis, fishing cruisers, rental tackle and bait. The point off the hotel has a long right break.
14	**Playa Chileno**. This is a public beach, with fenced parking. Bahía Chileno has rocky reefs alternating with sandy areas and shoals of colorful tropical fish. A night dive here is a special treat. The bay provides a partly protected anchorage in normal weather, but the bottom is rocky and the surge can be heavy. Cabo Acuadeportes, at the western end of the bay near the parking lot, has air, dive equipment rentals and repairs, tank inspection, rental cameras and trips

with bilingual guides. Two single-tank no-decompression boat dives are run daily, as well as two guided snorkel tours. No spearfishing is permitted on their trips, but one-of-a-kind dead shelling is allowed. Although they are available to rent, the shop recommends that visiting divers bring their own mask, snorkel, fins, regulator and buoyancy compensator. Instruction and certification are available, ranging from introductory courses to full certification and open-water check-outs. In addition, sailboards, Sunfish and small cats are for rent, and whale-watching trips are available January through March.

12	**Bahía Santa María**. Public beach with fine diving on coral heads, brilliant tropical fish. Drive 1/2 mile west of KM 13, turn south, drive 1/3 mile, park at the gate, and walk five minutes to the beach. Fair anchorage in good weather.
9+	"Wreck Beach." This public beach got its name from the Japanese tuna-fishing vessel *Inari Maru 10*, which stranded here in 1966. This was once the most popular campground at the Cape, and it was not uncommon to encounter a hundred RVs and trailers parked in the area during holidays, some apparently on a semi-permanent basis with wooden fences defining territorial claims. However, things finally got out of hand, and overnight camping is now (1991) prohibited. Reefs along the beach provide the best diving in the vicinity, and parts of the wreck lie in five to forty feet. Moorish idols and fantastic Indo-Pacific reef fish with an ornate black, yellow and white color scheme and long trailing fins inhabit the area, often in pairs or small schools, and occasional longnose butterfly fish can be seen. Thoughtless people anchoring on the reef are damaging the corals, and the bottom is becoming littered with beer cans, cast-off rope and fishing line.
5+	"Monuments." Left reef break. This small area is in just the right place to catch northwest swells refracted around Cabo San Lucas, providing the most consistent surfing in the area. Turn south at the H-shaped concrete monument, signed "Mirador del Médano," drive 0.4 mile southeast and hike for two minutes to the sandy cove. The dirt road has been improved and sedans can make it with little difficulty.
5	El Arco Trailer Park. Full hookups, showers, toilets, restaurant, ice, pool.
4	Cabo Cielo RV Park. Full hookups, toilets, showers.
3	Vagabundos del Mar RV Park. Full hookups, pool, showers, restrooms, laundry machines, bar, cafe. Ice-making plant, north side of road.
0	**Cabo San Lucas**. This is it, the end of the Transpeninsular!

CABO SAN LUCAS

There seems to be a greater percentage of Americans and Canadians in the day-to-day population of Cabo San Lucas than any other town in Baja. Crews from the vast fleet of yachts at anchor in the harbor wander the streets at all hours, wearing studied uniforms of faded T-shirts emblazoned with the logos of ritzy handball emporiums, frayed white shorts and rotted running shoes. Subconsciously wishing to call public attention to the fact that they have survived the perilous voyage from San Diego, they walk slowly through town with a slight but still rakish swagger, faint whiffs of alcohol and pretended massive indifference permeating the air. Hemingway would have understood. An almost continuous parade of vans, daisy-painted ex-school buses and magnificent motor coaches clogs the narrow lane-and-a-half streets, their occupants often pouring out to invade the Giggling Marlin (1) in search of beers and burgers.

Time is not being kind to those who love the place for what it was in the old days. In an effort to make a good first impression, officials have caused several hundred yards of new four-lane, mercury-lighted highway to be built into the eastern outskirts of town, only to plunge traffic abruptly into its crowded center. Construction of hotels and condominiums threatens to overwhelm the place and will certainly change its character. A gigantic new hotel looms over the marina, no structure in North America less suited architecturally to its surroundings. Its exterior color, previously unknown to all but professors of optical physics, can only be described as "shocking terra cotta." Even so, Cabo San Lucas is still the most lively and thoroughly amiable town in Baja, although one wonders how long it can last, for certainly the growing hustle and bustle must someday bring gridlock.

The waters around Cabo San Lucas provide some of the finest fishing in the world. The winter of 1985-86 was the premier year in its marlin history, most boats getting multiple hookups each day. In April and May it was not uncommon to see five or six finning stripers within a circle a hundred yards across, and many fishermen reported active competition among the fish over which would be first to take the bait. Several light-tackle fishermen in a *panga* reportedly collected twenty-two hookups in one day (none boated due to their ultra-light tackle), and a group of three men in a small trailerboat reported eighty-five marlin caught and released in five days. There is year-round fishing for stripers, sailfish, wahoo and dolphins, the warm months being best, and in addition to these species, roosters and yellowfin tuna often move into the area. Yellowtail that have migrated from the cold waters of the northern Cortez are found between January and May.

Four of the best marlin areas are Banco San Jaime, 18 miles, 252° from Cabo Falso; Banco Golden Gate, 19 miles, 293° from Falso; Banco Gorda Primero, 8 1/2 miles, 095° from the San José del Cabo lighthouse; and Banco Gorda Segundo, 11 miles, 095° from the San José del Cabo lighthouse. Run 23 miles, 056° from Cabo San Lucas for Gorda Primero. The "95 Spot" and "The Dropoff," 9 miles, 106° and 12 miles, 160°, respectively, from Los Frailes (the large granite rocks that seem to form the "end" of the peninsula) are also good but harder to find. Many marlin also are caught between Frailes and Falso, where the 100-fathom line comes within a mile of shore. Fishermen with cartoppers or inflatables have an excellent chance for a marlin by drifting live bait in this area, as described in Chapter 3. Yachtsmen coming from Mazatlan report large numbers of sailfish at Cabrillo Seamount, 26 miles, 110° from the San José del Cabo lighthouse.

There are, of course, numerous other species in Cape waters. Dolphin are often taken incidentally by marlin fishermen. Bancos Gorda Primera and San Jaime produce many

Cabo San Lucas and Los Frailes.

Los Frailes

Bahía San Lucas

Playa de Amor

Playa el Medano

To La Paz

Bahía San Lucas

Blvd. Marina

Madero

Guerrero

M. de León

Farias

Mendoza

Vicario

Morelos

Zaragoza

Ocampo

Abasolo

To Todos Santos

Matamoros

Hidalgo

San Lucas

Mateos

Green

Miguel

Ortega

Morelos

Anikan

12 de Oct.

Obregón

Carranza

Revolución

20 de Nov.

Libertad

16 de Sept.

Niños

Constitución

5 de Mayo

Carranza

Serdan

Zapata

Camino de Cerro

CABO SAN LUCAS

STATUTE MILES

0   0.25

fine wahoo, and when water temperatures are normal (non-El Niño years) they may come close to shore between Bahía Chileno and Bahía Santa María, and between Frailes and Falso. The area just west of Punta Palmilla, known locally as "Red Hill," is also excellent for wahoo, often in water less than 200 feet deep. Trollers sometimes work roosters right in front of the Hotel Solmar (2), but be careful of the waves—more than one boat has been tossed here. Excellent wahoo and dolphin fishing can be found in 125-300 feet along the beach from Falso to Punta los Arcos (Punta San Cristobal). The beach immediately west of Frailes can be a hot spot for shorecasters, and yellowtail, roosters and even dolphins are possible.

A large fleet of sportfishing boats is available. The Solmar has a fleet of cruisers ranging from twenty-six to sixty feet. A fishing trip/cruise to Isla Socorro, 250 miles south, may be available. The Finisterra Tortuga Sportfishing Fleet has information and reservations desks at the Hotel Finisterra (3) and Hotel Mar de Cortez (4). Pisces Fleet (5) has a variety of boats, ranging from *pangas* to a thirty-four-foot cruiser, fishing equipment, box lunches and live and frozen bait. Admirably, Pisces encourages catch-and-release, and will provide a trophy for fish given their freedom. Both fleets have U.S. reservation and information offices, listed in Appendix A. Freelance boat operators will be found at the docks.

One of the most interesting SCUBA dives in Baja can be made in the outer harbor. The narrow strip of land leading out to Frailes is overtopped by waves during storms, carrying sand into the bay. Several tributaries of an enormous underwater canyon begin between the mouth of the inner harbor and Frailes. Starting with a rather modest slope, the canyon begins to descend at an average of 75% within a few hundred feet. It then levels off to a slope of 10%, which it maintains until the water is 6,000 feet deep. Granite walls tower over the bottom of the canyon, and at a depth of 5,400 feet the walls are over 3,000 feet high. Long rivers of excess sand from the beach flow down the tributaries of the canyon at a rate of 0.1 mile an hour, forming sandfalls when they reach cliffs. The sandfalls should be visited only by certified divers with deep water experience. The best place to start a dive is half-way between the mouth of the inner harbor and Frailes, where an islet with a flat top will be seen sixty yards from shore. Follow the slope down and start watching for falls at 100 feet. Most sandfalls are intermittent, but the chances of seeing at least one cascading over the cliffs are good. Rocky areas are covered with lush growths of corals and gorgonians, and there are many species of fish to be seen, but touch nothing, for the bay is an underwater ecological reserve.

Banco Gorda Primero is another excellent dive site, although it is too deep for all but the most experienced divers, since its shallowest areas are about 110 feet. Nautical charts show one area at eight fathoms, but local black-coral divers insist it does not exist. The primary diving attractions at Gorda are the large numbers of heavy-duty gamefish, plus the chance to see black coral. In addition, Gorda is frequented by whale sharks. Some gray whales continue past the Cape during their annual migration, and divers have occasionally been able to swim with them.

There are other, less demanding dives in the area. An interesting wreck can be found in fifty feet of water on a sand bottom just southwest of the most southerly rock at Frailes. It is badly disintegrated, but is home to a number of interesting fish, including an occasional longnose butterfly fish. Be careful diving here, for sightseeing and fishing boats studiously ignore diver's flags. The wreck is often festooned with fishing lures, some quite expensive, a small treasure for the taking. Big jewfish occasionally visit the wreck in the summer months, and sea lions living nearby often accompany divers.

Amigos del Mar (6) has complete SCUBA equipment rentals and limited repairs, snorkeling equipment rentals and sales, compressed air, local snorkel tours, SCUBA tours of Pulmo and Gordo with bilingual guides, an open water certification course and a resort/refresher diving course. No spearfishing is permitted, although one-of-a-kind dead shelling is allowed. The shop operates two large trimarans, a pontoon boat and several *pangas*, and also offers sightseeing and whale-watching trips. Cabo Acuadeportes at the Hotel Hacienda Beach Resort (7) has the same basic service, instruction and rentals as their facility at Chileno described earlier, and offers local trips, including sandfalls dives.

The inner harbor has a concrete launch ramp (8) suitable for large trailerboats, although parking can be a problem. This ramp was damaged by rain in late 1990, but with luck should be repaired soon. Another concrete ramp (9) is available. The inner harbor is often crowded, especially from December to May, and the docks are almost always jammed. The accompanying city map shows the location of the COTP, customs, immigration and Pesca offices, as well as several outboard mechanics. There are long-standing plans to consolidate the COTP, customs and immigration offices at the main dock area, but nothing ever seems to happen. Yachties should check with the COTP about fueling arrangements. The ferry that once ran to Puerto Vallarta is out of operation (1991) and the terminal is deserted.

Although weather at the Cape is usually benign, at least during the non-*chubasco* months from mid-November to mid-May, occasional freak weather is possible. On December 8, 1982, a southeast gale caught the fleet of yachts anchored

Mike's first marlin, taken at Banco Gorda after a ninety-minute fight. It was released unharmed.

off Playa el Médano unprepared, wrecking twenty-two of them. Boaters headed for areas west of Falso should take care, for weather there is often very different—usually worse—from that observed off the harbor. Unofficial weather reports are broadcast on VHF channel 22 each morning.

Many other activities are possible. Los Frailes are an attraction for climbers. The easternmost rock is 222 feet high, the western 291 feet. Dotted with weird dikes and pockets, these solid, high-friction miniature mountains offer practice in face, crack and chimney climbing in an unusual setting, with routes at almost every skill level. El Trono Blanco it's not, but Frailes has something no other climb in Baja can claim; should you become prostrate from too much exertion, your buddies can carry you to the bar at the nearby Solmar for replenishment and rejuvenation. That thin vertical spire nearby rising 80 feet out of the water has been conquered, the climber taking the fast way down—he dove. In addition to diving, Cabo Acuadeportes offers sailboard rentals and instruction, and the Pisces Water Sport Center (10) offers water skiing, jet skis, Hobies, sailboards, kayaks and snorkeling trips. Playa el Médano is within walking distance of town and provides fine swimming, without undertow or heavy surf, and excellent conditions for novice boardsailors. A favorite activity of many visitors is a boat trip to Frailes, and boats leave from Playa el Médano and from the dock in the inner harbor all day. A glass-bottom boat also frequents the area.

Los Frailes is reputed to be the southernmost part of the

Barbara Busse climbs Los Frailes, undoubtedly the most southerly climbing location in Baja.

peninsula, but the real tip lies to the west. Perfectionists should proceed west from Frailes, 2.48 miles. This "point," virtually unnoticeable along an almost straight beach, is 437 yards south of Frailes. In fact, Frailes is only in third place; Falso, 1.86 miles further west, extends 327 yards south of Frailes.

There are numerous places to stay in Cabo San Lucas. The new Hotel Melia San Lucas (11) has rooms and suites with balconies and ocean views, restaurants, bars, coffee shop, beach, pools, tennis, volleyball, all water sports and a travel agency. The Solmar has rooms and suites with beach entrances or balconies, restaurant, bar, gift shop and car rental agency, and offers many recreational activities, including horseback riding, tennis, volleyball, swimming, SCUBA diving and fishing. The Hacienda has rooms, suites, cabanas and townhouses, restaurant and several bars, and offers a nice sand beach, swimming pool, volleyball, tennis, boardsailing, boating, water skiing, putting green, horseback riding, fishing trips, a dive shop (described earlier) and car rentals. The Finisterra has rooms, suites and villas, restaurant, bars, a boutique and a health spa, and such activities as swimming and tennis. There are sportfishing, sightseeing and car rental desks in the lobby. The Mar de Cortez has relatively inexpensive rooms and suites with baths, swimming pool, restaurant and bar, and offers SCUBA diving, sportfishing and Jeep and car rentals. There are a number of good RV parks on the Transpeninsular east of town. There are many other places to stay—consult with the travel agents listed on page 81. Besides the Giggling Marlin and those in the hotels mentioned earlier, there are almost fifty restaurants in town, in every price range and food preference possible, including seafood, steak, pizza, L.A.-deli, Japanese, Chinese, Italian, American, French, Spanish and even Mexican.

In Cabo San Lucas, heading northwest for Todos Santos

Although this paved road crosses many arroyos, most grades are gentle and only a few are very long. There are many spur roads to fine beaches and good camping. Bicyclists will find the trip to Todos Santos enjoyable and undemanding. Birders should keep a sharp eye out for the dramatic crested

A near-miss at Pescadero.

caracara and uncommon pyrrhuloxia, Swainson's hawk, painted and lazuli bunting, and dickissel, and the endemic Xanthus hummingbird and Belding's yellowthroat. More ordinary species include gray flycatcher, Cassin's kingbird, purple martin, varied bunting, common raven, water pipit, white-wing dove, Wilson's warbler and northern cardinal. The groove-billed ani has been considered extinct since before 1900, but who knows . . . ?

KM	LOCATION
124	Begin at the intersection of Av. Cardenas (main drag) and Av. Morelos. Set odometer and drive northwest on Morelos. At Mile 0.7 the road swings left (260°), at Mile 1.1 right (330°), and at Mile 1.2 you will be at KM 122 on Route 19.
107+	**Playa San Cristobal**. Public beach.
102	Public beach.
97	**Migriño**. Beautiful public beach, right breaks on point. A sandy road parallels the beach for miles, providing access to many fine campsites.
91	Road left (205°) to Boca el Barranco. Right reef breaks, sand beach.
86	**Cabo el Cajoncito**. Public beach.
81+	**Las Cabrillas**. Public beach.
78	**Plutarco Elias Calles**. Settlement.
73+	**Punta Gasparino**. Good right point breaks on large waves.
71+	Western end of the Naranjas Road, signed "Sp. de la Soledad."
64	Road left (219°) 1.6 miles to Playa los Cerritos. Public beach, point and beach breaks. Although the abandoned RV park here has no facilities or services it is becoming an increasingly popular stop anyway. The water in a cistern just east of the park building is allegedly good to drink.
62	**El Pescadero**. Cafes, groceries, *tortilla* factory, water. The main part of town lies east of the road. The reef and beach breaks in this vicinity consistently produce fine surfing, with steep faces and short, fast rides. Boardsailors also love the place. Road east to Santo Domingo.

SIDETRIP TO SANTO DOMINGO

As noted earlier in this chapter, the roadhead at Santo Domingo is the end point of the Cañon San Bernardo backpack trip. Turn east (095°) 0.4 mile northwest of the KM 62 marker. Set odometer, and at Mile 0.4 take the left (070°) fork near the village stadium, take the right (056°) fork at Mile 0.8, and the left (006°) fork at Mile 5.8. Take the left (320°) fork at Mile 6.1, turn right (065°) at Mile 6.8, and right (074°) at Mile 7.5. The grading ends here and the road requires a pickup. Take the left (058°) fork at Mile 9.2, and go straight ahead (107°) at Mile 12.3, and straight ahead (030°) at Mile 12.9, arriving at the settlement at Mile 13.3.

Back on Route 19 at KM 62

| 59 | Sedan road west to public beach and San Perdito RV Park. This popular park has full hookups, restaurant, |

bar, pool, restrooms, showers, laundry. Surfers like the beach break.

| 55+ | Road east to Rancho San Juan del Aserradero. |

SIDETRIP TO SAN JUAN DEL ASERRADERO

This ranch is often the starting point for backpacking and mule forays to La Laguna. Although steep, the trail is only about seven miles long and it may be cooled by fogs and winds off the ocean. The trip up by mule will take only about four hours, making it a temptation to try to make the trip a one-day affair, but make it an overnighter, for there is much to see. A round-trip afoot should take at least three days, including exploring time. To get to the ranch, turn northeast (059°) 0.3 mile north of the KM 55 marker, cross a cattle guard and set odometer. The steep face seen at 045° at this point is Cerro la Aguja. Go straight ahead (140°) at Mile 2.2, pass a forest-fire tower at Mile 2.7, go left (043°) at Mile 3.9, straight ahead (030°) at Mile 8.8, left (015°) at Mile 10.8, straight ahead (090°) at Mile 12.7 and arrive at the ranch at Mile 13.5. The road can handle sedans, although a 21% downgrade at Mile 12.3 may cause problems on the way out.

The trail departs the ranch in an easterly direction, quickly swinging north and continuing up the north side of Cañada San Matías. At the half-way point a water source may be encountered. On the ridge above Cañon El Frijolar, Picacho Cerro La Laguna can be seen just over a mile to the north. As the altitude gets higher oaks and then pines appear, providing welcome shade. Mexican 1:50,000 topos Las Cuevas F12B24 and El Rosario F12B23 show a close approximation of the route, the first also showing the route from Rancho San Dionisio. "El Rosario" shows the ranch on its lower margin; the next topo to the south, Todos Santos F12B33, shows the roads and intersections on the way to the ranch from Route 19, as described above.

Back on Route 19 at KM 55

| 51+ | **Todos Santos**. PEMEX (MND), stores, groceries, motel, laundry, auto parts, telephone, telegraph, mail, mechanic, tires, bank, medical, dental, pharmacy, liquor, cinema, *tortilla* factory, water from spigots. There are a half-dozen small restaurants, some of them offering locally grown organic produce. Some claim that the Santa Monica Restaurant, on Route 19 just south of the main part of town, has the best oysters in North America. The historic Hotel California has rooms with baths, pool, restaurant and cantina. El Molino RV Park, just west of the PEMEX, occupies the grounds of an old sugar mill and offers full hookups, restrooms, showers and laundry, all shaded by avocado, papaya and eucalyptus. There is also a *palapa* restaurant, and the Sunday brunch is popular. A pleasant agricultural town, once the site of a Jesuit mission, Todos Santos is now the home of a number of painters, potters, woodcarvers and other artists. There is even a tiny museum; the Casa Cultura has red-dyed skulls of Pericru Indians, pottery, baskets and other local crafts, historical displays, photos of the old sugar days, and a |

small collection of rocks and minerals. To the west are a number of good beach breaks and several freshwater esteros. The highway north is easy biking. Although parts are fenced, you should have little trouble finding a sideroad leading to a flat spot to camp.

0   Junction with the Transpeninsular Highway at KM 185.

****

LAS CUEVAS DE LOS INDIOS. A number of years ago I stopped at La Ciéneguita, a tiny settlement on the newly bulldozed Naranjas Road across the Victorias. The local people were having a volleyball game, but as I drove up the women and children ran in terror and the adult men formed a small arc and approached my van with grim looks. The place had been almost totally isolated until the road was constructed, and it was obvious that the inhabitants were not used to strangers and had no intention of becoming so. They appeared to be rather unsophisticated, almost the image of the traditional American hillbilly. Some of the men had dental work that appeared homemade, with equal amounts of tooth enamel and gold showing, the latter worked into fleur-de-lis and other heraldic devices.

I was scouting for "new" caves, and when I asked whether there were any in the vicinity they said no, rather too emphatically. Hoping to pry out the information with an ancient device, I opened a large cooler full of Dos Equis and a gallon of home made wine, and within minutes I had their rapt attention and full cooperation. There was perhaps a small cave of little consequence up the road, they admitted, and as the alcohol flowed the cave assumed grander proportions. There were actually three of them, known as "Las Cuevas de los Indios," and they were so large that entire tribes of ancient Indians used to gather in them for magic ceremonies. When I announced, just at the end of the fifth six-pack, that I wanted to explore the caves and needed a guide, there was a rush for the van and before I could protest it was jammed with the entire male population of La Ciéneguita. The weight was so great that we barely made it up the first small grade, a problem somewhat relieved when half of my guides demanded a stop for a call of nature. Singing and joking, we

continued on our journey, but there was soon a call for another stop and the other half relieved themselves. This place, however, was also the closest approach to the caves.

None of my guides were in any condition to perform their duties, but two of the more sober got out of the van, promising the grandest of all caves. However, as we climbed down a steep gorge I began to notice that it was increasingly hard to keep them on the subject of caves; they wanted to talk about deer hunting. As we approached the caves the reason became apparent—the tribes must have been elves. Instead of the grand Cuevas de los Indios I had been promised, we found several small grottos, distinguished only by the presence of a few emaciated bats hanging dejectedly from the ceilings. The third grotto could be approached only by rappelling down from above, but given the diluted state of the blood of those who would be on belay, I was not about to stretch my luck.

As we hiked up the gorge toward the sound of music coming from the van, my guides sheepishly turned the conversation back to deer hunting. When that didn't work they started a short seminar on native medicine. Every few yards they dismantled a bush or uprooted a shrub, assuring me that the sap, leaf or bark was good for cancer, rheumatism, piles and/or impotence, apparently hoping that I suffered from one or more and thereby gaining my interest. I was surprised to find that one medicine actually did work, rather dramatically in fact. When I scraped my hand on a thorn they gleefully broke a branch from a low, woody shrub with reddish bark they called lomboy colorado *and rubbed the clear astringent sap on the wound. Within seconds the bleeding stopped and by the next day the scrape could hardly be seen. When we reached the van the medical seminar ended and one of my guides returned to the subject of caves. With a golden grin he said that it was a shame that I had chosen not to explore the third cave, for it was the one the Indians really had used. A real shame! With everyone singing raunchy songs, we returned to La Ciéneguita, party-time continuing until the cooler was empty. My new friends were perhaps a bit unsophisticated and given to exaggeration, but they proved to be friendly, intelligent and well-informed about their small part of the world.*

****

CHAPTER 16
TECATE TO SAN FELIPE

By necessity the organization of this chapter will be more complex than its predecessors. We will follow Route 2 from Tijuana to Mexicali, with five sidetrips south: (1) Route 3 to Ensenada, (2) the Alvarez-Ojos Negros road, (3) Parque Nacional Constitución de 1857, (4) the La Rumorosa-Parque 1857 road, and (5) the Palm Canyon area. From Mexicali we will head south on Route 5 to Crucero la Trinidad. From this point we will return to Ensenada and cover Route 3 back to Route 5, then travel south through San Felipe, Puertecitos and Bahía Gonzaga, ending the chapter on the Transpeninsular. Use the regional map in Chapter 10. Maps of the Sierra de Juárez/Palm Canyon area and the San Felipe-Puertecitos area will appear when needed.

On Route 2 at Tijuana

KM	LOCATION
185	**Tijuana**.
136	PEMEX (N).
132	**Tecate**. This small, tourist-oriented city has a variety of supplies and services. The border crossing is generally uncrowded, at least by Tijuana standards, and is open from 6 a.m. to midnight. There is a *Migración* office where tourist cards can be obtained and validated, but it is often closed on Sundays. Local information can be obtained from the office of the State Secretary of Tourism on the south side of the park at the corner of Route 3 (Av. Benito Juárez) and Av. Ortiz Rubio.

SIDETRIP TO ENSENADA ON ROUTE 3

This route is very scenic, with rolling hills and large boulders. Bicyclists will find it challenging, with headwinds and long grades. There are many small stores, and thirsty bikers will find everything from tequila to orange juice, but increased fence-building is making it difficult to find places to camp.

10+	**Tanamá**. Pyrites have been found nearby.
27	**Valle las Palmas**. Tires, cafes, groceries, ice, medical.
35	Begin moderate upgrades, averaging 7%.
40	Highest point on this section of Route 3, 2,130 feet. Begin downgrades to KM 47.
64	Possible place to camp among the oaks, but noisy.
73	Road east to Rancho Agua Caliente.

SIDETRIP TO THE CUEVAS DE AGUA CALIENTE

The area surrounding Rancho Agua Caliente consists of plutonic rocks, but the ranch itself is on limestone and is the site of two fine solution caves. In recent years a gate has occasionally blocked the way, and permission to visit the caves has sometimes been refused when requested at the ranch to be noted shortly. There is no way to determine this in advance, and no phone where current information can be obtained, so the only course of action is to try to get in and see what happens.

Opposite the Domecq winery warehouse, turn east on a sedan road and set odometer. At Mile 1.1 turn north, at Mile 1.9 east, and at Mile 4.0 encounter a stream, which most vehicles should be able to ford safely in dry weather. However, at Mile 5.2 another crossing has soft sand where even four-wheel-drives sometime have problems. Park, ford the stream and hike up the canyon. At Minute 30 arrive at the ranch, identified by meteorological and hydrological apparatus. Stop, pay your respects and ask permission to continue, while simultaneously jutting forth a cold six-pack.

At Minute 20 (from the ranch) encounter a cliff on the south side of the stream. A tributary stream in a small arroyo above the cliff sometimes forms a fine waterfall. The caves are in this arroyo. Continue up the main stream 150 feet past the cliff, scramble up the steep, rocky slope and hike up the tributary stream for fifteen minutes. The first cave is 30 feet above the streambed on the right side. A climb down through a 2-by-3-foot entrance leads to a multilevel maze cave several hundred feet long. This cave has chambers up to 30 feet high, and hidden passages, squeezes, breakdown blocks, ledges, drops, flowstones, ceiling domes and a number of natural

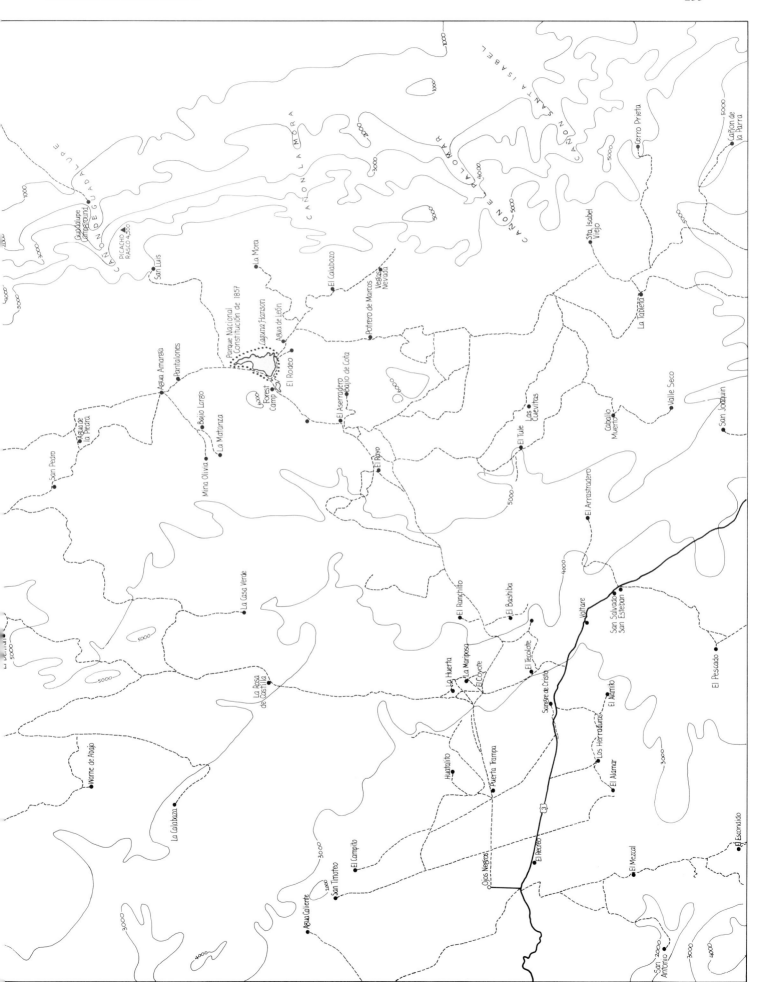

Modest Mike insisted that his dad take this photograph of him skinny-dipping in a tiny pool above the Río Guadalupe from a *long* distance away.

bridges. Cavers have sometimes found it necessary to dig through breakdown clogs. The second cave is on the right side 90 feet farther upstream, 100 feet above the streambed. A 3-by-4-foot entrance leads to an L-shaped chamber 125 feet long, 20 feet wide and 10 feet high.

Back on Route 3 at KM 73

77   **Guadalupe junction**. Tires, cafe, groceries, liquor. The paved road right (210°) leads into the village, where a PEMEX (MN), mechanic, bakery, auto parts, doctor, pharmacy, post office, meat market and hardware will be found. Fleeing persecution in Russia, a religious sect known as the Malakans founded a colony here in 1905, but today little differentiates the village other than an occasional head of blond or red hair.

83   Trailer park with full hookups, but open for business only erratically.

93   Restaurant, mechanic, tire repairs, small RV park with full hookups and showers.

94   **Villa de Juárez**. Grocery store. Cuprite, silver and gold have been found nearby.

98   Long downgrades to Route 1.

105   Junction with Route 1.

Back on Route 2 at Tecate

Bicyclists heading east will not appreciate the heavy traffic, rolling hills and increasing elevation, but occasional stores sell cold sodas to help ease the pain.

122   **San Pablo**. PEMEX (MND). An old caver's publication noted a large gypsum cave in this vicinity, but it seems to have become "lost" in recent years.

109+   Possible source of bicycle repairs and used parts.

109   PEMEX (MND), tiny cafe, groceries, tire repair.

98   **Ejido Luis Echeverria Alvarez**. Road south to Ojos Negros.

SIDETRIP ON THE ALVAREZ-OJOS NEGROS ROAD

This pleasant trip crosses fine rolling chaparral country dotted with pine-rimmed meadows and groves of oaks. The area is heavily mineralized, and collectors could look for pegmatites. The road is generally in good condition, with no bad grades, not much change in altitude and only two sizable stream crossings, both of which are sandy and flat, so almost any vehicle except low-slung sedans can make it. Although there are many minor forks and intersections, the correct road is usually obvious and there is little danger of becoming lost. The appropriate 1:50,000 topographic maps for the area along this road and west to the Palm Canyon area are La Rumorosa I11D63, El Centinela I11D64, Nejí I11D73, La Poderosa I11D74, San Juan de Dios I11D83, Arroyo de Sauz I11D84,

Members of Baja's Club Pedal y Fibre swing past Guadalupe.

Real del Castillo Nuevo H11B13 and El Rayo H11B14.

The road starts south 0.1 mile east of the KM 98 marker. Set odometer. The pavement ends at Mile 4.7. At Mile 8.8 continue straight ahead (183°) at the fork. Rancho Nejí is reached at Mile 11.3. Continue straight ahead (125°) at Mile 12.4, and at Mile 18.8 turn right (140°), passing through El Compadre, a small settlement graced by enormous oaks. The road then crosses several streams, passes large meadows and several ranches on either side of San Faustino at Mile 29.0, and runs through a series of majestic oak groves, offering fine places to camp. At Mile 36.7 wheel tracks lead two miles north to a tungsten deposit.

After you pass more oak groves, La Rosa de Castilla, a tiny ranching community, is reached at Mile 42.6. The tailings of Mina el Fenómeno can be seen on the ridge to the west. As its name implies, the mine was a phenomenon of its time, producing over 2% of the world's supply of tungsten during its short working life. By 1943 the 100,000-ton ore body was exhausted, and today the mine is a totally deserted but fascinating place. The west flank of the ridge has cool, mysterious mine shafts. Look for thousands of cast iron balls used in the mill to crush scheelite. Minerals to be found include apophyllite, garnet, calcite, quartz, malachite, azurite, schorl, actinolite, arsenopyrite, bismuth, pyrite, chalcopyrite, clinozoisite, diopside, scheelite, hedenbergite, idocrase, pyrrhotite, axinite, epidote and prehnite. Surrounding areas contain many mine shafts, tailing dumps and signs of pegmatites. A pegmatite on a ridge about 500 yards east has yielded small yellow-to-lavender tourmaline crystals, and sapphire has been found to the southwest.

La Huerta, a small settlement, is reached at Mile 50.8, and at Mile 52.1 El Coyote, an important junction, unmarked except for a barbed-wire fence with metal posts, a rarity in Baja. To continue on to Ojos Negros, drive straight ahead (255°), arriving at Mile 61.1. If you intend to head for Parque Nacional Constitución de 1857 turn left (110°), and you will encounter the KM 55+-Parque 1857 road in three miles.

Back on Route 2 at KM 98

89+   The La Jollita pegmatites, an extension of well-known mineral deposits in the U.S., are located to the north. Turn onto the road signed "Jacumé," turn east below the power lines at Mile 0.2, and park at Mile 0.4. The light-colored rocks on the hillsides are remnants of pegmatite dikes, yielding green tourmaline, blue topaz, cleavelandite, muscovite, beryl, microcline, apatite and lots of schorl.

83   **El Cóndor.** PEMEX (MND), restaurant, road south.

SIDETRIP TO PARQUE NACIONAL CONSTITUCIÓN DE 1857

An ever-changing maze of roads from El Cóndor to the park makes a compass useful, and there are enough rough spots that sedans are not recommended. The road running north from KM 55+ on Route 3 into the park is in better condition, allowing those in sedans easier access.

The road from El Cóndor heads south next to the PEMEX station. Set odometer, and take the left (145°) fork at Mile

STEPHEN PETERSON

Climbers work their way up El Trono Blanco.

11.4. The surrounding areas are among the most heavily mineralized in Baja, with many gold, tungsten, manganese and cobalt mines. Collectors have found clinozoisite, quartz, axinite, grossularite garnet, blue tourmaline and epidote. Keep left (123°) at the intersection at Mile 12.0. La Mesquita, near Mile 13.0, is known for beryl, aquamarine and apatite mined from vugs in a pegmatite. At the crossroads at Mile 17.0 note the sign "*Evite Incendios*" and continue straight (141°) ahead. (The right (179°) fork leads to the Las Margaritas and Gavilanes mineral areas.) Take the left (128°) fork at Mile 17.5, and at Mile 18.0 join the La Rumorosa-Parque 1857 road; continue southeast (125°). The sideroad east at Mile 20.0 leads to the Rancho San Ignacio-La Milla area, jumping-off point for hikes into Cañon Tajo.

SIDETRIP TO CAÑON TAJO

The upper reaches of Cañon Tajo approach this point.

A Cañon Tajo swimming hole.

Largest of the canyons in the Juárez escarpment, Tajo is also the most colorful, with broad bands of white, green, black, red, brown, beige and tan frozen into its rocks. Thousands of palms line the canyon, firewood is plentiful and there are many campsites, some next to fine swimming holes. El Trono Blanco, Baja's supreme technical climbing challenge, lies at the head of the canyon at the confluence of its northwest and south forks.

The easiest approach to El Trono Blanco and into the main canyon is by way of "Bell Dome" campground. Turn east at Mile 20.0 onto a pickup road signed "Rancho San Ignacio-La Milla," set odometer and turn right (160°) at Mile 1.1. You will pass a tiny ranch on the right, and the road will begin to meander. Stay left at every fork, and at Mile 3.8 you will arrive at the small, clean campground (no facilities). A canyon will be noted bearing 095°, with a bell-shaped dome on the left, a steep rock cliff on the right. The uphill foot route east from the campground soon passes through an area of massive boulders requiring a great deal of scrambling and even some travel on hands and knees through dark passages. In fact, if you need some bouldering practice this is the place to do it. After about forty-five minutes the pass is reached and there are glimpses of what lies ahead, the bottom of a gigantic canyon 2,300 feet below and a great wall of rock to the left. The canyon ahead is Tajo's south fork, about a mile from its junction with the main east-west canyon. As you drop into the canyon it becomes steeper, and although the brush grows thicker little heed will be given to it as the proportions of the awesome 1,600-foot wall become more apparent. Composed of lightly weathered granite with large feldspar crystals, it

provides excellent climbing conditions, so much so that one San Diego climber has made fifty ascents. The descent from the campground will take about three hours, and there is no water until the bottom of the canyon.

An eagle's-eye view of Tajo can be found by hiking from the La Milla campground to a ridge overlooking the canyon. Return to the fork at Mile 1.1, reset your odometer and drive northwest (320°). The road will meander north and then east toward the Juárez escarpment. Swing right (090°) at the forks at Miles 0.6 and 0.7, left (090°) at Mile 0.8, and arrive at the campground at Mile 1.7 (no facilities). There is no trail to the ridge, but the country is fairly open and hiking is easy. Simply head east from the campground for about an hour, avoiding dropping too deeply into the northwest fork of the canyon, which approaches the campground.

Backpackers wishing to experience one of Baja's most challenging trips can drop down into the main canyon by way of the northwest fork. This trip is shorter but more difficult than Cañon del Diablo, described beginning on page 245. Since the return trip back to the campground involves stretches of technical climbing, virtually everyone making the trip arranges to be picked up at the mouth of the canyon. The horizontal distance involved, about eight miles from the campground to the head of the road leading west from the Laguna Salada area, is deceptive, and at least three days should be set aside for a one-way trip, including some loafing and exploring time. Careful route finding will keep it a marginal class 3, and it would be well to bring a rope to allow lowering backpacks down chasms. The appropriate 1:50,000 Mexican topo is La Poderosa I11D74. Though not labeled, the canyon is shown along the bottom margin.

The northwest fork of the canyon is entered by hiking 165° from the campground. The open and relatively level terrain during the first half-hour will instill undue confidence, but the moment of reckoning will soon approach. The terrain quickly becomes steeper and the underbrush denser, and by the time you see the first palms you will be wishing you had taken the route from Bell Dome. Horizontal progress is irrelevant; it's the vertical that matters. Great boulders lie jumbled, one on top of the other, and the term "boulder-hopping" becomes meaningless—you don't hop but rather struggle from one down to the next, sliding on seat bottoms, securing hand- and footholds as they present themselves, and skidding your pack along. The first pools will be encountered within an hour. There are rewards for all this work; a number of beautiful, thready waterfalls drop into crystal-clear pools, some a dozen feet deep, slowing the progress of those who can't resist a skinny-dip in each one. Working around the first thirty-foot waterfall is a real challenge, but greater ones lie below, including a sixty-footer. Watch for tourmaline crystals. Incredibly, it will take a long, hard day to arrive at the bottom of the main canyon, less than 1 1/2 miles from the campground.

The main canyon, lying east of El Trono Blanco, is less steep than the northwest fork but is still challenging. Great numbers of palms continue for the next three miles, amid huge piles of boulders and pools of water, after which the canyon floor becomes broader and more sandy. Fill all canteens, for the stream soon disappears under the sand, and no surface water will be found to the east. Considerable effort can be saved by hiking on cattle trails along the south side of the canyon. You will arrive at the roadhead sore, sweating and thoroughly tired but happy with a new experience.

Back on the Parque 1857 Road at Mile 20

A tungsten mine was once located southeast of Mile 20.0. Starting at this point there are great views of "Picacho Row," a line of miniature granite spires rising up to 500 feet above the tableland, with many spires, chimneys and domes (one of which is Bell Dome), some offering fine rock climbing. Continue straight ahead (150°) at the intersection at Mile 24.0. Mina el Topo near Mile 24.5 produced gold and cuprite. "Rough stuff" is encountered between Miles 25.5 and 28 as the road climbs a ridge. Take the left (114°) fork at the intersection at Mile 30.6.

At Mile 34.5 a pickup road leads 3 1/2 miles southwest to Mina Olivia, producing scheelite. In 1964 an odd spherical formation of axinite was uncovered there, and within several months 1,200 pounds had been removed. Most crystals were flawed, but 50 pounds were of gem quality, and one crystal, cut into a beautiful flawless gem of almost twenty-four carats, is in the National Museum in Washington, D.C. The mine owner estimates the crystals sold for $400,000 at retail, but laments that little was realized by him or the lucky miners. When news of this world-class find reached the outside world a mob of collectors and opportunists headed for the mine, but no more crystals were found and the excitement quickly died out. However, small amounts of axinite and clinozoisite are found nearby, and the owner is friendly and may provide collecting suggestions.

At Mile 35.5 encounter an abandoned forest-fire camp, and at Mile 37.3 a pickup road (signed) northeast to Rancho San Luis, seven miles. This ranch is near the upper reaches of Cañon de Guadalupe, only four miles from the Guadalupe campground as the crow flies. Since there are no established trails, a trip into the canyon is strictly a compass-and-topo proposition. The reward at the end will be a soak in a hot tub. See Arroyo del Sauz I11D84 for this and other hikes in the vicinity of Laguna Hanson.

El Trono Blanco from the floor of the canyon.

REEVE PETERSON

Much of the park is above 4,000 feet, and the chaparral of lower regions has given away to the cool pine forests and dry meadows of the Sierra de Juárez. Shallow and muddy Laguna Hanson, at Mile 38.9, is less than a mile across but home to many water birds. Campsites are available around the shores of the lake, a few with tables. Potable water can be obtained from a tiny seep at the forest camp 1/2 mile southwest. You will rarely see more than a half-dozen campers, but during Easter vacation it can become a scene from Hell: hundreds of people sitting in pickups, swilling beer and roasting chunks of meat over fires, with ATVs and trail bikes splitting the blue air. A week later all is quiet again.

A POT OF TROUBLE

Most place names in Baja California are, of course, in Spanish, and many are after saints—the index lists over 150 names beginning with "San. . ." and "Santa. . ." Place names in English are unusual, and one that immediately strikes the eye is "Laguna Hanson." "Lake Hanson" got its name from a strange incident in the minor history of Baja.

The discovery of gold at Real del Castillo, located east of Ensenada, in 1870 attracted a horde of international adventurers to northern Baja and the Sierra de Juárez. However, not everyone there was gold-crazy. In 1872 an American named Hanson drifted into the area. Twenty-four years old and something of a dreamer, he was attracted to the beauty of the forest and its wildlife, and he "discovered" the lake that now bears his name (the local Indians knew it well, of course). Popular with the locals, he assumed the management of Rancho El Rayo, located on the southwestern outskirts of what is now the national park.

One morning in 1880 the local people awoke with a sense of foreboding—during the night the livestock had broken out of the corrals, and a white calf had been seen running into the woods, a bad omen to the superstitious people. They soon noticed that Hanson was not to be found, although a fire was still burning beneath a huge iron caldron near his home. Inexplicably, an American friend of Hanson's named Harvey appeared. He was uncharacteristically friendly and generous, distributing gifts of clothes and *huaraches* to the adults, and passing out handfuls of sugar cubes to the children. Scarcely noticed was a strange odor coming from the cauldron.

Several weeks passed and concern for Hanson faded—the locals simply assumed he had suddenly decided to leave Baja and return home. One afternoon mounted police arrived, tied and gagged Harvey and dredged up the contents of the cauldron into a bag. The human bones found there were to be used as evidence in his trial. However, Harvey was too rich not to be able to buy his freedom, evidence or not, and within several months he was freed and fled to the United States.

Because of its altitude the park is cooler than surrounding areas, and there is little underbrush, making hiking enjoyable. There are no marked trails and no maps are available from rangers. The six-mile hike around the lake through the pines and meadows is pleasant. A number of granite peaks offer excellent climbs, and slabs, cracks and beautifully carved chimneys abound. You can see much of the surrounding country from class 3 formations rising to several hundred feet 500 yards northwest of the buildings at Mile 39.4. Picacho del Diablo, seventy-eight miles away, bears 140°. East is the Juárez escarpment, dropping precipitously to the desert floor. The escarpment can be approached on either of two roads south of the lake. Rolling waves of rock are passed before the sudden drop. Views from the top of the sharp-pointed peaks six miles east of the lake are smashing. The highest peak in the Juárez is 6,435-foot Cerro Colorado, somehow out of place in much lower tablelands forty-two miles southeast.

As might be expected, the Laguna Hanson area provides fine birding. Check lists might include the following: eared grebe, double-crested cormorant, tundra swan, mallard, northern pintail, northern shoveler, gadwal, American wigeon, canvasback, ring-necked and ruddy ducks, osprey, red-shouldered hawk, golden eagle, prairie falcon, Virginia rail, American coot, spotted sandpiper, Allen's hummingbird, Lewis's and acorn woodpeckers, red-breasted and Williamson's sapsuckers, black phoebe, western kingbird, purple martin, house wren, American robin, Townsend's warbler, western tanager, lazuli bunting, chipping, Brewer's, black-chinned and Lincoln's sparrows, and purple and Cassin's finches.

The road south starts near the buildings at the southwest end of the lake. Reset odometer. At Mile 0.4 pass the forest camp and another small lake, at Mile 1.1 a tree farm, at Mile 2.5 a ranch, and at Mile 3.9 arrive at El Aserradero (The Sawmill). The place is almost deserted, but you may be able to buy a meal at the first house on the left, and collectors can purchase mineral samples. The road from here on is in good condition, with many long downhill stretches. At Mile 6.6 pass more ranches and a small lake. A fine shaded campsite is at Mile 14.8.

Encounter a fork at Mile 16.5. Mina Verde, famous for huge crystals of danburite, among the largest in the world, is located less than a mile southeast of this point. Although the fork is important, it is unmarked and looks like just another place where drivers have made parallel roads to avoid bad spots, and if you don't look sharp it is easy to miss. If you are headed south (including those on the Two Parks Loop Trip), take the left branch, which immediately turns southeast to a fork reached in 0.8 mile. Take the right (180°) turn here and arrive on Route 3 at KM 55+.

Those on the Laguna Hanson Loop Trip and those headed for Ojos Negros should go straight ahead at the fork at Mile 16.5. The road immediately swings west, then drops through

A peaceful scene on Laguna Hanson.

WILL ASHFORD

a canyon and arrives at El Coyote, another important intersection, at Mile 19.4. Those on the Laguna Hanson Loop Trip should turn right (065°). The route north from this point to KM 98 on Route 2 was described beginning on page 336. Those heading for Ojos Negros should turn left (255°).

Back on Route 2 at El Cóndor, KM 83

KM   *LOCATION*
72   Road south to Cerro Teta de la India and Parque 1857.

SIDETRIP ON THE LA RUMOROSA-PARQUE 1857 ROAD

Turn southeast 0.2 mile east of the KM 72 marker, its location marked by three brick columns, and set odometer. Stop and sight 125°; Mexican cartographers gave the mountain 6 1/2 miles southeast the name "Cerro Teta de la India" (Indian Tit Hill) because of its shape, but less delicate locals call it simply "Chi Chi." The mountain serves as a useful landmark throughout the northern Sierra de Juárez. At Mile 1.9 encounter a park owned by the local *ejido*, with trees, fireplaces and a pavilion. Unfortunately it is often badly littered, and the water and sanitary facilities are usually inoperative. A pickup road runs east from Mile 7.3, shortening the approach to Chi Chi. After a class 2 scramble, a climber will be greeted with the best views in the Juárez. A naive friend of mine once set out to climb it, but the photos he produced upon his return showed he had chosen the less shapely mountain just to the west, apparently oblivious to the meaning of Chi Chi's official and unofficial names. A number of minerals have been reported nearby, including quartz, tourmaline, jasper and chalcedony. Arrive at the intersection with the El Cóndor-Parque 1857 Road at Mile 16.0, previously described.

Back on Route 2 at KM 72

71   **La Rumorosa**. PEMEX (MND, unreliable), stores, mail, restaurants, cafe, auto parts, tires.
68   There are fifteen miles of twisting downgrade averaging 5% between here and KM 44.
40   Pinto Wash, well known to U.S. mineral collectors, crosses the border into Baja north of this point.
28   Road south to the Palm Canyon area (signed "Cañon Guadalupe").

SIDETRIP TO THE PALM CANYON AREA

A series of wildly beautiful canyons are eroded into the Juárez escarpment. The road west of Laguna Salada passes through typical desert scrub, but in the canyons California fan palms, blue fan palms, smoke trees, cottonwoods and elephant trees can be found. The largest canyons, Tajo, El Carrizo, Guadalupe, La Mora and El Palomar, have surface water, often inhabited by such unlikely creatures as tree frogs, water striders and giant water bugs. Large emerald pools make fine swimming holes. Indians used the canyons as routes between the desert and the pine forests above. Virtually all portable artifacts were carried off long ago, but petroglyphs, pictographs, chipping waste, *metates* and pottery shards are common in the palm groves and around watered sites. The best time of year to visit is November through March, since temperatures at other times go well over 100 degrees.

A two-lane sedan road heads south at KM 28. Set odometer. At Mile 14.7 encounter Rancho La Poderosa, at Mile 20.7 shacks and a water tank, and at Mile 21.4 a road leading west toward the mouth of Cañon Tajo. El Trono Blanco is in plain view, looking deceptively close because of its massive size; it is actually over eight miles away. Pickups can get 1 1/2 miles west on this road before it becomes too soft, four-wheel-drives somewhat more.

Continue southeast to Mile 26.8 and turn southwest between irrigated fields. Note the pointed peak dominating the skyline ahead, Picacho Rasco, 4,500 feet, and the sharp spire, which is the Virgin of Guadalupe, named for a fancied likeness to the Madonna. Arrive at the campground at Mile 34.6. Although not on Tajo's grand scale, Guadalupe has three major blessings over it: a road into the mouth of the canyon, a campground, and hot tubs full of highly mineralized water at exactly the right temperature for loosening tight muscles and removing desert dust.

A small fee is charged for day use and camping. A year-round stream cascades through hundreds of palms and disappears in the alluvial fan below. A steep wash north of the campground has a group of twenty-foot boulders which offer excellent boulder problems. Views from the ridge above are well worth the class 3 climb to elevation 1,800 feet; the view of the mouth of the canyon is breathtaking. The Pool of the Virgin can be found two miles upstream. Bounded on three sides by white granite cliffs, surrounded by cottonwoods, willows, ferns and mosses, and fed by a slender waterfall, it seems out of place. Guadalupe can also be entered from the vicinity of Rancho San Luis, as noted earlier in this chapter.

Back on Route 2 at KM 28

24   **El Oasis**. PEMEX (MND), refreshment stand. Laguna Salada can be seen about six or eight miles south. In 1987, when the first edition of this book was completed, the lake was at a much higher level due to heavy flows of the Río Colorado. A road led a short distance to a camp on its shores, where fishermen could rent boats to pursue bass, crappie, carp and huge catfish. The continuing drought has reduced the size of the lake to where the shoreline is miles to the south; the change in only four years is remarkable.
0   Intersection of Routes 2 and 5. North-bound drivers headed for the U.S. border crossing at Calexico should head through Mexicali northwest on Calzada Benito Juárez (the extension of Route 5), turn half-right (north) onto Calzada Justo Sierra, and then turn left (west) on Av. Cristobal Colon, a one-way, west-bound street immediately south of the border fence. The border crossings are open twenty-four hours a day, seven days a week. Drivers headed south from the border crossing will find route signs directing them onto Calzada Lopéz Mateos at the first stoplight encountered after entering Mexico. Lopéz Mateos is the "main drag" running southeast through

town and crossing Benito Juárez at Mile 5.5 from the border. Signs noting the location of *Migración* and customs offices will be seen immediately south of the border crossing. No Mexicali driver in the city's history has ever been known to yield the right-of-way to another vehicle, and travelers should expect sulfurous fumes, suicidal pedestrians, supersonic taxis and sado-masochistic truckers. Mexicali is the capital of the state of Baja California [Norte] and has most supplies and services. Local information can be obtained from the office of the Mexicali Tourism and Convention Bureau (1). There is also an office of the Attorney General for the Protection of Tourists (2).

On Route 5 south of Mexicali

0   Start KM numbering sequence.

31   PEMEX (MND).

49   Pickup road west to the Mina Promontorio sulfur area. Set odometer. At Mile 1.0 a grade of 15% is encountered, the most difficult obstacle. At Mile 6.3 take the north fork, and arrive at Mile 9.4. The mine is fenced, but deposits are found throughout area, largely small crystals on rocky substrates. Quartz

thundereggs have been reported in the surrounding Sierra Cucapa.

52   A number of modest RV camps are found along the Río Hardy for the next few miles. The road passes fine marshes, with immense populations of pelicans, coots, cranes, egrets and a dozen or more species of ducks. It is not uncommon to see thirty egrets solemnly surveying a single pond twenty yards across.

57   Groceries, cold sodas.

65+   The road starts across Laguna Salada on a causeway. In 1991 this end of the lake was dry, with no water to be seen for miles, but in 1987 it was the scene of a thriving freshwater fishery, with large numbers of catfish to twenty pounds and other fish being taken by dozens of commercial fishermen, whose trucks and camps crowded the highway.

87+   South end of Laguna Salada.

TOO LITTLE AND THEN TOO MUCH

In the early part of this century two strange tragedies occurred in northeastern Baja, one caused by too little water, the other by too much.

In the summer of 1902 a group of forty-two Chinese laborers arrived in San Felipe aboard the small steamer

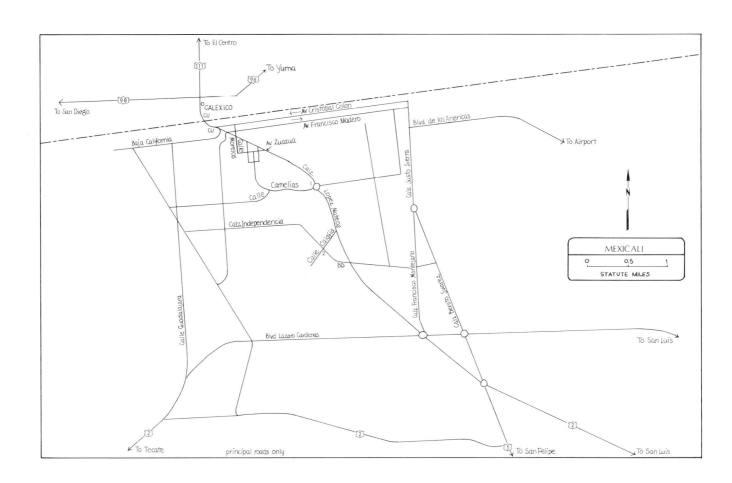

Topolobampo. They found no work, but heard rumors of vast irrigation projects that were underway to the north. No transportation existed, so they hired a Mexican guide and on August 26 set out on foot for Mexicali, 130 miles of sand, stones and 120° heat away. They had virtually no equipment and little food. Some did not even have shoes or hats, and the only water they had was carried in cans and old liquor bottles. They headed for a well thirty miles to the north in the vicinity of a volcanic butte now called Cerro El Chinero (Chinese Hill). One man died on the way, but panic did not set in until it became certain that the well was not where the guide said it was. Pressing on, they turned northwest toward the optimistically named Tres Pozos (Three Wells), located to the west of this point. Thirty-three men died en route. No water could be found and two more men promptly died of shock. Nine days after leaving San Felipe, the guide and five Chinese reached the Río Hardy and were rescued. Another man was subsequently found safe.

Although the area where the Chinese died is the hottest and driest on the continent, the nearby Río Colorado provided one of nature's great phenomena involving the movement of water: the great Colorado River Tidal Bore. When the thirty-one-foot tides of the Cortez met the swift current of the Colorado, a huge wave was produced that moved far upstream. It had been first reported by Francisco Ulloa in 1539 and was seen by explorer James Pattie in 1826 and by Joseph Ives of the Corps of Topographical Engineers in 1857. In 1864 the schooner *Victoria* was damaged by the bore, and in 1893 R.E.L. Robinson and a party of adventurers witnessed the bore, claiming it was fifteen feet high and twenty miles wide. Their sailboat was swept along and deposited on the mud flats far inland.

With the completion of Laguna Dam the river's current was reduced, but apparently the bore still retained much of its power. On the evening of November 18, 1922, twenty years after the Chinese-laborer tragedy, the captain of the *Topolobampo*, the same ship involved in that earlier incident, decided to stop for the night and ordered anchors set fore and aft near La Bomba, many miles north of the mouth of the river. The steamer had departed Guaymas with 125 Mexican workers and their families bound for Mexicali, where work was available in the cotton fields. All seemed secure and the crew and passengers made their meals and dozed off—after all, what could happen on a tranquil moonlit night on the muddy Colorado? A number of hours later, no one really knows when, a deafening roar brought a stampede of sleepy people to the deck. Stunned, they saw a gigantic wall of water approaching them from downriver. Before anyone could react, the ship rolled over and sank. Days later rescuers were still finding bodies and half-crazed survivors, their skins blistered by the sun, riddled by hordes of mosquitoes and blasted by a sandstorm. Eighty-six people lost their lives. New dams and silting of the now-slowly-moving river have tamed the bore and it is now little more than a ripple lost among the wind-driven waves.

105	**La Ventana.** PEMEX (MN), cold drinks, small store.
113	The hill to the east is a source of Apache tears.
120	Picacho del Diablo, Baja's highest mountain, dom-

Guadalupe Ruiz works a small gold claim near the historic town of El Alamo.

inates the skyline at 192°.

| 123 | Sedan road west to Mina la Escondida. Set odometer. Take the left (270°) fork at Mile 2.7, and arrive at the mine at Mile 4.1. The area is highly mineralized with gold, silver, lead and copper. To visit Mina Jueves Santo, return to the fork at Mile 2.7, take the right (305°) fork, drive as far as possible and walk the trail to the mine, where an American company has been taking gold out of a quartz vein. |
| 140 | **Crucero la Trinidad** (Crucero El Chinero). |

At Ensenada on Route 3

KM	LOCATION
0	Start new KM numbering sequence. Once out of town the road makes a moderate and nearly unbroken climb to near the Ojos Negros turnoff. The sides of the road are fenced almost continuously for the next hundred miles, and campsites are scarce. Those mentioned in later sections are modest indeed, most of them little more than places to pull off the road.
39+	Paved road (signed) north to Ojos Negros, 1.3 miles, which has a PEMEX (MND), groceries, post office, limited auto parts, tire repairs, medical and pharmacy. The Los Casian Trailer Camp advertised along the highway will be found 0.7 mile east of the PEMEX. Although it has shaded campsites and brick barbecues, it is badly littered and the restrooms and showers have not seen monkey wrench, paintbrush nor PineSol for many years. To drive north on the Alvarez-Ojos Negros road or to Parque 1857, set

odometer at the PEMEX and drive east. At Mile 4.0 note the road ahead winding into the hills and steer for it, arriving at El Coyote junction at Mile 7.7, described earlier.

49   Place to camp off south side of road, 200 yards west of the KM marker. Some privacy behind the rocks, but lots of road noise.

52   Moderate upgrades to KM 69.

55+   Sedan road north to Parque 1857, signed "Laguna Hanson." About 0.6 mile to the north the fencing ends and camping is possible.

59   A chance for a bath in the stream in wet years, campsite, often littered.

62   From a point 100 yards southeast of KM marker a bulldozer road leads south to possible campsites.

69   Gently rolling hills, low to moderate up- and down-grades to KM 114.

71+   **Rancho Cerro Colorado**. Pickup road southwest to Rancho el Porvenir, six miles, known for pale yellow labradorite, and Rancho Tres Hermanos (Santa Clara), eleven miles, known for chiastolite.

75   **Pino Solo**. The small tree at 250 yards, 222° is the new replacement for a famous pine that used to inhabit the spot. This is a celebrated pegmatite dike area, yielding ilmenite, quartz, tourmaline and gem-quality epidote, and some believe it to be the most important sphene area in the world. The pegmatites start 20 yards south of the tree.

85   A dirt road leading southwest to campsites will be found three-tenths of a mile southeast of the KM marker.

86   Sedan road southwest (signed) to El Alamo, eleven miles.

SIDETRIP TO EL ALAMO

The nearby Santa Clara gold placers were discovered in 1888, and El Alamo soon had more than 5,000 inhabitants, a newspaper, a pool hall and a cantina. Unwashed miners had another source of entertainment: the first captured louse to scurry out of a circle won a poke of gold dust for his handler. Gold seemed unlimited, and a one-ounce nugget was found in the gizzard of a chicken. Famous mystic Eilley Orrum, the Washoe Seeress, soon appeared. In earlier years, aided by a crystal ball, she had provided Nevada miners with advice on where to stake their claims, and which way and how deep to dig. Her advice had made her and a number of miners wealthy. At one point she owned a mansion in Virginia City, but when she arrived in El Alamo she was an elderly widow down on her luck. Pitching her tent and polishing her ball, she went into business again. Her first "seeing" demonstrated that she knew the commercial value of positive thinking; the ball showed El Alamo's gold fields to be extensive, spreading all the way to San Diego, and the specifics could be known for a price. Finding gold in Nevada was one thing, in El Alamo another, and even Eilley's talents could not sustain the boom, and today El Alamo is almost a ghost town. Mineral collectors have found magnetite, specularite, pyrrhotite, sphalerite, chalcopyrite, galena, pyrite, marcasite and, of course, gold and gold inclusions in quartz. A few miners still are at work,

and gold can be purchased at market prices.

Back on Route 3 at KM 86

92   **Heroés de la Independencia**. Gas station (MN), cafes, auto parts, tires, groceries, fruit market, stores, medical, pharmacy.

95+   Road south.

SIDETRIP TO MINAS EL SOCORRO AND LAS DELICIAS

Two of the most famous mineral sites in Baja are located nearby. Turn southeast 0.2 mile east of the KM marker and you will immediately encounter a Y. Set odometer, take the left (200°) fork, stop at Mile 1.3 and sight 230°. The light-colored hill 1,000 yards away is El Socorro. The mine is cut into a classic pegmatite dike, and schorl, mica, biotite, beryl, topaz, muscovite, quartz and green, blue, rose and watermelon tourmaline have been found.

The old direct route to Las Delicias has been cut by washouts and by fence-building farmers. If you are willing to do some exploring, take the right (240°) fork at the Y. The road will begin to meander radically in a southerly direction. Take the left forks at Miles 1.9 and 2.0. From this point explicit directions are impossible. Using your compass, try to drive south as much as possible. At Mile 3.0 start looking for a prominent rock-strewn hill with sparse vegetation. At Mile 4.0 a road will be found at the north end of the hill, running east-west and turning south along the hill's western side. At Mile 5.1 stop and hike south up the trail to the mine. A deep canyon running roughly east-west lies 1/3 mile to the south of the mine, and the highway lies five miles to the north, so you should not get really lost. Forming a complex and beautiful pegmatite dike, the area's light-colored rocks are shot with fan patterns of black schorl, and quartz, garnet, sphene, beryl, topaz, epidote, aquamarine and blue, pink, green and watermelon tourmaline have been found. So much mica lies about that reflections can be dazzling.

Back on Route 3 at KM 95

110   Cattle guard, dirt road northeast to modest campsites.

114   Downgrade to KM 125.

121   **Valle de Trinidad**. PEMEX (N, located southeast side of town), mechanic, auto parts, tires, stores, groceries, restaurants, medical, dental, post office, bakery, ice.

138   Sedan road south (signed) to Mike's Sky Ranch, twenty miles.

SIDETRIP TO MIKE'S SKY RANCH AND THE OBSERVATORY ROAD

Located at 4,000 feet elevation near the northwestern outskirts of Parque Nacional Sierra San Pedro Mártir, Mike's Sky Ranch is perhaps the most unusual resort in Baja; it is the highest in elevation, the only one with a trout stream and the only one catering largely to motorcyclists and off-road racing enthusiasts. Although graded and generally fairly smooth, the road has up- and downgrades to 26% and there are some rough stretches. People get trailers and motorhomes in here, but it takes time, patience and some very low gears. The route is signed all the way. Perched on a knoll above the year-round Río San Rafael and surrounded by pine-covered mountains, it offers motel accommodations, bar service, family-style meals and shaded campsites. Using worms dug along the riverbank, less mechanically inclined visitors can try to catch extremely wary trout. Good hiking can be found up and down the river among the pines and interesting rock formations, and there are a number of swimming holes upstream.

A road heads west immediately in front of the resort buildings, climbs precariously out of the canyon and joins the Observatory Road, making it a key section in the Two Parks Loop Trip. The road is best driven in a four-wheel-drive, although lightly loaded two-wheel-drive pickups can make it with some difficulty. Other than shortness of breath and sweaty eyes, bicyclists will have no undue problems.

MILE	LOCATION
0.0	In front of resort buildings. Set odometer.
0.1	Fork, take left (195°), begin 21% upgrade in loose rock.
1.6	On top.
5.1	Fork, go right (280°). The next mile has excellent shaded campsites among the oaks, possible streams in wet years.
11.3	Rough stuff. 34% downgrade into canyon.
12.2	Gate in barbed wire fence.
12.8	Gate in barbed wire fence.
13.5	Junction, go right (242°).
14.3	Junction, go left (180°), cross cattle guard.
14.6	Junction, go straight (190°).
19.2	Junction, go right (200°).
19.4	Junction with Observatory Road at Mile 29.7. Go left (090°) for Parque Nacional Sierra San Pedro Mártir, right (240°) for Transpeninsular.

Back on Route 3 at KM 138

142	**San Matías.** Gas station (N), cafe.
147	Unfenced area (1991), possible campsites. Begin moderate-to-gentle downgrades to KM 164+.
152	Soft, sandy road west to flat spots, best campsites in area.
164+	Road south to Laguna Diablo, signed "Col. San Pedro Mártir."

SIDETRIP TO LAGUNA DIABLO AND CAÑON DEL DIABLO

A road south from KM 164+ crosses Laguna Diablo and eventually swings east, joining Route 5 at KM 179. Except for a few stretches of sand and minor washboard the road is easily passable by sedans in normally dry years, and is an interesting and adventurous way to get to San Felipe. The road also permits driving to the mouth of Cañon Diablito, the jumping-off place for backpacking ventures up Cañon del Diablo and an alternate approach to the ascent of Picacho del Diablo, described in Chapter 9.

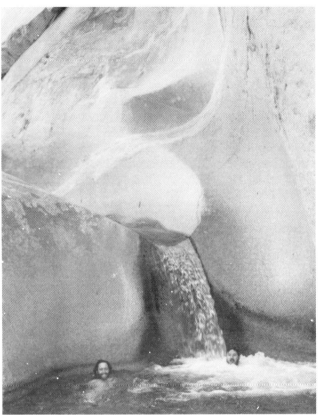
Will Ashford and Rick Tinker enjoy a beautiful pool in Cañon del Diablo.

Close your doors and windows and set odometer. At Mile 4.0 take the left (170°) fork. At Mile 6.5 the road starts across the dry lake. The bed of the lake is so hard and flat that dope smugglers have been known to land their four-engine DC-4s here after flights from Colombia. If you are headed for Route 5, the road will begin to rise out of the dry lake at Mile 18.7. At Mile 19.5 encounter a ranch building; take the left (110°) fork. At Mile 21.4 go left (100°) at the fork, at Mile 27.3 go straight (040°), arriving at Route 5 at Mile 40.7.

Those headed for Cañon del Diablo should stop at Mile 14.3 (from KM 164+) and locate the observatory perched on the rim of the mountains. Continue on until it bears 240°. At this point the observatory will be perched right over the mouth of Cañon del Diablo, and Picacho will bear 204°. Sight 232°: this is the mouth of Cañon Diablito and the roadhead where you will park. Continue on to Mile 15.4 and look for wheel tracks leading west. Reset odometer. At Mile 0.9 pass a corral and ranch building, and at Mile 1.2 take the right (226°) fork. Arrive at the roadhead at Mile 6.5, elevation 2,100 feet, marked by a plywood shack. The local rancher has indicated he will close the area if the parking area is littered or vandalized, or if access is blocked by parked vehicles.

The most musically talented coyotes in all Baja live nearby. During a trip a number of years ago we were treated to a concert of glorious howling at dusk. Later that night the members of the chorus paid a visit, and there was a great deal of scurrying and snarling over food we had left out. Secure in my van, I thought the event was hilarious, but Rick Tinker and Will Ashford didn't appreciate the humor from the confines of their pup tents.

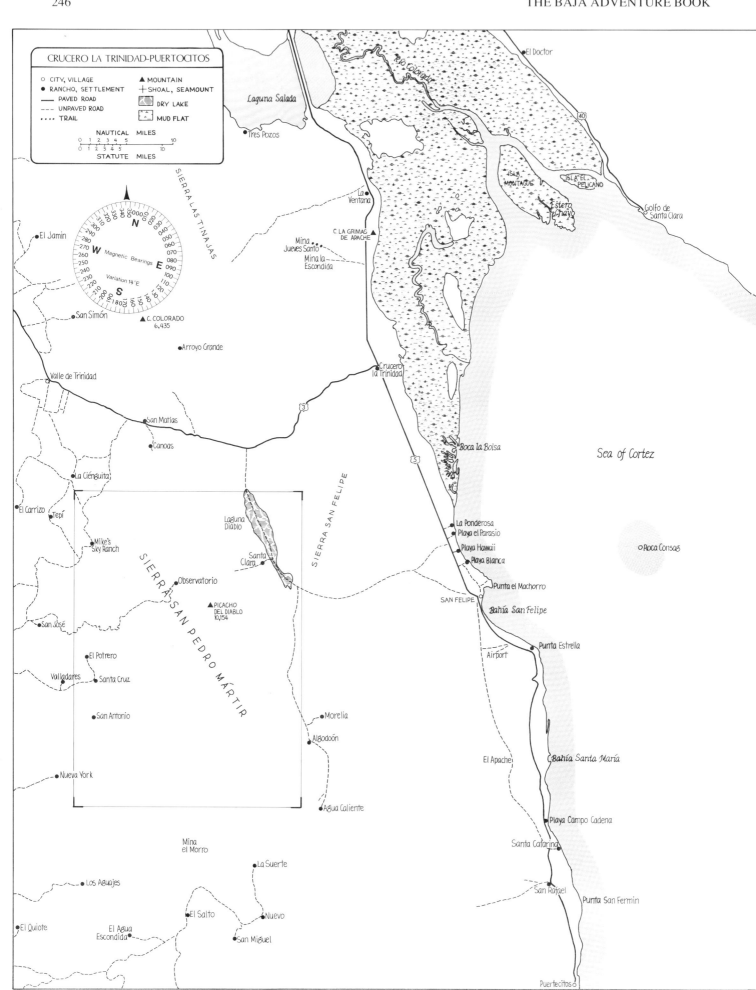

CRUCERO LA TRINIDAD-PUERTOCITOS

○ CITY, VILLAGE
● RANCHO, SETTLEMENT
▬ PAVED ROAD
--- UNPAVED ROAD
•••• TRAIL

▲ MOUNTAIN
+ SHOAL, SEAMOUNT
▨ DRY LAKE
▨ MUD FLAT

NAUTICAL MILES
0 1 2 3 4 5   10
0 1 2 3 4 5   10
STATUTE MILES

Magnetic Bearings
Variation 14°E

N W E S

SIERRA LAS TINAJAS

▲ C. COLORADO
6,435

El Jamin

San Simón

Arroyo Grande

Valle de Trinidad

San Matías

Canoas

La Ciénguita

El Carrizo   Tepí

Mike's
Sky Ranch

Observatorio

San José

El Potrero

Valladares   Santa Cruz

San Antonio

Nueva York

SIERRA SAN PEDRO MÁRTIR

▲ PICACHO
DEL DIABLO
10,154

Laguna
Diablo

Santa
Clara

Morelia

Algodoón

Agua Caliente

Mina
el Morro

Los Aguajes

La Suerte

El Salto   Nuevo

El Quiote   El Agua
Escondida   San Miguel

Laguna Salada

Tres Pozos

La
Ventana

Mina
Jueves Santo
Mina la
Escondida

C. LA GRIMAS
DE APACHE ▲

Crucero
la Trinidad

SIERRA SAN FELIPE

La Ponderosa
Playa el Parasio
Playa Hawaii
Playa Blanca

Punta el Machorro

SAN FELIPE

Bahía San Felipe

Airport

Punta Estrella

El Apache   Bahía Santa María

Playa Campo Cadena

Santa Catarina

San Rafael
Punta San Fermín

Puertecitos

Río Colorado

El Doctor

140

ISLA
MONTAGUE   ISLA EL
PELICANO

Estero
el Chayo

Golfo de
Santa Clara

Boca la Bolsa

Sea of Cortez

○ Roca Consag

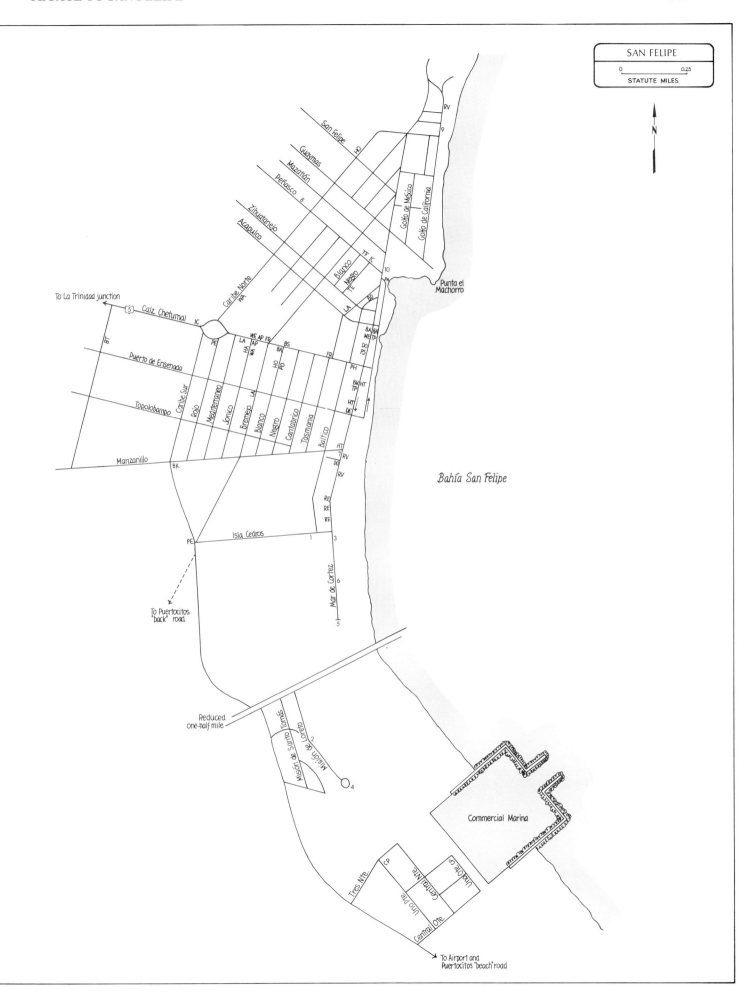

SAN FELIPE

0   0.25
STATUTE MILES

N

To La Trinidad junction

Calz. Chetumal

San Felipe

Guaymas

Mazatlán

Peñasco

Zihuatanejo

Acapulco

Caribe Norte

Golfo de México

Golfo de California

Punta el Machorro

Blanco

Negro

Puerto de Ensenada

Topolobampo

Manzanillo

Caribe Sur

Rojo

Mediterraneo

Jonico

Bremejo

Blanco

Negro

Cantabrico

Tasmania

Baltico

Bahía San Felipe

Isla Cedros

Mar de Cortez

To Puertocitos "back" road

Reduced one-half mile

Misión de Santa Tomás

Misión de Loreto

Tres Nte.

Uno pte.

Central Nte.

Uno Ote.

Commercial Marina

To Airport and Puertocitos "beach" road

After crossing a boulder-strewn wash, contour northwest to Cañon del Diablo, an easy forty-five minute hike across fairly smooth and open desert. Turn west into the canyon and after about 1/2 mile you will encounter what is often the most difficult single obstacle on the entire journey: a beautiful waterfall at elevation 2,250 feet cascading through steep, smoothly curving granite walls into a pool with a sandy bottom. Sand carried by storms sometimes fills the pool, allowing one to clamber up the falls with few problems. At other times you can almost see over the top but can't quite make it, for the walls are smooth and lack handholds; so near and yet so far! Creative climbers have improvised ladders out of tree branches and even constructed human pyramids. In 1984 someone installed an expansion bolt and a wire rope, allowing climbers to hand-over-hand up the wall and pendulum over above the falls. If this is gone and nothing else works, simply climb the north ridge.

At Mile 1.0 (from the waterfall), elevation 2,660 feet, the canyon turns south. Stay left at the major forks encountered at Mile 4.5, elevation 4,090, at Mile 5.0, elevation 4,420, and at Mile 5.8, elevation 4,880. Cañon del Diablo is much larger than any of its tributaries, so the choice is usually obvious. After the first fork the canyon again swings left, to about 140°. In its lower reaches fantastic water-carved granite sculptures surround deep, sandy-bottomed swimming holes and fine waterfalls. The changes in vegetation are striking, starting with palo verdes and cardóns and going through agaves and barrel cactuses to willows, aspens, oaks and cedars. The route is well ducked, but waterfalls may require creative route-finding. At Mile 7.0, elevation 6,300, you will find Campo Noche. The ascent from this point was described in Chapter 9. Two days should be allowed for the climb to the camp, and 1 1/2 days for the return to the roadhead.

Back on Route 3 at KM 164+

The road from here to Crucero la Trinidad is generally unfenced, with numerous sideroads leading to camping areas. Upgrades to KM 168, then gentle ups-and-downs to KM 187, followed by downgrades to Crucero at KM 197.

On Route 5 at Crucero la Trinidad, KM 140, headed south

141+   PEMEX (MND). Except for the pumps, no valve, pipe, tank, nail, board or brick in this station seems to have started its career as part of a gas station. There ought to be a place in Guinness for it. Note the antique glass-barrel gas pump. Many beach camps and RV parks are located between here and San Felipe.

179   Road to Laguna Diablo and KM 164+ on Route 3 (already described). Take the right (230°) fork 13 1/2 miles west of this point.

189   **San Felipe**.

SAN FELIPE

When the first roads connected San Felipe with the outside world in the 1920s, it was little more than a collection of

shacks. A large commercial fishery was established in the 1930s and 40s, primarily for 200-pound totuaba, and the town started to grow. During the 1950s tourism became important, and sportfishermen began to arrive in large numbers, but by the late 60s the totuaba were gone. In the 60s and 70s a holiday or three-day weekend would draw hundreds of off-road racers, a species occasionally given to excess in dress, drink and deportment. Today the town has matured, and a wide variety of American and Canadian visitors seem to be able to coexist, providing a fascinating mix of sights and sounds: a mariachi band struggling to make "*La Golondrina*" audible as a motorcycle tears past; gentle old Mom and Pop, spending the day sitting under the awning of their Winnie talking about their previous trip and planning the next; boardsailors flitting around the bay like a covey of bright marine butterflies; a fat woman with enormous breasts bouncing around an improvised slalom on a three-wheel ATV, unaware that the combined effects of gravity, inertia and centrifugal force are making her the center of attention. It's all great fun. Holidays still bring chaos, but otherwise the town is lively, pleasant and tourist-oriented, with vendors hawking everything from ironwood carvings to fresh shrimp. Sadly, the Clam Man expired recently, proof that the restorative properties of his favorite bivalve don't last forever.

San Felipe is a tourist city, and there are many hotels, motels, RV parks, restaurants, trinket shops and other facilities. Hotel Riviera (1) has rooms with bath, pool, jacuzzi, restaurant and bar. Hotel Las Misiónes (2) offers rooms and suites with baths, most rooms with a view of the Cortez, plus pools, tennis, basketball, restaurant, bars, gift shop and beach. El Cortez Motel (3) has rooms with baths, some two-bedroom units, pool, picnic area, gift shop, restaurant, bar, disco and *palapas* on the beach. Mar del Sol RV Park (4) has full hookups, restrooms, showers, laundry, ice, restaurant, tennis, pool, beach and *palapas*. Club de Pesca Trailer Park (5) has RV sites (many permanent) with electrical and water hookups, dump station, tent sites, restrooms, showers, laundry, recreation room, store, ice, restaurant and beach. Victor's RV Park (6) offers full hookups, restrooms, showers, recreation room and beach.

"Restaurant Row" is a section of Av. Mar de Cortez with numerous restaurants offering fish, shrimp, clams, lobster, steak, chicken and almost anything else you could possibly want to eat—even frog's legs and quail. See the accompanying map for the locations of more of the town's many hotels, RV camps, restaurants, stores, etc.. The office of the State Secretary of Tourism (7) also has many brochures, fliers and maps. The office of the Attorney General for the Protection of Tourists is located in the same building. At present (early 1991) there is no *Migración* office in San Felipe and those headed south will not find it possible to obtain tourist cards or to have them validated.

The two PEMEX stations (both MN) have been known to run out of gas during holidays, resulting in lines at every station all the way to Ensenada. Diesel is available at the commercial marina south of town, but you must bring a large funnel, since the nozzle is too large to fit an automotive tank.

The famous fishery continues to decline, and small corbina, cabrilla and occasional sierra are about all that remain. Even corvina, mainstay of San Felipe fishing until the late

1970s, are scarce. Roca Consag, seen on the horizon to the east, seventeen miles, 062° from the lighthouse on Punta el Machorro, used to be one of the fabled Baja hot spots. Today fishing there is fair at best, with a mixed bag of small cabrilla, triggerfish and sierra. If you are having a really good day you might pick up a halibut, and if the gods are pleased with your recent behavior, a white sea bass. There are numerous *pangas* for rent, and limited tackle is available at hardware stores and sportfishing offices. If you don't catch anything no one need know—there is a fish market in town (8). Skin diving is poor and there are no dive shops. Yes, climbers, Consag has been conquered.

San Felipe has miles of fine white-sand beaches. Hobies and sailboards are popular, and jet skis are for rent at several places along the waterfront. San Felipe is not often visited by cruising yachts because of its distance from the Cape, although some yachts are now being berthed at the commercial harbor. The harbor has not been dredged adequately, and areas go dry at low tide. Concrete launch ramps are located at the El Cortez Motel and Club de Pesca, but both are subject to wave damage and are often covered by deep sand. Several rusted high-rise trucks based at Ruben's Trailer Park (9) can facilitate over-the-beach launches for sizable trailerboats. Due to the enormous tides the shoreline can extend a half-mile at low tide, and launches, whether on ramps or over the beach, must be planned for high tide. Winds tend to blow in the afternoon, so head out early. A security compound for cars, boats and trailers is located across the street from Ruben's. This trailer park is renowned for incredibly loud, uninterrupted, unstoppable rap music, so persons valuing their hearing and sanity are cautioned to avoid the place by at least a half-mile. A hardware store (10) carries some marine parts and supplies, has service and common parts for Evinrude and Johnson outboards and has a limited selection of Coleman products.

Because of its proximity to the border and excellent road access, the town is often the starting point for the 160-mile cruise to Bahía de los Angeles and the Midriff, the first anchorage south being the open roadstead at Puertecitos, 48 miles away. Kayakers and small-boat sailors will find numerous camps where water may be obtained, and many sand beaches and pebble beaches for landings.

On the road south from San Felipe to KM 229+ on the Transpeninsular Highway

The road south to Puertecitos and Bahía San Luis Gonzaga and ending on the Transpeninsular is one of the most interesting in Baja. Bicyclists will find it a fairly demanding six- to eight-day ride, January and February often being the only months cool enough to be really enjoyable. Water is not difficult to obtain from homes and camps along the way, and many beach campsites will be found. Start south at the intersection of Calz. Chetumal and Av. Caribe Sur. Set odometer.

MILE   LOCATION

0.75   You have the choice at this point, just south of the town's second PEMEX, of taking either the "back" road or the "beach" road. Since some deep sand will be encountered and there is little to see, few take the back road. However, mineral collectors may wish to

check out the El Apache sulfur area, found on both sides of the road for 1/2 mile starting 21.4 miles from the fork. Some deposits are reported to be fumarolic, so perhaps you will find something new! The beach road will be reached 35.9 miles from the fork. To take the beach road continue straight ahead from Mile 0.75.

6.1   Junction; take left (100°) fork (right goes to airport).

9.2   **Punta Estrella**. Faro Beach Trailer Park has full hookups, tent sites, restrooms, showers, laundry, pool, bar and tennis. A "hole" a mile off the point in eighty feet of water is the first outpost of good fishing south of San Felipe, mostly for a mixed bag of cabrilla, corbina, sierra, grouper and an occasional white sea bass. Just after slack tide, when the currents are moving but not roaring along, the fishing in shallow water several hundred yards offshore can be excellent. There are numerous camps, resorts and private homes along the beach for many miles to the south. The road to Puertecitos was paved recently, but the job was done so poorly that it quickly deteriorated into a moonscape of potholes; in places it is hard to tell that it was ever paved at all.

38.8   Junction with "back" road. Continue south.

43.0   A four-wheel-drive road meanders west far into Arroyo Matomí, which bears 255198. Rancho San Rafael is 200 yards south of the fork. Marine chart 21008 and Mexican 1:500,000 topo Ensenada 11R-II show the "Cuevas de Santa Rosa" at about latitude 30° 01' north, five miles or so west of the shoreline. This places them about five miles northwest of the ranch in the Sierra San Fermin. A reconnaissance geology map of the area suggests volcanic rock can be expected; could they be lava tubes? (There are also sedimentary areas in the vicinity.) Although large-scale topos do not show references to caves and nothing further is known, cavers could have a fine time searching. The appropriate 1:50,000 topos are Bahía Santa María H11B67 and Puertecitos H11B77.

51.4   A dense outcropping of quartz with crystals to eight inches has been found near the first foothills to the west.

53.2   **Puertecitos**. This small village has a PEMEX (N, not always open during business hours), modest motel and RV sites, restaurant, cantinas, store with limited produce, ice maybe, and many retired Americans. Diving is poor, but fishing is a noticeable improvement over San Felipe; in 1988 a 103-pound "grouper" was caught. There are several natural hot tubs in the rocky beach near the point, each having a different temperature. A steep, rough launch ramp and a concrete dock can be found at the point. Although the ramp extends into fairly deep water, the tidal range here is still extreme, so use your tables. The anchorage, some of it a mud flat at low tide, is protected from all but south winds. Commercial fishing vessels like to anchor behind a spur of land 3/4 mile south. The next anchorages south are Isla San Luis and Gonzaga. Kayakers and

The worst of the "Terrible Three" as it was in 1967. The surface had been firmed up by dumping bags of cement. Any help was welcome.

pargo and snapper. Cartoppers can be launched at Cristina or at Mile 11.2, trailerboats at El Huérfanito, Mile 17.3.

11.2   Access to a sand-and-cobble beach with a natural breakwater. Beware of the 26% grade coming out.
16.6   Site of infamous grade in the "old" road.

"THE TERRIBLE THREE"

Steep grades, loose rock, sharp turns and yawning chasms made the eleven-mile stretch in this area a bane to travelers and an attraction to the daring for many years, the most celebrated "off-road" road in Baja. Three of the worst grades, the "Terrible Three" (some insist there were a "Terrible Six"), tested the metal and mettle of every vehicle and driver. No one seems to know the least-capable type of automobile to ever survive the trip to Gonzaga before improvements were made, but the dividing line seems to be somewhere between the levels of a Corvair and of a Gremlin; the rusted remains of a Corvair still lie at the bottom of one grade, but I met a man who claimed to have made it in a Gremlin, with considerable damage. Many years ago Reeve and I drove it in a VW van, but at the bottom of the most terrible of the "Terrible Three" we had to unload and carry everything to the top; the van didn't have the power to make it any other way. With burning rubber, flying stones and screaming engine we barely made it to the top. The road has now been graded, greatly easing the difficulty of passage, but also reducing its character and the feeling of accomplishment in survival. The accompanying photo was taken on the worst of these grades, seen today by looking south from Mile 16.6.

17.3   **El Huérfanito** (Nacho's Camp). There are just a few homes here, opposite a tiny island. A rough concrete launch ramp leads to a pebble beach. Kids will have a ball with the hordes of small spotted bass.

small-boat sailors will encounter numerous sand beaches and pebble beaches along the thirty-nine-mile coastline to Gonzaga.

On the road to Gonzaga, south of Puertecitos

The road south from Puertecitos has been improved, although washouts, rough spots and washboard can be expected. There are no upgrades over about 14% going north or south, but underpowered three-speed vehicles, especially those with heavy loads or towing trailers, may encounter difficulty. Many people drive far too fast along this stretch—a man recently bragged to me that his wife had made the forty-eight mile run between Puertecitos and Alfonsina's in an hour in her "hot-rod sand rail." There have been a number of accidents, so take your time and drive defensively. Use the regional map in Chapter 10 for areas south of Puertecitos. Reset odometer.

MILE   LOCATION
4.6   **Playa la Costilla** ("Playa Cristina"). Camping, sand beach with stretches of gravel.
9.3   The dark hill to the east is Volcán Prieto ("Black Mountain"). The shallows offshore are great for leopard grouper, and the small indentation in the shoreline just to the south has excellent corvina,

ENCHANTED ISLANDS

The Islas Encantadas are a group of six small islands stretching along the coast for eighteen miles, the most northerly lying offshore at this point. Their collective name stems from the facts that mirages are often seen, currents on their eastern and western sides run in opposite directions, some of the beaches are black (lava sand), some rocks float (pumice) and others are made of glass (obsidian). The first four, El Huérfanito, El Muerto, Lobos and Encantada (El Huérfanito, Miramar, Lobos and El Muerto, respectively, on some charts) were formed by fault blocking of Miocene volcanic rock during the Pleistocene epoch. Huérfanito, Lobos and Encantada provide little shelter for boats, but Muerto has several small coves on its southwestern side. Although kayakers will find no adequate place to camp on Huérfanito or Lobos, there are good campsites in the coves on Muerto (keep the DEET handy), Encantada has a rocky beach on its southwest end, and San Luis has a number of good locations.

The area east of Encantada is the focus of fishing in the area. About 700 yards to the east of the island is a tiny islet, covered with bird droppings and unworthy of a name, and even farther to the east is a large reef. Studded with pinnacles, this reef is loaded with gulf grouper, yellowtail, cabrilla and moderate numbers of white sea bass. The reef is generally too deep for free-divers, so spearfishing is very limited. The eastern margin of the reef is marked by a wash rock that bares to three feet at low tide.

San Luis (Encantada Grande), the largest and most southern of the islands, is also the most interesting. As you near the island, its western side gives few hints as to its violent volcanic birth during the Holocene, but as you round the southern coast, layers of ash and pumice are encountered, and the east side proves to be far more dramatic than the west. Even those without a graduate degree in geology will recognize that the semi-circular bluff encountered there is the inside curve of a volcano, and that the fifty-foot cone of dark, rough lava in the center is a vent plug, formed as volcanic activity ended. The eastern half of the volcano is missing, blasted into oblivion when it exploded. The coast on both sides of the volcano is a fantastic sculpture of volcanism and erosion.

Boaters and kayakers should set aside a day to explore San Luis and its companion, Isla Pomo. A long sand spit sticks out from San Luis' southwestern side, providing exposed anchorages on either side, as well as a place to land and camp. The volcano site, with its sloping beach of pumice and pebbles, provides a good place to camp, the looming bluffs providing welcome afternoon shade. The aid-to-navigation

Reeve with a dandy white seabass, caught off a rocky point near Isla San Luis.

Bill Gibson quenches a mighty thirst during a trip south of San Felipe.

tower here, askew on its foundation, has been dubbed "The Leaning Tower of Pumice." A pebble beach on the east side, just south of the north tip of the island, provides another place to camp. Rounding the north tip counterclockwise, you soon see a snug little harbor, but beware—the entrance may be awash at low tide, the rocks are sharp and the place stinks to high heaven. Just to the south sun will be seen glinting off huge boulders of low-grade obsidian. Nearby is a "lunch cave," a small sea cave providing a cool, dark place to take a break if tidal conditions permit. There are numerous sand beaches and pebble beaches along the west coast which provide good camping.

Isla Pomo, just to the northeast, also of Holocene volcanic origin, has another lunch cave on its south side, but there are few good places to land and camp. Above and adjacent to the cave is a mystery—are those white objects cactus covered by bird droppings, natural sculptures created by artistic birds using the same material, or stalagmites produced by an as-yet unknown geologic process? The cove on the east side is less protected than it appears, but camping might be possible in periods of low tides.

Fishing is good around the islands; trollers working yellowtail may have trouble keeping the numerous cabrilla off their bait. Try the south and east sides of San Luis, the shallow channel across to Pomo and several reefs a half-mile or so north of both San Luis and Pomo. Diving is uninspiring, the bottom being generally featureless cobble and gravel, but spearfishing might prove rewarding. Visibilities range between six and twenty-five feet, varying widely in only short distances. Mineral collectors will find all the obsidian they could ever want. The islands are home to may sea birds, including ospreys, Heermann's gulls, frigates, and brown and blue-footed boobies. Hundreds of pelicans often inhabit the sand spit on San Luis. There are large deposits of guano on both islands, and during a recent circumnavigation, most of the guano flies left their normal habitat and landed on my brother, a week from his last bath. Do they know something?

21.4 **Arroyo el Volcán.** Good quality sphene crystals, possibly washed down from the El Mármol area, have been found at the mouth of the canyon.

24.4 Gas, water, food, sodas.

36.3 **Las Encantadas** (signed). Sportfishing, food, drink, sand beach.

37.8 **Campo Bufeo** (signed). Restaurant, camping, cabins, gas, diesel. The long sand beach here is a good jumping-off place for visits to San Luis and Pomo.

42.9 **Campo El Faro**, sportfishing.

43.2 Papa Fernández', one mile east (signed), may have gas, oil, food, drink and rental boats. Launch over a fairly hard sand-and-pebble beach. The twin bays of Ensenada San Franciscquito and Bahía Gonzaga provide an excellent all-weather anchorage, although you may have to move around to keep out of the chop. Fishing, diving and shelling continue to improve as you go farther south from San Felipe. Fishing can be good in the spring and fall for barracuda, leopard grouper, sierra, snapper and spotted bass, and the area is frequently the northernmost range of significant numbers of migratory yellowtail. Hot spots include the waters off Punta Willard and along the shoreline just to the north. Commercial boats anchored in the bay may have fresh shrimp for sale. The next all-weather anchorage south is Puerto Refugio on the north end of Guardian Angel Island, forty-seven miles. Kayakers and small-boat sailors following the coast will find that the seventy-five-mile trip to Bahía de los Angeles requires caution, for the coastline has long stretches of high bluffs. The anchorage at Puerto Calamajué is open to the north. It has a sand beach, and the camp here may be the last source of water until Bahía de los Angeles. Ensenada Blanca is an open roadstead, with a gravel beach. Punta Bluff provides a bit of protection from prevailing weather, and there is a sand beach. Tidal currents in the Canal las Ballenas can be heavy. There is an open anchorage south of Punta Remedios, providing fair shelter in prevailing weather, with a beach. Short stretches of pebble beach will be found south from Remedios to Bahía de los Angeles.

45.8 Road east (signed) to Alfonsina's, two miles. This resort has rooms, restaurant, gas, water, limited supplies, rental boats and possible mechanical repairs. Boats can be launched easily over the beach. There is a growing community of Americans.

50.9 Junction, take the right (210°) fork. The other fork leads to Punta Final.

62.0 Pickup road southwest to a turquoise and chrysocolla site. You can drive five miles, but the last mile must be hiked.

64.5 **Las Arrastras.** Ranch, cold sodas, tire repairs.

68.0 Intersection, go left (045°) for Puerto Calamajué or right (164°) for the Transpeninsular.

80.9 Arrive at the Transpeninsular Highway at KM 229+.

****

OFF-ROAD ADVENTURES. Having read of the vast and mysterious wasteland to the south, Reeve and I finally mustered up enough courage to take our first trip to Baja. The broken axles and shredded tires plaguing other drivers would not catch us unprepared! We visited a Volkswagen dealer and bought so many spare parts we could have almost built a new van. Enough insect repellent, first-aid supplies, aerial flares, emergency water, shovels and sunburn glop to support a platoon of Marines in Kuwait were then collected. The van became so packed that we were forced into a difficult choice; something had to stay, our cooler of ice and beer or our half-dozen SCUBA tanks. A neighbor saved us by offering a roof rack.

SCUBAS on the roof, beer at the ready, we pulled out of San Diego rehearsing what action we would take in every conceivable emergency situation. The scorching flats south of Mexicali shimmered in the heat, reminding us that this was the real Baja, where people actually died from unpreparedness or even from simple mistakes like turning the wrong way at a fork. We passed through San Felipe and knew that the first of the Terrible Three was just seventy miles ahead. We could not find the road to Puertecitos shown on our maps, but finally we approached the end of the pavement. The road ahead certainly looked like what we imagined a Baja road should look like: deep sand and ruts. Having read that speed and power were necessary to overcome such situations, I shifted to a lower gear and pushed the accelerator to the floor. Slightly overestimating the required velocity, we shot across the first dip and ricocheted over a rise with such force that my head hit the ceiling of the van, momentarily stunning me. The van swerved violently left, its spinning steering wheel almost tearing off one of my thumbs. It then hit a bump so hard that the roof rack collapsed, scattering SCUBAS in every direction and causing Reeve's door to fly open, his seat belt saving him from ejection. The violent deceleration threw us against the dashboard, and there was an avalanche of equipment from the rear of the van. Fortunately nothing was hard or sharp.

Staggering out of the van, we found it sunk to the axles, exactly fifty-seven feet from the end of the pavement. During the next four hours we reorganized the shambles in the back, collected our SCUBAS and dug away tons of sand in an attempt to build a road to firmer ground. Every twenty minutes or so a car or pickup would whiz by about fifty yards ahead of our excavations. We finally got underway, pulling onto the freshly graded road to Puertecitos that we had missed earlier.

****

APPENDIX A
DIRECTORY

The telephone companies plan changes to various area codes, including locations now served by 213, 415 and 714. If you encounter a problem consult your directory or call an operator.

Aero California
213-322-2644
213-322-7080 fax
800-258-3311

Aerolineas California Pacifico, S.A.
Blvd. Emiliano Zapata No. 15
Apdo. Postal 64
Guerrero Negro, BCS, Mexico
011-526-857-0055
011-526-877-0666 fax

Aeromexico
800-237-6639

Agriculture Canada
Communications Branch
Ottawa, Ontario
Canada K1A 0C7

Air-Evac International, Inc.
8665 Gibbs Drive, Suite 202
San Diego, CA 92123
619-278-3822
800-854-2569 outside CA

Airstream, Inc.
419 West Pike Street
Jackson Center, OH 45334
513-596-6111

Alaska Airlines
800-426-0333

Alfredo's Sport Fishing
Benito Juárez y Callejon Dos
Apdo. Postal 39
Loreto, BCS, Mexico
011-526-833-0165
011-526-833-0590 fax

Almar Dive Shop
Av. Macheros No. 149
Ensenada, BCN, Mexico
011-526-678-3013

American Alpine Institute, Ltd.
1212 24th Street
Bellingham, WA 98225
206-671-1505

American Cetacean Society
Box 2639
San Pedro, CA 90731-0943
213-548-6279
213-548-6950 fax

Amigos del Mar
Apdo. Postal 43
Cabo San Lucas, BCS, Mexico
011-526-843-0505
011-526-843-0887 fax
800-447-8999

Aquamarina RV Park *See* La Paz Diving Service

Arcos, Hotel Los
Av. Obregon 498
Apdo. Postal 112
La Paz, BCS, Mexico
011-526-822-2744
800-347-2252

Arenas, Hotel Las
16211 East Whittier Blvd.
Whittier, CA 90603
213-943-0619
213-943-4078 fax
800-423-4785

Arturo's Sports Fishing Fleet
Apdo. Postal 5
Loreto, BCS, Mexico
011-526-833-0409

Attorney General for the Protection of Tourists, State of Baja California [Norte]

Ensenada Office
Lopéz Mateos No. 135-13B
Ensenada, BCN, Mexico
011-526-676-2222

Mexicali Office
Plaza Baja California
Calzada Independencia y Calle Calafia, Local #4
Mexicali, BCN, Mexico
011-526-556-1072

San Felipe Office
Av. Mar de Cortez y Calle Manzanillo s/n
San Felipe, BCN, Mexico
011-526-577-1155

Tijuana Office
Centro de Gobierno 2nd Piso
Zona del Río
Tijuana, BCN, Mexico
011-526-684-2138

Attorney General for the Protection of Tourists, State of
Baja California Sur

KM 5 1/2 Carretera Transpeninsular (FIDEPAZ)
Apdo. Postal 419
La Paz, BCS Mexico
011-526-822-7975

16 de Septiembre y Alvaro Obregon
La Paz, BCS, Mexico
011-526-822-5939

Backroads Bicycle Touring
1516 5th Street, Suite Q333
Berkeley, CA 94710-1713
415-527-1555
415-527-1444 fax
800-245-3874

Baja Beach & Tennis Club
1655 Broadway, Suite 17
Chula Vista, CA 91911
619-283-8519
800-842-3118 from SoCal
011-526-673-0220, Ensenada office

Baja California Tours, Inc.
6986 La Jolla Blvd., #204
La Jolla, CA 92037
619-454-7166
619-454-2703 fax

Baja Discovery
P.O. Box 152527
San Diego, CA 92115
619-262-0700
800-829-2252

Baja Diving & Service
Independencia 107-B
Apdo. Postal 179-B
La Paz, BCS, Mexico
011-526-822-1826

Baja Ensenada RV and Beach Club
1105 Broadway, Suite 214
Chula Vista, CA 91911
619-422-2864
800-982-2252 from CA
800-356-2252 elsewhere
Call collect from Mexico

Baja Expeditions
2625 Garnet Avenue
San Diego, CA 92109
619-581-3311
619-581-6542 fax
800-843-6967 outside CA
or
Expediciones Turisticas de Baja Californianas, S.A. de C.V.
Calle Sonora entre Abasolo y Topete
La Paz, BCS, Mexico
011-526-822-3828

Baja Experience Club, La
2630 E. Beyer, Suite 676
San Ysidro, CA 92173
619-423-3830 information
011-526-678-2062 reservations

Baja Hotel Reservations
4422 Cerritos Avenue
Los Alamitos, CA 90720
213-583-3393
714-827-3933
800-347-2252 reservations only

Baja Naval, S.A. de C.V.
Av. de la Marina
Apdo. Postal 1408
Ensenada, BCN, Mexico
011-526-674-0020
011-526-674-0028 fax
or
3040 E. Beyer, Box #1
San Ysidro, CA 92173

Baja Outfitter
223 Via de San Ysidro, Suite 7
San Ysidro, CA 92173
619-428-2164
800-696-2164 from CA

Baja Safari
P.O. Box 1827
Monterey, CA 93942
408-375-3544
408-646-0270 fax
800-248-9900 from CA
800-347-6847 elsewhere

Baja Sur Internacional
Guerrero e/ Revolución y Serdan
La Paz, BCS, Mexico
011-526-822-7154

Baja Surf Club
P.O. Box 9388
Canoga Park, CA 91309
818-883-2049
818-340-3745 fax
800-551-8844

Baja Trail Publications, Inc.
P.O. Box 6088
Huntington Beach, CA 92615
714-969-2252

Bicycling West, Inc.
P.O. Box 15128
San Diego, CA 92175-0128
619-583-3001

Binational Emergency Committee
401 H Street, Suite 6
Chula Vista, CA 91910
619-691-7634 24 hours

Biological Journeys
1696 Ocean Drive
McKinleyville, CA 95521
800-548-7555

Bob Butler Baja Fishing
P.O. Box 417
Palm Springs, CA 92263
619-325-1379
011-526-822-1313 in La Paz

Bodegas de Santo Tomás
Av. Miramar #666
Ensenada, BCN, Mexico
011-526-678-2509

Brisa del Mar Trailer Park
Apdo. Postal 45
Los Cabos, BCS, Mexico
011-526-842-0660

Bufadora Dive, La
Dale Erwin
Apdo. Postal 102
Maneadero, BCN, Mexico

Cabo Acuadeportes, S.A. de C.V.
Apdo. Postal 136
Cabo San Lucas, BCS, Mexico
011-526-843-0662

Cabo Pulmo Beach Resort
P.O. Box 2294
Ketchum, Idaho 83340
208-788-3353
208-788-9133 fax

Cabo San Lucas, Hotel
Box 48008
Los Angeles, CA 90048
800-282-4809 from CA
800-421-0777 elsewhere

Calmarinos
Av. 7A No. 1564 E. Hildalgo
Colonia Obrera
Ensenada, BCN, Mexico
011-526-677-1880

Campistre La Pila Trailer Park
Apdo. Postal 261
Ciudad Constitución, BCS, Mexico

Campo de Lorenzo
811 E. 11th Street, Suite 205
Upland, CA 91786
714-946-6692

Canadian Consulate
German Gedovius No. 5-201
Condominio del Parque
Tijuana, BCN, Mexico
011-526-684-0461

Canadian Department of External Affairs
Ottawa, Ontario
Canada K1A 0G2

Cardón Trailer Park, El
Apdo. Postal 104
La Paz, BCS, Mexico
011-526-822-0078

Casa Diaz
Bahía de los Angeles
Apdo. Postal 579
Ensenada, BCN, Mexico

Casitas, Hotel Las
Fco. Madero No. 50
Apdo. Postal 3
Mulegé, BCS, Mexico
011-526-853-0019

Castro's Fishing Place
Apdo. Postal 974
Ensenada, BCN, Mexico
011-526-676-2895

Centra Publications
4705 Laurel Street
San Diego, CA 92105

Club de Pesca Trailer Park
Apdo. Postal 90
San Felipe, BCN, Mexico
011-526-577-1180

Club Deportivo "Bahía Kino"
Apdo. Postal 84
Bahía Kino, Sonora, Mexico
011-526-242-0024

Compania Mexicana Acrofoto, S.A. de C.V.
11 de Abril 338
C.P. 11800
Mexico, DF, Mexico
011-525-516-0740

Concha Beach Resort, La
KM 5 Carretera a Pichilingue
La Paz, BCS, Mexico
011-526-822-6544
213-543-1369
800-999-2252

Consulate General of the United States
Avenida Tapachula 96
Col. Hipódromo
Tijuana, BCN, Mexico
011-526-681-7400
011-526-681-8016 fax
    or
P.O. Box 439039
San Ysidro, CA 92143
619-585-2000 24 hour answering service

Corona Hotel
Blvd. Costero #1442
Ensenada, BCN, Mexico
011-526-676-0901
011-526-676-4023 fax
    or
4630 Border Village Road
Suite 0-303 San Ysidro, CA 92173

Corrcaminos Trailer Park
Cascade Travel Service
111 Oak Street
Hood River, OR 97031
503-386-6800
503-386-4899 fax
800-426-4981 U.S. and Canada

Cortez, Motel El
P.O. Box 1227
Calexico, CA 92232-1227
011-526-577-1056

Cortez Motor Hotel
Apdo. Postal 396
Ensenada, BCN, Mexico
011-526-678-2307
011-526-678-3904 fax
800-528-1234
800-268 8993 Canada

Cortez Yacht Charters
7824 Longdale Drive
Lemon Grove, CA 91945
619-469-4255

Critical Air Medicine
4141 Kearny Villa Road
San Diego, CA 92123
619-571-0482
800-247-8326

Cruise America
5959 Blue Lagoon Drive
Suite 250 Miami, FL 33126
800-327-7778
800-327-7799 from Canada and Alaska

Cruising Charts
P.O. Box 976
Patagonia, AZ 85624

Dawson's Book Shop
535 North Larchmont Blvd.
Los Angeles, CA 90004
213-469-2186

Defense Mapping Agency, CSC
Attn: PMSR
Washington, DC 20315-0020
800-826-0342

Deportes Blazer
Hildalgo No. 18
Loreto, BCS, Mexico
011-526-833-0006

Desert Enterprises
Box 286
Ontario, CA 91762

Dive Palmilla *See* Hotel Palmilla

Diving Charters, Inc.
P.O. Box 6374
San Diego, CA 92106
619-224-4997

Dorado Velez Fleet
Apdo. Postal 402
La Paz, BCS, Mexico
011-526-822-2744, ext. 637

Earth Observation Satellite Co.
4300 Forbes Blvd.
Lanham, MD 20706
301-552-0500
800-344-9933

East Cape Divers *See* Rancho Leonero

Ensenada Clipper Fleet
2630 E. Beyer, Suite 676
San Ysidro, CA 92173
011-526-678-2062

Ernesto's Resort Motel
Apdo. Postal 54
San Quintín, BCN, Mexico

Estero Beach Hotel
Apdo. Postal 86
Ensenada, BCN, Mexico
011-526-676-6225
800-762-2494

Excursions Extraordinaires
P.O. Box 3493
Eugene, OR 97403
503-484-0493
503-343-7507 fax
800-678-2252

Faro Beach Trailer Park
Apdo. Postal 107
San Felipe, BCN, Mexico

Fantasia Destinations, Inc.
Box 79714
Houston, TX 77279-9714
713-558-9524
713-558-9587 fax
800-336-3483

Finisterra, Hotel
Apdo. Postal 1
Cabo San Lucas, BCS, Mexico
011-526-843-0000
800-347-2252

Finisterra Tortuga Sportfishing Fleet
Hotel Mar de Cortez
Cabo San Lucas, BCS, Mexico
011-526-843-0366
    or
18700 MacArthur Blvd.
Irvine, CA 92715
714-752-9010

Fisherman's Landing
2838 Garrison Street
San Diego, CA 92106
619-2221-8500

Fisherman's Paradise
3800 N.W. 27th Avenue
Miami, FL 33142
800-327-2507

Fishing International
4010 Montecito Avenue
P.O. Box 2132
Santa Rosa, CA 95405
707-542-4242
707-542-1804 fax
800-950-4242 reservations

Foundation For Field Research
787 South Grade Road
P.O. Box 2010
Alpine, CA 91903
619-445-9264

Fraser Charters, Inc.
2353 Shelter Island Drive
P.O. Box 60099
San Diego, CA 92166
619-225-0588
619-225-1325 fax

Fritz's Landing Boat House
Apdo. Postal 553
Ensenada, BCN, Mexico
011-526-674-0294

Glendale Community College
1500 N. Verdugo Road
Glendale, CA 91208
818-240-1000

Good Sam Club
P.O. Box 500
Agoura, CA 91376
818-991-4980

Gordo's Sportfishing Fleet
Apdo. Postal 35
Ensenada, BCN, Mexico
011-526-678-3515

Green Tortoise
Box 24459
San Francisco, CA 94124
415-821-0803
800-227-4766

H & M Landing
2803 Emerson Street
San Diego, CA 92106
619-222-1144

Hacienda Beach Resort, Hotel
P.O. Box 48872
Los Angeles, CA 90048
213-205-0015
800-282-4809 from CA
800-421-0645 elsewhere

Hyperbaric Medicine Center
University of California, San Diego
225 Dickinson Street
San Diego, CA 92103
619-543-5222 (24 hours)

Instituto Nacional Indigenista
Domicilio Conocido
Bahía Kino, Sonora, Mexico
011-526-212-0106

International Game Fish Association
3000 E. Las Olas Blvd.
Fort Lauderdale, FL 33316
305-467-0161

International Gateway Insurance Brokers
3450 Bonita Road, Suite 103
Chula Vista, CA 92010-3209
619-422-3028
619-422-2671 fax
800-423-2646 from CA

Jolla Beach Camp, La
Apdo. Postal 953
Ensenada, BCN, Mexico

Kino Bay RV Park
Apdo. Postal 857
Hermosillo, Sonora, Mexico
011-526-242-0216

La Paz Diving Service
#10 Calle Nayarit y Playa
Apdo. Postal 133
La Paz, BCS, Mexico
011-526-822-3761
011-526-825-6228 fax

La Siesta Press
P.O. Box 406
Glendale, CA 91209
818-244-9305

Lee Palm Sportfishers
1403 Scott Street, Suite 201
San Diego, CA 92106
619-224-3857

Loremar RV Park
Colonia Zaragoza
Loreto, BCS, Mexico
011-526-833-0711

Lucero, Alberto
Apdo. Postal 7
San Ignacio, BCS, Mexico

Manriquez Trasviña, Cirilo
Rancho San Dionisio
Santiago, BCS, Mexico
Buena Vista 5-36-36, ask for 166

Map Centre, Inc.
2611 University Avenue
San Diego, CA 92104-2894
619-291-3830
619-291-3840 fax

Mar de Cortez, Hotel
Apdo. Postal 1 ı
Cabo San Lucas, BCS, Mexico
011-526-843-0032
408-375-4755
800-248-9900 from CA

Mar de Sol RV Park
Box 120637
Chula Vista, CA 91912
800-336-5454

Marina de La Paz, S.A. de C.V.
Topete 3040 y Legaspi
Apdo. Postal 290
La Paz, BCS, Mexico
011-526-825-2112
011-526-825-5900 fax

Marina Palmira, S.A. de C.V.
KM 2.5 Carretera a Pichilingue
Apdo. Postal 34
La Paz, BCS, Mexico
011-526-825-3959
011-526-825-6242 fax

Marisla *See* La Paz Diving Service

Martin Verdugo Trailer Park
Apdo. Postal 477
La Paz, BCS, Mexico

Melia San Lucas, Hotel
Playa el Médano s/n
Cabo San Lucas, BCS, Mexico
011-526-843-1000
011-526-843-0420 fax
800-336-3542

Mexican Consulate General
610 A Street
San Diego, CA 92101
619-231-8414
619-231-4802 fax

Mexican Ferry System
    Guaymas
    011-526-222 3394

    La Paz
    011-526-825-3833

    Mazatlan
    011-526-784-1198

    Pichilingue terminal
    011-526-822-9485

    Santa Rosalía
    011-526-852-0013

Mexican Government Tourism Office
10100 Santa Monica Boulevard, Suite 224
Los Angeles, CA 90067
213-203-8191

Mexicana Airlines
800-531-7921

Mexico Department of Fisheries
2550 5th Avenue, Suite 101
San Diego, CA 92103
619-233-6956
619-233-0344 fax

Mexico Resorts International
Box 120637
Chula Vista, CA 91912
800-336-5454

Mexico West Travel Club, Inc.
3450 Bonita Road, Suite 107
Chula Vista, CA 91910
619-585-3033
619-422-2671 fax

Mike's Sky Ranch
P.O. Box 435376
San Ysidro, CA 92143
011-526-685-4995

Misión de Loreto, Hotel
Blvd. Lopéz Mateos No. 1
Apdo. Postal 49
Loreto, BCS, Mexico
011-526-833-0048
011-526-833-0648 fax

Misión Santa Isabel, Hotel
Blvd. Lazaro Cardenas y Av. Castillo
Apdo. Postal 76
Ensenada, BCN, Mexico
011-526-678-3616
619-942-9108

Misiónes, Hotel Las
Av. Misión de Loreto 148
San Felipe, BCN, Mexico
011-526-577-1280
800-336-5454

Mr. Bill's Boardsailing Adventures
Cascade Travel Service
111 Oak Street
Hood River, OR 97031
503-386-6800
503-386-4899 fax
800-426-4981 U.S. and Canada

Molino RV Park, El
Rangele Villarino y Verduzco
Todos Santos, BCS, Mexico
011-526-824-0140
818-986-7420 reservations

Molino Viejo Motel
Apdo. Postal 90
Valle de San Quintín, BCN, Mexico

Monday International Sports, Inc.
P.O. Box 99120
San Diego, CA 92109
619-275-1384

Monte RV Center, El
12061 E. Valley Blvd.
El Monte, CA 91732
818-443-6158
818-443-3549 fax
800-367-3687

Moorings, The
1305 US 19 South, Suite 402
Clearwater, FL 34624
800-535-7289

Mulegé Divers
Madero No. 45
Mulegé, BCS, Mexico

Mustang Aviation
1424 Continental
Brown Field
San Diego, CA 92073
619-661-6113
800-266-1414

National Audubon Society
950 Third Avenue
New York, NY 10022
212-832-3200

National Outdoor Leadership School
Box AA
Lander, WY 82520
307-332-6973

Oasis, Hotel
Apdo. Postal 17
Loreto, BCS, Mexico
011-526-833-0112

Oasis Club de Playa
211 Church Street, Suite B
Chula Vista, CA 91910
011-526-613-3255
619-476-1666
800-225-6001

Oasis Los Aripez Trailer Park
KM 15 Transpeninsular Norte
La Paz, BCS, Mexico

Ocean Voyages
1709 Bridgeway
Sausalito, CA 94965
415-332-4681
415-332-7460 fax

Oceanic Society Expeditions
Fort Mason Center, Building E
San Francisco, CA 94123
415-441-1106
800-326-7491

Outback Expeditions
P.O. 16343
Seattle, WA 98116
206-932-7012
206-935-1213 fax

Pacific Sea Fari Tours *See* H & M Landing

Paddling South
4510 Silverado Trail
Calistoga, CA 94515
707-942-4796 June-September
707-942-4550 October-May

Palmas de Cortez, Hotel
P.O. Box 9016
Calabasas, CA 91372
818-887-7001
800-368-4334

Palmilla, Hotel
4343 Von Karman Avenue
Newport Beach, CA 92660-2083
714-833-3033
800-637-2226

Palmira, Hotel
Blvd. Alberto Alvarado s/n
La Paz, BCS, Mexico
011-526-822-4000
800-262-2656

Palomar Trailer Park, El
Apdo. Postal 595
Ensenada, BCN, Mexico

Pan-American Hotels International, Inc.
P.O. Box 2776
Chula Vista, CA 91911
619-422-6918
619-422-3274 fax
800-678-7244

Paz Trailer Park, La
Apdo. Postal 482
La Paz, BCS, Mexico
011-526-822-8787

Perez, Raul
Bahía de los Angeles
Apdo. Postal 579
Ensenada, BCN, Mexico

Pisces Fleet
Apdo. Postal 137
Cabo San Lucas, BCS, Mexico
011-526-843-1288
fishing hot line 408-375-3554
408-646-0270 fax
800-248-9900 from CA
800-347-6847 elsewhere

Pisces Water Sport Center
011-526-843-1288

Pinta Hotels, La *See* Mexico Resorts International

Playa de Oro RV Resort
3106 Capa Drive
Hacienda Heights, CA 91745
818-336-7494

Playa Hermosa, Hotel
P.O. Box 1827
Monterey, CA 93942
408-375-2251
408-646-0270 fax
800-347-6847

Point Loma Sportfishing
1403 Scott Street
San Diego, CA 92106
619-223-1627

Point South R.V. Tours, Inc.
11313 Edmonson Avenue
Moreno Valley, CA 92560
714-247-1222
800-421-1394

Posada Don Diego
Apdo. Postal 126
Colonia Guerrero
Valle de San Quintín, BCN, Mexico
011-526-666-2181

Posada Real Cabo, Hotel
Malecón s/n
Zona Hotelera
San José del Cabo, BCS, Mexico
011-526-842-0155
800-528-1234

Punta Chivato, Hotel
Apdo. Postal 18
Mulegé, BCS, Mexico
011-526-853-0188

Punta Colorada, Hotel
P.O. Box 9016
Calabasas, CA 91372
818-887-7001
800-368-4334

Punta Pescadero, Hotel
P.O. Box 1044
Los Altos, CA 94023
415-948-5505

Rancho Buena Vista
P.O. Box 673
Monrovia, CA 91017
818-303-1517
818-303-3860 fax
800-258-8200 outside CA

Rancho Leonero
223 Via de San Ysidro, Suite 7
San Ysidro, CA 92173
619-428-2164
619-428-6269 fax
800-696-2164 from CA

Rancho San José
Apdo. Postal 1326
Ensenada, BCN, Mexico

Recreation Industries Co.
P.O. Box 68386
Oak Grove, OR 97268
503-653-2833
503-654-0052 fax

Riviera, Hotel
Av. Mar Baltico s/n
San Felipe, BCN, Mexico
011-526-577-1185

Rueda, Mario
Apdo. Postal 139
Guerrero Negro, BCS, Mexico

Safety Seal Tire Repair Products
800-888-9021

Scorpio Surfing Tours
P.O. Box 4184
Chula Vista, CA 91909
619-425-8154

Sea Trek Ocean Kayaking Center
85 Liberty Ship Way
Sausalito, CA 94965
415-332-4457

See & Sea Travel Service, Inc.
50 Francisco St., Suite 205
San Francisco, CA 94133
415-434-3400
415-434-3409 fax
800-348-9778

Serenidad, Hotel
Apdo. Postal 9
Mulegé, BCS, Mexico
011-526-853-0111
011-526-853-0311 fax

Soc. Coop. de Producción Pesquera
Av. Ryerson 17
Ensenada, BCN, Mexico
011-526-678-1166
    and
Aeropuerto El Ciprés
Ensenada, BCN, Mexico
011-526-676-6076

Solmar, Hotel
P.O. Box 383
Pacific Palisades, CA 90272
213-459-9861
213-454-1686 fax

Southwest Sea Kayaks
1310 Rosecrans
San Diego, CA 92106
619-222-3616

Spa Buenavista, Hotel
Apdo. Postal 574
La Paz, BCS, Mexico
011-526-822-1962
    or
P.O. Box 218
Placentia, CA 92670
714-524-6656
800-752-3555

Special Expeditions, Inc.
720 Fifth Avenue
New York, NY 10019
212-765-7740
800-762-0003

State Secretary of Tourism of Baja California [Norte]

Av. Lopéz Mateos No. 1350-13B
Edificio Pronaf
Ensenada, BCN, Mexico
011-526-676-2222

Calzada Independencia y Calle Calafia
Centro Comercial Baja California Local 4-C
Mexicali, BCN, Mexico
011-526-556-1172
011-526-556-1282 fax

Av. Mar de Cortez y Calle Manzanillo s/n
San Felipe, BCN, Mexico
011-526-577-1155

Callejon Libertad #1305
Tecate, BCN, Mexico
011-526-654-1095

Blvd. Diaz Ordaz y Avenida las Americas
Edificio Plaza Patria 3er Nivel
Tijuana, BCN, Mexico
011-526-681-9494
011-526-681-9579 fax

7860 Mission Center Court, Suite 202
San Diego, CA 92108
619-298-4105
800-522-1516 from CA
800-225-2786 elsewhere

State Secretary of Tourism of Baja California Sur
KM 5 1/2 Carretera Transpeninsular (FIDEPAZ)
Apdo. Postal 419
La Paz, BCS, Mexico
011-526-822-7975

Stouffer Presidente Hotel
Blvd. Misión Loreto
Loreto, BCS, Mexico
011-526-833-0700
011-526-833-0377 fax
800-468-3751

Stouffer Presidente Hotel
Blvd. Mijares s/n
Apdo. Postal 2
San José del Cabo, BCS, Mexico
011-526-842-0038
011-526-842-0232 fax
800-468-3751

Sun Tours
8055 W. Manchester Avenue, Suite 535
Playa del Rey, CA 90293
213-578-9680
213-578-9682 fax
800-829-0510

Thompson Voyages
P.O. Box 217
Laguna Beach, CA 92652
714-497-1055
714-497-6911 fax

Tijuana Tourism and Conventions Bureau
7860 Mission Center Court, Suite 202
San Diego, CA 92108
619-298-4105
800-522-1516 from CA
800-225-2786 elsewhere
011-526-684-0537

Tony Reyes Fishing Tours
4010 East Chapman Avenue #D
Orange, CA 92669
714-538-8010

Touring Exchange
P.O. Box 265
Port Townsend, WA 98368
206-385-0667

Tracks to Adventure
2811 Jackson, Suite K
El Paso, TX 79930-9985
915-565-9627
800-351-6053

TRIPUI RV Park
Apdo. Postal 100
Mulegé, BCS, Mexico
011-526-833-0818
    or
P.O. Box 839
Port Aransas, TX 78373
512-749-6070

U. S. Coast Guard Rescue Coordination Center
400 Oceangate
Long Beach, CA 98022-5395
213-499-5370

U. S. Customs Service
Box 7407
Washington, DC 20044
202-566-8195

U. S. Fish and Wildlife Service
Department of Interior
Washington, DC 20240
202-343-9242

U. S. State Department
Citizen's Emergency Center
202-647-5225

University of Arizona
Publishing Support Services
102 West Stadium
Tucson, AZ 85721
602-621-2571
602-621-6478 fax

Vagabundos del Mar Boat and Travel Club
P.O. Box 824
Isleton, CA 95641
707-374-5511
707-374-6843 fax

Vela HighWind Center
125 University, No. 40
Palo Alto, CA 94301
415-322-0613
415-322-3817 fax
800-223-5443

Viajes Mario's
Blvd. Emiliano Zapata s/n
Apdo. Postal 144
Guerrero Negro, BCS, Mexico
011-526-857-0888
011-526-857-0788 fax

Victor's Aquatics *See* Hotel Posada Real Cabo

Villa Marina, Hotel
Apdo. Postal 28
Ensenada, BCN, Mexico
011-526-678-3351

Vista Hermosa, Hotel
Camino al Puerto s/n
Mulegé, BCS, Mexico
011-526-853-0222
800-829-0510

Wagner, Bob
12430 Royal Road
El Cajon, CA 92021
619-443-2532

Wave-Trak
P.O. Box 197
Surfside, CA 90741
900-246-7873, then dial 2-3

Wilderness: Alaska/Mexico
1231 Sundance Loop
Fairbanks, AK 99709
907-479-8203

Yaqui Dive Shop, El
C.C. Valle Dorado, Local No. 3
Ensenada, BCN, Mexico
011-526-676-6344

APPENDIX B
MAP KEY, MEASUREMENTS AND DISTANCES

CITY MAP KEY

Airline office	AO
Auto/truck parts	AP
Bakery	BK
Bank	BA
Bicycle shop	BS
Bus depot/stop	BD
Butane	BT
Captain of the Port	CP
Car rental	CR
Customs	CU
Dentist	DE
Doctor	DO
Ferry	FE
Fruit/vegetables	FR
Groceries	GR
Hardware	HA
Hospital/clinic	HO
Hotel/motel	HT
Ice	IC
Immigration	IM
Laundry	LA
Meat	ME
Mechanic	MC
Motorcycle shop	MO
Optical	OP
Outboard parts/repairs	OB
Pangas, fishing guides	PA
PESCA (fishing license) office	PS
PEMEX	PE
Pharmacy	PH
Post office	PO
Restaurant/cafe	RE
RV park/campsites	RV

Showers	SH
Sporting goods	SG
Storage	ST
Taxi	TA
Telegraph	TE
Telephone	TP
Tire sales, repair	TS
Tortilla factory	TF
Tourist office	TO
Veterinarian	VE
Welding	WE
Water	WA

MEASUREMENTS

1	pound	=	0.454 kilogram
1	kilogram	=	2.2046 pounds
1	gallon	=	3.784 liters
1	liter	=	0.264 gallon
1	liter	=	1.0567 liquid quarts
1	liquid quart	=	0.946 liter
1	meter	=	39.37 inches
1	meter	=	3.281 feet
1	foot	=	0.305 meter
1	inch	=	2.54 centimeters
1	centimeter	=	0.393 inch
1	kilometer	=	3,280.8 feet
1	kilometer	=	0.621 statute mile
1	kilometer	=	0.54 nautical mile
1	statute mile	=	1.61 kilometers
1	statute mile	=	5,280 feet
1	nautical mile	=	6,076.1 feet
1	nautical mile	=	1.15 statute miles
1	nautical mile	=	1.85 kilometers

MILEAGE BETWEEN POINTS—TRANSPENINSULAR HIGHWAY

TIJUANA	ENSENADA	SAN VICENTE	SAN QUINTÍN	EL ROSARIO	CATAVIÑA	PARADOR PUNTA PRIETA	GUERRERO NEGRO	VIZCAÍNO	SAN IGNACIO	SANTA ROSALÍA	MULEGÉ	LORETO	CIUDAD CONSTITUCIÓN	LA PAZ	SAN LUCAS
69															
125	56														
186	117	61													
226	157	101	40												
299	230	174	113	73											
365	296	240	179	139	66										
447	378	322	261	221	148	82									
492	423	367	306	266	193	127	45								
536	467	411	350	310	237	171	89	44							
581	512	456	395	355	282	216	134	89	45						
619	550	494	433	393	320	254	172	127	83	38					
703	634	578	517	477	404	338	256	211	167	122	84				
792	723	667	606	566	493	427	345	300	256	211	173	89			
923	854	798	737	697	624	558	476	431	387	342	304	220	131		
1057	988	932	871	831	758	692	610	565	521	476	438	354	265	134	

A BAJA BOOKSHELF

Aschmann, Homer, *Central Desert of Baja California*. Riverside (CA): Manessier Publishing Co. 1967.

Baegert, Johann Jakob, *Observations in Lower California*. Translated by M. M. Brandenberg and Carl L. Bauman. Berkeley: University of California Press. 1952.

Bostic, Dennis L., *A Natural History Guide to the Pacific Coast of North Central Baja California and Adjacent Islands*. Vista (CA): Biological Educational Expeditions. 1975.

Browne, John Ross, *A Sketch of the Settlement and Exploration of Lower California*. San Francisco: H. H. Bancroft & Co. 1869.

_____, *Explorations in Lower California*. Studio City (CA): Vaquero Books. 1966.

Brusca, Richard C., *Common Intertidal Invertebrates of the Gulf of California*. Tucson (AZ): University of Arizona Press. 1980.

Cannon, Ray, *The Sea of Cortez*. Menlo Park (CA): Lane Books. 1966.

Case, Ted J., and Martin L. Cody, eds., *Island Biogeography in the Sea of Cortez*. Berkeley: University of California Press. 1983.

Clavigero, Francisco Javier, *The History of Lower California*. Translated by Sara E. Lake. Edited by A. A. Gray. Palo Alto (CA): Stanford University Press. 1937.

Crosby, Harry, *The King's Highway*. Salt Lake City: Copley Books. 1974.

_____, *The Cave Paintings of Baja California*. Salt Lake City: Copley Books. 1984.

_____, *Last of the Californios*. Salt Lake City: Copley Books. 1981.

Dunne, Peter Masten, *Black Robes in Lower California*. Berkeley: University of California Press. 1952.

Grant, Campbell, *Rock Art of Baja California*. Los Angeles: Dawson's Book Shop. 1974.

Gardner, Erle Stanley, *The Land of Shorter Shadows*. New York: William Morrow and Company. 1948.

_____, *Hunting The Desert Whale*. New York: William Morrow and Company. 1960.

_____, *Hovering Over Baja*. New York: William Morrow and Company. 1961.

_____, *The Hidden Heart of Baja*. New York: William Morrow and Company. 1962.

_____, *Off the Beaten Track in Baja*. New York: William Morrow and Company. 1967.

_____, *Mexico's Magic Square*. New York: William Morrow and Company. 1968.

Gastil, R. Gordon, et al., *A Guidebook to the Geology of Peninsular California*. Pacific Sections AAPG, SEPM and SEG. 1974.

Gastil, R. Gordon, Richard R. Phillips, and Edwin C. Allison, "Reconnaissance Geology of the State of Baja California." In *Geological Society of America Memoir 140*. 1975.

Gotshall, Daniel W., *Marine Animals of Baja California*. Los Osos (CA): Sea Challengers. 1982.

Grant, Campbell, *Rock Art of Baja California*. Los Angeles: Dawson's Book Shop. 1974.

Hale, Howard, *Long Walk to Mulegé*. Santee (CA): Pinkerton Publishing Co. 1980.

Hancock, Ralph, *Baja California*. Los Angeles: Academy Publishers. 1953.

Henderson, David A., *Men and Whales at Scammon's Lagoon*. Los Angeles: Dawson's Book Shop. 1972.

Huycke, Harold D., *To Santa Rosalía: Further and Back*. Newport News (VA): Mariners Museum. 1970.

Kerstitch, Alex, *Sea of Cortez Marine Invertebrates: A Guide to the Pacific Coast, Mexico to Ecuador*. Monterey (CA): Sea Challengers. 1989.

Lamb, Dana, *Enchanted Vagabonds*. New York: Harper and Brothers, Publishers. 1938.

Leigh, Randolph, *Forgotten Waters*. New York: J. B. Lippincott Company. 1941.

Lewis, Leland R., *Baja Sea Guide*. Newport Beach (CA): Sea Publications, Inc. 1971.

Martinez, Pablo L., *A History of Lower California*. Mexico, D.F.(Mexico): Editorial Baja California. 1960.

Murray, Spencer, *Cruising the Sea of Cortez*. Palm Desert (CA): Desert-Southwest, Inc. 1963.

North, Arthur W., *Camp and Camino in Lower California*. New York: Baker and Taylor Co. 1910.

Roberts, Norman C., *Baja California Field Plant Guide*. La Jolla (CA): Natural History Publishing Co. 1990.

Robinson, John W., *Camping and Climbing in Baja*. Glendale (CA): La Siesta Press. 1979.

Steinbeck, John, and Edward R. Ricketts, *The Log from the Sea of Cortez*. New York: Viking Press. 1941.

Thompson, Donald A., Lloyd T. Findley and Alex N. Kerstitch, *Reef Fishes of the Sea of Cortez*. New York: John Wiley & Sons. 1979.

Thompson, Donald, and Nonie McKibbin, *Gulf of California Fishwatcher's Guide*. Tucson: Golden Puffer Press. 1976.

Wiggins, Ira L., *Flora of Baja California*. Stanford, CA: Stanford University Press. 1980.

Wilbur, Sanford R., *Birds of Baja California*. Berkeley: University of California. 1987.

Wilson, Ivan F., "Geology and Mineral Deposits of the Boleo Copper District, Baja California, Mexico." *Geological Survey Professional Paper 273*, Washington: U.S. Government Printing Office. 1955.

Wong, Bonnie, *Bicycling Baja*. San Diego: Sunbelt Publications. 1988.

In addition, Baja Trail Publications, Inc. and La Siesta Press publish a number of interesting books on Baja California. Dawson's Book Shop offers books on such disparate Baja subjects as history, ethnology, linguistics, Indian art, whales, pirates, the Gold Rush, railroads, and cattle drives and brands, and publishes a number of books under their own imprimatur. They will send a book list upon request.

INDEX

Grocery stores, doctor's offices, vehicle parts and repair, banks, post offices, fuel sales and other services and facilities only indirectly related to the adventure travel theme of the book are not included in the index and can be found on the city maps and road logs in Chapters 9-16. Regional names have been abbreviated as follows:

TJSQ   Tijuana-San Quintín
ELRBLA   El Rosario-B. de los Angeles
MIDRIFF   Midriff
GNSI   Guerrero Negro-San Ignacio
SRLORETO   Santa Rosalía-Loreto
BMAGLAPAZ   Bahía Magdalena-La Paz
CAPE   Cape
TECATESF   Tecate-San Felipe

ClubMex de Occidente, S.A.
International Gateway Insurance
3450 Bonita Rd., Suites 100 and 103
Chula Vista, California 91910-3209
P.O. Box 609 • Bonita, California 91908-0609
619/422-3028 • 1-800/423-2646
Fax 619/422-2671

THE BAJA ADVENTURE BOOK
Application for Mexican Auto Insurance
Aseguradora Mexicana, S.A.
Multiple Entry Coverage

ASEMEX
ASEGURADORA MEXICANA, S.A.

ClubMex   DATE OF ENTRY INTO MEXICO _____

PERSONAL DATA Please Print (Press Firmly) or Type

Name _____ Date of Birth _____ Telephone (___) _____
Address _____ City _____ State _____ Zip _____
Driver's License # _____ State _____ Member # _____ Other Driver(s) _____

VEHICLE DATA
AUTO/RV—ONE SELF-PROPELLED VEHICLE PER POLICY

Make _____ Year _____ Model _____ Length (Motorhome) _____
Vehicle ID_____ License # _____ State _____
U.S. Auto Insurance Company_____ Expiration Date _____ Current Market Value $ _____

BOAT / BOAT TRAILER / OTHER TRAILER—*It is mandatory, by Mexican law, to list all towed units.*

	MAKE	YEAR	MODEL	LENGTH	ID NUMBER	STATE	VALUE
BOAT							$
OUTBOARD MTR							$
BOAT TRAILER							$
OTHER UNIT 1							$
OTHER UNIT 2							$

USE TOTAL VALUE OF ALL ITEMS LISTED TO DETERMINE PREMIUM: $ _____

NOTE: BOATS INSURED UNDER THIS APPLICATION ARE ONLY COVERED WHILE TOWED BY OR ATTACHED TO TOWING VEHICLE.
— NO COVERAGE WHILE BEING LAUNCHED OR AFLOAT —

Limits are quoted in U.S. currency and are based on current market value (ACV). Losses are paid in U.S. currency. For full coverage, place an "X" in the box corresponding to the current market value of your vehicle(s). For Civil Liability only, place an "X" in box J. Coverage does not apply to Mexican nationals nor Mexican registered vehicles. See territory maps on reverse side for zones of coverage.

PLAN A: Limited Territory
COVERAGE
Collision; Fire; Total Theft; Glass; Liability; $25,000 Property Damage; $40/80,000 Bodily Injury; $4/20,000 Medical Payment; $10 membership includes Tour Aid services.

CURRENT MARKET VALUE

A.	Less than $5,000 Premium	$145
B.	$5,001–$9,999 Premium	$165
C.	$10,000–$14,999 Premium	$182
D.	$15,000–$19,999 Premium	$198
E.	$20,000–$24,999 Premium	$228
F.	$25,000–$29,999 Premium	$240
G.	$30,000–$35,000 Premium	$263
H.	Each $5,000 over $35,000 add:	$20

+Additional Premium $ _____
=Total Premium $ _____

J.	Liability only Premium	$120
K.	Excess Liability	$20

Increases Bodily Injury and Property Damage Liability to $200,000 Total

L.	Boat Liability	$95

WARNING
MEXICAN INSURANCE LAW
MANDATES THAT ALL ACCIDENTS OR LOSSES UNDER THIS POLICY MUST BE REPORTED *IN MEXICO* PRIOR TO YOUR RETURN TO THE U.S.

INTERNATIONAL GATEWAY INSURANCE BROKERS
ASEMEX
ASEGURADORA MEXICANA

PLAN B: Full Territory
COVERAGE
Collision; Fire; Total Theft; Glass; Liability; $25,000 Property Damage; $40/80,000 Bodily Injury; $4/20,000 Medical Payment; $10 membership includes Tour Aid services.

CURRENT MARKET VALUE

A.	Less than $5,000 Premium	$245
B.	$5,001–$9,999 Premium	$265
C.	$10,000–$14,999 Premium	$282
D.	$15,000–$19,999 Premium	$298
E.	$20,000–$24,999 Premium	$328
F.	$25,000–$29,999 Premium	$340
G.	$30,000–$35,000 Premium	$363
H.	Each $5,000 over $35,000 add:	$20

+Additional Premium $ _____
=Total Premium $ _____

J.	Liability only Premium	$220
K.	Excess Liability	$20

Increases Bodily Injury and Property Damage Liability to $200,000 Total

L.	Boat Liability	$95

FOR COMPANY USE

Membership ▸ $ _____
Premium → $ _____
Total Due → $ _____

*NOTE: Premiums quoted include policy fee and 15% Mexican government tax.

I, the undersigned, hereby request coverage under the fleet policy for Mexican Tourist Auto insurance written by Aseguradora Mexicana, S.A. I accept the terms and conditions of said policy.

ACCEPTED BY—AGENT _____ DATE _____   INSURED'S SIGNATURE—PLEASE SIGN IN ALL CASES. _____ DATE _____

NOTE: POLICY FOR TOURISTS ONLY—*POLIZA DE SEGURO SOBRE AUTOMOVIL ESPECIAL PARA TURISTAS*
POLICY PREMIUM IS TOTALLY EARNED AFTER 30 DAYS. PREMIUMS AND OPTION AMOUNTS QUOTED ARE FOR A PERIOD OF ONE YEAR

JB2606a 3/91

NOT A BINDER OF INSURANCE

COVERAGE DOES NOT APPLY TO USE WITH COMMERCIAL CARAVANS.

SPECIFICATIONS OF RISKS AND LIMITS

Risk 1. Collision, Upset, and Glass Breakage (obligatory deductible*) covers damage to the insured unit.

Risk 2. Fire & Total Theft (obligatory deductible*), Lightning, Strikes, Popular Uprisings, Windstorms, Cyclone, Hurricane, Hail, Earthquake, Volcanic Eruption, Flood, Explosion, Landslide, and Cave-in, covers damage to insured vehicle.

Risk 3. Property Damage to parties other than the insured (third party)—$25,000 (U.S.).

Risk 4. Public Liability and bodily injury to those other than the insured, covers damages resulting from the use of the insured vehicle-$40,000 (U.S.) per person/$80,000 (U.S.) per accident. (Coverage does not apply to occupants of the insured vehicle.

Risk 5. Medical Payment covers expenses incurred by the occupants of the insured vehicle as a result of bodily injuries sustained aboard said vehicle caused by fire, collision, and/or upset (limited to $4,000 U.S. per person, $20,000 (U.S.) per occurrence). The Mexican Insurance company shall pay funeral expenses (to a maximum of 25% of the per person limit), and ambulance service.

It is mandatory that any accident and/or loss in Mexico be reported immediately—IN MEXICO. FAILURE TO DO SO MAY JEOPARDIZE YOUR CLAIM.

Current Market Value

In case of a total loss, ASEMEX will adjust on the basis of the actual cash value at the time of the accident. It is imperative that a realistic current market value of your vehicle be determined. **Under-insuring your vehicle(s) may result in financial penalties in the event of a loss.**

Deductible

There is an Obligatory Deductible for Collision, Upset and Glass Breakage that is applied for each accident and each described vehicle, boat, or trailer as follows:

A. $300 (U.S.) on all Private Passenger Cars, Pick-ups, up to 1/2 ton and Passenger Panels (Vans) (without conversions of any sort)

B. $400 (U.S.) on all Trailers, Campers, Motorhomes, and other vehicles that have Conversions of any type (i.e.Modified to be a Camper)

Total theft—$400 (U.S.) per loss.

Fire, lightning, strikes, popular uprisings, cyclone, hurricane, windstorms, hail, earthquake, volcanic eruption, flood, landslide, cave-in, and explosion—$200 (U.S.) per loss.

Important: Immediately after the occurrence of an accident covered by your policy, please contact the nearest claims agent (adjuster), and refrain from entering into agreements and arrangements with the other party until the adjuster is present.

Claims may be reported to any adjuster on your adjuster list in Mexico. The required premiums must be paid on or prior to the effective date of this policy.

IMPORTANT: Boat coverage under this certificate is limited to physical damage sustained while boat is being towed by or attached to the towing vehicle.

This policy applies only within the Republic of Mexico.
COVERAGE DOES NOT APPLY TO USE WITH COMMERCIAL CARAVANS.

COVERAGE TERRITORY ZONES: Coverage applies only in areas shown.

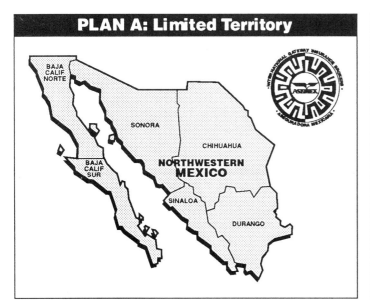

WARNING The Insurance company, Aseguradora Mexicana, S.A., is not legally obligated under the terms and conditions of this policy to repair or replace your vehicle in the United States.